In the Lives of People with Intellectu

Community Living/ Employment	Family Support	Bioethics	Aging	Quality of Life	Health
pp. 293, 303–304; 332–333	pp. 355–360	pp. 83; 158–159; 168–170; 373	pp. 327, 332–333	p. 373	pp. 139; 204; 327
pp. 293, 303–304	pp. 355–360	p. 373		pp. 288; 373	
p. 23	pp. 23; 112–114, 115–118, 122; 320	pp. 83; 158–159; 168–170	pp. 23; 320–321	pp. 23; 53–54; 320–321, 330–331	pp. 112–113; 139; 204; 330–331
pp. 22–23; 267–268; 302–305	pp. 22–23; 355–360	p. 373		p. 373	
	pp. 194, 204				
	pp. 194, 204				

Intellectual Disabilities Across the Lifespan

Ninth Edition

Clifford J. Drew
University of Utah

Michael L. Hardman
University of Utah

Upper Saddle River, New Jersey
Columbus, Ohio

Library of Congress Cataloging-in-Publication Data

Drew, Clifford J.
Intellectual disabilities across the lifespan/by Clifford J. Drew, Michael L. Hardman.—9th ed.
p. cm.
Includes bibliographical references and index.
ISBN 0-13-170734-5 (alk. paper)
1. People with mental disabilities. 2. Mental retardation. 3. People with mental disabilities—United States. I. Hardman, Michael L. II. Title.
HV3004. D74 2007
362.2—dc22 2005029501

Vice President and Executive Publisher: Jeffery W. Johnston
Senior Editor: Allyson P. Sharp
Editorial Assistant: Kathleen S. Burk
Production Editor: Sheryl Glicker Langner
Production Coordination: Norine Strang, Carlisle Publishing Services
Design Coordinator: Diane C. Lorenzo
Photo Coordinator: Sandy Schaefer
Cover Designer: Terry Rohrbach
Cover Image: PhotoDisc
Production Manager: Laura Messerly
Director of Marketing: David Gesell
Marketing Manager: Autumn Purdy
Marketing Coordinator: Brian Mounts

This book was set in Garamond by Carlisle Publishing Services. It was printed and bound by Edwards Brothers Malloy.

Photo Credits: Laura Bolesta/Merrill, pp. 2, 48, 70, 232; Ross Anania/Getty Images, Inc.—PhotoDisc, p. 4; Anne Vega/Merrill, pp. 10, 110, 192, 268, 301; Scott Cunningham/Merrill, pp. 19, 258, 374; Todd Yarrington/Merrill, pp. 27, 242; UN/DPI Photo, p. 52; Anthony Magnacca/Merrill, p. 79; Photo Researchers, p. 82; David Mager/Pearson Learning Photo Studio, p. 98; Barbara Schwartz/Merrill, p. 117; Shirley Zeiberg/PH College, pp. 128, 157, 182; PH College, p. 136; Keith Brofsky/Getty Images, Inc.—PhotoDisc, p. 162; courtesy of Clifford Drew, p. 164; Stockbyte, p. 173; courtesy of the Medical Radiology Program at the University of Western Ontario, p. 172; George Dodson/PH College, pp. 205, 224; Michal Heron/PH College, pp. 207, 318; Mark Richards/PhotoEdit, p. 273; AP Wide World Photos, pp. 286, 356; Greenlar/The Image Works, p. 294; Randy Olson/Aurora & Quanta Productions, Inc., p. 325; EMG Education Management Group, p. 344; Laura Dwight/PhotoEdit, p. 360; Bubbles Photolibrary/Alamy, p. 364; Bill Burlingham/Prentice Hall School Division, p. 379.

Pearson Education Ltd.
Pearson Education Singapore, Pte. Ltd.
Pearson Education Canada, Ltd.
Pearson Education—Japan
Pearson Education Australia Pty, Limited
Pearson Education North Asia Ltd.
Pearson Educación de Mexico, S.A. de C.V.
Pearson Education Malaysia, Pte. Ltd.

10 9 8 7
ISBN: 0-13-170734-5

Preface

We are pleased to present the ninth edition of *Intellectual Disabilities Across the Lifespan*. Our intent with this book is to provide an introduction to intellectual disabilities that tells the wide array of human stories associated with intellectual disabilities in a manner that is readable and comprehensive. Three basic concepts form the framework of this book. The first is human development. We discuss the relationship between intellectual disabilities and development from the time of conception to old age. The second concept involves the many different disciplines associated with the field of intellectual disabilities—no single field can address all the needs and issues of those who have this condition. Finally, the third concept is that, first and foremost, intellectual disability is an intensely personal event that lasts a lifetime and involves human stories that are emotional, complicated, and affect many people. We have tried to capture elements of these stories in order to provide a glimpse into the lives of those people having intellectual disabilities and those around them who care and support them.

This text is designed primarily for students in education and the social and behavioral sciences who are at the upper-division undergraduate or beginning graduate level. Students in general and special education, psychology, educational psychology, sociology, rehabilitation, and social work will find the book particularly relevant to their preparation. Premed students and individuals anticipating professional work in nursing, law, and administration will also find a great deal that facilitates their careers.

CHANGES IN THIS EDITION

This edition includes many changes suggested by our students and reviewers. We have combined, reorganized, eliminated, and rewritten topics where needed. These changes reflect an expanded understanding of a complex condition that has many intertwined causes, many developmental trajectories, and a growing array of interventions and supports. Additionally, this new edition also has updated and expanded coverage of a number of growing areas related to people with intellectual disabilities.

Our chapter on multicultural issues (Chapter 2) continues to evolve as the literature in this area matures. In addition to material in this chapter, other topics in the book have enormous significance to multicultural issues, including assessment bias and social and educational supports. In many cases these topics are integrated throughout the text in places where they can be discussed in appropriate depth.

Other areas of discussion also continue to mature in ways that permit a more complete attainment of our original goals when this book was originally conceived. For example, the text continues to focus on the full cycle of human development. Consequently, as the body of research on infants, toddlers, adults, and senior citizens with intellectual disabilities has grown, our examination of these individuals has expanded. The commitment to understanding intellectual disabilities within the framework of human development is much more complete in this edition than was possible when we wrote the first edition more than 30 years ago. The field has changed, new topics have emerged as science accumulated, and societal emphases have fluctuated. We have tried to reflect those changes while retaining our fundamental goals.

In addition to the information presented in the text narrative, there are a number of pedagogical features to engage the reader actively and to provide instructors with a wider variety of teaching options. Each chapter begins with a brief chapter preview, a personal human story related to the chapter focus, followed by some reflective questions that can be used in several ways by the instructor and the students. These reflective questions may be helpful as a guide to reading the chapter, as well as revisiting them at the end to see if reader opinions have changed. If so, how, and why? We have also included a *Tips for Professionals* feature that takes the reader into a context where the information is translated into a practical setting for professionals. Three sections at the end of each chapter are aimed at further engaging the reader and also offering instructional flexibility. *Core Questions* and *Roundtable Discussions* present issues and topics in varying formats aimed at stimulating dialogue. Instructors can use these in multiple ways. Finally, at the end of each chapter there is a new feature called *Parent and Professional Organization Positions on Key Issues in the Lives of People with Intellectual Disabilities.* This feature summarizes how organizations are addressing key issues in the field. It is linked to a larger matrix found on the inside cover of the book. All of these features have been incorporated to encourage active participation and interaction with the material.

ACKNOWLEDGMENTS

The changes in this edition were made on the basis of suggestions from many sources and on our own observations of growth within the field. We are most appreciative for the guidance provided by our reviewers, colleagues, and students, who have contributed immensely to the development of this project. To those of you who gave so generously of your time reviewing earlier versions of this manuscript, we thank you. In particular, we appreciate the assistance of Carrie Ann Blackaller, California State University, Dominguez Hills; Douglas Carothers, Florida Gulf Coast University; Sheryl R. Glausier, William Carey College, Hattiesburg Campus; Harold Griffin, East Carolina University; Beth Hair, Greensboro College; Maribeth Kasik, Governors State University; Kathleen McCoy, Arizona State University; and Dalum Zhang, Clemson University. Their careful review of the manuscript and cogent comments helped greatly. We are grateful for the invaluable efforts of our able research assistants, Lacy Egbert and Jayne McGuire, who labored tirelessly to help ensure the accuracy and presentability of our documents. For the extra help in reading the manuscript when we couldn't find the time, for accepting or ignoring our frequent whining, and for providing encouragement, support, and generally putting up with us, we once again thank our families.

Clifford J. Drew
Michael L. Hardman

Teacher Preparation Classroom

See a demo at
www.prenhall.com/teacherprep/demo

Your Class. Their Careers. Our Future. Will your students be prepared?

We invite you to explore our new, innovative and engaging website and all that it has to offer you, your course, and tomorrow's educators! Organized around the major courses pre-service teachers take, the Teacher Preparation site provides media, student/teacher artifacts, strategies, research articles, and other resources to equip your students with the quality tools needed to excel in their courses and prepare them for their first classroom.

This ultimate on-line education resource is available at no cost, when packaged with a Merrill text, and will provide you and your students access to:

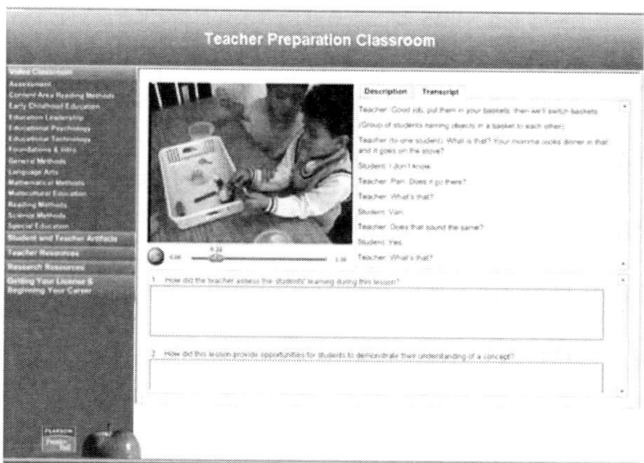

Online Video Library. More than 150 video clips—each tied to a course topic and framed by learning goals and Praxis-type questions—capture real teachers and students working in real classrooms, as well as in-depth interviews with both students and educators.

Student and Teacher Artifacts. More than 200 student and teacher classroom artifacts—each tied to a course topic and framed by learning goals and application questions—provide a wealth of materials and experiences to help make your study to become a professional teacher more concrete and hands-on.

Research Articles. Over 500 articles from ASCD's renowned journal *Educational Leadership*. The site also includes Research Navigator, a searchable database of additional educational journals.

Teaching Strategies. Over 500 strategies and lesson plans for you to use when you become a practicing professional.

Licensure and Career Tools. Resources devoted to helping you pass your licensure exam; learn standards, law, and public policies; plan a teaching portfolio; and succeed in your first year of teaching.

How to ORDER Teacher Prep for you and your students:
For students to receive a *Teacher Prep* Access Code with this text, instructors must provide a special value pack ISBN number on their textbook order form. To receive this special ISBN, please email **Merrill.marketing@pearsoned.com** and provide the following information:

- Name and Affiliation
- Author/Title/Edition of Merrill text

Upon ordering *Teacher Prep* for their students, instructors will be given a lifetime *Teacher Prep* Access Code.

Discover the Merrill Education Resources for Special Education Website

Technology is a constantly growing and changing aspect of our field that is creating a need for new content and resources. To address this emerging need, Merrill Education has developed an online learning environment for students, teachers, and professors alike to complement our products—the *Merrill Education Resources for Special Education* Website. This content-rich website provides additional resources specific to this book's topic and will help you—professors, classroom teachers, and students—augment your teaching, learning, and professional development.

Our goal with this initiative is to build on and enhance what our products already offer. For this reason, the content for our user-friendly website is organized by topic and provides teachers, professors, and students with a variety of meaningful resources all in one location. With this website, we bring together the best of what Merrill has to offer: text resources, video clips, web links, tutorials, and a wide variety of information on topics of interest to general and special educators alike. Rich content, applications, and competencies further enhance the learning process.

The *Merrill Education Resources for Special Education* Website includes:

- Video clips specific to each topic, with questions to help you evaluate the content and make crucial theory-to-practice connections.
- Thought-provoking critical analysis questions that students can answer and turn in for evaluation or that can serve as basis for class discussions and lectures.
- Access to a wide variety of resources related to classroom strategies and methods, including lesson planning and classroom management.
- Information on all the most current relevant topics related to special and general education, including CEC and Praxis standards, IEPs, portfolios, and professional development.
- Extensive web resources and overviews on each topic addressed on the website.
- A search feature to help access specific information quickly.

To take advantage of these and other resources, please visit the *Merrill Education Resources for Special Education* Website at

http://www.prenhall.com/drew

Clifford J. Drew

Clifford J. Drew is associate dean for research, technology, and outreach in the College of Education at the University of Utah. He is also a professor in the Departments of Special Education and Educational Psychology. Dr. Drew came to the University of Utah in 1971, after serving on the faculties of the University of Texas at Austin and Kent State University. He received his master's degree from the University of Illinois and his Ph.D. from the University of Oregon. His professional interests include research methods in education and psychology, human development and disabilities, applications of information technology, and outreach and continuing education in higher education.

Dr. Drew has published on many topics in education and related areas, having made over 110 contributions to the professional literature on subjects including mental retardation, research design, statistics, diagnostic assessment, cognition, evaluation related to the law, and information technology. His most recent book, *Understanding Child Behavior Disorders* (Wadsworth, 2003), is Dr. Drew's 25th text. Dr. Drew has served on the board of directors of the Far West Laboratory for Research and Development in Education, chaired the National Ethics Committee of the American Association on Mental Retardation, and is a fellow of that organization. He is listed in several honorary biographical volumes, including *Who's Who in America*.

Michael L. Hardman

Michael L. Hardman is the department chair and professor in special education at the University of Utah. He is also the chief education adviser to the Joseph P. Kennedy, Jr., Foundation in Washington, D.C. Dr. Hardman, who completed his doctorate in educational administration, has published in national journals throughout the field of education and authored 10 college textbooks. His coauthored textbook *Human Exceptionality* (7th ed.) has been adopted by over 300 universities and colleges throughout the United States. He has also written *Introduction to Persons with Severe Disabilities* (2nd ed.). As a researcher, he has authored numerous publications and has directed international and national demonstration projects on mental retardation/developmental disabilities, school reform and professional development, inclusive education, transition from school to adult life, the future of the Individuals with Disabilities Education Act, and training future leaders in special education. Dr. Hardman is the recipient of the 2000 National Distinguished Service Award from the Council for Exceptional Children, Division of Teacher Education.

Contents

Part 1 Introduction 1

Chapter 2 Diversity Issues 48

Part 2 Identifying People with Intellectual Disabilities 69

Chapter 3 Assessment Issues and Procedures 70

Chapter 9 The Adolescent with Intellectual Disabilities and the Transitional Years 258

Part 5 Adulthood and Aging 285

Chapter 10 The Adult Years 286

Part 6 Family and Social Issues 343

Chapter 12 Families 344

Chapter 13 Social and Ethical Issues 364

NOTE: Every effort has been made to provide accurate and current Internet information in this book. However, the Internet and information posted on it are contantly changing, so it is inevitable that some fo the Internet addresses listed in this textbook will change.

Introduction

Chapter 1

Understanding Intellectual Disabilities

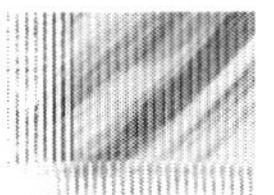

Chapter Preview

At the completion of this chapter, you will have a better understanding of intellectual disabilities as:

- Representing complex, fluid concepts that are influenced by many societal factors, and involving an array of behaviors and abilities.
- A condition requiring multiple disciplines for research, assessment, and effective collaboration in service interventions.
- A field that examines the interactions between individuals and their environment that are essential to our understanding of how to provide opportunities for personal independence, thriving, and optimal development.

Advocating for Tommy

Tommy Young's mother was a frustrated single mother. She sat at the kitchen table trying to reconcile and collect her thoughts. With no one to talk to, it seemed like her problems were insurmountable. Tommy had brought a note home from his first-grade teacher that both frightened Jerilyn Young and confused her. The note indicated that his teacher wanted to refer Tommy for testing because he was behind his classmates in his classwork, primarily reading. Tommy had progressed through his early years at what seemed a reasonable rate, although he seemed a little slow walking and talking. When Jerilyn had asked their pediatrician about these matters a few years earlier, the doctor indicated that he was possibly a little slow but that perhaps she was a worrywart. Jerilyn had taken that information with some relief but a lingering concern. Now, with the teacher's note in hand, she was more anxious than before. She wanted to believe what the doctor had said earlier, that nothing was wrong, but Jerilyn still worried that Tommy's limited language skills reflected a developmental problem.

Jerilyn faces a situation common for many parents of children who have mild intellectual disabilities. While there may be some indicators of slow development during the early years, they are not significant enough to show up until the child reaches school age and is confronted with an environment that focuses on academic abilities. Health care professionals are often the primary group consulted during the early years, and they may be ill equipped to identify mild developmental limitations because there is often no obvious physical indicator. But now, as Tommy is in school, his developmental limitations may become more evident because schoolwork has a greater emphasis on abstract and conceptual thinking than he has encountered before.

Multiple disciplines may be called on to provide services and supports to Tommy, including education, psychology, and health care. As this occurs, it will be a continuing challenge to ensure that these professionals are centered on the child, serving his needs in a coordinated fashion. It is hoped that such coordination will become collaboration with Jerilyn as a continuing team member. She cannot be passive in this process; she must be a proactive, thoughtful, and informed advocate for Tommy's best interests.

- *What do you think Jerilyn should do? Should she agree to allow Tommy's teacher to refer him for testing? Should she contact the teacher to engage in*

Jerilyn will have to be Tommy's best advocate.

a conversation about Tommy's welfare and progress through the school system, making clear that she is her son's advocate?

- *Jerilyn feels alone. Where might she turn for information about testing, and how schools work (particularly related to Tommy's issues)? Where might she turn for discussion of her fears and other emotions as she orchestrates Tommy's future, to the degree that she can?*

People differ greatly in many ways, yet for the most part, there is a range of variability that is considered "normal." Outside this range, differences are often extreme enough to attract attention. As we saw in our opening vignette, some developmental differences may be so subtle at one point that they do not attract attention but may become more evident at another time in the developmental lifespan. Further, what may be considered a developmental limitation by one profession at one point in time may be viewed otherwise by another profession at another time. The challenges presented to parents and professionals who provide services and supports for children with developmental differences are significant (Abbeduto et al., 2004; Neely-Barnes & Marcenko, 2004; Shin & Crittenden, 2003).

People have been interested in individuals with physical, mental, and behavioral differences throughout recorded history. The perspectives that religion, psychology, education, and various branches of medicine offer on such phenomena have been prominent throughout history, and perceptions of what is normal have varied widely over time and from one discipline to another. Definitions and concepts associated with human differences continue to change as knowledge expands and societal values shift. Like other conditions, the history of intellectual disabilities follows a changing path.

HISTORICAL PERSPECTIVES

The history of intellectual disabilities is enormously important because it has had such a powerful impact. Parents and family members of those with intellectual disabilities have led, promoted, and participated in change movements that have altered society's view of people with disabilities. Without these efforts many federal and state laws would not have been passed, the idea of a free and appropriate public education would differ from what it is today, and quite possibly, society's fundamental views of how people should treat others would be less caring and supportive. Advances have been built on the accomplishments of a few insightful and caring people who worked diligently for improved circumstances and a more evenhanded world for those with intellectual disabilities.

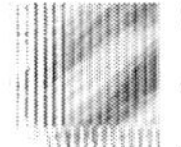

Core Concept

The concept of intellectual disabilities is continually influenced by economic, societal, and situational factors.

Societies throughout the ages have been affected by intellectual disabilities, although the way people have viewed those having this condition has changed significantly over time. Many diverse concepts and varying characteristics have influenced different descriptions of people with intellectual disabilities, depending on society's views and situational influences during any given time period. In fact, as one looks at the history of intellectual disabilities, the picture is chameleonlike and its appearance changes with the attitudes and convictions of the time (Otani, 2002; Stone, 2003).

The concept of intellectual disabilities has been fluid and elusive for a variety of reasons, not the least of which have been the influences of economic, social, and political climates of various cultures throughout history. Such shifting viewpoints have influenced attitudes toward disabilities and had a significant impact on treatment approaches, just as they do in today's society (Campbell, Gilmore, & Cuskelly, 2003; Coopman, 2003; Vehmas, 2004).

Before 1800, with a few notable exceptions, having intellectual disabilities was not considered an urgent social problem in any society because those with more severe intellectual disabilities were either killed or died of natural causes at an early age. In some cases, those with disabilities were viewed as a drain on society and targeted for elimination, even in relatively recent times such as the mid-1900s (Mostert, 2002). Those considered to have mild intellectual disabilities could function fairly well in an agrarian society. Although the earliest written reference to intellectual disabilities is dated 1552 B.C., some anthropological studies have found evidence of intellectual disabilities substantially pre-dating that time. Severe head injuries were not uncommon during early times, and they most certainly resulted in behavior that was not considered normal. Human skulls dating to the Neolithic Age indicate that crude brain surgery had been performed. The surgical procedures apparently were intended to cure abnormal behavior. The methods used may have been based on an assumption that evil spirits caused strange behavior and that opening a hole in the skull permitted them to escape. Not all such operations were performed on people with intellectual disabilities, but regardless of the reason, the treatment often resulted in behavior resembling diminished intellectual ability.

Socioeconomic conditions have influenced human understanding and treatment of people with intellectual disabilities as well. Primitive tribes often looked on mental and physical differences with fear or as signs of disgrace, largely because of the stigma associated with such conditions. Superstitions and myths also bolstered this view. In a more pragmatic sense, those with disabilities often represented an unbearable economic drain on the tribe. In particular, nomadic tribes could ill afford to be burdened by members who consumed limited food and water supplies but did not tangibly contribute to the common welfare. Individuals with intellectual disabilities were frequently viewed as a wasteful extravagance the group could not afford, even when tribal civilization progressed and a less nomadic existence prevailed. The advent of farming and grazing could not dispel the threat of famine, which remained constantly on the horizon. The economic usefulness of people with disabilities was similar to what it had been during more nomadic times. Neither the religious nor the economic perspective was conducive to the care of those with diminished intellectual capacity; nonproductive citizens were expendable.

Throughout history, political authority has also been a force in determining the lot of people with intellectual disabilities. Sometimes, authority supported harsh treatment of individuals with disabilities while at other times more humane approaches were in favor. For example, in the 6th century, Pope Gregory I issued a decree instructing the faithful to assist those who were crippled. During this period, various types and degrees of care were provided for people with disabilities, including those with intellectual disabilities, who commonly were referred to as "idiots." England enacted special legislation for these citizens under the rule of King Henry II in the 12th century. Individuals who were "natural fools" became wards of the king, and for the first time the law distinguished between those having intellectual disabilities and those with mental illness. These were isolated efforts on behalf of people with intellectual disabilities. Unfortunately, history is also replete with examples of extremely discriminatory and repressive practices. Individuals with intellectual disabilities and those with other disability conditions have long been at the mercy of the more able majority.

Although one may view the attitudes of earlier societies as primitive and uninformed, a serious examination of current thinking and practices results in a less complacent perspective. Battles waged by advocacy groups in the courts and other arenas are public testimony that many challenges remain. Economic downturns and competition for funding frequently place the support of research and service for intellectual disabilities in jeopardy. Future societies probably will think that the present efforts are nearly as primitive as we consider those of the past.

Reproductive sterilization has periodically been a prominent topic in the history of intellectual disabilities. The sterilization issue has been entangled with a number of other questions: the nature-versus-nurture dispute, political and economic issues, and moral and social debates. Some early genealogical studies were very influential in generating the sterilization controversy in the United States. One such study by Henry Goddard (1913) received particularly widespread attention. Goddard traced the descendants of a Revolutionary War soldier to whom he gave the pseudonym Martin Kallikak. At one time in his life, Kallikak had sexual relations with a barmaid and fathered a child. The descendants of this union were reported to be primarily thieves, prostitutes, and other social undesirables. Kallikak later married a "normal" woman; their descendants were purportedly normal and, in some cases, superior. The resulting conclusion was that because of genetics, one group was doomed to a life of degeneracy, whereas the other was almost certainly destined to be successful. Current research methods do not allow such a simplistic interpretation because, even if the resulting offspring were as described, the outcomes could easily be attributed to environmental as well as biological influences (Gelfand & Drew, 2003; Goodwin, 2005). The descendants of Martin Kallikak and the barmaid were probably victims, at least in part, of their social situation. The descendants of Kallikak and his "normal" wife no doubt benefited from better educational and social opportunities.

Reports such as Goddard's fostered a sterilization movement in the early part of the 20th century (Griffiths, Watson, Lewis, & Stoner, 2004). Fear of intellectual disabilities promoted widespread support for methods that would "control" it, among them sterilization and isolation. Institutions became custodial in order to "protect" society and to prevent reproduction. This was a considerable philosophical backlash because previously there had been at least guarded optimism that institutions would be able to provide education and training. Societal fears, therefore, have influenced the nature, role, and function of such institutions.

With the shift in purpose, people with intellectual disabilities in institutions were viewed as permanent residents. They were not trained for any eventual return to society. Such actions represented the simplistic solution of preventing problem members of society from having children who, in turn, also might become "problem" citizens. With this solution, people could at once both deny responsibility for an undesirable social condition like intellectual disabilities and allow expenditures for the care and well-being of those affected by it.

Although sterilization remains an issue in some circumstances, a reevaluation has been prompted by expansion of the knowledge of heredity and advances in the education of those with intellectual disabilities. The viewpoints related to those with intellectual disabilities are less frequently influenced by inadequate knowledge. Perspectives are still fluid but are more likely influenced by economic priorities combined with society's philosophy about helping others.

DISCIPLINES AND PROFESSIONS

Disciplinary Perspectives and Contributions

The question of what is an intellectual disability seems rather simple, yet it has plagued educators, psychologists, and other professionals for years. Like questions in many areas of behavioral science, its simplicity is deceiving; any complete answer is highly complex.

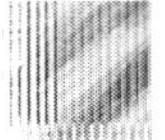

Core Concept

People with intellectual disabilities often need services and supports from many different professionals.

In many ways, people with intellectual disabilities are similar to the individuals without disabilities. Their need for love, independence, support, and respect is the same as everyone else's. Additionally, everyone benefits from the services and contributions of such professions as medicine, education, psychology, sociology, anthropology, and social work. Yet individuals with intellectual disabilities will likely benefit to an even greater degree.

During their lifetimes, citizens with intellectual disabilities likely will receive services from a broader range of professions than those who are not disabled. As children, like Tommy in our opening vignette, they may learn from both general education and special education teachers, while also receiving support from a school psychologist and speech and language specialist. As adolescents or young adults they may interact with these professionals plus others who teach employment. These examples highlight a need to consider the multiple professions involved in the field of intellectual disabilities. The delivery of services and understanding of individuals with intellectual disabilities are far beyond the scope of any single discipline (Hulgin, 2004; Routh & Schroeder, 2003). As a social phenomenon, intellectual disabilities falls within the purview of a number of professions, and many are stakeholders in serving those with this condition (Freeman, 2003; Wagner, 2002).

Core Concept

No single discipline has the breadth and depth of expertise and resources necessary to fully support people who have intellectual disabilities.

Professions are organized naturally around a specific body of knowledge. However, their territories are somewhat arbitrary, and information often crosses disciplinary boundaries. Communication and collaboration are crucial for professionals in all disciplines. This communication process depends on building trust and being committed to information sharing as well as improving the child's program. These are pieces that can be seen in the description of family–professional partnerships in the Tips for Professionals feature.

Societal challenges do not readily align themselves according to the convenience of individual professions. Still, the academic model of establishing a disciplinary focus has been an effective method for building a knowledge base in particular areas. Before addressing the challenge of better interdisciplinary cooperation, we will briefly examine terminology and then explore the contributions of various professions.

Terminology

The term *intellectual disabilities* has a ring of precision to many people; that is, it would seem that a person either has intellectual disabilities or does not. This perceived precision is due, in part, to the scientific orientation of Western culture, in which constancy, regularity, and predictability are assumed. Past definitions of intellectual disabilities show that perceptions of the phenomenon have changed over time. From characterizing intellectual disabilities as a genetically determined and incurable condition, professionals have moved toward a more fluid conceptualization that

Core Concept

The term *intellectual disabilities* encompasses a wide range of characteristics; it is both a label of fact and a label of conjecture.

Tips for Professionals

Summers, Nelson, & Beegle (2001) identified elements that parents and professionals consider important in building positive partnerships. Over 30 focus groups were conducted in North Carolina, Louisiana, and Kansas. Some groups were comprised of only families of children with disabilities, while others included families of children without disabilities. The researchers also conducted focus groups with service providers and held private interviews with families.

These researchers found that "relationships" emerged as the most important thing to most parents and providers. Relationship quality between parents and the service provider(s) was key to the success of the partnership. They identified six factors as being crucial to the success of the relationship of the service provider and the parents. They are:

1. Equality—Parents want equal influence in decisions related to their child. They want the service provider to seek their opinion about the child and the services provided.
2. Communications—This involves the sharing of resources, being open and honest, avoiding "jargon" in an attempt to maintain clarity in the sharing of information, and a service provider who is willing to listen as well as talk.
3. Commitment—Parents respond well to service providers who give the extra measure of service to the family. They like people who go the extra mile.
4. Trust—Families want to be sure their child is safe both physically and emotionally (confidentiality). Also, they want to be able to count on the service provider to follow through on what they say.
5. Skills—Parents desire a service provider who makes things happen for their child. They want to see progress being made, needs being met. They want the service provider to have the needed training and be able to use it to help their child.
6. Respect—Parents want the service provider to respect and value both them and their child. The service provider must treat parent and child politely and courteously regardless of race, religion, or economic class.

These researchers emphasized that relationships have to be nurtured and grown. It takes effort on the part of all parties to build good partnership relationships. Each participant should examine his on her role in the relationship and find ways to emphasize the most important activities.

Source: Adapted from "Family-Professional Partnerships: Win-Win Benefits for Parents, Students, and Teachers" by J. A. Summers, L. L. Nelson, and G. P. Beegle, 2001. *CEC Today*. Retrieved from http://www.cec.sped.org/bk/cec_today/may-june_2001/index.html.

includes biomedical causes as well as environmental and social factors in determining whether someone has or does not have intellectual disabilities at a given time (American Association on Mental Retardation [AAMR], 2002; Wehmeyer & Garner, 2003). This change is the result of a number of factors, including advances in the natural and social sciences, economics, and the use of less pejorative terms.

The term *intellectual disabilities* is an encompassing one that includes a wide range of behavior. It shares with other such "people-labeling terms" the attribute of being a convenient, generalized expression about persons or groups (Hardman, Drew, & Egan, 2006). Intellectual disabilities is both a label of fact and a label of conjecture. A label of fact must be quantifiable and verifiable, whereas a label of

Professionals from different disciplines need to work as team members with parents to plan appropriate services for children with intellectual disabilities.

conjecture may include concepts that are as yet only hypothesized. As a label of fact, intellectual disabilities must demonstrate observed characteristics that are verifiable and quantifiable, perhaps determined by biomedical diagnosis. Down syndrome, Tay-Sachs disease, and anencephaly are examples of conditions that can be verified through observation and medical techniques, although existing tests can quantify only approximate intelligence levels. Only about 20% of intellectual disabilities is caused by biomedical factors, however. For the remaining 80%, the actual cause is uncertain. Therefore, intellectual disabilities is also a label of conjecture. The influence of environment has been a major source for speculation because the incidence of milder forms of intellectual disabilities is much higher for people from lower socioeconomic backgrounds.

The framework that a discipline uses to describe intellectual disabilities affects society's perception of the nature and extent of the challenge. A technologically oriented society, such as that in the United States, responds to "breakthroughs," "cures," and "innovations" much more enthusiastically than it does to the social complexity and ambiguous nature of cultural challenges. The so-called natural sciences, on the one hand, tend to be more favored by people from such countries because the results seem more tangible and dramatic. Social sciences, on the other hand, are viewed with more caution because they work with the more fluid values, perceptions, and beliefs of society.

Eye on Technology

Information Technology to Help Manage Services?

Information technology (IT) has been identified as a means of helping coordinate service delivery among agencies for those with intellectual disabilities. In this context, the need and the potential application of IT involves the exchange of information, including budgets, procurement or purchasing of data and sources, a coordinated and common access point (easily accessed one-stop shopping for the parent or caregiver), coordinated or even collaborative planning processes, and others. The need is rapid and easy communication both among agencies and between users of services and those who deliver them. IT tools can facilitate this process, and questions are being raised regarding the system architecture that can best accomplish this (Holburn et al., 2004; Lenton et al., 2004; Liu, 2004). Such questions are important, but they not the core issues, nor the solutions. Technology will not solve the needs; people will.

Anyone who has ever participated in interagency collaboration knows only too well the challenges involved. While it is fashionable to suggest that IT will resolve the communication problems, such solutions will not function if the root cause(s) of interagency territorialism is unresolved. The following list barely scratches the surface:

1. Agencies and professionals from different disciplinary groups are in competition with one another for funding, and to the degree that one succeeds, another often has funding reduced.
2. Agencies, and particularly professionals, sometimes feed off interagency competition for personal esteem and self-fulfillment. While most managers in both private and public sectors want their employees to have a high level of job ownership to promote productivity, that same ownership should be centered on serving the client rather than accomplishing an agency triumph over another agency that should be working together to deliver service.
3. Agencies and professionals often worry about sharing client information because of privacy issues. While this is an important matter, it may be used as an unnecessary and artificial roadblock to client-centered delivery of service.

It is easy to make the case that IT can help resolve interagency communication challenges. It is true that IT can be a helpful tool, but it will not solve the problems that exist. As professionals that have been involved in enterprisewide IT activities, we have found that solutions for communication and resulting cooperation or collaboration lie in the people undertaking the effort. If they are unwilling to work together, technology will not function. If they fail to turn on the equipment and input the appropriate content (information), IT cannot do any work. People solve problems; technology can help, but not by itself.

The orientation of a discipline affects its view of people with intellectual disabilities. Physicians look for medical causes, psychologists seek psychological factors, and sociologists are interested in group influences on the behavior of individuals. Each discipline, at least initially, sees a person with intellectual disabilities from its own perspective. Such a view should not, however, preclude different professions from at least being aware of and appreciating the contributions of their colleagues in related areas. Full and effective service delivery requires interdisciplinary and interagency collaboration (Holburn, Jacobson, Schwartz, Flory, & Vietze, 2004; Lenton,

Franck, & Salt, 2004; McDonnell, Hardman, & McDonnell, 2003). Facilitating such collaboration requires an explicit decision to promote cooperation and communication among the agencies providing service to those with intellectual disabilities. Information technology (IT) as seen in the Eye on Technology feature, represents a tool with powerful potential for helping with complex information (Ashbaugh, 2001). However, tools are only as helpful as the people that use them. The focus must be on the core issues and problems to be solved, not on the technology itself.

Contributions of Biological and Medical Sciences

Core Concept

The medical profession has a long history of involvement in the field of intellectual disabilities.

An intellectual disability as a label of fact is best exemplified by an identifiable condition that is most frequently related to a biomedical cause. However, even when the condition is readily identifiable, the cause is not always clear. For example, some chromosomal abnormalities are not always inherited (Down syndrome, microcephaly), and environmental factors, such as lead poisoning and infection, can contribute to or even cause neurological problems.

Medical professionals have long been involved with intellectual disabilities in a number of ways. A physician is frequently the first professional to identify, diagnose, and counsel parents of children with intellectual disabilities. When diminished intellectual ability is evident at birth, as in the more severe cases caused by birth trauma or by a congenital condition, a physician is usually the first professional consulted.

It is not unusual for physicians to view intellectual disabilities from a physiological perspective. Although changes in this viewpoint are evident in the medical field, physicians frequently have not had sufficient background to understand the nonmedical ramifications of this condition. This limited view may limit their effectiveness in working with the family. It certainly deters them from providing effective parent counseling, which often has been one of their tasks. Recent changes in medical training, however, promise considerable improvement in the physician's knowledge.

Medical research is another important area of medicine that warrants attention. Advances in medical research have had a dramatic impact in several areas related to intellectual disabilities (e.g., Hall & Marteau, 2003; Meininger, 2003; Sander & Castro, 2004). Because of intense efforts in investigating clinical syndromes, such as phenylketonuria and hypoparathyroidism, it has become possible to implement procedures that prevent some forms of intellectual disabilities. To reach this point, however, interdisciplinary collaboration was required. Once medical research had located the causal factor, it became necessary to turn to those skilled in chemistry and nutrition to implement preventive measures.

Advances in genetics have opened avenues that will allow professionals to prevent many forms of intellectual disabilities (e.g., Spinath, Harlaar, Ronald, & Plomin, 2004). Both positive and negative outcomes of such progress must be considered; such a process calls for input from multiple professions. At present, some forms of intellectual disabilities are preventable before conception. Prospective parents who may be carriers of defective genes can undergo genetic screening and receive counseling regarding the likelihood of their having offspring with the defect. Parents at risk then are faced with the decision of whether to have children. Similar options currently are available to parents who have conceived but face the probability of giving birth to an infant with the defect. Many moral and social issues surrounding such decisions are being debated nationally in legal and ethical forums as well as in the basic sciences.

Psychiatry has a lengthy history of dealing with intellectual disabilities. When the American Association on Mental Deficiency (AAMD, now the AAMR) was organized in 1876, it began with eight charter members, all psychiatrists. Psychiatrists, when they have dealt with intellectual disabilities, have focused primarily on those individuals who are more severely involved. This practice has resulted in a limited view of the spectrum of intellectual disabilities. Past approaches also have tended to operate from a curative, traditional medical model. In view of such a posture, it is little wonder that the psychiatric profession in general has become somewhat discouraged and disinterested in disabilities. Leaders and progressive thinkers in psychiatry, however, have advocated a shift away from the microscopic approaches of the past. Within the discipline there is considerable hope that territories will become less rigidly marked, which would be a potentially positive shift for more adequate delivery of services and supports.

Contributions of the Behavioral Sciences

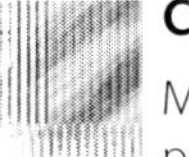

Core Concept

Many behavioral sciences, particularly psychology, have been concerned with intellectual disabilities.

Behavioral sciences have also made many important contributions to the understanding and treatment of intellectual disabilities (e.g., Mumley, Tillbrook, & Grisson, 2003; Neihart, 2003; Wagner, 2002). Most, however, have dealt with it in only a limited fashion. Each field generally has operated independently and within the confines of its own terminology and parameters. The consequent reduction in effective contributions to education about and treatment of intellectual disabilities exemplifies the importance of interdisciplinary collaboration. Still, each of the behavioral fields has added to our store of knowledge about intellectual disabilities.

Psychology has been the behavioral science most directly involved in the scientific study of intellectual disabilities. Three important areas to which psychology has contributed are (a) intelligence theory and testing, (b) learning theory research, and (c) interpersonal social aspects (e.g., Brinkley, Newman, & Widiger, 2004; Laws & Gunn, 2004; van Vonderen, 2004). Knowledge about intellectual disabilities would not have progressed as far without the data and knowledge generated by experimental psychology. Likewise, the testing and evaluation provided by psychometric researchers and school psychologists have long been a part of the overall picture in providing programs for children with intellectual disabilities and other disabilities (Batshaw, 2001; Katims, 2001; White, 2000). This discipline, however, like others, frequently has operated independently, within the confines of its own terminology and perspective.

Historically, anthropology has focused relatively little attention on intellectual disabilities. Yet it has offered some extremely important insights into the broader perspective of the condition (Gonzalez, 2004). Early work by Edgerton (1968) described the anthropological study of intellectual disabilities as nonexistent and argued for drastically expanded efforts. Edgerton's continued effort (e.g., 2001) represents important anthropological contributions and has added considerable information about the adaptation of people with intellectual disabilities to their environments. Although the limited data provided by anthropologists are important in and of themselves, the research approach has far-reaching implications in other ways and the study of cultural elements of intellectual disabilities for other professions (e.g., Gonzalez, 2004; Kane, Avila, & Rogers, 2001).

Anthropology offers some intriguing possibilities from the standpoint of research methodology. The major anthropological approach to research represents qualitative research methods, emphasizing the observation and recording of information about people in their natural environment (Gelfand & Drew, 2003; Gonzalez, 2004). This is a substantially different approach from that historically used in the study of intellectual disabilities. Often researchers have emphasized the research methods of experimental psychology, which studies the person in an artificial laboratory situation. Consequently, relatively little is known about the performance or adaptation of individuals with intellectual disabilities in a variety of natural environments. Anthropological research using qualitative methodology provides useful information to complement the existing knowledge base. Educational planning in particular might profit substantially from qualitative research generating knowledge about how people with diminished intellectual abilities operate in a natural setting (Holburn & Vietze, 2002; Mertens, 2004; Sofaer, 2005). Thus, anthropology is a discipline that has not been broadly involved in intellectual disabilities but one that may make substantial contributions in an interdisciplinary effort.

Sociology has been investigating intellectual disabilities, at least tangentially, for a number of years. A number of authors have examined disabilities from sociological perspectives and concepts of social competence and deviance (Greenwood, Walker, & Utley, 2002; Hardman et al., 2006; Pillay, 2003). In many cases, these authors discuss the need to view disabilities from a sociological perspective rather than from the traditional clinical model. Such issues should become increasingly important in the years ahead as the world continues to face the complex challenges of intellectual disabilities. But the full contribution of sociology to the understanding of intellectual disabilities in a larger societal framework remains untapped.

The law has also been an important force in the area of intellectual disabilities. The legal profession, in comparison to other professions, tends to operate in an adversarial role. The case of *Covarrubias v. San Diego Unified School District* (1971), which challenged special class placements, offers an example of the legal role. In this case, an injunction negated further placements until procedural changes had been made. Only recently have collaborative alliances been formed between the legal and other professions (Kinsler, Saxman, & Fishman, 2004; Luckasson, 2001).

The preceding discussion of selected professions has both given examples of disciplinary perspectives and stressed the absence of interaction between professions. We could easily have selected other areas for inclusion because of their attention (or lack of it) to intellectual disabilities.

Contributions of Education

Core Concept

Education has been integrally involved with the challenges associated with intellectual disabilities.

Many areas have contact, as need or interest arises, with individuals who have intellectual disabilities. However, education—specifically, special education—is involved perhaps more comprehensively by virtue of its nature and delegated role in society. Educators do not have the luxury of viewing the world from a restricted framework or retreating behind disciplinary fences when faced with the multidisciplinary needs of those with intellectual disabilities (Hardman et al., 2006). The role of education in intellectual disabilities is primarily one of providing effective research-based instruction (e.g., Bates, Cuvo, Miner, & Korabek, 2001; Calhoon & Fuchs, 2003; Stokes, Cameron, & Dorsey, 2004). The contributions of education in aiding the understanding of intellectual disabilities has been to (a) identify needs, (b) stimulate research and theory, and (c) coordinate and deliver instruction and related services.

Identifying children with intellectual disabilities was one of the earliest efforts of education. The first intelligence test worthy of the name was developed by Alfred Binet at the request of the French minister of public education. The task was to develop a way to determine which children are likely to fail in school programs and, thus, need special help; therefore, the measurement of intelligence has been influenced largely by educational needs rather than by the interests of the discipline. Over the years, first educators and then theorists and test makers recognized that social factors were also important in determining a child's present and future performance levels. Professionals have since been introduced to the concepts of adaptive behavior and social intelligence. The involvement of education in intellectual disabilities greatly facilitated the development of these and other constructs. In other areas, the great strides in differential diagnosis, individualization of instruction, task analysis, and contingency management techniques were enhanced by educators and their interest in providing better services for students with intellectual disabilities. For example, the need to understand mild intellectual disabilities has influenced research efforts to increase knowledge about the importance of environmental influences on intelligence. The development of secondary school programs has created a need for appropriate curricula and has prompted research on many different factors related to community placement for adolescents and young adults with intellectual disabilities (e.g., Clark, Olympia, Jensen, Heathfield, & Jenson, 2004; Robertson et al., 2004).

Without proactive recognition of the needs of those with intellectual disabilities, educators would not be where they are today in either understanding or providing services. Educators often have been a catalyst core, stimulating the efforts of the disciplines and then using their findings for the betterment of society.

Core Concept

To better support individuals with intellectual disabilities, professionals must coordinate efforts and involve the family.

Disciplinary Collaboration

Our discussion thus far outlined a number of disciplinary perspectives. It is evident that isolated efforts within a profession, without interdisciplinary collaboration, often result in less effective service delivery to people with intellectual disabilities. Although change has been slow, the different professions are making progress toward bridging the gaps among their perspectives. At least two factors have prompted this progress. First, experience has shown that people with intellectual disabilities being served are the ultimate beneficiaries of improved cooperation. Improvements in service have provided a considerable impetus toward increasing cooperation. A second factor promoting change is the realization that something can actually be done to promote interdisciplinary collaboration (Bronstein & Abramson, 2003; Dosser, Handron, McCammon, Powell, & Spencer, 2001; Holburn et al., 2004). When knowledge is limited to a single field, differences in perspective result. The acquisition of enough information to understand another perspective broadens professional viewpoints and focuses efforts on the person needing service. Fortunately, advances are being made in collaboration, although much remains to be accomplished (Bronstein & Abramson, 2003; Holburn et al., 2004).

Beyond the professional and discipline level, similar cooperative efforts are essential in state service and political arenas. Agencies frequently compete for limited funds to operate their programs, and lobbying techniques may aim to improve the lot of one group but do so at the expense of another. Unfortunately, the real reason for agency operation may be overlooked, that is, to serve those citizens with intellectual disabilities. Proper service to citizens with intellectual disabilities requires interagency collaboration.

It is not surprising that interdisciplinary cooperation is also important at the practitioner level—the contact point between the service-delivery system and the person with intellectual disabilities. A teacher needs the school psychologist to provide information that is helpful for instruction in a timely fashion. The psychologist must effectively communicate with the teacher to make the assessment information useful and also to obtain data regarding student behavior and performance in class. The communication is a two-way interaction and, in fact, multidimensional when one considers the information flow between the parents and various professional service providers.

Core Concept

Serving children in an inclusive educational setting emphasizes the need for collaboration among professionals.

Implementing the principle of **inclusion** for all children with disabilities involves placing a significant number of such children in general education classrooms. This approach to educating children with disabilities requires significant collaborative efforts among general and special educators as well as other team members, such as school psychologists. In today's schools, many general education teachers have students with intellectual disabilities placed in their classes. When this has been accomplished properly, it has been based on a thorough functional analysis of the child's skills and abilities along with an examination of the curriculum, personnel, and other elements present in the classroom (Matson et al., 2003; McAdam, DiCesare, Murphy, & Marshall, 2004). For example, one of these elements should involve an assessment of the teacher's strengths and capacity to successfully merge the child into the classroom program. A particular profile of strengths and challenges for both child and teacher may result in differing support planning among various child–teacher dyads. As we analyze the context, information about the family and other environmental elements are included in the planning. This becomes a complex set of variables and emphasizes the crucial nature of effective collaboration among all participants.

CONCEPTS, DEFINITIONS, AND CLASSIFICATION

The remainder of this chapter examines the concepts, definitions, and classification systems of intellectual disabilities. By reviewing the material in this and the following chapters, the reader will have a comprehensive overview of intellectual disabilities. Intellectual disabilities multifaceted challenge education, medicine, psychology, law, society in general, and always the family involved. In this volume, we have attempted to place the concept of intellectual disabilities in its broadest perspective—squarely in the center of human existence—because, above all, it is a human challenge. It cannot be viewed from a narrow focus if one wishes to obtain an accurate and comprehensive perspective.

INTELLECTUAL DISABILITIES AS A CONCEPT

The literature on intellectual disabilities indicates that conceptual issues are complicated and continually evolving (Blacher, 2001; Cuskelly, 2004; Hardman et al., 2006). Over the years definitions have encountered difficulties trying to incorporate advances in conceptual understanding and social progress while attempting to maintain measurement usefulness and accuracy. Clarifying the concept of intellectual disabilities has become more complex as previously unknown factors are taken into account.

Core Concept

The concept of intellectual disabilities is made more complex because the varying professions that deal with it hold widely divergent viewpoints.

Earlier in this chapter, we sketched the long historical interest in intellectual disabilities. References to people with such a condition are found in the ancient history of various civilizations, which raises some interesting questions about definitions (Brady, 2001; Carpenter, 2000). If people have been studying it for so long, why does confusion about classification and definition still remain?

Many factors contribute to this lack of precision. Intellectual disabilities always implies a reduced level of intellectual capacity, and the concept of intelligence has played a central but variable role in defining intellectual disabilities (Kittler, Krinsky-McHale, & Devenny, 2004; Wehmeyer & Garner, 2003). Every controversy about the nature of intelligence has a direct impact on the field of intellectual disabilities. Thus part of the difficulty in defining intellectual disabilities relates to the notion of permanence and measurement of intelligence. Social competence has also been an important element of most recent definitions of intellectual disabilities. Relationships between intelligence and social competence have varied considerably across different definition and classification schemes (Routh & Schroeder, 2003; Switzky, 2001).

Intellectual disabilities has always been an area of interest and study for many professions. This has also contributed to the challenges of definitional and conceptual clarity. Psychiatrists, sociologists, psychologists, educators, anthropologists, and others—each with their own perspective and language—have all studied the challenges of intellectual disabilities. The various definitions and classification systems of these disciplines tend to focus on the constructs of a particular profession rather than on the affected individual. Sociologists set out to study intellectual disabilities as a social challenge, psychologists examine it as a psychological condition, physicians treat it as a medical condition, and so on. Even wide variations are evident within professional areas, such as clinical, developmental, and experimental psychology. We do not deny the value of a multidisciplinary approach; in fact, we strongly subscribe to its value. We do, however, assert that the central focus—the individual with intellectual disabilities—is in danger of being ignored. We will present intellectual disabilities from a multidisciplinary perspective while focusing on the individual.

Preparation of professionals who work with those having intellectual disabilities has been hampered by definitional issues. Education and training is much more difficult in the absence of a concept of intellectual disabilities that is logical, theoretically sound, and yet functional in field settings. While significant sophistication has developed in some technical aspects of programming for children (e.g., diagnosis, behavior management), the lack of an effective general concept of intellectual disabilities has impeded the overall progress of service delivery. Professional expertise often consists of a great deal of technical skill in certain areas but with limited knowledge about individuals with intellectual disabilities in their total environment. Efforts are now under way to formulate conceptual frameworks that will facilitate more effective professional preparation. Individuals with intellectual disabilities must be viewed as developing human beings with varying needs and characteristics, living in a fluid and complex society.

From our viewpoint, human development is an excellent framework for examining intellectual disabilities. Human development serves effectively across disciplines, causes, and the full range of human life. This book rests on the development conceptual cornerstone. As you read this volume, you will find that its overall structure is the life cycle, from conception through old age. Certain topics tend to stand somewhat alone, and in most cases you will find minidiscussions of those topics in the context of development. We hope that the perspective of human development will be as useful and interesting to you as it has been to us.

INTELLECTUAL DISABILITIES: A DEFINITION IN TRANSITION

Definitions of intellectual disabilities have varied widely over the years among disciplines. The definition of intellectual disabilities is currently in a transition period. Similarly, the language being employed is evolving with different descriptions of this complex condition. The various definitions include those of the American Association on Mental Retardation (AAMR), the American Psychiatric Association (APA), and the Individuals with Disabilities Education Act. Recent definitions published by the AAMR (2002) and APA (2000) reflect similar views of intellectual disabilities.

Core Concept

The 2002 AAMR definition employs intellectual functioning and adaptive behavior.

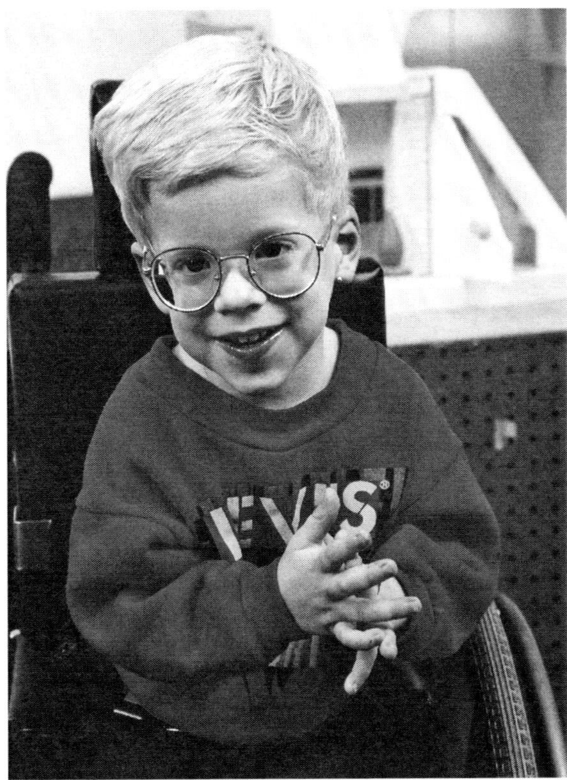

Intellectual disabilities is a human problem that affects this child and all of us.

The AAMR definition of intellectual disabilities states that

> Mental retardation is a disability characterized by significant limitations both in intellectual functioning and in adaptive behavior as expressed in conceptual, social, and practical adaptive skills. This disability originates before age 18. (AAMR, 2002, p. 1).

Add to this definition five assumptions that are essential considerations in applying the definition:

> *Assumption 1.* Limitations in present functioning must be considered within the context of community environments typical of the individual's age peers and culture. This means that the standards against which the individual's functioning must be measured are typical community-based environments. . . . Typical community environments include homes, neighborhoods, schools, businesses, and other environments in which people of similar age ordinarily live, play, work, and interact. The concept of age peers should also include people of the same cultural or linguistic background.
>
> *Assumption 2.* Valid assessment considers cultural and linguistic diversity as well as differences in communication, sensory, motor, and behavioral factors. This means that in order for assessment to be meaningful, it must take into account

> the individual's diversity and unique response factors. The individual's culture or ethnicity, including language spoken at home, nonverbal communication, and customs that might influence assessment results, must be considered in making a valid assessment.
>
> *Assumption 3.* Within an individual, limitations often coexist with strengths. This means that people with mental retardation are complex human beings who likely have certain gifts as well as limitations. Like all people, they often do some things better than other things. . . . These may include strengths in social or physical capabilities, strengths in some adaptive skill areas, or strengths in one aspect of an adaptive skill in which they otherwise show an overall limitation.
>
> *Assumption 4.* An important purpose of describing limitations is to develop a profile of needed supports. This means that merely analyzing someone's limitations is not enough, and that specifying limitations should be a team's first step in developing a description of the supports the individual needs in order to improve functioning.
>
> *Assumption 5.* With appropriate personalized supports over a sustained period, the life functioning of the person with mental retardation generally will improve. This means that if appropriate personalized supports are provided to an individual with mental retardation, improved functioning should result. A lack of improvement in functioning can serve as a basis for reevaluating the profile of needed supports. In rare circumstances, however, even appropriate supports may merely maintain functioning or stop or limit regression. . . . Improvement in functioning should be expected from appropriate supports, except in rare cases. (AAMR, 2002, pp. 8–9).

This definition and the expansion provided by its assumptions stress the functioning of a person with intellectual disabilities within home, school, and community environments. The 2002 AAMR definition document emphasizes environmental circumstances that may influence an individual's performance level, such as language or ethnic differences and the development of an effective support plan.

The importance of adaptive behavior and inclusion in the community (with supports) has been evident in the intellectual disabilities literature for some time. However, the **measurement** of adaptive behavior has always been a challenge, not achieving the desired precision despite significant and continuing research efforts (e.g., Cuskelly, 2004; McBrien, 2003). Adaptive behavior is a very important concept in the most recent AAMR definition. Concerns about assessment accuracy continue, as do apprehensions regarding implementation and growing evidence regarding overrepresented ethnic minorities among those diagnosed with intellectual disabilities (Gelfand & Drew, 2003; Hatton, 2002; Moore, Feist-Price, & Alston, 2002). Response to these concerns is reflected in the narrative of the 2002 AAMR definition; future implementation of this definition will determine the degree to which it can be translated into effective action.

Including adaptive behavior in definitions of intellectual disabilities first occurred during the early 1960s and represented a rather dramatic broadening of formally stated criteria. Professionals had largely ignored adaptive behavior in previous definitions, depending almost exclusively on measured intelligence in defining intellectual disabilities. Individuals' behaviors are considered adaptive to the degree they manage personal needs, display social competence, and avoid problem behaviors (Blair, 2003; Goodman, 2003; McHale, Dariotis, & Kauh, 2003).

The AAMR definition focuses adaptive behavior assessment by specifying that it be "expressed in conceptual, social, and practical adaptive skills" (AAMR, 2002, p. 1). The manifestation of the adaptive behavior skills emphasizes how well an individual actually shows adaptation in the context of his or her environment. Diagnosing an individual as having intellectual disabilities using this definition means that the assessment of adaptive behavior must focus on the expression of adapting in practical terms. This requires some significant assumptions about adaptation and its measurement, as summarized in Table 1–1.

Table 1–1
2002 AAMR Adaptive Behavior Assumptions

- Adaptive behavior is a construct that has multiple domains.
- No existing measure of adaptive behavior completely measures all adaptive behavior domains.
- For a person with mental retardation, adaptive behavior limitations are generalized across domains of conceptual, social, and practical skills.
- Some adaptive behaviors are particularly difficult to measure using a rating scale and are not contained on existing standardized instruments.
- Low intellectual abilities may be responsible for problems in acquiring adaptive behavior skills as well as the appropriate use of skills that have been learned.
- Assessment about typical behavior for the individual requires information that goes beyond what can be observed in a formal testing situation.
- It is unlikely that a single standardized measure of adaptive behavior can adequately represent an individual's ability to adapt to the everyday demands of living independently.
- Maladaptive behavior is not a characteristic or dimension of adaptive behavior, although it often influences the acquisition and performance of adaptive behavior.
- Adaptive behavior must be examined in the context of all developmental periods.
- Adaptive behavior scores must be examined in the context of the individual's own culture.
- Limitations in adaptive behavior should be considered in light of the four other dimensions of:
    - Intellectual abilities
    - Participation, interactions, and social roles
    - Health
    - Context

Source: Adapted from *Mental Retardation: Definition, Classification, and Systems of Supports* (10th ed., pp. 74–75). Washington, DC: American Association on Mental Retardation. Copyright 2002 by the American Association on Mental Retardation, by permission.

Figure 1–1
Graphic Conceptualization of the 2002 AAMR Definition of Intellectual Disabilities

Source: From *Mental Retardation: Definition. Classification, and Systems of Supports* (10th ed., p. 10). Washington, DC: American Association on Mental Retardation. Copyright 2002 by the American Association on Mental Retardation, by permission.

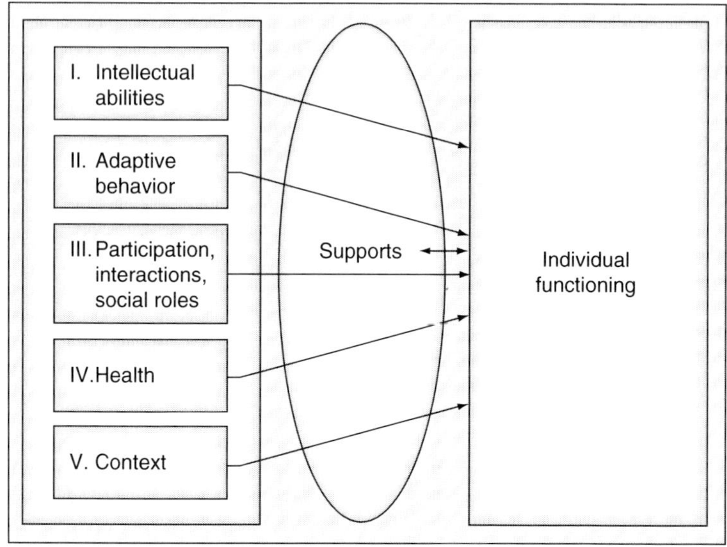

One perspective of a person with intellectual disabilities is a person who relies on some protection and support from the family or community. Two factors usually enter into this perception: (a) the deficits or level of functioning of the individual with intellectual disabilities and (b) the threshold of community tolerance. The kind of action taken depends on the degree to which an individual deviates significantly from community norms—from those zones of behavior or performance society deems acceptable. The 2002 AAMR definition conceptualizes intellectual disabilities in this manner: in the context of his or her environment and the supports that are in place. Figure 1–1 captures the framework graphically.

People with intellectual disabilities often come to the attention of someone in their community because they act or look differently enough from the norm to be noticeable. This is true regardless of the degree of disability. Identification of the individual with a more severe disability may occur at birth or very early in life. This identification usually happens because a physical or behavioral anomaly is already evident at this stage of development. For those who differ less obviously from the norm, identification may not occur until they begin to develop language or enter school. What may have been only parental worries or suspicions may be investigated further through diagnostic evaluation and clinical observation by professional personnel.

Recently, there has been an intense focus on the person with intellectual disabilities within the community. An organization known as TASH (formerly the Association for Persons with Severe Handicaps) has developed advocacy position statements relating to life in community settings and the supports that should be available for inclusive and integrated life in the community (TASH, 2000). Although these perspectives are based on philosophies of civil rights, dignity, and social justice, they are also aligned with human development research that has emerged over the years. TASH supports realistic life in the general community, inclusive and early educational experiences, as well as promoting quality and best practices in all services, and the development of inclusive public policy on health care matters (TASH, 2004).

Another important organization working in intellectual disabilities is the International Association for the Scientific Study of Intellectual Disabilities (IASSID). The IASSID also reflects a perspective that emphasizes issues facing an individual within the community. For example, IASSID sponsors special-interest groups on aging, families, health issues, parenting, and quality of life. These perspectives take the study of intellectual disabilities directly into the community and emerge with some of the same issues facing all of us.

INCIDENCE AND PREVALENCE

Two terms frequently have been confused in the field of intellectual disabilities—**incidence** and **prevalence.** *Incidence* refers to the number of new cases identified during a given time period (often 1 year). Tabulating incidence involves a count of all individuals newly identified as having intellectual disabilities during that period, whether newborns or youngsters diagnosed in school. *Prevalence* refers to all cases existing at a given time, including both newly identified cases and cases still labeled as having intellectual disabilities from some earlier diagnosis. Figure 1–2 illustrates how incidence and prevalence differ and how they relate to each other. Obviously, these two kinds of

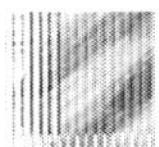

Core Concept

It is important to distinguish between incidence and prevalence and to consider other factors, such as socioeconomic status (SES), severity, and age, when determining how frequently intellectual disabilities occurs.

Figure 1–2
Incidence and Prevalence of Intellectual Disabilities

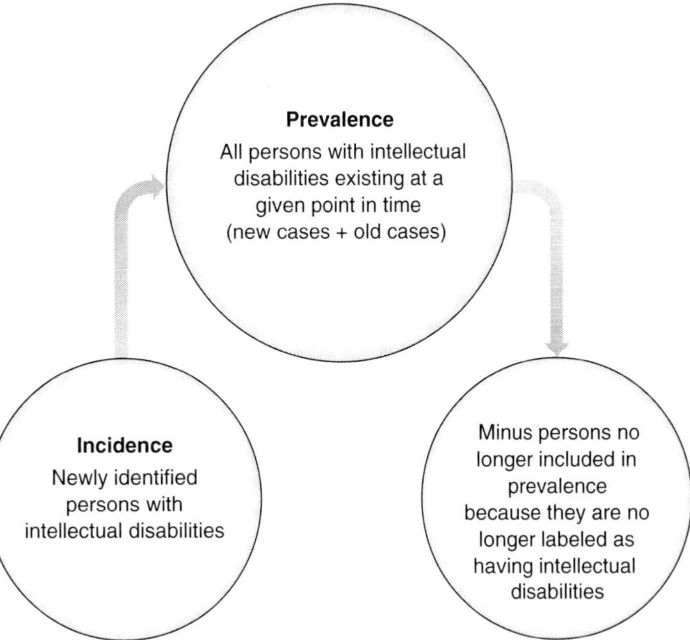

counting do not result in the same number. But the terms have often been used rather loosely, sometimes interchangeably, in the literature. Wherever possible, we examine incidence and prevalence separately.

How frequently do individuals evidence sufficient deviancy to be considered to have intellectual disabilities? A precise answer to this question is difficult to obtain. Accurate accounting is neither easy nor economically feasible. Inconsistent definition and classification schemes over the years have made the problem of determining frequency of intellectual disabilities even more formidable, particularly from a cross-cultural perspective and for those who have other disabilities that are co-occurring (Bradley, Summers, Wood, & Bryson, 2004; Gelfand & Drew, 2003). Estimates of the prevalence of intellectual disabilities in the United States historically have ranged from about 1% to 3% of the general population, with the 3% figure being most consistently cited. In its *24th Annual Report to Congress*, the U.S. Department of Education (2002) estimated that 11% of the children with disabilities (ages 6–21) in U.S. public schools have intellectual disabilities.

Translating estimated U.S. percentages into numbers of individuals with intellectual disabilities is interesting, albeit difficult. According to the U.S. Department of Education (2002), 612,978 youngsters ages 6 to 21 with intellectual disabilities were served under the Individuals with Disabilities Education Act (IDEA) during 2000–2001. Beyond the school years covered by specific federal laws, however, such figures become much more difficult to determine and are based on population projections. The President's Committee on Mental Retardation, now called the President's Committee for People with Intellectual Disabilities (PCPID; 2000), estimated that 6.2 to 7.5 million Americans had intellectual disabilities. Which figures are accurate? We cannot choose with any confidence. In discussing numbers of affected individuals, AAMR (2002) emphasizes that intellectual disabilities is a multidimensional construct and estimates are often focused on a single area, such as intelligence.

Those with a more mild disability represent by far the largest proportion of the intellectual disabilities population. Hardman et al. (2006) estimated that about 0.75% of the total population was mildly affected, which represents about 90% of those diagnosed as having intellectual disabilities. The moderate level of intellectual disabilities is generally thought to involve about 0.3% of the total population, and the severe and profound levels combined account for approximately 0.25%. These figures do not total exactly 3% for a variety of reasons. For example, some individuals have other co-occurring disabilities that are reflected in a primary diagnosis, depending on which seems most prominent to the clinician in a given circumstance. It should be noted that the 2002 AAMR definition does not employ a classification system regarding degree of disability based on IQ level (mild, moderate, severe/profound), electing to focus on the intensities of supports needed. The approach taken suggests varying levels of intensity for the supports needed by an individual with intellectual disabilities. Four intensity levels of supports are outlined in the following manner: (a) *intermittent*—the supports are provided as needed, which is characteristically periodic and for short durations; (b) *limited*—supports are provided more consistently (not intermittently), but they are not typically intense; (c) *extensive*—regular assistance, perhaps daily, is provided in some environments, such as at work, and is not time limited (i.e., long-term support); and (d) *pervasive*—supports are of high intensity, constant, and needed across environments and may be life sustaining in nature (AAMR, 2002, p. 152). It is likely that the prevalence of intellectual disabilities is highest at the intermittent support level and progressively less as one moves toward the pervasive level. However, this definition document has not been available long enough for implementation to provide such information.

Variation is found in the incidence of intellectual disabilities at different chronological ages. Research has indicated consistently that the incidence of intellectual disabilities is highest during the school years, approximately 5 to 18 years of age, with much lower numbers at both preschool and postschool levels. This distribution relates both to the level of disability and to the tasks presented to the individual at different ages. Before children enter the formal school environment, all but the more severely affected can perform as expected. Youngsters identified as having intellectual disabilities before about age 6 are often more seriously involved, reflecting levels of disability that constitute only a small percentage of all individuals with intellectual disabilities. As children enter school, they encounter an emphasis on abstract learning, such as the acquisition of academic skills. In such an environment, children with intellectual disabilities become highly visible because abstract skills make up their area of greatest difficulty. A majority of youngsters identified as having intellectual disabilities at this stage function in the mild range of intellectual deficit. The identification of intellectual disabilities decreases dramatically after formal schooling has ended. A majority of individuals with intellectual disabilities have been identified by the time they leave school. If no one has so identified a person during the school years, when tasks emphasize abstraction, identification is unlikely in less demanding postschool environments.

The prevalence of intellectual disabilities also varies a great deal as a function of age. Across all levels of IQ, the highest prevalence occurs in the 6-to-19 age range—over 97% of those with intellectual disabilities served under IDEA, an estimated 70% of the total population with intellectual disabilities (U.S. Department of Education, 2002). The pattern of prevalence is similar for those with intellectual disabilities but who have IQs of 50 and above, except that an even higher percentage falls in the 6-to-19 age range and smaller percentages in the preschool and postschool ranges. Several factors contribute to this pattern. The years of formal schooling are particularly taxing for those with intellectual disabilities because the tasks require conceptual performance in areas in which they are most deficient. The drop in prevalence after school years is interesting and occurs for reasons related to but somewhat different from incidence influences. After formal education, many individuals with intellectual disabilities (particularly those in the 50+ IQ range) are placed back in an environment where the demands focus less on their areas of greatest difficulty. They seem more able to adapt in the postschool environment. In addition to a lower incidence during postschool years, prevalence also is reduced because some individuals may no longer be functioning as disabled and are thus "declassified." This reduction in prevalence has often been referred to as the phenomenon of "disappearing" or "6-hour" disability (referring to the time spent in

Table 1–2
Intellectual Disability Prevalence per 1,000 School-Age Children by SES and IQ Level

Degree of Impairment	Socioeconomic Status		
	High	**Middle**	**Low**
IQ below 20	1	1	1
IQ 20 to 50	4	4	4
IQ 50 to 75 or 80	10	25	50
IQ 75 or 80 to 90	50	170	300

Note: IQ ranges are given for the convenience of the reader. They represent ranges that vary to some degree, depending on the source of data.

school each day). This may indicate that the school curriculum is out of phase with later life and may not represent effective education, at least for these people. The prevalence patterns also differ as a function of age for the lower IQ ranges. A much lower rate of prevalence occurs in children between the ages of 6 and 19. This pattern is influenced by a higher incidence during the early years of life and a higher mortality rate among more severely affected individuals when they are young.

Finally, intellectual disabilities prevalence also varies across different levels of Socioeconomic Status (SES). Various estimates have suggested considerable prevalence differences as a function of SES and degree of impairment. Table 1–2 presents a summary of approximate prevalence rates of intellectual disability per 1,000 school-age children by SES level and IQ level. As indicated in Table 1–2, no difference appears in prevalence as a function of SES level at the two lower levels of functioning (IQ 20–50 and below 20). The two higher levels of functioning (IQ 50–75 or 80 and IQ 75 or 80–90), however, show an increasing prevalence as SES decreases. These figures suggest that in the lower levels of intellectual disabilities, where greater central nervous system damage pervades, different SES levels are equally vulnerable. The prevalence of milder impairments seems more sensitive to environmental influences. Because the majority of individuals with intellectual disability are mildly impaired, the social dimensions of intellectual disabilities stand out.

Core Concept
Multiple classification systems are used by the 2002 AAMR definition document to address grouping individuals by (a) service reimbursement or funding, (b) research services, and (c) communication about selected characteristics. These classification systems are based, for example, "on the intensities of needed supports, etiology, levels of measured intelligence, or levels of assessed adaptive behavior" (AAMR, 2002, p. 99).

CLASSIFICATION

Classification schemes for intellectual disabilities have varied over the years in much the same fashion that definitions have. Before the 1990s, the AAMR classification focused primarily on two major parameters: (a) severity of the disability and (b) causation or etiology. Terminology such as *mild*, *moderate*, and *severe* or *profound intellectual disabilities* related primarily to disability severity with respect to both measured intelligence and adaptive behavior. Etiology classification was based mainly on the biomedical causes of intellectual disabilities (e.g., infection,

Effective assessment must use a variety of types of measurement, often including observation of specific skills.

trauma, metabolism, nutrition). The two parameters of severity and etiology have been so prominent in the field of intellectual disabilities that some have claimed they have actually generated two distinct research cultures—one focusing on etiology and one on severity of impairment (Gelfand & Drew, 2003; Hardman et al., 2006).

The *Diagnostic and Statistical Manual of Mental Disorders* (*DSM–IV–TR*) classification system continues to describe those with intellectual disabilities in terms of degrees of severity that reflect the measured level of intellectual functioning (APA, 2000). Four degrees of severity are employed, with a fifth category reflecting situations in which the person's intelligence is untestable. As outlined in *DSM–IV–TR*, these severity classifications are as follows: (a) mild intellectual disabilities, with IQ levels of 50–55 to approximately 70; (b) moderate intellectual disabilities, with IQ levels of 35–40 to 50–55; (c) severe intellectual disabilities, with IQ levels of 20–25 to 35–40; (d) profound intellectual disabilities, with IQ levels below 20 or 25; and (e) intellectual disabilities, severity unspecified, for which a strong presumption of intellectual disabilities exists but the individual's intelligence is not testable by use of standard instruments. This latter category exists for circumstances in which the person functions at a level too low for testing, is uncooperative, or is too young for reliable assessment, such as infants (APA, 2000, pp. 42–43). This classification varies from that of the AAMR (2002), which does not employ such terms as *mild*, *moderate*, *severe*, and *profound* to suggest degree of intellectual impairment. A measured IQ of "approximately two standard deviations below the mean" is set as the ceiling by AAMR with caveats that consideration be given to the error of measurement for the instrument used and the instrument's strengths and limitations (2002, p. 58). The AAMR also gives attention to other dimensions of functioning.

With the publication of its 2002 manual, the AAMR expanded the dimensions considered in assessing intellectual disabilities. Five dimensions are outlined and intended for use in the processes of diagnosing, classifying, and determining what support is needed for an individual: (a) Dimension I—intellectual abilities; (b) Dimension II—adaptive behavior (conceptual, social, and practical skills); (c) Dimension III—participation, interactions, and social roles; (d) Dimension IV—health (physical health, mental health, and etiological factors); and Dimension V—context (environments and culture). These dimensions provide the overall organizing concept for examining someone suspected of having intellectual disabilities.

A diagnosis of intellectual disabilities means an individual is determined to have intelligence and adaptive behavior that are significantly below average and that this was found before age 18, which is considered to be the developmental period by the AAMR (2002). Assessments of intelligence and adaptive behavior are characteristically done individually for diagnosis purposes and always involve clinical judgment on many factors related to the assumptions of the definition. As noted, intelligence that falls two standard deviations below the mean is viewed as the upper level for a diagnosis of intellectual disabilities. Adaptive behavior is conceived as including conceptual, social, and practical skill areas, which include the example skills outlined in Table 1–3.

Assessment of adaptive behavior has always been a concern. The 2002 AAMR definition document notes that particular attention must be paid to this issue. The purpose of the diagnosis (e.g., service eligibility, funding) must be considered as

Table 1–3
Example Skills in AAMR Adaptive Behavior Areas

Adaptive Behavior Area	Example Skill
Conceptual	Language Reading and writing Money concepts Self-direction
Social	Interpersonal Responsibility Self-esteem Gullibility Naïveté Follows rules Obeys laws Avoids victimization
Practical	Activities of daily living Occupational skills Maintains safe environments

Source: Adapted from *Mental Retardation: Definition, Classification, and Systems of Supports* (10th ed., p. 82). Washington, DC: American Association on Mental Retardation. Copyright 2002 by the American Association on Mental Retardation, by permission.

assessment is undertaken. Adaptive behavior measurement must also be done in a technically adequate manner that is appropriate for the person being evaluated. Furthermore, the AAMR asserts explicitly that multiple assessment approaches will be required to adequately evaluate the full spectrum of individuals needing assessment (2002).

The final step in the AAMR's diagnosis, classification, and program planning process involves developing a plan of the supports needed by the person with intellectual disabilities. This framework for diagnosis, classification, and planning builds on the multiple dimensions of the definition, employs the varying assessment protocols appropriate for the person, and plans the supports in terms of intensity and context in which the individual lives. Table 1–4 summarizes the framework for assessment and use of tools to develop the indivdual's family service plan, education program, transition, and other planning to provide appropriate services (AAMR, 2002).

CROSS-CATEGORICAL ISSUES

Intellectual disabilities is one category among several that refer to atypical conditions involving ability or behavior. Others include such examples as learning disabilities and behavioral disorders or emotional disturbance, among many more. The use of such categories has had a long history among professionals working in the various fields of disabilities. Considerable interest has emerged in the literature regarding perspectives on disabilities that cross traditional categorical boundaries—often called "cross-categorical views." Some authors contend that traditional categories fail to adequately distinguish among different disability conditions and do not serve the needs of individuals from a service-delivery standpoint. In contrast, some believe that cross-categorical views are not functional and see the traditional categories as being more appropriate. The issues of categorical and cross-categorical approaches to defining disabilities have received substantial attention and continue to be controversial (Biklen & Schein, 2001; Hardman et al., 2006; Thelen, Burns, & Christiansen, 2003).

Core Concept

Cross-categorical definition and classification models have emerged because conventional categories are not always effective and functional.

Interest in cross-categorical definitions arose primarily because, in certain circumstances, the traditional categories did not clearly distinguish among people with disorders carrying different labels. In some instances, those with disparate categorical labels did not appear all that different; they seemed to have a number of characteristics in common. Additionally, treatment or interventions for some individuals with different labels appeared to be quite similar or at least to have a number of similar elements. What has become evident is that categorical labels for various disabilities are functional for some purposes with some conditions but that for other circumstances do not serve well (Angermeyer & Schulze, 2001; Barlow, 2004; Baum & Olenchak, 2002). It is important to consider the purposes and uses of definition and classification schemes.

Cross-categorical models have often been based on the concept of symptom severity with terminology such as *mild learning and behavior disorders*, *moderate*

Table 1–4
AAMR Framework for Assessment, Classification, and Planning

Function	Purposes	Measures and Tools	Considerations for Assessment
Diagnosis	Establishing eligibility: • Services • Benefits • Legal protections	IQ tests[a] Adaptive behavior scales[a] Documented age of onset[a]	Match between measures and purpose Psychometric characteristics of measures selected Appropriateness for person (age-group, cultural group, primary language, means of communication, gender, sensorimotor limitations) Qualifications of examiner Examiner characteristics and potential for bias Consistency with professional standards and practices Selection of informants
Classification	Grouping for: • Service reimbursement or funding • Research • Services • Communication about selected characteristics	Support intensity scales IQ ranges or levels Special-education categories Environmental assessments Etiology–risk factor systems Levels of adaptive behavior Mental health measures Funding levels Benefits categories	Relevant context and environments Social roles, participation, interactions Opportunities/experiences Clinical and social history Physical and mental factors Behavior in assessment situation Personal goals Team input
Planning Supports	Enhancing personal outcomes: • Independence • Relationships • Contributions • School and community participation • Personal well-being	Person-centered planning tools Self-appraisal Assessment of objective life conditions measures Support intensity scales Required individual plan elements (IFSP, IEP, ITP, IPP, IHP)	

Note: IFSP = individualized family service plan; IEP = individualized education program; ITP = individualized transition plan; IPP = individualized program plan; and IHP = individualized habilitation plan.

[a]Required assessments to establish diagnosis of mental retardation.

Source: From *Mental Retardation Definition, Classification, and Systems of Supports* (10th ed., p. 12), Washington, DC: American Association on Mental Retardation. Copyright 2002 by the American Association on Mental Retardation, by permission.

learning and behavior disorders, and *severe and profound/multiple disorders*. Definitions for such broad categories include a range of ability and behavioral deficits and a variety of assessment approaches. Although any framework of this nature is necessarily general, the focus of this scheme is on functional and behavioral specificity, articulated and evaluated for intervention purposes on an individualized basis (Hardman et al., 2006). It is also clear that cross-categorical models do not supplant conventional categories totally. But where categories do not serve well, cross-categorical models are worthy of consideration.

Cross-categorical models appear most applicable to individuals who are mildly affected by a disability. People with mild behavioral disorders and mild learning disabilities have many shared characteristics. In terms of those with intellectual disabilities, the same can be said when their disability is also mild or the supports needed are less intense, depending on which classification scheme is used. Youngsters at the mild disability level of functioning have a great deal of performance and skill overlap in the classroom regardless of their specific labels. Service delivery from a cross-categorical model, based on functional skills, may be most reasonable for these individuals (Hardman et al., 2006).

More severely involved disabilities have greater distinctiveness, and conventional categories are more relevant. Individuals with moderate to severe disabilities have fewer shared characteristics, although some remain, and these are typically acknowledged by cross-categorical models. Primary disabling conditions are more easily identified as impairment severity increases. People with more severe intellectual disabilities are also more likely to be affected by multiple challenges. This likelihood is particularly true for those at the lowest level of functioning. Those with profound intellectual disabilities have a relatively high incidence of congenital heart disease, epilepsy, respiratory distress, sensory impairments, and poor muscle tone. From a definition or classification standpoint, these are often viewed as associated conditions and would require pervasive supports using the AAMR model (2002). From the perspective of intervention or treatment, each must be addressed on a case-by-case basis. Treatment is the ultimate outcome of any diagnosis and therefore of any definition or classification regardless whether a categorical or cross-categorical approach is used (Barlow, 2004). An appropriate choice of classification scheme depends on the use context.

PURPOSES AND USES OF DEFINITIONS AND CLASSIFICATIONS

There are a variety of reasons for development of definitions and classifications. At times, they provide a conceptual picture of the entity being defined or classified and facilitate communication among professionals. Beyond these roles, however, is the vital reason for defining and classifying: translating statements into action and thereby delivering appropriate service across the lifespan (Blacher, 2001; Hardman et al., 2006).

Core Concept

The purposes and uses of definition and classification schemes must be considered and related to assessment procedures employed and to the impact of labels.

The adequacy with which a classification scheme translates into practice is the acid test of the system. A number of factors influence the ease with which this translation can occur; two are particularly evident from the preceding discussion of definitions and classification. The first is how faithfully a scheme reflects reality; the second relates to how well the purposes or objectives of the group using a classification are served. If a classification or definition is out of touch with actual circumstances, it is of little value and will likely fall into disuse.

One also must consider the second factor: How well served are the purposes or objectives of the group using a scheme? Purposes and objectives have been nearly as numerous and diverse as the professions involved with intellectual disabilities. Many past attempts at defining and classifying individuals with intellectual disabilities have approached this process with grouping as a principal goal. Grouping, or placing likc individuals together on some dimension, serves certain types of purposes well, yet others are addressed only minimally or not at all. For example, grouping may serve administrative convenience quite efficiently. It makes individuals easy to count, funds easy to allocate by type of individual, and services easy to justify to legislatures. Grouping also serves legal purposes well. Placing an individual in a particular category facilitates decisions about legal responsibility for action or guardianship. The reader should realize that we are writing from the perspective of a service professional or agency. In both cases, a certain degree of impersonality is involved in decision making. Administrative personnel, legislators, and staff at legal agencies are often working with numbers and names rather than with the individuals the numbers and names represent. We are not addressing the question of how well the individual is served by such decisions. For the individual, service or justice may be marginal or absent.

We do not intend to detract from the value of grouping or the progress that the field of intellectual disabilities has made because of it. In fact, the impetus from legislation and administration of funds at local, state, and federal levels has permitted dramatic service improvements over the years. The issue is that one classification framework may be effective in one sector but serve poorly another sector whose purposes are different.

Educational classifications of intellectual disability have most often followed the grouping approach. Unfortunately, such an approach may not be effective for purposes of instruction, particularly with at-risk learners. The evidence consistently indicates this, and educators of youngsters with intellectual disabilities are recognizing the challenges of group classification for instructional purposes. Problems arise when educational programs focus on grouping rather than on specifying purposes, objectives, and resulting classificatory schemes more in harmony with the instructional process. The literature demonstrates a long-standing awareness of such problems. Concern has arisen when evaluation indicates that the curriculum for individuals with intellectual disabilities reflects convenience in administrative arrangement as much as consideration for the student's needs.

An interesting phenomenon begins to emerge when one reviews a number of sources discussing intellectual disabilities. Because classification and definition are related to diagnosis and evaluation, one serious deficit is evident with respect to both assessment and conceptualization. The conceptual weakness revolves around the relationship of evaluative assessment, classification, and, ultimately, programming. We have evaluated, and this is the classification. Now what? Early approaches to this topic often suggested that nature should be allowed to take its course, that one can "predict a typical course and outcome with a fair degree of confidence." Diagnostic purposes are adequately served here if the only inclination is a passive response; no active education or instruction is implied. Current trends in instructional philosophy and technique do not support a passive predictive approach but dictate active intervention with specific behavioral objectives. A logical and functional link must exist between assessment and intervention (Joshi, 2003; Katims, 2001; White, 2000).

Criterion-Referenced Versus Norm-Referenced Measurement

Definitions are not always precise; definitions of intellectual disabilities have suffered difficulties compounded by the demand for measurement. This imprecision is one facet of the AAMR definition that has had questions raised about it: How are the conceptualizations going to be translated into practical measurement and such measurement into diagnosis and service delivery (Linn & Gronlund, 2001; Merrell, 2002)? Placing individuals into groups—often IQ groupings in the field of intellectual disabilities—has been predominant in definition and classification for years. The measurement approach most often used for this scheme is known as **norm-referenced assessment.** Historically, norm-referenced evaluation has not been of much value for educational programming. More conceptually sound and pragmatically oriented evaluation approaches have been developed in areas other than intellectual disabilities. It is necessary to explore these approaches about instruction for persons with intellectual disabilities in order to make educational programming more effective.

Norm-referenced evaluation is the single type of psychological testing with which most people are familiar. Probably the best-known assessment of this nature is the intelligence test. The goal of norm-referenced evaluation is to measure an individual's functioning in comparison with some standard or group norm. A test score indicates whether the person stands above or below another student or some hypothetical average student. This type of evaluation is of value for purposes of grouping and, beyond that, has relevance for certain educational decisions. But the approach has limitations for overall instructional programming, and it cannot be expected to yield all the information necessary for the actual teaching process. Global acceptance of the norm measure in the past has led to diminished educational effectiveness for those with intellectual disabilities and much frustration with psychometric information in general.

During the past 25 years, a counterpart evaluation concept has developed to meet a variety of needs not addressed by norm-referenced assessment. This concept, known as criterion-referenced evaluation, does not place the individual's performance in comparative context with either other students or a normative standard. **Criterion-referenced assessment** often focuses on specific skills and looks at absolute level of performance. It attends to the actual level of mastery that an individual exhibits or, from a different perspective, the level at which a student becomes unable to perform a given task. This type of information is more useful to a teacher because it indicates the level at which to begin instruction. Criterion-referenced evaluation has become very popular in recent years, but despite its obvious usefulness for instruction, it does not by itself provide all the information needed for a well-reasoned total educational effort. The development of effective total evaluation models related to learning has become a high priority. Such models are discussed in detail in Chapter 3.

Labeling

In examining classification, it is important also to consider labeling. Labeling has been a source of controversy and concern for many years. The problems of labeling and interest in the difficulties associated with such designations have continued (see Angermeyer & Schulze, 2001; Hardman et al., 2006; Johnson-Glenberg & Chapman, 2004). Classification and labeling are not necessarily synonymous. However, assigning a child to a category typically results in a public communication about that categorization and therefore a label. It is difficult to imagine a case in which an individual would be referred, evaluated, and classified without having some label attached. The nature of human communication involves giving names to phenomena we observe. To speak about something causes us to label it, whether by a given name, a type name, or an impression that the phenomenon gives to the speaker. Labeling occurs more commonly than most of us consciously realize. There are many labels, types of labels, and sources of labeling (e.g., societal, official, and unofficial labeling). What a label is intended to signify may differ from the meanings associated with the term. It is clear that terms evoke a variety of responses from different individuals and result in many types of services for those labeled (Hardman et al., 2006). This set of circumstances is certainly the case for labels of deviance, illustrating the complexity of the relationship between labeling and other factors related to categorization and treatment, as well as part of the difficulty in determining the effects of labeling. For many, it has become fashionable to denounce labels and labeling with strong statements regarding their detrimental effects or lack of usefulness. Many have rallied to the cause of eliminating labels. The idea behind most of these efforts is that labeling has a negative impact on those labeled. This belief has great emotional appeal. But empirical evidence of the effects of labeling is difficult to obtain because of the complex interrelationship of labeling with other factors. If we are to continue and progress in research on the effects of labeling, we must be able either to isolate the effects or to study the problem in the context of its complexities.

One of the most frequently discussed issues is that of the impact of a label on the individual who bears it, even though definitive evidence about this influence is much less available than folklore would suggest. But the topic certainly warrants discussion because it is so central to the controversy.

The idea of the self-fulfilling prophecy has played a prominent role in controversies related to labeling impact. This notion springs from an assumption that expectations and the treatment of the labeled individual resulting from those expectations largely determine the individual's behavior. The label, it is assumed, substantially influences expectations. This perspective came to popularity because of the widely cited works by Rosenthal and Jacobson (1966, 1968), although the idea had been presented long before. Despite its intuitive appeal, solid empirical evidence supporting the notion of the self-fulfilling prophecy has been limited. The Rosenthal and Jacobson (1966, 1968) works have been severely criticized for serious methodological flaws, and the controversy continues unresolved (Diekmann, Tenbrunsel, & Galinsky, 2003; Gelfand & Drew, 2003).

Considerable research has been unable to replicate Rosenthal and Jacobson's findings, likely because of the serious flaws in their research methods (Gelfand & Drew, 2003). Such evidence seems to question the self-fulfilling prophecy notion. It is important to emphasize, however, that these studies were unable to replicate only the findings of Rosenthal and Jacobson. It is most unfortunate that such an important problem was studied with such flawed methodology, particularly when it drew so much attention. There is little question that people, such as teachers, form certain expectations of students with intellectual disabilities and that such expectations affect their perceptions and assessment of competence (Good & Nichols, 2001; Thelen et al., 2003; Zohar, Degani, & Vaakin, 2001). Yet it remains unclear what information people use in forming their expectations, and the precise effect that expectations (and labels) have is uncertain (Ma, 2001; Maynard, 2001). Personal impressions that trigger biases may be formed on the basis of very little information (sometimes a single cue), even in the face of evidence to the contrary. Attention to this area and its broad impact in several contexts continues (e.g., Epstein & Van Voorhis, 2001; Johnson-Glenberg & Chapman, 2004).

NEW ISSUES AND FUTURE DIRECTIONS

We began this chapter with an opening vignette on Tommy Young and his mother Jerilyn. Two significant points stood out in this piece. First, Tommy, like the vast majority of children with intellectual disabilities, did not stand out as diagnosable before he entered school. Second, Jerilyn Young faced a significant challenge of working with multiple disciplines to provide a coordinated and meaningful service program for Tommy.

> **Core Concept**
>
> A number of cultural changes among and within professions are needed to enhance collaboration on challenges of those with disabilities.

Several considerations are pertinent and should be examined when considering cooperation among professions. Certainly, one is the knowledge or database; another is service delivery, and the collaboration among different disciplines that presents significant challenges (Dosser et al., 2001; Hulgin, 2004). The Tips for Professionals feature early in the chapter pointed to some of the communication and collaboration challenges in forming an effective service team. These challenges are so significant that to observe or be part of such a team is a true accomplishment. Efforts must include and focus on the diagnosis and classification efforts as they lead toward individualized planning in all contextual arenas with particular attention to designing and implementing programs of supports that serve individual needs (Towell & Sanderson, 2004). We can best approach the accumulation of data and supports planning through both multidisciplinary and interdisciplinary models. **Multidisciplinary** models are those in which various professions approach a particular condition from their own focus (e.g., psychological aspects of intellectual disabilities or medical aspects of intellectual disabilities). Each discipline's database grows, but future efforts must include explicit attention to sharing information in consolidated and individualized planning focusing on the individual and across disciplinary boundaries. Unlike the multidisciplinary method, the **interdisciplinary** model attempts to develop "knowledge bridges" among professions. From these efforts, subdisciplinary areas such as social psychology, sociolinguistics, and neuropsychology have developed.

A serious movement has gained considerable momentum in special education to refrain from labeling disability conditions. Such terms as *intellectual disabilities, behavior disorders,* and *learning disabilities,* although convenient for communication, often tell little about a person's characteristics or skill level. Likewise, these terms, when used in social contexts, often create flawed perceptions, imprecise applications, and inaccurate generalizations (Biklen & Schein, 2001; Johnson-Glenberg & Chapman, 2004). Tradition also has designated professions by labels (psychology, education, psychiatry) that are extremely convenient for communication. In fact, society could not operate without terminology and classifications. Disciplinary labels, however, do generate certain difficulties. Although they may help communicate in restricted settings, they also generate myriad connotations for each discipline. As a result, the same type of stereotyping that disability labels produce also emerges from the use of disciplinary labels. The labels all too frequently serve primarily to specify and promote boundaries—to assert territorial rights. And territorialism is a strong deterrent to effective interdisciplinary collaboration.

We suggested earlier that a broader knowledge base appears to facilitate interdisciplinary collaboration. In retrospect, this seems logical—perhaps simplistic. Without at least some information about another person's profession, it is extremely difficult even to communicate, much less to collaborate. Professionals are all quite experienced at obtaining information by reading journals and books. In many cases, however, such approaches are not enough to break down interdisciplinary barriers. Frequent personal contact with individuals from other professions is more valuable. In fact, some would maintain that such contact is not only helpful but also prerequisite to facilitating interdisciplinary efforts.

When the topic of interdisciplinary collaboration is raised, people often indicate that attitudes must change before it can occur. Although most would agree with such a statement, few would be able to specify how to accomplish this. Attitude is an extremely elusive concept, and it is far from easy to tell how one knows when an attitude has changed. It is somewhat easier, however, to speak in terms of altering certain behaviors.

One important behavioral change for interdisciplinary collaboration involves reaction to terminology differences. Frequently, dramatic differences in terminology are found among professions. A person's use of a different terminology often generates negative reactions, sometimes even openly derogatory remarks, from individuals with different disciplinary perspectives. It is easy to see how such reactions lend themselves to friction and antagonism rather than to cooperation. Individuals working in an interdisciplinary setting must minimize their negative reactions to differences in terms. This does not mean adopting another's terms, concepts, and approaches, but it does imply that value judgments about the approach of the other discipline should be set aside. For example, Person A may not choose to incorporate the term *ego strength* into his or her vocabulary or conceptualization. If that is an important term in Person B's disciplinary perspective, however, Person A can understand its meaning and judge it as different—but not inappropriate—terminology. Certainly, the acceptance of "differentness" is a goal of people working for the benefit of individuals with intellectual disabilities, and improvements in interactions among professionals can reduce friction and ultimately promote greater effectiveness in terms of interdisciplinary collaboration.

A second major behavioral change relates to the delivery of services to those with intellectual disabilities. We have discussed how the various professions, operating through their applied branches, work independently of one another. Educators often have been left with a series of tests and reports that are mostly meaningless for planning a given child's educational program. In an interdisciplinary service approach model, although assessments are derived independently, the program parameters are decided on in collaboration. This approach, however, also has some drawbacks. Hardman et al. (2006) pointed out that, too often, professional cooperation diminishes after initial program development, and efforts at coordinating services often are limited.

A third approach, called the **transdisciplinary** model, was conceived as an effort to overcome some of the problems of the other two models. This approach emphasizes the role of a primary therapist, who acts as the contact person for service provisions, so the number of professionals with direct child contact is minimal. In a transdisciplinary plan, no discipline is dominant; all should support each other and make their own contributions. This approach requires a mature professional attitude that recognizes and allows for relevant disciplinary contributions. The emphasis is on the person with intellectual disabilities and that person's needs rather than on the professions working independently or without coordination. The role of the teacher (whether general or special education) in this method becomes predominant because the teacher sees the children on a daily basis and is most conversant with their skills, aptitudes, and needs. The teacher, then, would be the primary therapist and the focal point for diagnoses and direct service to the child.

One of the crucial points of a chapter on disciplinary collaboration involves the purpose of the professional effort. Often, people in the various professions have lost sight of the reason for their effort—the citizen with intellectual disabilities. Too much time and attention are devoted to professional self-preservation, sometimes to the detriment of the individuals being served. Those being served must remain the focal point and include attention to elements that maximize their growth and

Core Concept

New issues and future directions in the definition and classification of intellectual disabilities may include a better balance between individual and environmental factors.

development. In many cases, individualized planning must include significant elements of self-determination and self-advocacy as contextually appropriate. This reflects a cultural change development in some professional arenas where history has emphasized the preeminance of knowledge and goal setting by those providing the service and little inclusion of the perspectives of those with intellectual disabilities who are being served.

Intellectual disabilities, like most other phenomena associated with human development and performance, is an enormously complex condition. It is not a unidimensional disorder; to capture the vital elements and contributors adequately in a single definition or classification system is far from simple. In this chapter, we have examined some of the issues pertaining to intellectual disabilities definitions. Many changes have occurred over the years as theories have been discarded and replaced by others that have also been subjected to the rigorous tests of applicability. As definitions evolve, there is a seemingly continual progression from the laboratory to the daily world environment—from a relatively restrictive view of ability and capability based on measured intelligence to a more inclusive perspective of functioning within an environment with a distinct emphasis on support functions needed for success in that environment. This certainly has not made the conception of intellectual disabilities simpler; quite the opposite. This field is as complicated as the people being studied.

The 2002 AAMR definition has presented such a perspective. Although it is not a definition that will simplify matters, neither is a person's functioning in his or her environment a simple matter. We know that people do not function in a vacuum and that environment significantly influences their performance. Throughout this volume are references to the vital influence of environmental circumstances on the development of abilities, performance, and behavior. One major challenge at this point is to continue examining how well the AAMR scheme can be translated into practice.

One of the major elements of intellectual disabilities—intelligence—has been reformulated by some theorists in a manner that considers some broader components, including practical contextual abilities and a person's ability to planfully pursue goals (Bates, 2004; Sternberg, 2001; Sternberg et al., 2001). Some of these conceptual elements are important in the field of intellectual disabilities because they represent distinct functional limitations for this population (e.g., the abstraction of planning ahead). Others capture important contributors to the level of functioning for those with intellectual disabilities (contextual functioning). Theoretical and empirical research must explore the extension of such thinking to issues of definition and classification. The important note here is that intelligence is seriously being reexamined, and this may have significant impacts on the field of intellectual disabilities.

Another component requiring examination and attention relates to planning and programming of supports for the person with intellectual disabilities. This involves a focus that has existed before but requires largely unprecedented planning and implementation intensities (AAMR, 2002). Table 1–5 illustrates support functions and activities potentially involved in an individualized plan.

Table 1–5
Illustrative Support Functions and Representative Activities

Support Function[a]	Representative Activities		
Teaching	Supervising Giving feedback Organizing the learning environment	Training Evaluating Supporting inclusive classrooms	Instructing Collecting data Individualizing instruction
Befriending	Advocating Carpooling Supervising Instructing	Evaluating Communicating Training Giving feedback	Reciprocating Associating and disassociating Socializing
Financial planning	Working with SSI-Medicaid Advocating for benefits	Assisting with money management Protection and legal assistance	Budgeting Income assistance and planning/considerations
Employee assistance	Counseling Procuring/using assistive technology devices	Supervisory training Job performance enhancement	Crisis intervention/ assistance Job/task accommodation and redesigning job/work duties
Behavioral support	Functional analysis Multicomponent instruction Emphasis on antecedent manipulation	Manipulation of ecological and setting events Teaching adaptive behavior	Building environment with effective consequences
In-home living assistance	Personal maintenance/care Transfer and mobility Dressing and clothing care Architectural modifications	Communication devices Behavioral support Eating and food management Housekeeping	Respite care Attendant care Home-health aides Homemaker services
Community access and use	Carpooling/rides program Transportation training Personal protection skills	Recreation/leisure involvement Community awareness opportunities Vehicle modification	Community use opportunities and interacting with generic agencies Personal protection skills
Health assistance	Medical appointments Medical interventions Med Alert devices	Emergency procedures Mobility (assistive devices) Counseling appointments Medication taking	Hazard awareness Safety training Physical therapy and related activities Counseling interventions

[a]The support functions and activities may need to be modified slightly to accommodate individuals of different ages.

Source: Mental Retardation: Definition, Classification, and Systems of Supports (10th ed., pp. 153–154). Washington, DC: American Association on Mental Retardation, Copyright 2002 by the American Association on Mental Retardation, by permission.

One of the foremost questions confronting the 2002 AAMR definition is utility in the field. Definition and classification must translate into practical applications of diagnosis and treatment. While this definition document emphasizes practical aspects, such as supports and individualized planning, translation into practice will remain the important test of its soundness. Definition documents do little if they are no more than theories in the pages of scientific journals. Diagnosis and treatment, to be widely accepted, must not become so burdensome that they are avoided. Experience with well-conceived assessment systems, which are complex and time consuming, has suggested that lack of convenience is a deterrent to broad usage. Utility must receive attention in reconceptualization efforts that translate into field application. Additionally, evidence suggests that an overwhelming number of minority children are classified as having intellectual disabilities even under assessment systems designed to avoid such problems (Gelfand & Drew, 2003; Hatton, 2002; Hosp & Reschly, 2004).

Chapter Review

Throughout this chapter you encountered Core Concepts inserted at key points in the margin. These Core Concepts summarize important information presented in the narrative. At the end of each chapter you will find questions related to the Core Concepts to help you review and enhance your acquisition of these key points. Review these questions and self-test to prepare for your examinations. Additionally you will find a Roundtable Discussion section that includes topics that are framed in a manner suitable for group discussion or examination. These topics reinforce the information presented in the chapter and represent another mechanism for learning.

Core Questions

1. How did politics, economics, and basic lifestyles affect the lives of persons with intellectual disabilities before 1900?
2. What were some of the factors that influenced the development of institutions in the United States for persons with intellectual disabilities?
3. Why is the term *intellectual disabilities* considered to be linguistically influenced?
4. Why is intellectual disabilities both a label of fact and a label of conjecture?
5. What are three areas in which psychology has contributed to the understanding of those with intellectual disabilities?
6. What are the primary contributions of education in helping the understanding of the phenomenon of intellectual disabilities?
7. What are some of the challenges facing disciplinary collaboration in serving people with intellectual disabilities?

8. What can be done to enhance collaboration between disciplines and professions involved with persons with intellectual disabilities?
9. How has the concept of intellectual disabilities differed among professions, and how might this difference affect an individual with a disability?
10. What five assumptions are essential in applying the 2002 AAMR definition of intellectual disabilities?
11. What is the difference between incidence and prevalence?
12. When considering the question of how frequently intellectual disabilities occurs, how do SES, age, and severity affect the answer?
13. How has the involvement of many disciplines studying intellectual disabilities been both an advantage and a disadvantage?
14. How do the three adaptive behavior areas and related skills identified in the 2002 AAMR definition document enter into diagnosis, classification, and program planning?
15. How can definition and classification systems serve some purposes well and yet be inappropriate for others?
16. Why is it important that a relationship exist between definitions, classifications, assessment, and programming?
17. What difficulties may be encountered when using a grouping-oriented classification system and criterion-referenced assessment?
18. What difficulties may be encountered when using norm-referenced assessment in conjunction with a definition that does not focus on grouping but that instead emphasizes functional skill levels?

Roundtable Discussion

1. *As a concept, intellectual disabilities has been known throughout recorded history. The perception of what is and what is not deemed intellectual disabilities has changed continually. With the development of scientific approaches to the study of human behavior, many disciplines and professions emerged and began to identify areas of primary investigation, concern, and service.*

   In a discussion group, consider the societal influences on intellectual disabilities and how present-day attitudes toward persons with intellectual disabilities may or may not reflect them. What would be some realistic approaches to overcoming disciplinary and professional friction?
2. *When discussing or otherwise considering any phenomenon, the definition of what is being addressed is the foundation on which discussion is based. Communication between you and your student colleagues would be difficult indeed if some of you were talking about automobile transportation and others were considering air travel while you all were using the same term, say,* mustifig. *You would encounter difficulty agreeing on cost per mile, miles easily traveled in an hour, and many other factors. This is an exaggerated illustration, but in some*

ways it is not all that different from intellectual disabilities as it is defined, categorized, counted, and served.

In your study group or on your own, examine intellectual disabilities from the perspective of, for example, sociology, medicine, psychology, education, and politics. Describe the phenomenon, discuss service, and address various aspects of how it should be conceptualized. Examine parameters of classification, labeling, and assessment. After completing this exercise, determine how you will conceptualize the phenomenon of intellectual disabilities to best learn all that must be known about it and how those affected can best be served. Reflect on the information in this chapter and consider the task facing early professionals working in intellectual disabilities. They did (and do) not have a simple assignment. We hope you will do better.

Parent and Professional Organization Positions on Key Issues in the Lives of People with Intellectual Disabilities

The inside front cover of this text presents a matrix that includes several key issues in the lives of people with disabilities, the positions of various parent and professional organizations on each issue, and the chapter and page number where the information is addressed. Table 1–6 below is a summary of the organizations and key issues addressed in this chapter.

Table 1–6
Key Issues and Organizations Discussed in This Chapter

Organization/Website	Key Issues Addressed	Chapter Heading
American Association on Mental Retardation (http://www.aamr.org)	Purposes and use of terminology Assessment issues	Intellectual Disabilities: A Definition in Transition Classification
TASH (http://www.tash.org)	Inclusion Early intervention Community living & employment Family support	Intellectual Disabilities: A Definition in Transition Early intervention Inclusive education Community Living/Employment Family support
International Association for the Scientific Study of Intellectual Disabilities (http://www.iassid.org)	Health issues Community living & employment Family & parenting support Aging Quality of life	Intellectual Disabilities: A Definition in Transition Health issues Community living & employment Family & parenting support Aging Quality of life

References

Abbeduto, L., Seltzer, M. M., Shattuck, P., Krauss, M. W., Orsmond, G., & Murphy, M. M. (2004). Psychological well-being and coping in mothers of youths with autism, Down syndrome, or fragile X syndrome. *American Journal on Mental Retardation, 109,* 231–236.

American Association on Mental Retardation (AAMR). (2002). Mental retardation: Definition, classification, and systems of supports (10th ed.). Washington, DC: Author.

American Psychiatric Association (APA). (2000). Diagnostic and statistical manual of mental disorders (4th ed., Text Rev.). Washington, DC: Author.

Angermeyer, M. C., & Schulze, B. (2001). Reducing the stigma of schizophrenia: Understanding the process and options for interventions. *Epidemiologia e Psichiatria Sociale, 10,* 1–7.

Ashbaugh, J. (2001). Better managing the delivery of services and supports to people with developmental disabilities using information technology. *Mental Retardation, 39,* 322–326.

Barlow, D. H. (2004). Psychological treatments. *American Psychologist, 59,* 869–878.

Bates, P. E., Cuvo, T., Miner, C. A., & Korabek, C. A. (2001). Simulated and community-based instruction involving persons with mild and moderate mental retardation. *Research in Developmental Disabilities, 22*(2), 95–115.

Bates, T. (2004). Models of intelligence: International perspectives. *Applied Cognitive Psychology, 18,* 481–482.

Batshaw, M. L. (2001). Mental retardation. In M. L. Batshaw (Ed.), *When your child has a disability: The complete sourcebook of daily and medical care* (Rev. ed., pp. 203–216). Baltimore: Paul H. Brookes Publishing.

Baum, S. M., & Olenchak, F. R. (2002). The alphabet children: GT, ADHD, and more. *Exceptionality, 10,* 77–91.

Biklen, D., & Schein, P. L. (2001). Public and professional constructions of mental retardation: Glen Ridge and the missing narrative of disability rights. *Mental Retardation,* 39, 436–451.

Blacher, J. (2001). Transition to adulthood: Mental retardation, families, and culture. *American Journal on Mental Retardation, 106,* 173–188.

Blair, C. (2003). Physiological and neurocognitive correlates of adaptive behavior in preschool among children in Head Start. *Developmental Neuropsychology, 24,* 479–497.

Bradley, E. A., Summers, J. A., Wood, H. L., & Bryson, S. E. (2004). Comparing rates of psychiatric and behavior disorders in adolescents and young adults with severe intellectual disability with and without autism. *Journal of Autism and Developmental Disorders, 34,* 151–161.

Brady, S. M. (2001). Sterilization of girls and women with intellectual disabilities: Past and present justifications. *Violence Against Women, 7,* 432–461.

Brinkley, C. A., Newman, J. P., & Widiger, T. A. (2004). Two approaches to parsing the heterogeneity of psychopathy. *Clinical Psychology: Science and Practice, 11,* 69–94.

Bronstein, L. R., & Abramson, J. S. (2003). Understanding socialization of teachers and social workers: Groundwork for collaboration in the schools. *Families in Society, 84,* 323–330.

Calhoon, M. B., & Fuchs, L. S. (2003). The effects of peer-assisted learning strategies and curriculum-based measurement on the mathematics performance of secondary students with disabilities. *Remedial and Special Education, 24,* 235–245.

Campbell, J., Gilmore, L., & Cuskelly, M. (2003). Changing student teachers' attitudes towards disability and inclusion. *Journal of Intellectual & Developmental Disability, 28,* 369–379.

Carpenter, P. K. (2000). The Victorian small idiot homes near Bath. *History of Psychiatry, 11*(44, Pt. 4), 383–392.

Clark, E., Olympia, D. E., Jensen, J., Heathfield, L. T., & Jenson, W. R. (2004). Striving for autonomy in a contingency-governed world: Another challenge for individuals with developmental disabilities. *Psychology in the Schools, 41,* 143–153.

Coopman, S. J. (2003). Communicating disability: Metaphors of oppression, metaphors of empowerment. In P. J. Kalbfleisch (Ed.), *Communication Yearbook* (Vol. 27, pp. 337–394). Mahwah, NJ: Erlbaum.

Covarrubias v. San Diego Unified School District, 7-394, Tex. Rptr. 1971.

Cuskelly, M. (2004). The evolving construct of intellectual disability: Is everything old new again? *International Journal of Disability, Development and Education, 51,* 117–122.

Diekmann, K. A., Tenbrunsel, A. E., & Galinsky, A. D. (2003). From self-prediction to self-defeat: Behavioral forecasting, self-fulfilling prophecies, and the effect of competitive expectations. *Journal of Personality and Social Psychology, 85,* 672–683.

Dosser, D. A., Jr., Handron, D. S., McCammon, S. L., Powell, J. Y., & Spencer, S. S. (2001). Challenges and strategies for teaching collaborative interdisciplinary practice in children's mental health care. *Families, Systems, & Health, 19,* 65–82.

Edgerton, R. B. (1968). Anthropology and mental retardation: A plea for the comparative study of incompetence. In H. J. Prehm, L. A. Hamerlynck, & J. E. Crosson (Eds.), *Behavioral research in mental retardation* (pp. 75–87). Eugene, OR: Rehabilitation Research and Training Center in Mental Retardation.

Edgerton, R. B. (2001). The hidden majority of individuals with mental retardation and developmental disabilities. In A. J. Tymchuk, C. K. Lakin, & R. Luckasson (Eds.), *The forgotten generation: The status and challenges of adults with mild cognitive limitations* (pp. 3–19). Baltimore: Paul H. Brookes Publishing.

Epstein, J. L., & Van Voorhis, F. L. (2001). More than minutes: Teachers' roles in designing homework. *Educational Psychologist, 36,* 181–193.

Freeman, S. F. N. (2003). Early childhood inclusion: Focus on change. *American Journal on Mental Retardation, 108,* 435–436.

Gelfand, D. M., & Drew, C. J. (2003). *Understanding child behavior disorders* (4th ed.). Pacific Grove, CA: Wadsworth.

Goddard, H. H. (1913). *The Kallikak family.* New York: Macmillan.

Gonzalez, N. (2004). Disciplining the discipline: Anthropology and the pursuit of quality education. *Educational Researcher, 33,* 17–25.

Good, T. L., & Nichols, S. L. (2001). Expectancy effects in the classroom: A special focus on improving the reading performance of minority students in first-grade classrooms. *Educational Psychologist, 36,* 113–126.

Goodman, J. F. (2003). "Maladaptive" behaviours in the young child with intellectual disabilities: A reconsideration. *International Journal of Disability, Development and Education, 50,* 137–148.

Goodwin, C. J. (2005). *Research in psychology: Methodology and design* (4th ed.). Hoboken, NJ: Wiley.

Greenwood, C. R., Walker, D., & Utley, C. A. (2002). Relationships between social-communicative skills and life achievements. In H. Goldstein & L. A. Kaczmarek (Eds.), *Promoting social communication: Children with developmental disabilities from birth to adolescence.* Communication and language intervention series (Vol. 10, pp. 345–370). Baltimore: Paul H. Brookes Publishing.

Griffiths, D. M., Watson, S. L., Lewis, T., & Stoner, K. (2004). Sexuality research and persons with intellectual disabilities. In E. Emerson, C. Hatton, T. Thompson, & T. R. Parmenter (Eds.), *The international handbook of applied research in intellectual disabilities* (pp. 311–334). Hoboken, NJ: Wiley.

Hall, S., & Marteau, T. M. (2003). Causal attributions and blame: Associations with mothers' adjustment to the birth of a child with Down syndrome. *Health and Medicine, 8,* 415–423.

Hardman, M. L., Drew, C. J., & Egan, M. W. (2006). *Human exceptionality: School, community, and family* (8th ed.). Needham Heights, MA: Allyn & Bacon.

Hatton, C. (2002). People with intellectual disabilities from ethnic minority communities in the United States and the United Kingom. In L. M. Glidden (Ed.), *International review of research in mental retardation (Vol. 25,* pp. 209–239). San Diego: Academic Press.

Holburn, S., Jacobson, J. W., Schwartz, A. A., Flory, M. J., & Vietze, P. M. (2004). The Willowbrook Futures project: A longitudinal analysis of person-centered planning. *American Journal on Mental Retardation, 109,* 63–76.

Holburn, S., & Vietze, P. M. (2002). *Person-centered planning: Research, practice, and future directions.* Baltimore: Paul H. Brookes Publishing.

Hosp, J. L., & Reschly, D. J. (2004). Disproportionate representation of minority students in special education: Academic, demographic, and economic predictors. *Exceptional Children, 70,* 185–199.

Hulgin, K. M. (2004). Person-centered services and organizational context: Taking stock of working conditions and their impact. *Mental Retardation, 42,* 169–180.

Johnson-Glenberg, M. C., & Chapman, R. S. (2004). Predictors of parent-child language during novel task play: A comparison between typically developing children and individuals with Down syndrome. *Journal of Intellectual Disability Research, 48,* 225–238.

Joshi, R. M. (2003). Misconceptions about the assessment and diagnosis of reading disability. *Reading Psychology, 24,* 247–266.

Kane, W. M., Avila, M. M., & Rogers, E. M. (2001). Community and culture: World views and natural affiliations as the basis of understanding, trust, assistance, and support. In A. J. Tymchuk, C. K. Lakin, & R. Luckasson (Eds.), *The forgotten generation: The status and challenges of adults with mild cognitive limitations* (pp. 55–83). Baltimore: Paul H. Brookes Publishing.

Katims, D. S. (2001). Literacy assessment of students with mental retardation: An exploratory investigation. *Education and Training in Mental Retardation and Developmental Disabilities, 36,* 363–372.

Kinsler, P. J., Saxman, A., & Fishman, D. B. (2004). The Vermont Defendant Accommodation project: A case study. *Psychology, Public Policy, and Law, 10,* 134–161.

Kittler, P., Krinsky-McHale, S. J., & Devenny, D. A. (2004). Sex differences in performance over 7 years on the Wechsler Intelligence Scale for Children–Revised among adults with intellectual disability. *Journal of Intellectual Disability Research, 48,* 114–122.

Laws, G., & Gunn, D. (2004). Phonological memory as a predictor of language comprehension in Down syndrome: A five-year follow-up study. *Journal of Child Psychology and Psychiatry and Allied Disciplines, 45,* 326–337.

Lenton, S., Franck, L., & Salt, A., (2004). Children with complex health care needs: Supporting the child and family in the community. *Child: Care, Health & Development, 30,* 191–192.

Linn, R. L., & Gronlund, N. E. (2001). *Measurement and assessment in teaching* (8th ed.). Upper Saddle River, NJ: Merrill/Prentice Hall.

Liu, M. (2004). Examining the performance and attitudes of sixth graders during their use of a problem-based hypermedia learning environment. *Computers in Human Behavior, 20,* 357–379.

Luckasson, R. (2001). The criminal justice system and people with mild cognitive limitations. In A. J. Tymchuk, C. K. Lakin, & R. Luckasson (Eds.), *The forgotten generation: The status and challenges of adults with mild cognitive limitations* (pp. 347–356). Baltimore: Paul H. Brookes Publishing.

Ma, X. (2001). Participation in advanced mathematics: Do expectations and influence of students, peers, teachers, and parents matter? *Contemporary Educational Psychology, 26,* 132–146.

Matson, J. L., Kuhn, D. E., Dixon, D. R., Mayville, S. B., Laud, R. B., Cooper, C. L., et al. (2003). The development and factor structure of the functional assessment for multiple causality (FACT). *Research in Developmental Disabilities, 24,* 485–495.

Maynard, T. (2001). The student teacher and the school community of practice: A consideration of "learning as participation." *Cambridge Journal of Education, 31,* 39–52.

McAdam, D. B., DiCesare, A., Murphy, S., & Marshall, B. (2004). The influence of different therapists on functional analysis outcomes. *Behavioral Interventions, 19,* 39–44.

McBrien, J. (2003). The intellectually disabled offender: Methodological problems in identification. *Journal of Applied Research in Intellectual Disabilities, 16,* 95–105.

McDonnell, J., Hardman, M., & McDonnell, A. P. (2003). *Introduction to persons with moderate and severe disabilities.* Boston: Allyn & Bacon.

McHale, S. M., Dariotis, J. K., & Kauh, T. J. (2003). Social development and social relationships in middle childhood. In R. M. Lerner & M. A. Easterbrooks (Eds.), *Handbook of psychology: Developmental psychology* (Vol. 6, pp 241–265). New York: Wiley.

Meininger, H. P. (2003). Intellectual disability, ethics and genetics—A selected bibliography. *Journal of Intellectual Disability Research, 47,* 571–576.

Merrell, K. W. (2002). *Behavioral, social, and emotional assessment of children and adolescents* (2nd ed.). Mahwah, NJ: Erlbaum.

Mertens, D. M. (2004). *Research and evaluation in education and psychology: Integrating diversity with quantitative, qualitative, and mixed methods* (2nd ed.). Thousand Oaks, CA: Sage.

Moore, C. L., Feist-Price, S., & Alston, R. J. (2002). VR services for persons with severe profound mental retardation: Does race matter? *Rehabilitation Counseling Bulletin, 45*(3), 162–167.

Mostert, M. P. (2002). Useless eaters: Disability as a genocidal marker in Nazi Germany. *Journal of Special Education, 36,* 155–168.

Mumley, D. L., Tillbrook, C. E., & Grisson, T. (2003). Five year research update (1996–2000): Evaluations for competence to stand trial (adjudicative competence). *Behavioral Sciences and the Law, 21,* 329–350.

Neely-Barnes, S., & Marcenko, M. (2004). Predicting impact of childhood disability on families: Results from the 1995 national health interview survey disability supplement. *Mental Retardation, 42,* 284–293.

Neihart, M. (2003). Contrasts in children's development: An interview with Nancy Robinson. *Roeper Review, 25,* 106–111.

Otani, H. (2002). University students' attitudes toward persons with mental retardation. *Japanese Journal of Special Education, 40,* 215–222.

Pillay, A. L. (2003). Social competence in rural and urban children with mental retardation: Preliminary findings. *South African Journal of Psychology, 33,* 176–181.

President's Committee for People with Intellectual Disabilities (PCPID). (2000). Mission. Retrieved from http://www.acf.dhhs.gov/programs/pcmr/mission.htm

Robertson, J., Emerson, E., Pinkney, L., Caesar, E., Felce, D., Meek, A., et al. (2004). Quality and costs of community-based residential supports for people with mental retardation and challenging behavior. *American Journal on Mental Retardation, 109,* 332–344.

Rosenthal, R., & Jacobson, L. (1966). Teacher expectancies: Determinants of pupils' IQ gains. *Psychological Reports, 19,* 115–118.

Rosenthal, R., & Jacobson, L. (1968). *Pygmalion in the classroom.* New York: Holt, Rinehart & Winston.

Routh, D. K., & Schroeder, S. R. (2003). A history of psychological theory and research in mental retardation since World War II. In L. M. Glidden (Ed.), *International review of research in mental retardation* (Vol. 26, pp. 1–59). San Diego, CA: Academic Press.

Sander, H. W., & Castro, C. (2004). Neurocysticercosis. *New England Journal of Medicine, 350,* 266.

Shin, J. Y., & Crittenden, K. S. (2003). Well-being of mothers of children with mental retardation: An evaluation of the Double ABCX model in a cross-cultural context. *Asian Journal of Social Psychology, 6,* 171–184.

Sofaer, B. (2005). *Qualitative methods in health services and policy research.* Hoboken, NJ: Wiley.

Spinath, F. M., Harlaar, N., Ronald, A., & Plomin, R. (2004). Substantial genetic influence on mild mental impairment in early childhood. *American Journal on Mental Retardation, 109,* 34–43.

Sternberg, R. J. (2001). Successful intelligence: Understanding what Spearman had rather than what he studied. In J. M. Collis & S. Messick (Eds.), *Intelligence and personality: Bridging the gap in theory and measurement* (pp. 347–373). Mahwah, NJ: Erlbaum.

Sternberg, R. J., Nokes, C., Geissler, P. W., Prince, R., Okatcha, F., Bundy, D. A., et al. (2001). The relationship between academic and practical intelligence: A case study in Kenya. *Intelligence, 29,* 401–418.

Stokes, J. V., Cameron, M. J., & Dorsey, M. F. (2004). Task analysis, correspondence training, and general case instruction for teaching personal hygiene skills. *Behavioral Interventions, 19,* 121–135.

Stone, S. D. (2003). Disability, dependence, and old age: Problematic constructions. *Canadian Journal on Aging, 22,* 59–67.

Summers, J. A., Nelson, L. L., & Beegle, G. P. (2001). Family-professional partnerships: Win-win benefits for parents, students, and teachers. *CEC Today.* Retrieved from http://www.cec.sped.org/bk/cec_today/may-june_2001/index.html

Switzky, H. N. (2001). *Personality and motivational differences in persons with mental retardation.* Mahwah, NJ: Erlbaum.

TASH (2000). TASH resolutions on services and supports in the community. Retrieved from http://www.tash.org

TASH (2004). TASH resolutions. Retrieved from http://www.tash.org/resolutions/

Thelen, R. L., Burns, M. K., & Christiansen, N. D. (2003). Effects of high-incidence disability labels on the expectations of teachers, peers, and college students. *Ethical Human Sciences and Services, 5,* I183–193.

Towell, D., & Sanderson, H. (2004). Person-centered planning in its strategic context: Reframing the Mansell/Beadle-Brown critique. *Journal of Applied Research in Intellectual Disabilities, 17,* 17–21.

U.S. Department of Education. (2002). To assure the free appropriate public education of all children with disabilities. *Twenty-Fourth Annual Report to Congress on the Implementation of the Individuals with Disabilities Education Act.* Washington, DC: Author.

Van Vonderen, A. (2004). Effectiveness of immediate verbal feedback on trainer behaviour during communication training with individuals with intellectual disability. *Journal of Intellectual Disability Research, 48,* 245–251.

Vehmas, S. (2004). Ethical analysis of the concept of disability. *Mental Retardation, 42,* 209–222.

Wagner, G. A. (2002). Enduing contributions of behavioral science. In R. L. Shalock & P. C. Baker (Eds.), *Embarking on a new century: Mental retardation at the end of the 20th century* (pp. 111–132). Washington, DC: American Association on Mental Retardation.

Wehmeyer, M. L., & Garner, N. W. (2003). The impact of personal characteristics of people with intellectual and developmental disability on self-determination and autonomous functioning. *Journal of Applied Research in Intellectual Disabilities, 16,* 255–265.

White, S. H. (2000). Conceptual foundations of IQ testing. *Psychology, Public Policy, and Law, 6,* 33–43.

Zohar, A., Degani, A., & Vaakin, E. (2001). Teachers' beliefs about low-achieving students and higher order thinking. *Teaching and Teacher Education, 17,* 469–485.

Chapter 2

Diversity Issues

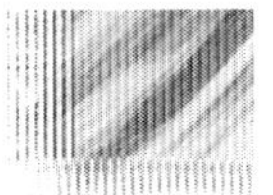

Chapter Preview

At the completion of this chapter, you will have a better understanding of intellectual disabilities and how:

- Cultural, environmental, and language diversity surface as critically important issues and are associated in complicated ways.
- Economic factors are very influential in many ways as a child grows and develops, and emerge as impacting children's well-being enormously.
- Assessment challenges appear as diversity issues surface and how together they can become divisive as bias, or problems to be solved by science.

Denise's Dilemmas

Denise is a 9-year-old African American girl in the fourth grade. Her elementary school is in a midsized city in the southeastern United States. Denise lives with her parents and two older brothers in an apartment complex in a working-class African American neighborhood. Because of recent redistricting, Denise is being bussed from an all-black school in her neighborhood to a predominantly middle-class white elementary school across town. This is her first year in the school, and Denise is one of only five African American girls in the fourth grade.

Denise has never been a troublesome student and she has good social skills. This had been the case when she started the year at her new school. Recently, however, Denise has gotten into fights with several of her classmates. She has also been failing to complete her classwork and has been talking back to her teacher.

The teacher suggests that the school counselor meet with Denise. She suspects that Denise might be having some problems at home that may be causing her behavior to change in school.[1]

- *Denise is in the fourth grade, but in a new school environment, one that is substantially different from what she experienced before. Reportedly she did not have academic difficulties before, but she is in this new environment. Why is that the case? Are the academic expectations so different, or is she performing more poorly because she is now in a different environment—one that is less conducive to her success because of the ethnic or economic composition of the student body?*
- *Did the previous school let her down, or is the current school presenting her with a biased or ethnically hostile environment? Denise is also experiencing social problems that she did not experience in her other school. Is this related to her academic frustrations or is it also reflecting a biased or ethnically hostile environment?*

[1] *Source:* Adapted from Locke (1995, pp. 26–27), with permission.

These questions are among several that can and should be raised by Denise's situation, and none of them are easily answered. Care must be taken to avoid evaluating Denise with procedures that are culturally unfair and labeling her with a disability because of cultural matters rather than her ability. However, if Denise needs extra help and specialized programming, we should do all we can to provide her with an appropriate education so that she can succeed. These are not simple questions, nor are they simple circumstances. This chapter examines some of the confusing and difficult dilemmas pertaining to multicultural issues and intellectual disability.

Departures from normal functioning are part of the nature of intellectual disabilities. People with intellectual disability exhibit lower intellectual performance, accompanied by reduced functioning in social skills (Kemp & Carter, 2002; Matson, Luke, & Mayville, 2004; Souza & Kennedy, 2003). The perspective and expectations for intellectual and social functioning emanate from the context of society, and definitions of intellectual disabilities emerge from societal expectations and service supports (AAMR, 2002; APA, 2000). Standards of performance are broadly defined by the social majority. The source of these general performance standards gives rise to several concerns related to ethnic and cultural diversity that have existed for years and that continue to present potential problems (Hatton, 2002; Naglieri & Rojahn, 2001; Shapiro, Monzo, Rueda, Gomez, & Blacher, 2004; Watts & Erevelles, 2004).

Countries with multiple cultures, such as the United States, are always faced with circumstances in which definitions of acceptable behavior differ among various groups. Yet broad and general standards that cross cultural boundaries also operate and must be determined in some way. Typically, such definitions emanate from sources and institutions that primarily represent the views of the cultural majority (Ben-Ari & Lavee, 2004; Ruvolo, Peterson, & LeBoeuf, 2004). Scientists, public officials, and others in positions of authority more often reflect the perspectives of the cultural majority than those of smaller groups or population segments.

Core Concept

Cultural diversity involves critically important differences that require attention as one examines intellectual disability both as a concept and in the context of individual assessment.

Issues related to cultural diversity are integrated into topical discussions in this volume, where they play a major role. These issues pervade many aspects of intellectual disability, such as causation, assessment, prevention, and placement and treatment. In this chapter, however, we examine certain subjects separately. One serious problem is that of poor assessment, misdiagnosis, and classification of individuals as having intellectual disability when, in fact, their behavior or performance is related to cultural difference rather than to significantly reduced functioning. The concept of the self-fulfilling prophecy (the idea that one becomes what one is labeled) is prominent in this area. The self-fulfilling prophecy suggests that if a person is labeled as having intellectual disability, over time he or she will begin to function as a person who has intellectual disability—even if the initial assessment was inaccurate.

The self-fulfilling prophecy was brought into widespread prominence in the 1960s although it continues to be of interest (e.g., Diekman, Tenbrunsel, & Galinsky, 2003; Snyder, 2003). The early conceptions of the self-fulfilling prophecy suggested that children's performance levels reflect the expectations of their teachers and others of significant influence to a substantial degree. This research generated a great deal of controversy, and topics related to expectations remain of considerable interest in a number of areas (Holguin & Hansen, 2003; Mezulis, Abramson, Hyde, & Hankin, 2004; Sprott, Spangenberg, & Fisher, 2003). As professionals, we still have much to learn before the effects of expectation are fully understood. It is clear, however, that the self-fulfilling prophecy represents an area of concern, particularly for youngsters who may be identified as having intellectual disability more on the basis of cultural background than on performance level. Evidence continues to emerge suggesting that matters such as ethnicity are associated with a youngster's being identified as having a disability and receiving special education (Hatton, 2002; Shapiro et al., 2004).

ASSOCIATED INFLUENCES

Many factors contribute to what we are and how we function in the world around us. We inherited certain genetic material from our parents that affects how we look and act. We also are greatly influenced by both our current environment and the one in which we grew up. All these contributions come together in a complex, interactive manner to affect the person that each of us is now.

Certain influences contributing to lowered intellectual functioning are related to culturally different populations in this country. They are associated with intellectual disability by virtue of environmental conditions beyond the control of the people shaped by them (e.g., poor health care and poverty). Other influences are inherent where there is cultural and ethnic diversity, such as social customs or mores and language differences. These are more purely cultural influences and come into play with respect to a literal perspective of the term *differences* in the sense that behavior and performance that are predominant in one culture may not play the same role in another. All these factors concern workers in the area of intellectual disability. The Tips for Professionals feature outlines a series of questions that need further examination every time children from different cultures are considered as referrals for specialized help.

Poverty

Poverty is one of the strongest influences on sociocultural environment today, and impoverished economic circumstances are found more often among ethnic minorities than among their white counterparts (Chow, Jaffee, & Snowden, 2003; Durant, 2004; Yali & Revenson, 2004). The U.S. Bureau of the Census indicated that 7.5% of the non-Hispanic white population lived below the poverty level in 2000. As shown in Figure 2–1, the proportions of African American and Hispanic populations in this economic condition, however, are much higher: 22.1% and 21.2%, respectively (U.S. Bureau of the Census, 2000). Other

Core Concept

Poverty exists at a rather high level among many culturally different groups and creates a number of environmental disadvantages that may impair a child's mental development.

Tips for Professionals

The points below were outlined by a panel of professionals reviewing a January 2002 report by the National Research Council on Minority Children in Gifted and Special Education programs. These items were crafted in the context of additional research needed on English language learners with special needs. However, they also are essential questions that professionals should ask every time a culturally diverse child is referred for specialized instruction. The question simply is directed at *this particular* case and situation rather than a general statement.

1. How does culture and history affect an English language learner's development?
2. What do we know about the differences within an ethnic group? How does a family's legal status or reason for immigration affect a child's success in school?
3. What happens to children once they enter special education, and what happens to those who stay in regular classrooms?
4. How do impoverished families look for help within the schools?
5. Why are English language learners highly overrepresented in special education, especially for learning disabilities and speech and language disorders?
6. What conflicts arise when a teacher and student are from different ethnic groups?

Source: Adapted from "Experts Respond to Study on Minority Students" by D. Sashine, 2002. *CEC Today.* Retrieved from http://www.cec.sped.org/bk/cec_today/may_2002/index.html. Panel members included Asa Hilliard, Georgia State University; Alfredo Artiles, Vanderbilt University; Alba Ortiz and James Yates, University of Texas at Austin; Kathy Froelich and Sandra Wolf, Sitting Bull University; Phil Chinn, California State University; and Gloria Taradash, Association for the Gifted.

Poverty affects the health care of this youngster and the nutrition that builds her physical systems during important developmental periods.

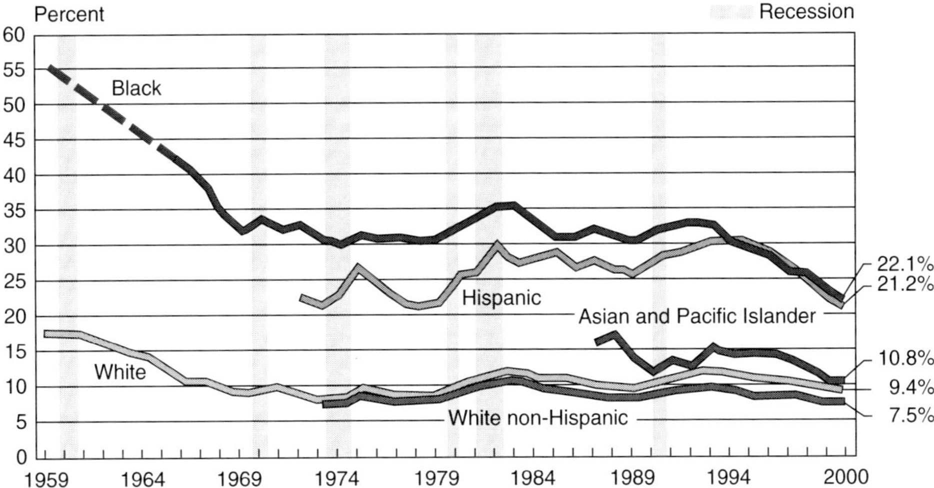

Note: The data points represent the midpoints of the respective years. The latest recession began in July 1990 and ended in March 1991. Data for blacks are not available from 1960 to 1965. Data for the other race and Hispanic origin groups are shown from the first year available. Hispanics may be of any race.

Figure 2–1
Poverty Rates by Race and Hispanic Origin: 1959–2000

Source: U.S. Bureau of the Census (2000, p. 4).

sources confirm the gravity of poverty as a problem, with nearly 12 million children being poor and therefore in a high-risk environment for multiple difficulties (Crockett, 2003).

While the conditions portrayed in Figure 2–1 suggest improvement over time, the situation still places many members of ethnic minorities at a considerable disadvantage. For example, minority children from poor environments tend to have lower educational and occupational expectations than their Caucasian counterparts from more advantaged neighborhoods (Barnett & Camilli, 2002; Yali & Revenson, 2004). Some researchers even assert that poverty is a threat to scholastic functioning and that it is clear that there is a strong relationship between poverty and poor school performance (Ackerman, Brown, & Izard, 2004; Farkas, Lleras, & Maczuga, 2002). Despite this strong relationship, it is important to note that poverty does not exert a simple, singular influence. The effects of poverty represent a complex interaction of factors, including such matters as detrimental physical components of the environment (e.g., poor health care, increased health and development risks), the children's self-perception of competence, teachers' assessment of their effort, and other influences within the environment (Evans, 2004; Guttmann & Dick, 2004; Yali & Revenson, 2004). Poverty emerges as a significant topic of concern in many discussions of educational problems, educational and social reform, and early intervention efforts (e.g., IASSID, 2003). Research suggests that early, preschool programs have a beneficial effect on poor children's cognitive development and school success (Barnett & Camilli, 2002).

Poverty increases the probability of childhood malnutrition as well as the risk of detrimental exposure to such toxic agents as lead and other harmful environmental substances. Extreme poverty may also lead to homelessness, which contributes to irregular school attendance, chronic health problems, and a number of developmental delays (Evans, 2004; Flouri, 2003; Serbin & Karp, 2004). These same factors are also interrelated with each other and with migrancy and homelessness, which emphasizes the difficulty of isolating the impact of single variables in the area of cultural diversity (Ackerman et al., 2004; Yali & Revenson, 2004).

Poverty affects the type and level of health care that people receive as youngsters and the nutrition that builds their physical systems during important developmental periods, both before birth and during the first few years of life. Evidence suggests that during these periods, ethnic minorities suffer from more health complications than their white counterparts. Gelfand and Drew (2003) examined these issues and noted that about 5% of white upper-class infants experience birth complications, whereas birth complications emerge in 15% of the deliveries for low-SES whites and 51% of nonwhites. Ethnic and cultural background substantially influences nutritional intake and other environmental risk factors for young children, which is likely to affect their health status (Crockett, 2003; Evans, 2004; IASSID, 2003). Children who begin their developmental years in unfavorable circumstances have a substantial probability of continued slower or abnormal development and of being labeled as having intellectual disability. The environment continues to present a context of health risk, health risk behaviors, and increased jeopardy for premature mortality for young people from some racial backgrounds (Gelfand & Drew, 2003; Guttman & Dick, 2004). Finally, poor adults from racial minority backgrounds and parents of children with intellectual disability show evidence of significant chronic stress, perhaps suffering the cumulative effects of such influences over a long period (Hughes & Ng, 2003; Richter, 2003; Siddiqui & Pandey, 2003). Symptoms of chronic stress and elevated depression appear related to poverty and further magnify the overall risk for children in these environments (Dennis, Parke, Coltrane, Blacher, & Borthwick-Duffy, 2003; Reading, 2004; Robinson & Emde, 2004). While such effects are not necessarily surprising, they present a serious risk because many of these parents do not have health care resources that are often available to other populations and are important to help buffer the negative effects of such conditions.

Cultural–Social Mores

Core Concept

Social values that differ from culture to culture may result in behavioral or performance deviation from the cultural majority, which some might view as reflecting intellectual disability.

Certainly, social and cultural mores do not contribute to a person's intellectual disability in the same way as genetic abnormality. They do, however, play a significant role in how others view the person's performance in particular areas and in the person's demeanor (Hardman, Drew, & Egan, 2006; Sanson, Hemphill, & Smart, 2004). And these matters influence the overall view of a person's level of functioning, making a direct impact on whether that individual is seen as having intellectual disability.

Different cultures view education and formal schooling quite differently. The U.S. educational system follows the value system of the white cultural majority. It does not equally reflect the beliefs of the members of various subcultures who spend time in U.S. schools. Belief structures are very different in American subcultures, and sources of knowledge, values, expectations, wisdom, and attitudes toward achievement are quite diverse. Such belief systems are also extremely potent, and understanding them may be a key factor in the success or failure of an intervention (Chen, Mo, & Honomichl, 2004; Ruvolo et al., 2004; Yang, Chung, Chen, & Chen, 2004). The impact of deep-seated cultural beliefs is understandable, particularly when one considers that these ideas have permeated children's early developmental years and have shaped their views of the world. This type of culture-specific value system can and often does substantially control how a youngster approaches, acts, and performs in school. It takes little imagination to see how a child with different cultural priorities might do poorly and be assessed as having intellectual disability.

Cultural and social mores may also significantly influence the treatment of individuals with health problems and disabilities and the services sought by their families (Conyers, 2003; Szymanski et al., 2003; Webb, 2004). Intellectual disability is a condition that many cultures recognize, but how it is conceptualized, how it is treated, and its social interpretation are as diverse as the cultures. Accepting certain disability conditions is very difficult for some groups. Culturally related beliefs and superstitions often play a significant role in the way people view abnormality and have a considerable impact on acceptance (Dein, 2003; Harrison & Kahn, 2004; McArdle, 2004). And for the different family structures of various cultural subgroups, care-giving for family members with disability conditions varies. For example, the extended families common to some cultural groups affect beliefs about where care for such individuals should come from and may result in anxiety or even suspicion regarding special services from outside the family (Shapiro et al., 2004). This presents an interesting challenge as educators and other professionals attempt to engage parents in planning for their child's education as required by federal laws such as IDEA. Parents from some cultural minority groups may be reluctant to join with school personnel in such planning because they do not trust such government organizations or have other views that impede such collaboration. Parents of youngsters with disabilities may feel great shame, may be unwilling to seek or accept outside assistance, or may have actually been left behind during clandestine emigration. Thus, interacting with the educational system is not an easy matter for parents of children from other cultures. Such difficulties are compounded in some circumstances in which the parents' communication with the system is further inhibited by language differences.

Cultural and social mores clearly affect how individuals approach and interact with institutions that represent authority and reflect the belief systems of the cultural majority. Because of this diversity, different demeanors and behaviors have different meanings in various population subgroups (Angermeyer, Buyantugs, Kenzine, & Matschinger, 2004; El-Islam, 2004; Mercer, 2004). Behavior that is highly regarded, seen as reflecting intelligence, or viewed as reflecting an attitude that is positively valued by one culture may be viewed as offensive, unwise, or even unintelligent in another. The magnitude of such differences is highlighted in the context of achievement goals and intrinsic achievement motivation often associated with success in our educational system (Edward, 2003; Kuroishi, 2004; Van Houtte, 2004). Matters such as facial expressions, emotional expressions, and proper behavior often have culture-specific meaning (Elfenbein & Ambady, 2002; Gauthier, 2003). Including information on these complex cultural influences is vital when one considers the overall phenomenon of intellectual disability (Pentland et al., 2003). Cultural influences are of great practical impact as children from cultural minority groups are educated. They also challenge professionals to prove the conceptual soundness and utility of intellectual disability definitions.

Language

Core Concept

Language differences that create academic difficulties for some culturally different children may place them in jeopardy of being considered as having intellectual disability.

Cultural diversity also results in a number of language differences that often contribute to academic challenges in a school system designed and operated by the cultural majority (Datnow, Borman, Stringfield, Overman, & Castellano, 2003; Morrison, Cosden, O'Farrell, & Campos, 2003). Academic problems stemming from language differences may result in referral, assessment, and inappropriate labeling of a child as having intellectual disability if consideration is not given to cultural factors. Language differences may be absolute, as when a youngster's family speaks a language other than English. Additional differences may be found when the youngster's linguistic patterns represent what is known as nonstandard language or nonstandard English. Nonstandard language is evident in the communication patterns of some cultural or racial subgroups and may result in biased perceptions and assessment (Blake & Cutler, 2003; Boone, 2003; Zhiming, 2003).

Language patterns emerging from the speech configurations in nonstandard English are sufficiently different from those of the cultural majority to cause considerable academic difficulty for a youngster in the school system. It is easy to see how a teacher from the dominant culture might find it difficult to understand the child. It is also easy to see how teachers and others might think that the child had a language deficiency or disorder and might therefore refer the child for testing for intellectual disability. Once into the referral–assessment cycle, the child using nonstandard language could be diagnosed and placed into special education service patterns that could label that individual for life. This is a particularly unfortunate outcome if the diagnosis of intellectual disability is erroneous and due to a cultural difference rather than actual intellectual status. Consideration of cultural background in communication disorder diagnosis is complex, differing in some significant ways among cultural groups (Battle, 2002; Saenz & Huer, 2003; Stow & Dodd, 2003). Such consideration, however, grows increasingly essential by educators at all levels as school populations become more culturally diverse (Hardman et al., 2006).

Classification errors based on language differences place assessment in a critical position. Language differences and inaccurate or biased assessment have received considerable attention in the literature (e.g., Denton, Anthony, Parker, & Hasbrouck, 2004; Moseley, 2004; Stow & Dodd, 2003). Issues pertaining to the fairness of assessment for children with language and cultural differences continue to perplex evaluation specialists and are not easily resolved (Everatt, Smythe, Ocampo, & Gyarmathy, 2004; Jesse, Davis, & Pokorny, 2004). Minimizing assessment error and interpretation bias appears to be the most satisfactory approach in order to provide the most effective instruction possible to all children.

ISSUES OF ASSESSMENT AND INTERVENTION

Core Concept

Personnel and procedures involved in the assessment and intervention process may all contribute to a biased overrepresentation of culturally different children as having intellectual disability.

Assessment has played a central role in dealing with culturally different people and intellectual disability (Bainter & Tollefson, 2003; Merrell, 2003). Testing for deficiencies or differences is at the core of the process by which one determines whether an individual has intellectual disability. If this process is unfavorably biased against cultural differences, then the likelihood increases that a child who actually reflects diversity rather than deficiency will be labeled with intellectual disability. Youngsters from minority backgrounds do appear more frequently in disability categories than would be expected on the basis of the proportion of culturally different people in the population. This disproportionately high rate of identification frequently involves deficiencies diagnosed through psychoeducational assessment, which suggests that the evaluation process and the uses of assessment information may include serious bias (e.g., Geisinger, 2003; Meyer, Bevan-Brown, Harry, & Sapon-Shevin, 2004; Saenz & Huer, 2003). It should also be noted that there have been continuing concerns regarding the various definitions with respect to the possibility that definitions themselves may magnify the problem of minority overrepresentation (Hatton, 2002). This is reflected in recent changes in the AAMR (2002) definition.

Measurement bias can occur in many fashions. Cultural bias in assessment leads to inaccurate results based on cultural background. Such results are testing artifacts—conclusions from an evaluation that reveal cultural background rather than actual mental abilities or skills (Fox, 2003; Oakland & Hatzichristou, 2003). This type of error in psychological assessment has been of concern to professionals for many decades, and arguments about the causes of such bias, its effects, and resolutions of it continue in the scientific literature (Bainter & Tollefson, 2003; Merrell, 2003; Morgan & Mehta, 2004).

Norm-referenced measurement procedures, which often employ normative data, language patterns, and knowledge or content based on the cultural majority, are highly vulnerable to assessment bias. Under the conditions presumed by norm-referenced tests, individuals from minority and culturally different backgrounds may have a built-in performance disadvantage (Hardman et al., 2006; Morgan & Mehta, 2004; Oakland & Hatzichristou, 2003). Such a disadvantage may occur because their performance scores are compared with those of a large group of individuals who are tested as a part of instrument development (the norm group). The norm group may not include an appropriate number of minority individuals and therefore not be adequately representative. Further, the conditions of testing may reflect procedures more comfortable for those of the cultural majority. This type of inequitable assessment has played a dominant role in widely publicized court cases involving Hispanic and African American students (*Diana v. State Board of Education*, 1970; *Larry P. v. Riles*, 1972, 1979). Such cases have had a major impact on the manner in which testing is viewed.

Attempts to design culturally fair test instruments have been made for many years but have met with little success. Certain improvements were achieved with respect to minimizing conspicuous culture-specific components and developing complex systems of assessment that attempt to consider cultural background through multiple measures. Difficulties remain, however, and concerns regarding minority children's disadvantage continue to appear in the literature (e.g., Bainter & Tollefson, 2003; Merrell, 2003; Morgan & Mehta, 2004).

Attention to the instruments of assessment without concern for the people and processes involved in evaluation leaves room for considerable cultural bias in psychological assessment. People often make classification decisions on the basis of specific data and form impressions from scant information. Efforts must be undertaken to minimize the personal bias of professionals involved in psychological assessment. These efforts will require additional training or different preparation specifically incorporating information about cultural factors, language background, and curriculum or intervention plans into the evaluation (Boyd, 2003; Kritikos, 2003). Some have argued that attention must be given to a variety of protocol issues (Denton et al., 2004; Everatt et al., 2004; Jesse et al., 2004).

Earlier, we examined the influences associated with minority and culturally different status. Knowledge of such information about each individual child is extremely important in any assessment and often must be obtained through interviews with parents and other significant people in the youngster's environment. Determining such matters as the language spoken in the home, who the child's caretakers are, and what activities are undertaken all add to the picture of the world the child lives in. Professionals must obtain this background information in a manner sensitive to differences in cultural attitudes and mores, or it, too, has the potential for being inaccurate or biased (Merrell, 2003). An accurate understanding of the child requires contextual understanding of that youngster in the family. Table 2–1 summarizes important points of consideration during the assessment process with children from diverse backgrounds.

Psychological assessment plays a vital role in assessing intellectual disability. It is an important component in the process of identifying and serving those

Table 2–1
Process Checklist for Serving Children From Diverse Backgrounds

This checklist provides professionals with points to consider in the process of educating children from culturally diverse backgrounds. These matters should be considered during each of the following: referral and testing or diagnostic assessment; classification, labeling, or class assignment change; teacher conferences or home communication.

Process	Issues	Question to Be Asked
Referral, testing, or diagnostic assessment	Language issues	Is the native language different than the language in which the child is being taught, and should this be considered in the assessment process? What is the home language? What is the normal conversational language? In what language can the student be successfully taught or assessed—academic language?
	Cultural issues	What are the views toward schooling of the culture from which the child comes? Do differences exist in expectations between the school and family for the child's schooling goals? What are the cultural views toward illness or disability?
	Home issues	What is the family constellation, and who are the family members? What is the family's economic status?
Classification, labeling, or class assignment change	Language issues	Does the proposed placement change account for any language differences that are relevant, particularly academic language?
	Cultural issues	Does the proposed placement change consider any unique cultural views regarding schooling?
	Home issues	Does the proposed change consider pertinent family matters?
Teacher conferences or home communication	Language issues	Is the communication to parents or other family members in a language they understand?
	Cultural issues	Do cultural views influence communication between family members and the schools as a formal governmental organization? Is there a cultural reluctance of family members to come to the school? Are home visits a desirable alternative? Is communication from teachers viewed positively?
	Home issues	Is the family constellation such that communication with the schools is possible and positive? Are family members positioned economically and otherwise to respond to communication from the schools in a productive manner? If the family is low SES, is transportation a problem for conferences?

Source: From *Human Exceptionality: School, Community, and Family* (8th ed.), by M. L. Hardman, C. J. Drew, and M. W. Egan, 2006. Needham Heights, MA: Allyn & Bacon.

who need specialized treatment. Assessment must not, however, become a mechanism for discrimination or an expression of cultural prejudice. To allow such misuse runs counter to the basic purpose of intervention to help those who need treatment. Chapters 3 and 4 are devoted solely to assessment. As you read and study these chapters, it is important to keep multicultural issues firmly in mind.

Core Concept

Cultural diversity may result in some influences that generate actual developmental disadvantages as well as differences.

HUMAN DEVELOPMENT AND MULTICULTURAL ISSUES

A wide variety of factors as diverse as inherited genetic material and environmental influences, such as nutrition, disease, and toxic substances, affect the course of human development. All these factors may have favorable or unfavorable consequences on the rate and quality of a young person's developing abilities, depending on how they come in contact with the individual and when the contact occurs. Many of these factors are discussed in more detail in later chapters as we address the developmental abnormalities resulting in intellectual disability. In this section, we address how some of these influences are associated with cultural diversity and how they may, in this context, have an impact on the development of children and youths from minority cultures.

Earlier in this chapter, we discussed impoverished economic circumstances as a condition often associated with ethnic minority status in this country. For example, poverty occurs much more frequently among African American and Hispanic populations than it does in those of the cultural majority (Chow et al., 2003; Yali & Revenson, 2004). Nearly three times as many members of these groups live in conditions below the poverty level as do members of the dominant culture (U.S. Bureau of the Census, 2000). Such circumstances severely limit accessibility to quality health care, adequate nutrition, early stimulation, and a variety of other environmental features that promote favorable growth and development in youngsters. These matters dramatically influence maturation both prenatally and during the important growth periods after birth. During these times in the life cycle, crucial physical, neurological, and cognitive structures undergo their most rapid growth. The foundations of a person's development are laid at this point and play a very strong role in determining how later maturation proceeds. To the degree that inadequate health care, nutrition, and other circumstances exist in culturally diverse populations, children in these groups are placed at risk for delayed or otherwise abnormal development that may result in intellectual disability (Gelfand & Drew, 2003). Chapters 6 and 7, in particular, discuss such unfavorable developmental circumstances and their potential outcomes.

The influences just mentioned may generate serious developmental disadvantages for culturally different youngsters, adversely affecting basic neurological and cognitive structures. In addition to these factors, what is learned during the formative years plays a pivotal role in later behavior. The content of what is learned may produce sociocultural differences that set minority youngsters apart from their peers in the cultural majority (Cloninger, 2003; Danoff-Burg, Prelow, & Swenson, 2004). Earlier, we noted that cultural and social mores influence the view of education and formal schooling. Different cultures display divergent belief structures, with varying opinions about the sources of wisdom and knowledge and attitudes toward achievement. For example, certain Native American cultures view group cooperation for excellence more favorably than individual striving or competition for achievement. This perspective has a significant impact on school performance where the dominant culture places a high value on individual achievement and behavior. These and other types of social values are learned very early in the developmental life cycle and have a powerful influence on how children approach and engage the world around them. Many subgroups have beliefs and cultural mores that differ from the cultural majority. Some are reflected in racial groups (e.g., Asian or African American), whereas others have geographic elements or pieces of both (such as Hawaiian or Alaskan natives). The impact of these beliefs on how culturally different children perform in institutions designed and operated by the cultural majority should not be underestimated. Such early learning is extremely durable and often creates serious conflict as youngsters encounter varying belief systems in the world beyond their cultural background.

Society's role in changing the circumstances of human development is not clear. Few would argue that it is important to alter the contingencies that present developmental disadvantages to children. To do otherwise runs counter to the basic philosophy of a society that explicitly promotes the well-being of its entire people. Serious philosophical questions arise, however, about the degree of conformity society should require. Most would not subscribe to a basic doctrine that requires culturally diverse belief systems to be brought into conformity with those of the cultural majority. The dimension of developmental differences presents a complicated challenge, one that is not easily solved.

NEW ISSUES AND FUTURE DIRECTIONS

The face of behavioral science, including education, is undergoing tremendous changes in its basic research models. Quantitatively oriented experimental and clinical psychology have formed the foundations of traditional research methodologies used in the study of intellectual disability. These methodologies usually have had a quantitative, norm-referenced framework as their context. The largest body of research in intellectual disability reflects investigation of the phenomenon as a concept of performance or ability deficit viewed predominantly in relation to normative abilities derived from the cultural majority. Historically, only isolated researchers have pursued investigations of intellectual disability emphasizing the study of individuals in the context of their environment (see Klotz, 2004; Mactavish & Schleien, 2004).

Core Concept

Professionals in the field of intellectual disability must change basic models of research on intellectual disability so that the influences of cultural diversity on human development can be more fully understood.

We cannot address the challenges that Denise faces in our opening vignette just based on the research models that have predominated behavioral science in the past. It is clear that we do not have enough information to determine how we can help Denise. But it is clear that the few questions we posed earlier require a careful and thorough examination of the environment Denise was in before and the school she is in now. Assessment steps necessarily will include attention to her family circumstances, how the parents interact with the school personnel (previously and now), and how all these matters combine to present us with a child that is not doing well in school (see again Table 2–1 and reconsider the Tips for Professionals item at the first part of the chapter). From this type of analysis, we can begin to determine what type of intervention might be appropriate.

Professionals' understanding of intellectual disability is only as adequate as the research models. It is important to realize that intellectual disability occurs not in the laboratory but in the context of the broader society. Although the laboratory has provided considerable information, that information must be placed in context to achieve understanding, which, from the perspective of this chapter, means consideration of cultural diversity issues. Educational, social, and cultural environments must become integral in the study of child development both generally and with regard to developmental deviations such as intellectual disability (Johnson-Glenberg & Chapman, 2004; Rimmerman, Turkel, & Crossman, 2003).

The study of intellectual disability as a part of the social and cultural environment is gaining considerable momentum. Qualitative research models, like those of ethnography, hold great promise for future understanding of this multidimensional problem (Denzin, 2003; Maxwell, 2004; Northcutt & McCoy, 2004). Where once little was written about methodology, now volumes are beginning to rival those available in quantitative research (Cassell & Symon, 2004; Flick, Steinke, & Von Kardoff, 2004; Sofaer, 2005).

As these changes are occurring, it is important to realize that the choice of methods is expanding, not that one is supplanting another. There is little reason to think that the future will involve discarding the strengths of quantitative investigation. What will be needed is the strength of multiple methods studying the same questions with the same populations. Future research will require investigators to be thoughtful eclectics, incorporating the necessary rigor while shedding the narrow perspective of a single model. Such an approach holds great promise for improving the understanding of the complex interactions of cultural diversity and intellectual disability.

Core Questions

1. How does cultural diversity result in differences that one must address when considering intellectual disability conceptually?
2. How does cultural diversity result in differences that one must consider when diagnosing an individual as having intellectual disability?

3. How does poverty create environmental circumstances that might impair a child's mental development?
4. How might social values emerge in the behavior or performance of a culturally different individual and suggest a diagnosis of intellectual disability?
5. How might language differences place a child in jeopardy of being diagnosed as having intellectual disability?
6. How do assessment procedures potentially place a culturally different individual at an unfair disadvantage, with the possible result of a label of intellectual disability?
7. How might assessment personnel influence diagnostic evaluation in a manner that inaccurately identifies a culturally different individual as having intellectual disability?
8. How might the environmental circumstances of cultural diversity have such an adverse influence on human development that they help cause intellectual disability?
9. How have traditional research models in intellectual disability failed to account for the influences of cultural diversity in human development?

Roundtable Discussion

Intellectual disability is a problem that by definition involves differences from normal functioning. Individuals with intellectual disability perform poorly from both intellectual and social perspectives. In examining intellectual disability, it is important to consider who sets the norms of behavior and performance. For the most part, society shapes these norms on the basis of the views of the cultural majority, without much reflection of the belief structures of ethnic minority populations.

In your study or discussion group, examine the potential effects of having one segment of the population set the standards for another group; focus on a subgroup that does not share the belief systems of the majority. Remember that ethnic minorities represent a greater proportion of those labeled handicapped with disabilities than would be expected. Does this fact represent discrimination? How do you separate discrimination from actual disadvantages associated with cultural diversity? Should performance or behavior reflecting cultural differences be considered in applying the label of intellectual disability?

Parent and Professional Organization Positions on Key Issues in the Lives of People with Intellectual Disabilities

The inside front cover of this text presents a matrix that includes several key issues in the lives of people with disabilities, the positions of various parent and professional organizations on each issue, and the chapter and page number where the information is addressed. Table 2–2 on page 64 is a summary of the organizations and key issues addressed in this chapter.

Table 2–2
Key Issues and Organizations Discussed in This Chapter

Organization/Website	Key Issues Addressed	Chapter Heading
American Association on Mental Retardation (http://www.aamr.org)	Definitions and societal expectations Minority overrepresentation Measurement bias Health care, poverty	Introduction Issues of Assessment and Intervention Associated Influences
International Association for the Scientific Study of Intellectual Disabilities (http://www.iassid.org)	Health care Development risks and poverty Malnutrition and poverty	Poverty

References

Ackerman, B. P., Brown, E. D., & Izard, C. E. (2004). The relations between persistent poverty and contextual risk and children's behavior in elementary school. *Developmental Psychology, 40,* 367–377.

American Association on Mental Retardation (AAMR). (2002). *Intellectual disability: Definition, classification, and systems of supports* (10th ed.). Washington, DC: Author.

American Psychiatric Association (APA). (2000). *Diagnostic and statistical manual of mental disorders* (4th ed.). Washington, DC: Author.

Angermeyer, M. C., Buyantugs, L., Kenzine, D. V., & Matschinger, H. (2004). Effects of labelling on public attitudes towards people with schizophrenia: Are there cultural differences? *Acta-Psychiatrica-Scandinavica, 109,* 420–425.

Bainter, T. R., & Tollefson, N. (2003). Intellectual assessment of language minority students: What do school psychologists believe are acceptable practices? *Psychology in the Schools, 40,* 599–603.

Barnett, W. S., & Camilli, G. (2002). Compensatory preschool education, cognitive development, and "race." In J. M. Fish (Ed.), *Race and intelligence: Separating science from myth* (pp. 369–406). Mahwah, NJ: Erlbaum.

Battle, D. E. (2002). Language and communication disorders in culturally and linguistically diverse children. In D. K. Bernstein & E. Tiegerman-Farber (Eds.), *Language and communication disorders in children* (5th ed., pp. 354–386). Boston: Allyn & Bacon.

Ben-Ari, A., & Lavee, Y. (2004). Cultural orientation, ethnic affiliation, and negative daily occurrences: A multidimensional cross-cultural analysis. *American Journal of Orthopsychiatry, 74,* 102–111.

Blake, R. A., & Cutler, C. (2003). AAE and variation in teachers' attitudes: A question of school philosophy? *Linguistics and Education, 14,* 163–194.

Boone, P. R. (2003). When the "Amen Corner" comes to class: An examination of the pedagogical and cultural impact of call-response communication in black college classroom. *Communication Education, 52,* 212–229.

Boyd, S. (2003). Foreign-born teachers in the multilingual classroom in Sweden: The role of attitudes to foreign accent. *International Journal of Bilingual Education and Bilingualism, 6* (3–4), 283–295.

Cassell, C., & Symon, G. (2004). *Qualitative methods and intervention in organizational research: A practical guide.* Thousand Oaks, CA: Sage.

Chen, Z., Mo, L., & Honomichl, R. (2004). Having the memory of an elephant: Long-term retrieval and the use of analogues in problem solving. *Journal of Experimental Psychology: General, 133,* 415–433.

Chow, J. C. C., Jaffee, K., & Snowden, L. (2003). Racial/ethnic disparities in the use of mental health services in poverty areas. *American Journal of Public Health, 93,* 792–797.

Cloninger, C. R. (2003). Completing the psychobiological architecture of human personality development: Temperament, character and coherence. In U. Lindenberger & U. M. Staudinger (Eds.), *Understanding human development: Dialogues with lifespan psychology* (pp. 159–181). Dordrecht, Netherlands: Kluwer Academic Publishers.

Conyers, L. M. (2003). Disability culture: A cultural model of disability. *Rehabilitation Education, 17,* 139–154.

Crockett, D. (2003). Critical issues children face in the 2000s. *School Psychology Quarterly, 18,* 446–453.

Danoff-Burg, S., Prelow, H. M., & Swenson, R. R. (2004). Hope and life satisfaction in black college students coping with race-related stress. *Journal of Black Psychology, 30,* 208–228.

Datnow, A., Borman, G. D., Stringfield, S., Overman, L. T., & Castellano, M. (2003). Comprehensive school reform in culturally and linguistically diverse contexts: Implementation and outcomes from a four-year study. *Educational Evaluation and Policy Analysis, 25,* 143–170.

Dein, S. (2003). Psychogenic death: Individual effects of sorcery and taboo violation. *Mental Health, Religion and Culture, 6,* 195–202.

Dennis, J. M., Parke, R. D., Coltrane, S., Blacher, J., & Borthwick-Duffy, S. A. (2003). Economic pressure, maternal depression, and child adjustment in Latino families: An exploratory study. *Journal of Family and Economic Issues, 24,* 183–202.

Denton, C. A., Anthony, J. L., Parker, R., & Hasbrouck, J. E. (2004). Effects of two tutoring programs on the English reading development of Spanish-English bilingual students. *Elementary School Journal, 104,* 289–305.

Denzin, N. K. (2003). Performance ethnography: Critical pedagogy and the politics of culture. Thousand Oaks, CA: Sage.

Diana v. State Board of Education, C-70-37 R.F.P. (N.D. California, Jan. 7, 1970).

Diekman, K. A., Tenbrunsel, A. E., & Galinsky, A. D. (2003). From self-prediction to self-defeat: Behavioral forecasting, self-fulfilling prophecies, and the effect of competitive expectations. *Journal of Personality and Social Psychology, 85,* 672–683.

Durant, N. A. (2004). Mental health professionals, minorities, and the poor. *American Journal of Psychiatry, 161,* 382–383.

Edward, N. S. (2003). First impressions last: An innovative approach to induction. *Active Learning in Higher Education, 4,* 226–242.

Elfenbein, H. A., & Ambady, N. (2002). On the universality and cultural specificity of emotion recognition: A meta-analysis. *Psychological Bulletin, 128,* 203–235.

El-Islam, M. F. (2004). Culture in the clinical practice of psychiatry. *Arab Journal of Psychiatry, 15,* 8–16.

Evans, G. W. (2004). The environment of childhood poverty. *American Psychologist, 59,* 77–92.

Everatt, J., Smythe, I., Ocampo, D., & Gyarmathy, E. (2004). Issues in the assessment of literacy-related difficulties across language backgrounds: A cross-linguistic comparison. *Journal of Research in Reading, 27,* 141–151.

Farkas, G., Lleras, C., & Maczuga, S. (2002). Does oppositional culture exist in minority and poverty peer groups? *American Sociological Review, 67,* 148–155.

Flick, U., Steinke, I., & Von Kardoff, E. (2004). *Qualitative research: Paradigms, theories, methods, practice and contexts.* Thousand Oaks, CA: Sage.

Flouri, E. (2003). Social work and child and adolescent mental health. *Journal of Adolescence, 27,* 217.

Fox, J, D. (2003). From products to process: An ecological approach to bias detection. *International Journal of Testing, 3,* 21–47.

Gauthier, M. (2003). The inadequacy of concepts: The rise of youth interest in civic participation in Quebec. *Journal of Youth Studies, 6,* 265–276.

Geisinger, K. F. (2003). Testing and assessment in cross-cultural psychology. In J. A. Naglieri & J. R. Graham (Eds.), *Handbook of psychology: Assessment psychology* (Vol. 10, pp. 95–117). New York: Wiley.

Gelfand, D. M., & Drew, C. J. (2003). Understanding child behavior disorders (4th ed.). Fort Worth, TX: Harcourt Brace.

Guttmann, A., & Dick, P. (2004). Infant hospitalization and maternal depression, poverty and single parenthood—A population-based study. *Child: Care, Health and Development, 30,* 67–75.

Hardman, M. L., Drew, C. J., & Egan, M. W. (2006). *Human exceptionality: School, community, and family* (8th ed.). Needham Heights, MA: Allyn & Bacon.

Harrison, T. C., & Kahn, D. L. (2004). Disability rites: The cultural shift following impairment. *Family and Community Health, 27,* 86–93.

Hatton, C. (2002). People with intellectual disabilities from ethnic minority communities in the United States and the United Kingdom. In L. M. Glidden (Ed.), *International review of research in mental retardation* (Vol. 25, pp. 209–239). San Diego, CA: Academic Press.

Holguin, G., & Hansen, D. J. (2003). The "sexually abused child": Potential mechanisms for adverse influences of such a label. *Aggression and Violent Behavior, 8,* 645–670.

Hughes, D. C., & Ng, S. (2003). Reducing health disparities among children. *Future of Children, 13,* 153–167.

International Association for the Scientific Study of Intellectual Disabilities (IASSID). (2003). Health SIRG news. *Newsletter, 20,* 13.

Jesse, D., Davis, A., & Pokorny, N. (2004). High-achieving middle schools for Latino students in poverty. *Journal of Education for Students Placed at Risk, 9,* 23–45.

Johnson-Glenberg, M. C., & Chapman, R. S. (2004). Predictors of parent-child language during novel task play: A comparison between typically developing children and individuals with Down syndrome. *Journal of Intellectual Disability Research, 48,* 225–238.

Kemp, C., & Carter, M. (2002). The social skills and social status of mainstreamed students with intellectual disabilities. *Educational Psychology, 22,* 391–411.

Klotz, J. (2004). Sociocultural study of intellectual disability: Moving beyond labelling and social constructionist perspectives. *British Journal of Learning Disabilities, 32,* 93–104.

Kritikos, E. P. (2003). Speech-language pathologists' beliefs about language assessment of bilingual/bicultural individuals. *American Journal of Speech-Language-Pathology, 12,* 73–91.

Kuroishi, N. (2004). Motivational psychology in the context. *Japanese Psychological Review, 46,* 5–11.

Larry P. v. Riles, 343 F. Supp. 1306 (N.D. California 1972); 343 F. Supp. 1306, 502 F.2d 963 (N.D. California 1979).

Locke, D. C. (1995). Counseling interventions with African American youth. In C. C. Lee (Ed.), *Counseling for diversity* (pp. 21–40). Boston: Allyn & Bacon.

Mactavish, J. B., & Schleien, S. J. (2004). Re-injecting spontaneity and balance in family life: Parents' perspectives on recreation in families that include children with developmental disability. *Journal of Intellectual Disability Research, 48,* 123–141.

Matson, J. L., Luke, M. A., & Mayville, S. B. (2004). The effects of antiepileptic medications on the social skills of individuals with mental retardation. *Research in Developmental Disabilities, 25,* 219–228.

Maxwell, J. A. (2004). *Qualitative research design: An interpretive approach* (2nd ed.). Thousand Oaks, CA: Sage.

McArdle, P. (2004). Attention-deficit hyperactivity disorder and life-span development. *British Journal of Psychiatry, 184,* 468–469.

Mercer, J. A. (2004). The Protestant child, adolescent, and family. *Child and Adolescent Psychiatric Clinics of North America, 13,* 161–181.

Merrell, K. W. (2003). Behavioral, social, and emotional assessment of children and adolescents (2nd ed.). Mahwah, NJ: Erlbaum.

Meyer, L. H., Bevan-Brown, J., Harry, B., & Sapon-Shevin, M. (2004). School inclusion and multicultural issues in special education. In J. A. Banks & C. A. M. Banks (Eds.), *Multicultural education: Issues and perspectives, Update* (4th ed., pp. 327–352). New York: Wiley.

Mezulis, A. H., Abramson, L. Y., Hyde, J. S., & Hankin, B. L. (2004). Is there a universal positivity bias in attributions? A meta-analytic review of individual, developmental, and cultural differences in the self-serving attributional bias. *Psychological Bulletin, 130,* 711–747.

Morgan, S, L., & Mehta, J. D. (2004). Beyond the laboratory: Evaluating the survey evidence for the disidentification explanation of black-white differences in achievement. *Sociology of Education, 77,* 82–101.

Morrison, G. M., Cosden, M. A., O'Farrell, S. L., & Campos, E. (2003). Changes in Latino students' perceptions of school belonging over time: Impact of language proficiency, self-perceptions and teacher evaluations. *California School Psychologist, 8,* 87–98.

Moseley, D. (2004). The diagnostic assessment of word recognition and phonic skills in five-year-olds. *Journal of Research in Reading, 27,* 132–140.

Naglieri, J. A., & Rojan, J. (2001). Intellectual classification of Black and White children in special education programs using the WISC-III and the Cognitive Assessment System. *American Journal on Mental Retardation, 106,* 359–367.

Northcutt, N., & McCoy, D. (2004). *Interactive qualitative analysis: A systems methods for qualitative research*. Thousand Oaks, CA: Sage.

Oakland, T., & Hatzichristou, C. (2003). Issues to consider when adapting tests. *Psychology: The Journal of the Hellenic Psychological Society, 10,* 437–448.

Pentland, W., Walker, J., Minnes, P., Tremblay, M., Brouwer, B., & Gould, M. (2003). Occupational responses to mid-life and aging in women with disabilities. *Journal of Occupational Science, 10,* 21–30.

Reading, R. (2004). Maternal depression, changing public assistance, good security, and child health status. *Child: Care, Health and Development, 30,* 398.

Richter, L. M. (2003). Poverty, underdevelopment and infant mental health. *Journal of Paediatrics and Child Health, 39,* 243–248.

Rimmerman, A., Turkel, L., & Crossman, R. (2003). Perception of child development, child-related stress and dyadic adjustment: Pair analysis of married couples of young children with developmental disabilities. *Journal of Intellectual and Developmental Disability, 28,* 188–195.

Robinson, J., & Emde, R. N. (2004). Mental health moderaters of early head start on parenting and child development: Maternal depression and relationship attitudes. *Parenting: Science and Practice, 4,* 73–79.

Ruvolo, C. M., Peterson, S. A., & LeBoeuf, J. N. G. (2004). Leaders are made, not born. The critical role of a developmental framework to facilitate an organizational culture of development. *Consulting Psychology Journal: Practice and Research, 56,* 10–19.

Saenz, T. I., & Huer, M. B. (2003). Testing strategies involving least biased language assessment of bilingual children. *Communication Disorders Quarterly, 24,* 184–193.

Sanson, A., Hemphill, S. A., & Smart, D. (2004). Connections between temperament and social development: A review. *Social Development, 13,* 142–170.

Sashine, D. (2002). Experts respond to study on minority students. *CEC Today.* Retrieved from http://www.cec.sped.org/bk/cec_today/may_2002/index.html

Serbin, L. A., & Karp, J. (2004). The intergenerational transfer of psychosocial risk: Mediators of vulnerability and resilience. *Annual Review of Psychology, 55,* 333–363.

Shapiro, J., Monzo, L. D., Rueda, R., Gomez, J. A., & Blacher, J. (2004). Alienated advocacy: Perspectives of Latina mothers of young adults with developmental disabilities on service systems. *Mental Retardation, 42,* 37–54.

Siddiqui, R. N., & Pandey, J. (2003). Coping with poverty by an urban poor minority group. *Psychological Studies, 48,* 66–71.

Snyder, C. R. (2003). "Me conform? No way": Classroom demonstrations for sensitizing students to their conformity. *Teaching of Psychology, 30,* 59–61.

Sofaer, B. (2005). *Qualitative methods in health services and policy research.* Hoboken, NJ: Wiley.

Souza, G., & Kennedy, C. H. (2003). Facilitating social interactions in the community for a transition-age student with severe disabilities. *Journal of Positive Behavior Interventions, 5,* 179–182.

Sprott, D. E., Spangenberg, E. R., & Fisher, R. (2003). The importance of normative beliefs to the self-prophecy effect. *Journal of Applied Psychology, 88,* 423–431.

Stow, C., & Dodd, B. (2003). Providing an equitable service to bilingual children in the UK: A review. *International Journal of Language and Communication Disorders, 38,* 351–377.

Szymanski, E. M., Parker, R. M., Ryan, C., Merz, M. A., Trevino-Espinoza, B., & Johnston-Rodriguez, S. (2003). Work and disability: Basic constructs. In R. M. Parker & E. M. Szymanski (Eds.), *Work and disability: Issues and strategies in career development and job placement* (2nd ed.), (pp. 1–25). Austin, TX: PRO-ED.

U.S. Bureau of the Census. (2000). Poverty in the United States: 2000. Retrieved from http://www.census.gov/dmd

Van Houtte, M. (2004). Why boys achieve less at school than girls: The difference between boys' and girls' academic culture. *Educational Studies, 30,* 159–173.

Watts, I. E., & Erevelles, N. (2004). These deadly times: Reconceptualizing school violence by using critical race theory and disability studies. *American Educational Research Journal, 41,* 271–299.

Webb, F. J. (2004). Mental health professionals, minorities, and the poor. *Journal of Behavioral Health Services and Research, 31,* 343.

Yali, A. M., & Revenson, T. A. (2004). How changes in population demographics will impact health psychology: Incorporating a broader notion of cultural competence into the field. *Health Psychology, 23,* 147–155.

Yang, P., Chung, L. C., Chen, C. S., & Chen, C. C. (2004). Rapid improvement in academic grades following methylphenidate treatment in attention-deficit hyperactivity disorder. *Psychiatry-and-Clinical-Neurosciences, 58,* 37–41.

Zhiming, B. (2003). Social stigma and grammatical autonomy in nonnative varieties of English. *Language in Society, 32,* 23–46.

Part 2

Identifying People with Intellectual Disabilities

Chapter 3

Assessment Issues and Procedures

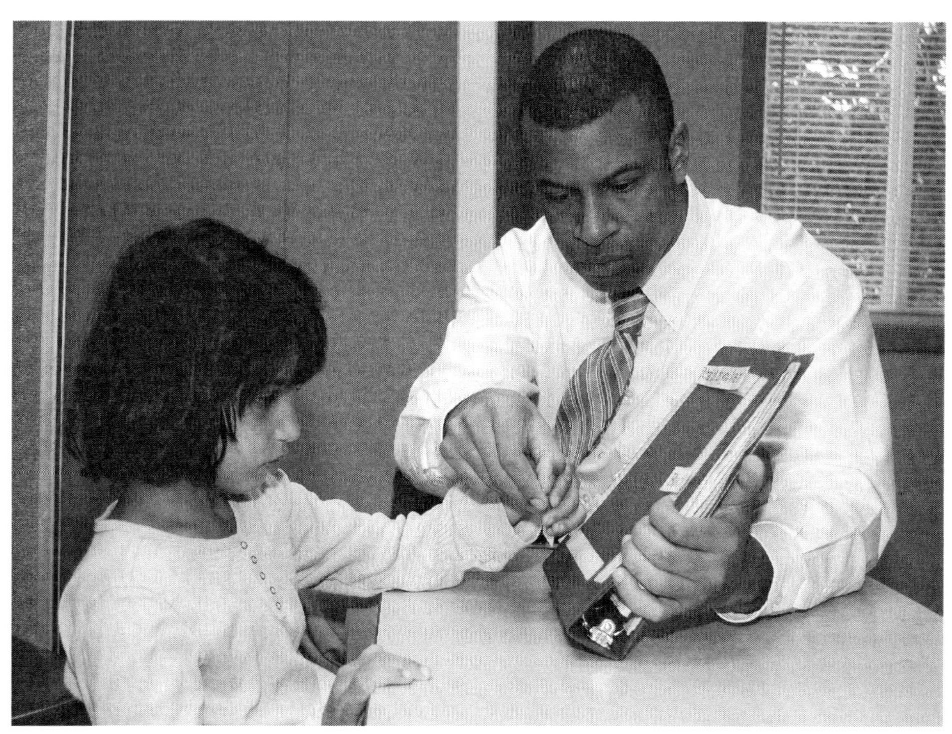

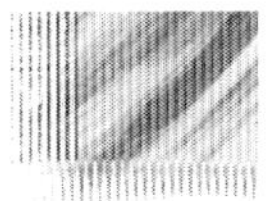

Chapter Preview

At the completion of this chapter, you will have a better understanding of the challenges involved in assessment of those having intellectual disabilities. You will encounter:

- The challenges of designing an appropriate instrument for assessment and how the proper use of assessment instruments has a great impact on the results of measurement.
- How the purpose of any assessment greatly influences the procedure(s) employed and the way data are interpreted.
- How assessment procedures are different depending on the age of the person and the performance area being evaluated.

The Beginning Evaluation

My baby boy came early, around 3:00 in the morning of April 16, 1960. The delivery was pretty easy although I was pretty much out of it at first in the recovery room. My head had begun to clear when the obstetric doctor showed me little Charles in the small crib and said the words that changed my life forever. "Your son is mentally retarded. You can see by his eyes and hands. I'm sorry to have to tell you." Our family was never the same. This was nearly 50 years ago and we were told that Charley would be better off in an institution with others like himself. Things would be different now. There are a lot more cultural support systems for parents of children with intellectual disabilities. (Margery Johnson, parent)

- *The "beginning evaluation" vignette looks back many years. This seemingly simple approach was based on very incomplete and imperfect assessment information (e.g., "you can see by his eyes and hands") and often had a profound impact on the developmental future of the child. What do you think the feelings and emotions of the parent are when these words are said aloud? In 1960 when a figure of authority said something like "your son will be mentally retarded" it was typically taken at face value (even the terminology was different).*

The basis for assessment and diagnostic statement by an obstetrician, as shown in the opening vignette, was neither fictional nor outlandish 50 years ago. Historically there has been an inclination for assessments of intellectual capacity to be pronounced by physicians, at very early ages, with very little data except observations. This continues to some degree today. Many parents and others have for years been accepting of such judgments as accurate and true because of a certain level of unquestioning deference to the physician. It may well have been the case that what the physician was saying in this vignette was accurate. However, in today's world we are more likely to undertake a more comprehensive assessment process before labeling a newborn as having intellectual disabilities.

Viewed broadly, psychological assessment has a lengthy history when compared with other areas of behavioral science. Within the specialty of psychological assessment, the measurement of intelligence has received a great deal of attention over the years. Work in the measurement of intelligence has been a major force in all psychological assessment, and the roots of psychological assessment go deep into the field of intellectual disabilities. Alfred Binet began the serious efforts to measure intelligence in 1904. Binet was commissioned by school officials in Paris to develop a means by which those children who were "truly dull" could be identified. Although interest had been expressed in psychological measurement before this, Binet's assignment generally is viewed as an important beginning.

The influence of development in psychological assessment is evident far beyond the area of intellectual disabilities, and its methodology has become increasingly complex, sophisticated, and, some would say, elegant. In certain areas, however, its sophistication may be no more than superficial. This chapter discusses assessment issues, frameworks, and procedures from the perspective of intellectual disabilities and in terms of the various phases of the human life cycle.

ISSUES AND CONCEPTS

Research on the measurement of intelligence has a very long history. Likewise, efforts to evaluate other areas of functioning—personality, language, and social development—also have been under way for a long time (e.g., Gruenewald, 2004; Van-Geert, 2003; Zigler, Bennett-Gates, Hodapp, & Henrich, 2002). Although significant effort has been directed at such measurement, much of the work has not been undertaken in as thoughtful a manner as might be appropriate or desirable. In some cases the development of assessment instruments has been driven by commercial motives rather than the cautious and systematic investigations of science.

Assessment Use

Core Concept

Careful attention to the proper use of assessment instruments has a great impact on the results of measurement.

One difficulty plaguing behavioral evaluation over the years has been the misuse of assessment procedures. Instrument development has occurred at a very rapid rate, often at the expense of careful and deliberate thought about the purposes and uses of the tests. Assessment literature reflects serious concern about usage over many years (e.g., Erbas, Ozen, & Acar, 2004; Everatt, Smythe, Ocampo, & Gyarmathy, 2004; Glenn, Jones, & Hoyt, 2003). Much of this concern emerged because over the years, many practitioners seemed to have a fixation on instruments of assessment with much less attention to questions of why the testing was being done. Because this was a driving force for the commercial market of testing materials, technical precision in psychological assessment seemed always to be ahead of conceptual considerations for practical assessment. Technical precision in this context relates to instrument construction; conceptual considerations relate to the underlying purposes for assessment and the use of the resulting information. Some questions also have been raised about how much technical precision generally has been achieved, but the use problem is fundamental and even may be more serious because, logically, concepts need to be in place before an evaluation can take place. Evidence regarding the relationship between assessment data and decisions made by placement teams raises serious questions. In some cases, concerns have been raised about limited relationships between assessment information and instructional planning (including individualized education programs or IEPs) designed for children (Fuchs & Fuchs, 2001; Neubert, 2003; Shriner & Destefano, 2003). These concerns raise the crucial question, Why should one test if the information is not directly used for instruction or other intervention? The conceptual problems related to purpose and usage may be reflected also in the practical applications of assessment as seen in the Tips for Professionals.

There has been a significant proliferation of psychoeducational instruments during the past 30 years. In today's market there is most likely an instrument available that purports to measure every facet of human behavior that one would want to evaluate. New instrumentation is being developed continually at what seems to be an accelerating rate. Yet questions arise about the degree of technical precision of much psychoeducational assessment. This concern is an appropriate one. But the problems related to technical precision are not the result of insufficient knowledge or theory about instrument development and measurement. Measurement theory has become a rather highly developed area in behavioral science and has been studied for many years (e.g., Aiken, 2003; Airasian, 2005; Merrell, 2003). Unfortunately, many instruments on the market do not give adequate attention to sound measurement practices. The great demand from the field appears to have resulted in inadequate instruments.

Assessment Referencing

Development and articulation of measurement concepts regarding the reference used for data interpretation represents one of the more important developments in the field of assessment. Practically speaking this refers to what standards or comparisons are used for a child's performance. Is his or her performance compared to those of others or is it compared to some specified learning or skill goal that might be set? Most prominent in this work is the distinction between norm- and criterion-referenced evaluation. Clarification of these concepts forced the field to be clear about at least one dimension of how test information is to be used. It should also be noted that different referents or performance standards might be employed for the same data. That is, a child's score on a 10-item test might be compared with the scores of others or it simply might represent an important instructional goal to be reached. Using different referents does not necessarily mean that different test items are employed, just that the performance data are compared with a different standard.

Core Concept

The purpose of any assessment greatly influences the procedure(s) employed and the way data are interpreted. Recognition of this has led to the articulation of such important concepts as norm and criterion referencing and formative and summative evaluation.

Tips for Professionals

Instructional planning that joins assessment and instruction can be adapted to link any district's general education curriculum objectives with the goals and objectives delineated in a student's individual education plan (IEP).

Seven Steps to Retooling the Classroom

Determine Present Level of Performance

First, select the goal on the student's IEP you wish to measure. Once this is done, list the student's strengths and weaknesses in relation to the goal. Then identify if and how the student is currently exhibiting skills related to the goal and document this.

Plan Activities for Instruction

Once the goal is selected, determine if the student needs to develop prerequisite skills or is ready for instructional activities directly addressing the goal. For example, if a student is not ready to begin a task such as naming and describing, you should choose a point at which to begin instruction. The student might learn to demonstrate this skill as follows:

- Use a picture attendance chart to name others in the class.
- Match picture cards to objects in the classroom.
- Use a picture card class schedule, and take the card to the appropriate class.
- Learn words, increasing the number of words the student knows.
- Name familiar people and objects, i.e., mom, dad, things the student likes.

Choose the Setting for Instruction

Some students may be able to learn skills in an artificial setting, such as a special or general education classroom. But for students learning functional skills, generalizing to real world settings usually requires community-based instruction such as a restaurant, post office, or home. Some of these instructional activities will be one-on-one and tailored to a specific student's needs, while others will be integrated into existing class activities.

Describe the Support Needed

Supports are the resources a student needs to overcome the effects of a disability. Examples of ongoing supports are communication devices, assistive technology, specially designed equipment, switches, computers, braille, sign language, wheelchairs, and assistive listening devices. Ongoing supports, which are needed by a student on a daily basis, should be determined by the IEP team.

Identify Data Collection Methods

To track a student's progress throughout the year on the selected goals and generate evidence for a portfolio, you, collaboratively with others, will need to collect data in relation to each goal. If you or a colleague will observe the student performing the skill, then charting and graphing the student's performance may be appropriate.

If the student's demonstration of the goal results in work samples or products, you may keep these as evidence. If the student is on a work site, interviews with the job coach, rehabilitation counselor, or supervisor may be helpful. Anecdotal records, videotapes, audiotapes, or photographs may also be appropriate.

Document Student Performance

Depending on the instructional activities and data collection method you select, documentation for the portfolio may take various forms. The items in the portfolio must tell the story of the student's performance to those who were not present. When a specific instructional activity or performance demonstration is used, documentation for the portfolio will consist of a description of the activity, the student's performance, the setting, the level of instructional assistance, and the ongoing supports. The examples included in the portfolio should represent different times and settings in which the student demonstrated the skill throughout the school year. For example, you could develop a chart showing when a student independently completes certain tasks.

Rate the Student's Performance

When you have accumulated student performance data on educational activities throughout the school year and documented it in the portfolio, you can then rate the student's performance on the selected goal when other students participate in state-wide standardized testing. At the time mandated by your individual state, you will rate the student on his or her level of performance on the goal based on the categories delineated.

We must have high expectations for all students and not put students with disabilities in a different category but bring them into the learning process. All stakeholders, students, parents, teachers, administrators, and policy makers benefit from linking assessment and instruction, thus truly impacting our nation's schools.

Source: Excerpted from "Retooling the Classroom to Incorporate Alternate Assessment" by A. Richards, 2000. *CEC Today.* Retrieved from http://www.cec.sped.org/bk/cec_today/nov_dec_2002.

Norm Referencing. Early assessment developments focused on how an individual performed, compared with others, particularly in the area of intelligence. A child's test score was viewed in relation to his or her age-mates or some standard norm. Research and repeated testing of individuals at various ages usually establish norms or databases for comparison. Similar procedures are used in assessment of factors other than intelligence. Personality measures usually compare one person's response to certain questions with those of other people who have particular personality descriptions. Educational achievement often is measured by the amount of information a child has accumulated, as demonstrated by correct responses on a variety of test questions. The child's performance then is compared with that of other children who are about the same age or grade level.

Assessment in which the performance of an individual is compared with that of others is known as **norm-referenced evaluation.** The term is self-explanatory; how well an individual performs is compared or referenced to the scores of others by using established norms. Mental age (MA) is a concept that is norm referenced, and Binet and Simon (1908) intended it to be so when they first defined MA. Many other areas of assessment, particularly those using standardized tests, are also norm referenced.

The norm-referenced approach has been predominant for many years. For the most part, professionals involved in all types of assessment (e.g., developmental status, intelligence, personality) have interpreted performance relative to norms. Norm referencing has served some purposes well. During the development of assessment as a science, it was the foundation for both researchers and practitioners working in all areas of human behavior. But gradually some serious problems emerged.

As the science of human behavior progressed, measurement problems that obviously needed attention developed. Standardized tests provided information that was useful for some purposes but not for others. Educators, for example, frequently found that scores from norm-referenced evaluation did not translate easily into teaching plans. A single score often was used for decisions about educational placement, with little or no additional information about the child. Such single scores gave the teacher, at best, meager guidance concerning activities and specific areas to target in instruction. A global score or a psychologist's report did not indicate where to begin in teaching specific mathematics or reading skills. This lack left teachers with many practical problems to solve in trying to teach the child. No logical link connected evaluation and instruction.

Similar problems emerged in working with individuals with intellectual disabilities and other disabilities in social-vocational efforts and other aspects of the adult world. Norm-referenced assessment information did little to facilitate placement, planning, and programming. Professionals working in such social agencies as welfare and employment departments and sheltered workshops soon found that they had to augment such information with their own, more specific evaluations. Sheltered workshop directors, for example, had to determine what specific skills a client with retardation already had and which needed to be taught for the individual to perform productively. The difficulties with norm-referenced assessment described here do not mean that it lacks value. To suggest that would be inaccurate and add fuel to a debate that has continued for some time. The examples noted above reflect purposes for which norm-referenced assessment is ill suited.

Criterion Referencing. **Criterion-referenced evaluation** is nearly synonymous with what norm-referenced evaluation is not. Individual performance is not compared with some norm. Criterion-referenced evaluation assesses specific skill areas individually, rather than generating a score based on a composite of several skills.

Criterion-referenced evaluation does not compare an individual's performance with that of others. Assessment tasks or test items are usually arranged in a sequence of increasing difficulty, and a person's functioning is viewed in terms of absolute performance level or the actual number of operations completed. If a child being tested on counting skills is able to progress successfully through counting by twos but no farther, that is his or her absolute performance. The child counts by twos with 100% accuracy, but by threes with 0% accuracy. This level of performance may be referenced in one or both of two ways. The first way involves the evaluator and the teacher (frequently the same person) asking, Is this level of proficiency adequate for this child at this time? The level of proficiency necessary for the child is the criterion (hence the term *criterion-referenced evaluation*). If a child needs to be able to count by threes, the teacher knows exactly what instruction to give. As the child progresses, he or she may need to perform at a more advanced skill level, depending on environmental requirements, and the criterion for this skill will change accordingly.

The second way that performance or skill level is referenced involves comparison of the individual's performance in one area with performance in others; for example, a child may perform well in letter recognition but poorly in sound blending. The evaluator examines performances in various skill areas, frequently constructs a profile of the child's strengths and weaknesses, and pinpoints instructional effort from the profile. The referent for evaluation data is still in one individual's performance, but now between skill areas. Usually the measurement involves performance on specific tasks. The evaluator draws no inferences about such abstract concepts as intelligence, instead relating performance measurement directly to instruction. Criterion-referenced evaluation has improved the relationship between evaluation and teaching, changing the way education is conceived and executed.

Past years have witnessed a theoretical difference of opinion in child assessment. Obviously, norm- and criterion-referenced evaluations operate from different approaches. Proponents of each viewpoint have spent much time and effort defending their positions, often without careful examination of what the other approach has to offer. This is unfortunate; such professional wrangling has little positive result. Although arguments continue to some extent, attention to basic measurement principles and reasoned applications have begun to replace rhetoric (Chafouleas, Riley-Tillman, & Eckert, 2003; Rust, Price, & O'Donovan, 2003).

Criterion-referenced evaluation has been applied in a wide variety of settings, one of the most pertinent applications being the direct linkage between assessment and classroom instruction. This use has evolved into an application that has received considerable attention in the field—curriculum-based assessment. **Curriculum-based assessment** uses the sequential objectives of the student's curriculum as the referent or criterion for evaluating progress. Consequently the curriculum that a student is being taught is the referent for evaluation. The objectives associated with the curricular activities represent the standard for success as the youngster's performance is assessed. This approach emphasizes the link between instructional objectives and assessment, improving the potential for instructional decision making (Chafouleas et al., 2003; Gronlund, 2004; Nelson & Van Meter, 2002). Curriculum-based assessment also provides a natural and efficient process for screening assessment, a topic examined later in this chapter. Curriculum-based assessment is a specific application of referencing evaluation for a particular purpose. In some cases, other terms, such as **objectives-referenced measurement**, have been used, although distinctions are less crucial once the more general concept of assessment referencing is understood (Nelson & Van Meter, 2002; Shermis & Daniels, 2003).

Analysis of the usefulness of criterion- and norm-referenced assessment over time has led many to conclude that neither approach in isolation results in a totally effective evaluation process. Criterion-referenced evaluation is useful for specific instructional programming, a need not served well by norm-referenced evaluation. Many children with intellectual disabilities, however, ultimately must function in a larger world, perhaps in a regular educational setting on a partial basis. This broader world usually operates on a competitive basis, with children's performances compared with each other, so it is largely a norm-referenced world. To maximize a child's chances for success, information that will indicate how the child's performance compares with others in the larger world must be obtained. It would be disastrous to bring a child's skill level from Point A to Point B (criterion-referenced evaluation) and find that Point C was necessary for success in a regular educational setting. Those working with individuals who have intellectual disabilities cannot afford to be rigid in using only some of the tools available to them. Because they serve different purposes, both norm- and criterion-referenced evaluation must be used. Referencing of assessment information clearly depends on the use or application intended.

Formative and Summative Evaluation

Other conceptual developments look directly to the purposes of evaluation and have led to the articulation of two broad categories: formative and summative. **Formative evaluation** in this framework is assessment that focuses not on a desired ultimate behavior but rather on the next step in an instructional program. Formative evaluation is frequently an integral part of the instructional program. **Summative evaluation** is quite different. It involves assessment of terminal behaviors and evaluates a child's performance at the end of a given program. These conceptualizations also have been combined with norm- and criterion-referenced evaluation and other measurement models to develop functional and comprehensive views of assessment that have been applied in a broad range of settings (e.g., Brown & Kiernan, 2001; Rees & Sheard, 2004; Shermis & Daniels, 2003). Myopic views of evaluation and psychological assessment seem to be giving way to more thoughtful approaches to the broad field. This change is promising because it means that workers in the field are being more thorough and reasoned in their consideration of assessment.

Assessment Bias

Discriminatory testing is another concern in the assessment field, an issue examined in the context of multicultural issues in Chapter 2. Questions about discriminatory assessment surface particularly often with respect to the standardized, norm-referenced testing of minority group children. African Americans, Hispanics, and Native Americans, as well as others, have legitimately claimed that evaluation instruments contain cultural bias and prejudice (Bailey, 2004; Clark, Chein, & Cook, 2004). Likewise, they have raised serious concerns regarding the absence of assessment specialists with appropriate training and background (Aiken, 2003; Everatt et al., 2004; Jesse, Davis, Pokorny, 2004). Assessment bias, whether due to instrumentation or administration, generates inaccurate results that are at least partially due to cultural background, rather than to actual mental abilities or skills (Geisinger, 2003; Gregory, 2004; Saenz & Huer, 2003). Because psychoeducational assessment instruments usually are devised by individuals from the cultural majority, test items are probably more representative of that group than others. Likewise, norms and the scientists who develop them are more frequently reflecting the cultural majority than the minority subgroups (e.g., Meyer, Bevan-Brown, Harry, & Sapon-Shevin, 2003; Shapiro, Monzo, Rueda, Gomez, & Blacher, 2004; Watts & Erevelles, 2004). When minority children's scores are compared with norms established on other populations, the children are often at a disadvantage because of cultural differences. Such bias in psychological assessment has been evident for many years, although only in recent decades have significant efforts begun to address the problem (Cohen, 2002; Gregory, 2004; Moseley, 2004).

Attempts to construct unbiased instruments have been largely disappointing. Widespread concerns regarding the disadvantage of minority children in testing

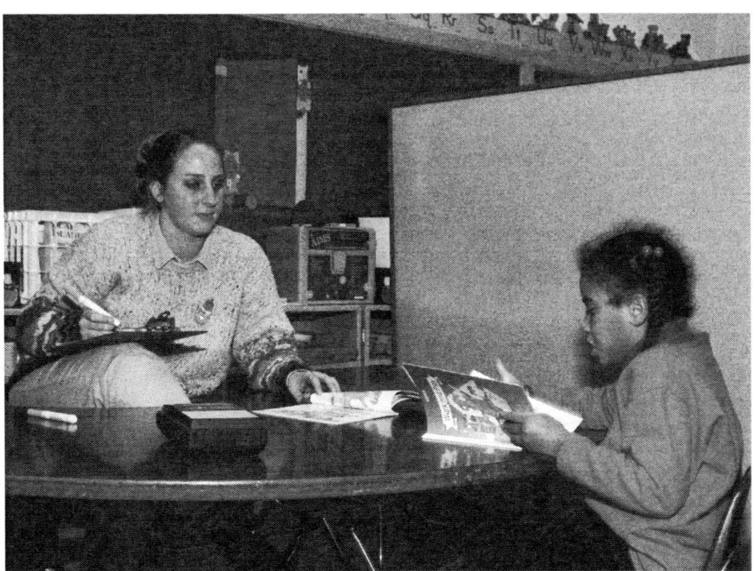

Assessment with this child may result in a biased performance score that does not accurately reflect the child's ability.

continue to appear on a regular basis (e.g., Battle, 2002; Geisinger, 2003; Saenz & Huer, 2003). Some of the efforts undertaken, however, are beginning to place the assessment of minority children on firmer ground. In part, this bolstering has meant more appropriate applications of norm- and criterion-referenced assessment procedures, as well as formative, summative, and other assessment protocols useful for instruction (Airasian, 2005; Greene, 2003; Gronlund, 2004). Much research remains to be done in this area, however, because a full understanding of bias, its effects on assessment outcomes, and a resolution of the problem remain elusive (Aiken, 2003; Gregory, 2004).

Evidence continues to indicate that factors such as ethnicity influence a youngster's likelihood of being diagnosed as having a disability, and minority children still represent a disproportionately large segment of the population identified as having intellectual disabilities (Epps, 2002; Lau et al., 2003; Valdez, 2003). Some authors claim that basic reform in educational purpose is needed in addition to work in assessment development (Hardman, Drew, & Egan, 2006; Jones & Menchetti, 2001). The problem of cultural unfairness remains, whether the problem is one of assessment bias or one of prejudice in the educational system. The reader can find a more complete examination of the range of environmental and cultural factors associated with minority status in Chapter 2. From the discussion there, it is clear that some factors, such as poverty, are broad societal problems far beyond the scope of psychoeducational assessment.

Although the issues in the preceding discussion have been articulated in the past, the reader should not assume that these problems have evaporated with the passage of time. The problems of educational uses and misuses of norm-referenced assessment have been addressed only in a limited fashion and, some believe, inappropriately (Chafouleas et al., 2003). Issues arising from the use of criterion-referenced assessment have yet to be broadly explored and merit much more attention. Further, professional training in diagnostic assessment remains limited and needs to be reformed (Crespi & Politikos, 2004). The need for basic reform in professional training is crucial and ocassionally there are positive initiatives in this regard (APA, 2003; Murray, 2002). Ordinary human frailty leaves plenty of room for racial and cultural bias on the part of psychodiagnosticians.

EARLY LIFE

Core Concept

Assessment procedures are quite different, depending on the age of the person and the performance area being evaluated.

Assessment procedures are necessarily quite different at various stages in the life of a child. This section examines approaches to evaluation during the early years of life, from birth to about 2 years of age. Evaluation at this point in the life of children is conducted for at least two related purposes: (a) identification of children who already show intellectual disabilities in their development and (b) identification of children who have a high probability of showing intellectual disabilities later. These purposes are two essential components of early screening assessment. In the discussion that follows, we first examine the idea of screening, then look at reasons for identification, and finally explore potential results. Identification cannot stand alone, or else it would be merely an exercise.

Screening Concepts

Core Concept

Screening assessment is very important throughout a person's lifespan, but it is crucial in early life.

Screening is somewhat like sorting sizes for things like fruit. For example, oranges might be rolled across a screen with certain-sized holes. These holes would permit oranges of an acceptable size or smaller to fall through. Those that are larger than the acceptable marketable size will not fall through the screen and will be sorted out for other purposes (special gift packages). Those that fall through would include oranges of marketable size plus those that are much smaller. A second screening process might then be used. This second phase would involve a screen with holes that were much smaller than the first screen's. The only oranges that would fall through the second screen are those that are unmarketable because they are too small (these could be used for frozen orange juice). This process leaves only those oranges that are in the size range that the buying public prefers. Screening for intellectual disabilities is somewhat like this. Only those who now have intellectual disabilities or exhibit behaviors that suggest that they will later have intellectual disabilities are sorted out by early screening.

High-risk situations like those noted above may trigger assessment and actual intervention aimed at prevention. Prevention in this circumstance may involve pregnancy prevention if genetic screening of the parents indicates a problem or pregnancy termination if screening information indicates the unborn fetus is negatively affected. Genetic counseling may be employed in a wide range of circumstances where developmental abnormalities are probable and may result in advice that a pregnancy should be avoided or closely monitored if the potential parents decide to proceed (Barr & Millar, 2003). Matters such as genetic counseling, prenatal assessment, and selective abortion have long been controversial and continue to raise many questions regarding ethics and moral beliefs (e.g., Parens & Asch, 2003).

For some children, the possibility of preventing intellectual disabilities or lessening the impact may be minimal. These are the children who have severe intellectual disabilities, frequently because of a birth defect or congenital malformation. Such conditions make identification easier, but because of the severity of the problems, positive action is more difficult. Even in these situations, early identification plays a vital role in terms of planning for the future of the child and the family. Certain problems persist in accomplishing early screening assessment for intellectual disabilities. One serious difficulty in assessing young children is accuracy of prediction (Friend & Keplinger, 2003; Naar-King, Ellis, & Frey, 2004). The behavioral repertoire of the infant is much different from that of the child at age 6 or 10 years. The infant is functioning primarily in a motor-skill world. Grasping, rolling over, sitting, and crawling are a few of the baby's behaviors. Infant vocalizations are quite limited and frequently focus on such physiological factors as hunger, pain, and fatigue. Early screening tries to predict later behaviors that are very different. Because the best predictor of performance on a given task is performance on a sample of that task or a similar one—in most cases, impossible with an infant—prediction is not so accurate as one would like.

However, this does not mean that prediction is impossible. If this were so, there would be little reason even to consider early screening. Fortunately for child care workers, developmental status and progress in the psychomotor areas that dominate the world of the infant do predict, though grossly, later levels of functioning (Berk, 2005; Driscoll & Nagel, 2005). Accuracy of prediction is much greater with the infant who has a severe disability and exhibits clearer signs of impairment earlier. The mild disability presents the greatest challenges to early screening.

Another concern in early screening assessment involves the factors evaluated. Recent research and thinking in this area have made some changes in the indicators that early screening assesses. Valuable predictive information may be obtained by evaluating environmental factors in addition to examining the child's developmental status directly. Professionals traditionally have used such indicators as socioeconomic status and parental education and occupation to differentiate between environments, but now other factors have been shown to be more important influences on a child's development. Some of these are parents' language style, their attitudes about achievement, and general involvement with the young child. Research is beginning to study these areas, which promise to become even more important in the future (Berk, 2005; Bernstein & Levey, 2002; Gleason, 2005).

Genetics, Other Assessment, and Prevention Issues. The early identification of disability or risk conditions is very important and, in many cases, enhances the probability of a favorable intervention outcome (Harbin et al., 2004; Peterson et al., 2004; Yoshinaga-Itano, 2003). In certain cases the ultimate impact of a disability condition can be reduced substantially with early treatment or intervention. Certain disabilities even may be prevented if action is taken early enough.

Prenatal assessment of this young fetus is important since this represents a vulnerable period.

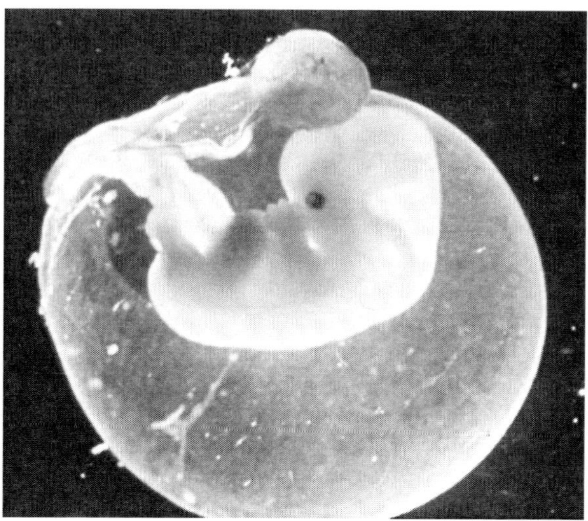

The idea of prevention focuses particularly on pregnancies, anticipated pregnancies, or newborn children who are thought to be at risk for intellectual disabilities. Certain pregnancy situations are at greater risk for developmental accidents or disruption of the normal developmental processes than others. Such circumstances involve trauma to the fetus that might come from environmental circumstances, such as high levels of environmental toxins like drugs, alcohol, radiation, and others (Mayes & Lombroso, 2003; Willford, Richardson, Leech, & Day, 2004). Other risk circumstances might emerge from known genetic conditions that have some probability of being transmitted to the child and that cause some level of intellectual disabilities. Genetic conditions such as **phenylketonuria** represent this type of abnormality and represent a circumstance that is amenable to prenatal screening and intervention. Finally, high-risk circumstances may also occur that seem to be related to parental status such as age. In some cases, such as certain types of Down syndrome, actual genetic anomalies occur in the developing fetus that appear to be related to matters like maternal age.

Early screening generally has been discussed in terms of its positive value for the child faced with the possibility of intellectual disabilities and for the child's parents. In a broader societal context, certain ethical issues arise. One of the negative outcomes of early assessment is labeling. Labels and their impact on children have been a serious concern in special education for some time. The potential for harm is even greater if a label is attached to a youngster in infancy. To avoid labeling, child care workers must move to behavior- and skill-oriented descriptions. And here we should say once more that assessment, evaluation, or early screening cannot be justified if its only purpose is identification. During the school years, evaluation and education must be linked. Purposive evaluation is even more crucial in the early years. The negative effect of assessing a young child, stigmatizing the child with a label, and doing nothing in the form of positive action beyond that is unimaginable.

We do not support evaluation at any time in the life of an individual if it is only for categorization.

Earlier, we mentioned the problems involved in evaluation of minority groups. These problems are of even greater concern in early assessment, for issues of poverty, race, and environment play a large role in early screening (e.g., Sahler & Carr, 2003; Seguin, Xu, Potvin, Zunzunegui, & Frohlich, 2003). As professionals gain skill in dealing with these issues, not only early childhood assessment but also early childhood education should become increasingly important in treating intellectual disabilities.

Early Life Assessment

Prenatal. Advances in medical science and health care techniques during the past decade have had a significant impact on the field of intellectual disabilities. One area in which dramatic developments have occurred involves prenatal assessment and detection of intellectual disabilities that have resulted. Such very early assessments are now considered essential to monitoring fetal status. In cases where problems are detected these assessments may result in very early intervention, but also may generate ripples of bioethical controversy as one might expect. However, they are suggested by many disciplines and organizations working in intellectual disabilities (AAMR, 2002; IASSID, 2003).

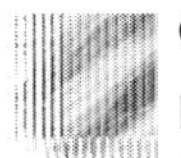

Core Concept

Prenatal evaluation can provide extremely important information about the fetus.

During pregnancy the most common assessment involves routine monitoring of the physical condition of mother and fetus by the obstetrician or other trained health care personnel. Some of this prenatal assessment employs technology to access information about the fetus such as that described in the Eye on Technology feature. Another portion of this assessment basically employs low levels of technology and includes a detailed record of the mother's family and medical history. In addition to the history, the mother's blood pressure, uterus size, urine status, and other indicators are monitored throughout the pregnancy to ensure that no symptoms are present that would signal danger for the fetus, as well as for the mother. At this level of examination, the mother's physical condition is the primary source of information for assessment. The obstetrician also examines the fetus by various means as the pregnancy proceeds. This ongoing monitoring is crucial to maximize the probability of a healthy baby being born. The mother's diet frequently is altered, and occasionally medication is administered to correct minor deviations from the optimum situation for fetal development. Women who do not have access to good health care run a much higher risk of giving birth to a child with a defect. High-risk pregnancies are more frequent among women who cannot afford adequate health care or who for some other reason do not have adequate medical resources available to them (e.g., Cook & Cook, 2005; Gelfand & Drew, 2003).

Routine, ongoing prenatal assessment is generally adequate as long as a healthy mother and fetus are involved. Certain danger signs, however, prompt more extensive evaluation. If the family or medical history suggests that a particular problem may occur (e.g., an inheritable disorder), routine monitoring is not sufficient.

Eye on Technology

The Importance of Health Care Assessment During Pregnancy

Deborah Burkholder

My husband and I have grown accustomed to having prenatal sonograms performed as we have had our children and our family took shape. It has become a routine assessment process and the image below is our oldest child at our 20-week visit. This is always an exciting event for expectant parents. For many fathers, visually seeing the baby for the first time provides a connection they had not yet experienced. For the mother, it is a confirmation of the little being she has been nourishing and watching grow (from the outside).

However, the sonogram provides more than this emotional high. Some parents choose to discover the gender of their baby. And while this information is important to many, the sonogram is a medical checkpoint to see if the baby is developing normally.

My brother's second child was born with many physical problems. This was a heart-wrenching thing for our family to watch. As a consequence, the sonograms that any of our family members have had since that time have a more weighted feeling. Some regard the sonogram as just a time to find out the gender of their baby, and a routine part of pregnancy. And while it is routine, the real reason for the sonogram should not be forgotten, because it truly is a status-check on how the unborn baby is doing.

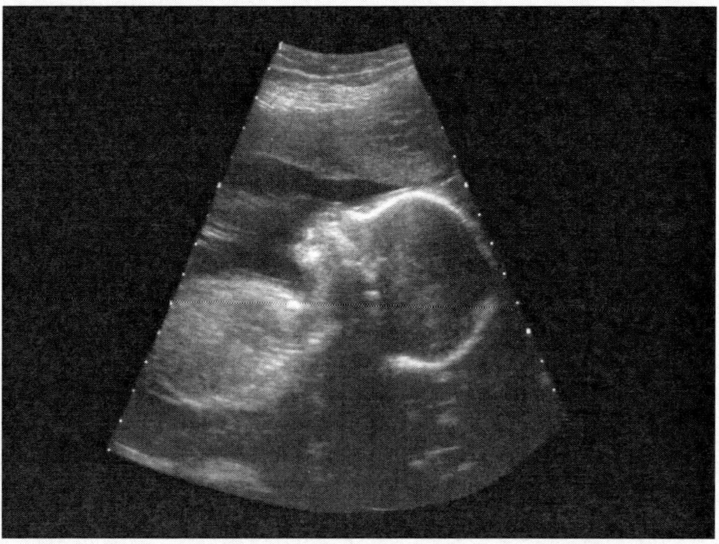

If the mother's or fetus' physical condition is deviant, more extensive evaluation and action are in order. In such cases, evaluation becomes diagnosis aimed at the prenatal assessment of fetal status (Posner, Learman, Gates, Washington, & Kuppermann, 2004). Certain biological and chemical characteristics of the fetus can be measured. Diagnostic analyses of this type are not possible with every type of retardation, and work has focused on clinical syndromes that involve genetic metabolic disorders resulting in severe intellectual disabilities.

Accurate diagnosis is possible for a variety of hereditary disorders, and the list expands continually (e.g., Down syndrome, **galactosemia,** Gaucher's disease, maple syrup urine disease, PKU, Tay-Sachs disease) (e.g., Antshel, Brewster, & Waisbren, 2004; Diamond & Kontos, 2004). Some of these disorders are rare, but in an entire society, the ability to detect and take action is a major contribution to the field of intellectual disabilities. Even more significant is the ability to prevent the personal tragedies resulting from the birth of children with such devastating disorders and to provide intervention and support for parents (Read, 2004). In most cases, parents of these children are forced to watch a progressive deterioration from what appeared to be a healthy normal baby to a child destined for a passive existence or premature death.

Significant portions of this kind of prenatal assessment are not yet routine (e.g., Cook & Cook, 2005; Posner et al., 2004). For the most part, the general obstetric monitoring mentioned suffices for a first level of screening, like the first screening in our orange-sorting analogy. In certain cases, however, metabolic or genetic disorders have a higher probability of occurrence, and in these cases current thinking recommends routine diagnostic prenatal evaluation. Tay-Sachs disease, for example, is a disorder transmitted genetically and found primarily in individuals of Ashkenazi Jewish origin. When two individuals with this background plan to have children, it is wise to always evaluate fetal status from a prenatal diagnostic standpoint. Strong arguments also can be made for evaluation of all pregnant women over 40 years of age. Maternal age is important in the birth of children with Down syndrome as well as other conditions associated with more severe levels of intellectual disabilities (Chapman, Scott, & Mason, 2002; Roesch, Schetter, Woo, & Hobel, 2004). The detection process for prenatal identification of Down syndrome is still being refined. As this work progresses, it is quite possible that such diagnostic screening will be recommended even for others younger than 40 years.

Core Concept

Assessment of the newborn can identify problems and prompt immediate intervention to prevent intellectual disabilities.

Newborn. A variety of assessment techniques are used with the newborn (Cook & Cook, 2005; Gleason, 2005). Clinical assessment at this time is vital. Immediately after a birth, several factors are noted and rated by using what is known as the Apgar score. This procedure generally is completed by delivery room staff at 1 and 5 minutes after birth and may be repeated, if needed, until the infant's condition has stabilized. Five factors are included in the Apgar scoring: heart rate, respiratory effort, muscle tone, reflex irritability, and color. Each is rated by giving a score of 0, 1, or 2 (0 indicating low or weak, 2 indicating high or strong). The separate scores are added together. Extremely low Apgar scores at the 5-minute measure suggest a potential problem and is considered an indicator for a variety of developmental difficulties (e.g., Ginsberg, 2003; Reading, 2004). Newborns with a 5-minute score of 3 or below have three times as many neurological problems at age 1 as babies of similar birth weights with Apgar scores of 7 to 10. Apgar scores of 6 or lower are viewed with concern. Infants with such scores usually are monitored closely for the first several days, with interventions as necessary.

Other assessment procedures can be conducted during the very early part of a child's life. Some evaluate neurological status and reflex behaviors such as their sucking responses (Gardner, Karmel, & Freedland, 2001; Korner & Constantinou, 2001; Schubert & McNeil, 2004). Other procedures attempt to detect inherited or congenitally present abnormalities (they overlap with some of the procedures discussed above in the section on prenatal assessments). As with the prenatal evaluation process, biological-chemical analysis is frequently the means for newborn screening. Table 3–1 lists a number of inherited abnormalities that are identifiable through the analysis of blood specimens alone.

As indicated in Table 3–1, a number of these anomalies are treatable conditions. Treatment can prevent or substantially diminish the developmental problem that would result if the condition were unknown or ignored. These treatable disorders make up most of those we have listed, a fact that seems to support neonatal screening. Yet such assessment is not necessarily routine. Diagnosis of these disorders can be made from analysis of a dried blood spot, and in each case completely or partially automated analysis is possible, which streamlines the process and permits cost-effective mass screening. It is hoped that health care services in the future will routinely include biological-chemical analysis.

Core Concept

Evaluation beyond the newborn stage includes many assessment areas not previously amenable to measurement.

Certain other abnormalities are detectable from clinical observation at the newborn stage. Medical examination of conditions such as Down syndrome and cranial anomalies can indicate with considerable accuracy the existence of a problem. Such effective evaluation, however, involves only conditions that are present and observable either at birth or in the first few days of the infant's life.

Table 3–1

Inherited Abnormalities Identifiable Through Blood Analysis

Phenylketonuria[a]
Maple syrup urine disease[a]
Tyrosinemia[a]
Homocystinuria[a]
Histidinemia[a]
Valinemia[a]
Galactosemia transferase deficiency[a]
Argininosuccinic aciduria[a]
Orotic aciduria[a]
Hereditary angioneurotic edema
Galactosemia transferase or kinase deficiency[a]
Emphysema (adult)
Liver disease (infant)
Sickle cell anemia

[a]Treatable conditions.

Beyond the Newborn Stage. Certainly, no widespread agreement can be reached concerning when one stage of development ends and another begins. In fact, it is misleading even to suggest that a "stage" is an identifiable and discrete entity. Stage theories of development have been somewhat controversial and continue to kindle interest and debate (Austrian, 2002; Cook & Cook, 2005; Gleason, 2005). Usage of terms like *newborn, infant,* and *early childhood* is fluid, at best. In the previous section, the term *newborn* meant the time shortly after birth. The use of this term was not intended to suggest that the term covered a stage; it was used for convenience. Henceforward, we place evaluation in an age context instead of using terms that connote stages.

Certain measurements are difficult to make from birth through the first few years of life. This is particularly true when attempting to predict later intelligence. Before the child acquires language, his or her sensorimotor development is necessarily the basis for evaluation (Gleason, 2005; Owens, 2005; Reed, 2005). Because later intelligence measures are heavily weighted according to verbal performance, prediction difficulty is natural. Progress in this area of assessment has been made, however.

Intellectual. A number of instruments and evaluation procedures attempt to assess intellectual functioning in young children. The revised Bayley Scales of Infant Development represent one such instrument. The Bayley Scales have certain strengths that should not be overlooked as one considers alternatives for assessing very young children. Research on the revised version (BSID-II) has been under way with clear evidence of need for restandardization (Colombo et al., 2004; Hess, Papas, & Black, 2004). The Bayley Scales include test items from 1 to 30 months after birth for children at risk; the items may be useful in situations where assessment of the very young or of older individuals functioning at a very low level is required. Further, the subscales (Mental, Motor, and Behavior Rating scale) have clinical appeal to some, although they may be misleading because they are only partial measures. Items include assessment of perception, memory, learning, problem solving, vocalization, gross motor skills and the development of hand and finger manipulation. The Bayley Scales rely heavily on the assessment of sensorimotor performance because there are few other means of performance evaluation at this age. The Bayley Scales are reasonably accurate for certain high-risk populations such as premature babies, although some researchers believe they should be supplemented with other assessments (Aiken, 2003; Lawson & Ruff, 2004).

Other techniques have been developed and are used by many professionals for early assessment of a child's intellectual functioning. Most of these are not widely known because of the difficulty involved in assessing intelligence in the very early years. Instruments that have been employed at this age include the Brazelton Neonatal Behavioral Assessment Scale (3 days through 4 weeks), the Griffiths Scale (birth through 4 years), and the Revised Gesell Scale (birth through 5 years) (Aiken, 2003; Gregory, 2004). We return to intellectual assessment at the preschool level.

Language. Although closely related to cognitive development, some distinct efforts have focused on early language assessment. The assessment of language at this very early age is challenging, and much of the work has been of an experimental nature. In certain cases, the experimental assessment procedures developed for research purposes have not been developed further and therefore have not been brought to the broader marketplace. We examine a few of these evaluation techniques and how they fit within broader models of assessment in order to provide the reader with some concept of the approaches involved and the difficulties encountered.

Robinson and Robb (2002) note that two broad models are prominent in the literature on language assessment for very young children. One model promotes an evaluation that is generally called naturalistic assessment, where the child's language status is observed and evaluated in natural settings. These circumstances might be situations such as play in routine settings wherein the child's language facility is evaluated as he or she participates in natural environments. Such observation requires a period of time during which the evaluator collects data that, it is hoped, represent the child's language status in a natural setting. This type of information is viewed quite favorably by professionals in the field of language development but is also costly in terms of the time necessary to gather assessment information, and also requires considerable training of observers who represent the language assessment mechanism (Gleason, 2005; Owens, 2005).

An alternative model to naturalistic assessment is one where an instrument is employed to assess language development status. Such an instrument might be a language test or a time-limited standardized protocol for evaluating language development status of the child. Selected early language assessment instruments are listed in Table 3–2.

The trade-off between naturalistic assessment and evaluation instruments developed for determining language status are fairly clear. Criticism of the instrument administration approach is often directed at the limited scope of evaluation that is imposed, and also at the circumstances for assessment, which do not indicate language status in natural circumstances (which has much greater flexibility and therefore increased ecological validity and utility) (Robinson & Robb, 2002). On the other front, using instruments to assess language status often does not involve as much time for the evaluation as the more lengthy naturalistic assessment approach. Language assessment during the very early years is a significant challenge. Often it must include consideration of other matters in the child's life as well, such as his or her physical status and socioeconomic circumstances (Cook & Cook, 2005; Owens, 2005; Silliman & Diehl, 2002).

Evaluation of language development is an increasingly important area of interest in terms of early assessment, particularly with respect to developmental intellectual disabilities. As professionals continue to refine skill description, specific areas of performance level will become more important. Language assessment may represent only language skill, rather than measure the abstract concept of mental development. It is already clear that an area like language will be broken down further into component behaviors. As this occurs, efforts in evaluation, screening, and diagnosis probably will take on a very different description, increase professionals' predictive ability, and certainly lead more directly to intervention and modification (Gleason, 2005; Reed, 2005).

Table 3–2
Early Language and Communication Assessment Tools for Infants and Toddlers

Developmental/Traditional Assessment Tools	Naturalistic/Dynamic Assessment Tools
Minnesota Child Development Inventory (Ireton & Thwing, 1974)	Assessing Prelinguistic and Linguistic Behaviors (Olswang, Stoel-Gammon, Coggins, & Carpenter, 1987)
Preschool Language Scale–3 (Zimmerman, Steinger, & Pond, 1992)	Neonatal Behavioral Assessment Scale, 2d ed. (Brazelton, 1973)
Battelle Developmental Inventory (Newborg, Stock, & Wnek, 1984)	Assessment of Mother–Child Interaction (Klein & Briggs, 1987)
The Language Development Survey (Rescorla, 1989)	MacArthur Child Development Inventories, Infant and Toddler forms (Fenson et al., 1993)
Reynell Developmental Language Scales (Reynell, 1985)	Parent–Child Interaction Assessment (Comfort & Farran, 1994)
Bayley Scales of Infant Development (Bayley, 1993)	Communication and Symbolic Behavior Scales (Wetherby & Prizant, 1993)
Infant-Toddler Language Scale (Rossetti, 1990)	Communication Matrix (Rowland, 1996)
Receptive-Expressive-Emergent Language Scale–2 (Bzoch & League, 1991)	Integrated Developmental Experiences Assessment (Norris, 1992)
Clinical Linguistic and Auditory Milestones Scale (Capture & Accardo, 1978)	Assessment Evaluation and Programming System (Bricker, 1993)
Hawaii Early Learning Profile (Furuno et al., 1987)	Syracuse Assessments for Birth to Three (Ensher et al., 1997)
Sequenced Inventory of Communicative Development–Revised (Hedrick, Prather, & Tobin, 1984)	Communication Play Protocol (Adamson & Bakeman, 1999)
Early Language Milestone Scale (Coplan, 1993)	Transdisciplinary, Play-Based Assessment (Linder, 1993)
Mullen Scales of Early Learning (Mullen, 1997)	
Infant/Toddler Checklist for Communication and Language Development (Wetherby & Prizant, 1998)	

Source: "Early Communication Assessment and Intervention: An Interactive Process" by N. B. Robinson and M. P. Robb, 2002, in D. K. Bernstein and E. Tiegerman-Farber (Eds.), *Language and Communication Disorders in Children* (5th ed., p. 137). Boston: Allyn & Bacon.

Social/Adaptive Behavior. Evaluation of social-emotional development presents a challenge to those working with young children (Carter, Briggs-Gowan, & Davis, 2004; Lawson & Ruff, 2004). All of the instruments that try to assess this area of behavior have a common problem: the reliability of the assessment itself. In terms of standardized instrumentation, we limit examination in this section to the Vineland Adaptive Behavior Scale. Although it suffers from some mixed reliability results, it is one of the few instruments useful at this young age.

The Vineland Adaptive Behavior Scales (VABS) represent a revision of the original Vineland Social Maturity Scale, which was used in the intellectual disabilities field for many years. Standardization information about the revision is still emerging from field applications and research. Early results are promising, although caution is always warranted as new instrumentation matures. The VABS is administered individually by a person who is very familiar with the person being evaluated. Three forms are available: two are interview editions, and the third is a classroom edition. The four domains of assessment are communication, daily living skills, socialization, and motor skills. This instrument is norm referenced, based on national samples of subjects (ages newborn to 18 years 11 months for the interview editions; 3 to 12 years 11 months for the classroom edition). Although the norming appears good and discriminant validity is termed good, reliability varies. The various forms of the Vineland are used in a variety of settings with a broad range of children including those with autism, intellectual disabilities, low-birth-weight status at birth, and youngsters at risk for other reasons. Although all instrumentation is subject to limitations, the VABS appear to be a useful assessment of a child's developmental status in the targeted areas of functioning (Cohen, 2003; Nachshen, Woodford, & Minnes, 2003; Taylor, 2003).

Assessment during the very early part of life is also accomplished by observational protocols that do not represent standardized instrumentation. These procedures, for want of a better term, have been labeled the "functional analysis approach." This work rests on the basic principles of applied behavior analysis and is highly relevant to issues of early childhood assessment. The functional analysis approach to assessment requires direct observation of the child, rather than reliance on behavioral description reported by an informant. Observation is conducted of children who are referred for behavioral or developmental problems; it takes place in the setting in which the problem occurs. Data typically are divided into three categories: behavioral deficits, behavioral excesses, and inappropriate stimulus control. Within these general categories, the behavioral description of the child's functioning is very specific, permitting precise intervention, rather than a broad spectrum treatment approach (Flood & Gredler, 2004). Its specificity is a definite strength of the functional analysis assessment framework, but observation requires substantial training in applied behavior analysis. Either professional or paraprofessional staff members with the proper preparation can conduct the evaluation. A second strength of functional analysis assessment is its use of direct observation, rather than such indirect methods as interviews. Interviews have long been viewed as problematic and have added substantially to the difficulties of reliability and validity of assessment.

Multiple Domain Assessment. Thus far, our discussion has focused on instruments and techniques that assess a child's developmental status in a limited area (e.g., language). Although the boundaries of performance areas are far from distinct, many professionals have attempted to assess intellectual development, language development, and social-emotional development discretely, as well as to consider the early health status and possible presence of inheritable disorders. Assessment from a somewhat broader framework, including infant-environment interactions, has attracted some attention in recent years, and developmental screening techniques that evaluate several factors simultaneously while still providing specific information in each area have been designed. These techniques have become popular for several reasons, one certainly being the greater efficiency of using a single instrument to assess several performance areas.

One rather well-known multifactor instrument is the Revision of the Denver Developmental Screening Test (DDST)—the Denver II—developed due to a number of difficulties with the earlier DDST. This instrument is useful from birth to 6 years of age and scores a child's status in four areas of development: gross motor, fine motor, language, and personal-social. Test developers are careful to mention that this should be used only as a screening mechanism and should not be used to determine a diagnostic label such as intellectual disabilities. It is easily administered in about 20 minutes (including scoring and interpretation) and requires little special training. Considerable research has been conducted on the earlier version of the Denver scale's standardization and prescreening procedures. There has been less opportunity for investigation of the Denver II and caution should be exercised since the two versions have a number of differences. This instrument is intended to provide a preliminary estimate of developmental delay that should lead to a more thorough diagnosis if results warrant (Gregory, 2004; Mirrett, Bailey, Roberts, & Hatton, 2004).

Another developmental battery used in the early years is the Battelle Developmental Inventory. This procedure evaluates developmental skills from birth to age 8, is individually administered, and is intended for use by those who teach young children from the infant level through preschool. Five domains are assessed: personal-social, adaptive, motor skills, communication, and cognitive. The evaluation includes observations of the child, parental interviews, and administration of standardized items to the child. The screening version of the Battelle can be administered quickly—10 to 30 minutes for screening and 10 to 15 minutes for children under 3 years of age, although this protocol has been seriously criticized (Gregory, 2004). Like other multiple domain assessment techniques, the Battelle is used in a wide range of settings, although additional research on this procedure is needed (Mirrett et al., 2004; Smidt & Cress, 2004).

PRESCHOOL YEARS

From the discussion above, it is obvious that there is no clear-cut age at which certain instruments stop being used altogether and others become appropriate. Some assessment techniques discussed in the preceding section can be used during the preschool years, whereas others cannot. Likewise, certain evaluation procedures discussed in this section extend down to the early years. This section examines selected evaluation procedures used primarily during the years immediately preceding a child's school enrollment.

Core Concept

Functioning in intellectual, language, perceptual-motor, and social/adaptive behavior is important in evaluating the status of preschool youngsters. Proper assessment must employ procedures appropriate for this age range.

Intellectual Functioning

One assessment most frequently associated with intellectual disabilities is the measurement of intelligence. Although many people think of intelligence as a concrete entity, it is really an abstraction, something inferred to exist to a greater or lesser degree, depending on an individual's performance on selected tasks. Continuing developments in evaluation have prompted the conceptual clarification that a particular score on an intelligence test is representative of various performances and that the concept of intelligence, as a general ability, is an inferred, rather than a known, observable entity.

Part of the conceptualization of intelligence results from the framework of early instrumentation. Binet's early work was based on the idea that intelligence was a general ability factor. Consequently, his approach involved a mixture of items and aimed at an assessment that represented a composite measure, presumably including performances related to the notion of general intelligence. The fourth edition of the Stanford-Binet test still generates a composite measure, although some uses in clinical and diagnostic settings have resulted in attempts to isolate various performances (Seung & Chapman, 2004).

The Stanford-Binet test is recommended as appropriate for ages 2 through 23 years of age. Frequently, however, other instruments are used for individuals over 12 years of age because of the longer administration time required for older people. The Stanford-Binet frequently has been viewed as the standard against which intelligence measurement is compared. Its norms, validity, and reliability appear good, and the new edition is seen as an improvement over its predecessor (Caruso, 2001; Kay et al., 2003; Quereshi, 2003).

Another instrument frequently used with preschool children to assess intelligence is the Wechsler Preschool and Primary Scale of Intelligence–Revised (WPPSI-R). The WPPSI-R is recommended for use with children from 3 through 7 years of age. Designed somewhat differently from the Binet test, the WPPSI-R organizes items into 13 subtests (Information, Comprehension, Similarities, Arithmetic, Vocabulary, Sentences, Picture Completion, Picture Arrangement, Block Design, Object Assembly, Animal Pegs, Mazes, and Geometric Designs). This organization encourages the use of the instrument as a measure of more specific skill areas, although it should be noted that reliabilities on the subtests are much lower than for the full-scale scores. The WPPSI-R is being used increasingly with the preschool child for whom evaluation of intellectual performance is required. Restandardized in 1989 (with 50% new items from the WPPSI), a more complete picture of field use is continuing to emerge (Aiken, 2003; Gregory, 2004).

Over the years, picture vocabulary tests have been a rather widely used approach to assessing children's intelligence. Although often used in this fashion, it is important to emphasize that picture vocabulary tests are not measures of intelligence in the same manner as those discussed above. They tend to assess receptive vocabulary, which generally is considered to be only one dimension of intelligence. Some researchers have investigated picture vocabulary tests in relation to intelligence (e.g., Brooks-Gunn, Klebanov, Smith, Duncan, & Lee, 2003; Campbell, Bell, & Keith, 2001). Although some picture vocabulary tests have certain psychometric elements that are technically sound, it is not unusual for others (e.g., validity) to be completely ignored.

Language Functioning

As the child grows older, the distinction between assessing language development and assessing intellectual functioning becomes increasingly blurred, to the point of imperceptibility. This results from several factors. First, at least in terms of normal language development, the child's language structure rapidly grows more sophisticated. By the time normal children reach 3 or 4 years of age, they can typically use all of the basic syntactic structures in language (Bernstein & Levey, 2002; Gleason, 2005; Reed, 2005). A different response mode becomes possible from when the very young child was operating almost totally as a sensorimotor organism. Test developers working with children of this age range are quick to take advantage of this new response mode. The assessment of intellectual status includes a much heavier verbal component as the child gets older, so the relationship between language and intellectual assessment grows closer.

Evidence of this close link is found in the Peabody Picture Vocabulary Test–Third Edition (PPVT-III), which is used by some as an estimate of intelligence (Campbell et al., 2001; Speece, Ritchey, Cooper, Roth, & Schatschneider, 2004). Although the PPVT is occasionally described as an intelligence test, many professionals view it more as a receptive language measure. In fact, some characterize it primarily as such a measure (Kastner, May, & Hildman, 2001; Spencer, 2004). Because of the way the items are presented, the view of the PPVT-R as measuring receptive language is more plausible. However, caution should be exercised in most interpretation of assessment results that attempt to infer extensively regarding subdomains. As noted earlier, picture vocabulary tests as presently constructed probably should be viewed only as preliminary screening procedures.

Developed in the 1960s, the Illinois Test of Psycholinguistic Abilities (ITPA) contributed perhaps more to a conceptual framework of disability assessment and intervention than actual measurement application. It was a highly complicated instrument that generated a profile of the child's performance in subtest areas. The ITPA was primarily associated with children who had learning disabilities but contributed to concepts of prescriptive education (pinpointing specific performance strengths and deficits) in many areas of disability. This has long been the position of those skilled in applied behavior analysis, but the ITPA fell psychometrically short in a number of fashions. Proponents of applied behavior analysis always desired much more precision in skill definition than the ITPA made possible. The ITPA is seldom given much attention in current assessment literature, more often treated as a historical contributor to assessment-treatment concepts (Estil, Whiting, Sigmundsson, & Ingvaldsen, 2003; Taylor, 2003).

Various other instruments provide language assessment procedures with differing degrees of precision and standardization. Instead of describing such instruments, however, we wish to discuss the larger question of evaluation approach. Many professionals concerned with practical application have viewed assessment as important only in its relation to intervention or instruction. Such a perspective does not place much value on scores unless they represent performance precisely related to specific instructional activities that will result in skill change. This approach tends to discount issues such as cause (except in the rare cases that can be rectified by surgery). Evaluation in this framework often reflects ongoing monitoring built into the instructional program or designed specifically for a given instructional program. This kind of assessment is in line with the concepts of prescriptive education (in fact, it represents a potent force in the development of those concepts) and is precise in pinpointing where instructional effort is most needed (Airasian, 2005).

Perceptual-Motor Functioning

Assessment of perceptual-motor skills is more commonly conducted with children suspected of having learning disabilities than with those thought to have intellectual disabilities. Yet perceptual-motor functioning is a crucial skill area in instruction for children with intellectual disabilities. Without the requisite visual-motor skills, a child can scarcely perform the basic tasks demanded in many instructional settings, let alone succeed from an academic standpoint. A child experiencing difficulty in these areas should be assessed for specific level of functioning and have instructional activities specifically designed to match these skills.

The Developmental Test of Visual Perception (DTVP) is one of the assessment techniques in the perceptual-motor area. This instrument was designed for use with children from about 4 to 8 years of age, but one can extend this age range for children who exhibit intellectual disabilities to a significant degree. The DTVP can be administered either individually or to groups and requires about 40 minutes to complete. It assesses five areas: eye-hand coordination, figure-ground perception, form constancy, position in space, and spatial relations. From a technical soundness standpoint, the DTVP has a number of problems. The subtests are not independent, and reliability and validity are unsatisfactory for diagnostic prescriptive teaching. Although the overall perceptual score is fairly reliable, this instrument is probably best used as a research tool, rather than for instructional purposes (Bearden et al., 2004; Schoemaker et al., 2001).

The Developmental Test of Visual-Motor Integration (VMI) also measures perceptual-motor skills but has a much more solid technical soundness. This instrument involves a paper-and-pencil performance by the child, to whom geometric forms are presented as stimuli to be copied. Although the VMI was designed primarily for use at the preschool and early primary levels, it can be administered to students from 2 to 19 years of age (e.g., Taylor, Minich, Klein, & Hack, 2004). The VMI was devised to assess how well motor behavior and visual perception are integrated. Like other perceptual-motor evaluations, it tries to identify fundamental skill deficits related to academic tasks. Such skills are pinpointed for remedial instruction. In reaching the final form for the 1989 edition, large standardization samples were used from a broad cross section of subjects. Although these norms were developed on a large cross-sectional sample, the makeup of the norm groups remains unclear. This vagueness causes some serious difficulty in using the test in a norm-referenced framework. Among the perceptual-motor instruments, the VMI stands out with fairly high reliability and validity.

Social/Adaptive Behavior

Evaluation approaches for assessing social skills were discussed in the section on very young children. In many cases, the upper age range of the measures extends far beyond the young child into preschool and elementary school years and even further. As the child progresses, judgments or ratings by others—caretakers, teachers, and parents—are often part of social skill assessment. It is important to remember that their ratings are not always reliable and in agreement. Such information sources are very important, however, and continued research is needed to resolve or minimize these difficulties.

Adaptive behavior is a concept involving skills that may be viewed generically as part of social competence. As mentioned in Chapter 1, adaptive behavior areas are a major element in the 2002 AAMR definition of intellectual disabilities. One of the major challenges continuing to face this definition is assessment in the area of adaptive skills (Bielecki & Swender, 2004; Hatton et al., 2001). Earlier development of an adaptive behavior scale by the AAMR (formerly the AAMD) led to a number of disappointments in terms of validity, reliability, and standardization. Second edition revisions are thought to be improved, although more validity data are needed (Taylor, 2003).

Also mentioned in the AAMR definition are the Scales of Independent Behavior which is now in a revised edition (SIB-R), which fares somewhat better from a technical soundness standpoint. The SIB-R may be used to assess adaptive functioning in individuals from infancy to adulthood. It is administered individually, and items generate four clusters or areas of functioning: (a) motor skills (gross and fine motor); (b) social interaction and communications (including social interaction, language comprehension, and language expression); (c) personal living skills (with five subscales pertaining to meal preparation and eating, dressing, toileting, self-care, and domestic skills); and (d) community living skills (time, money, work skills, home, and community). The SIB-R also includes maladaptive behavior indicators. Although there are some differences, the functioning clusters and subscales could serve the adaptive behavior areas defined by AAMR (2002). Validity evidence for the SIB-R, like its predecessor, appears to be satisfactory and reports about this instrument are rather positive (Gregory, 2004; Taylor, 2003).

Another instrument for assessing adaptive functioning is the Adaptive Behavior Inventory (ABI) which is used in a rather broad range of circumstances (Wood, Cowan, & Baker, 2002). The ABI is one of those procedures that blurs the age categories used here in that it is primarily for use with students from 6 to nearly 19 years of age. Agewise, it is more appropriate for the "Elementary School Years" section that immediately follows. It is presented here, however, to examine this instrument and the SIB in the context of the AAMR adaptive skill areas. The AAMR delineated three adaptive behavior areas: Conceptual, Social, and Practical Behavior areas. The ABI includes five subtests that are relevant to these adaptive behavior areas. These subtests can be administered independently and with little time investment: Self-Care Skills, Communication Skills, Social Skills, Academic Skills, and Occupational Skills.

Reviews of the ABI are rather positive, although more research is certainly warranted (Taylor, 2003).

The Comprehensive Test of Adaptive Behavior–Revised (CTAB-R) is used to assess one's ability to function independently in various environments. This instrument has standardization data on a wide range of samples from children through adults. Although the total score is thought appropriate for a diagnosis of intellectual disabilities, the scoring system does not fit neatly with the AAMR adaptive behavior areas (AAMR, 2002).

Table 3–3 summarizes the AAMR adaptive behavior areas related to specific assessment instruments. While some instruments fit better or less well with the AAMR scheme, these instruments do address the adaptive areas. It should be noted as well that these instruments appear to have reasonably sound psychometric properties and have a database developed on the general population.

Table 3–3
Correspondence Between Three Dimensions of Adaptive Behavior and Empirically Derived Factors on Existing Measures

Instrument	Conceptual Skills	Social Skills	Practical Skills
AAMR Adaptive Behavior Scale—School (Lambert, Nihira, & Leland, 1993)	Community self-sufficiency	Personal-social responsibility	Personal self-sufficiency
Vineland Adaptive Behavior Scales (Sparrow, Balla, & Cicchetti, 1984)	Communication	Socialization	Daily living skills
Scales of Independent Behavior–Revised (Bruininks, Woodcock, Weatherman, & Hill, 1996)	Community living skills	Social interaction and communication skills	Personal living skills
Comprehensive Test of Adaptive Behavior–Revised (Adams, 1999)	Language concepts and academic skills Independent living	Social skills	Self-help skills Home living

Note: All measures shown in this table are considered to have adequate psychometric properties and contain normative data on the general population. The purpose of this table is to illustrate that current adaptive behavior measures provide domain scores that represent the three dimensions of adaptive behavior skills in the 2002 AAMR definition. It is not intended to necessarily endorse these instruments or to exclude other measures that meet the guidelines for diagnosis.

Source: Mental Retardation: Definition, Classification, and Systems of Supports (10th ed., p. 77). Washington, DC: American Association on Mental Retardation. Copyright 2002 by the American Association on Mental Retardation, by permission.

ELEMENTARY SCHOOL YEARS

The elementary school child who has intellectual disabilities may be somewhat out of phase with the usual chronological age–formal education sequence. We use the phrase *elementary years* here only as a guideline. The overlap in age ranges for assessment approaches has already become obvious. Only techniques that become appropriate for this age range receive primary attention in this section. We also devote separate attention to emerging systems of assessment.

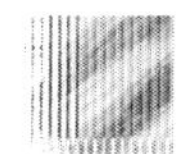

Core Concept

Multiple areas of functioning must be evaluated during the elementary years. Proper evaluation uses technically and conceptually sound procedures appropriate for this age range.

Intellectual Functioning

Several previously mentioned intellectual assessment instruments reached into the 5-to-12-year age range. In addition to these techniques, one of the best-known intelligence tests becomes age appropriate in this range: the Wechsler Intelligence Scale for Children–III (WISC-III). An updated version of the WISC-R, the WISC-III was developed for ages 6 to nearly 17, and has 13 subtests divided into two general areas: verbal and performance (Aiken, 2003; Taylor, 2003). Like most standardized instruments, the WISC is basically a norm-referenced instrument. Its score gives a composite IQ that indicates general ability. The instrument also provides for a profile of the child's performance in individual subtest areas, which generates more specific information than the composite IQ (e.g., Maller & French, 2004; Naglieri & Bornstein, 2003). Data from continuing accumulated field applications of the WISC-III will determine how it compares with previous editions, from a practical standpoint.

Although the recommended age range extends from about 6 to nearly 17 years (16 years–11 months), the WISC-III may not be the preferred instrument in this range. For general assessment of intellectual disabilities, the Stanford-Binet was viewed as stronger than the WISC-R up to age 8, mostly because of its standardization and clinical use. As data accumulate on the WISC-III, this preference may no longer hold.

Achievement

Many of the specific areas of assessment discussed for earlier age levels continue to be important during the elementary years. Determination of which areas require evaluation is based on a critical analysis of the areas in which a child has difficulty. One assessment area, however, becomes more important to evaluate than before: achievement. Many procedures assess academic achievement during the elementary years, including formal standardized instruments, as well as teacher-made assessment techniques for daily monitoring (Gronlund, 2004). Both norm- and criterion-referenced applications are used widely, as are individually and group-administered procedures. Each approach has its strengths, depending on the purpose of the evaluation. The following discussion is necessarily selective in those examined. Additional information regarding a more complete selection of instruments may be found in a number of sources devoted to this purpose (e.g., Aiken, 2003; Gregory, 2004).

Certain paper and pencil assessments are still used to evaluate functioning.

The revised edition of the Peabody Individual Achievement Test (PIAT-R) is an individually administered achievement test that assesses six content areas: mathematics, reading recognition, reading comprehension, spelling, general information, and written expression. The PIAT-R is designed for use from kindergarten through the 12th grade. Although the PIAT-R is a general achievement measure, it also may be used for instructional purposes. Easily administered, the PIAT-R results in a profile of the child's performance in the areas tested. The scores are presented in a variety of forms, including percentile ranks, age and grade equivalents, stanines, and normal curve equivalents. (Written Expression, a new subtest in this version, is scored differently by using scoring criteria provided in the manual.) Depending on the specific evaluation purpose, an examiner may select from these score formats as reporting dictates. Reliability is high for the objectively scored subtests. The manual provides information regarding reliability on the Written Language subtest, which is lower (Taylor, 2003). Validity, of course, is based on the correspondence of the items with the curriculum being used. Although developed as a norm-referenced instrument, skilled teachers may find criterion-referenced applications useful.

The seventh edition of the Metropolitan Achievement Test battery (MAT7) is an achievement battery that is group administered. The MAT7 is divided into two groups of tests: the Survey and Diagnostic batteries. The Survey battery assesses students' general achievement in reading, mathematics, language, social studies, and science. The Diagnostic battery addresses the three areas of reading, mathematics, and language. Both batteries are designed for students from about kindergarten through 12th grade (Diagnostic begins at K–5). By design, both the Survey and Diagnostic batteries may be used in norm- and criterion-referenced application. The Metropolitan is an example of how standardized instrumentation can be designed and used in a meaningful fashion for multiple purposes. Although the normed areas of evaluation are important, equally significant is what can be done with them. When analyzed in terms of the skills required by each item, the MAT7 can provide a vast amount of information about a child's functioning. This information then can be coordinated for specific determination of discrete activities for the child's instructional program. This kind of analysis demands considerable information and teacher training in task analysis and precision teaching. When such educational expertise is brought to the teaching task, instruments like the MAT7 are highly relevant for the education of both children with intellectual disabilities and others.

The achievement instruments discussed thus far have been general achievement measures, with some providing specific skill information. On certain occasions, it is necessary to use an instrument that focuses specifically on one content area and provides an in-depth assessment of subskills in that area. Such an instrument is the revised Keymath Diagnostic Arithmetic Test (Keymath-R). Keymath-R was developed for use with children as young as the kindergarten level and ranging upward through grade 9 (Taylor, 2003). Two forms (A and B) of Keymath-R are provided. Math performance is assessed in terms of three areas: basic concepts, operations, and applications. Scores create a profile of specific skills, although Keymath-R also may be scored on the basis of percentiles and standard scores.

Achievement assessment that results in only grade- or age-equivalency scores (as well as percentiles and standard scores) is norm-referenced information. In many cases, these same tests may be used in ways that make them criterion referenced, if the child's performance is not compared with other children's or with some norm. The more discrete and specific an assessment is, the greater its potential for drawing specific inferences for instruction. The highest relevance for instruction comes from assessment that is an integral part of the instructional program. Ideally, this type of achievement assessment continuously monitors a child's progress in specific skills. Instruction is aimed precisely at the child's level of functioning, permitting a highly efficient interface between evaluation and instruction. There is much in favor of such an approach for educating those who have intellectual disabilities.

Assessment Systems

Assessment procedures examined thus far have often had one area as their primary focus. Clinicians have often found it necessary to use several instruments to obtain a complete picture of an individual's capabilities. But some assessment development efforts evaluate a number of different attributes.

One evaluation system is the revised Woodcock-Johnson Tests of Cognitive Ability–Revised (WJTCA-III). This system covers an unusually wide age span (preschool to adult) and is designed to evaluate both academic achievement and cognitive ability (Bell, Rucker, Finch, & Alexander, 2002; Speece et al., 2004; Taub & McGrew, 2004). Academic achievement is assessed by using 14 subtests, and the Cognitive Ability battery includes 21 subtests (some of each group are standard; others are supplementary). Administration of the entire battery is very time consuming, and scoring is complicated. A relatively high level of skill is required for administration (Mather, Wendling, & Woodcock, 2001). The WJTCA-III is adequately standardized, although still a maturing instrument, and field applications will provide useful information.

ADOLESCENT AND ADULT YEARS

Core Concept

Assessment during adolescent and adult years involves use of age- or functioning-level-appropriate procedures. Attention also must be given to the changing purposes of evaluation in these years.

As we indicated at the beginning of each section, the age categories used must be viewed as guideposts. Consequently, the phrase *adolescent and adult years* is only a general reference that is used in this section to mean 13 years of age and older. Many of the evaluation techniques previously examined extend well into this age range.

Intellectual Functioning

The instrument frequently used in the middle adolescent and older years is the Wechsler Adult Intelligence Scale-III (WAIS-III). This is a substantially revised version of the earlier WAIS-R with three new subtests and an alternative scoring protocol (Gregory, 2004). The content is similar to the WISC and WPPSI (although age appropriate). The WISC-III, discussed earlier, extends into the early adolescent years (5 to 15 years). The WAIS-III is appropriate for assessing the intellectual functioning of people older than 15. The WAIS-R includes 13 subscales divided into verbal and performance categories plus an optional one to substitute for administration errors. The technical soundness of the WAIS-III appears to be quite positive—a good revision (Gregory, 2004).

Vocational Functioning

One area that becomes increasingly relevant as the person with intellectual disabilities grows older is his or her skill level for vocational training and placement. During adolescence and adulthood, the individual who has intellectual disabilities usually encounters vocational training as a part of formal education. In fact, the design of the vocational training received should be considered in detail both in the individualized education program (IEP) and the individualized transition plan (ITP) (AAMR, 2002; Airasian, 2005; Hardman et al., 2006). The nature of this training (as well as later placement) varies considerably, depending on the degree of impairment.

Assessment of vocational functioning, like other areas previously discussed, must be considered in the light of its purpose. One purpose of vocational assessment has nearly always been the prediction of vocational success. A second purpose involves determination of what skills are needed by the individual as the transition planners consider potential placements. And a third purpose is the evaluation of that training and placement success. Vocational assessment varies perhaps more than any other measurement area. There is an extremely broad range of potential placements (e.g., jobs, tasks) and an equally diverse range of individual skills.

Work samples seem to function very effectively for evaluating vocational functioning. Sometimes called "career simulation," work-sample observations have a very direct relationship to both job performance and the skills that need attention in preparing for the job (Roth, Huffcutt, & Bobko, 2003). Work-sample assessment is analogous to evaluation that uses applied behavior analysis techniques of observation and recording performance (Gelfand & Drew, 2003). This type of precise skill analysis has provided the most practically oriented information in other areas, and its utility in vocational assessment is not surprising. Evaluation takes place in a setting that is as nearly natural as possible. The close link between the assessment procedure and its purpose or referent setting provides the most useful and accurate data.

In addition to observing the individual's task performance, it is also important to evaluate other matters related to job success. Individuals with intellectual disabilities often exhibit different social interactions from their counterparts without retardation (Leffert & Siperstein, 2002). Such behaviors, and other "nonwork" factors like cultural influences, often contribute to vocational failure as much as actual job performance (Hardman et al., 2006). They are a part of the broader picture relating to overall success in a vocational setting. These factors require assessment just as the actual skills in performing job tasks do. Once again, behavioral observations in circumstances similar to that of the vocational setting are helpful. To the degree that the people and other stimuli can simulate an actual workplace, the utility of the evaluation data will be enhanced.

Perhaps the strongest deterrent to more widespread acceptance of direct observation and work-sample assessment is convenience. Work sampling and direct observation as assessment procedures tend to be cumbersome in terms of development and administration. Considerable time and effort are involved, to say nothing of the training of observers and evaluators. However, the alternatives for vocational assessment of those with intellectual disabilities are limited. A variety of standardized vocational-type assessments are available as diverse as testing for graduate school and general aptitude and finger dexterity. It is clear in many cases, however, that these have limited relevance for adolescents and adults with intellectual disabilities. It is also important to note that work-sample and observational assessment techniques are not nearly so inconvenient when they are designed as an integral part of a training program. Many successes in vocational assessment remain somewhat unknown because they are an integrated part of training, rather than a separate published test on the market.

NEW ISSUES AND FUTURE DIRECTIONS

Many of the issues raised in assessment have historically paralleled prevailing debates and issues in intellectual disabilities. This was illustrated by the early nature-versus-nurture controversy on development and the source of intelligent behavior, and continues today in more abstract questions about fundamental conceptions of intellectual disabilities (e.g., AAMR, 2002; Heffelfinger, 2002; Lickliter & Honeycutt, 2003). Assessment in intellectual disabilities is moving from its position as a somewhat isolated, almost laboratory-based activity into the center of culture, society, and environment.

It is no longer acceptable merely to test people's ability in a "stimulus-free environment" to determine how they will adapt and function in the broader world in which they live. Assessment and program planning and implementation are rapidly becoming matters of serious collaboration between disciplines that scarcely interacted a decade ago (Edmondson & Cain, 2002; Gronlund, 2004; Kronenberger & Dunn, 2003). Additionally, emerging qualitative research methodology tries to study people in the context of their environment more than ever before (Bartunek & Seo, 2002; Mertens, 2004; Sofaer, 2005). Social and cultural environments will become integral in the study and assessment of intellectual disabilities.

Such changes serve some very important purposes in the field of psychoeducational measurement. From one standpoint, they should present a more accurate view of how an individual functions and what his or her ability is in the relevant environmental context. We hope that such an assessment will also have greater utility than previously has been the case (e.g., ability testing that has little usefulness for instruction). Often called "authentic" or "alternative" assessment in current terminology, the field is moving away from sterile test scores to information that has the most likelihood of relating to the task (Gronlund, 2004). Some work is beginning to view assessment as more than a static evaluation, with more of a view of what is being termed dynamic assessment (Elliot, Lidz, & Shaughnessy, 2004). From another perspective, assessment in context also may hold promise for alleviating some of the problems of evaluating individuals from minority subgroups. Integrating information about family stress, environmental circumstances, culture, language, and other pertinent factors into a child's evaluation has considerable potential for producing more appropriate assessment in a variety of contexts (Lauchlan, 2001; Saenz & Huer, 2003).

Better methods, however, will not solve certain assessment difficulties. Designing environmentally contexted measurement will not do away with prejudice. Improvement will not be so great that assessment inaccuracies are solely the result of racial bias on the part of the examiner. This is a problem of professional ethics. Additionally, placing assessment in environmental context is not simple. It is likely to be both difficult and cumbersome. This result must be of concern to those working in the area of measurement, for if assessment is not user-friendly, it will not be used. Finally, we return to the Tips for Professionals feature and our opening vignette. Communicating the outcomes of assessment with the people it makes the most difference to—parents or other family members—is a sensitive and challenging task. Not only is the information important but the reporting of that information is equally vital.

Core Questions

1. Why are the uses of assessment procedures so important in the outcome of evaluation?
2. Why is it essential to clarify the purposes involved in assessment before one embarks on a testing effort?
3. Many conceptual developments have been important in the field of assessment during the past years. Among them have been the notions of formative and

summative evaluation and the distinctions between norm- and criterion-referenced assessment. How do these concepts fit into the evaluation picture, and why were they important?

4. What are some difficulties encountered in predicting later functioning from infant assessment procedures?
5. Outline potential assessment instruments or procedures that you would find important during the prenatal period. Describe conditions that would prompt such assessment.
6. Describe assessment procedures you might employ for early life (neonatal) and preschool years. Discuss conditions that would prompt you to undertake such assessment.
7. How might you prepare an appropriate evaluation plan for children during the elementary school years? What considerations would come into play in your assessment plan?
8. Outline relevant assessment considerations for the adolescent and adult years. How are these different from earlier considerations?
9. In reviewing the lifespan perspective, how do purposes change, and what considerations must be given to selection of an assessment approach?

Roundtable Discussion

Assessment is much more complex than merely picking up a test and administering it to a child. Careful consideration must be given from the outset to why one is evaluating and what is to be the result. Throughout the assessment process, one must exercise care in the choice of techniques, in how to undertake procedures, and in how to interpret data. Proper assessment must also consider the age of the individual being evaluated because different domains become relevant at different ages and because techniques diverge widely.

In your study group or on your own, design an evaluation plan that will attend to the considerations raised in this chapter. If you are working with others, have each person be responsible for a different age level and one or two individuals attend to the conceptual issues related to assessment. Compare your final plan with an existing one, such as that used in a school district. Full consideration of the lifespan must extend beyond the school years to health and social service agencies.

Parent and Professional Organization Positions on Key Issues in the Lives of People with Intellectual Disabilities

The inside front cover of this text presents a matrix that includes several key issues in the lives of people with disabilities, the positions of various parent and professional organizations on each issue, and the chapter and page number where the information is addressed. Table 3–4 on page 104 is a summary of the organizations and key issues addressed in this chapter.

Table 3–4
Key Issues and Organizations Discussed in This Chapter

Organization/Website	Key Issues Addressed	Chapter Heading
American Association on Mental Retardation (http://www.aamr.org)	Prenatal assessment Bioethics, early intervention Broadened definition scope and related assessment challenges	Early Life Assessment Social/Adaptive Functioning
International Association for the Scientific Study of Intellectual Disabilities (http://www.iassid.org)	Prenatal assessment Bioethics, early intervention	Early Life Assessment

References

Aiken, L. R. (2003). *Psychological testing and assessment* (11th ed.). Boston: Allyn & Bacon.

Airasian, P. W. (2005). *Classroom assessment: Concepts and applications* (5th ed.). New York: McGraw-Hill.

American Association on Mental Retardation (AAMR). (2002). *Mental retardation: Definition, classification, and systems of supports* (10th ed.). Washington, DC: Author.

American Psychological Association (APA). (2003). Guidelines on multicultural education, training, research, practice, and organizational change for psychologists. *American Psychologist, 58*, 377–402.

Antshel, K. M., Brewster, S., & Waisbren, S. E. (2004). Child and parent attributions in chronic pediatric conditions: Phenylketonuria (PKU) as an exemplar. *Journal of Child Psychology and Psychiatry, 45*, 622–630.

Austrian, S. G. (2002). Infancy and toddlerhood. In S. G. Austrian (Ed.), *Developmental theories through the life cycle* (pp. 7–68). New York: Columbia University Press.

Bailey, D. S. (2004). Developmental needs missing from desegregation. *Monitor on Psychology, 35*(8), 67.

Bangs, T., & Dodson, S. (1986). Birth to Three Developmental Scales. Allen, TX: DLM Teaching Resources.

Barr, O., & Millar, R. (2003). Parents of children with intellectual disabilities: Their expectations and experience of genetic counselling. *Journal of Applied Research in Intellectual Disabilities, 16*, 189–204.

Bartunek, J. M., & Seo, M. G. (2002). Qualitative research can add new meanings to quantitative research. *Journal of Organizational Behavior, 23*, 237–242.

Battle, D. E. (2002). Language and communication disorders in culturally and linguistically diverse children. In D. K. Bernstein & E. Tiegerman-Farber (Eds.), *Language and communication disorders in children* (5th ed., pp. 354–386). Boston: Allyn & Bacon.

Bearden, C. E., van-Erp, T. G. M., Monterosso, J. R., Simon, T. J., Glahn, D. C., Saleh, P. A., et al. (2004). Regional brain abnormalities in 22q11.2 deletion syndrome: Association with cognitive abilities and behavioral symptoms. *Neurocase, 10*, 198–206.

Bell, N. L., Rucker, M., Finch, A. J., Jr., & Alexander, J. (2002). Concurrent validity of the Slosson Full-Range Intelligence Test: Comparison with the Wechsler Intelligence Scale for Children–Third Edition and the Woodcock Johnson Tests of Achievement—Revised. *Psychology in the Schools, 39*, 31–38.

Berk, L. E. (2005). *Infants and children: Prenatal through middle childhood* (5th ed.). Boston: Allyn & Bacon.

Bernstein, D. K., & Levey, S. (2002). Language development: A review. In D. K. Bernstein & E. Tiegerman-Farber (Eds.), *Language and communication disorders in children* (5th ed., pp. 27–94). Boston: Allyn & Bacon.

Bielecki, J., & Swender, S. L. (2004). The assessment of social functioning in individuals with mental retardation: A review. *Behavior Modification, 28*, 694–708.

Binet, A., & Simon, T. (1908). Le développement de l'intelligence chez les enfants. *L'Année Psychologique, 14,* 1–94.

Brazelton, T. (1973). *Neonatal Behavioral Assessment Scale.* Philadelphia: Lippincott.

Brooks-Gunn, J., Klebanov, P. K., Smith, J., Duncan, G. J., & Lee, K. (2003). The black–white test score gap in young children: Contributions of test and family characteristics. *Applied Developmental Science, 7,* 239–252.

Brown, J. L., & Kiernan, N. E. (2001). Assessing the subsequent effect of a formative evaluation on a program. *Evaluation and Program Planning, 24,* 129-143.

Bzoch, K., & League, R. (1991). Receptive-Expressive-Emergent-Language Test (REEL-2). Los Angeles: Western Psychological Services.

Campbell, J. M., Bell, S. K., & Keith, L. K. (2001). Concurrent validity of the Peabody Picture Vocabulary Test–Third Edition as an intelligence and achievement screener for low SES African American children. *Assessment, 8,* 85–94.

Carter, A. S., Briggs-Gowan, M. J., & Davis, N. O. (2004). Assessment of young children's social-emotional development and psychopathology: Recent advances and recommendations for practice. *Journal of Child Psychology and Psychiatry and Allied Disciplines, 45,* 109–134.

Caruso, J. C. (2001). Reliable component analysis of the Stanford-Binet: Fourth Edition for 2- to 6-year-olds. *Psychological Assessment, 13,* 261–266.

Chafouleas, S. M., Riley-Tillman, T. C., & Eckert, T. L. (2003). A comparison of school psychologists' acceptability, training, and use of norm-referenced, curriculum-based, and brief experimental analysis methods to assess reading. *School Psychology Review, 32*, 272–281.

Chapman, D. A., Scott, K. G., & Mason, C. A. (2002). Early risk factors for intellectual disabilities: Role of maternal age and maternal educaton. *American Journal on Mental Retardation, 107*, 46–59.

Clark, K. B., Chein, I., & Cook, S. W. (2004). The effects of segregation and the consequences of desegregation. *American Psychologist, 59,* 495–501.

Cohen, I. L. (2003). Criterion-related validity of the PDD Behavior Inventory. *Journal of Autism and Developmental Disorders, 33,* 47–53.

Cohen, M. N. (2002). An anthropologist looks at "race" and IQ testing. In J. M. Fish (Ed.), *Race and intelligence: Separating science from myth* (pp. 201–223). Mahwah, NJ: Lawrence Erlbaum.

Colombo, J., Shaddy, D. J., Richman, W. A., Maikranz, J. M., Blaga, O. M., & Colombo, J. (2004). The developmental course of habituation in infancy and preschool outcome. *Infancy, 5,* 1–38.

Comfort, M., & Farran, D. C. (1994). Parent–child interaction assessment in family-centered intervention. *Infants and Young Children, 6,* 33–45.

Cook, J. L., & Cook, G. (2005). *Child development: Principles and perspectives.* Boston: Allyn & Bacon.

Coplan, J. (1993). *Early Language Milestone Scale* (2nd ed.). Austin, TX: Pro-Ed.

Crespi, T. D., & Politikos, N. N. (2004). Respecialization as a school psychologist: Education, training, and supervision for school practice. *Psychology in the Schools, 41*, 473–480.

Diamond, K. E., & Kontos, S. (2004). Families' resources and accommodations: Toddlers with Down syndrome, cerebral palsy, and developmental delay. *Journal of Early Intervention, 26,* 253–265.

Driscoll, A., & Nagel, N. G. (2005). *Early childhood education, birth-8: The world of children, families, and educators* (3rd ed.). Boston: Allyn & Bacon.

Edmondson, C. A., & Cain, H. M. (2002). The spirit of the Individuals with Disabilities Education Act: Collaboration between special education and vocational rehabilitation for the transition of students with disabilities. *Journal of Applied Rehabilitation Counseling, 33*, 10–14.

Elliot, J., Lidz, C., & Shaughnessy, M. F. (2004). An interview with Joe Elliot and Carol Lidz. *North American Journal of Psychology, 6*, 349–360.

Epps, E. G. (2002). Summary comments: Race, class, gender, and exceptionality of African American learners. In B. A. Ford & F. E. Obiakor (Eds.), *Creating successful learning environments for African American learners with exceptionalities* (pp. 217–223). Thousand Oaks, CA: Corwin Press.

Erbas, D., Ozen, A. & Acar, C. (2004). Comparison of two approaches for identifying reinforcers in teaching figure coloring to students with Down syndrome. *Education and Training in Developmental Disabilities, 39*, 253–264.

Estil, L. B., Whiting, H. T. A., Sigmundsson, H., & Ingvaldsen, R. P. (2003). Why might language and motor impairments occur together? *Infant and Child Development, 12,* 253–265.

Everatt, J., Smythe, I., Ocampo, D., & Gyarmathy, E. (2004). Issues in the assessment of literacy-related difficulties across language backgrounds: A cross-linguistic comparison. *Journal of Research in Reading, 27*, 141–151.

Fenson, L., Dale, P., Reznick, S., Thal, D., Bates, E., Hartung, J., et al. (1993). *MacArthur Communicative Development Inventories.* San Diego: Singular.

Flood, J., & Gredler, G. R. (2004). Practitioner's guide to empirically based measures of school behavior. *Psychology in the Schools, 41*, 814–816.

Friend, M., & Keplinger, M. (2003). An infant-based assessment of early lexicon acquisition. *Behavior Research Methods, Instruments and Computers, 35*, 302–309.

Fuchs, L. S., & Fuchs, D. (2001). Computer applications to curriculum-based measurement. *Special Services in the Schools, 17*, 1–14.

Gardner, J. M., Karmel, B. Z., & Freedland, R. L. (2001). Determining functional integrity in neonates: A rapid neurobehavioral assessment tool. In L. Twarog & P. S. Zeskind (Eds.), *Biobehavioral assessment of the infant* (pp. 398–422). New York: Guilford Press.

Geisinger, K. F. (2003). Testing and assessment in cross-cultural psychology. In J. A. Naglieri & J. R. Graham (Eds.), *Handbook of psychology: Vol. 10. Assessment psychology* (pp. 95–117). New York: Wiley.

Gelfand, D. M., & Drew, C. J. (2003). *Understanding child behavior disorders* (4th ed.). Belmont, CA: Wadsworth.

Ginsberg, D. L. (2003). Selective serotonin reuptake inhibitor use during pregnancy associated with premature delivery. *Primary Psychiatry, 10*, 25–26.

Gleason, J. B. (2005). *The development of language* (6th ed.). Boston: Allyn & Bacon.

Glenn, L. M., Jones, C. G., & Hoyt, J. E. (2003). The effect of interaction levels on student performance: A comparative analysis of Web-mediated versus traditional delivery. *Journal of Interactive Learning Research, 14*, 285–299.

Greene, M. M. (2003). Program evaluation. In M. Hersen & J. C. Thomas (Eds.), *Understanding research in clinical and counseling psychology* (pp. 209–242). Mahwah, NJ: Erlbaum.

Gregory, R. J. (2004). *Psychological testing: History, principles, and applications* (4th ed.). Boston: Allyn & Bacon.

Gronlund, N. E. (2004). *How to write and use instructional objectives* (7th ed.). Columbus, OH: Merrill/Prentice Hall.

Gruenewald, D. A. (2004). At home with the other: reclaiming the ecological roots of development and literacy. *Journal of Environmental Education, 35*, 33–43.

Harbin, G. L., Bruder, M. B., Adams, C., Mazzarella, C., Whitbread, K., Gabbard, G., et al. (2004). Early intervention service coordination policies: National policy infrastructure. *Topics in Early Childhood Special Education, 24*, 89–97.

Hardman, M. L., Drew, C. J., & Egan, M. W. (2006). *Human exceptionality: School, community, and family* (8th ed.). Needham Heights, MA: Allyn & Bacon.

Hatton, C., Emerson, E., Robertson, J., Gregory, N., Kessissoglou, S., Perry, J., et al. (2001). The Adaptive Behavior Scale–Residential and Community (Part I): Towards the development of a short form. *Research in Developmental Disabilities, 22*, 273–288.

Hedrick, D., Prather, E., & Tobin, A. (1984). *Sequenced Inventory of Communication Development (Revised).* Los Angeles: Western Psychological Services.

Heffelfinger, A. K. (2002). The development of psychopathology: Nature and nurture. *Child Neuropsychology, 8*, 144–145.

Hess, C. R., Papas, M. A., & Black, M. M. (2004). Use of the Bayley Infant Neurodevelopmental Screener with an environmental risk group. *Journal of Pediatric Psychology, 29*, 321–330.

International Association for the Scientific Study of Intellectual Disabilities (IASSID). (2003). Health SIRG news. *Newsletter, 20*, 13.

Jesse, D., Davis, A., & Pokorny, N. (2004). High-achieving middle schools for Latino students in poverty. *Journal of Education for Students Placed at Risk, 9*, 23–45.

Jones, L., & Menchetti, B. M. (2001). Identification of variables contributing to definitions of mild and moderate intellectual disabilities in Florida. *Journal of Black Studies, 31*, 619–634.

Kastner, J. W., May, W., & Hildman, L. (2001). Relationship between language skills and academic achievement in first grade. *Perceptual and Motor Skills, 92*, 381–390.

Kay, D. W. K., Tyrer, S., Margallo-Lana, M. L., Moore, P. B., Fletcher, R., Berney, T. P., et al. (2003). Preliminary evaluation of a scale to assess cognitive function in adults with Down's syndrome: The

Prudhoe Cognitive Function Test. *Journal of Intellectual Disability Research, 47*, 155–165.

Korner, A. F., & Constantinou, J. C. (2001). The neurobehavioral assessment of the preterm infant: Reliability and developmental and clinical validity. In L. Twarog & P. S. Zeskind (Eds.), *Biobehavioral assessment of the infant* (pp. 381–397). New York: Guilford Press.

Kronenberger, W. G., & Dunn, D. W. (2003). Learning disorders. *Neurologic Clinics, 21*, 941–952.

Lau, A. S., McCabe, K. M., Yeh, M., Garland, A. F., Hough, R. L., & Landsverk, J. (2003). Race/ethnicity and rates of self-reported maltreatment among high-risk youth in public sectors of care. *Child Maltreatment: Journal of the American Professional Society on the Abuse of Children, 8*, 183–194.

Lauchlan, F. (2001). Addressing the social, cognitive, and emotional needs of children: The case for dynamic assessment. *Educational and Child Psychology, 18*, 4–18.

Lawson, K. R., & Ruff, H. A. (2004). Early attention and negative emotionality predict later cognitive and behavioural function. *International Journal of Behavioral Development, 28*, 157–165.

Leffert, J. S., & Siperstein, G. N. (2002). Social cognition: A key to understanding adaptive behavior in individuals with mild mental retardation. In L. M. Glidden (Ed.), *International review of research in mental retardation* (Vol. 25, pp. 135–181). San Diego, CA: Academic Press.

Lickliter, R., & Honeycutt, H. (2003). Evolutionary approaches to cognitive development: status and strategy. *Journal of Cognition and Development, 4*, 459–473.

Maller, S. J., & French, B. F. (2004). Universal nonverbal intelligence test factor invariance across deaf and standardization samples. *Educational and Psychological Measurement, 64*, 647–660.

Mather, N., Wendling, B. J., & Woodcock, R. W. (2001). *Essentials of WJ III–Super I tests of achievement assessment*. New York: Wiley.

Mayes, L. C., & Lombroso, P. J. (2003). Genetics of childhood disorders: LV. Prenatal drug exposure. *Journal of the American Academy of Child and Adolescent Psychiatry, 42*, 1258–1261.

Mayfield, J. W., & Reynolds, C. R. (1997). Black–white differences in memory test performance among children and adolescents. *Archives of Clinical Neuropsychology, 12*, 111–122.

Merrell, K.W. (2003). *Behavioral, social, and emotional assessment of children and adolescents* (2nd ed.). Mahwah, NJ: Lawrence Erlbaum.

Mertens, D. M. (2004). *Research and evaluation in education and psychology: Integrating diversity with quantitative, qualitative, and mixed methods* (2nd ed.). Thousand Oaks, CA: Sage.

Meyer, L. H., Bevan-Brown, J., Harry, B., & Sapon-Shevin, M. (2003). School inclusion and multicultural issues in special education. In J. A. Banks & C. A. M. Banks (Eds.), *Multicultural education: Issues and perspectives, update* (4th ed., pp. 327–352). New York: Wiley.

Mirrett, P. L., Bailey, D. B. Jr., Roberts, J. E., & Hatton, D. D. (2004). Developmental screening and detection of developmental delays in infants and toddlers with fragile X syndrome. *Journal of Developmental and Behavioral Pediatrics, 25*, 21–27.

Moseley, D. (2004). The diagnostic assessment of word recognition and phonic skills in five-year-olds. *Journal of Research in Reading, 27*, 132–140.

Murray, B. (2002). Psychology training gets major recognition. *Monitor on Psychology, 33*(3), 22–23.

Naar-King, S., Ellis, D. A., & Frey, M. A. (2004). *Assessing children's well-being*. Mahwah, NJ: Erlbaum.

Nachshen, J. S., Woodford, L., & Minnes, P. (2003). The Family Stress and Coping Interview for families of individuals with developmental disabilities: A lifespan perspective on family adjustment. *Journal of Intellectual Disability Research, 47*, 285–290.

Naglieri, J. A., & Bornstein, B. T. (2003). Intelligence and achievement: Just how correlated are they? *Journal of Psychoeducational Assessment, 21*, 244–260.

Nelson, N. W., & Van Meter, A. M. (2002). Assessing curriculum-based reading and writing samples. *Topics in Language Disorders, 22*, 35–59.

Neubert, D. A. (2003). The role of assessment in the transition to adult life process for students with disabilities. *Exceptionality, 11*, 63–75.

Olswang, L., Stoel-Gammon, C., Coggins, T., & Carpenter, R. (1987). *Assessing linguistic behavior*. Seattle: University of Washington Press.

Owens, R. E., Jr. (2005). *Language development: An introduction* (6th ed.). Boston: Allyn & Bacon.

Parens, E., & Asch, A. (2003). Disability rights critique of prenatal genetic testing: Reflections and recommendations. *Mental Retardation and Developmental Disabilities Research Reviews, 9*, 40–47.

Peterson, C. A., Wall, S., Raikes, H. A., Kisker, E. E., Swanson, M. E., Jerald, J., et al. (2004). Early head start: Identifying and serving children with disabilities. *Topics in Early Childhood Special Education, 24,* 76–88.

Posner, S. F., Learman, L. A., Gates, E. A., Washington, A. E., & Kuppermann, M. (2004). Development of an attitudes measure for prenatal screening in diverse populations. *Social Indicators Research, 65,* 187–206.

Quereshi, M. Y. (2003). Absence of parallel forms for the traditional individual intelligence tests. *Current Psychology: Developmental, Learning, Personality, Social, 22,* 149–154.

Raack, C. (1989). *Mother/infant communication screening.* Schaumburg, IL: Community Therapy Services.

Read, C. Y. (2004). Using the Impact of Event Scale to evaluate psychological response to being a phenylketonuria gene carrier. *Journal of Genetic Counseling, 13,* 207–219.

Reading, R. (2004). Visual function at school age in children with neonatal encephalopathy and low Apgar scores. *Child: Care, Health and Development, 30,* 558–559.

Reed, V. A. (2005). *Introduction to children with language disorders* (3rd ed.). Boston: Allyn & Bacon.

Rees, C. E., & Sheard, C. E. (2004). The reliability of assessment criteria for undergraduate medical students' communication skills portfolios: The Nottingham experience. *Medical Education, 38,* 138–144.

Robinson, N. B., & Robb, M. P. (2002). Early communication assessment and intervention: An interactive process. In D. K. Bernstein & E. Tiegerman-Farber (Eds.), *Language and communication disorders in children* (5th ed., pp. 126–180). Boston: Allyn & Bacon.

Roesch, S. C., Schetter, C. D., Woo, G., & Hobel, C. J. (2004). Modeling the types and timing of stress in pregnancy. *Anxiety, Stress and Coping: An International Journal, 17,* 87–102.

Rossetti, L. (1990). *The Rossetti Infant-Toddler Language Scale.* Moline, IL: Lingua Systems.

Roth, P. L., Huffcutt, A. I., & Bobko, P. (2003). Ethnic group differences in measures of job performance: A new meta-analysis. *Journal of Applied Psychology, 88,* 694–706.

Rust, C., Price, M., & O'Donovan, B. (2003). Improving students' learning by developing their understanding of assessment criteria and processes. *Assessment and Evaluation in Higher Education, 28,* 147–164.

Saenz, T. I., & Huer, M. B. (2003). Testing strategies involving least biased language assessment of bilingual children. *Communication Disorders Quarterly, 24,* 184–193.

Sahler, O. J. Z., & Carr, J. E. (2003). *The behavioral sciences and health care.* Ashland, OH: Hogrefe & Huber.

Salvia, J., & Ysseldyke, J. E. (1995). *Assessment* (6th ed.). Boston: Houghton Mifflin.

Schoemaker, M. M., van der Wees, M., Flapper, B., Verheij-Jansen, N., Scholten-Jaegers, S., & Geuze, R. H. (2001). Perceptual skills of children with development coordination disorder. *Human Movement Science, 20* (1–2), 111–133.

Schubert, E. W., & McNeil, T. F. (2004). Prospective study of neurological abnormalities in offspring of women with psychosis: Birth to adulthood. *American Journal of Psychiatry, 161,* 1030–1037.

Seguin, L., Xu, Q., Potvin, L., Zunzunegui, M. V., & Frohlich, K. L. (2003). Effects of low income on infant health. *Canadian Medical Association Journal, 168,* 1533–1538.

Seung, H. K., & Chapman, R. (2004). Sentence memory of individuals with Down's syndrome and typically developing children. *Journal of Intellectual Disability Research, 48,* 160–171.

Shapiro, J., Monzo, L. D., Rueda, R., Gomez, J. A., & Blacher, J. (2004). Alienated advocacy: Perspectives of Latina mothers of young adults with developmental disabilities on service systems. *Mental Retardation, 42,* 37–54.

Shermis, M. D., & Daniels, K. E. (2003). Norming and scaling for automated essay scoring. In J. Burstein & M. D. Shermis (Eds.), *Automated essay scoring: A cross-disciplinary perspective* (pp. 169–180). Mahwah, NJ: Erlbaum.

Shriner, J. G., & Destefano, L. (2003). Participation and accommodation in state assessment: The role of individualized education programs. *Exceptional Children, 69,* 147–161.

Silliman, E. R., & Diehl, S. F. (2002). Assessing children with language learning disabilities. In D. K. Bernstein & E. Tiegerman-Farber (Eds.), *Language and communication disorders in children* (5th ed., pp. 181–255). Boston: Allyn & Bacon.

Smidt, M. L., & Cress, C. J. (2004). Mastery behaviors during social and object play in toddlers with physical impairments. *Education and Training in Developmental Disabilities, 39,* 141–152.

Sofaer, B. (2005). *Qualitative methods in health services and policy research.* Hoboken, NJ: Wiley.

Speece, D. L., Ritchey, K. D., Cooper, D. H., Roth, F. P., & Schatschneider, C. (2004). Growth in early reading skills from kindergarten to third grade. *Contemporary Educational Psychology, 29,* 312–332.

Spencer, P. E. (2004). Individual differences in language performance after cochlear implantation at one to three years of age: Child, family, and linguistic factors. *Journal of Deaf Studies and Deaf Education, 9,* 395–412.

Taub, G. E., & McGrew, K. S. (2004). A confirmatory factor analysis of Cattell-Horn-Carroll theory and cross-age invariance of the Woodcock-Johnson Tests of Cognitive Abilities III. *School Psychology Quarterly, 19,* 72–87.

Taylor, H. G., Minich, N. M., Klein, N., & Hack, M. (2004). Longitudinal outcomes of very low birth weight: Neuropsychological findings. *Journal of the International Neuropsychological Society, 10,* 149–163.

Taylor, R. L. (2003). *Assessment of exceptional students: Educational and psychological procedures* (6th ed.). Boston: Allyn & Bacon.

Valdez, C. M. (2003). Placement of ethnic minority students in special education: A study of over and under-representation issues. *Dissertation Abstracts International Section A: Humanities and Social Sciences, 64* (5-A), 1602.

Van-Geert, P. (2003). Measuring intelligence in a dynamic systems and contextualist framework. In J. Lautrey & R. J. Sternberg (Eds.), *Models of intelligence: International perspectives* (pp. 195–211). Washington, DC: American Psychological Association.

Watts, I. E., & Erevelles, N. (2004). These deadly times: Reconceptualizing school violence by using critical race theory and disability studies. *American Educational Research Journal, 41,* 271–299.

Willford, J. A., Richardson, G. A., Leech, S. L., & Day, N. L. (2004). Verbal and visuospatial learning and memory function in children with moderate prenatal alcohol exposure. *Alcoholism: Clinical and Experimental Research, 28,* 497–507.

Wetherby, A., & Prizant, B. (1993). *Communication and symbolic behavior scales*. Chicago: Riverside.

Wood, J. J., Cowan, P. A., & Baker, B. L. (2002). Behavior problems and peer rejection in preschool boys and girls. *Journal of Genetic Psychology, 163,* 72–88.

Yoshinaga-Itano, C. (2003). Early intervention after universal neonatal hearing screening: Impact on outcomes. *Mental Retardation and Developmental Disabilities Research Reviews, 9,* 252–266.

Zigler, E., Bennett-Gates, D., Hodapp, R., & Henrich, C. C. (2002). Assessing personality traits of individuals with mental retardation. *American Journal on Mental Retardation,* 107.

Zimmerman, I., Steinger, V., & Pond, R. (1992). *Preschool Language Scale–3.* San Antonio, TX: Psychological Corporation.

Chapter 4

Understanding Intelligence and Adaptive Skills

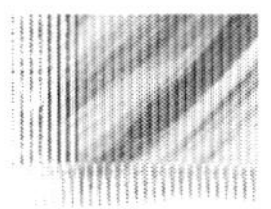

Chapter Preview

At the completion of this chapter, you will have a better understanding of the challenges involved in assessment of those having intellectual disabilities. You will encounter:

- The development of intelligence and the contributions of genetics and environmental influences have been of interest for many years.
- The definition of intelligence and the ways in which social competence is involved continue to be of interest for both researchers and practitioners working in the area of intellectual disabilities.
- The assessment and conceptualization of intelligence are vitally important in the field of intellectual disabilities.

Wanting the Best for Our Unborn

It had been 1 month since Sonia had heard from her physician—she was pregnant. She and her husband were delighted. It had been planned and somewhat scheduled, like most of their life together had been. Randy was a new faculty member in engineering, and Sonia had just finished her master's degree in psychology. Although they weren't exactly sure when they wanted their first baby, they had talked a lot about it over the past several years and definitely wanted it before too long.

Sonia and Randy had both spent much of their lives on a university campus, each being a third-generation faculty member. For the most part, their worlds had always been logical, rational, and scientifically oriented. They discussed at considerable length the development of intelligence from conception on, including matters of genetics and environmental influences. These discussions had been like most of their visits, laced with references from literature and science.

Yet both of them had done some things the past month that were unusual and different. It seemed to start when Randy came home one evening with a list of do's and don'ts for pregnant mothers. Some were only logical, or even based on science, but others were less sound. Maybe it wasn't known for sure that the microwave oven could hurt the baby, but Sonia had started casually leaving the kitchen when she turned it on. And Randy, of all people, had started worrying about having sex because of the pregnancy. Sonia was hardly showing yet and comfort was not at all an issue.

Beyond the possibility of harm, there were other behaviors that Sonia did not mention to anyone. She had started listening to classical music instead of her long-time favorite folk artists. She kept to herself the fact that she had heard this on a television tabloid story indicating that such exposure would raise the IQ of unborn babies. At times she wondered what was going on with the thought processes of both of them—but she still privately thought about reading aloud to her unborn baby, wondered about the high-protein diet that was also supposed to promote the baby's intelligence, and waited eagerly for their baby to start kicking and moving in her womb.

- *What are your thoughts regarding the intelligence potential of Sonia and Randy's baby? What do you know about their background that would inform you about what the youngster is likely to inherit, and what impacts the environment might have on his or her intelligence?*

- *How do you evaluate the evidence around you such as the reports of scientific study? Where do you find the information that helps influence your ideas about human development of intelligence or other matters?*

Sonia and Randy are certainly not the first to be caught up in the emotional aspects of a first pregnancy in ways that diverge from their previous belief systems, whether that earlier viewpoint was shaped by science, religion, or some other perspective. Most mothers can reflect back on some elements of their pregnancy period with questions about how much of what they experienced was predictive of their baby's intelligence. Did the overall activity level predict an inquisitive, active, intelligent youngster that will grow into an intelligent adult? (Remember the baby kicking every time you tried to take a nap?) Were there maternal choices made that significantly promoted or detracted from the cognitive growth of the baby and his or her ability to adapt to the social and physical environment? (Remember the social choices you made about seltzer water instead of a glass of wine?)

Answers to these questions are somewhat varied. Yes there are some predictors, and yes there are some choices that parents can make that make a difference. However, some of the differences are perhaps not as direct or strong as some parents would like to think. In some cases the relationships are in the myth category, whereas in others there is a grain of science mixed with a substantial amount of creative fiction. Fetal activity at various prenatal periods does appear to have a relationship to a baby's temperament, and even the early fussiness. But linkages between some prenatal measures and infant behavior are not as strong as laypeople might want to infer. Further, as we saw in the previous chapter, linkages between assessments during infancy and later abilities are also modest at best. What is clear is that mothers should have good nutrition and not partake of certain substances during pregnancy in order to give their developing baby the best possible chance—that is, avoid potential injury. More subtle control such as making your baby very intelligent, or creative, or socially adept at adapting, are quite difficult. Part of the baby's intelligence and adaptive capability are due to genetic inheritance from the parents, and part from the environment. (Sonia and Randy probably transmitted important genes that more positively influence the baby's intelligence than the music.) Likely the best we can do as parents is to try to avoid environmental contributors that might cause damage (e.g., toxic substances, drugs, alcohol). It is also important to promote environmental circumstances that are known to promote healthy growth, such as healthy food, reasonable rest, and other lifestyle choices (IASSID, 2003). Healthy nutrition during and after pregnancy does not need to be complicated as suggested by the Tips for Professionals.

Core Concept

Of all the ways people differ, none have generated as much continuing interest and speculation as has intelligence.

Physical differences in humans are easily seen through variation in height, weight, skin and hair coloring, physical

Tips for Professionals

Simple Nutrition Guidelines

Enhanced nutrition is recommended by many professional sources. Part of the challenge for all of us is making the rules sufficiently simple that they can be remembered and made an automatic part of our daily life. Most people know in a general way a healthy diet should include at least five fruits and vegetables. However, they're not making the most nutritious choices because messages about what to eat are unclear, according to research in the March 2005 issue of the *Journal of the American Dietetic Association*.

How do you know which fruits and veggies have the most power in keeping you healthy? There are some relatively simple tips according to the acting director of the Obesity Prevention Center at Saint Louis University.

The veggies and fruits that do the best job in reducing the health risk for chronic disease are dark green leafy vegetables, yellow/orange citrus, and cruciferous.

Think about color to pack nutritional power in your diet:

1. White: Eat cauliflower more often than potatoes, onions, and mushrooms.
2. Green: Add more dark lettuces, such as romaine and red leaf lettuce, spinach, broccoli and Brussels sprouts to replace iceberg lettuce and green beans.
3. Yellow/orange: Substitute more carrots, winter squashes, sweet potatoes, cantaloupe, oranges and grapefruit for corn or bananas.
4. Red: Select tomatoes, red peppers and strawberries in favor of apples.

These do not necessarily represent traditional choices, but they represent good nutritional choices and good nutritional choices enhance the environment for development of intelligence.

Source: Adapted from a news release issued by Saint Louis University dated March 5, 2004, titled *Will an apple a day keep the doctor away? There are better food choices.*

coordination, gender, and many other distinctive attributes that make individuals recognizable. You can also see more subtle differences in people with respect to creativity, personality, and intelligence, to name a few of the more abstract human traits. All of these abilities are interesting, but none have been so controversial as intelligence. Intelligence has been an intriguing subject for philosophers, psychologists, and laypeople for a variety of reasons. In Western culture, few concepts have been studied as intensely as that of intelligence, both in definition and in measurement. At times, scientists and test developers have been so caught up in quantifying intelligence that they have experienced difficulty keeping the concept in focus. It is important to keep a firm grasp on the conceptual identity of what is being measured as one collects data on an ability or characteristic. Otherwise, it may be difficult to assign meaning to the data or information obtained (Aiken, 2003; Gregory, 2004).

At least two factors have contributed to the problem: (a) a tendency to rush the development and marketing of instruments that purport to measure intelligence and (b) a simplistic notion that test performance is valid and reliable regardless of cultural or motivational influences. There certainly has been no lack of awareness about these influences. Investigators in all behavioral sciences have pointed out definitional problems and the impact of behaviors that are not easily quantified, subject to situational influences and short-term changes (e.g., Aiken, 2003; Ardelt, 2004; Gronlund, 2004). Psychologists' "success" in developing tests actually presents a significant problem, particularly if the instruments neglect other relevant aspects of intelligent behavior, such as the influence of social and cultural mores, language, early environmental influences, physical development, and sex role expectations.

Core Concept

Interest in the development of intelligence increased as people moved from primarily hunting, gathering, and agrarian societies.

There has been an interest in the phenomenon of intelligence for centuries. As humans formed social groupings the need to specify skills and competencies of group members became necessary to facilitate the efficient division of labor. The need to prepare individuals for group membership emerged when people saw that some were more skilled in certain areas than others. As societies developed and became more complex, the need to explain individual differences also increased in importance. The development of theories of intelligence parallels society's progress from hunting groups through agrarian communities, the industrial age, and into the atomic, space, and information ages. The rapid progress in this information-oriented society, with expanding computer use, places a renewed emphasis on the importance of intelligence.

The advent of the space and computer ages and the development of world markets made the need to identify those with high intellectual ability more pronounced. Governments of industrial nations have undertaken searches and provided rewards for the intellectually capable through grants for higher education, merit scholarships, and the promise of exciting, well-paid positions in a variety of areas. Conversely, this emphasis also has brought increased attention to those whose intellectual capabilities are limited. Such individuals constitute a concern in technologically advanced societies because they frequently become social liabilities. In less mechanized times, individuals with limited intellectual ability often could make significant contributions to society by performing work that did not require a high level of skill. As technology has advanced and influenced the entire spectrum of society, the need for unskilled and semiskilled individuals has diminished. Machines now more efficiently perform the work formerly done by individuals with little formal education. This change has not been a great problem for those who have the requisite intellectual ability but simply lack the necessary training to undertake more skilled labor. But for those who cannot profit educationally to the same extent as their more intelligent peers, opportunities for high status and a fulfilling life have decreased sharply. Any humane society must explore ways to reduce the social and economic liability of all of its less gifted citizens, including those with intellectual disabilities, while also providing educational opportunities appropriate to their intellectual abilities. Individual self-respect often depends on developing resources through education. A society that does less than it is able degrades and demeans both its citizens and the society itself.

In these circumstances, the need to identify and isolate particular characteristics associated with limited mental ability, both from biological and environmental causes, becomes paramount. Much of the public controversy surrounding intelligence pertains to its measurement or the manner in which the assessment of intelligence has been implemented. Major difficulties relate to intellectual assessment in the context of our culturally diverse society, as outlined in Chapter 2. In some states, such as California and Texas, the issues of discrimination in assessing intelligence and other psychoeducational factors have resulted in legal intervention regarding assessment (see the discussion in Chapter 2). In these cases the implementation experience in measuring intelligence will significantly impact the overall view and conceptualization of a major human performance area, heretofore termed intelligence (Ardelt, 2004; Cohen, 2002; Kaufmann, 2003). Intellectual disabilities clearly involve matters other than measured intelligence (AAMR, 2002). Limited intellectual ability is central, however, and intelligence is a topic that warrants examination. The need to understand, define, and measure this phenomenon remains an important task as attempts are made to provide better care for those with intellectual disabilities in this society.

THE CONCEPT OF INTELLIGENCE

There are about as many ways to define intelligence as there are people interested and motivated enough to try. Early scientists encountered hundreds of widely varying definitions being used to classify children related to intelligence. Interest in this area continues across the spectrum from those considered gifted to many differing disability areas (e.g., Baron-Cohen & Wheelwright, 2004; Reis & Moon, 2002; Sarouphim, 2004). Likewise, the concept of intellectual disabilities, at the other end of the intellectual spectrum, has produced a plethora of definitions. The number of definitions for these two intellectual extremes has led many people to think of intelligence in a quantitative sense. Intelligence, however, cannot be considered solely as a simple linear phenomenon ranging from more to less or from bright to intellectual disabilities. The complexity of human intelligence dictates that its qualitative aspects must also be considered. An appreciation of the many determinants affecting intelligence is necessary if professionals are ever fully to understand and appreciate the phenomenon. From genetic selection at conception through the adult and advanced years, an almost infinite number of variables exists that can affect intellectual abilities of the developing human organism (Godfrey-Smith, 2002; Stankov, 2003; Verri et al., 2004). As scientists continue to grapple with the concept of intelligence two questions consistently stand out: How is intelligence developed? and How can scientists gain some understanding of its composition in order to make predictions about future behavior? Neither question has been completely answered.

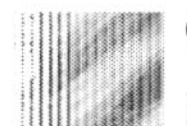

Core Concept

Intelligence has too frequently been conceived in a linear fashion because of the development of quantitative measures; qualitative factors also must be considered.

DEVELOPMENT OF INTELLIGENCE

Questions about how intelligence develops contributed to what is commonly known as the nature-versus-nurture controversy, which was directly stimulated by the

Core Concept

Discussion regarding the causes of intellectual disabilities stimulated debates about whether intelligence is primarily genetically determined or environmentally influenced.

phenomenon of intellectual disabilities. Is intelligence genetically determined with little or no contribution from later environmental conditions and influences, or is it primarily dependent on environmental factors, with only a limited genetic contribution? Advocates of both positions have, at times, been very vocal in championing their view and claiming the naïveté of their opponents. The controversy has persisted in the United States since the turn of the century, with varying social and economic factors affecting the way society views and provides for people with intellectual disabilities. A more reasoned approach, one that attempts to establish the interrelatedness and interaction of heredity and environment, has emerged from this controversy (deCastro, 2004; Heffelfinger, 2002; Lickliter & Honeycutt, 2003). This attempt signals a certain level of theoretical maturity, with a trend away from extreme perspectives toward a middle position that recognizes and draws on the facts established by both sides.

The question that spurs such heated debates is not really whether hereditary factors or environmental conditions play the major role in intellectual disabilities but their presumed effect. It is well established that some conditions are caused by hereditary factors—for example, microcephaly, neurofibromatosis, and Tay-Sachs disease. Similarly, it has been shown that environmental conditions can affect the level of mental functioning. It is therefore no longer a matter of debate whether genetics affects human intelligence or whether environmental factors play a part in the dynamics of intelligence. Both play a role in which each depends on the other for intelligence to be manifested. The contributions of heredity in setting the limits of intelligence are recognized, and the influence of environmental factors is accounted for in determining the range of intelligence.

Although the concept of interaction between heredity and environment is acceptable to almost all scientists, a controversy remains about how much each aspect contributes. Scientists presently are unable to accurately partition genetic and environmental contributions into percentages to indicate the precise amount that each contributes to individual performance. Attempts to ascertain the relative contributions of each continue, ranging from "best guesses" to stringently controlled research. Studies using twins have generally found that identical twins, whether raised together or apart, are more similar than random pairs of nonrelated persons (e.g., Cook & Cook, 2005; deCastro, 2004). Problems arise, however, even with this research methodology because all variables cannot be controlled and because twins often are placed in similar environments when raised apart (Gelfand & Drew, 2003).

The nature-nurture debate has persisted for many years. Periodically these arguments and related social issues surface in the public's eye, often raising issues of considerable importance to parents as the stewards of young children's environment (Forman, Aksan, & Kochanska, 2004; Lickliter & Honeycutt, 2003). The contexts for the nature-nurture discussion cover many areas beyond the development of intelligence as scientists seek explanations of how various human conditions evolve. Research continues to explore such topics as talent development, criminal behavior, cognitive ability, nearly all disability areas, and many others in the context of genetic and environmental influences (Cook & Cook, 2005; deCastro, 2004; Lickliter & Honeycutt, 2003).

A variety of factors influence intelligence, or performances that most people would agree contribute to the measurement of intelligence. Certainly, intelligent behavior in people's daily lives is not pure, without many sources of influence. In fact, most initial concerns about schoolchildren have to do with inappropriate behavior, not a perceived lack of intelligence. The AAMR definition of intellectual disabilities (see Chapter 1) focuses significantly on adaptive behavior areas, which attempt to address these important influences on personal and social success. Behaviors generally associated with the social aspect of intelligence have often been the focus of research and scientific literature in intellectual disabilities and many other fields of study (e.g., Bass, 2002; Radvanyi, 2003; Rosner, Hodapp, Fidler, Sagun, & Dykens, 2004). A wide variety of behaviors are involved in the performance area broadly termed **social intelligence** and **social, or personal, competence.** For example, interpersonal interaction and forming relationships, communication, and self-regulation and reacting appropriately to the subtle cues in one's environment fit into such areas of performance (Griffin, Scheier, Botvin, & Diaz, 2001; Kyratzis, 2004; Rhule, McMahon, & Spieker, 2004). Although measurement presents some challenges, many of these behaviors reliably appear as limitations in the behavioral repertoire of those with intellectual disabilities (e.g., Edeh & Hickson, 2002; Hodapp, 2003; Rosner et al., 2004).

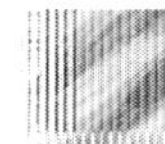

Core Concept

The need to know about the influence of a person's expectations, motivations, and social intelligence has stimulated research on the relationship between sociopersonal factors and intelligence.

Social interaction and experience may have a significant influence on a youngster's intellectual development.

Expectation of an event, often called expectancy, has a considerable effect on how a person behaves. Expectancies are simply attitudes or one's outlook that prompts a person to decide whether something may or may not occur. They are related to previous experiences. A person with an expectancy of failure in a certain situation, for example, cannot be expected to enter the same or similar situations with a positive expectation of success. Those with intellectual disabilities often have a lifetime of experiences that shape their expectations toward failure and success in a wide variety of circumstances (Stancliffe, Hayden, Larson, & Lakin, 2002). Motivation is related to expectancies, as well as to competence and anxiety (Lecavalier & Tasse, 2002; Routh & Schroeder, 2002). A person who expects to fail and who does not feel competent generally has little motivation to engage in new or different tasks. Low motivation can influence test results by preventing the test taker from diligently trying to perform the tasks.

Social intelligence reflects a person's ability to understand and engage effectively in social situations. Adaptive behavior is a corollary of social competence. Professionals have recognized for some time that social behavior is one of the primary factors in determining whether a person is viewed as having intellectual disabilities or not. Virtually everyone is familiar with people who, despite a low IQ, are socially aware enough to function adequately in society. A number of attributes (subcomponents) of social intelligence have been identified and continue to be studied (e.g., Bass, 2002; Rosner et al., 2004).

MEASUREMENT OF INTELLIGENCE

Core Concept

Attempts to measure it have generated considerable controversy about definitions of intelligence.

Questions about the measurement of intelligence elicit controversy over definition. The manner in which intelligence is defined influences the methods used to determine relative degrees of intelligence for prediction purposes (Fish, 2002; Gruenewald, 2004; van-Geert, 2003). Basically, there are two extremes in how people think about intelligence. Some people take a factorial approach, attempting to isolate and identify the component parts of the intelligence concept. Others conceptualize intelligence as a holistic construct that is either hypothetical or so intermingled with total personality that it cannot be conceived of as a separate and distinct entity. Most definitions fall between these two extremes.

It is one thing to theorize about the nature of intelligence and another to attempt to measure its parts. First, one must make a decision about the essential components of the phenomenon. If, for example, prospective test makers believe that intelligence cannot be understood apart from personality, then their test will likely include measures of emotions, experiences, physical condition, age, and other factors involved in personality development. The obvious difficulty with this approach is that it is difficult to construct tests to include all of the factors that might be required. Because of this, intelligence tests can measure only limited samples of behavior at a given time in a given place. As we examine the measurement of intelligence, we should also observe some aspects of the technology of assessing intelligence as seen in the Eye on Technology.

Eye on Technology

Most of the time we think of electronic devices or some type of mechanical mechanism when the term *technology* is used. This type of view has become more common as we all have become increasingly comfortable with computer applications and using electronic devices like cell phones, various and continually evolving music players, and other items that have similar uses or meaning for us as individuals.

There are some applications of electronic technology that have been involved in assessment that is related to or reflective of intelligence. For example, the Science and Technology Corporation at the University of New Mexico has been developing a specialized application of magnetic resonance spectroscopy (MRS). The MRS scans for specific chemicals and provides a quantitative assessment of their concentration in the brain. These values are then compared with normative data to estimate intelligence or IQ.

The MRS application noted above may provide a significant advance in our ability to reliably measure intelligence. This procedure, however, is not in widespread use across the country. More often than not, intelligence assessment occurs using procedures that employ an interaction between a test administrator and the person being tested. The process generally involves the interaction between these people and the person's intelligence score depends on the number of correct responses he or she gives to questions. In most people's view this involves what would be considered "low tech" approaches to assessment. The future of techniques like the MRS will depend on ease of application, cost, reliability, and most certainly the acceptability to practitioners in the field.

The best tests of intelligence presently available cannot and should not be considered the right way or the only way of measuring intellectual ability. Intelligence cannot be measured directly. As with any other concept, its primary components must be identified before any inferences can be made. The measurable attributes must be isolated, evaluated, and subjected to experimental analysis. This analysis is what early test constructors did, for example, in deciding that judgment was involved in intellectual functioning. Successful test development occurs to the degree that a test maker effectively identifies measurable attributes (often referred to as subtests), standardizes them, and provides validity and reliability data. Current intelligence tests include attributes that test makers believe are the best of the measurable aspects of intelligence now available. How well a person performs on the components of a test (e.g., vocabulary, judgment, analogies) determines how much one can infer about the individual's relative intelligence. The question of how far a test of intelligence can measure attributes of intelligence adequately is a source of continuing debate. Such matters as a child's persistence and attention definitely have an impact on test score.

As the use of intelligence tests with different groups increased over the years, it became clear that many factors argue against the indiscriminate use of tests and quick stereotyping of a person by IQ. We hope that a renewed call for consideration of the rights of others has raised a new consciousness. Many of the early psychologists and educators in the mental-testing movement in the United States warned against indiscriminate use of intelligence and IQ tests and against belief in their sanctity.

At the beginning of the 21st century, those in the field of intelligence testing find themselves in a position of having promised too much; slighted some important aspects of the intelligence puzzle, such as social and motivational aspects; and allowed practical considerations to outdistance sound theoretical development. There is a need to reconsider the development of theory and its relationship to the testing movement.

Most tests have emanated from the factorialists, rather than from those who have taken the holistic approach toward intelligence. Charles Spearman (1863–1945) initiated the factorial approach and believed that intelligence could best be expressed through two factors: (a) a general or *g* factor and (b) a specific or *s* factor. Spearman (1904) assumed that the *g* factor represented "true intelligence" in that the various tests of intelligence were consistently interrelated. He then hypothesized that a *g* factor was present in all valid tests of intelligence because it appeared to be a constantly recurring entity. But because the correlations were not perfect among tests, Spearman further hypothesized that an *s* factor was also present—though to a lesser degree than the *g* factor—and that the *s* factor resulted from those activities that could be associated with particular situations.

A contemporary of Spearman, Edward L. Thorndike (1874–1949), took a broader view in developing a multifactor theory. He believed that intellectual functioning could be divided into three overall factors: (a) abstract intelligence, in which a facility for dealing with verbal and mathematical symbols is manifested; (b) mechanical or concrete intelligence, in which the ability to use objects in a meaningful way is stressed; and (c) social intelligence, in which the capacity to deal with other persons is paramount. Thorndike took issue with Spearman's two-factor theory, maintaining that the correlations among tests, although demonstrably high, were not necessarily attributable only to a *g* factor. Further, Thorndike believed that neural interconnections in the brain influence intelligence and that whether the number of these interconnections is high or low can be inferred from a person's performance capabilities.

Core Concept

Guilford and Piaget presented two different approaches to the complex task of understanding the nature of intelligence.

A considerable amount of debate arose as a result of the apparent disagreement between Spearman and Thorndike. Research during the next 40 years suggested that much of the presumed difference between their data was due to divergent research techniques, rather than to substantive differences between their theories. But the debate remains unresolved. Proponents of the multiple-factor theory versus the single-factor theory are still at odds; the issue is still important. The work of J. P. Guilford and Jean Piaget, two theorists who have approached the problem from different theoretical frameworks, offers a perspective on the complex task of defining intelligence.

Guilford and his associates at the University of Southern California developed a program of research on the factorial approach to identifying the primary elements of intelligence. Guilford (1982) proposed a three-dimensional theoretical model that specifies parameters (content, products, and operations), incorporates previously identified primary factors, and assumes the existence of yet unidentified factors. This model (Figure 4–1) postulates the existence of 150 possible primary intellectual abilities. In Guilford's structure of intelligence (SOI), the intent is to identify discrete factors and to distinguish them from one another. Guilford indicated that the model should not be seen as a collection of independent factors but as a model to stimulate thinking about intelligence.

Guilford's model viewed human thought processes as involving five major categories in the content dimension: (a) visual (having a visual or tactile form, e.g., books, trees, houses, clouds); (b) auditory (involving the processing of sounds into meaningful symbols); (c) symbolic (possessing a summarizing quality, e.g., numbers, musical notes, codes); (d) semantic (requiring that meanings be attached to intangibles, e.g., the word *pencil* refers to object); and (e) behavioral (involving nonverbal qualities, e.g., perceptions, desires, moods).

The product aspect of Guilford's intelligence model includes six major types or categories that serve to organize figural, symbolic, and semantic content. The subdivisions are (a) units (the processing of a single item, e.g., a number, a letter, a word); (b) classes (the classification of sets of items or information by common properties, e.g., figure symbols); (c) relations (the activity of developing relationships between a product subdivision and a content subdivision or even relationships between relations); (d) systems (an aggregate of interacting parts, e.g., in sentence diagramming, numerical operations, social situations); (e) transformations (the more abstract and creative activity of transforming material into results, conclusions, or physical

Figure 4–1
The Structure-of-Intellect Model with Three Parameters

Source: Adapted from *The Nature of Human Intelligence* by J. P. Guilford, 1967. New York: McGraw-Hill. Copyright 1967 by McGraw-Hill Book Co. Adapted by permission.

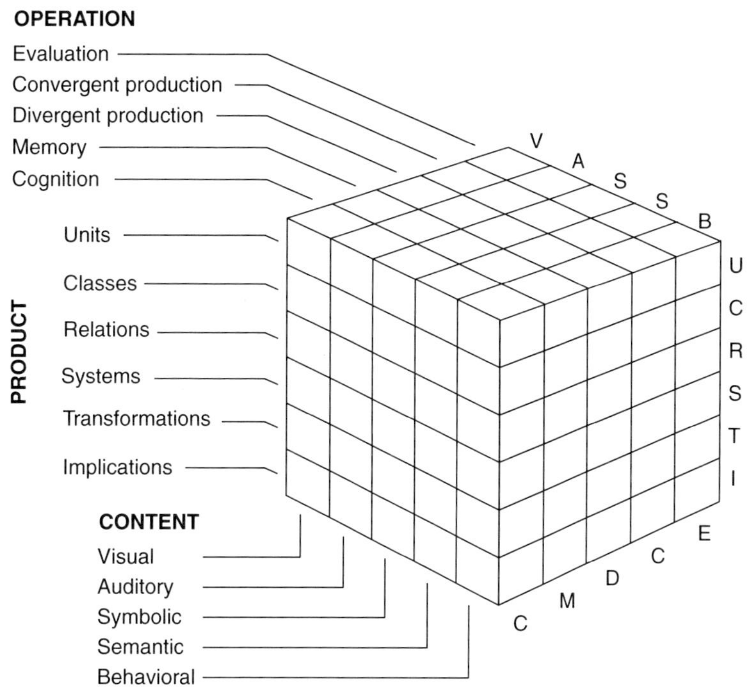

configurations different from those anticipated); and (f) implications (the most abstract of the product subdivisions, one that involves anticipation and making predictions).

The third aspect of Guilford's model—intellectual operation—includes the mental processes involved in using the information or content with which it works. Guilford defined five types of operations: (a) cognition (the process of comprehension, knowing, understanding, familiarity; the comprehension of interesting material in a nonthreatening atmosphere, e.g., games, television); (b) memory (the ability to recall specific information, e.g., arithmetical steps, telephone numbers; both short- and long-term memory are included in this subdivision); (c) divergent production or thinking (the process of being able to generalize and produce alternatives based on information possessed or provided); (d) convergent production or thinking (the process of being able to produce an acceptable response derived, it is assumed, from a large quantity of material); and (e) evaluation (mental activities, e.g., judging, comparing, contrasting, making decisions). Guilford's model continues to receive some attention in the literature (e.g., Guyette & Kock, 2002; Michael, 2003; Sternberg & Grigorenko, 2001).

Jean Piaget (1896–1980) is unique among theorists in that he approached the problem of understanding intellectual functioning from an entirely different framework. Instead of developing various tasks and then evaluating the correctness of the response, Piaget focused on the psychological process that led to the response. He was concerned primarily with interpreting the development of behavior.

Whereas Guilford was influenced by early work in factorial statistical analysis, Piaget's early preparation was in biology and zoology. His approaches have evolved over more than 50 years. During this time, his work has gone through three distinct phases. In the first phase, he investigated children's language and thought, judgment and reasoning, conception of the world, conception of physical causality, and moral judgments. During this phase, Piaget questioned the view that child development resulted completely from either environmental or genetic influences. His concepts suggested that mental growth was influenced neither entirely by nature nor solely by nurture, but rather by the continuous interaction of both aspects (Lautrey, 2003; Lickliter & Honeycutt, 2003; Tiwari & Srivastava, 2004). In the second phase, Piaget attempted to observe intelligence and development of the idea of reality in his three children by observing their behavior in situations involving objects and persons. Piaget demonstrated a genius for observation that was continually guided by his theoretical formulations, and in his observations he accumulated evidence to support his theories on the development of cognitive structures. In the third phase of Piaget's research, he and his associates investigated a number of issues that had arisen in his early theories: concrete operations, conservation, relations, preconceptual symbolization, formal operations, sensorimotor stages, probability, perceptions, illusions, and logical operations.

Piaget postulated a series of intellectual developments. The order of their appearance is important but not the age at which they appear. He believed that intelligence is an adaptive process and is only one aspect of all biological functioning. The environment places an individual simultaneously in the position of adapting to it and modifying it. The term **accommodation** was used by Piaget to describe the adaptation of an individual to the environment; he used the term **assimilation** to describe an individual's modification of the environment to fit his or her perceptions. An organism is considered to have adapted when equilibrium (balance) is reached between accommodation and assimilation. Piaget used this biological concept of equilibrium in describing learning activities. A child at play uses assimilation: The stick becomes a fishing pole, a rifle, or a baton; the shoe becomes a car or a boat. When the child is playacting, however, accommodation becomes predominant: The youngster becomes an astronaut, a rock star, a movie star, or a champion tennis player in an attempt to imitate the desired model through accommodating ephemeral perceptions. Assimilation and accommodation are complementary and antagonistic functions. Each creates alternate states of disequilibrium until the two are gradually resolved into a state of equilibrium.

Piaget postulated a sequence of developmental periods and substages that he believed to be generally the same for everyone. According to Piaget (1960), maturation and experience influence a child's rate of progress through the following sequences. The four main periods and their substages are as follows:

1. *Sensorimotor period.* This period is from birth to about 1½ to 2 years of age. In this period, the child is involved in a number of behavioral activities leading to a stable imagery.
2. *Preoperational period.* This period is divided into two substages: preconceptual and intuitive.
   a. *Preconceptual substage.* This substage occurs from about 1½ to about 4 years of age. Symbolic thought and language manifest themselves, indicating the child's awareness of objects and realization of his or her relation to and interrelation with them. The child is now able to initiate actions.
   b. *Intuitive substage.* From about 3 to 7 years of age, the child's thought is restricted to what is directly perceived. The child enters this stage unable to understand constancy, believing that, for example, the amount of liquid is less and not the same in a bowl than in a narrow cylinder. By the end of this stage, the child is able to recognize other points of view but is not able to transfer generalizations to other situations.
3. *Concrete operations period.* This period falls roughly between 7 and 11 years of age. During this stage, the child moves toward the ability to understand the conservation of quantity, length, and number. The youngster now understands, for example, the constancy of the amount of liquid regardless of the size or shape of the container and is able to generalize about other situations.
4. *Formal operations period.* From approximately 11 years of age onward, the child is involved in a continuous refinement of approaches to complex problems. The child engages in reasoning activities that are beyond a concrete operational approach. Children are now hypothesizing and making correct deductions. Words, which provide the developing human being with increasingly abstract concepts to manipulate, are now a primary tool used to solve problems.

Piaget advanced a developmental theory of intelligence. He envisioned both qualitative and quantitative differences as the person develops. His orientation differed from that of other theorists engaged in studying intelligence and represented a different way of looking at children's intellectual growth. Piaget's concepts still prompt attention in cognitive development although advances in many areas of science have altered the view of intelligence and cognitive functions (Andreucci, 2003; Lautrey, 2003; Myers, Shaffner, & Briggs, 2002).

Mental Age and Intelligence

Core Concept

Mental age and IQ historically have been central in assessment of intellectual disabilities, although many other factors are emerging as important for full evaluation.

Two additional concepts require brief attention. Neither is new to the field of psychological assessment or intellectual disabilities. In fact, both have great historical significance and have been particularly prominent in the assessment of intelligence. These are the ideas of mental age (MA) and intelligence quotient (IQ). They serve as convenient summaries of an individual's performance on tasks that presumably tap behavior representing intelligence. Both have caused difficulties, however, primarily from the ways people have used them.

Mental Age. The concept of **mental age (MA)** was developed by Binet and Simon (1908) as a means of expressing a child's intellectual development. An MA score represents the average performance of children with chronological age (CA) equal to that score. For example, a child who obtains an MA of 5 years 6 months has performed in a manner similar to the average performances of children whose CA is 5 years 6 months. MA has been a useful concept, especially in intellectual disabilities, because it is norm referenced to average intellectual development at various CA levels. The general idea of mental development expressed by MA is easy to grasp. MA provides a convenient means of communication with parents and others about children with intellectual disabilities. Most parents and other laypeople have had opportunities to observe children at various ages, so they have behavioral reference points that help them generally understand the abilities of individuals with intellectual disabilities.

The MA concept has been less useful in other contexts. Because it is a summary score derived from performance on various types of test items, it is a composite measure. The single score provides little information about specific skill levels. Two children may obtain the same MA and have very different patterns of skill strengths and deficits. For example, an MA of 7 years might be attained by a child who is chronologically 5 years old and by another who is chronologically 9 years old. These children might be labeled as being "bright," having "intellectual disabilities," or a number of other terms. The same MA may have been obtained from very different specific performances. The developmentally advanced child (CA 5) more frequently succeeds in verbal reasoning and abstract items. The slower child (CA 9) more frequently responds correctly on performance items or those for which previous learning was highly repetitive. Equivalent MAs do not indicate similar skill capabilities; the usefulness of the concept is limited in terms of teaching, particularly when instruction is pinpointed to skill deficits. Analysis of mental age remains of interest to researchers despite limitations in the way it may have been used or misused in the past (Lichten, 2004; Peled, Larocci, & Connolly, 2004).

Intelligence Quotient. The **intelligence quotient (IQ)** came into use somewhat later than MA. Originally, IQ was derived by dividing an individual's MA by his or her CA and multiplying the result by 100. Thus, a child 6 years old who obtained an MA of 6 would have an IQ of 100 ($6/6 = 1 \times 100 = 100$). This approach to IQ calculation was known as ratio IQ. Certain difficulties developed in the use of the ratio IQ, prompting its decline beginning about the mid-1940s. Since that time, the deviation IQ has been used as an alternative to the ratio calculation. This approach uses a statistical computation known as the standard deviation to derive the IQ. The deviation approach to determining IQ offered several advantages. The ratio calculation was quite unstable from age level to age level, making IQ comparison between ages difficult. The deviation approach for deriving IQ is a standard score with much more stability along the age continuum. The ratio calculation also became problematic as the individual approached adulthood. As CA increased, an apparent leveling or even a decline occurred in measured intelligence, even when more items were answered correctly. The ratio IQ thus was less viable for assessing individuals other than developing children. Because deviation IQ is referenced to a standard score, it circumvents these difficulties and is more consistent at all ages. The Bell Curve feature summarizes how standard deviation is used, particularly in psychoeducational assessment in the context of measured intelligence. It illustrates how different levels of performance result in varying individual perspectives.

Like MA, IQ is a composite measure derived by performance in several skill areas. The problems noted for MA and IQ are similar in this regard. The global score, though providing an overall assessment of performance, does not indicate specific skill strengths and deficits, a problem that may have been more acute with IQ than with MA (Reiss & Reiss, 2004). Because of its single score and apparent simplicity, users of IQ have tended to forget the component performance of the score and have treated it instead as a unitary concept. Also, people began to look on the score as sacred and permanent, rather than as a reflection of performance on a variety of tasks. This misconception led to considerable misuse and eventual disenchantment with the concept.

IQ remains in use today, and in many cases the abuses continue. We hope, however, that people using IQ now have a better perspective on what it actually assesses and less often see it as a permanent status marker resulting in labels that themselves become entities. Modification of the IQ concept, plus expansion of evaluation concepts in general, appears to have prompted movement in the direction of more realistic use of the IQ score. Research aimed at refining its assessment, analyzing its various components, and examining how the concept emerges in various disability conditions continues (Gregory, 2004; Luciano, Leisser, Wright, & Martin, 2004; Taylor, 2003).

The Bell Curve

Everything You Ever Wanted to Know About a Standard Deviation

Standard deviation is a *measure* of the amount that an individual score differs from the average. Put another way, standard deviation gives us a way to measure the difference between the average score of a group of people and how well a given individual performed in comparison to that average.

Let's take, for example, an intelligence test. Questions are put together by a group of researchers that for the sake of our discussion, measure the construct known as *intelligence*. Once the questions have been developed, this test is administered to a group of people to see how well they do on each of the questions. When all the scores are added up and divided by the number of people who have taken the exam, the average scores turn out to be 100. This certainly doesn't mean that everyone scored 100, it is merely a mathematical way of establishing what is average.

When we look at individual scores on the intelligence test, we find that some people actually do score 100, whereas others score either higher or lower. Johnny, for example, has a score of 83. So just what does the score of 83 mean in comparison to the scores of the rest of the people who have taken this test?

We can now use a mathematical procedure to determine the extent to which Johnny's score differs from the average score of 100. The measurement is called a standard deviation from the average. Again, for the sake of discussion. We find that on this intelligence test, each standard deviation is about 15 points. Now, looking at the chart for reading standard deviations, we can see that, because Johnny scored 83. he is more than one standard deviation *below* the average score on the test. Mary on the other hand, scored 50. Looking at the chart, we see that she is more than three standard deviations below the average. William scored 104 on the test, so he is less than one standard deviation above the average. Susan scored 134, so she is more than two standard deviations above the average.

We now know how many standard deviations each of these individuals is away from the average but the information is still not very meaningful. Let's convert these standard deviations into percentages. The mathematical procedure used to determine a standard deviation also reveals the *percentage* of people taking the test who score at each of the standard deviation levels. The chart reveals that Johnny's score of 83 means that he performed better than only 16 percent of all the people who took the test. In other words, 84 percent of the people taking the test had better scores than Johnny. Mary's score of 50 is better than the scores of less than 1 percent of everyone taking the test. Susan's score of 134 is better than about 98 percent of all the scores.

The standard deviation is simply a means of measuring percentages. Whether a test is a measure of intelligence, academic achievement, behavior, weight, height, age, or some other characteristic, the idea is the same.

Source: From *Human Exceptionality: Society, School, and Family* (6th ed.) by M. L. Hardman, C. J. Drew, and M. W. Egan, 1999. Needham Heights, MA: Allyn & Bacon.

One final point needs mention in this section. A very important link exists between assessment and treatment. In some situations, it has seemed that testing was being conducted with no clear notion of possibilities or plans for intervention. In others, the assessment is represented by a single snapshot of global performance rather than a dynamic evaluation that identifies specific intervention areas as targets for intervention (Neubert, 2003; Shriner & Destefano, 2003). Such assessment is lacking in functionally contributing to intervention. A second issue related to the assessment-treatment link is this: Some practitioners claim that the amount of testing required detracts significantly from instructional time. This is a serious problem, particularly when the time available is limited (the school year). A balance clearly is needed because assessment is ancillary to the primary goal of effective intervention. If assessment and intervention are not in balance, service-delivery needs are not being met.

Our discussion has explored certain issues and conceptual developments in psychological assessment. The examination was by no means exhaustive, but it does provide a backdrop for the study of assessment procedures.

NEW ISSUES AND FUTURE DIRECTIONS

All of the early work of the theorists discussed here represents foundation material in some way for future developments in cognition and the understanding of intelligence. For example, Guilford's SOI model might serve as a guide to future thinking and development in the field. One of Piaget's primary contributions might have been the way he examined the process of developing intelligence rather than his actual theories. A variety of questions continue to explore Piaget's developmental stage concepts and other elements of his work (e.g., Holbrook, 2002; Lautrey, 2003). In some cases researchers have not found the stage notions helpful whereas others find them useful concepts (Cohn & Westenberg, 2004; Goswami, 2001).

The field of assessment appears to be moving away from test development per se and toward a reconceptualization of what we know about intelligence and testing. There are a number of promising trends that appear in the literature suggesting this. One is a recognition of the importance of various affective elements in any attempt to understand intelligence (Bass, 2002; Rosner et al., 2004). Another appears as an interest in better understanding achievement in relation to intelligence, rather than a view of them as distinct (e.g., Aronson, Fried, & Good, 2002; Supplee, Shaw, Hailstones, & Hartman, 2004). And still another is a continuing interest in the association between learning and development (e.g., Forman et al., 2004; Marazita & Merriman, 2004; Montgomery, 2002). This association represents an attempt to make a connection between a quantitative, psychometric approach and a qualitative, developmental view in understanding learning and, consequently, intelligence.

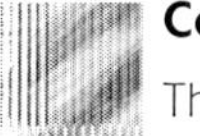

Core Concept

The trend toward a reconceptualization of intelligence includes a renewed interest in affect, achievement, and qualitative factors.

Two theorists who have received considerable recognition in recent years are Robert J. Sternberg and Howard Gardner. Sternberg has developed what he terms a "triarchic" theory of human intelligence which has been applied in a number of different contexts (Sternberg, 2002, 2003; Sternberg, Castejon, Prieto, Hautamaeki, & Grigorenko, 2001). His theory has three elements: contextual, experiential, and componential. The contextual element addresses the importance of culture and the behaviors that the culture considers intelligent. Sternberg maintains that intelligent behavior in contextual situations involves being able to adapt to the environment, selecting another environment, or shaping the present environment to meet better

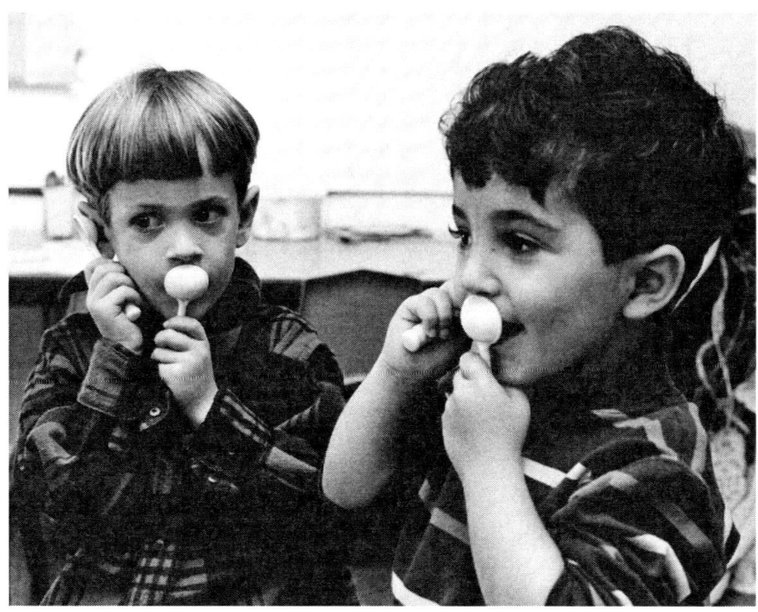

Experience with imaginary telephones and others helps children develop social skills.

personal attributes (skills, interests, values). The way a person goes about adapting, selecting, or shaping varies from one culture to the next. Each culture identifies what types of activities are acceptable, important, and valued. Therefore, being able to interact in a purposeful way with one's culture is an indication of contextual intelligence.

Sternberg's experiential element is related to the learning experiences a person faces. Intelligence is involved (a) when the events a person engages in are either themselves novel or present new problems or (b) when people practice responses so that they can respond quickly and easily. Intelligence may be determined by the way individuals approach new or novel tasks, as long as they have some experiential background that prepares them to undertake the task. Sternberg maintains that a person's ability to learn needed material to an automatic level facilitates intelligence. At the automatic level, the learned material becomes part of memory. Sternberg believes that this allows a person to devote more processing capabilities to learning new or novel tasks.

The componential element attempts to identify those internal cognitive factors that underlie intelligent behavior. This subtheory is related to the environments in which a person lives. Three aspects, or components, are involved. First are metacomponents, the processes people use in deciding how to solve a problem, in monitoring the process being used to solve it, and in evaluating the results. Second are performance components, which are the activities a person uses to carry out the strategy for solving the problem. Knowledge-acquisition components are the third part of the componential subtheory. These components selectively encode new information, combine this new information, and then make comparisons between the newly learned material and previously learned material.

Sternberg's triarchic theory has interesting implications for intellectual disabilities because the breadth of factors addressed helps account for the many causes and ramifications of individual performance. The theory forces a more comprehensive look at behavior, including intellectual disabilities, than many past approaches have required. Most workers in the field would agree that intellectual disabilities alone may not seriously impair a person from adapting to the environment. If the environment is related to and supportive of a person's skills and abilities, then there is little reason to believe that a person cannot function at an acceptable level.

The triarchic theory is a much broader theory of intelligence than many previously proposed. The theory goes beyond intelligence—as exemplified by the ability to perform scholarly work—to extend the horizons of the concept of intelligence. It runs counter to the *g* conception of intelligence and has been examined in a number of contexts and a practical attainment of goals within a person's environment. Although Sternberg discussed a number of measurement and prediction effectiveness issues, a great deal of work remains before his theories are given the acid test of application (Sternberg, 2002, 2003).

Howard Gardner's multiple intelligence theory is another broad-based concept that focuses on varying areas of competence, rather than on a general factor approach. Gardner became dissatisfied with both Piagetian intelligence theory and the orientation of schools toward linguistic and logicomathematical symbolization (Gardner, 2002, 2003). His research convinced him that the mind is modular and capable of working with many symbolic systems (numerical, linguistic, spatial) independently. A person may be particularly adept at one symbolic system (say, music) without having concomitant skills in other systems. By measuring only one or two aspects of intelligence (linguistic and logical), existing tests define intelligent behavior very narrowly. Gardner defined intelligence very broadly to include solving problems and creating products that have value in at least one cultural setting. As a result of extensive research and analysis of the work of others, Gardner developed a list of seven types of intelligence. He believes that everyone possesses all seven cognitive elements but does not display them uniformly because of both hereditary and environmental influences. The types of skills that people possess direct their future endeavors as long as the culture accepts and is responsive to the importance of that skill. For example, a person with excellent linguistic aptitude may flourish in a society that values such abilities but be frustrated in developing these skills in a culture that is more logicomathematically oriented.

Gardner and his colleagues have proposed seven intelligences. Each is distinct from the others, although they are related and complementary.

1. *Logicomathematical* intelligence relates to the ability to carry out numerical and reasoning tasks and is a critical skill for mathematicians and scientists.
2. *Linguistic* intelligence focuses on language and its uses. Writers and poets have high skill levels in this domain.
3. *Musical* intelligence is associated with the composition and performance of music. Composers and performers exhibit a high degree of ability in this area.
4. *Spatial* intelligence relates to the ability to see objects clearly in a visual-spatial sense and to manipulate them on the basis of dimensional perceptions.

Artists (particularly sculptors), astronauts, pilots, and others demonstrate a high degree of this type of intelligence.

5. *Bodily-kinesthetic* intelligence is translated into bodily movement, both fine- and gross-motor ability. Examples of individuals with high levels of this skill are dancers, athletes, and surgeons.
6. *Interpersonal* intelligence includes the ability to perceive the feelings and attitudes of others. Individuals who successfully interact with others are skilled in this area—for example, politicians, therapists, salespeople.
7. *Intrapersonal* intelligence can be summarized as the ability to know oneself. Persons in touch with their feelings, strengths, and weaknesses demonstrate a high capacity in this area. Psychiatrists and clinical psychologists are expected to possess this skill to a high degree.

Gardner's work has been examined in a number of contexts, including religion, cultural differences, and scientific theory construction (e.g., Bates, 2004; Chen, 2004; Edwards, 2003). Some attention also has been given to Gardner's theory with respect to assessment, although additional effort is clearly needed in order to move toward an application level (Garcia, Sanchez, Martinez, & Garcia, 2004).

Considerable movement is occurring in the areas of theory and testing at the present time. The recognition that affect is important and that different intelligences are possible is producing a renewed vigor in the area of cognition and learning (Aiken, 2003; Gregory, 2004). The next decade should see advances in the field of theory and testing. Some believe that by the early part of the 21st century, the field of psychometrics (psychoeducational assessment) will address the measurement of intelligence in vastly different ways than has been the case in past history (e.g., Cohen, 2002; Kaufmann, 2004; Mayer, Salovey, & Caruso, 2004). Professionals must proceed with caution, however, in order not to embrace every new theory or test without thoughtful analysis. We should learn at least that much from past errors. The broadening of intelligence theory to include such things as culture and experience follows closely on calls for reconceptualizing intellectual disabilities, perhaps as what we have seen in the AAMR definition (2002). Rethinking the concepts of intellectual disabilities has been encountered in nearly every facet of what we have discussed thus far and is likely to emerge again as we proceed.

Core Questions

1. How have societal changes affected the concepts of intelligence?
2. What is meant by the nature-versus-nurture controversy, and why is it important?
3. Why is social intelligence an important aspect of intelligence?
4. Why can't intelligence be measured directly?
5. What is the orientation of factorialists toward understanding intelligence?
6. What approach did Piaget take in his study of intellectual development? How does it differ from the factorial approach?

7. In what ways are the theories of Sternberg and Gardner similar to and different from earlier theories of intelligence?
8. What next steps remain as acid tests for the theoretical work of both Sternberg and Gardner?

Roundtable Discussion

Humankind's search for the critical aspects of and keys to the development of intelligence has been carried out rigorously by many scientists. Scientists have moved from simplistic views of what intelligence is to complex theories about its characteristics. In doing so, we have identified both quantitative and qualitative aspects of intelligence. For those interested in the study of intellectual disabilities, an understanding of past history, present formulations, and future considerations about intelligence is both important and necessary.

In a study group, discuss the development of knowledge about intelligence to the present day. As a part of the discussion, members should relate what they believe were important developments and what they were surprised to learn. Further discussion should focus on what individuals believe about the different approaches and how their perception of persons with intellectual disabilities has been influenced by using one or another approach.

Parent and Professional Organization Positions on Key Issues in the Lives of People with Intellectual Disabilities

The inside front cover of this text presents a matrix that includes several key issues in the lives of people with disabilities, the positions of various parent and professional organizations on each issue, and the chapter and page number where the information is addressed. Table 4–1 is a summary of the organizations and key issues addressed in this chapter.

Table 4–1
Key Issues and Organizations Discussed in This Chapter

Organization/Website	Key Issues Addressed	Chapter Heading
American Association on Mental Retardation (http://www.aamr.org)	Definition and assessment	Introduction
	Definition, assessment, and adaptive behavior	Development of Intelligence
	Reconceptualizing intelligence and related assessment	New Issues and Future Directions
International Association for the Scientific Study of Intellectual Disabilities (http://www.iassid.org)	Parents and health promotion	Introduction

References

Aiken, L. R. (2003). *Psychological testing and assessment* (11th ed.). Boston: Allyn & Bacon.

American Association on Mental Retardation (AAMR). (2002). *Mental retardation: Definition, classification, and systems of supports* (10th ed.). Washington, DC: Author.

Andreucci, C. (2003). How children get the notion that volume varies. *Enfance, 55,* 139–158.

Ardelt, M. (2004). Wisdom as expert knowledge system: A critical review of a contemporary operationalization of an ancient concept. *Human Development, 47,* 257–285.

Aronson, J., Fried, C. B., & Good, C. (2002). Reducing the effects of stereotype threat on African American college students by shaping theories of intelligence. *Journal of Experimental Social Psychology, 38,* 113–125.

Baron-Cohen, S., & Wheelwright, S. (2004). The empathy quotient: An investigation of adults with Asperger syndrome or high functioning autism, and normal sex differences. *Journal of Autism and Developmental Disorders, 34,* 163–175.

Bass, B. M. (2002). Cognitive, social, and emotional intelligence of transformational leaders. In R. E. Riggio, S. E. Murphy, & F. J. Pirozzolo (Eds.), *Multiple intelligences and leadership* (pp. 105–118). Mahwah, NJ: Erlbaum.

Bates, T. (2004). Models of intelligence: International perspectives. *Applied Cognitive Psychology, 18,* 481–482.

Binet, A., & Simon, T. (1908). Le développement de l'intelligence chez les enfants. [The development of intelligence in children]. *L'Année Psychologique, 14,* 1–94.

Chen, J. Q. (2004). Theory of multiple intelligences: Is it a scientific theory? *Teachers College Record, 106,* 17–23.

Cohen, M. N. (2002). An anthropologist looks at "race" and IQ testing. In J. M. Fish (Ed.), *Race and intelligence: Separating science from myth* (pp. 201–223). Mahwah, NJ: Erlbaum.

Cohn, L. D., & Westenberg, P. M. (2004). Intelligence and maturity: Meta-analytic evidence for the incremental and discriminant validity of Loevinger's measure of ego development. *Journal of Personality and Social Psychology, 86,* 760–722.

Cook, J. L., & Cook, G. (2005). *Child development: Principles and perspectives.* Boston: Allyn & Bacon.

deCastro, J. M. (2004). When identical twins differ: An analysis of intrapair differences in the spontaneous eating behavior and attitudes of free-living monozygotic twins. *Physiology and Behavior, 82,* 733–739.

Edeh, O. M., & Hickson, L. (2002). Cross-cultural comparison of interpersonal problem-solving in students with intellectual disabilities. *American Journal on Mental Retardation, 107,* 6–15.

Edwards, A. C. (2003). Response to the spiritual intelligence debate: Are some conceptual distinctions needed here? *International Journal for the Psychology of Religion, 13,* 49–52.

Fish, J. M. (2002). *Race and intelligence: Separating science from myth.* Mahwah, NJ: Erlbaum.

Forman, D. R., Aksan, N., & Kochanska, G. (2004). Toddlers' responsive imitation predicts preschool-age conscience. *Psychological Science, 15,* 699–704.

Garcia, C. F., Sanchez, M. D. P., Martinez, P. B., & Garcia, M. R. B. (2004). Validity and reliability of the multiple intelligences assessment instruments in the preschool and primary school. *Psicothema, 16,* 7–13.

Gardner, H. (2002). Learning from extraordinary minds. In M. Ferrari (Ed.), *The pursuit of excellence through education* (pp. 3–20). Mahwah, NJ: Erlbaum.

Gardner, H. (2003) Three distinct meanings of intelligence. In J. Lautrey & R. J. Sternberg (Eds.), *Models of intelligence: International perspectives* (pp.43–54). Washington, DC: American Psychological Association.

Gelfand, D. M., & Drew, C. J. (2003). *Understanding child behavior disorders* (4th ed.). Belmont, CA: Wadsworth.

Godfrey-Smith, P. (2002). Environmental complexity and the evolution of cognition. In R. J. Sternberg & J. C. Kaufman (Eds.), *The evolution of intelligence* (pp. 223–249). Mahwah, NJ: Erlbaum.

Goswami, U. (2001). Cognitive development: No stages please—we're British. *British Journal of Psychology, 92,* 257–277.

Gregory, R. J. (2004). *Psychological testing: History, principles, and applications* (4th ed.). Boston: Allyn & Bacon.

Griffin, K. W., Scheier, L. M., Botvin, G. J., & Diaz, T. (2001). Protective role of personal competence skills in adolescent substance use: Psychological well-being as a mediating factor. *Psychology of Addictive Behaviors, 15*(3), 194–203.

Gronlund, N. E. (2004). *How to write and use instructional objectives* (7th ed.). Columbus, OH: Merrill/Prentice Hall.

Gruenewald, D. A. (2004). At home with the other: Reclaiming the ecological roots of development and literacy. *Journal of Environmental Education, 35,* 33–43.

Guilford, J. P. (1967). *The nature of human intelligence.* New York: McGraw-Hill.

Guilford, J. P. (1982). Cognitive psychology's ambiguities: Some suggested remedies. *Psychological Review, 89,* 48–59.

Guyette, J., & Kock, C. (2002). Object-recognition tasks: Comparing paper versions to computerized laboratory methods. *Perceptual and Motor Skills, 94,* 333–337.

Hardman, M. L., Drew, C. J., & Egan, M. W. (2006). *Human exceptionality: School, community, and family* (8th ed.). Needham Heights, MA: Allyn & Bacon.

Heffelfinger, A. K. (2002). The development of psychopathology: Nature and nurture. *Child Neuropsychology, 8,* 144–145.

Hodapp, R. M. (2003). A reemergence of the field of mental retardation. *Contemporary Psychology, 48,* 722–724.

Holbrook, J. E. (2002). Bringing Piaget's preoperational thought to the minds of adults: A classroom demonstration. In R. A. Griggs (Ed.), *Handbook for teaching introductory psychology: Vol. 3. With an emphasis on assessment* (pp. 231–233). Mahwah, NJ: Erlbaum.

International Association for the Scientific Study of Intellectual Disabilities (IASSID). (2003). Health SIRG news. *Newsletter, 20,* 13.

Kaufmann, G. (2003). What to measure? A new look at the concept of creativity. *Scandinavian Journal of Educational Research, 47,* 235–251.

Kaufmann, G. (2004). Two kinds of creativity: But which ones? *Creativity and Innovation Management, 13,* 154–165.

Kyratzis, A. (2004). Talk and interaction among children and the co-construction of peer groups and peer culture. *Annual Review of Anthropology, 33,* 625–649.

Lautrey, J. (2003). A pluralistic approach to cognitive differentiation and development. In J. Lautrey & R. J. Sternberg (Eds.), *Models of intelligence: International perspectives* (pp. 117–131). Washington, DC: American Psychological Association.

Lecavalier, L., & Tasse, M. J. (2002). Sensitivity theory of motivation and psychopathology: An exploratory study. *American Journal on Mental Retardation, 107,* 105–115.

Lichten, W. (2004). On the law of intelligence. *Developmental Review, 24,* 252–288.

Lickliter, R., & Honeycutt, H. (2003). Evolutionary approaches to cognitive development: Status and strategy. *Journal of Cognition and Development, 4,* 459–473.

Luciano, M., Leisser, R., Wright, M. J., & Martin, N. G. (2004). Personality, arousal theory and the relationship to cognitive ability as measured by inspection time and IQ. *Personality and Individual Differences, 37,* 1081–1089.

Marazita, J. M., & Merriman, W. E. (2004). Young children's judgment of whether they know names for objects: The metalinguistic ability it reflects and the processes it involves. *Journal of Memory and Language, 51,* 458–472.

Mayer, J. D., Salovey, P., & Caruso, D. R. (2004). Emotional intelligence: Theory, findings, and implications. *Psychological Inquiry, 15,* 197–215.

Michael, W. B. (2003). Guilford's structure of intellect and structure-of-intellect problem-solving models. In J. Houtz (Ed.), *The educational psychology of creativity* (pp. 167–198). Cresskill, NJ: Hampton Press.

Montgomery, J. W. (2002). Understanding the language difficulties of children with specific language impairments: Does verbal working memory matter? *American Journal of Speech Language Pathology, 11,* 77–91.

Myers, J. E., Shaffner, M. F., & Briggs, M. K. (2002). Developmental counseling and therapy: An effective approach to understanding and counseling children. *Professional School Counseling, 5*(3), 194–202.

Neubert, D.A. (2003). The role of assessment in the transition to adult life process for students with disabilities. *Exceptionality, 11*(2), 63–75.

Peled, M., Larocci, G., & Connolly, D. A. (2004). Eyewitness testimony and perceived credibility of youth with mild intellectual disability. *Journal of Intellectual Disability Research, 48,* 699–703.

Piaget, J. (1960). The general problems of the psychobiological development of the child. In J. M. Tanner & B. Inhelder (Eds.), *Discussions on child development* (pp. 3–27). London: Tavistock.

Radvanyi, K. (2003). Relations between intelligence, social competence (adaptive behaviour), and home environment in Down's syndrome children. *Pszichologia: Az MTA Pszichologiai Intezetenek folyoirata, 23,* 393–408.

Reis, S. M., & Moon, S. M. (2002). Models and strategies for counseling, guidance, and social and emotional support of gifted and talented students. In M. Neihart & S. M. Reis (Eds.), *The social and emotional development of gifted children: What do we know?* (pp. 251–265). Waco, TX: Prufrock Press.

Reiss, S., & Reiss, M. M. (2004). Curiosity and mental retardation: Beyond IQ. *Mental Retardation, 42,* 77–81.

Rhule, D. M., McMahon, R. J., & Spieker, S. J. (2004). Relation of adolescent mothers' history of antisocial behavior to child conduct problems and social competence. *Journal of Clinical Child and Adolescent Psychology, 33,* 524–535.

Rosner, B. A., Hodapp, R. M., Fidler, D. J., Sagun, J. N., & Dykens, E. M. (2004). Social competence in persons with Prader-Willi, Williams and Down's syndromes. *Journal of Applied Research in Intellectual Disabilities, 17,* 209–217.

Routh, D. K., & Schroeder, S. R. (2002). A history of psychological theory and research in mental retardation since World War II. In L. M. Glidden (Ed.), *International review of research in mental retardation* (Vol. 26, pp.1–59). San Diego: Academic Press.

Sarouphim, K. M. (2004). Discover in middle school: Identifying gifted minority students. *Journal of Secondary Gifted Education, 15,* 61–69.

Shriner, J. G., & Destefano, L. (2003). Participation and accommodation in state assessment: The role of individualized education programs. *Exceptional Children, 69,* 147–161.

Spearman, C. E. (1904). General intelligence: Objectivity determined and measured. *American Journal of Psychology, 15,* 201–293.

Stancliffe, R. J., Hayden, M. F., Larson, S. A., & Lakin, K. C. (2002). Longitudinal study on the adaptive and challenging behaviors of deinstitutionalized adults with intellectual disabilities. *American Journal on Mental Retardation, 107,* 302–320.

Stankov, L. (2003). Complexity in human intelligence. In J. Lautrey & R. J. Sternberg (Eds.), *Models of intelligence: International perspectives* (pp. 27–42). Washington, DC: American Psychological Association.

Sternberg, R. J. (2002). Successful intelligence: A new approach to leadership. In R. E. Riggio, S. E. Murphy, & F. J. Pirozzolo (Eds.), *Multiple intelligences and leadership* (pp. 9–28). Mahwah, NJ: Erlbaum.

Sternberg, R. J. (2003). Our research program validating the triarchic theory of successful intelligence: Reply to Gottfredson. *Intelligence, 31,* 399–413.

Sternberg, R. J., Castejon, J. L., Prieto, M. D., Hautamaeki, J., & Grigorenko, E. L. (2001). Confirmatory factor analysis of the Sternberg Triarchic Abilities Test in three international samples: An empirical test of the triarchic threory of intelligence. *European Journal of Psychological Assessment, 17,* 1–16.

Sternberg, R. J., & Grigorenko, E. L. (2001). Guilford's structure of intellect model and model of creativity: Contributions and limitations. *Creativity Research Journal, 13*(3–4), 309–316.

Supplee, L. H., Shaw, D. S., Hailstones, K., & Hartman, K. (2004). Family and child influences on early academic and emotion regulatory behaviors. *Journal of School Psychology, 42,* 221–242.

Taylor, R. L. (2003). *Assessment of exceptional students: Educational and psychological procedures* (6th ed.). Boston: Allyn & Bacon.

Tiwari, P. S. N., & Srivastava, N. (2004). Schooling and development of emotional intelligence. *Psychological Studies, 49,* 151–154.

van-Geert, P. (2003). Measuring intelligence in a dynamic systems and contextualist framework. In J. Lautrey & R. J. Sternberg (Eds.), *Models of intelligence: International perspectives* (pp. 195–211). Washington, DC: American Psychological Association.

Verri, A., Maraschio, P., Uggetti, C., Pucci, E., Ronchi, G., Nespoli, L., et al. (2004). Late diagnosis in severe and mild intellectual disability in adulthood. *Journal of Intellectual Disability Research, 48,* 679–686.

Development and Causation

Chapter 5

Basic Principles of Early Development

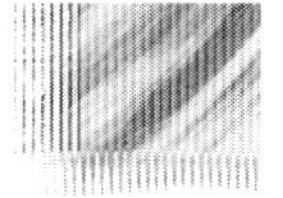

Chapter Preview

At the completion of this chapter, you will have a better understanding of the fascinating complexities involved in early development and how vital this period is for an individual's future. You will encounter how:

- The development of humans during the prenatal and newborn periods is rapid, very complex, and has direct impacts on the individual that emerges later.
- Because of the rapid growth during the earliest periods the risk of injury and other types of insults are very high.
- The progress of science on human development during the earliest periods holds great promise for diagnosis and treatment while also raising serious social questions.

The Red Flags

"I'll quit smoking and drinking when I get pregnant" Janine said as she and her roommates were discussing one of their frequent topics for weekend parties—men, why have them around, relationships, and future lifestyles. Like her friends, Janine has some pretty strong views about what she wants out of life. Right now they are talking about intimacy with their boyfriends, and are certain that they are fully aware of the world they live in. Janine has begun her psychology sequence and next week is starting the material on human development. There have already been some red flags popping up that have personal meaning and may suggest some changes in personal behavior. Janine had no idea that there were such risks to a baby during early pregnancy.

Janine left home for college and found certain parts of this new world to be rather wonderful. Her mother wasn't there every time she came home from a party and her father's stone-faced evaluation of her friends was a full 763 miles away. She could decide when to study, when to go out with her girlfriends, and when to see a movie with Bob. There were other matters too, like smoking and drinking which were very adult and physically quite pleasant. But they were also part of a long-standing taboo in her family environment. Betty and Richard would not approve (she now called her parents by their names from a distance—it seemed to put them in a different category than when they were labeled Mom and Dad). And they would have a total come-apart if they knew about the other stuff—the little pills that made the parties really fun.

The red flags from the psych class related directly to smoking and drinking, but there was nothing there about the pills. Maybe they were not harmful. When she got to the point of having a baby she would quit the cigarettes and liquor.

- *What are your thoughts about Janine's concerns regarding her parties? Certainly she is not planning a pregnancy at this point and she has committed to eliminating some risky behaviors when that type of planning becomes reality. Or are there other steps she might consider?*

- *How much information do you and your peers have about prenatal development? How can you access information that might have importance to you personally?*

Janine's psychology class is giving her some good information. It is probably a good idea to not smoke or drink alcohol while pregnant. It is certainly a laudable goal, but the timing may not be as precise and easily determined as Janine might think. A lot happens very quickly once fertilization occurs. For the most part, you can't even weigh the small mass in the first month. However, the cells are dividing rapidly and by 2 weeks after conception some changes have occurred that already begin changing parts of the tissue into selected portions of the body. While many young mothers claim to "know" when they got pregnant, some will also note that they may be 3 weeks to a month off in their calculations. By the end of this period the initial stages of the heart, the nervous system, and some sensory organs have been accomplished. If toxic agents are introduced during these developments, particularly in large or continuous amounts, there may be serious negative outcomes for the small mass of tissue that was destined to become a baby.

So, these are good thoughts Janine. But perhaps a little more preliminary planning should be given for several reasons. There may be some physical and social risks involved in Janine's pattern of partying. From a physical standpoint, an unborn fetus is most vulnerable when it is most rapidly developing, and that portion most rapidly growing is the part that is most vulnerable.

This chapter examines certain human development concepts that form the basis for the book's organization as a whole. The developmental life cycle is our fundamental perspective of intellectual disabilities. The reader already has seen that intellectual disabilities are multidimensional conditions. Myriad factors contribute to their occurrence and have been studied and treated by many disciplines, as discussed earlier in Chapter 1. In this chapter we examine the biological, psychological, and educational dimensions of intellectual disabilities from a developmental perspective and explore the complex interactions of these seemingly disparate topics from a developmental approach.

Developmental pathology is a relatively recent area of study that has evolved into the investigation of problems and detrimental events that emerge in human development. Developmental psychopathology represents the productive combination of methods and content from multiple fields, brought together to focus on a variety of human disabilities and disorders that have their roots in the errors occurring in human developmental processes (Hertzig & Farber, 2003; Phares, 2003; Pine, 2004). Although developmental psychopathology is relatively new, child development traditionally has held a very prominent position in psychology and education and has employed the rigors of the scientific method only during the last century (Behar & Borkovec, 2003; Ehrenreich & Gross, 2003; Goodwin, 2005). Above all, studying the course of human development is a quest for understanding human behavior, a conceptual organizer through which explanations are sought to comprehend why people behave as they do. Developmental psychology is a way of looking at things and an extremely useful means of examining such abnormalities as intellectual disabilities. Developmental psychopathology—the developmental study of psychological differences—has become increasingly visible in recent years. But as a field of study, it is still maturing with respect both to its knowledge base and to its research methodology.

This chapter introduces principles of early development that have particular relevance to intellectual disabilities. Applying the basic concepts of child development to the study of intellectual disabilities is important for a number of reasons. For many subgroups of the population with intellectual disabilities, developmental factors are central to intellectual, physical, and psychological status. From a basic biological standpoint, many of the clinical syndromes are integrally related to human development. Beyond biology, the broad psychological view of the population having the mildest form of intellectual disabilities has long spotlighted child development within the nature-versus-nurture controversy (Berkson, 2004; Garlick, 2003; Keogh, Bernheimer, & Guthrie, 2004), and this group represents the largest proportion of people with intellectual disabilities. Acquaintance with the concepts of child development is essential for the student of intellectual disabilities.

HUMAN DEVELOPMENT: TERMINOLOGY, CONCEPTS, AND THEORY

Human growth and development has become a more complex field as research and technology in all of its contributing sciences have advanced. The information base has expanded dramatically because of rapidly emerging research from biology, embryology, genetics, psychology, and many other areas. Evidence from all of these fields of study have been molded into a body of highly technical knowledge with unique properties beyond those of the contributing areas.

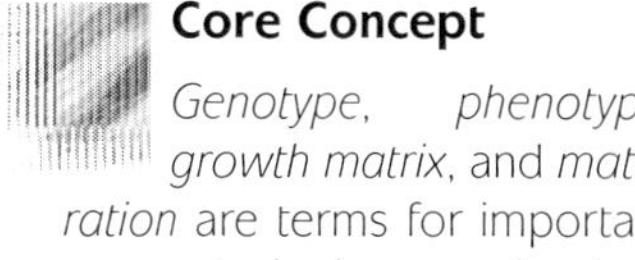

Core Concept

Genotype, *phenotype*, *growth matrix*, and *maturation* are terms for important concepts in human development.

Concepts and Terms

Many different factors influence a person's life status at any given time. As used here, life status refers broadly to one's physical, psychological, and behavioral attributes, as well as to talents and abilities. All of these personal elements are influenced by genetic material inherited from parents plus environmental circumstances that have nourished or impeded development (AAMR, 2002; IASSID, 2003). These components combine and interact in a unique fashion to produce the person one sees at a particular point. In some cases advances in genetic science have potential for enormously important interventions or treatments as suggested in the Eye on Technology.

As we begin this discussion of early development it is important to become acquainted with certain terms and concepts pertaining to the elements in this complex human equation. Parents transmit genetic material to their offspring that strongly influences what the offspring become. This genetic material can be likened to a computer chip that encodes a number of messages. These messages are activated to influence many aspects of physical and psychological growth. Geneticists use the term **genotype** to refer to the genetic message makeup of an individual. Established at conception by the combining of sperm and ovum, the genotype is usually constant. Only rarely does this constancy fail, as when a mutation or other error in cell division alters subsequent cell divisions. The human genotype is not readily accessible for actual inspection, but the **phenotype,** a term that refers to observable

Eye on Technology

Genetic targeting was developed in the early 1980s by Mario Capecchi and allows manipulation of an individual gene (KUER, 2005). It allows removal of a specific gene which can then be replaced by another that has very specific characteristics, like the ability to "turn on" certain types of biological conditions. This approach is employed in thousands of laboratories around the world as scientists have revolutionized the study of diseases of many types.

Gene targeting has the potential for interventions in a variety of diseases that seem to be triggered by a particular gene that switches on a particular growth process. Some examples are more well known because they receive attention in the popular press, such as various forms of cancer. Others, however, have not surfaced to the lay public to the same degree, but may begin development because of a particular genetic configuration. Examples of conditions relating to intellectual disabilities include some types of Down syndrome, phenylketonuria or PKU, and others. While gene targeting represents a very exciting line of research, it also generates potential controversy and ethical questions as the knowledge is translated to intervention or treatment. Some are most uncomfortable with knowledge about and manipulation of the basic building blocks of human development. For scientists like Capecchi however, knowledge itself is not a bad thing (KUER, 2005).

physical traits, may be used to draw inferences about the genotype. The phenotype is the observable result of interaction between the genotype and the environment.

Another related term in child development is **growth matrix.** The growth matrix is also the result of interactions between heredity and environment. Although partially observable (because it includes the phenotype), the growth matrix also includes all of the internal aspects of a child that generate a given response in a particular situation. The growth matrix is more than a simple combination of phenotype and genotype, however. One distinction is that whereas genetic concepts are relatively constant, the growth matrix changes as interactions occur between the organism and its environment. The growth matrix is a product of that interaction and at the same time determines or regulates individual response patterns.

Maturation is a term also used in child development in a way that requires definition. Although some difference in usage exists, maturation generally signifies any development or change in the status or underlying process of a behavioral trait that takes place in the demonstrable absence of specific practical experience. In the present context, one additional restriction is added: the absence of specific instruction. Thus, in this context, maturation is distinguishable from **learning,** which refers to changes associated with specific practice or instruction. In many situations, it is difficult to discriminate between changes resulting from maturation and changes resulting from learning. A history of maturation and of learning and a combination of the two are involved in any child's current developmental status. This developmental status and its components are related to the notion of readiness.

Readiness exists when the child is at a point in development (including previous maturation and learning) where he or she might be expected to profit from a particular situation. A familiar example is "reading readiness." From the present standpoint, reading readiness refers to the point in a child's development at which one could expect progress as a result of exposure to reading experience or instruction. Of course, if the status from either a maturational or previous learning standpoint were deficient (inadequate to establish readiness), the child is not expected to progress as a result of a given stimulation. There is no magic formula "X amount of maturation plus Y amount of previous learning equals readiness." Although developmental readiness includes both, widely varying amounts and types of each may exist in different children who have reached readiness for an experience.

Developmental Theories

The complexities of human development have been of interest since the beginning of recorded history. Some of the most common theoretical positions have an extremely long history. Certain prescientific explanations of human growth and development, although amusing in retrospect, were quite popular in the past.

Core Concept

Theories of human development have differed dramatically about the importance of influences, ranging from prepotency of genetic material to total environmental shaping.

Preformationist Perspective. The preformationist theory of human growth and development had a substantial early following. According to preformationism, the human organism is preformed before birth; this theory proposed that the foundation elements of human behavior are intact from the beginning and do not qualitatively develop or change during life. The preformationists thus denied the importance of growth and development except in the sense of quantity, or growing larger. The early homuncular theory of human reproduction exemplified the preformationist position. This theory held that a completely formed, tiny person existed in the sperm. This tiny person, called a homunculus, began to grow in size at conception but did not change in the sense that tissue changes occurred qualitatively, such as in the formation of various organs.

Environmental effects on human development were largely discounted by the preformationist position. Prenatal as well as postnatal environment was of little consequence as far as development went from this viewpoint. The concessions usually made to environmental effects involved only expansion of existing abilities, drives, and behaviors. Preformationists thought that neither new growth nor directional influence of development did much to change the preformed organism.

Predeterministic Perspective. Predeterministic theorists' assumptions appear similar to that of the preformationists, at first glance. Although their outcome is much the same, some significant differences are discernible between the two theoretical positions. Predeterministic positions did not view human development as a simple accentuation of a preformed organism. Qualitative growth and tissue differentiation played a substantial role in most theories of predeterminism. An example of this is found in the doctrine of recapitulation, which was described in great detail by G. Stanley Hall (1904). Recapitulation hypothesized that the development of the child from conception to maturity progressed through all of the evolutionary phases of the human race. Although quite popular for a period around the turn of the century, this theory fell into disfavor primarily because of the absence of objective or observable data to support its sweeping hypotheses.

The outcome of predeterministic theories was essentially the same as preformationism in that environmental influence was thought to be minimal, perhaps limited to restricting development. Growth patterns were viewed as innate or internally regulated. More recently, the disciplines of biology, genetics, and embryology have provided factual knowledge supporting the notion that certain development is regulated primarily internally (e.g., prenatal growth and certain infantile behavioral development). Former predeterministic contentions of innate control, however, involved broad applications that have received no scientific support.

Tabula Rasa Perspective. In the context of human development, **tabula rasa** refers to approaches that emphasize the prepotency of environmental influences. The term means "blank slate" and was popularized by John Locke in the 17th century. For purposes of this discussion, *tabula rasa* is used generically to represent positions emphasizing extreme environmental impact.

Tabula rasa theories differed substantially from the approaches of preformationism and predeterminism. Tabula rasa positions minimized the influence of internal factors (e.g., heredity) on human development. Environment was seen as playing a predominant role in nearly all aspects of development. Tabula rasa theorists considered the human organism plastic and infinitely amenable to molding by external influences. Thus, an individual's ability was dependent on what was "written" on the blank slate through experience. The weakness of this framework, like that of preformationism and predeterminism, was the extreme to which proponents of the position went.

Neither tabula rasa nor predeterministic approaches to child development were satisfactory. Belief in preformed human functioning at birth has little logical or empirical support. With the exception of very simple reflex responses, few human behavioral dimensions are not influenced by environment. The fundamental error of predeterministic proponents was their disregard for the impact of experience. Tabula rasa theorists caught the pendulum at the opposite end of its swing. The assumption that environmental impact is a significant contributor to human growth and development does represent reality, but tabula rasa theorists emphasized the impact of this factor far too strongly.

Interactional Perspectives. Human development specialists now generally subscribe to the notion of an interaction between heredity and environment (Berk, 2005; Cook & Cook, 2005). Both genetic and environmental factors set limits for growth, as well as selectively influence each other. Genetic material determines limits even under the most favorable environment conceivable. Likewise, environment limits the fulfillment of genetic potential. Genetic material determines which factors in the environment are more potent by rendering the organism more sensitive to some than to others. Similarly, environmental factors such as culture and ecology operate on genetic expression by providing selective influences on ability development.

The interactional approach to human growth and development emphasizes analysis of relationships between heredity and environment (Cook & Cook, 2005; Gelfand & Drew, 2003; Lickliter & Honeycutt, 2003). This emphasis represents a substantial difference from earlier positions, which assumed the prepotence of one over the other. Although other approaches may be conceptually simpler, the interactional position seems to represent reality better.

THE DEVELOPMENTAL PROCESS

The emergence of an interactional view of human development generated a more intense focus on developmental processes. Researchers and theoreticians began to ask questions that were more amenable to study than were the philosophical positions exemplified by former views. A number of interesting questions have focused on the nature of the developmental process and have become rather controversial. This section presents an examination of some of these questions.

Continuity Versus Discontinuity of Growth

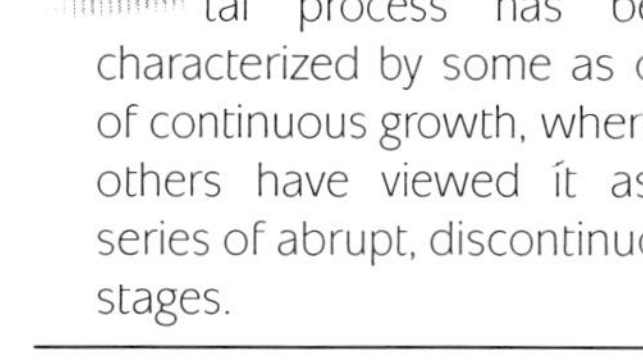

Core Concept

The human developmental process has been characterized by some as one of continuous growth, whereas others have viewed it as a series of abrupt, discontinuous stages.

One area that has generated substantial discussion involves the continuity or discontinuity of human growth. The question is, Does development proceed by gradual continuous quantitative change or in stages typified by abrupt discontinuous changes in quality?

Theories emphasizing stages encouraged the discontinuity view of human development. Early developmental stage theories implied little or no process overlap from one stage to the next. Each developmental stage was specifically and qualitatively different from the others. The first developmental theorist to dismiss the notion of discontinuity was Piaget (1926). From his background in biology and zoology, Piaget formulated a theory of stages of cognitive development that incorporated the occurrence of immature and mature responses at all developmental levels. His concept of intelligence included three global developmental periods: (a) the period of sensorimotor intelligence, (b) the period of preparation for and organization of concrete operations, and (c) the period of formal operations. Sensorimotor intelligence development, he thought, began at birth and continued for about the first 2 years of life. Piaget viewed the development of intelligence in the second period, from about 2 to 11 years of age, as involving the essential formation of a conceptual framework that the child uses in interaction with the environment. The third period, from 11 years of age on, is the time, Piaget contended, during which an individual works with abstract thought. During this period (formal operations), the person begins to think of hypothetical possibilities instead of relying exclusively on concrete operations, in which cognition depends on a concrete or real object as a basis. Piaget conceived the total developmental picture as one of a dynamic interaction, with the organism operating on the environment, as well as being molded by it. His theory has come under heavy fire, and issues involving the plasticity of human growth and critical periods continue to be debated in the literature (e.g., Berk, 2005; Berkson, 2004; Owens, 2005).

The continuity position contends that growth is a gradual process, rather than a series of abrupt changes followed by periods of less rapid change (plateaus). A variety of factors can be mentioned in support of the theory of growth continuity. First, it is well known that both mature and immature responses are made by children at all levels of development. Second, theories of continuity test hypotheses generated from general behavior theories more effectively than do discontinuous stage theories.

Both continuity and discontinuity theories of development have had strong proponents. Growth and development specialists, however, have largely progressed beyond the point where polarized thinking prevails. No one believes that theoretically formulated stages are precise definitions involving exact ages, behaviors, and response levels. They are convenient approximations based on averages and are useful in conceptualizing developmental processes and suggesting directions for research, although methodologically sound research is very difficult to conduct on critical periods in human development (Austrian, 2002).

Critical Periods and Developmental Vulnerability

Core Concept

Certain periods of development are critical both for growth and because of the organism's vulnerability to injury and developmental risk during them.

Developmental difference is a central concern in the field of intellectual disabilities, as it is in other disability areas. The concept of developmental vulnerability is related to developmental difference and is of vital importance to those studying intellectual disabilities. Here we use *vulnerability* to refer to how susceptible the organism is to being injured or altered by a traumatic incident. Traumatic incident is defined broadly to include such occurrences as exposure to toxic agents (poisons) and cell division mutations, as well as other deviations from the usual sequence of development.

Biology and embryology have provided a great deal of information about how human growth occurs (Berk, 2005). From the time of conception, a series of complex cell divisions occurs that ultimately results in the entity called a human being. During the early part of this developmental process, the original fertilized cell divides repeatedly to form a mass no larger than the point of a sharp pencil (at about 14 days) and eventually (at about 9 months) to the size of a newborn child. Obviously, this implies a very dramatic growth process. Cell division occurs extremely rapidly in the first few days after the ovum is fertilized by a sperm. The mass that is to become the fetus does not actually become implanted or attached to the mother's uterus until about 2 weeks after fertilization. In this short period, cell division has progressed with considerable speed and has begun the process of tissue differentiation. Both the speed of cell division and the process of tissue differentiation are important with regard to the vulnerability to trauma.

After cell division begins, chemical reactions occur that generate new cells of different types (tissue differentiation). These cells multiply, forming three different layers of tissue: the ectoderm, the mesoderm, and the endoderm. Figure 5–1 pictorially represents the three cell tissue layers. Although the tissue layers are named because of their early developmental position (ectoderm, outer layer; mesoderm, middle layer; endoderm, inner layer), they eventually form different parts of the organism. Parts of the ectoderm become nervous tissue, various types of muscle come from the mesoderm, and so on. During the time that a particular organ or system is being formed, the cells generating that system divide very rapidly. During specific periods, for instance, the central nervous system is the primary part of the organism that is developing. During that time, the cells that constitute the central nervous system divide more rapidly than other types of cells, and at this time the central nervous system is most vulnerable to trauma. If a toxic agent or infection occurs in the mother at this time, the developing central nervous system (or some particular part of it) probably will be the most affected.

Other critical periods occur during prenatal development. These periods are biologically important for the healthy growth of the fetus. Some professionals have long suspected that critical periods also exist after birth. Hypotheses regarding postnatal critical periods and vulnerability have varied considerably. In some cases, the "critical periods" of early childhood have been viewed as those times that are optimal for the child to learn or experience certain things. Others have conceived the

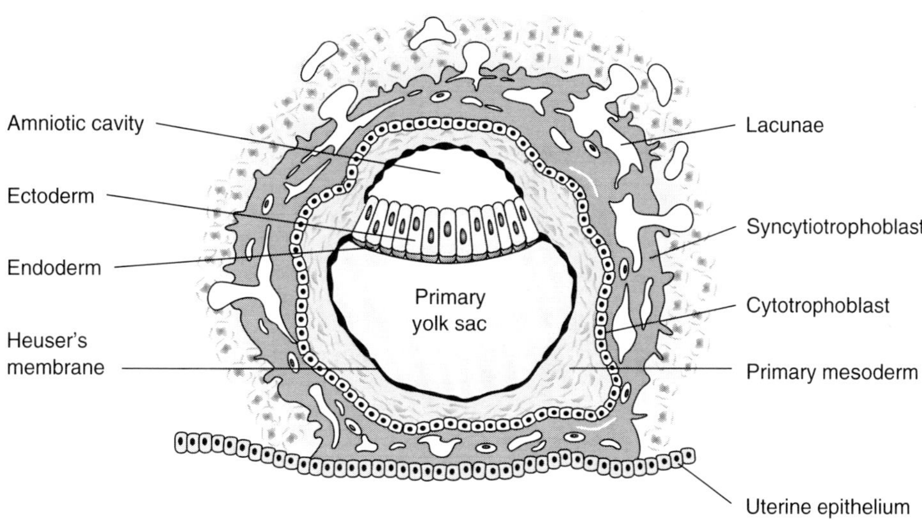

Figure 5–1
Conceptus at About 12 Days, Showing Cell Tissue Layers

critical-period idea in terms of irreversibility, holding that if a child does not acquire certain skills or fails to experience certain stimuli at the appropriate time, development will be altered in some way that is irreversible. Under some circumstances, the theoretical outcome of either viewpoint is the same. The child, if not taught at the critical time, may fail to learn given material as well as might be possible. The critical-period concept has had considerable effect in both research about and education of very young children. Educational programs like Montessori have flourished because of the intuitive appeal of the critical-period concept. Research evidence supporting the importance/irreversibility view, however, has been fragmentary and results mixed, and the topic remains difficult to investigate (Austrian, 2002).

PRENATAL DEVELOPMENT

The prenatal period of human development has long been recognized as highly important. Very early explanations of prenatal development tended to be more philosophical and metaphysical than scientific in orientation, illustrated by the prescientific homunculus notion. Contemporary advances in research methods have permitted at least limited glimpses of this previously unexplored region. Although much of our information about prenatal development has come from studies with animals, direct knowledge about the human organism is continually increasing. This section surveys the sequence of prenatal development. Information about this subject facilitates a broader understanding of developmental deviations as they relate to intellectual disabilities.

Practical information about prenatal development and health is what Janine is seeking. Seeking such information is important and the March of Dimes outlines a number of points related to prenatal health care in the Tips for Professionals.

Core Concept

Cephalocaudal and proximodistal growth trends begin very early in prenatal development and also can be observed during the first few years of life.

Early cell division occurs at different rates, depending on which portion of the organism is mainly being formed at that time. Additionally, two important general growth trends warrant mention. The first is known as the **cephalocaudal developmental trend,** or growth gradient. As the term suggests, the fetus develops more rapidly in the head area (*cephalo-*) first, with maturation in the lower extremities (*caudal*) or "tail" following. At almost all stages of a young child's development, the upper regions (and behaviors associated with these regions) are more nearly complete than the lower regions. Dramatically evident prenatally, the cephalocaudal trend also is present after birth. A young child is skilled in a behavior involving the arms before developing a similar skill in the legs. The second general developmental trend is the **proximodistal gradient.** This term refers to the fact that more rapid growth and development occur near the center of the organism (*proximo-*), with extremities (*distal*) maturing later. This trend is also present both prenatally and during the first few years of infant life.

Very soon after fertilization occurs, the cell division process commences that ultimately results in a fully formed human. As noted earlier, it takes about 2 weeks for the dividing cell mass to become attached to the uterus. Even before this

Tips for Professionals

Prenatal Health Care

The March of Dimes outlines a number of points related to prenatal health care. Some of the information relates to consultation matters and areas of question for Janine. These points become important tips for conversations between health care professionals and their clients.

Prenatal care can bring piece of mind. It's reassuring to find out that you and your baby are doing just fine.

During prenatal visits, the health care provider:

- Teaches the woman about pregnancy
- Monitors any medical conditions she may have (such as high blood pressure)
- Tests for problems with the baby
- Tests for health problems in the woman (such as gestational diabetes)
- Refers the woman to services such as support groups, the WIC program or childbirth education classes

A Typical Prenatal Care Schedule

A typical prenatal care schedule for a low-risk woman with a normally progressing pregnancy is:

- Weeks 4 to 28: 1 visit per month (every 4 weeks)
- Weeks 28 to 36: 2 visits per month (every 2 to 3 weeks)
- Weeks 36 to birth: 1 visit per week

A woman with a chronic medical condition or a "high-risk" pregnancy may have to see her health care provider more often. Make sure you go to all your prenatal care appointments, even if you're feeling fine.

What Happens at a Prenatal Care Visit?

During your first prenatal care visit, your provider will ask you a lot of questions and do some tests. Most of your other visits will be much shorter.

At the first visit your health care provider will:

- Ask you about your health, your partner's health and the health of your close family members. Don't worry if you don't know all the answers.
- Identify medical problems.
- Discuss with you any medications you are taking.
- Do a physical exam and a pelvic (internal) exam.
- Weigh you.
- Check your blood pressure.
- Check a urine sample for infection.
- Do some blood tests to check for anemia and see if you have had certain infections. You will be asked if you want a test for HIV, the virus that causes AIDS.
- Do a pap smear to check for cervical cancer and other tests for vaginal infections.
- Figure out your due date: an estimate of the day your baby will be born. Most babies are born within two weeks (before or after) their due date.
- Make sure you're taking a prenatal vitamin with folic acid.

continues on next page

continues from previous page

During later prenatal visits your provider will:

- Weigh you.
- Check your blood pressure.
- Measure your belly to see how the baby is growing (middle and late pregnancy).
- Check your hands, feet and face for swelling.
- Listen for the baby's heartbeat (after the 12th week of pregnancy).
- Feel your abdomen to assess the baby's position (later in pregnancy).
- Do any tests that are needed, such as blood tests or ultrasound.
- Ask you if you have any questions or concerns. It's a good idea to write down your questions and bring a list with you so you don't forget.

Source: Excerpted from March of Dimes (2005). *Prenatal Care.* Pregnancy & NewBorn Health Education Center. Retrieved from http://www.marchofdimes.com. Used by permission.

Table 5–1
Cell Tissue Layers of the Embryo

Endoderm	Mesoderm	Ectoderm
Epithelium of pharynx, tongue, root, auditory tube, tonsils, thyroid	Muscles (all types)	Epidermis, including cutaneous glands, hair, nails, lens
Larynx, trachea, lungs	Cartilage, bone	Epithelium of sense organs, nasal cavity, sinuses
Digestive tube	Blood, bone marrow	Mouth, including oral glands, enamel
Bladder	Lymphoid tissue	Anal canal
Vagina	Epithelium of blood vessels, body cavities	Nervous tissue
Urethra	Kidney, ureter, gonads, genital ducts	
	Suprarenal cortex	
	Joint cavities	

Source: Adapted from *Developmental Anatomy* (7th ed.) by L. B. Arey, 1974. Philadelphia: W. B. Saunders Co. Copyright 1974 by W. B. Saunders Co. Reprinted by permission.

implantation occurs, the cells begin to differentiate. As the ectoderm, mesoderm, and endoderm are initially formed, considerable flexibility remains in what individual cells within those layers can become. Thus, at the 14-day stage, a given cell within the mesoderm still could grow into something besides the parts of the body usually formed from the mesoderm. Determination of resulting organs at this point is more a function of layer position than of the composition of the cell. Cell flexibility disappears, however, as growth proceeds. The layers themselves become increasingly differentiated; as this occurs, individual cells become more specialized (Berk, 2005). Table 5–1 is a summary of some types of structures associated with each tissue layer.

The embryo is still very small at the time of implantation. Despite all that has gone on, the mass is little larger than a dot made by a sharp pencil. The estimated size is about that of a ball 2 millimeters in diameter, and the weight cannot even be estimated. It is difficult to conceive that such a tiny piece of matter not only is living but also has already begun to differentiate in anticipation of forming such structures as eyes, a brain, and muscles. After implantation (14 days), activity continues at an extremely rapid pace. By about the 18-to-24-day point (from the time of fertilization = fertilization age), weight is still undeterminable; size is portrayed in Figure 5–2. At this point, blood cells much like those that will serve in later life have begun to form (Carrera, Chervenak, & Kurjak, 2003; Sadler, 2003).

Several developments have occurred by the time the embryo has reached the 4-week point (fertilization age). Weight is detectable, at about 0.4 gram. Figure 5–2 portrays the embryo's approximate size and shape at this point. A primitive circulatory system has developed, and the heart structure has begun pulsation (Berk, 2005; Carrera et al., 2003; Sadler, 2003). The initial formative stages of other systems, such as trunk muscles and muscles necessary for respiratory and intestinal functions, also occur in the 4th week. Limb buds appear at this time, and the nervous system reaches a point that is crucial for development of both the sense organs and the area that later will become the spinal cord. Figure 5–2 illustrates that the tiny embryo already has assumed the curved shape of the unborn human. This shape is generated primarily at the 4-week period by a very rapid lengthening of the neural tube (spinal area), which is not matched by growth on the front (ventral) side.

The embryo has grown and developed to a considerable extent at 6½ weeks fertilization age. Figure 5–2 illustrates the approximate embryonic size and shape at this time. The circulatory system and heart are now more nearly complete. You can also see the positioning of the eyes on either side of the head area. Later, these will assume the more frontal position characteristic of the human infant. Lungs and intestinal system are more complete, and for the first time a primitive form of the gonad is observable. Differentiation of this tissue has not occurred yet with respect to gender (Berk, 2005). Figure 5–2 also portrays the embryo at about 7½ weeks fertilization age. The embryo begins to develop openings for waste systems at this point (both urethral and anal). The circulatory system reaches a stage at which heart valves develop, and sensory nerve tissue in the upper region progresses.

The embryo is essentially complete as the fertilization age reaches the 8th week. Beyond this point, it commonly is referred to as a fetus. There is some difference with regard to when this term is applied. Although most use it in the 9th week, some consider the fetal period to begin earlier, and others define it somewhat later (Berk, 2005; Broderick & Blewitt, 2003). Figure 5–2 also illustrates the size and shape of a fetus at about the 9th week. The eyes have begun to assume frontal position. The fetus has noticeably changed its posture. The head region at this point constitutes nearly half the total mass, and the cerebral cortex has formed.

Core Concept

Prenatal fetal development during weeks 10 through 12 is particularly important because of the tissues being formed at that time.

Particularly crucial growth occurs in the head region during weeks 10 through 12. From about this time through the 13th week, the palate completes fusion. The forehead is

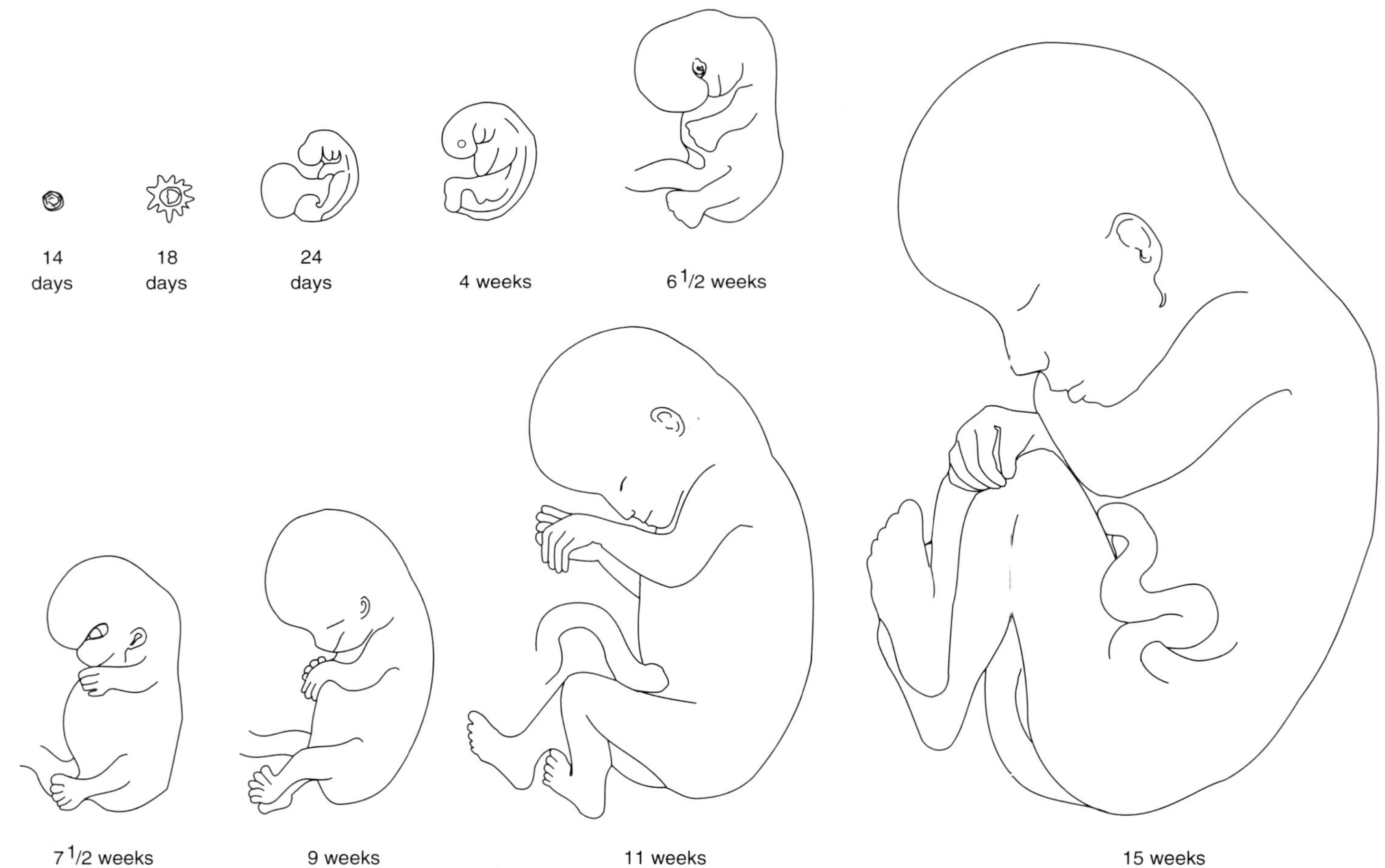

Figure 5–2
The Actual Size of Human Embryos at Early Stages of Development and a Comparison of the Relative Stages of External Development

somewhat outsized in comparison with the rest of the head (see Figure 5–2) and at this point contains a brain that is essentially complete in configuration. Inspection of the external organs permits determination of the gender of the fetus. The skeleton begins the process of becoming bone matter (ossification), and the vital structures of the eyes are nearly formed (Berk, 2005).

At 12 weeks, a fetus has completed one of the most crucial periods in its developmental lifespan. By no means is the tiny fetus ready to take on the outside world, but the primary body structures are formed. In Chapter 6, we refer repeatedly to the first trimester of prenatal life. From our discussion of vulnerability and its relationship to tissue growth, it is very easy to see why this period is so vital. Trauma occurring during these first weeks is most likely to injure the essential body structure being formed at this time. The fetus at 12 weeks has a weight of about 19 grams. It has a long way to go, but has made a lot of progress since the mass was so tiny that it could not be weighed.

The fetus reaches a weight of approximately 600 grams during the second trimester of prenatal life (weeks 12 through 24). At this point, appearance leaves no doubt that the fetus is a tiny human. The second trimester is also the time when the mother first experiences fetal movement. Fetal bodily proportions change, as illustrated in Figure 5–2 (15 weeks). Several important internal developments occur during the second trimester. Various glands mature to the point that metabolic functions can begin. The lungs become complete, although not until the third trimester are they adequate to sustain life. The extremely important function of myelinization also begins during the second trimester. **Myelinization** refers to the development of a sheathlike material that covers and protects the nervous system. During the second trimester, development of the myelin covering begins in the spinal cord area. This process continues during the third trimester, when the myelinization of higher cortical matter begins. Completion of the myelin covering of the cerebral cortex is accomplished primarily after birth (Carrera et al., 2003; Sadler, 2003). The progression of the myelin covering also relates to the child's vulnerability to trauma (see Chapter 7).

Development that occurs during the final trimester of prenatal life is essential for sustaining life outside the mother's body. One vital change involves the final development of the lung structures. Changes continue right up to the last month of gestation. The fetus is also growing larger and stronger at a rapid rate. By the time term is reached, at about 40 weeks gestational age, the average fetus weighs somewhere around 3,200 grams. Brain and sensory organs continue to develop, reaching functional stage at birth (Berk, 2005). Thus, although the basic structural components have long since been formed, the third trimester of gestation involves developments that are crucial for survival.

BIRTH

After about 280 days of gestation, the fetus leaves the intrauterine environment of the mother's body and begins its life in the outside world. Despite the vast improvements in delivery techniques that have occurred over the years, many facets of

Core Concept

The birth process represents another important time when potential risk to the child is high.

childbirth are still not well understood. This section presents a survey of the salient aspects of this dramatic event.

Preparation for childbirth does not occur at the last moment. Certain changes in the mother's anatomy that are necessary for birth to proceed smoothly have been under way since about midpregnancy. The muscle structure of the uterus has been rearranged substantially to facilitate fetal expulsion. Another change that is essential to permit passage of the fetus through the birth canal has occurred in the cervical area. Figure 5–3 illustrates an advanced fetus in the uterine environment. In the latter days of pregnancy and during the onset of labor, expansion occurs in the upper part of the cervical area. By the time the fetus is moving down the birth canal, the cervical muscle structure has expanded to the point where the tubelike structure shown at the bottom of Figure 5–3 no longer exists. The loosening of the cervix, called effacement, is an important change in the muscle structure that must occur for the fetus to be expelled.

The exact mechanism that triggers labor remains mysterious. Many possibilities have been investigated, including both chemical (hormones) and mechanical (degree of uterine expansion) agents. The usual and desirable fetal position at the onset of labor is with the head toward the cervix, as illustrated in Figure 5–3. This position occurs in more than 80% of all childbirths. As the fetus begins to move

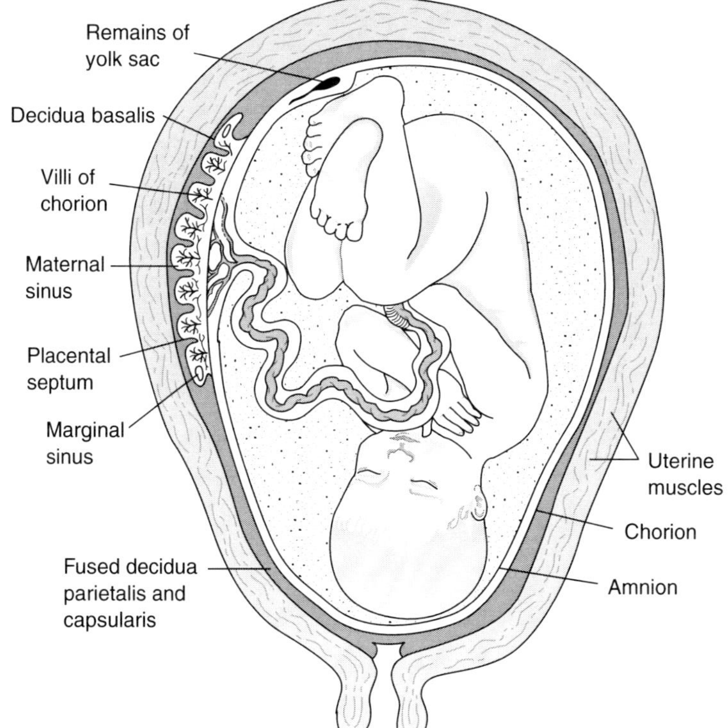

Figure 5–3
Advanced Fetus in Uterine Environment

Source: From *Child Health Maintenance: Concepts in Family Centered Care* (2nd ed., p. 109) by P. L. Chinn, 1979, St. Louis: Mosby. Copyright 1979 by C. V. Mosby Co. Reprinted by permission.

downward into the birth canal, the pelvic girdle stretches more. The pressure of the pelvic girdle also molds the head of the fetus, so newborns often have strangely shaped heads. Later, the head returns to its natural shape.

All of this movement is generated by labor, the muscle contractions of the uterus. At the same time that the fetus moves downward, it turns counterclockwise from the effect of the uterine muscle action. Figure 5–4 shows a series of fetal positions during the birth process.

The infant's delivery usually is followed by expulsion of the placenta a few minutes later. The placenta has transmitted oxygen and nourishment to the developing child and disposed of waste during the prenatal period. Now the infant must accomplish these functions in the outside world. The respiratory tract is immediately cleared of the remaining amniotic fluid and mucus, and the infant begins to breathe. This is the time that most new mothers and fathers remember as the first cry of their newborn. This crying serves an important function, and if the infant does not begin it spontaneously, the physician must provide stimulation. Crying expands the infant's lungs with air for the first time, causing the circulatory changes that accompany the use of the lungs and the loss of the placenta.

The birth process is very complex and, unfortunately, does not always proceed smoothly. Difficulties can arise that result in intellectual disabilities. Some of the possible problems are discussed in Chapter 6.

NEONATAL DEVELOPMENT

The term **neonate** often is applied to the baby during the first 2 months after birth. Beyond that period, the terminology is varied and less specific. Here we examine early life, some of whose principles apply beyond the neonatal period. Later chapters treat development of the infant and the older child.

The first few weeks of extrauterine life are crucial, and many authorities view the first month as being among the most dangerous in the entire lifespan (Berk, 2005; Broderick & Blewitt, 2003). Many of the developmental functions begun in utero are continuing but without the protective agents available before. In addition to physiological changes, a variety of forces initiate the neonate's rapid development in psychological and behavioral areas. As development proceeds, previous and ongoing physiological changes fuse with changes generated by environmental stimuli (e.g., learning) to form the integrated complex of responsiveness called a human being.

Core Concept

Many consider the time immediately following birth as the most dangerous period of human life.

From a behavioral standpoint, the neonate seems to be little more than a mass of reflex actions, and at this age, assessment of reflexes is the primary method of evaluation by health care professionals. The infant's movements seem primarily nonpurposeful and nonspecific and more often than not involve nearly the entire body. This movement pattern usually involves gross-motor movements often accompanied by verbal output (crying). The frequency and intensity of movements rise between feedings and tend to diminish as the hungry neonate becomes satisfied. Cephalocaudal and proximodistal developmental trends continue after birth. These are perhaps best

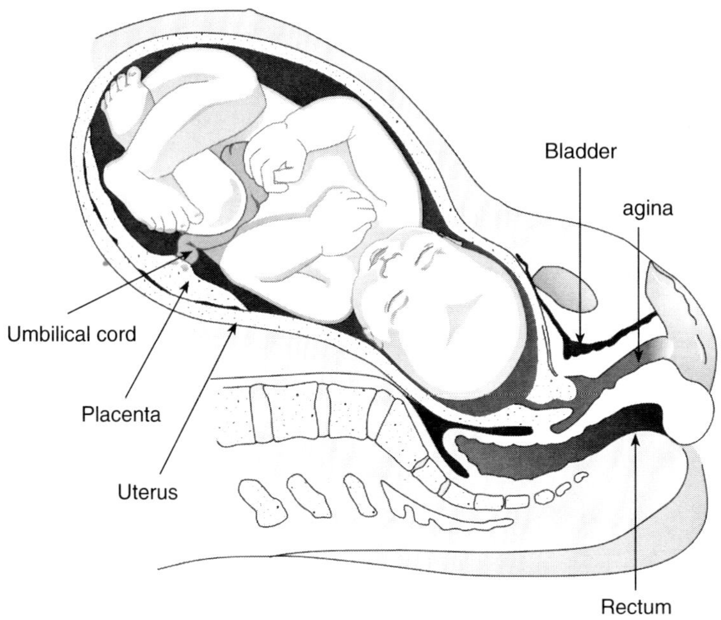

A, Engagement

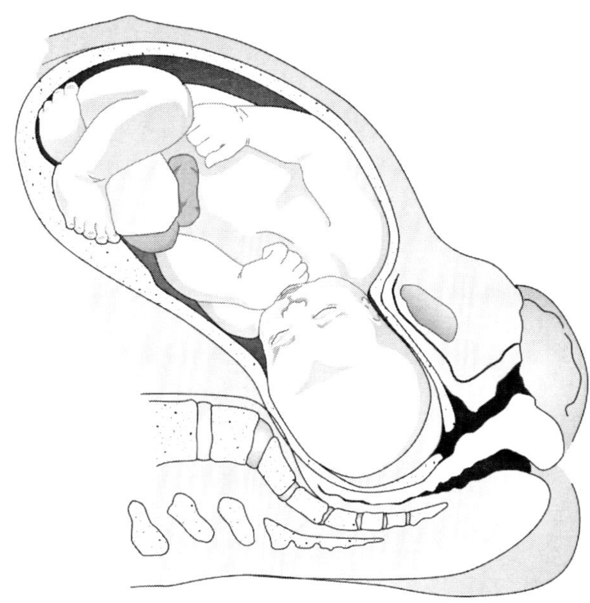

B, Descent with Flexion

Figure 5–4
Stages of the Birth Process

Source: From *Childbirth: Family Centered Nursing* by J. Iorio, 1975, St. Louis: Mosby. Copyright 1975 by C. V. Mosby Co. Reprinted by permission.

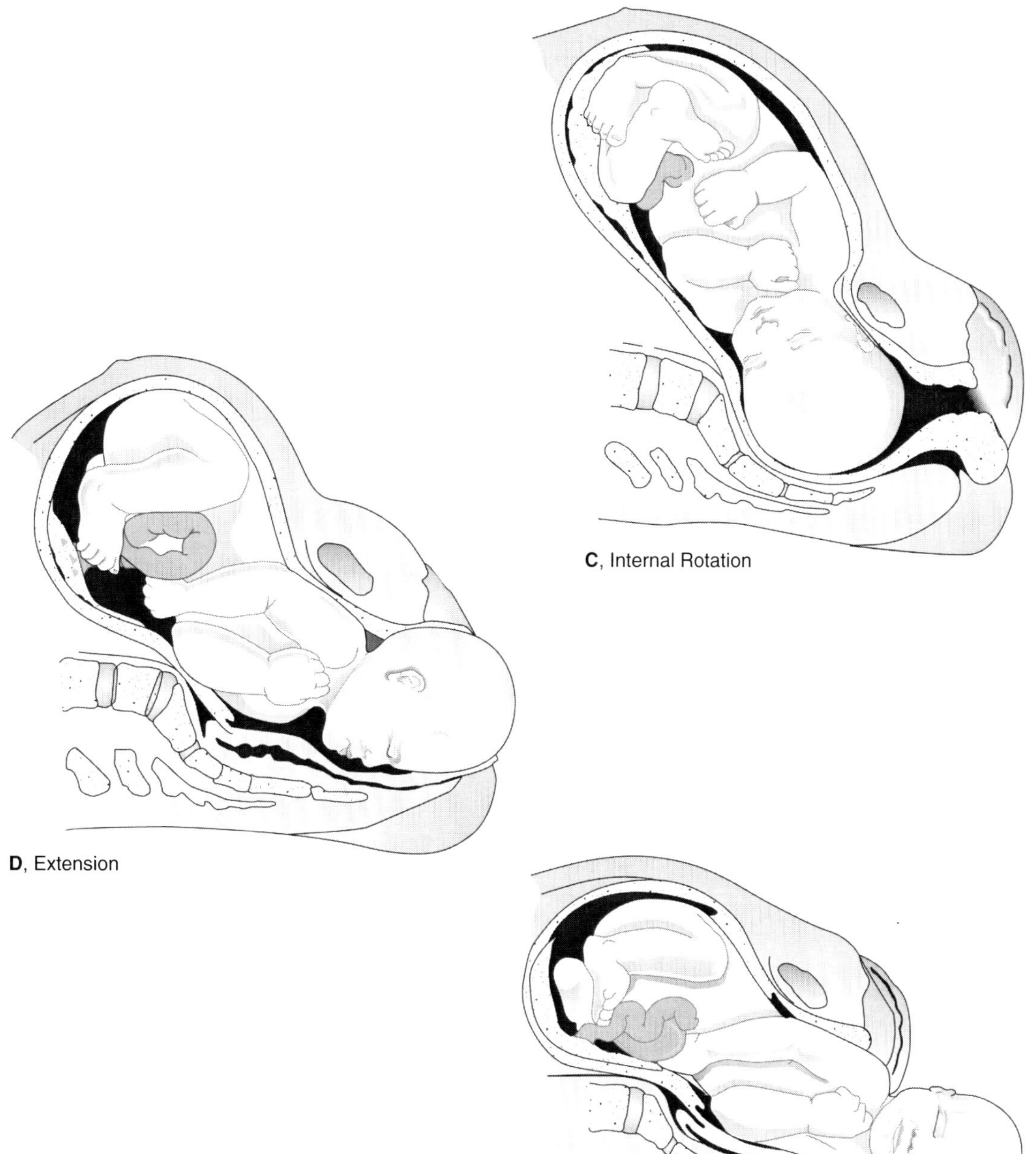

Figure 5–4
Continued

Figure 5–4
Continued

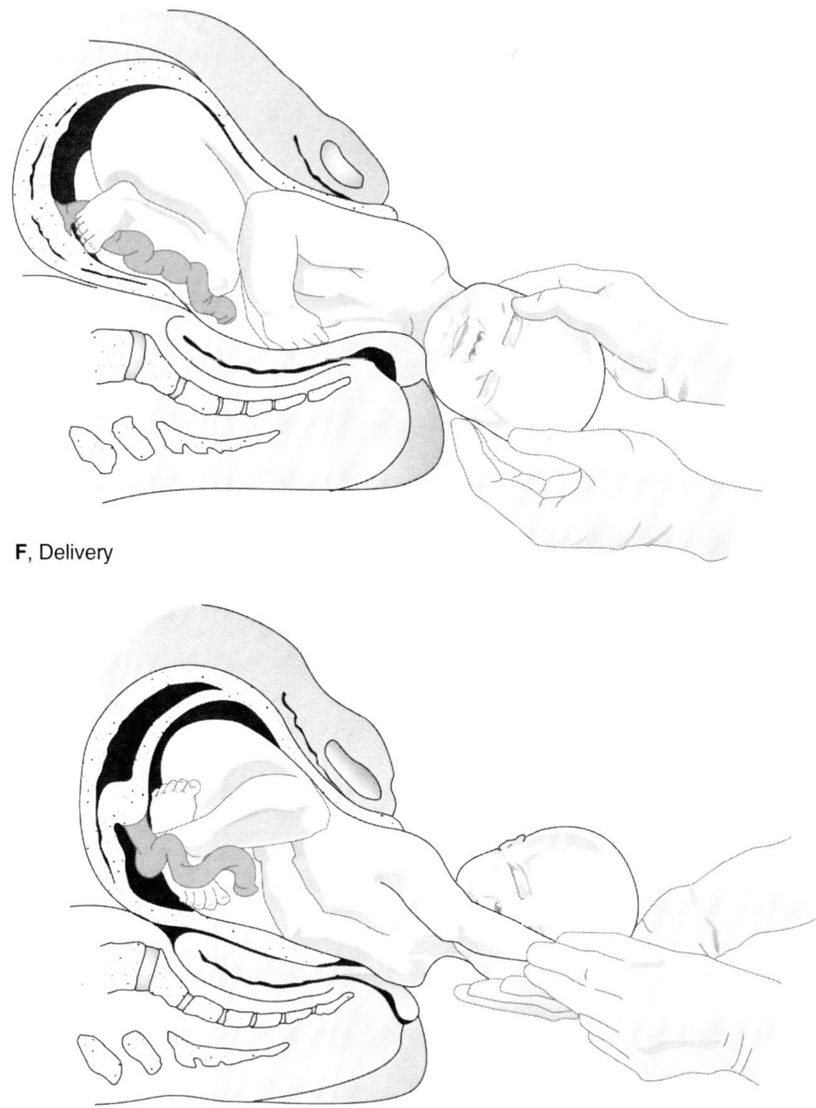

F, Delivery

G, Lateral Flexion

observable in the behavior patterns of the first 2 years of life. More mature responses tend to appear earlier in areas closest to the brain (e.g., eye movement) and progress downward and outward. The neonate's gross-motor movements precede any control of more distal movements, such as those of the fingers. Infants can also usually reach for and grasp objects accurately long before they can walk.

Certain physiological changes occur very rapidly during the first period of postnatal life. The central nervous system exhibits dramatic growth during the first 4 years, with acceleration leveling off in later childhood. For example, during this growth period, brain weight increases nearly 400% over what it was at birth. In addition to quantitative changes, the brain matter is rapidly developing convolutions or folds and is developing in a number of ways that are vital to later cognitive function (Berk, 2005; Broderick & Blewitt, 2003).

The progress of myelinization, which began prenatally, continues during the first 12 months after birth and declines thereafter. The progression of the myelin sheath follows the course of central nervous system development to some degree. At birth the lower or subcortical portion of the central nervous system (spinal cord, brainstem) governs the neonate, and this part of the central nervous system is first to receive the myelin covering. Later, the higher cerebral matter is involved in myelinization and likewise begins to take charge of the child's behavior. For example, functioning of the frontal lobe of the brain may be influential in developing emotional regulation (Berk, 2005). The myelin sheath is essentially complete at age 2, although fragmentary myelinization apparently continues through adolescence and perhaps even middle adult life. In our consideration of intellectual disabilities, the myelinization process becomes important when considering possible injury to the central nervous system (see Chapter 6).

The sensory organs, particularly the eyes and the ears, are nearly complete in structure at birth. Certain parts of the retina are yet to be completed, but basic sight exists at birth. For the first few weeks, the infant's eyes tend to operate independently, rather than together. By about 6 weeks, however, eye fixation is pretty well coordinated. Visual acuity appears to be imperfect during the neonatal and infant periods. Early images are blurred forms, patterns, and shapes, but visual acuity improves rather rapidly from about 20/400 at the neonate stage (Berk, 2005; Broderick & Blewitt, 2003).

Hearing is apparently intact at birth. The neonate responds to a wide variety of auditory stimuli, suggesting that probably the full range of humanly detectable sound is available quite early. Additionally, the neonate seems able to identify where sounds come from. The development of auditory discrimination needs much more investigation. Part of the ability to discriminate sounds may be a learned or acquired skill.

Many environmental stimuli in this baby's world affect development.

The sense of taste is difficult to study in a very young child. However, evidence indicates that even at the neonatal stage an infant makes gross taste discriminations. Such discrimination, however, is primarily observable in different behavioral reactions to sweetness versus other tastes, such as sourness and bitterness. This sense improves with experience. The sense of smell is even more difficult to study than that of taste, so we have very little evidence about it in the neonatal period. It does seem, however, that the neonate is responsive to very dramatic or intense odors and that sensitivity increases during the infant stage.

The sucking response is an important component of neonatal behavior. In addition to its obvious value to the child in terms of feeding, it remains an important early check of well-being (Berk, 2005; Broderick & Blewitt, 2003). A weak sucking response is a signal for concern. The neonate tends to suck in response to a variety of stimuli, both in terms of the type of stimulus and of the body part stimulated. Later, responsivity diminishes and can be elicited primarily around the mouth.

The behavioral repertoire of the newborn is limited as noted earlier. During the first few weeks of postnatal life, verbal output is limited primarily to crying. Crying seems to be associated mostly with discomfort of some sort, although at times the source of discomfort is not evident, as parents well know. From birth, hunger is the standard stimulus for crying. Later, the young child learns to use crying as a means of communicating in a wide variety of situations that are unpleasurable. Other verbal output (e.g., gurgling, cooing, general noise) seems to develop considerably later, often not becoming a significant part of the behavioral repertoire until the infant is several months old.

NEW ISSUES AND FUTURE DIRECTIONS

Core Concept

The knowledge gained from scientific advances both holds great promise for improving the early developmental fortunes of children and raises serious social questions.

Most of this chapter has addressed matters pertaining to development from the prenatal period through birth and influential factors impinging on the young human during this time. Perhaps nowhere in the developmental life cycle have the advances of technology and research information generated so many potential treatments for health and other problems as in this time frame (IASSID, 2003). This progress has created both optimism and uncertainty.

The past 30 years have seen unprecedented scientific advancement in understanding genetic function. Many of the findings have led to interventions that would have been unimaginable in the past. The level of detailed description of genetic material now possible holds enormous potential for a variety of treatments, many with implications for the field of intellectual disabilities. Society has begun to witness early work in predicting and correcting certain genetic lesions. Such a capability provides the eventual capacity for removal of specific genes (e.g., those causing sickle cell anemia or phenylketonuria) and replacement with synthetic genes able to function normally. Although such suggestions seem like science fiction on one level, it was not long ago that in vitro fertilization was front-page news. Now thousands of children have been born as a result of in vitro fertilization, and such events hardly warrant attention.

Such advancements create marvelous possibilities, but they also cause uncertainty and controversy. One constant concern is the ethics of such interventions and, further, the possibility that the science that creates opportunities also has the potential for social and moral abuse. Many of these procedures *can* be performed, but *should* they be? Genetic engineering may hold promise for eliminating certain diseases, which might mean that more people would survive and have a better quality of life. Is such improvement of the human gene pool appropriate when the world population as a whole cannot be properly nourished? Who will decide which genetic defects should be corrected, determining who lives and who dies? Technological capability has outstripped human wisdom and the refinement of ethical thinking. This is not the first time such ethical dilemmas have had to be faced, and they continue to raise a variety of questions (e.g., Harris, 2003; Simpson, 2004; Zucker, 2004). These questions demand serious attention and examination of how such progress affects public policy (AAMR, 2002; IASSID, 2003).

Core Questions

1. Compare the concepts of genotype and phenotype and discuss how they relate to the growth matrix.
2. The tabula rasa approach to explaining human growth and development differed significantly from both the preformationist and predeterministic positions. Compare and contrast these three approaches. How do you think their proponents would differ in their explanations of intellectual disabilities, and why might the interactional view be more helpful for a major portion of those with intellectual disabilities?
3. How are the notions of discontinuous growth and critical stages related? Discuss the views of continuous and discontinuous human growth in terms of prenatal and neonatal development.
4. In what manner does the speed of cell reproduction influence vulnerability to trauma that might cause intellectual disabilities? How does this relate to the often noted "first trimester" of pregnancy, particularly with respect to weeks 10 through 12?
5. Why would you expect a new baby's head and arm movements to be more mature than those of its legs? What other growth gradient is also typical of early development?
6. What important physical changes in the mother prepare her for giving birth? How is the baby physically influenced during birth?
7. Why is the neonatal period a time of risk for the baby, and what important physical developments are continuing at this time?
8. How do scientific advances present technical capabilities that contribute to moral or ethical dilemmas?

Roundtable Discussion

A basic understanding of early human development is important background for the study of intellectual disabilities. Many prenatal influences have a substantial impact on a child's status. During this time, many vital organs are being formed, and tissue growth occurs at a phenomenal rate. This is all occurring in the womb during a relatively short period of about 9 months. Biological and embryological information suggests that such processes as myelinization are taking place, central nervous system tissue is being formed, and many other matters essential to the well-being of a young child are going on.

In your study group or on your own, examine these processes as if through the eyes of a preformationist, predeterminist, tabula rasa theorist, and interactionist. Using the material presented in this chapter, as well as in other sources, explain the prenatal developments mentioned (e.g., myelinization, central nervous system development, brain development). Try to integrate the concepts of continuous/discontinuous growth and critical periods into your arguments from each theoretical perspective. Push your explanations and arguments to extremes, as early developmental theorists did. Do you find taking an extreme position the most difficult part of your tasks, or are the fundamental premises more problematic? After this examination of the basic principles of development, where do you stand theoretically as you prepare to push ahead with your study of intellectual disabilities?

Parent and Professional Organization Positions on Key Issues in the Lives of People with Intellectual Disabilities

The inside front cover of this text presents a matrix that includes several key issues in the lives of people with disabilities, the positions of various parent and professional organizations on each issue, and the chapter and page number where the information is addressed. Table 5–2 is a summary of the organizations and key issues addressed in this chapter.

Table 5–2
Key Issues and Organizations Discussed in This Chapter

Organization/Website	Key Issues Addressed	Chapter Heading
American Association on Mental Retardation (http://www.aamr.org)	Genetics, environment, and human development Intervention ethics	Human Development: Terminology, Concepts, and Theory New Issues and Future Directions
International Association for the Scientific Study of Intellectual Disabilities (http://www.iassid.org)	Genetics, environment, and human development Prenatal health promotion Intervention ethics	Human Development: Terminology, Concepts, and Theory New Issues and Future Directions New Issues and Future Directions

References

American Association on Mental Retardation (AAMR). (2002). *Mental retardation: Definition, classification, and systems of supports* (10th ed.). Washington, DC: Author.

Arey, L. B. (1974). *Developmental anatomy* (7th ed.). Philadelphia: W. B. Saunders.

Austrian, S. G. (2002). Infancy and toddlerhood. In S. G. Austrian (Ed.), *Developmental theories through the life cycle* (pp. 7–68). New York: Columbia University Press.

Behar, E. S., & Borkovec, T. D. (2003). Psychotherapy outcome research. In J. A. Schinka & W. F. Velicer (Eds.), *Handbook of psychology: Research methods in psychology* (Vol. 2, pp. 213–240). New York: Wiley.

Berk, L. E. (2005). *Infants and children: Prenatal through middle childhood* (5th ed.). Boston: Allyn & Bacon.

Berkson, G. (2004). Intellectual and physical disabilities in prehistory and early civilization. *Mental Retardation, 42,* 195–208.

Broderick, P. C., & Blewitt, P. (2003). *The life span: Human development for helping professionals.* Upper Saddle River, NJ: Pearson/Prentice Hall.

Carrera, J. M., Chervenak, F. A., & Kurjak, A. (2003). *Controversies in perinatal medicine: Studies of the fetus as a patient.* Boca Raton, FL: CRC Press.

Cook, J. L., & Cook, G. (2005). *Child development: Principles and perspectives.* Boston: Allyn & Bacon.

Didio, L. J. A. (1970). *Synopsis of anatomy.* St. Louis: Mosby.

Ehrenreich, J. T., & Gross, A. M. (2003). Group designs. In J. C. Thomas & M. Hersen (Eds.), *Understanding research in clinical and counseling psychology* (pp. 133–159). Mahwah, NJ: Erlbaum.

Garlick, D. (2003). Integrating brain science research with intelligence research. *Current Directions in Psychological Science, 12,* 185–189.

Gelfand, D. M., & Drew, C. J. (2003). *Understanding child behavior disorders* (4th ed.). Belmont, CA: Wadsworth.

Goodwin, C. J. (2005). *Research in psychology: Methods and design* (4th ed.). Hoboken, NJ: Wiley.

Hall, G. S. (1904). *Adolescence: Its psychology and its relation to physiology, anthropology, sociology, sex, crime, religion, and education.* New York: Appleton-Century-Crofts.

Harris, J. (2003). Consent and end of life decisions. *Journal of Medical Ethics, 29,* 10–15.

Hertzig, M. E., & Farber, E. A. (2003). *Annual progress in child psychiatry and child development: 2000–2001.* New York: Brunner-Routledge.

International Association for the Scientific Study of Intellectual Disabilities (IASSID). (2003). Health SIRG news. *Newsletter, 20,* 13.

Iorio, J. (1975). *Childbirth: Family centered nursing.* St. Louis: Mosby.

Keogh, B. K., Bernheimer, L. P., & Guthrie, D. (2004). Children with developmental delays twenty years later: Where are they? How are they? *American Journal on Mental Retardation, 109,* 219–230.

KUER. (2005). *The life and career of Mario Capecchi.* Five-part series on genetic science. Salt Lake City, UT.

LeFrancois, G. R. (2001). *Of children—An introduction to child development* (9th ed.). Belmont, CA: Wadsworth/Thompson Learning.

Lickliter, R., & Honeycutt, H. (2003). Evolutionary approaches to cognitive development: Status and strategy. *Journal of Cognition and Development, 4,* 459–473.

Owens, R. E., Jr. (2005). *Language development: An introduction* (6th ed.). Boston: Allyn & Bacon.

Phares, V. (2003). *Understanding abnormal child psychology.* New York: Wiley.

Piaget, J. (1926). *The language and thought of the child.* New York: Harcourt Brace.

Pine, D. (2004). Editorial. *Journal of Child Psychology and Psychiatry, 45,* 1039–1040.

Sadler, T. W. (2003). *Langman's medical embryology with simbryo CD-ROM.* Philadelphia: Lippincott Williams & Wilkins.

Simpson, E. (2004). Harms to dignity, bioethics, and the scope of biolaw. *Journal of Palliative Care, 20,* 185–192.

Zucker, A. (2004). Law and ethics. *Death Studies, 28,* 803–806.

Chapter 6

Early Influences and Causation

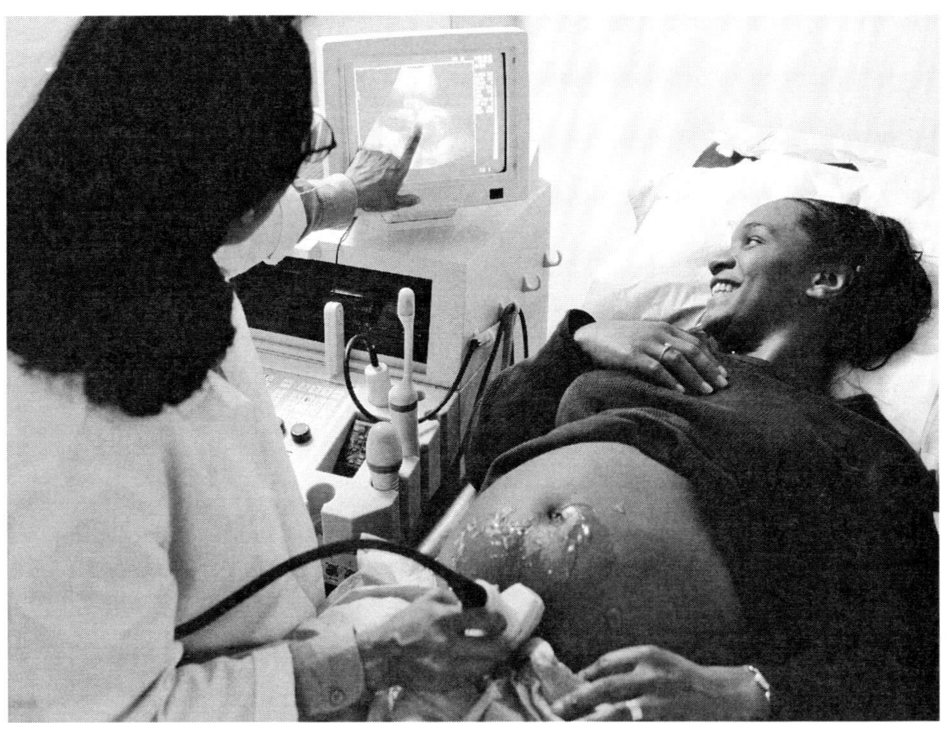

Chapter Preview

In Chapter 5 we examined the many complexities of very early development. This chapter will turn to some of these developmental processes where errors can occur. At the completion of this chapter, you will have a better understanding of developmental errors that can result in intellectual disabilities. You will encounter:

- How genetic errors can result in subsequent development leading to, or increasing the risk of, intellectual disabilities.
- How prenatal development can result in a marginal or inadequate birth weight and gestational age, and how this can present a developmental risk for potential intellectual disabilities.
- How the birth process itself may present a risky situation for the baby, with potential for damage that can cause intellectual disabilities.

The Scary Risks of Pregnancy

We met Janine briefly as we began the last chapter. A lot has transpired since her self-assured statement that she will quit smoking and drinking when she gets pregnant. What was a confident assertion to her roommates has become a concern and reality. She married her sweetheart although maintaining close ties with her college friends, and now she examines the somewhat fuzzy image below with considerable anxiety. She hadn't realized that she was pregnant during the December party circuit with family, old college girlfriends, and certainly the New Year's Eve bash. Now she worries that their baby has been seriously damaged by all this party activity. She searches the image again, looking for any sign that will relieve her concern, or confirm her worries.

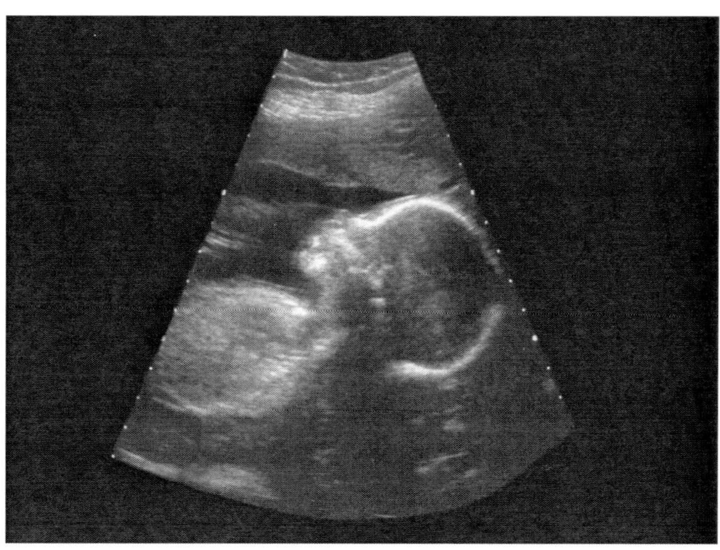

As most parents know, sonograms are frequently used in consultations with young parents who are expecting. They provide some very basic information regarding the health of the unborn baby, but the concerns that swirl in Janine's mind have not been either put to rest, or confirmed by this somewhat routine assessment. She has harbored her worries and this image shows her 20-week, growing baby. As we proceed through this chapter we will encounter a number of diagnostic processes that might help inform her. But she will need to talk about her concerns to her doctor and her husband, and together they will need to undertake further prenatal assessment.

- *What are your thoughts now about Janine's worries? Certainly she needs to talk with her physician and her spouse. If nothing else, this process of sharing and discussing the concerns can bring them to the surface rather than being a constant but private anxiety.*
- *How do you undertake these types of discussions—the dreaded ones? Some people seem to handle them with ease on the surface but everyone has areas where it is difficult to prompt a conversation. What do you think can be done to make productive discussion of topics like Janine's more approachable?*

Early life is very important in human growth and development and deserves considerable attention in the study of intellectual disabilities. The young human is almost wholly at the mercy of the environment and is vulnerable to its impact both prenatally and after birth. Normal developmental processes during this period were examined in Chapter 5. The current chapter considers influences and causes of intellectual disabilities in the same period (conception through early infancy).

Examination of the causes of intellectual disabilities during prenatal and neonatal periods requires attention to certain physiological conditions and, when possible, the treatment of these conditions. Medical professionals are often the first to interact with a child at risk for intellectual disabilities during this early period. Instead of an in-depth examination of the medical aspects of intellectual disabilities, however, we wish to make the reader aware of influences on mental development during this period. We discuss more common types of intellectual disabilities beginning at this time, as well as certain rare conditions for which intervention can prevent disabilities or reduce their impact. A variety of developmental and ongoing life processes can go away at this time and can result in reduced intellectual functioning. In fact, the beginning student occasionally wonders how any child ever manages to get through this period at all without deviation or abnormality. The vast majority of children, however, do develop to a level of functioning that is considered normal or average.

Maternal and fetal conditions both play central roles in healthy fetal development. Similarly, various maternal and fetal conditions contribute to intellectual disabilities during early life. These influences may result in intellectual disabilities that ranges from profound or severe to only mild deviations from normal. Such varying degrees of disability can be conceived of as a *continuum of reproductive causality*. This notion views the child with a mild disability at the less extreme end of the causality range; individuals with more severe disabilities and stillborn infants are at the more extreme end. Spontaneous abortion occurring early in pregnancy may represent one extreme of the continuum; mild or slight disabilities in basically normal children represent the other.

EARLY CAUSATION: THE FETUS AND INFANT AT RISK

The first portion of the life cycle is extremely important, as we have already mentioned. Many view developments during the prenatal period and immediately after birth as among the most critical in the entire lifespan (e.g., Berk, 2005; Cook & Cook, 2005). Fortunately, most infants enter life outside the womb after a full, successful gestational period, with no labor and delivery complications and no factors during the first month of life that lead to serious illness or disability. When a serious problem does occur in these early months, however, the family often must adjust to having a child with a permanent mental or physical disability. Several conditions are known to place the fetus or infant at high risk for development of serious illness or permanent disability.

Genetic Causation

Chromosomal and genetic errors contribute to a number of problems that occur during the prenatal period. In many cases, intellectual disabilities resulting from such difficulties fall into well-known syndrome classes.

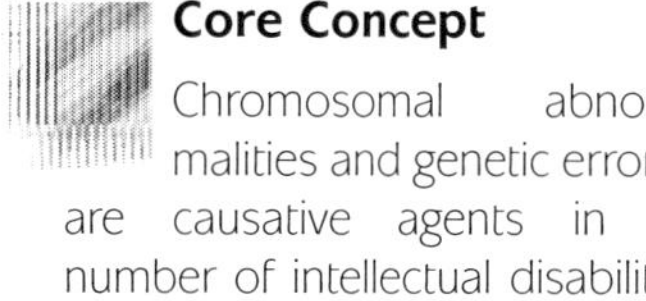

Core Concept

Chromosomal abnormalities and genetic errors are causative agents in a number of intellectual disability syndromes.

Chromosomal Aberrations. Chromosomal aberrations occur when some abnormality emerges in the number or configuration of the chromosomes in the body. Figure 6–1 illustrates a **karyotype,** or classification of photographed human chromosomes obtained from a blood or skin sample. The chromosomes in the sample have been stained to bring out transverse bands; chromosomes with matching bands then can be paired. The karyotype is obtained by cutting individual chromosomes out of photographs and pasting them into place. By convention, the pairs are arranged and numbered from longest to shortest and are separated into seven groups labeled A through G. In this way, determinations of the particular chromosomal anomaly causing an abnormal condition can be identified. The karyotype shown in Figure 6–1 is a normal chromosomal configuration with 44 autosomal and 2 sex chromosomes. One kind of abnormal condition involves extra chromosomes, such as 3 chromosomes in position 21 or 2 or more X or Y chromosomes. Another type of common aberration involves abnormally shaped chromosomes—for example, an excessively long "arm" on number 15.

When 45 chromosomes are present with only a single X sex chromosome, the child has the condition called **Turner syndrome,** or gonadal aplasia. The child is nearly always female because the Y chromosome conveys maleness to the individual. Gonads are rudimentary, no secondary sex characteristics develop at puberty, and there may or may not be accompanying physical signs, such as bowleggedness or webbed neck and abnormalities of the kidneys and heart (Collaer, Geffner, Kaufman,

Figure 6–1
Karyotype Classification of Human Chromosomes

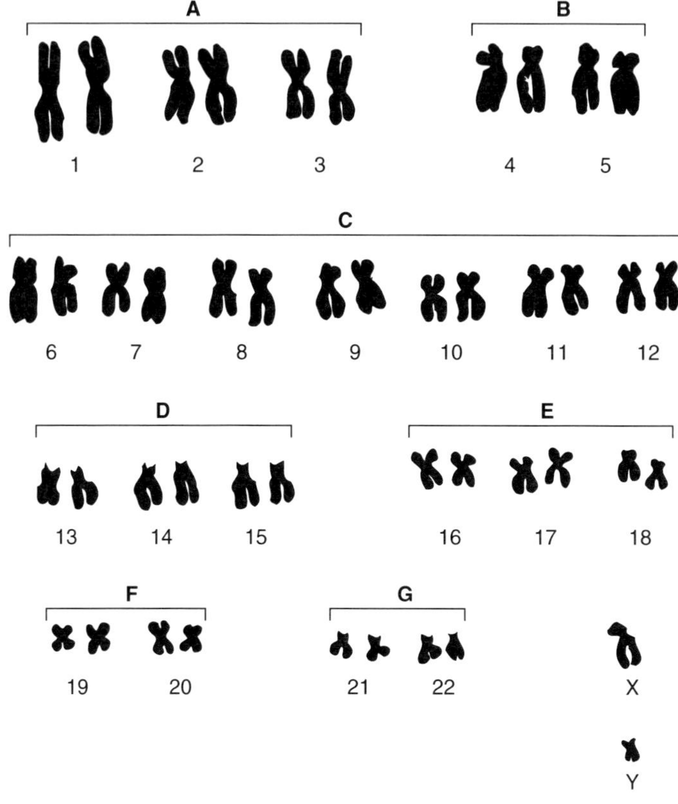

Buckingham, & Hines, 2002; Hines, 2004; Nijhuis-VanderSanden, Eling, Van Asseldonk, & Van Galen, 2004). A substantial number of individuals with this problem who survive the prenatal period and reach the newborn stage have developmental difficulties and intellectual disabilities.

A number of abnormalities occur on the chromosomes of Groups A through G. These chromosomes are referred to as autosomal because they contain genetic material that does not involve sexual characteristics. Down syndrome can occur from any one of three different aberrations of the autosomal chromosomes. The first type is **trisomy,** or nondisjunction, in which an extra chromosome occurs in Group G. This is the most common cause of Down syndrome and has a definite correlation with maternal age. The risks increase from 0.69 per 1,000 births for mothers in their early 20s, to 1 per 336 at 35, and further, to about 1 per 97 in mothers at 40. Research on fetal diagnostic procedures is ongoing, aimed at early detection of trisomy Down syndrome (e.g., Chapman, Scott, & Mason, 2002; Hengstschlager et al., 2004; Simensen, Colby, & Corning, 2003).

A second type of chromosomal difficulty resulting in Down syndrome is **translocation,** occurring in 9% of affected infants born to mothers under the age of 30 and in 2% of affected infants born to mothers over the age of 30. In translocation, some of the chromosomal material of the 21st pair in Group G detaches and becomes attached to a chromosome of the 15th pair in Group D, causing an extra long chromosome in the karyotype. A parent is sometimes the carrier of this condition, as can be detected through genetic studies of both parents and child. When the aberration is not inherited, it occurs as a result of a chance chromosomal error (e.g., Yoshida, Yamada, & Sakaguchi, 2003).

The third condition resulting in Down syndrome is **mosaicism.** In this case, the cells of the individual's body are identified as mixed. Some contain trisomies; others are normal. This error occurs during the very early cell divisions after fertilization, with some cell groups forming normally before the error occurs. Such individuals tend to exhibit milder manifestations of the condition, which may reflect the stage of development at which the chromosomal error began. As with other types of Down syndrome, research on the causal mechanism for this condition continues (e.g., Hird, 2004; Simensen, Colby, & Corning, 2003).

The physical features evident in Down syndrome vary, but are similar enough that most individuals with Down syndrome resemble one another more than they resemble their own family members. Characteristics include a lateral upward slope of the eyes; protruding tongue because of a small oral cavity; short nose with flat bondage caused by underdevelopment of the nasal bone; flattened head front and back; shortness of fingers, especially the fifth; wide space between the first and second toes; and short, stocky build. These children are more likely than the general population to have congenital heart defects and leukemia and are more susceptible to respiratory infections. Intellectual disabilities almost always accompanies Down syndrome, with IQ scores in the moderate to severe retardation ranges (APA, 2000). A few individuals have IQs in the normal range, and the effect of early stimulation and education programs results in improved mental and neurological functioning for some with Down syndrome. Down syndrome occurs across all three types in about 1 to 1.5 cases per 1,000 live births. Considerable research continues on Down syndrome, including such topics as academic performance, self-help and adaptive behaviors, various aspects of cognitive performance, and maternal/family matters (e.g., Hamill, 2003; Hodapp, 2004; Lewis & Kritzinger, 2004). Individuals with this condition continue to capture the attention of a significant group of researchers in intellectual disabilities, as they have for many years.

Genetic Errors. Genetic errors are conditions resulting from inheritance factors involving specific genes. Such disorders are rather poorly understood, and investigation of these problems is somewhat restricted because of some limitations encountered when studying human genetic material. Some areas of genetic research have achieved enormous advances while others have languished because of funding or methodological limitations (Hodapp, 2004). Although genetic disorders can be identified through study of family inheritance patterns, examination and identification of these problems can sometimes be difficult. Such conditions cannot be studied the way chromosomal disorders are.

Most genetic errors are rare, but a few that result in intellectual disabilities happen often enough that diagnostic and treatment approaches have been developed.

One example of such a condition is Prader-Willi syndrome, which occurs about once in every 15,000 births and results in mild to moderate intellectual disabilities (Descheemaeker et al., 2002; Einfeld, 2004). Another example is phenylketonuria (PKU), which has become a heavily studied condition among the genetic defects related to intellectual disabilities (Channon, German, Cassina, & Lee, 2004; Read, 2004; Welsh, 2002). It occurs about once in every 10,000 live births. It is transmitted by an autosomal recessive gene that appears with highest frequency in northern European ethnic groups; it is rare in African and Jewish groups. Affected individuals produce less of the enzyme necessary for metabolism of phenylalanine, leading to an accumulation of this product in the blood serum, cerebrospinal fluid, tissues, and urine. The effect of this metabolic malfunction on the central nervous system is grave; all untreated individuals will reach a level of severe intellectual disabilities within the first few months of life. Elevated phenylalanine in the blood or urine can be detected within a few weeks after consumption of milk, which contains the substance. Many states have established mandatory screening procedures for all infants in order to institute early treatment measures and to minimize or prevent the serious effects of the untreated condition (Baieli, Pavone, Meli, Fiumara, & Coleman, 2003; Huijbregts et al., 2002). It is now possible to diagnose PKU prenatally although like other prenatal assessment, the resulting decision-making and ethical issues are complex, and the technique is not widely employed (Shaw-Smith, Hogg, Reading, Calvin, & Trump, 2004; Williams, Alderson, & Farsides, 2002). In addition to intellectual disabilities, affected children develop some degree of microcephaly and have blond hair, blue eyes, and very sensitive skin. Early assessment provides information of great importance to parents and health care personnel in order to maximize consideration of prenatal intervention if needed and the difficult ethical questions that may also emerge (AAMR, 2002; IASSID, 2005). Once again, the March of Dimes questions on genetic counseling become relevant in the Tips for Professionals. However, in this case the issue is not lifestyle but more on the typical points of such consultation.

Specific recessive genes play a causal role in a number of other disorders. In these cases, the parents are carriers of a deficient gene but are phenotypically normal. When the recessive genetic material combines, however, the children may develop conditions that result in intellectual disabilities. One such disorder is galactosemia, which occurs when an infant cannot properly metabolize galactose, a chemical generated during digestion of milk products. Newborns with this condition who are on milk diets rapidly develop symptoms that can become life threatening—jaundice, vomiting, and a tremendously heightened vulnerability to infection. Intellectual development also may suffer. Early detection and treatment through strict dietary means can dramatically improve the infant's potential development, although some difficulties may persist. Longitudinal research on treatment effectiveness remains inexact because of the disorder's relative rarity, a common difficulty with such genetic problems.

Prenatal Causation

A variety of problems can emerge during the prenatal period that lead to a risk condition for an infant. In some cases, circumstances result in an inadequate or

Tips for Professionals

What to Expect in Genetic Counseling

The March of Dimes outlines a number of questions for people related to genetic counseling. These points are important tips for conversations between health care professionals and their clients.

Is Genetic Counseling for You?

Anyone who has unanswered questions about origins of diseases or traits in the family should consider genetic counseling. People who may find it valuable include:

- Those who have, or are concerned that they might have, an inherited disorder or birth defect.
- Women who are pregnant or planning to be after age 35.
- Couples who already have a child with mental retardation, an inherited disorder or a birth defect.
- Couples whose infant has a genetic disease diagnosed by routine newborn screening.
- Women who have had babies who died in infancy or three or more miscarriages.
- People concerned that their jobs, lifestyles or medical history may pose a risk to outcome of pregnancy. Common causes of concern include exposure to radiation, medications, illegal drugs, chemicals or infections.
- Couples who would like testing or more information about genetic conditions that occur frequently in their ethnic group.
- Couples who are first cousins or other close blood relatives.
- Pregnant women whose ultrasound examinations or blood testing indicate that their pregnancy may be at increased risk for certain complications or birth defects.

What Happens at a Genetic Counseling Appointment?

When you go to see a genetic counselor, he or she:

- Will record your family history (for instance, if your parents, grandparents or siblings had heart disease, diabetes, etc.) and your own medical background.
- May arrange appointments for blood tests, physical exams, or amniocentesis.
- Will try to put together a picture of how your family's health may affect your children.
- Will help you interpret medical information about any risks present and explain the role of genetics in these conditions.

Often genetic counselors can determine the risk of occurrence or recurrence of a condition and the availability of tests for it.

Evaluation of tests results usually is coordinated between the genetic counselor, the person or couple and the doctor. In the occasional case of troubling results, the counselor will provide information to help you make decisions (for instance, on the risk of having a child or more children). The counselor or the doctor can refer you to resources in your community that deal with a specific genetic condition, or to medical specialists, educational specialists or family support groups.

How To Find a Genetic Counselor

A family can seek genetic counseling directly or be referred by a physician. Comprehensive genetic services centers are available in the United States, usually located within large medical centers or teaching hospitals. Smaller areas may be served by satellite clinics.

continues on next page

continues from previous page

If you think you could benefit from genetic counseling:

- Call your local chapter of the March of Dimes for information on services in your area.
- Ask your physician or nearest hospital associated with a medical school.
- Contact the National Society of Genetic Counselors.
- Locate the name of clinic on the GeneTests Website.

Source: Excerpted from March of Dimes (2005). *Genetic Counseling.* Pregnancy & Newborn Health Education Center. Retrieved from http://www.marchofdimes.com. Used by permission.

incomplete development and the baby is born before he or she is ready to thrive in the outside world. Each difficulty discussed here is a condition that places the infant in one risk category or another.

Core Concept

Inadequate birth weight and gestational age are the problems that most commonly place an infant at developmental risk. They can be caused by a number of factors.

Birth Weight and Gestational Age. The most prevalent of prenatal risk problems involve inadequate birth weight and gestational age, which result in a number of developmental difficulties. Although these problems occasionally do exist alone, there is more often an accompanying maternal, genetic, or traumatic condition (Mick, Biederman, Prince, Fischer, & Faraone, 2002; Shenkin, Starr, & Deary, 2004). Inadequate birth weight and gestational age may be the result of a number of different specific developmental difficulties, either in combination or operating singly. Although some infants with gestational age deficiencies exhibit a "catch-up" growth spurt after birth, a significant portion do not who experience serious difficulties including intellectual disabilities (Akisu et al., 2004; Shenkin et al., 2004). Human development at this early stage is an extremely fragile and delicate process.

Babies delivered before the 38th week of gestation generally are classified as *preterm;* those born between the 38th and 42nd weeks are referred to as *term;* and those delivered after the 42nd week are known as *postterm* infants. Great progress has been made in infant survival through improved obstetric care, even under difficult circumstances. Approximately 98% of infants born after the 32nd week of gestation now survive. Survival rates diminish substantially, however, for infants born before that time. Birth weight is a second important factor in infant mortality and neurodevelopmental deficits. Depending on the gestational age, an infant may be considered "small for gestational age," "appropriate for gestational age," or "large for gestational age." Current medical care suggests that both gestational age and birth weight should be taken into account. Because it is now possible to estimate the maturity of a newborn by physical signs of maturation, care for the infant can be more adequately geared to the particular needs that occur according to gestational age. Such improved care has led to a dramatic decrease in neonatal mortality in the United States.

Predisposing Factors. Several factors have been identified that are related to low birth weight and inappropriate gestational age (Akisu et al., 2004; Shenkin et al., 2004).

Each of the problems discussed in later sections (on infant chromosomal aberrations, maternal-infant interaction problems, and early pregnancy trauma) can be associated with early termination of pregnancy. But several other conditions also appear to lead to early pregnancy termination and inadequate birth weight.

A mother's age and pregnancy history are significant factors in risks to the fetus. Mothers under age 20 or over 35 are more likely to suffer early pregnancy termination than are women between those ages. Likewise, women who have a history of miscarriages, stillbirths, or premature deliveries tend to have as much as a 30% chance of recurrence. Socioeconomic factors also are related to the incidence of preterm and low gestational weight infants and those at risk for intellectual disabilities (Shenkin et al., 2004).

Premature birth rates have also been associated with ethnicity, although this factor is probably more closely aligned with extremes of socioeconomic status (wealth, poverty) than with ethnic differences per se (Landry, Miller-Loncar, & Smith, 2002; Stoelhorst et al., 2003). The percentage of infants born prematurely to white Americans is consistently about half the percentage born prematurely to nonwhite Americans. Viewing the extremes of socioeconomic status more specifically, 51% of all nonwhite (who have lower incomes as a group) births have complications, whereas only 5% of white upper-class births are so affected (Gelfand & Drew, 2003).

Mothers who have had multiple pregnancies account for a high percentage of infants born with low gestational age and birth weight and their concomitant problems. The reasons are complex and numerous, mainly including difficulties of placental problems that lead to ineffective transfer of nutrients across the placenta late in pregnancy and hence to fetal malnutrition. Labor and delivery often commence before term, and the infant is usually small for gestational age. Placental problems are not clearly understood and, when no other cause can be identified, often are attributed to inadequate intrauterine growth. Placental insufficiency implies an impaired exchange between mother and fetus through the placenta. Several well-defined placental lesions are associated with fetal and infant disorders (e.g., blockage of fetal vessels in the placenta, early placenta separation, a single umbilical artery).

Another factor that has long been associated with inadequate growth during fetal life is maternal smoking (Choo, Huestis, Schroeder, Shin, & Jones, 2004; Rauh et al., 2004). Pregnant mothers who smoke more than a pack of cigarettes daily tend to have infants who are growth retarded substantially more often than pregnant mothers who do not smoke (Wang et al., 2002). The precise reasons for this difference have not yet been completely delineated, although evidence suggests two probable factors: (a) smoking mothers tend to eat less, and (b) the vascular constriction caused by smoking restricts uterine blood flow. Other related factors, however, may be as important as the actual problem of maternal smoking. Recent literature raises some research methods questions, and suggests that additional study is needed on several elements related to smoking (Klerman, 2004). It remains clear, however, that there is risk involved in maternal smoking, regardless of the specific manner in which the effect occurs.

Eye on Technology

Spina bifida is a condition where the neural tube forming the spine does not close properly or grows in some abnormal fashion. This may leave the nervous system exposed or even permit it to grow in a way that does not appropriately complete the circuitry. In some cases this can be seen in a prenatal radiological scan such as shown in the sonogram. The arrow points to an abnormal widening of the spine area where the neural tube has failed to close.

Source: Courtesy of the Medical Radiology Program at the University of Western Ontario, http://www.med.uwo.ca/ume/radiology/year3/OBGYN.

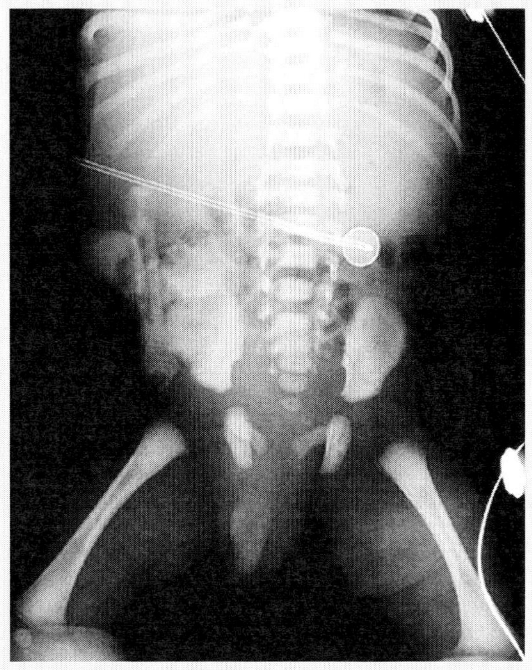

Advancing technology is very useful in determining developmental problems.

Alcohol consumption during pregnancy can seriously injure the fetus. In its most severe form, alcohol-induced fetal injury is known as **fetal alcohol syndrome**. Some problems linked to fetal alcohol syndrome are facial abnormalities, cardiac defects, various cognitive deficits, neurological abnormalities, autism, behavioral deficits, and intellectual disabilities. Even moderate alcohol consumption by pregnant women can result in fetal problems, although the exact amounts and risk have not been well established. It is clear, however, that alcohol consumption during pregnancy can cause decrements in measured intelligence, and fetal alcohol syndrome is associated with specific memory impairments and verbal fluency (Cohen-Kerem & Koren, 2003; Cook & Savva, 2004). Cases in which less severe damage results are now being recognized as **fetal alcohol effect**, and children who suffer from it exhibit milder but clearly evident forms of developmental problems (Burd, Klug, Martsolf, & Kerbeshian, 2003; French, 2004). The effect of maternal alcohol consumption has been recognized for nearly a century, although research on the problem was rather scarce, and fetal alcohol syndrome was first described only in the early 1970s.

Maternal nutrition is crucial to the developing fetus.

Neurological development during the prenatal period is obviously crucial to the health and well-being of the fetus. Risk factors can emerge from inherited or environmental sources, creating potential for physical and cognitive hazards (AAMR, 2002; IASSID, 2005). In some cases the development does not proceed properly and may result in intellectual disabilities. Prenatal assessment may show such developmental problems as that discussed in the Eye on Technology feature.

Maternal nutrition is another incompletely understood factor, although evidence thus far has indicated it is very important to fetal health (Gelfand & Drew, 2003; Leavitt, Tonniges, & Rogers, 2003). Many families who eat poorly belong to less affluent socioeconomic groups, and the dietary practices of a subculture often influence them. Thus, it seems difficult to put a finger on the factors in this complex set of interacting variables that have contributed primarily to increased rates of low-birth-weight and gestational-age problems. A pregnant woman has greater nutritional requirements than a nonpregnant woman. For example, caloric requirements increase by about 300 calories per day during the third trimester, which may result in about a 25-pound maternal weight gain. Additionally, both the protein and calcium requirements of a pregnant mother increase. Maternal malnutrition, which often reflects a lifelong state of inadequacy, has been implicated in damaging the fetus, particularly the fetal central nervous system. Such findings are difficult to evaluate and substantiate, however, because the direct transfer of nutrients to the fetus cannot be examined nor can the fetus' exact nutritional requirements be determined.

Associated Problems. Newborns at risk, especially those with inadequate birth weight and gestational age, tend to be susceptible to serious stress after birth. Problems are primarily complications of respiratory and cardiac failure, infection, and nutritional disorders. They account for many of the conditions associated with birth-weight and gestational-age inadequacies (e.g., Shenkin et al., 2004; Vicari, Caravale, Carlesimo, Casadei, & Allemand, 2004).

Respiratory and cardiac difficulties lead to serious interference with the delivery of oxygen to the developing fetal tissues. The central nervous system is particularly vulnerable, for even though a newborn can tolerate longer periods of anoxia (low oxygen level) than can an adult, a continuing lower level of oxygen to the tissues interferes with critical development occurring during the preterm period. Central nervous system tissue cells are still developing until about the 44th week after fertilization, and the tissue depends on oxygen for adequate development. An infant who is born at risk before term and who develops such oxygen delivery interference is particularly jeopardized with respect to developing adequate neural tissue, although the relationship between such interference and future development is not yet fully understood. With continuing improvements in neonatal care, however, including prevention of respiratory and cardiac complications and improved care for the infant with these complications, medical personnel anticipate reducing the serious neurological impact of prematurity.

Infection represents another serious complication for infants with low-birth-weight or gestational-age problems. The fetus and the preterm infant are extremely susceptible to infection from organisms that ordinarily do not cause illness for older individuals, and infants have few physiological mechanisms with which to combat infection. An infection that begins in the skin can progress rapidly to serious illness—pneumonia, septicemia (widespread infection of the blood), or meningitis (infection of the central nervous system). And because an infant does not exhibit the usual signs of infection—for example, fever—diagnosing an infection may be difficult or impossible until it has become serious. Infection of the central nervous system in particular leads to grave and permanent consequences, affecting the child's neurological capacity in later life.

Nutrition and oxygen intake are significant problems for infants of low birth weight and inadequate gestational age. Such infants miss the optimal nutritional source of the mother through the placenta and suffer from inadequate intake of basic metabolic nutrients. Particularly important during the last few months of gestation is the supply of glucose, proteins, and oxygen through the placenta. These materials nourish all growing tissues, particularly those of the central nervous system. Central nervous system tissue depends on each of these nutrients not only for growth and development but also for survival. When an infant is born with fetal malnutrition from placental insufficiency, nutrition to help the child recuperate must be incorporated into the routine care. Oxygen administration is most complicated for infants of low birth weight or inadequate gestational age because transfer of the ambient oxygen across the lung-blood barrier cannot be measured directly. An infant may be underoxygenated while receiving large percentages of oxygen or be overoxygenated while receiving relatively low concentrations of oxygen. Excessive oxygenation causes damage to the retina of the eye and, eventually, blindness, a process known as *retrolental fibroplasia.*

Psychological and Educational Impact. Precise determination of the psychological and educational impact of inadequate birth weight and gestational age has been difficult. Part of the problem is separating these influences from the confounding variables of low socioeconomic status and racial minority groups, which consistently have more births in this category. Groups in which greater numbers of infants are born with gestational-age and birth-weight problems also have a higher percentage of educational and psychological problems among their young children (Gelfand & Drew, 2003; Hardman, Drew, & Egan, 2006). Comparison of investigations is difficult because of varying definitions of prematurity, low birth weight, and gestational age. Findings of long-term studies, which are necessary in order to determine ultimate educational impact, are often outdated by the time the data can be collected. That is, by the time a child who was born prematurely reaches 6 years of age or older, medical and nursing care for preterm infants will have progressed so much that the findings are not germane for infants born several years earlier. For example, 20 years ago, little was known about the administration of oxygen to preterm infants for the treatment of lung disorders or the prevention of anoxia. Today, great advances have been made in these and related areas, so most infants cared for in a high-risk specialty center receive optimal oxygenation of body tissues throughout the critical period of instability. It is hoped, therefore, that the seriously detrimental effects of anoxia, which may have caused many of the psychological and educational problems reported for children born in the previous two or three decades, can be offset.

Research has generally shown a number of developmental difficulty areas associated with low birth weight and prematurity (Akisu et al., 2004; Mick et al., 2002; Shenkin et al., 2004). General findings support the conclusion that premature youngsters are a high-risk group in several areas. In some cases, it appears that effects may be long term, although this is not universal; in certain circumstances, early risk appears reversible, and intervention may be rather successful. Evidence has accumulated over time that low birth weight and gestational age present substantial difficulty and are related to intellectual disabilities.

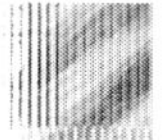

Core Concept

Various types of interactions between the mother and the unborn fetus can cause damage resulting in intellectual disabilities.

Influences from Maternal-Fetal Interaction. Several abnormal maternal-fetal interactions have serious consequences for the infant. Infants of diabetic mothers, for example, are always high-risk babies because of their excessive birth weight for gestational age and their usually low gestational age. Physical anomalies are also more common among infants of diabetic mothers, and the infants are prone to several serious illnesses during the neonatal period—for example, lung disorders, seizures, hypoglycemia (low blood glucose), and hyperbilirubinemia (resulting in jaundice). The mother's diabetic condition places the child at serious risk from several standpoints. The incidence of neurological impact is largely dependent on the severity of the maternal diabetes and the neonatal course, including **gestational age** and complications during this period.

The problem of maternal-fetal Rh-factor incompatibility has a more direct effect on the infant's neurological capacity. In this instance, the mother has a negative Rh blood factor and the infant a positive Rh factor. The mother reacts to the infant's positive factor by developing antibodies that destroy the infant's blood cells, leading to serious consequences during fetal life and the neonatal period. The infant's condition is known as **erythroblastosis fetalis.** The higher the level of antibodies in the mother's blood, the more serious the effect on the fetus. In the most severe form, known as fetal hydrops, the fetus develops severe anemia, enlargement of the heart, liver, and spleen, and deterioration of the body tissues. In most cases, the fetus dies during the late second or early third trimester and is stillborn. If the child is born alive, survival is unlikely. A moderate form of erythroblastosis fetalis, known as icterus gravis, occurs more frequently because, in many instances, the infant's delivery is induced before term to prevent progression of the disease to the more severe form. When this preventive measure occurs, an infant is placed in the disadvantageous position of being delivered preterm, but the hazards are less than those of a more severe form of erythroblastosis fetalis. Such an infant, in addition to low gestational age, may be of low birth weight because of the condition's effect in utero. The infant is typically anemic, jaundiced, and has an enlarged spleen and liver. The high level of bilirubin, occurring from the metabolism of red blood cells, accounts for the jaundice and for any central nervous system damage. As the bilirubin level rises rapidly, adequate excretion cannot occur, and molecules enter the skin tissue, with a toxic effect known as kernicterus. If the infant survives the first week of life, outlook for survival is good. The possibility of impact on the neurological system, however, depends on the severity of the hyperbilirubinemia and accompanying illnesses occurring during the neonatal period. When the blood factor incompatibility effects are minimal, as is usual for the first or second infants of most Rh-negative mothers, neonatal problems are minimal and no neurological impacts are evident. Research on various aspects of the Rh factor continues, including considerable work on prevention (Berk, 2005).

Core Concept

Fetal damage causing reduced mental functioning may occur from such factors as maternal infection and drug ingestion.

Trauma During Early Pregnancy. A variety of influences can result in trauma to the fetus during the first trimester, including drug or chemical ingestion and maternal infection. The teratogenic effects of such exposures are poorly understood, but it is known that although the exact effect of most teratogens is not specified, the timing of exposure probably leads to specific kinds of anomalies. Thus, when a mother contracts rubella during the first trimester of pregnancy, resulting anomalies probably are related more to the timing of fetal exposure than to the specific effects of the virus. Teratogenic effects on the fetus include intrauterine growth retardation, central nervous system infection, microcephaly, congenital heart disease, sensorineural deafness, cataracts and/or glaucoma, and anomalies of the skin. There is a wide range of severity and variability in the occurrence of each possible condition. Again, range of severity probably is related to the timing of the infection, as well as to the possible individual susceptibility of a particular mother and fetus to the effects of the infection. The infant is likely to have a number of physical, behavioral, and intellectual disabilities.

Perinatal and Postnatal Causation

A variety of physical traumas and developmental deviations may result in intellectual disabilities. This section focuses on influences that occur following prenatal development, during what is termed the perinatal and postnatal periods. As we address this time we begin with influences that may place a baby at risk during the birth process.

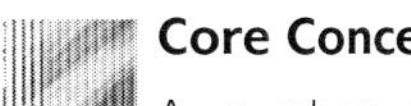

Core Concept

A number of problems during the delivery of a baby may cause damage that results in intellectual disabilities.

The Birth Process. The birth process has long been characterized as an extremely traumatic event in the life of the human organism. Birth trauma has been described as the basis for many psychological problems. Early proponents of the psychoanalytical school attributed a great deal of later life anxiety to the separation shock felt at birth. A variety of other phenomena, such as the content of adult dreams, have been thought, at times, to reflect birth trauma. Although there is little doubt that birth is a stressful occurrence, recent thinking places much more emphasis on its physical than its psychoanalytical aspects. From a physical trauma perspective, abnormal birth processes were a major source of later physical and mental difficulties during the early part of the 20th century. However, improvements in obstetrical procedures and practices have drastically reduced such trauma as we enter the 21st century (Berk, 2005; Cook & Cook, 2005).

Chapter 5 outlines briefly the sequence of events that occur during the birth of a baby. Although the birth process is a stressful time, danger is minimal if the baby is positioned head first, facing downward, and if the mother's pelvic opening is adequate for the child. This description assumes, of course, that fetal development has progressed without mishap to this point. Two general types of problems during birth can result in intellectual disabilities: (a) physical trauma or mechanical injury and (b) anoxia or asphyxia. The first is almost self-explanatory. Physical trauma or mechanical injury refers to some occurrence during birth that injures or damages the baby so as to impair mental functioning (Berk, 2005). In anoxia or asphyxia, the baby is deprived of an adequate oxygen supply for a period long enough to cause brain damage, reducing mental functioning and contributing to other disorders (Brenner, 2003; Shah, Al-Adawi, Dorvlo, & Burke, 2004). Many conditions can be responsible. Although these problems are given different labels and appear to be quite dissimilar, they frequently are interrelated.

It has been mentioned that the danger of birth injury is relatively low if the fetus is positioned correctly. When labor begins, the most favorable position is head first and facing toward the mother's back. Other fetal positions are considered abnormal and can cause numerous problems, depending on the situation. Both mechanical injury and anoxia can result from abnormal fetal presentation.

The breech presentation represents one widely recognized abnormal position. Breech presentation occurs when the buttocks, rather than the head, present first. Figure 6–2 illustrates a breech presentation and can be compared with the more normal presentation illustrated earlier in Chapter 5, Figure 5–3. Physicians are becoming increasingly reluctant to deliver babies in breech position through the birth canal. Except when the delivery is conducted by extremely skilled personnel, the danger to the baby is substantial. More and more frequently, a baby lying breech within the uterus is delivered by cesarean section, which involves abdominal surgery and extraction of the baby through the uterine wall.

A number of difficulties are encountered in breech birth if delivery is executed through the birth canal. Because the head presents last, it reaches the pelvic girdle (the bony hip structure of the mother) during the later, more advanced stages of labor. Contractions are occurring rapidly at this point, and the head does not have an opportunity to proceed through the slower molding process possible earlier in labor. Additionally, the molding may occur in an abnormal and damaging fashion because the skull is receiving pressure in an atypical manner (Berk, 2005; Cook & Cook, 2005).

The abnormal pressure generated in a breech birth can result in mechanical injury to the brain matter in at least two general ways. In one way, because the skull is still quite soft, rapid compression, which crushes a portion of the brain, can cause an injury. Such damage is less likely in normal presentation because the skull is molded more gently, permitting protective fluid to absorb the pressure. In a second way, the rapid pressure and shifting of cranial bones may be severe enough to damage the

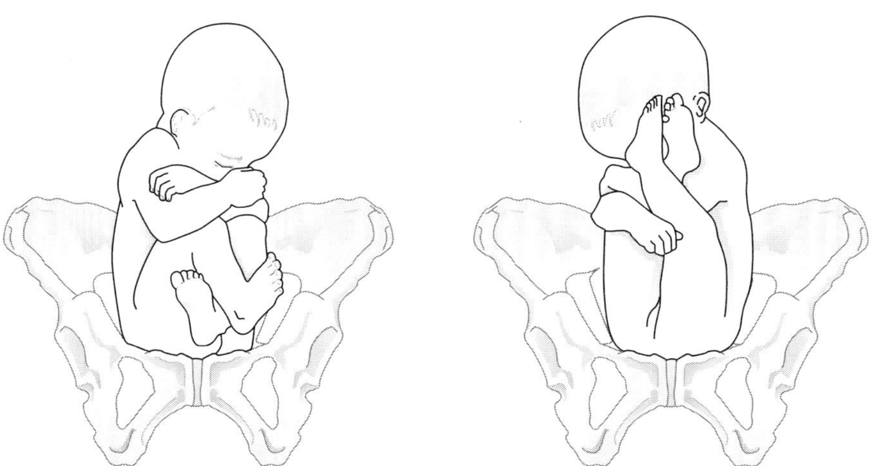

Figure 6–2
Examples of Breech Fetal Position

Source: From *Childbirth: Family Centered Nursing* (3rd ed.) by J. Iorio, 1975, St. Louis: Mosby. Copyright 1975 by the C. V. Mosby Co. Reprinted by permission.

circulatory system around the brain and lead to a hemorrhage in the skull, which, in turn, damages brain tissue.

Fetal anoxia may occur in a breech delivery. Because the skull is the last part of the body delivered, the baby must depend entirely on the umbilical cord as a source of oxygen until birth is complete. But the positioning can make the cord too short to remain attached while the head is expelled. In this case, the placenta can become partially or completely detached while the baby's head is still in the birth canal. This separation, of course, eliminates the oxygen supply, and oxygen deprivation can happen if delivery is not completed quickly. Severe tissue damage can result if the head is not expelled and oxygen supplied through the baby's lungs. This possibility presents an extremely serious problem if the head becomes lodged in the pelvic girdle, preventing or substantially slowing progress down the birth canal. Anoxia may occur even if the cord is long enough to remain attached throughout delivery. We already have noted that the head is the tightest fit for the baby moving through the pelvic girdle. At the beginning of delivery, a section of the umbilical cord is necessarily drawn through. Depending on how tightly the skull fits into the bony pelvic structure, the cord can become pinched and the oxygen supply shut off. If this state lasts long (as in the situation of the lodged skull noted earlier), an anoxic condition will result just as if the cord had been cut. These descriptions are only a brief look at the difficulties of breech delivery and how they can cause damaged tissue and reduced mental functioning. Such problems, as well as numerous variations, are the reason why cesarean delivery is favored in breech presentations.

Another abnormal fetal position that presents serious difficulty is the transverse position, illustrated in Figure 6–3. In this presentation, the fetus lies across the birth canal. All of the injury problems noted with the breech position are potential difficulties with this presentation, depending on how delivery proceeds, and a multitude of other problems face the attending physician (Beck, 2004; Shorten, Donsante, & Shorten, 2002; Tolcos et al., 2003). If it is possible to rotate the fetus safely, then delivery through the birth canal may be attempted. This is particularly true if the baby can be moved into a normal or nearly normal head-down position. If the fetus cannot be satisfactorily rotated, a cesarean section is performed.

Abnormalities of fetal presentation can cause many difficulties during birth. Such problems may result in reduced mental functioning because of mechanical injury or anoxia or both. Abnormal presentation, however, is not the only type of problem to occur during the birth process. The initial stages of labor are important for several reasons. As the fetus proceeds into the birth canal, the pelvic girdle stretches. With a normally positioned fetus, the head also is molded to permit passage through the bony pelvic structure. This process occurs during early labor, when uterine contractions are less intense and less frequent than they later become. Consequently, normal molding and stretching occur without sufficient stress to cause injury to the baby. Molding and stretching take time. Delivery of a baby after a labor of less than about 2 hours is known as **precipitous birth** and causes considerable concern about the adequacy of time for gentle skull molding. Precipitous birth increases the risk of tissue damage and increases the probability of intellectual disabilities.

Figure 6–3
An Example of Transverse Fetal Position

Source: From *Childbirth: Family Centered Nursing* (3rd ed.) by J. Iorio, 1975, St. Louis: Mosby. Copyright 1975 by the C. V. Mosby Co. Reprinted by permission.

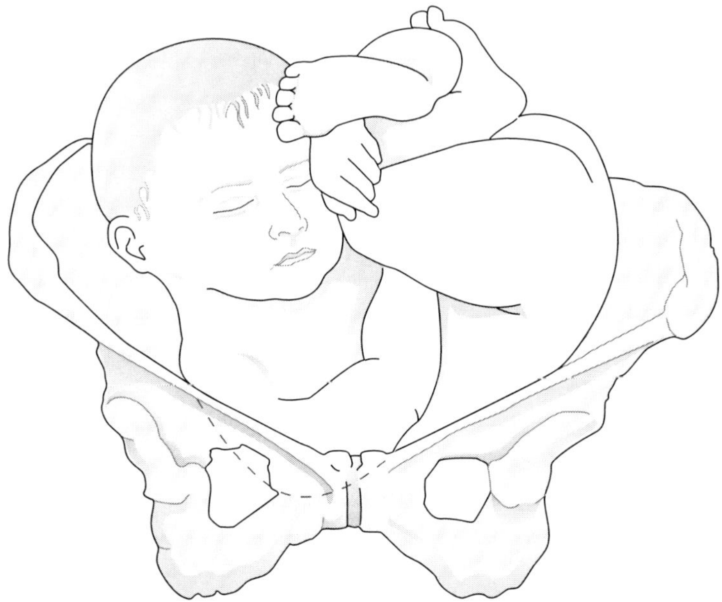

Time also may be a problem at the other end of the continuum—when labor is unusually prolonged (24 hours or more). Most deliveries do not approach 24 hours in length; 7 to 12 hours is average. A variety of conditions may accompany prolonged labor. Under certain circumstances, the uterine conditions deprive a fetus of oxygen, which after a lengthy labor results in either anoxia or a stillborn baby. This is a particular problem if the membranes have ruptured early and if labor is prolonged without delivery. Additionally, in a long period of advanced labor, the fetal skull is under an unusual amount of pressure, which can lead to intracranial hemorrhage. In either case, the probability of tissue damage and resulting intellectual disabilities substantially increases.

This section briefly reviewed influences and causes of intellectual disabilities occurring at birth. Our examples of conditions are the ones most prevalent, better known, and more easily understood. Even this abbreviated presentation can make readers who have just begun to study intellectual disabilities wonder how a normal birth ever happens, but perspective must be maintained. The vast majority of babies are born normally and are ready for the challenges of the postnatal world.

Postnatal Risk and Causation. Chapter 7 provides details regarding many facets of intellectual disability risks during infancy and early childhood. The current section briefly discusses selected risk factors that may surface during the time immediately after birth. Some of these risk factors, such as abuse and neglect by caregivers, are only recently receiving significant attention in the professional literature and represent areas where research evidence is not yet mature. As mentioned earlier, clear delineation of when one developmental period ends and another begins is, in many cases, arbitrary. Likewise, the risk factors presented here cross time-line boundaries. The current section discusses selected risk factors that may surface during the time immediately after birth. However, many of these risks are also present at other times, and statistics regarding occurrence at various specific ages are currently unclear.

The very young baby is quite vulnerable to various illnesses and disease states. Infections from many of the typical child sicknesses may have a more profound impact on the newborn simply because he or she is so fragile and just beginning the process of acclimating to the environment outside the womb. Of particular concern are sicknesses that may cause a high fever and damage the neurological system, which is still developing rather rapidly. Likewise, the very young baby is vulnerable to ingestion of toxic substances. For example, severe food allergies may result in an accumulation of toxins in the newborn's system and may damage the neurological system; or there may be circumstances in which the mother is being medicated and breast feeding can represent the transmission mechanism for potential toxic substances (e.g., American Academy of Pediatrics Committee on Drugs, 2001; Padgett, 2004; Schulpis et al., 2004). Any of these circumstances may lead to reduced mental functioning and intellectual disabilities, brain injury resulting in other disability states, or even death to the infant.

Accidents that result in neurological injury to a newborn also present significant risks for a child to have a variety of disabilities, including intellectual disabilities. Information from the National Institute of Mental Health indicates that fatal injuries most commonly occur from severe head traumas, shaken baby syndrome, trauma or injury to the abdomen and/or thorax, scalding, drowning, suffocation, and poisoning. These categories of trauma reportedly affect nearly 1 million children in the United States who are identified as substantiated victims of abuse or neglect (National Institute of Mental Health, 2000; Reece, 2004). Although it is currently difficult to narrow the age ranges to our current immediately postnatal focus, it appears that a vast majority of these cases that result in fatalities are youngsters under the age of 5 (Goldberg & Goldberg, 2002; King, MacKay, & Sirnick, 2003). Parents are often identified as the perpetrators of the abuse, followed by other relatives, and nearly two thirds of the total group are female. Many of the triggering events or circumstances relate to caregiver frustration with their very young charges in circumstances like an infant's crying and feeding difficulties.

There are various linkages between the above-noted risk factors and causal agents of intellectual disabilities. Abuse and neglect episodes occur in stressed family situations, with regard to parental stress as well as social and socioeconomic stressors such as poverty, substance abuse, and higher rates of domestic and community violence (Freisthler, 2004; Gelfand & Drew, 2003; Osofsky, 2004). These represent many of the circumstances where higher incidence of intellectual disabilities occurs and certainly high-risk situations for the neonate. However, research efforts and methods directly addressing these very young children remain inadequate. In many areas of the country, analyses of mortality rates for people with intellectual disabilities are inadequate in general and may even be weaker for many at the newborn stage.

PROFESSIONAL INTERVENTION

Core Concept

Many forms of professional intervention can prevent or minimize intellectual disabilities during the prenatal and neonatal periods.

We have examined a few conditions that can result in intellectual disabilities. Intellectual disabilities can be prevented, or at least curtailed in many instances, through various types of professional intervention. Children born at high risk because of inappropriate birth weight or gestational age are frequently predisposed to intellectual disabilities. As we have noted, problems often arise when prenatal care is either inadequate or nonexistent. Inadequacy or lack of prenatal care is often related to lack of financial resources, ignorance, a value system that does not include high regard for prenatal care, inefficient health care plans, or a combination of these factors.

Financial limitations may result in inadequate prenatal dietary intake, lack of necessary drugs and vitamins, and lack of supervision by health care specialists. Many mothers are uneducated about the necessity for prenatal care. Others who are informed do not always incorporate good prenatal care into their value systems, ignoring advice from health care specialists. Government-supported health care programs are frequently overburdened and inadequately staffed. Expectant mothers, frustrated by long waits and impersonal care, may become too discouraged to continue seeking prenatal care. Generally speaking, enhancing the mother's health has positive influences on the unborn child's well-being (Gelfand & Drew, 2003; Shenkin et al., 2004).

Professional intervention can greatly reduce the incidence of high-risk children. Low-income families lacking the financial resources for adequate prenatal care need to be directed to the proper agencies of government-supported health care. In addition,

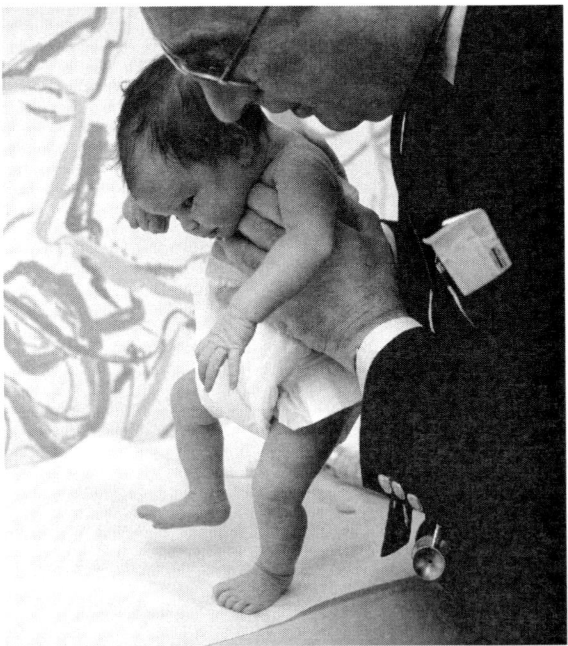

Routine health screening may detect abnormal conditions in developing infants.

to obtain supplemental foods, these families should be directed to various sources, such as agencies that distribute food stamps, maintain surplus food programs, and provide other types of resources to improve the diet of the entire family and especially the expectant mother. Social workers, public health staff, and other individuals working directly with the families can offer this information. It is imperative that families be advised how and where to apply for aid. Supplemental nutrition and care programs significantly improve the chances of many high-risk infants, and benefits may also extend to other family members. Many agencies require extensive documentation to verify financial need. Families should be tutored in the skills necessary to complete application forms, as well as to obtain documentation of financial need. Additionally, the heavy caseloads of physicians in government-supported programs could be much lightened by use of other health care specialists—for example, certified nurses and midwives. The growing corps of pediatric nurse practitioners can help families achieve better postnatal care.

Professional intervention can effectively address some genetic conditions and chromosomal aberrations. Because the majority of Down syndrome cases are of the nondisjunctive or trisomy variety, a high percentage tend to be related to advanced maternal age (Hengstschlager et al., 2004; Simensen et al., 2003). Health care specialists and social workers can encourage couples to have their children at an earlier age, preferably before the prospective mother is 35. Older couples might be urged to exercise birth control methods or at least to be informed of the possible consequences of having children at more advanced ages. Young mothers who have children with Down syndrome should have a chromosomal analysis to determine whether the condition is related to translocation. If a translocation exists, then the likelihood of a genetic or inherited etiology is high. These parents can be counseled and advised of the risks involved in having other children. Under such conditions, sterilization or other forms of birth control may be considered. Amniocentesis can show the existence of a translocation in the fetus, giving the parents a chance to make an informed decision about terminating the pregnancy by means of therapeutic abortion. Issues of abortion and euthanasia remain highly controversial (e.g., Shaw, 2002; Simpson, 2004; Zucker, 2004); we discuss them at length in Chapter 13. Although abortion may or may not be acceptable to the counselor, the counselor should avoid imposing personal values on parents, who are entitled to know what their alternatives are and that the decision regarding the alternatives is rightfully theirs.

Routine screening can diagnose certain disorders early, such as PKU. Screening for PKU can be accomplished by analyses that determine abnormal levels of phenylalanine in the urine. Other assessment also determines abnormal presence of phenylalanine through the examination of the patient's blood. Dietary restrictions often can prevent intellectual disabilities caused by PKU (Channon et al., 2004; Read, 2004). As early as possible, the child is placed on a diet that is essentially free of phenylalanine. Commercially prepared diets include such products as Ketonil and Lofenalac. The earlier a child is placed on a restricted diet, the greater the chances of avoiding intellectual disabilities. Although evidence suggests that a child with PKU may eventually be removed from the restricted diet, the appropriate time is specific to the individual.

Rh-factor incompatibility between mother and fetus can frequently lead to erythroblastosis fetalis and hyperbilirubinemia, which can cause brain damage and intellectual disabilities. Bilirubin levels can be monitored effectively by periodic testing through a variety of procedures that sample the bilirubin level in the amniotic fluid. When the fetus is affected by a high bilirubin content, professional intervention may take the form of induced labor so that the child is born before the bilirubin level reaches a critical point. Some efforts also have been made toward exchange transfusion through a fetal leg extended by surgery, and exchange transfusion immediately after birth has been effective in many instances. One of the most dramatic breakthroughs in medical intervention is the development of intrauterine transfusions. Guided by X-ray films, the surgeon extends a long needle through the mother's abdomen into the peritoneal cavity in the abdomen of the fetus. Blood of the same type as the mother's then is transfused into the fetus. Thus, the incompatibility factor is eliminated, and the fetal blood is immune from the mother's antibodies.

A desensitizing medication known as Rho immune globulin (RhoGAM) was introduced to the general public in 1968. If RhoGAM is injected into the mother within 72 hours of her first child's birth, it desensitizes her body to the Rh-factor antibodies, and she can begin her next pregnancy without the antibodies in her bloodstream. The procedure can be performed after the birth of each child and will largely preclude the development of antibodies, provided it is done faithfully after each birth. Between intrauterine transfusions and desensitization through RhoGAM, few incidents of death or intellectual disabilities resulting from Rh-factor incompatibility should occur in the future.

The first trimester of pregnancy is particularly vulnerable to any type of fetal insult or injury, as indicated earlier. During this period, expectant mothers must exercise extreme caution to avoid any exposure to irradiation, which may affect the fetus, or to infectious diseases. Rubella immunization is now available that can and should eliminate the possibility of widespread rubella epidemics. Parents can greatly reduce the possibility of rubella in their homes by immunizing all children in the family. This comprehensive immunization also protects future mothers from contracting the disease while pregnant.

Prevention of trauma during delivery is the major concern of adequate obstetrical management. Primary concerns include maintaining adequate fetal oxygenation during labor and delivery, ensuring appropriate delivery if a fetus-pelvis size disproportion occurs, and providing adequate observation and care of the infant during the first hour of life. Regional high-risk care centers for mothers provide an extremely high level of specialized care for both mothers and infants known to be in one of the risk categories described. These centers have significantly decreased maternal and infant mortality. One of the most important contributions that can be made in prevention of intellectual disabilities is early identification of at-risk mothers and infants to allow their transfer to a specialized center.

NEW ISSUES AND FUTURE DIRECTIONS

As we enter the 21st century, fetal and neonatal medicine offers both promise and challenge. On the favorable side, knowledge has increased phenomenally during the past several decades. Medical, biological, and genetics research continues to present us with new and exciting knowledge and procedures, seemingly on a daily basis. Prenatal screening and diagnosis now are available for several developmental problems relating to intellectual disabilities (e.g., Parmenter, 2003; Posner, Learman, Gates, Washington, & Kuppermann, 2004). Surgeons have progressed to the point of performing surgery to correct serious defects while the fetus is in utero and experimenting with gene therapy to correct some types of problems. However, our knowledge about many developmental errors is still incomplete and continued investigation is essential.

In many cases, advances in knowledge have been driven by progress in technology, which permits actions scarcely imaginable before; prenatal surgery is one illustration. However, some significant advances such as genetic engineering and gene therapy have occurred in the boundaries of knowledge that offer potential for preventing intellectual disabilities while sometimes treading on unstable ethical ground. Although prevention is clearly desirable, societal questions always arise when techniques have potential for abuse. Genetic mapping and its related technological capability present social and ethical issues that have yet to be fully addressed, let alone resolved (Field & Behrman, 2004).

Also challenging are the ethics of what professionals now can do to maintain life. Medical professionals are, through heroic efforts and applications of new technology, saving the lives of seriously endangered youngsters. One must ask—and many are asking—at what cost with respect to quality of life? In some cases, children are kept alive who would have died in earlier times. But in some instances, these youngsters, though alive, suffer severe mental or physical damage and may exist only in a vegetative state. This outcome raises serious ethical questions about withholding treatment. The questions are not new but remain evident in the literature and are becoming increasingly important as professionals continue to employ rapidly advancing knowledge and technology (Rosenfeld, 2004; Simpson, 2004). Chapter 13 examines in more detail some of these difficult social and ethical issues.

Other challenges presented by society are also significant, and many of them affect the prenatal and neonatal development of children. In some cases, even the widely heralded advances of technology will be sorely tried if professionals intercede and prevent developmental injury. It is well known that the use of certain substances during pregnancy creates risk for the unborn fetus. As indicated earlier, concern for fetal alcohol syndrome has expanded in recent years to include fetal alcohol effect, which causes less severe fetal damage but has observable detrimental effects as the youngster matures (Cook & Savva, 2004; French, 2004). Other substance use and abuse during pregnancy raise new questions almost daily as new drugs are developed and more is learned about diseases. Although drug and alcohol use by high school seniors peaked in the mid-1980s, it remains at a worrisome level. Effects of significant drug and alcohol use in young women during pregnancy are serious (Cook & Savva, 2004; French, 2004). Their babies are often exposed to the substance toxicity and appear to also be subjected to diminished positive parental behaviors, such as attentiveness, responsiveness, and interactions that promote cognitive development. On the brighter side, there are increasing reports of interventions that appear to be promising for both the young mothers and their infants (Gelfand & Drew, 2003).

Serious disease states continue to beset society and have significant implications for the health and development of young children. Perhaps the most publicized in the last part of the 20th century was human immunodeficiency virus (HIV), which is linked to AIDS. Increasing concern is evident regarding HIV and its transmission to the unborn fetus and newborn (Brocklehurst, 2002; Jourdain et al., 2004; Pollard, Savulescu, & Parker, 2004). Certainly there is much that is not known about the effects of HIV on infants, but HIV does appear to result in diminished neuropsychological functioning as physiological aspects of the disease progress. Such circumstances certainly lead the youngster through progressively impaired levels of mental functioning with features that may vary greatly with the individual. Future research is essential to more completely unravel the complexities of this disease and its enormous social and health impacts in our culture.

Core Questions

1. How do different types of Down syndrome occur? Why might they relate to differing levels of intellectual functioning?
2. What factors appear to contribute to inadequate birth weight and gestational-age problems? How do they place an infant at risk for intellectual disabilities? Give examples.
3. Why is maternal-fetal interaction important? How can it contribute to the proper development of a baby and to intellectual disabilities? Give examples.
4. Why is the first trimester of pregnancy so important to the developing fetus? How might maternal infection during this period influence the fetus?
5. Why is fetal positioning important in normal delivery of a baby? How might abnormal presentation cause intellectual disabilities?
6. How might professional intervention with respect to maternal nutrition during the first trimester of pregnancy be important in preventing intellectual disabilities?

Roundtable Discussion

Prenatal development is a very important phase in the life cycle of an individual, and a number of processes can malfunction during this time, to cause intellectual disabilities. Concern has been rising about drug and alcohol use, particularly among young people. Some claim that programs aimed at curtailing abuse of such substances represent moralistic "hype" and an intrusion on the individuals' rights to privacy. Others argue that, morals aside, such programs provide important knowledge related to the health of those involved, as well as to their future children.

In your study group or on your own, examine and reflect on the information this chapter contains about early development and intellectual disabilities. Consider this material in the light of substance abuse and discuss the pros and cons of educational and awareness programs like those you see on television.

Parent and Professional Organization Positions on Key Issues in the Lives of People with Intellectual Disabilities

The inside front cover of this text presents a matrix that includes several key issues in the lives of people with disabilities, the positions of various parent and professional organizations on each issue, and the chapter and page number where the information is addressed. Table 6–1 is a summary of the organizations and key issues addressed in this chapter.

Table 6–1
Key Issues and Organizations Discussed in This Chapter

Organization/Website	Key Issues Addressed	Chapter Heading
American Association on Mental Retardation (http://www.aamr.org)	Genetics and human development Prenatal assessment Parent and health care intervention Prenatal intervention ethics	Genetic Errors Predisposing Factors
International Association for the Scientific Study of Intellectual Disabilities (http://www.iassid.org)	Genetics and human development Prenatal assessment Parent and health care intervention Prenatal intervention ethics	Genetic Errors Predisposing Factors

References

Akisu, M., Balim, Z., Cetin, H., Kosova, B., Yalaz, M., Topcuoglu, N., et al. (2004). The role of angiotensin-converting enzyme and apolipoprotein-E gene polymorphisms on lipid compositions in newborn infants with intrauterine growth restriction. *Early Human Development, 78,* 95–103.

American Academy of Pediatrics Committee on Drugs. (2001). Transfer of drugs and other chemicals into human milk. *Pediatrics, 108,* 776–789.

American Association on Mental Retardation (AAMR). (2002). *Mental retardation: Definition, classification, and systems of supports* (10th ed.). Washington, DC: Author.

American Psychiatric Association (APA). (2000). *Diagnostic and statistical manual of mental disorders* (4th ed., Text Rev.). Washington, DC: Author.

Baieli, S., Pavone, L., Meli, C., Fiumara, A., & Coleman, M. (2003). Autism and phenylketonuria. *Journal of Autism and Developmental Disorders, 33,* 201–204.

Beck, C. T. (2004). Birth trauma: In the eye of the beholder. *Nursing Research, 53,* 28–35.

Berk, L. E. (2005). *Infants and children: Prenatal through middle childhood* (5th ed.). Boston: Allyn & Bacon.

Brenner, R. P. (2003). EEG in encephalopathy and coma. *American Journal of Electroneurodiagnostic Technology, 43,* 164–184.

Brocklehurst, P. (2002). Interventions for reducing the risk of mother-to-child transmission of HIV infection. *Cochrane Database System Review,* (1), CD000102.

Burd, L., Klug, M. G., Martsolf, J. T., & Kerbeshian, J. (2003). Fetal alcohol syndrome: Neuropsychiatric phenomics. *Neurotoxicology and Teratology, 25,* 697–705.

Channon, S., German, E., Cassina, C., & Lee, P. (2004). Executive functioning, memory, and learning in phenylketonuria. *Neuropsychology, 18,* 613–620.

Chapman, D. A., Scott, K. G., & Mason, C. A. (2002). Early risk factors for mental retardation: Role of maternal age and maternal educaton. *American Journal on Mental Retardation, 107,* 46–59.

Choo, R. E., Huestis, M. A., Schroeder, J. R., Shin, A. S., & Jones, H. E. (2004). Neonatal abstinence syndrome in methadone-exposed infants is altered by level of prenatal tobacco exposure. *Drug and Alcohol Dependence, 75,* 253–260.

Cohen-Kerem, R., & Koren, G. (2003). Antioxidants and fetal protection against ethanol teratogenicity I. Review of the experimental data and implications to humans. *Neurotoxicology and Teratology, 25,* 1–9.

Collaer, M. L., Geffner, M. E., Kaufman, F. R., Buckingham, B., & Hines, M. (2002). Cognitive and behavioral characteristics of Turner syndrome: Exploring a role for ovarian hormones in female sexual differentiation. *Hormones and Behavior, 41*(2), 139–155.

Cook, C. C. H., & Savva, S. (2004). Conceiving risk, bearing responsibility: Fetal alcohol syndrome and the diagnosis of moral disorder. *Addiction, 99,* 1069.

Cook, J. L., & Cook, G. (2005). *Child development: Principles and perspectives.* Boston: Allyn & Bacon.

Descheemaeker, M. J., Vogels, A., Govers, V., Borghgraef, M., Willekens, D., Swillen, A., et al. (2002). Prader-Willi syndrome: New insights in the behavioural and psychiatric spectrum. *Journal of Intellectual Disability Research, 46,* 41–50.

Einfeld, S. L. (2004). Behaviour phenotypes of genetic disorders. *Current Opinion in Psychiatry, 17,* 343–348.

Field, M. J., & Behrman, R. E. (2004). *Ethical conduct of clinical research involving children.* Washington, DC: National Academies Press.

Freisthler, B. (2004). A spatial analysis of social disorganization, alcohol access, and rates of child maltreatment in neighborhoods. *Children and Youth Services Review, 26,* 803–819.

French, L. A. (2004). Alcohol and other drug addictions among Native Americans: The movement toward tribal-centric treatment programs. *Alcoholism Treatment Quarterly, 22,* 81–91.

Gelfand, D. M., & Drew, C. J. (2003). *Understanding child behavior disorders* (4th ed.). Belmont, CA: Wadsworth.

Goldberg, K. B., & Goldberg, R. E. (2002). Review of shaken baby syndrome. *Journal of Psychosocial Nursing Mental Health Services, 40*(4), 38–41.

Hamill, L. B. (2003). Going to college: The experiences of a young woman with Down syndrome. *Mental Retardation, 41,* 340–353.

Hardman, M. L., Drew, C. J., & Egan, M. W. (2006). *Human exceptionality: School, community, and family* (8th ed.). Needham Heights, MA: Allyn & Bacon.

Hengstschlager, M., Prusa, A. R., Repa, C., Drahonsky, R., Deutinger, J., Pollak, A., et al. (2004). Patient with partial trisomy 9q and learning disability but no pyloric stenosis. *Developmental Medicine and Child Neurology, 46,* 57–59.

Hines, M. (2004). Psychosexual development in individuals who have female pseudohermaphroditism. *Child and Adolescent Psychiatric Clinics of North America, 13,* 641–656.

Hird, M. J. (2004). Chimerism, mosaicism and the cultural construction of kinship. *Sexualities, 7,* 217–232.

Hodapp, R. M. (2004). Studying interactions, reactions, and perceptions: Can genetic disorders serve as behavioral proxies? *Journal of Autism and Developmental Disorders, 34,* 29–34.

Huijbregts, S. C. J., de Sonneville, L. M. J., Licht, R., va Spronsen, F. J., Verkerk, P. H., & Sergeant, J. A. (2002). Sustained attention and inhibition of cognitive interference in treated phenylketonuria: Associations with concurrent and lifetime phenylalanine concentrations. *Neuropsychologia, 40,* 7–15.

International Association for the Scientific Study of Intellectual Disabilities (IASSID). (2005). *Aging SIRG mission.* Retrieved from http://www.iassid.org

Jourdain, G., Ngo-Giang-Huong, N., Coeur, S. L., Bowonwatanuwong, C., Kantipong, P., Leechanachai, P., et al. (2004). Perinatal-HIV-Prevention-Trial-Group TI: Intrapartum exposure to nevirapine and subsequent maternal responses to Nevirapine-based antiretroviral therapy. *New England Journal of Medicine, 351,* 229–240.

King, W. J., MacKay, M., & Sirnick, A. (2003). Shaken baby syndrome in Canada: Clinical characteristics and outcomes of hospital cases. *Canadian Medical Association Journal, 168,* 155–159.

Klerman, L. V. (2004). Protecting children: Reducing their environmental tobacco smoke exposure. *Nicotine and Tobacco Research, 6* (Suppl. 2), S239–S252.

Landry, S. H., Miller-Loncar, C. L., & Smith, K. E. (2002). Individual difference in the development of social communication competency in very low birthweight children. In D. L. Molfese & V. J. Molfese (Eds.), *Developmental variations in learning: Applications to*

social, executive function, language, and reading skills (pp. 81–112). Mahwah, NJ: Erlbaum.

Leavitt, C. H., Tonniges, T. F., & Rogers, M. F. (2003). Good nutrition: The imperative for positive development. In L. Davidson, L. Bornstein, & M. H. Bornstein (Eds.), *Well-being: Positive development across the life course* (pp. 35–49). Mahwah, NJ, Erlbaum.

Lewis, E., & Kritzinger, A. (2004). Parental experiences of feeding problems in their infants with Down syndrome. *Down Syndrome: Research and Practice, 9,* 45–52.

Mick, E., Biederman, J., Prince, J., Fischer, M. J., & Faraone, S. V. (2002). Impact of low birth weight on attention-deficit-hyperactivity disorder. *Journal of Developmental and Behavioral Pediatrics, 23,* 16–22.

National Institute of Mental Health. (2000, July 24). *Consortium on child and adolescent research.* Retrieved from http://www.nimh.nih.gov/childhp/

Nijhuis-VanderSanden, M. W. G., Eling, P. A. T. M., Van Asseldonk, E. H. F., & Van Galen, G. P. (2004). Decreased movement speed in girls with Turner Syndrome: A problem in motor planning or muscle initiation? *Journal of Clinical and Experimental Neuropsychology, 26,* 795–816.

Osofsky, J. D. (2004). Community outreach for children exposed to violence. *Infant Mental Health Journal, 25,* 478–487.

Padgett, D. A. (2004). Maternal vaccination: Is it effective in the face of stress? *Brain, Behavior and Immunity, 18,* 13–14.

Parmenter, T. R. (2003). The future of the disabled in liberal society, an ethical analysis—A commentary. *Journal of Intellectual Disability Research, 47,* 561–564.

Pollard, A. J., Savulescu, J., & Parker, M. (2004). Ethics in practice: Eligibility of overseas visitors and people of uncertain residential status for NHS treatment. *British Medical Journal, 329,* 346–349.

Posner, S. F., Learman, L. A., Gates, E. A., Washington, A. E., & Kuppermann, M. (2004). Development of an attitudes measure for prenatal screening in diverse populations. *Social Indicators Research, 65,* 187–206.

Rauh, V. A., Whyatt, R. M., Garfinkel, R., Andrews, H., Hoepner, L., Reyes, A., et al. (2004). Developmental effects of exposure to environmental tobacco smoke and material hardship among inner-city children. *Neurotoxicology and Teratology, 26,* 373–385.

Read, C. Y. (2004). Using the impact of Event Scale to evaluate psychological response to being a phenylketonuria gene carrier. *Journal of Genetic Counseling, 13,* 207–219.

Reece, R. M. (2004). The evidence base for shaken baby syndrome. *British Medical Journal, 328,* 1316–1317.

Rosenfeld, B. (2004). Where do we go from here? In B. Rosenfeld (Ed.), *Assisted suicide and the right to die: The interface of social science, public policy, and medical ethics* (pp. 165–175). Washington, DC: American Psychological Association.

Schulpis, K., Spiropoulos, A., Gavrili, S., Karikas, G., Grigori, C., Vlachos, G., et al. (2004). Maternal-neonatal folate and vitamin B-sub-1-sub-2 serum concentrations in Greeks and in Albanian immigrants. *Journal of Human Nutrition and Dietetics, 17,* 443–448.

Shah, M. K., Al-Adawi, S., Dorvlo, A. S. S., & Burke, D. T. (2004). Functional outcomes following anoxic brain injury: A comparison with traumatic brain injury. *Brain Injury, 18,* 111–117.

Shaw, A. B. (2002). Two challenges to the double effect doctrin: Euthanasia and abortion. *Journal of Medical Ethics, 28,* 102–104.

Shaw-Smith, C., Hogg, S. L., Reading, R., Calvin, J., & Trump, D. (2004). Learning and behavioural difficulties but not microcephaly in three brothers resulting from undiagnosed maternal phenylketonuria. *Child: Care, Health and Development, 30,* 551–555.

Shenkin, S. D., Starr, J. M., & Deary, I J. (2004). Birth weight and cognitive ability in childhood: A systematic review. *Psychological Bulletin, 130,* 989–1013.

Shorten, A., Donsante, J., & Shorten, B. (2002). Birth position, accoucheur, and perineal outcomes: Informing women about choices for vaginal birth. *Birth, 29,* 18–27.

Simensen, R. J., Colby, R. S., & Corning, K. J. (2003). A prenatal counseling conundrum: Mosaic trisomy 16. A case study presenting cognitive functioning and adaptive behavior. *Genetic Counseling, 14,* 331–336.

Simpson, E. (2004). Harms to dignity, bioethics, and the scope of biolaw. *Journal of Palliative Care, 20,* 185–192.

Singer, L. T., Siegel, A. C., Lewis, B., Hawkins, S., Yamashita, T., & Baley, J. (2001). Preschool language outcomes of children with history of bronchopulmonary dysplasia and very low birth weight. *Journal of Developmental and Behavioral Pediatrics, 22,* 19–26.

Stoelhorst, G. M. S. J., Rijken, M., Martens, S. E., van-Zwieten, P. H. T., Feenstra, J., Zwinderman, A. H., et al. (2003). Developmental outcome at 18 and 24 months of age in very preterm children: A cohort study from 1996–1997. *Early Human Development, 72,* 83–95.

Tolcos, M., Harding, R., Loeliger, M., Breen, S., Cock, M., Duncan, J., et al. (2003). The fetal brainstem is relatively spared from injury following intrauterine hypoxemia. *Developmental Brain Research, 143,* 73–81.

Vicari, S., Caravale, B., Carlesimo, G. A., Casadei, A. M., & Allemand, F. (2004). Spatial working memory deficits in children at ages 3–4 who were low birth weight, preterm infants. *Neuropsychology, 18,* 673–678.

Wang, X., Zuckerman, B., Pearson, C., Kaufman, G., Chen, C., Wang, G., et al. (2002). Maternal cigarette smoking, metabolic gene polymorphism, and infant birth weight. *Journal of the American Medical Association, 287*(2), 195–202.

Welsh, M. C. (2002). Developmental and clinical variations in executive functions. In D. L. Molfese & V. J. Molfese (Eds.), *Developmental variations in learning: Applications to social, executive function, language, and reading skills* (pp. 139–185). Mahwah, NJ: Erlbaum.

Williams, C., Alderson, P., & Farsides, B. (2002). "Drawing the line" in prenatal screening and testing: Health practitioners' discussions. *Health, Risk and Society, 4,* 61–75.

Yoshida, Y., Yamada, T., & Sakaguchi, H. (2003). Activation of protein kinase C by the error signal from a basal ganglia-forebrain circuit in the zebra finch song control nuclei. *Neuroreport: For Rapid Communication of Neuroscience Research, 14,* 645–649.

Zucker, A. (2004). Law and ethics. *Death Studies, 28,* 803–806.

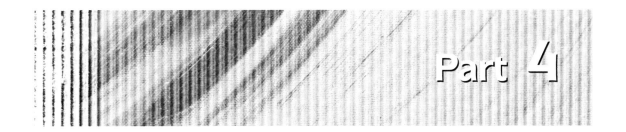

Intellectual Disabilities: Preschool and School Years

Chapter 7

Infancy and Early Childhood

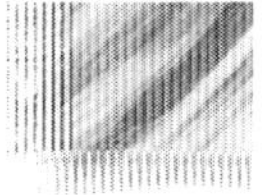

Chapter Preview

Chapters 5 and 6 examined many of the complexities of development during pregnancy and through the birth process. This chapter turns to the crucial and exciting developments after the child is born and during his or her early years. At the completion of this chapter, you will have a better understanding of some of the developmental processes for infants and young children with intellectual disabilities. You will encounter:

- How physiological and cognitive growth are important and how they interact during infancy and early childhood as well as how intellectual disabilities may emerge.
- The importance of the young child's environment as he or she develops.
- How developmental delays in social and emotional functioning can have a serious impact on a young child's ability to adapt and chances to succeed in school.

Helen and Joey

For the first time in the last 9 months Helen felt a small glimmer of hope. She was sitting at her computer, looking at a Web page that made some sense to her and talked about things that seemed to be pressing on her brain from all sides. Nine months ago her son was born and what should have been a time of joy had turned to misery. Joey had Down syndrome and that was obvious immediately. Tests had confirmed what Helen already knew. Since that time she had experienced a flood of feelings including guilt, shame, confusion about what she should do, and anger. Her husband of 5 years had left, and she felt totally alone with no guidance or direction.

Now she was looking at her computer screen at a website for families, for new parents of children with disabilities. Right there on the screen was written all the things she had felt, and where there was help available for her—help on how to survive, how to find help, ideas about what to do, and other things she desperately needed. Helen knew that this early period of life was important, that part she remembered from her college psychology class. But what *to do was a different story. She clicked on to the calendar page showing where to get help and reached for her pocket calendar. This was the first time in 9 months that she felt like doing anything.*

- *What are your thoughts regarding Joey's future? Because he has Down syndrome will he always be relegated to school in separate programs or is it possible for him to be included in general classes with his age-mates?*
- *What do you tell Helen as a new mom that is also a new single parent? Clearly she has her hands full, but what kinds of resources might be available to her?*

Helen's memory regarding the importance of this early development is generally correct although the details may be a little foggy given what she has been through. Growth and development during infancy and early childhood are vital to an individual's well-being. These are critical years for all children, and the importance of this time in a child's life cannot be overemphasized. Experiences during infancy and early childhood can promote the attainment of optimal development, or they can delay or even stifle learning. For some children, intellectual functioning may be enhanced so much that they function in the upper ranges of ability. For other children, experiences may detract from the developmental process in ways that permanently lower functioning. The effects of environmental influences during infancy and early childhood are often more lasting and pervasive than during any later phase of the life cycle (Berk, 2005; Broderick & Blewitt, 2003; Lightfoot, Lalonde, & Chandler, 2004). It is not surprising that this period causes stress and a variety of emotional responses in the families of children with intellectual disabilities like Joey. Seeking reassurance and help, Helen found a local resource through her home computer: Colorado Resources for Young Children and Families (http://www.rycf.org). She also found resource ideas on Web pages for the National Down Syndrome Congress (http://www.ndsccenter.org) and the National Down Syndrome Society (http://www.ndss.org). The National Down Syndrome Congress will provide Helen with new parent packets and facts about Down syndrome as well as a newsletter every other month (National Down Syndrome Congress, 2005). The National Down Syndrome Society is the largest national organization advocating for Down syndrome and has a hotline (National Down Syndrome Society, 2005). Interactions with parents are very important for professionals as suggested in the Tips for Professionals feature.

Helen will relearn the importance of early development—material covered in her college classwork. This time it will have new meaning from a different perspective, one of a parent whose child has intellectual disabilities. This time it will be very personal.

This chapter addresses development during infancy and preschool years and environmental influences that promote or detract from learning. We examine four broad areas of development: physical, language, cognitive, and psychosocial. Although interrelated, these also represent distinct areas of development that have been the focus of considerable research. Each is critical to a child's ability to learn. Pertinent research is reviewed on expected traits of development, traits evident in children with intellectual disabilities, and environmental influences.

PHYSICAL DEVELOPMENT

Core Concept

Physiological growth during infancy and early childhood plays a central role in the general development of an individual, laying the foundation for future learning.

Several major systems are involved in a discussion of physical development. Most often considered are the gastrointestinal, renal, endocrine, skeletal, reproductive, neurological, and muscular systems. Each has an important function, although those most closely related to the learning process are the neurological, skeletal, and muscular systems. These three systems are functionally related and occasionally are thought of as one—the neuromotor system. Neurological and motor functions are influenced by important stimuli, and responses are provided by the endocrine system (Garvey et al., 2003; Giegerich, 2002; Van De Graaff, 2002).

Tips for Professionals

Parent Relationships Are Vital to Effective Programming

Many professional organizations have publicly acknowledged parents as important partners in the design and implementation of educational programs. The Council for Exceptional Children has outlined guidelines for professional interactions with parents in their Code of Ethics as follows.

Parent Relationships

Professionals seek to develop relationships with parents based on mutual respect for their roles in achieving benefits for the exceptional person. Special education professionals:

1. Develop effective communication with parents, avoiding technical terminology, using the primary language of the home, and other modes of communication when appropriate.
2. Seek and use parents' knowledge and expertise in planning, conducting, and evaluating special education and related services for persons with exceptionalities.
3. Maintain communications between parents and professionals with appropriate respect for privacy and confidentiality.
4. Extend opportunities for parent education utilizing accurate information and professional methods.
5. Inform parents of the educational rights of their children and of any proposed or actual practices which violate those rights.
6. Recognize and respect cultural diversities which exist in some families with persons with exceptionalities.
7. Recognize that the relationship of home and community environmental conditions affects the behavior and outlook of the exceptional person.

Source: Excerpted from *Code of Ethics for Educators of Persons with Exceptionalities* by Council for Exceptional Children, 1997 Reston, VA: Author.

For the purposes of this text, we examine neuromotor development in order to become familiar with the physical dimensions of learning and the influences of the environment on this facet of development.

Neuromotor Development

Various parts of the neurological system are important to our understanding of early growth and development. The **neurological system** is composed of the brain, spinal cord, and peripheral neurons, including the autonomic system, which is functionally related to the endocrine system. Neurological pathways extend to muscle and skin tissues and provide for transmission of neurological sensations from the environment to the central nervous system. These pathways also serve as a means for neurological control and response between the central nervous system and the muscles, permitting movement and vocalization appropriate to various environmental stimuli. Neurological functioning cannot usually be studied directly, although technology developments continue to dramatically move forward in this area. Indirect investigation often occurs by observing a variety of performance areas and comparing a given child's functioning with age-appropriate levels. Neurological maturation is critical to a child's overall development and plays an important role in cognitive, language, and psychosocial development. More complete attention is given to these areas in later portions of this chapter. In the next section we focus directly on the development of the neuromotor system and examine certain conditions of physical development that can be detected in children with intellectual disabilities.

Head and Brain Characteristics. A child's neurological development and capacity are related to head and brain size. The brain grows very rapidly during the prenatal period. This rapid growth continues after birth; a 2-year-old's brain is approximately 90% of adult brain size. This growth may be assessed indirectly by measuring the head circumference. Normal circumference ranges have been established for each gender at each developmental stage. For example, the mean head circumference for male infants at birth is 34.5 centimeters and reaches 49 centimeters by the age of 2. Female infants have a mean head circumference of 34 centimeters at birth and reach 48 centimeters by the age of 2. Children with head sizes considerably larger or smaller will cause a concern on the part of health care professionals. In most cases, deviations of plus or minus two standard deviations from the expected mean head circumference at any age is enough to warrant concern (recall the bell curve and standard deviation discussion in Chapter 4). If this anomaly occurs, the child must undergo medical testing to determine whether a pathological condition is present that threatens physical health or intellectual functioning. An example of such a condition is microcephaly, in which the head circumference is below the norm by two standard deviations or more. (Children with microcephaly are characterized by several other physical abnormalities and typically have rather severe disabilities.) The child's brain size is limited, and abnormalities of brain tissue formation also may be present. Limited brain size, tissue abnormalities, or both may result from a genetic condition or from brain infections and other environmental circumstances that slow the growth of brain tissue. In either case, the neurological system is seriously impaired, and intellectual disabilities result (Ivanovic et al., 2004; Teicher et al., 2004).

A head circumference significantly larger than expected may also indicate a situation of serious concern. **Hydrocephalus,** for example, is a condition characterized by exceptionally large head size even though the brain may be inadequately developed or normal, depending on the precise cause of the condition. This condition is related to an increase in the amount of cerebrospinal fluid that circulates in the brain cavity and spinal column area. The excess fluid puts increased pressure on surrounding structures and leads to damage of brain tissue and ultimately to intellectual disabilities, regardless of initial capacity.

Brain development occurs rapidly during the early years. Sulci, or convolutions, in the lobes of the brain deepen and become more prominent and numerous during this period. These continue to develop throughout life, but more gradually than during the early years (Berk, 2005). It is thought that the development of sulci reflects processes of learning, memory, and the ability to reason and form conceptualizations. A child with inadequate neuromotor control and function or showing a developmental delay may suffer from some abnormality in brain form or function. However, the problem may not be directly detectable. Some information concerning the size and shape of the brain can be obtained by X-ray or MRI procedures. However, the primary cause of the child's lack of coordination, speaking difficulty, or limited ability to learn cannot usually be identified with certainty as faulty brain tissue.

Myelinization. As discussed in Chapter 5, myelinization is commonly accepted as an important developmental process. Myelinization involves the development of a protective insulating sheath surrounding the brain and neurological pathways. This sheath operates somewhat like the insulation on an electrical wire and allows nerve impulses to travel along the nerve pathway rapidly and without diffusion. The newborn has an incomplete myelin sheath; an incompleteness that accounts for nonspecific reactions to stimuli and a lack of motor coordination. Consequently, an infant may exhibit generalized body movement and crying in response to a painful stimulus to the foot, rather than specific withdrawal of the foot. As with other growth patterns, myelinization proceeds in a cephalocaudal and proximodistal fashion, which provides for the pattern of acquisition of gross-motor control before fine-motor control. By the age of 2, a major portion of the myelin sheath is formed, and the child's motor capacity is relatively mature (Brodsky & Martin, 2002; Carrera, Chervenak, & Kurjak, 2003; Sadler, 2003).

Reflexes and Voluntary Behavior. Reflex behavior is a primitive human response compared to many that are characteristic of general human functioning. Development of reflex behavior is thought to have evolved early in human history out of necessity for protection in a harsh environment. Sophisticated cognitive skills develop later, making possible voluntary action directed toward self-protection. Much of the reflexive behavior of early infancy gradually fades as voluntary control develops through association pathways of the nervous system. Some reflexes persist throughout life, such as the knee jerk, eye blink, and reaction of the eye pupil to light.

During early childhood, voluntary movement becomes predominant for the child who is neurologically healthy, although involuntary movement on one side of the body may mirror voluntary movement on the opposite side. This involuntary mirroring action is pronounced in children who suffer damage to the central nervous system. However, this phenomenon does not suggest damage unless it persists beyond the preschool years or is so pronounced that it interferes with the child's voluntary movements. Predominance of the one-sided voluntary function generally is established fully by the age of 4, and a child typically demonstrates a preference for right or left hand use in performing motor tasks.

Emotions and the Central Nervous System. The limbic system of the brain is located in the central portion of the tissue and surrounds the hypothalamus. This system functions specifically to mediate emotional and temperamental dimensions of behavior. Sensations such as pleasure or discomfort *and the individual meaning* *associated with such experiences, originate* and are stored in this system. Other behaviors related to these areas of functioning include excitement, anger, fear, sleep, and wakefulness. Maturity in these response areas progresses as a young child experiences a wider range of environmental stimuli and exercises more behavioral self-control, as well as control over the behavior of others. The feeling response rules most others in early childhood in terms of determining behavior, indicating that the limbic system is functioning and that associations with voluntary control areas are not fully accomplished. As growth continues and these associations mature, a child becomes more effective in disguising and voluntarily controlling emotional components of behavior.

Sensory Organs and Cranial Nerves. Development and integrity of cranial nerves and specialized sensory organs also play important roles in a young child's general functioning status. These maturational processes are essential to the child's ability to receive stimuli from the environment and integrate them into the perceptual and memory components of the central nervous system. **Cranial nerves** are distinct neural pathways that provide for the specialized sensory function and motor performance of the sensory and other essential organs and surrounding muscle structure. These nerves approach functional maturity by the age of 3 and can be tested by assessing sensory organ functions. Ears and eyes are particularly crucial for receiving stimuli related to learning. Other sensory functions, such as smell, taste, touch, and the sense of movement, however, are also important in providing essential neurological stimulation (Broderick & Blewitt, 2003; Garvey et al., 2003; Lightfoot, Lalonde, & Chandler, 2004).

Optimal functioning levels for taste and smell are reached during infancy. These senses also come under the influence of voluntary control and association with other sensory areas. A young child is able to, and often will, refuse to taste a food that looks unpleasant or that others have made negative comments about. The child is able to respond accurately to the sensation that a taste or smell arouses and learns associations between certain tastes and smells and culturally accepted values. Preferred foods in a child's culture become palatable, and foods that are not acceptable become displeasing. The role of these sensory capacities in terms of learning problems is not currently understood, but it does appear that significant learning stimuli come through these channels.

Hearing is a critical sense in the learning process. Children with hearing loss seem to have more difficulty with learning than children with other types of sensory disturbances. This effect obviously varies substantially, depending on the child and the nature and severity of the deficit (Loots & Devise, 2003; Williams & Rask, 2003). The sense of hearing relies on intact tissue structures between the external ear and the brain cortex, including the important cranial nerves involved in hearing functions. Functional structures of the ear also are related to the sense of balance and movement.

An infant's hearing apparatus is mature at birth except in two areas: (a) myelinization of the cortical auditory pathways beyond the midbrain and (b) resorption of the connective tissue surrounding the ossicles of the middle ear. The infant can hear and also can respond differently to loud noises (by crying) and to soft, soothing sounds (by relaxing and becoming calm). The child's reaction to sound at this stage is characteristic of reactions to most stimuli; it is generalized and involves movements of the entire body. Typically, these movements are of a gross-motor nature and are nonspecific; they tend to be characterized by a thrashing of the arms, body, and legs or by a generalized calming. As myelinization proceeds, the child begins to exhibit an ability to localize sound direction. By the age of 2 to 3 months, the child can respond by turning the head toward the sound (Berk, 2005; Broderick & Blewitt, 2003; Lightfoot, et al., 2004).

An infant does not have fully developed hearing like an adult's, however. Adult-like hearing is not present until about age 7 and involves complex cortical functioning, including the ability to listen, to respond with discrimination, to imitate sounds accurately, and to integrate the meaning of sounds. Identification of hearing loss during the first year of life is vital for maximally effective treatment and maintenance of optimal learning capacity (Guy, Nicholson, Pannu, & Holden, 2003; Van De Graaff, 2002). If a child's hearing loss can be identified at this time, intervention may enhance learning.

Visual acuity is rather limited at birth, although vision is fully developed by about age 6 (Berk, 2005; Cook & Cook, 2005). The newborn can differentiate only generally between light and dark. The development of visual acuity progresses rather rapidly during the neonatal period, however, and by the age of 6 months, an infant generally can recognize objects and people. A capacity to follow movement in the environment also begins to develop during the first months of life, and completely coordinated eye movements should be evident by the sixth month. The preschool child who is unable to see a single object when looking at it with both eyes (binocularity) has a condition known as **amblyopia.** Amblyopia creates some unusual difficulties with regard to a child's perceptual behavior (Jones, Westall, Averbeck, & Abdolell, 2003). Because the child sees two separate, overlapping objects instead of a single, unified perception, he or she begins to block the perception of one eye in order to see a single object through the preferred eye. Lack of use and stimulation of the other eye leads to gradual deterioration of the neural pathways from the eye to the central nervous system. This decline can cause permanent loss of function of the eye if it continues to be unused. The effects of amblyopia illustrate the vital role of adequate stimulation in order for neurological tissue to develop and maintain adequate function.

Integration of incoming visual stimuli with existing neurological functions is very important in early learning. By about 2 to 3 years of age, the child begins to remember and recall visual images. Along with an interest in pictures, the child begins to enjoy producing geometric shapes and figures. These abilities create a readiness to recognize symbols, or to read, which typically appears by the time the child is 4 years old. A further visual discrimination that has important implications for early learning processes is color recognition. For the most part, color recognition is established by the time the child is 5.

Summary. A variety of complex factors contribute to neuromotor developmental advances during early childhood. Growing muscles, practicing of motor skills, continuing organization of associations between established neural pathways, and the establishing of new pathways are only a portion of the developmental process that is under way. During this period, the ability to maintain focal attention, a hallmark of early childhood, also emerges. Incredible gains are evident in cognitive and intellectual functioning, memory, consciousness, and thought. The role of each structure in the nervous system with regard to the various forms of intellectual disabilities is not well understood. It is apparent, however, that an inadequacy in one dimension of the development of the nervous system is typically accompanied by inadequacies in the system generally. Thus, the child who has developmental delays in motor performance during early childhood frequently also exhibits delays in emotional development, language development, and cognitive development, because each of these dimensions of performance depends on the general adequacy of the nervous system (Owens, 2005; Shenkin, Starr, & Deary, 2004). Table 7–1 on pages 202–203 is a summary of selected developmental landmarks during the first 2 years of life in terms of a few motor, psychosocial, and verbal developmental features. It is important to remember that a child who is delayed in one area of development is likely also to exhibit signs of delay in others. The child's behavior may be generally more like that of children who are chronologically younger.

Effects of the Environment

Each of the child's neuromotor capabilities has an optimal time during the developmental cycle for appearance and integration into the system as a whole. The child's development of these specific capabilities during such periods is vulnerable to disruptions that can produce either temporary or permanent problems (e.g., Bendersky, Gambini, Lastella, Bennett, & Lewis, 2003; Berk, 2005). Some of these disruptions result from environmental influences. It is generally agreed that the effects of environmental conditions or stimuli on a young child are great, although the exact influences of many environmental conditions are poorly understood (Gelfand & Drew, 2003; Neiss & Almeida, 2004).

Investigations on the effects of early environmental experience represent important research in the field of intellectual disabilities and behavioral science in general. Studies supporting the importance of early stimuli have not accumulated enough evidence to draw firm conclusions, although certain trends are emerging. For example, extreme environmental deprivation, particularly during early childhood, appears to be a potent unfavorable influence (Fine et al., 2003; MacLean, 2003). Such extreme deprivation can result in pervasive developmental delays and potential intellectual disabilities.

Considerable evidence suggests how sensory deprivation of visual stimuli during early life affects a child. For example, significant delays appear in the development of both motor and cognitive performance in infants' and toddlers who are blind (Fine et al., 2003; Roder, Stock, Bien, Neville, & Rosler, 2003). Such extreme cases are difficult to relate to less severe sensory deprivation that might occur in less stimulating environments. It seems reasonable to expect that a child who lacks an opportunity to experience and practice certain sensorimotor skills will not develop these motor capacities. The effects of deprivation on later development of intellectual functioning, however, remain uncertain. One broadly held belief is that a wealth of sensory stimulation during the first 2 years, regardless of type, should promote favorable development of a child's cognitive and intellectual skills. Some evidence suggests that variety in stimulation is also important in cognitive development (Berk, 2005; Cook & Cook, 2005). Limited environmental stimulation, a lack of systematic or ordered interpretation and mediation, or limited motivation may bring about stimulus deprivation and, with it, limitations in the development of intelligence.

A number of factors prevent a systematic accumulation of data on the effects of deprivation. The ethics of using human subjects clearly and appropriately prevents experimental manipulation of stimulus deprivation in a manner that may harm subjects (Field & Behrman, 2004; Gelfand & Drew, 2003; Street & Luoma, 2002; Zucker, 2003). Occurrences of natural events that result in environmental deprivation are unsystematic and involve such situational variation that investigation of these instances provides data of only limited value. Studies like those on early visual deprivation are few and have become even more so as a result of advances in medical technology. Because of these impediments to studying deprivation, many researchers have turned to the study of stimulus enrichment in an effort to gather evidence about the influence of environmental sensory stimuli on the development of intellectual functioning. One approach to this type of investigation compares the functioning of young children who, as infants, received a natural wealth of sensory stimulation with that of children who were relatively deprived of such environmental stimulation. Although the evidence suggests some differential effect, the data are too global for inflexible conclusions. Even these investigations are not free of difficulties because, in many cases, it is unclear that presence or relative absence of environmental stimuli is the only influential variable.

Some investigators have examined various types of intensive sensory stimulation during the first few years of life (Abromeit, 2003; Bahrick, Lickliter, & Flom, 2004; Malekpour, 2004). Such research has investigated the influences of both visual and auditory stimulation during the early months of life and have demonstrated that controlled stimulation has marked effects on the rate and quality of specific aspects of development. Once again, the question whether such effects are lasting or significant with respect to the quality of future intellectual functioning remains unanswered in a clear fashion. Some results suggest that long-term effects are promising. One project generating considerable interest is the Carolina Abecedarian Project. This research involved comprehensive intervention in a variety of family environmental areas and also included direct infant stimulation (Campbell, Ramey, Pungello, Sparling, & Miller-Johnson, 2002; Ramey, Ramey, Lanzi, & Cotton, 2002). As with most longitudinal research of this type, results continue to emerge. However, the findings appear quite favorable regarding improvements in intellectual and social functioning. Additional investigation clearly is needed in this area.

As additional research is conducted on nervous system stimulation it may be possible to draw more accurate conclusions regarding relationships of system development and later intellectual functioning. Such information is vital in assessing the vulnerability of the nervous system to the environment during the first 2 years of life. At this time, we can safely conclude that sensory stimulation is beneficial in affecting the rate and perhaps the quality of all traits that depend on development of the neuromotor system.

Table 7–1
Selected Developmental Landmarks

	Months							
	1	2	3	4	5	6	7	8
Motor								
Sitting							Supported	
Walking								
Sucking								
Standing								
Crawling								
Creeping								
Bowel control								
Bladder control								
Head: prone		Lifts head						
sitting			Bobs					
Psychosocial								
Smiling				Spontaneous			Mirror image	
Reacting to others			Follows moving people				Discriminates	
Feeding					Solids			Holds
Socialization								
Verbal								
Crying								
Cooing								
Babbling, resembles one syllable							Tone	
Imitation of word sounds								
Some word understanding (dada, mamma)								
Word repertoire								

Table 7–1
Continued

Months															
9	10	11	12	13	14	15	16	17	18	19	20	21	22	23	24
							Without support								
		Supported						Without support							
			(Utility decreases with use of other feeding means)												
Supported							Without support								
									(Sex differences)						
		Sustains raised head													
			Steady												
Strangers							Waves good-bye								
Bottle		Cup					Partial self-feed								
Forms primary social relations and emotional attachments															
Differentiation															
							3 to 50 words					50 + begin phrases			

Professional and Parental Intervention

Core Concept

Early intervention is most effective when there are partnerships between professionals and parents.

Professionals working with infants and young children face multiple tasks in providing services (National Down Syndrome Congress, 2005; National Down Syndrome Society, 2005). Minimally, these include the identification of children with developmental delays, prevention of the occurrence of delays when possible, and assistance to family and child when a developmental problem is present. Health care workers are the professionals most often in contact with young children, particularly physicians and public health nurses. These individuals frequently depend on the aid and cooperation of social workers, nutritionists, and dietitians to assist in providing comprehensive services to families with multiple problems and needs.

Screening is a very important process in the overall evaluation scheme (see Chapter 3) and is crucial for identifying children who may be exhibiting delays in rate and quality of development. Routine health care is essential for the child's well-being and development. During the first 6 months of life, a youngster should receive monthly checkups, with intervals increasing gradually until the child is seen annually. Health care visits should include an assessment of the child's behavior at home since the last visit, health status, and eating patterns. Also, physical systems should be evaluated, including the neuromotor system, to determine whether development is adequate, and behavioral observations should be made to confirm the appearance of behavioral landmarks at each appropriate age (AAMR, 2002; IASSID, 2003). Each visit also should include discussion and guidance sessions with the child's parents on the subjects of developmental and health status. Finally, the child should receive immunizations to prevent serious contagious disease, and blood and urine tests should be made at regular intervals. The family should have developmental guidance to help prevent accidents and alleviate conditions that could lead to problems.

The routine health care just described is an important means of identifying unexpected developmental problems, but it becomes even more critical for the family of a child once a problem has been identified. Both the child with intellectual disabilities and the family need a great deal of support and assistance to meet the challenges of daily care and health maintenance. The health care team should be well equipped to provide such assistance.

Prevention of intellectual disabilities is a laudible goal. It is not, however, a subject whose principles are easy to grasp, nor is it one that is free of controversy as we will see in later discussions of social and ethical issues (see Chapter 13). One of the major difficulties in conceptualizing prevention lies with the field of intellectual disabilities. Intellectual disabilities, as a condition, is an extremely heterogeneous phenomenon. It varies greatly in terms of causation, severity, environmental circumstances, and professional disciplines concerned. By now, the reader is well aware that intellectual disabilities is a condition with many facets—sociocultural, psychological, biomedical, and much more. The complex nature of the condition makes conceptualizing prevention in any sort of global fashion most difficult. However, some notable, if limited, successes have occurred in prevention.

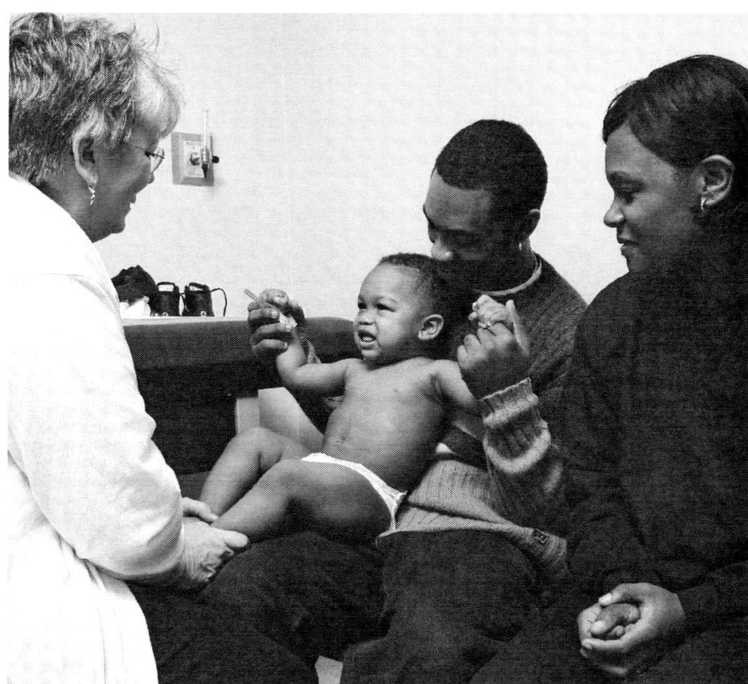

Health care assessment is important to the well-being of this child's development.

Screening and treatment for the enzyme-deficiency disease PKU (see Chapter 6) is a classic example of an instance in which a specific condition is identified and subsequent treatment results in preventing or reducing the effects of intellectual disabilities (Luciana, Hanson, & Whitley, 2004; Merrick, Aspler, & Schwarz, 2003). Continued assistance from the health care team is critical. The child must be placed on a very restricted and expensive diet to offset the enzyme deficiency. This expense puts certain pressures on the family, and maintenance of adequate and balanced nutrition for the child and the entire family can become a serious problem. The child's health also can be in jeopardy because of increased susceptibility to infection and other factors.

Well-defined prevention programs like those implemented with PKU are rare. However, theories and research results have stimulated considerable interest among health care workers in identifying family risk factors, including inadequate environmental stimulation (Annett, 2003; Repetti, Taylor, & Seeman, 2002). Health care workers are often the only professional people in contact with such families on any systematic basis, so the task of identification of problems is most logically approached from a health care standpoint. Nurses and child development specialists have begun programs of environmental stimulation and enrichment in many communities. As the programs develop, research evidence will be forthcoming and will add to our understanding of the effectiveness of this type of intervention.

The idea of enhanced stimulation is also generating increased interest in intervention beyond prevention. When a child is identified as already having intellectual disabilities and being developmentally disabled, health care workers and child development specialists have often begun infant stimulation programs to make the most of the child's development. As research findings suggest, such intervention in field settings has resulted in notable progress (Campbell et al., 2002; Hardman, Drew, & Egan, 2006). Children normally expected to be delayed in physical neuromotor development have shown impressive acceleration in physical development. For example, a child with Down syndrome is typically delayed by several weeks or months in all aspects of neuromotor development. These delays in young Down children and other youngsters with intellectual disabilities typically include sitting, crawling, walking, talking, eating, and a number of social behaviors (Diamond & Kontos, 2004; Erbas, Ozen, & Acar, 2004).

The focus of infant stimulation programs is systematic, planned stimulation of the infant in all sensory modalities. The desired result of such programming is acceleration of the child's development so that these skills appear at a time more nearly consistent with that of normal children of the same chronological age. All six perceptual systems should be stimulated, but multiple stimulation is not necessarily undertaken at any single session; one perceptual system at a time may be stimulated on a given occasion. This progression is often done to enhance clarity and specificity for parents, who frequently are involved heavily in program implementation and act as important interveners. At some point during the program, however, each of the senses is the focus of stimulation, including sight, hearing, touch, kinesthetic movement, smell, and taste. Thus, the parent may be instructed to strike a particular kitchen pot with a spoon near the infant, to rattle a toy, and generally to present as many hearing stimuli as possible to attract the infant's attention. As the infant responds, other perceptual systems may be stimulated, and the same stimuli are repeated but at different distances from the child. Frequently, the next step involves engaging the infant in active participation in the stimulation program. The child may be encouraged to hold the sound-producing spoon, to move the rattle, to manipulate soft cotton or a hard rock, and other such activities.

For many children, stimulation is a routine part of their environment and results from ordinary interactions and activities of the family. For the most part, these infants are wanted and loved; they are held and carried, cuddled, talked to, placed near the activities of the other children and adults in the family, and taken in the car for trips into the community. These are all a natural part of each day's activities. However, certain infants are born into environments lacking some or all of these features. During their early months, they may spend a great deal of time alone, in a room with little color, and with limited interaction with other people. When they are fed or changed, they may be handled only briefly, and the bottle often may be propped beside them instead of handheld. Early experience beyond this meager environment may not exist at all for many children.

Other situations may result in reduced stimulation. For example, a relative lack of stimulation may be offered to the child born with a significant physical disability, even if the family is not of limited means. Such a child may be difficult for the family to look at or to interact with and, consequently, may be excluded from some family activities. This child is not the beautiful baby the family anticipated, and they may not wish to carry him or her into the community.

Establishing a planned sequence of stimulation for such infants is one type of effort to provide an environment that more closely resembles the rich experience that children must have for normal development. It is based on the belief, reinforced by accumulating evidence, that stimulation and early intervention are of benefit to the child's intellectual development. Stimulation programs draw heavily on the child's home environment regardless of socioeconomic level. A family of limited income in a home with modest furnishings can provide interaction patterns and sensory stimulation as beneficial as those found in a family with greater means.

LANGUAGE DEVELOPMENT

Intellectual disabilities are manifested in a variety of ways and in a number of behavioral domains as evidenced by the current definition (AAMR, 2002). Perhaps the most serious and obvious deficit involves delayed language development (Emerson, Robertson, & Wood, 2004; Owens, 2005). Expressive language (the ability to produce language) may be completely absent. Parents and teachers commonly attribute most, if not all, of the child's learning problems to language deficiencies.

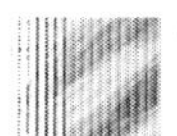

Core Concept

During the early childhood years, language deviations and delay are often evident in children with intellectual disabilities.

Normal Language Development

Table 7–2 provides some guidelines for normal developmental landmarks, including prelanguage and language behaviors. The normal progression of language development is an important indicator of general cognitive maturation. A newborn is expected to cry, to make other generalized sounds, and to be cooing and babbling by about 3 to 6 months. First words generally appear as babbling from 9 to 14 months,

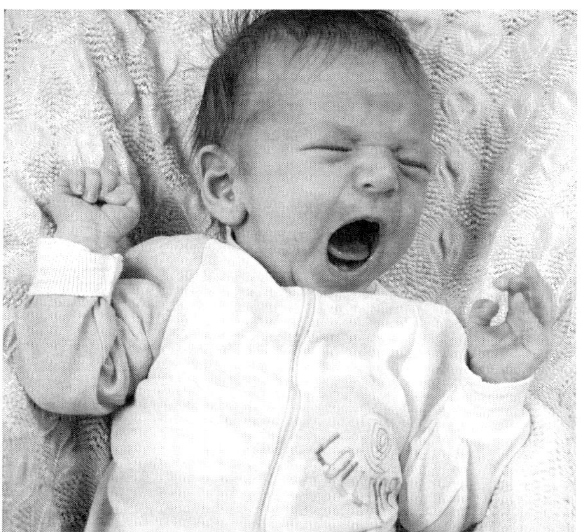

Early communication by an infant usually indicates a basic need.

Table 7–2
Normal Language and Prelanguage Development

Age	Behavior
Birth	Crying and making other physiological sounds
1 to 2 months	Cooing, as well as crying
3 to 6 months	Babbling, as well as cooing
9 to 14 months	Speaking first words, as well as babbling
18 to 24 months	Speaking first sentences, as well as words
3 to 4 years	Using all basic syntactical structures
4 to 8 years	Articulating correctly all speech sounds in context

and simple sentences are formed by 18 to 24 months. Basic syntactical structures are usually in place by 3 to 4 years, and speech sounds are articulated correctly, in context, by 4 to 8 years of age. This progression suggests that for a normal child, the basic language structure is largely complete sometime between 4 and 8 years of age (Berk, 2005; Owens, 2005). Certainly, as maturation continues beyond this point, language facility also tends to grow and expand, but such growth is largely an embellishment of existing structures.

The process involved in language development has been the source of considerable theoretical debate. A substantial portion of this debate began in 1957 with the publication of B. F. Skinner's *Verbal Behavior*. It was Skinner's contention that verbal behavior is reinforced by other people who have a prolonged history that has conditioned them in ways of "precisely" reinforcing the speaker (Skinner, 1957). The mediation of others and the reinforcing consequences continue to be important to maintenance of verbal behavior after initial acquisition. This view of language development is at variance with other theories that contend that language is an innate capacity specific to the human species and dependent on the maturation of the brain and nervous system. Part of the innate capacity argument is based on the fact that the onset of language occurs in children at a similar age in all cultures of the world despite enormous cultural differences. This view often carries the assumption that teaching cannot result in language acquisition unless an individual has the innate biological propensity for language. Compromise theories also presume a role for both learning and innate capacity (Bernstein & Levey, 2002).

Theoretical debates concerning language development have enriched our considerations of how it occurs. Although it is unfortunate that so much energy has been expended in controversy and refutation, the value of different opinions should not be overlooked. Each of the theories contributes substantially, and the various hypotheses will likely blend in some fashion in the future as the process of normal language development continues to be unraveled.

Delayed Language Development

Language development is commonly delayed among children with intellectual disabilities. Scales to measure language development of the child with intellectual disabilities specifically have not received widespread attention, although clinical assessment of language functioning has long been a concern (Owens, 2005; Silliman & Diehl, 2002; Young, Moni, Jobling, & van-Kraayenoord, 2004). Assessments of normative language development are useful insofar as they help identify the extent of the delay or deficiency. Numerous language development instruments have been constructed over the years (see Chapter 3). Some of these scales include the phonological (sound), semantic (meaning), morphological (word form), and syntactical (word order) skills acquired by normal children. All of these areas of assessment are important in evaluating language development both for children who appear to be progressing normally and for those who exhibit delay (AAMR, 2002; IASSID, 2003). For the most part, language development scales focus on the period from birth to 5 or 10 years of age. Such instrumentation provides a useful armory for those concerned with language development and particularly delayed or deficient language development.

Delayed language development presents a difficult challenge, particularly for those with intellectual disabilities in contemporary society (Owens, 2002, 2005). Exactly how delayed language relates to reduced intellectual functioning, or intellectual disabilities, is unclear. Delayed language development is not a simple characteristic and may be difficult to identify, particularly in children with primary languages other than English. It may be extremely obvious and debilitating, or it may be subtler (Bernstein & Levey, 2002; Butler & Silliman, 2002; Gleason, 2005). For children with intellectual disabilities, it presents some particular challenges.

For years, professionals have attempted to counteract language delay in children with intellectual disabilities. Unfortunately, language rehabilitation efforts with this population lagged for many years because of the attitudes and perceptions of many speech and language specialists. A substantial number of such specialists have opposed working with those having intellectual disabilities on the grounds that speech and language rehabilitation is almost impossible for these individuals. Such attitudes, although regrettable, are somewhat understandable in view of some of the theories about language development. If one believes that language development is innate to humans, many children with intellectual disabilities are inappropriate subjects for speech and language therapy because language may not appear to be innate to them. Other theoretical schemes offer a more optimistic outlook for children with intellectual disabilities. For example, B. F. Skinner's research provides a strong theoretical basis for working with children whose language skills fail to develop normally. Evidence is accumulating that language development during the early years is directly influenced by learning and social-experiential factors for children with intellectual disabilities, as it is for their normal peers (Gleason, 2005; Owens, 2005).

Skinner's ideas have been the basis for a number of efforts at language development for young children with intellectual disabilities. Several approaches have focused on the establishment of imitative repertoires in children with retardation in order to facilitate speech and language development. These procedures have often had promising results. Although details vary from technique to technique, major characteristics include the following:

1. Imitation apparently can be learned by children who initially did not have significant imitative behavioral repertoires.

2. Imitation combined with differential reinforcement can be used to train for both simple naming or labeling and generative repertoires of plurality, simple sentences, and verb tense usage.
3. Imitation can be regarded as a particular type of learning set that exemplifies the rule "Do as the model does."
4. Language development and consequent behavior that is rule-governed can be fairly directly related to the simple training procedures of differential reinforcement and fading, which teach a child to match a series of different behaviors that are modeled.
5. A child with a widely generalized imitative repertoire can be significantly influenced by language models in the environment. Such generalization is essential to the normal acquisition of speech and language.

Some of these results have prompted programming approaches to language development stimulation that can alter the course of progress for some with intellectual disabilities. Interestingly, it appears that effective language intervention occurs best when it is close to the natural environment, involving parents and others rather than depending only on language specialists (Kaderavek & Rabidoux, 2004; Weiss, 2002; Yoder & Warren, 2004).

COGNITIVE DEVELOPMENT

Core Concept

Cognitive development during infancy and early childhood involves many complex processes, including some in areas in which children with intellectual disabilities have great difficulty.

An individual's developing capacity to formulate thoughts is referred to as cognitive development. Ordinarily, perception refers to sensory experiences received from the environment, whereas cognition is used for the meaning and thought patterns that emerge as a result of combinations of perceptions. The purposes of this book are well served by these definitions, although the explanations vary, depending on the context and the authority consulted. In this section, we discuss the work of selected theorists who have examined cognitive development and its implications for intellectual disabilities.

Theories

Cognitive development theory has been substantially enriched by the work of Jean Piaget. We have briefly addressed his work in previous chapters. Despite certain theoretical criticisms, Piaget's work remains worthy of discussion in the context of cognitive development. Unlike most theorists, Piaget was interested primarily in the functions and structures of intelligent activity, rather than the content of intelligence per se. He outlined stages of intelligence development that change both quantitatively and qualitatively throughout the developmental period. It was Piaget's contention that although different children progress through various stages at different rates, the sequence is always the same. Piaget's developmental stages are marked by the most recently emerging capability of the child. It is important to remember, however, that behaviors and processes preceding a given stage continue to occur and may be more intense and frequent than the newly emerging function.

Piaget provides an interesting framework from which to view cognitive development in children with intellectual disabilities. It is speculated that these children, particularly those who are only mildly affected, do progress through Piaget's developmental stages, although somewhat more slowly than other children. The progression is demonstrable even though many individuals with intellectual disabilities do not seem to develop spontaneously beyond Piaget's first two periods—sensorimotor and concrete operations. Thus, children with intellectual disabilities often have cognitive structures more typical of chronologically younger children.

From Piaget's perspective, a child's cognitive capacities unfold naturally, although the influence of the environment is substantial. Through adaptation to the environment, a child shapes the exact nature of structures that unfold. His or her readiness to develop the next sequence of intellectual structures is governed largely by neurological capacity or readiness, whereas the stimulus for actual progression into the next stage comes from the environment. This view of cognitive development appears to have important implications for teaching children with intellectual disabilities because education should present an environment that stimulates development of maximum potential. For Piaget, conceptualization of an idea precedes verbalization. In other words, children must experience and understand a phenomenon actively in the real world before they are able to put the event into words and demonstrate mastery of the problem. Children who have opportunities to encounter life experiences appropriate to their stage of cognitive development can be assisted in growth and development of cognitive potential through environmental stimulation. As scientists continue sorting out the interactions between system maturation and the environment, we may find that developing cognitive abilities can be a more central focus of the teaching process than it has been in the past (Gifford, 2004; Lamb, Bornstein, & Teti, 2002; Venville, 2004).

The development of cognitive ability in individuals with intellectual disabilities has been of great interest to behavioral scientists for many years. As discussed in Chapter 4, a number of recent theoretical developments in the area of intelligence have occurred (e.g., Gardner, 2002, 2003; Sternberg, 2002, 2003). As these concepts receive additional attention from the research community, it will be interesting to see how they influence perceptions of the cognitive development in intellectual disabilities at various levels. For example, some earlier theories held that individuals with more severe intellectual disabilities fixate at the level of sensorimotor intelligence. From this view, such individuals simply repeat over and over the innate behaviors that are observed at birth, with very little knowledge of the objects with which they interact. Others who advance further in their development may be more closely oriented to the world around them, recognize familiar objects, and demonstrate intentionality in their behavior. They may be able to use trial-and-error experimentation with objects to produce a novel effect. Clearly, those who are less affected develop to more advanced stages, although they, too, are limited in their conceptions of such abstractions as time, space, and reality. It is anticipated that theoretical formulations of cognitive development for those with intellectual disabilities will change as the more current conceptions of intelligence mature. The development of conceptual knowledge by children with intellectual disabilities remains of interest to researchers and has both theoretical and practical implications (Butler & Silliman, 2002; Owens, 2005).

Implications for Professional Intervention

Early childhood specialists represent the professional group that is perhaps most concerned with the cognitive development of the preschool child, whether that child has intellectual disabilities or is of average intelligence. The primary goal of early childhood education is to provide an environment that stimulates maximum social and cognitive development. We already have examined the important implications of early environment for the development of optimal intellectual functioning later in life. As children progress beyond the age of 2, environmental stimulation appears to play a different role in their development. During the first 2 years, general stimulation in a wide variety of areas seems to affect individuals' ultimate level of functioning. For example, such factors as the involvement of family members are strongly related to many aspects of cognitive development (Berk, 2005; Cook & Cook, 2005; Weiss, 2002). As the child enters the preschool period at 3, 4, and 5 years of age, general sensory stimulation does not produce the same benefits. Instead, more specific experiences with particular and focused stimulation become influential in the child's progress. Conceptualization grows out of environmental experiences, and the child develops the capacity to represent events symbolically in both thought and language.

The objective of the early childhood education specialist is to provide specific tangible experiences that are consistent with the child's cognitive capacity and that stimulate development of cognitive structures. The initial challenge for the educational specialist working with a preschooler who has intellectual disabilities is to understand the child's level of cognitive development. If, for example, the child is functioning at a particular skill level but seems to have potential for development into a more advanced or complex skill set, the specialist may direct efforts toward preparing the child for that developmental progression. The child may be given experiences with a variety of spatial problems, such as physical activities that provide a contrast between objects in the environment and the child, and a recognition of how these objects can be manipulated and experienced in a consistent, predictable manner. Through such techniques, the education specialist may build a program for the young child that facilitates progression into the next cognitive stage of development. Early intervention programs are important to the developmental progression of young children with intellectual disabilities (e.g., Niccols, Atkinson, & Pepler, 2003; Siegler, 2003). Systematic early stimulation may be enhanced significantly by using readily available simple technology (Johnston, 2003; Owens, 2005) as suggested in the Eye on Technology feature.

Eye on Technology

Some popularly available toys can serve a very useful purpose as technology tools to stimulate and help in language development for young children. In some of these devices a switch is activated by the child pressing on a particular part of the toy. This then triggers a song or a word that can be imitated by the child (e.g., Playskool's Mr. Potato Head, Elmo's Boom Box by Fisher-Price). The imitation and rehearsal opportunities provided by these simple technologies can be very helpful in facilitating developmental experiences in language and other cognitive areas (Johnston, 2003).

PSYCHOSOCIAL DEVELOPMENT

A young child's growth and development involve many different components. All elements are essential to the whole with respect to development, and each is interrelated in complex ways. Psychosocial development, developing social and emotionally, is a vital process for all young children regardless of intellectual capacity. The development of social and emotional functioning has pervasive effects on children's intellectual functioning. When children have a serious problem in psychosocial development, it is likely to have a significant impact on their development of intellectual potential (Jaffee, 2002; Klin, & Kasari, 2004; Merrick, Kandel, & Vardi, 2004). Thus, the development of psychosocial functioning represents a growth component of importance. In what follows, we explore some theoretical positions that are of interest in the context of the preschool period. Although broad, sweeping theories have practical limitations, they do provide general frameworks for viewing development. We examine the potential intellectual functioning of children of average intelligence, as well as preschool-age children with intellectual disabilities, to provide contrasting viewpoints.

Core Concept

Developmental problems in social and emotional functioning can have a serious impact on a young child's ability to adapt and chances to succeed in school.

Theories

Theories of psychosocial development are somewhat different from those in other behavioral domains. In many cases, the topics under discussion are extremely abstract, less specific with respect to behavioral definitions, and more difficult to measure (Berk, 2005). However, they are still worth discussing, and very few readers will deny that these abstract concepts represent some behavioral reality.

Development of Trust, Autonomy, and Initiative. Erik H. Erikson viewed child development primarily from a psychoanalytical perspective. Erikson hypothesized that infancy is the time of the child's first social achievement: basic trust. To the extent that his or her parents provide nurturance, familiarity, security, and continuity of experience, an infant can develop a basic sense of trust in both the immediate environment and the people in it. An infant's behavior reflects constant testing, experimenting, and exploring of the world to discover its predictability or the extent to which it can be trusted. Erikson believed that when an adequate mothering relationship is not present, an infant develops a sense of mistrust of the environment and the people in it. He also contended that such an experience is irreversible and influences the evolution of all subsequent stages. Clearly, all infants experience trust and mistrust to some degree; it is the predominance of one over another that is critical for successful completion of this first stage.

The maturing of autonomy and initiative also is involved in Erikson's depiction of emotional development during early childhood. Initially, children undergo a struggle to attain autonomy—a sense of self and of separateness. As part of this process, they must overcome the hazards of doubt and shame. They learn to exercise control over the processes of having and letting go. The family environment offers restraint and freedom in an appropriate balance to permit young children to experiment without becoming the victims of indiscriminate use of the abilities to hold on and to let go. As this process evolves, children develop a sense of autonomy, which is important in further development of independent functioning. Development of independence is an important step in a youngster's maturation. Failure to do so may be due to a number of complex factors (e.g., parenting, interactions with others) and can result in a personality that is overly dependent (McClanahan, Kim, & Bobowick, 2003).

Erikson also conceived of a second stage in early childhood, beginning at about the end of the third year. This stage involves the struggle to gain a sense of initiative and to overcome the difficulties of guilt. The difference between this and the establishment of autonomy is likened to the difference between knowing oneself and knowing one's potential. At this point, children develop a sense of conscience, which is the regulatory or control function of the personality. If this function is overdeveloped, they may become too inhibited and even self-destructive, with a diminished capacity for creativity and initiative. As with all developmental processes, the desirable outcome is dominance of the positive task.

Development of Attachment. Another important emotional component of personality relates to attachment. Infancy is a crucial period for the emergence of attachment behavior (Berk, 2005; Cook & Cook, 2005). As attachment evolves, the behaviors of the mother and other significant individuals are often caretaking behaviors. The infant's behavior reflects efforts to maintain proximity to the mother first and then to other members of the family, who, in turn, reciprocate the expressed needs for proximity. An older infant maintains proximity in many specific ways, although five basic patterns emerge: sucking, clinging, following, crying, and smiling. Some of these behaviors are evident at birth but are not manifested as self-directed attachment behavior until about the age of 4 months. As development progresses, an infant exhibits sophisticated goal-directed systems of behavior to maintain proximity to the mother. These systems of behavior usually become apparent between 9 and 18 months.

Visual and tactile contacts are crucial for the development of attachment behavior. The nature of visual and tactile interactions provides an important indication of the adequacy of attachment formation. Using the mother as a base of security from which to operate, the infant explores the larger world but maintains visual contact during the process. Tactile contact is reestablished periodically, and then exploration continues. When the child becomes frightened, distressed, or uncomfortable for any reason, he or she tries to stay close to the mother by clinging and following. When a serious threat of separation occurs, intense anxiety, anger, and violent distress result. These feelings and behaviors remain strong throughout infancy and are quite apparent during early childhood, although they lessen in intensity.

Environment and Self-Esteem. There has long been an interest in better understanding the influence of environmental factors on emotional and social development. Theories in this area have typically not been oriented toward child development, although their implications for infants and young children are evident (Berk, 2005; Cook & Cook, 2005). Early theorists have suggested that individuals need a psychological atmosphere of unconditional positive regard in order to develop to their full potential. This type of atmosphere must come from the significant others in the environment and involves total and unconditional acceptance of the feelings and values of the young child. It does not mean, however, that others must always agree with the child; they must only accept the feelings and values as real to the child. Evaluative comparison, rejecting judgments, lack of trust, and harsh punishment lead to the development of a child's underlying doubts about worthiness and competence and may block the development of self-esteem, acceptance, and assurance.

Parents and other family members play important roles in the early development of self-esteem, as they do in other areas (Berk, 2005; Cook & Cook, 2005; Lamb et al., 2002). Children whose families give them the feeling that they mean a lot to their parents tend to develop high levels of self-esteem. Parental attention and concern, as well as restrictions on behavior, can convey such feelings. In this type of familial environment, the children are made aware of their successes, and they experience frequent success in their efforts toward development and learning. But children in these families are also made aware of situations in which they have not succeeded and are encouraged to develop the behavioral changes needed to achieve success and approval. High self-esteem seems to be related to a high level of stimulation, activity, and vigor in the family. Typically, members of the family maintain a high level of communication, including differences of opinion, dissent, and disagreement, leading to the development of mutual knowledge and respect.

Implications for Intellectual Functioning

Many of the factors of major concern in psychosocial development are also important components of intellectual functioning. For example, the role of early stimulation is immediately apparent in both psychosocial and intellectual domains (Berk, 2005; Cook & Cook, 2005). Personality theorists focus on the crucial relationship of the infant or young child with at least one significant adult who provides the necessary care and love for the child. The child receives this adult's attention and affection primarily through the sensory channels that are so critical in the development of intellectual functioning. Thus, it appears that a significant interaction or interdependence must occur between the development of psychosocial and intellectual functions, although the precise nature of this relationship is not known. Children who are victims of potential restriction of intellectual development through environmental deprivation are also likely to exhibit signs of attenuated emotional development. Such concomitant developmental inadequacies may be evident simply because of missing elements in vital sensory stimulation. A child who is unable to develop adequate emotional security, self-esteem, or social relationships with family members and peers is also likely to be inhibited in intellectual performance. Whether the inhibiting influence becomes permanent or significant is likely the result of interaction among a number of factors. We do know, however, that supporting optimal psychological development in early life has a favorable influence on the child's ability to function intellectually (Gelfand & Drew, 2003; Niccols et al., 2003; Siegler, 2003).

There is relatively little understanding of specific psychosocial development in the infant or preschooler with intellectual disabilities. These children seem to show developmental lags in the psychosocial features discussed. They remain dependent and relatively immature in social interactions for a prolonged period. It is not clear, however, whether this developmental lag arises from the intimately related neurological bases for both areas of development or whether an environmentally generated psychosocial delay arises from lack of interaction with significant adults. It seems reasonable to assume that young children with intellectual disabilities might exhibit psychosocial delays similar to their cognitive ones. Every effort should be made to sustain optimal psychosocial development for children with intellectual disabilities.

Professional Intervention

Psychosocial development is no less important for the child with intellectual disabilities than for the child of average intelligence. Professionals working with children who have retardation must be as concerned with this area of development as they are with cognitive domains (Klin & Kasari, 2004; Merrick et al., 2004). Such a child may be particularly at risk in terms of adverse environmental influences on emotional development because of unfavorable parental reactions. The family may need assistance from mental health specialists (psychologist, psychiatrist, psychiatric social worker) to facilitate the maintenance of optimal mental health and development for all family members. Both parents and child may have glaring needs. Professionals may provide short-term assistance and intervention during periods of crisis, such as at the time of the child's birth, when the diagnosis of intellectual disabilities is confirmed, or during periods of intense physical, social, or emotional stress in the family. Long-term assistance or intervention may be needed if the family experiences unusual or prolonged stress leading to disorganization of the family unit. It may be difficult for the family to accept such assistance because it threatens the emotional integrity of the family unit and the individual members. Accepting assistance often means recognizing a need that is most difficult to acknowledge and, for many families, represents a weakness or failure that they shun. Friends, health care professionals, and educators should be alert to signs of need for mental health intervention and should help the family accept such assistance. The process of adaptation and accommodation by family members to a child with intellectual disabilities is significant, multifaceted, and ongoing (Gray & Mohr, 2004; Hodapp, 2002).

In most cases, intellectual disabilities are not apparent at birth. A family may become aware of the child's disability during the first months or years of life or not until the child goes to school. It is not uncommon for family members to experience particular stress and crisis as they seek to allay their fears and restore their hopes for the normal, healthy baby they thought they had. These types of reactions are relatively common for several disability areas. The longer the family has lived with the belief that the child is healthy and normal, the more difficult the adjustment. Chapters 12 and 13 discuss further the difficult emotional problems that families of children with intellectual disabilities experience.

NEW ISSUES AND FUTURE DIRECTIONS

Changes in programs for young children with intellectual disabilities are sweeping, particularly with the enactment of IDEA 97 (Public Law 105-17, Individuals with Disabilities Education Act amendments of 1997). IDEA 97 Part C defines eligible infants and toddlers as those under the age of 3 needing early intervention for either (a) a developmental delay in one or more of the areas of cognitive development, physical development, communication development, social or emotional development or (b) a diagnosis of physical or mental condition that has a high probability of resulting in developmental delay (Sec. 632[1]). Early intervention services provided under IDEA 97 go beyond the child and are to be directed at the family's needs, aimed at informing and empowering the family to participate in the development of an individualized family service plan (IFSP) (Bailey, 2001; Harbin et al., 2004). The components of an IFSP are outlined in Table 7–3 and resemble an individualized education program (IEP) but with a broader scope.

As suggested by the elements outlined in Table 7–3, parents are becoming increasingly active partners in early intervention, promoting the development of children with disabilities and those who are at risk. They are an extremely important component in the young child's life and, as we saw with Helen in the opening vignette, many are desperately seeking some meaningful action they can take to help their child and thereby help themselves. Parents have moved from an ancillary role to more central involvement in collaborative planning and implementation of many aspects of intervention with their children. The IFSP considers the child's needs in the context of overall family needs and dynamics (Hardman et al., 2006). In the future, treatment and other interventions for young children with intellectual disabilities will continue to more centrally involve parents and other family members as participants in programming.

Any discussion of infancy and early childhood requires some attention to the effectiveness of early intervention programs aimed at enhancing children's development. This is particularly true for children with intellectual disabilities and other

Table 7–3
Components of an Individualized Family Service Plan

1. The infant's or toddler's present levels of physical development, cognitive development, communication development, social or emotional development, and adaptive development, based on objective criteria
2. The family's resources, priorities, and concerns relating to enhancing the development of the family's infant or toddler with a disability
3. The major outcomes expected to be achieved for the infant or toddler and the family and the criteria, procedures, and timelines used to determine the degree to which progress toward achieving the outcomes is being made and whether modifications or revisions of the outcomes or services are necessary
4. Specific early intervention services necessary to meet the unique needs of the infant or toddler and the family, including the frequency, intensity, and method of delivering services
5. The natural environments in which early intervention services shall appropriately be provided, including a justification of the extent, if any, to which the services will not be provided in a natural environment
6. The projected dates for initiation of services and the anticipated duration of the services
7. The identification of the service coordinator from the profession most immediately relevant to the infant's or toddler's or family's needs (or who is otherwise qualified to carry out all applicable responsibilities under this part) who will be responsible for the implementation of the plan and coordination with other agencies and persons
8. The steps to be taken to support the transition of the toddler with a disability to preschool or other appropriate services (IDEA 97, Sec. 636[d])

children at risk for developmental delay. Interpretation of early intervention outcomes, however, is not an easy task. The expectations placed on such programs as Head Start were probably unrealistic as we look back on them. But this does not mean that such programs or other early stimulation approaches are ineffective. Overall analyses of the influence of early intervention suggests substantial gains for both at-risk children and children with disabilities (Niccols et al., 2003; Siegler, 2003). Interpretations of individual studies must be viewed cautiously, and broad, sweeping generalizations about effects in single-study investigations are always suspect. Still, enthusiasm about the worth of early intervention remains high among professionals in early childhood development. We anticipate that early intervention programs will flourish in the future even as more caution is exercised with respect to expectations.

Future directions and issues for the young child with intellectual disabilities also include important contributions from the medical field. Medical technology for this group of youngsters, as for others, is developing at a dramatic pace. Medical management of these children continues to require attention to their higher incidence of chronic health problems: seizures, congenital abnormalities, and susceptibility to infectious diseases. Research and development efforts in drug and gene therapy, nutrition, and surgery (e.g., repair of birth defects, shunt implantations) will continue to have a significant impact on infants and young children with intellectual disabilities.

Some medical treatments are unconventional in the sense that they are either experimental or raise ethical questions and controversy (Field & Behrman, 2004). One such procedure involves facial surgery with Down syndrome children for cosmetic purposes and also to improve oral function (aiding speech). The appearance-normalization aspect of this procedure has raised questions by some who believe it unnecessary. Perhaps even more unconventional is the application of cell therapy with Down syndrome children. This procedure involves the injection of fresh fetal lamb brain tissue into the young child. Proponents claim dramatic alteration of developmental characteristics; others note that evidence for such change is not available and urge caution. Although such procedures may seem so unusual as to stretch the imagination, it is important to remember that altering genetic material was similarly unthinkable only a few years ago.

Core Questions

1. How does the brain develop during infancy and early childhood?
2. How can one trace the development of myelinization from a behavioral standpoint in very young children?
3. How does the early development of sensory organs influence a young child's learning?
4. How might environmental deprivation of stimuli affect the cognitive development of young children and result in intellectual disabilities?
5. How are parents potentially important in early childhood intervention programs?
6. How is early sensory stimulation important for both emotional and intellectual development?
7. How do parents and other family members influence the development of self-esteem in a child? How can they create an environment that promotes realistic views of self-worth for a young child?
8. How would Piaget see the cognitive developmental progress of individuals with and without intellectual disabilities as the same?

Roundtable Discussion

Human development during infancy and early childhood is extremely important. Much that occurs at this stage of life provides a foundation for many later skills and abilities. Physiological systems are developing, and they interact with aspects of cognition, language, and social development in a complex fashion that ultimately comes together to present an individual's sum potential.

In your study group or on your own, examine how physiological growth and development relate to language, cognition, and social competence. Explore the role of the environment during this time, including aspects of parental interaction and behavior. Examine how parents can be important interveners and how they might contribute to intellectual disabilities in a child. Describe how you might discuss early childhood development with potential parents in order to facilitate their lives as parents and field-based developmental specialists.

Parent and Professional Organization Positions on Key Issues in the Lives of People with Intellectual Disabilities

The inside front cover of this text presents a matrix that includes several key issues in the lives of people with disabilities, the positions of various parent and professional organizations on each issue, and the chapter and page number where the information is addressed. Table 7–4 below is a summary of the organizations and key issues addressed in this chapter.

Table 7–4
Key Issues and Organizations Discussed in This Chapter

Organization/Website	Key Issues Addressed	Chapter Heading
American Association on Mental Retardation (http://www.aamr.org)	Language delay and ID definition Language assessment Early health care	Language Development Delayed Language Development Professional and Parental Intervention
International Association for the Scientific Study of Intellectual Disabilities (http://www.iassid.org)	Language assessment Early health promotion Health care assessment Early child health care	Delayed Language Development Professional and Parental Intervention
National Down Syndrome Congress (http://www.ndsccenter.org)	Parent resources and support Early intervention	Introduction Professional and Parental Intervention
National Down Syndrome Society (http://www.ndss.org)	Parent resources and support Early intervention	Introduction Professional and Parental Intervention

References

Abromeit, D. H. (2003). The Newborn Individualized Developmental Care and Assessment Program (NIDCAP) as a model for clinical music therapy interventions with premature infants. *Music Therapy Perspectives, 21,* 60–68.

American Association on Mental Retardation (AAMR). (2002). *Mental retardation: Definition, classification, and systems of supports* (10th ed.). Washington, DC: Author.

Annett, M. (2003). Outcomes in neurodevelopmental and genetic disorders. *Infant and Child Development, 12,* 397.

Bahrick, L. E., Lickliter, R., & Flom, R. (2004). Intersensory redundancy guides the development of selective attention, perception, and cognition in infancy. *Current Directions in Psychological Science, 13,* 99–102.

Bailey, D. B., Jr. (2001). Evaluating parental involvement and family support in early intervention and preschool programs. *Journal of Early Intervention, 24,* 1–14.

Bendersky, M., Gambini, G., Lastella, A., Bennett, D. S., & Lewis, M. (2003). Inhibitory motor control at five years as a function of prenatal cocaine exposure. *Journal of Developmental and Behavioral Pediatrics, 24,* 345–351.

Berk, L. E. (2005). *Development through the lifespan* (5th ed.). Boston: Allyn & Bacon.

Bernstein, D. K., & Levey, S. (2002). Language development: A review. In D. K. Bernstein & E. Tiegerman-Farber (Eds.), *Language and communication disorders in children* (5th ed., pp. 27–94). Boston: Allyn & Bacon.

Broderick, P. C., & Blewitt, P. (2003). *The life span: Human development for helping professionals.* Upper Saddle River, NJ: Pearson/Prentice Hall.

Brodsky, D., & Martin, C. (2002). *Neonatology study guide.* Philadelphia: Lippincott / Williams & Wilkins.

Butler, K. G., & Silliman, E. R. (2002). *Speaking, reading, and writing in children with language learning disabilities: New paradigms in research and practice.* Mahwah, NJ: Erlbaum.

Campbell, F. A., Ramey, C. T., Pungello, E., Sparling, J., & Miller-Johnson, S. (2002). Early childhood education: Young adult outcomes from the Abecedarian Project. *Applied Developmental Science, 6,* 42–57.

Carrera, J. M., Chervenak, F. A., & Kurjak, A. (2003). *Controversies in perinatal medicine: Studies of the fetus as a patient.* Boca Raton, FL: CRC Press.

Cook, J. L., & Cook, G. (2005). *Child development: Principles and perspectives.* Boston: Allyn & Bacon.

Diamond, K. E., & Kontos, S. (2004). Families' resources and accommodations: Toddlers with Down syndrome, cerebral palsy, and developmental delay. *Journal of Early Intervention, 26,* 253–265.

Emerson, E., Robertson, J., & Wood, J. (2004). Levels of psychological distress experienced by family carers of children and adolescents with intellectual disabilities in an urban conurbation. *Journal of Applied Research in Intellectual Disabilities, 17,* 77–84.

Erbas, D., Ozen, A., & Acar, C. (2004). Comparison of two approaches for identifying reinforcers in teaching figure coloring to students with Down syndrome. *Education and Training in Developmental Disabilities, 39,* 253–264.

Field, M. J., & Behrman, R. E. (2004). *Ethical conduct of clinical research involving children.* Washington, DC: National Academies Press.

Fine, L., Wade, A. R., Brewer, A. A., May, M. G., Goodman, D. F., Boynton, G. M., et al. (2003). Long-term deprivation affects visual perception and cortex. *Nature Neuroscience, 6,* 915–916.

Gardner, H. (2002). Learning from extraordinary minds. In M. Ferrari (Ed.), *The pursuit of excellence through education* (pp. 3–20). Mahwah, NJ: Erlbaum.

Gardner, H. (2003). Three distinct meanings of intelligence. In J. Lautrey & R. J. Sternberg (Eds.), *Models of intelligence: International perspectives* (pp. 43–54). Washington, DC: American Psychological Association.

Garvey, M. A., Ziemann, U., Bartko, J. J., Denckla, M. B., Barker, C. A., & Wassermann, E. M. (2003). Cortical correlates of neuromotor development in healthy children. *Clinical Neurophysiology, 114,* 1662–1670.

Gelfand, D. M., & Drew, C. J. (2003). *Understanding child behavior disorders* (4th ed.). Belmont, CA: Wadsworth.

Giegerich, S. (2002). *Body of knowledge.* New York: Simon & Schuster.

Gifford, S. (2004). A new mathematics pedagogy for the early years: In search of principles for practice. *International Journal of Early Years Education, 12,* 99–115.

Gleason, J. B. (2005). *The development of language* (6th ed.). Boston: Allyn & Bacon.

Gray, K. M., & Mohr, C. (2004). Mental health problems in children and adolescents with intellectual disability. *Current Opinion in Psychiatry, 17,* 365–370.

Guy, R., Nicholson, J., Pannu, S. S., & Holden, R. (2003). A clinical evaluation of ophthalmic assessment in children with sensori-neural deafness. *Child: Care, Health and Development, 29,* 377–384.

Harbin, G. L., Bruder, M. B., Adams, C., Mazzarella, C., Whitbread, K., Gabbard, G., et al. (2004). Early intervention service coordination policies: National policy infrastructure. *Topics in Early Childhood Special Education, 24,* 89–97.

Hardman, M. L., Drew, C. J., & Egan, M. W. (2006). *Human exceptionality: School, community, and family* (8th ed.). Needham Heights, MA: Allyn & Bacon.

Hodapp, R. M. (2002). Parenting children with mental retardation. In M. H. Bornstein (Ed.), *Handbook of parenting: Vol. 1. Children and parenting* (2nd ed., pp. 355–381). Mahwah, NJ: Erlbaum.

International Association for the Scientific Study of Intellectual Disabilities (IASSID). (2003). Health SIRG news. *Newsletter, 20,* 13.

Ivanovic, D. M., Leiva, B. P., Castro, C. G., Olivares, M. G., Jansana, J. M. M., Castro, V. G., et al. (2004). Brain development parameters and intelligence in Chilean high school graduates. *Intelligence, 32,* 461–479.

Jaffee, S. R. (2002). Pathways to adversity in young adulthood among early childbearers. *Journal of Family Psychology, 16,* 38–49.

Johnston, S. (2003). Getting the most from single-switch technology: A primer. *Journal of Special Education Technology, 18*(2), 47–50.

Jones, D., Westall, C., Averbeck, K., & Abdolell, M. (2003). Visual acuity assessment: A comparison of two tests for measuring children's vision. *Ophthalmic and Physiological Optics, 23,* 541–546.

Kaderavek, J. N., & Rabidoux, P. (2004). Interactive to independent literacy: A model for designing literacy goals for children with atypical communication. *Reading and Writing Quarterly: Overcoming Learning Difficulties, 20,* 237–260.

Klin, A., & Kasari, C. (2004). The cradle of thought: Exploring the origins of thinking. *American Journal on Mental Retardation, 109,* 267–269.

Lamb, M., Bornstein, M. H., & Teti, D. (2002). *Development in infancy: An introduction* (4th ed.). Mahwah, NJ: Erlbaum.

Lightfoot, C., Lalonde, C., & Chandler, M. (2004). *Changing conceptions of psychological life.* Mahwah, NJ, US: Lawrence Erlbaum Associates.

Loots, G., & Devise, I. (2003). An intersubjective developmental perspective on interactions between deaf and hearing mothers and their deaf infants. *American Annals of the Deaf, 148,* 295–307,

Luciana, M., Hanson, K. L., & Whitley, C. B. (2004). A preliminary report on dopamine system reactivity in PKU: Acute effects of haloperidol on neuropsychological, physiological, and neuroendocrine functions. *Psychopharmacology, 175,* 18–25.

MacLean, K. (2003). The impact of institutionalization on child development. *Development and Psychopathology, 15,* 853–884.

Malekpour, M. (2004). Low birth-weight infants and the importance of early intervention: Enhancing mother-infant interactions—A literature review. *British Journal of Developmental Disabilities, 50* (99, Pt. 2), 78–88.

McClanahan, J. Z., Kim, S. A., & Bobowick, M. (2003). Personality disorders. In M. Hersen (Ed.), *Diagnostic interviewing* (3rd ed., pp. 173–202). New York: Kluwer Academic/Plenum.

Merrick, J., Aspler, S., & Schwarz, G. (2003). Phenylalanine-restricted diet should be life long. A case report on long term follow-up of an adolescent with untreated phenylketonuria. *International Journal of Adolescent Medicine and Health, 15,* 165–168.

Merrick, J., Kandel, I., & Vardi, G. (2004). Adolescents with Down syndrome. *International Journal of Adolescent Medicine and Health, 16,* 13–19.

National Down Syndrome Congress. (2005). *Parent resources.* Retrieved from http://www.ndsccenter.org

National Down Syndrome Society. (2005). *Hotline for information and referral sources.* Retrieved from http://www.ndss.org

Neiss, M., & Almeida, D. M. (2004). Age differences in the heritability of mean and intraindividual variation of psychological distress. *Gerontology, 50,* 22–27.

Niccols, A., Atkinson, L., & Pepler, D. (2003). Mastery motivation in young children with Down's syndrome: Relations with cognitive and adaptive competence. *Journal of Intellectual Disability Research, 47,* 121–133.

Owens, R. E., Jr. (2002). Intellectual disabilities: Difference and delay. In D. K. Bernstein & E. Tiegerman-Farber (Eds.), *Language and communication disorders in children* (5th ed., pp. 436–509). Boston: Allyn & Bacon.

Owens, R. E., Jr. (2005). *Language development: An introduction* (6th ed.). Boston: Allyn & Bacon.

Ramey, C. T., Ramey, S. L., Lanzi, R. G., & Cotton, J. N. (2002). Early educational interventions for high-risk children: How center-based treatment can augment and improve parenting effectiveness. In S. L. Ramey & J. G. Borkowski (Eds.), *Parenting and the child's world: Influences on academic, intellectual, and social-emotional development* (pp. 125–140). Mahwah, NJ: Erlbaum.

Repetti, R. L., Taylor, S. E., & Seeman, T. E. (2002). Risky families: Family social environments and the mental and physical health of offspring. *Psychological Bulletin, 128,* 330–366.

Roder, B., Stock, O., Bien, S., Neville, H., & Rosler, F. (2003). Speech processing activates visual cortex in congenitally blind humans. *European Journal of Neuroscience, 16,* 930–936.

Sadler, T. W. (2003). *Langman's medical embryology with simbryo CD-ROM.* Philadelphia: Lippincott/Williams & Wilkins.

Shenkin, S. D., Starr, J. M., & Deary, I. J. (2004). Birth weight and cognitive ability in childhood: A systematic review. *Psychological Bulletin, 130,* 989–1013.

Siegler, R. S. (2003). Thinking and intelligence. In L. Davidson & M. H. Bornstein (Eds.), *Well-being: Positive development across the life course* (pp. 311–320). Mahwah, NJ: Erlbaum.

Silliman, E. R., & Diehl, S. F. (2002). Assessing children with language disorders. In D. K. Bernstein & E. Tiegerman-Farber (Eds.), *Language and communication disorders in children* (5th ed., pp. 181–255). Boston: Allyn & Bacon.

Skinner, B. F. (1957). *Verbal behavior.* New York: Appleton-Century-Crofts.

Sternberg, R. J. (2002). Successful intelligence: A new approach to leadership. In R. E. Riggio, S. E. Murphy, & F. J. Pirozzolo (Eds.), *Multiple intelligences and leadership* (pp. 9–28). Mahwah, NJ: Erlbaum.

Sternberg, R. J. (2003). Our research program validating the triarchic theory of successful intelligence: Reply to Gottfredson. *Intelligence, 31,* 399–413.

Street, L. L., & Luoma, J. B. (2002). Control groups in psychosocial intervention research: Ethical and methodological issues. *Ethics and Behavior, 12,* 1–30.

Teicher, M. H., Dumont, N. L., Ito, Y., Vaituzis, C., Giedd, J. N., & Andersen, S. L. (2004). Childhood neglect is associated with reduced corpus callosum area. *Biological Psychiatry, 56,* 80–85.

Van De Graaff, K. (2002). *Human anatomy* (6th ed.). New York: McGraw-Hill.

Venville, G. (2004). Young children learning about living things: A case study of conceptual change from ontological and social perspectives. *Journal of Research in Science Teaching, 41,* 449–480.

Weiss, A. L. (2002). Planning language intervention for young children. In D. K. Bernstein & E. Tiegerman-Farber (Eds.), *Language and communication disorders in children* (5th ed., pp. 256–314). Boston: Allyn & Bacon.

Williams, M., & Rask, H. (2003). Literacy through play: How families with able children support their literacy development. *Early Child Development and Care, 173,* 527–533.

Yoder, P. J., & Warren, S. F. (2004). Early predictors of language in children with and without Down syndrome. *American Journal on Mental Retardation, 109,* 285–300.

Young, L., Moni, K. B., Jobling, A., & van-Kraayenoord, C. E. (2004). Literacy skills of adults with intellectual disabilities in two community-based day programs. *International Journal of Disability, Development and Education, 51,* 83–97.

Zucker, A. (2003). Laws and ethics. *Death Studies, 27,* 377–380.

Chapter 8

The Elementary School-Age Child with Intellectual Disabilities

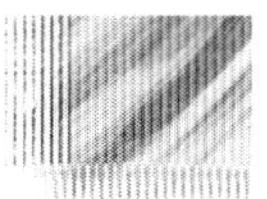

Chapter Preview

At the completion of this chapter, you will have a better understanding of elementary-age children with intellectual disabilities who:

- Are often delayed in their academic and adaptive skill learning but will achieve in school with appropriate services and supports.
- Are entitled to a free and appropriate public education under the Individuals with Disabilities Education Act (IDEA).
- Require individualized and intensive instruction in order to benefit from access to the general curriculum and demonstrate progress as mandated by the No Child Left Behind Act.
- May be successfully included in general education settings with the availability of both formal and natural supports.
- Come from many different cultural backgrounds and need educational experiences that focus on both academic and functional skills learning.

Including Scott

By the time Scott was 10 years old, he had been in five different schools. Because he has Down syndrome, he began his schooling at 18 months, attending the only public special education in the county once a week. At that time, all children [with intellectual disabilities] were bussed to this central location. Scott stayed at the special education school until he was 3½ years old. He could have stayed there until he was 21, but we wanted something different for him. . . . The transition to Coleridge Elementary School wasn't easy. . . . Scott spent most of the day working on academics in the special education classroom; he was included in the regular classroom for only short periods for art, music, lunch, and show-and-tell. At first, he didn't like going into the [general education] classroom, but before long it was the reverse: He didn't want to leave. . . . Scott is now fully included. Lately we've noticed that he is more verbal. . . . He is less dependent on an assistant at school and has started to develop independent work skills. (Bonn & Bonn [parents], 2000a, p. 174; 2000b, pp. 210–211)

- *Do you think Scott's parents made the right decisions for their son in seeking an inclusive education program for Scott? Why?*
- *Why do you think Scott is doing so well in the general education classroom?*

The beginning of elementary school is generally an exciting time for both children and their parents. It is a time to make new friends and begin associations. Even for the child without intellectual disabilities the beginning of school is filled with uncertainty, as well as anticipation. For many parents, the challenges of intellectual disabilities first become a reality when their child enters school. A 6-year-old child with mild intellectual disabilities may have a developmental delay of only about 1 year. This maturational lag may have been so slight during early childhood that it was viewed as insignificant or not even noticed by the parents and family physician. This often happens in the absence of physical or health problems. The child's differences surface when he or she is confronted with the academic and social demands of elementary school and may become compounded if proper educational services and supports are not provided. A teacher may attribute difficulties to immaturity and not refer the child for special education during early primary grades.

Whereas differences for children with mild intellectual disabilities may not be apparent by the beginning of elementary school, the physical, learning, and behavioral characteristics associated with children with moderate to severe intellectual disabilities are clearly evident. Such is the case for Scott in our opening vignette. Scott is a child with Down syndrome, a genetic condition that is diagnosed at birth. By the time Scott entered elementary school, he had been in special education for more than 3 years. He and his family had worked with professionals from many disciplines, including physicians, physical therapists, speech and language specialists, and educators.

For children such as Scott, the meaning of education extends far beyond the learning of basic academic skills. Before the passage of federal and state legislation in the 1970s, many children with intellectual disabilities were excluded from public schools because they were unable to meet academic or adaptive skills requirements. A different set of values has emerged over the past three decades, establishing two goals for public education: (1) raise the functioning level of the child to the next highest developmental level regardless of the severity of the disability and (2) develop an **adaptive fit** between the student and the learning environment (Hardman, Drew, & Egan, 2006). For children with severe intellectual disabilities, the emphasis is not on academic learning but on the development and application of skills that increase independence within the school, home, and community (such as self-help skills, mobility, and communication).

This chapter addresses cognitive development, learning personality, emotional development, motivation, and the physical health of children with intellectual disabilities. In most instances, these characteristics are not limited to school-age children with intellectual disabilities but may follow the individual throughout life.

COGNITIVE DEVELOPMENT

Core Concept

The cognitive development of the child with intellectual disabilities can be described in terms of stages or periods of growth.

To gain some understanding of the cognitive development of the school-age child, we briefly return to the theory of Jean Piaget (1969). Piaget referred to the span from 2 to 7 years as the period of preoperational thought and the span from 7 to 11 years as the period of concrete operation. During the preoperations subperiod, perceptions are the child's dominant mental activity. At about the age of 7, the child begins to move into a period in which perceptions are dominated by intellectual operations, the dominant mental activity of the concrete operations period. The ability to order and relate experiences to an organized whole begins to develop. Rather than being bound to irreversibility, as before, the child begins to develop mobility in thought processes and can reverse some mental operations and return to the starting point.

By 4 years old, the child is less self-centered and more able to take into account another person's point of view. Instead of centering on a one-dimensional property of a situation, the child is able to focus on several properties in sequence and to move quickly from one to another. This phase is termed "concrete" because the child's mental operations still depend on the ability to perceive concretely what has happened. No mental experimentation can take place without prior perception. The basic ability from which concrete operations develop is the ability mentally to form ordering structures, which Piaget called groupings and lattices. Lattices are a special form of groupings in which the focus is on the connection between two or more objects and the objects that are connected. Using lattices, the child can develop a classification hierarchy system in which he or she can understand that all humans are animals but that not all animals are human.

Children begin to conserve numbers around the age of 7 years, to conserve quantity (substance, amount of space occupied by an object) around ages 7 or 8 years, and to conserve weight around 9 years of age.

During the preoperational period, the child's egocentrism is evident in conversations with other children. During this developmental period, conversations with other children of the same age consist of collective monologues. Each child pursues a private, personal conversation regardless of what the other child says. During the concrete operational period, however, these children begin to take into account the other child's point of view and to incorporate these views into their own conversations. Thus, more meaningful communication emerges, and the children carry on dialogue, each responding to what the other has just said.

Children with intellectual disabilities move through the same states of development as their peers without disabilities but at a slower rate (Bray et al., 1999). School-age children with mild intellectual disabilities are slower in progressing from the preoperational stage into concrete operations, with delays as long as 3 to 4 years. Children with moderate intellectual disabilities may fixate at the preoperational level and not reach even the most basic stages of concrete operations until later adolescence. Children with severe levels of intellectual disabilities may fixate at the sensorimotor and preoperational stages and never reach the more advanced periods.

LEARNING CHARACTERISTICS

Children with intellectual disabilities perform well below average on tasks of learning and retention when compared to same-age peers without disabilities. In this section, we discuss the learning characteristics of children with intellectual disabilities. Our attention is directed not only to the pertinent research in this area, but to implications for classroom practice.

Core Concept

Memory problems are positively correlated with the severity of intellectual deficit.

Memory

Memory problems for individuals with intellectual disabilities have been attributed to several factors, including the inability to focus on relevant stimuli in a learning situation (Kittler, Krinsky-McHale, & Devenny, 2004; Westling & Fox, 2004).

The research on memory strongly indicates that ability is related to the type of retention task. **Short-term memory,** the ability to recall material over a period of seconds or minutes, has long been a topic of interest as it relates to children with intellectual disabilities. Early work in the area drew a somewhat confusing picture. Some research suggested the performance of children with intellectual disabilities was no different from that of individuals without disabilities; other work indicated quite the opposite. There is little question, however, that the child with intellectual disabilities may take longer to understand the nature of a task. However, the use of effective approaches to instruction will help compensate for such differences (Haager & Klinger, 2005; Smith, Polloway, Patton, & Dowdy, 2003). The following are some possible ways to enhance short-term memory skills in children with intellectual disabilities:

1. Teach as often as possible in the setting where you want the behavior(s) to occur.
2. Reduce extraneous environmental stimuli, which tend to distract students, and increase stimulus value of the task.
3. Present each component of stimuli clearly and with equivalent stimulus value initially.
4. Begin with simpler tasks, moving to the more complex.
5. Avoid irrelevant materials within the learning task.
6. Label all relevant stimuli.
7. Provide practice in short-term memory activities.
8. Integrate practice material with new subject fields, making use of the child's successful experiences.
9. Dramatize skills involving short-term memory, making them central to instruction.

Much of the thinking in cognitive psychology has turned to **information-processing theories** for exploration of long-term memory capabilities. Information-processing theorists study how a person processes information from sensory stimuli to motor output (Sternberg, 2003). Sternberg described the memory deficits of people with intellectual disabilities as the underdevelopment of metacognitive processes. Such processes are the strategies people use in trying to solve a problem, monitoring how well the strategy is working once implemented, and evaluating the results. Even though children with intellectual disabilities may be unable to use the best strategy when confronted with new learning situations, researchers have suggested that they can be taught ways to do so (Agran & Hughes, 1997; Mithaug, Wehmeyer, Agran, Martin, & Palmer, 1998).

Self-Regulation

Self-regulation is the ability to regulate one's own behavior by managing emotions constructively and keeping attention focused (Shonkoff & Phillips, 2000). In order to regulate behavior, a person must be able to develop efficient learning strategies, such as the ability to rehearse a task (practice a new concept over and over). While most people will rehearse to try to remember, it does not appear that individuals with intellectual disabilities are able to apply this skill. Children with intellectual disabilities appear to be unable to find, monitor, or evaluate the best strategy to use when confronted with a new learning situation. However, they can be taught to change their control processes (Bebko & Luhaorg, 1998).

Distribution of Practice

Many people appear to be able to function well by using massed practice, such as cramming for examinations. However, distributed practice enhances the learning performance of children with intellectual disabilities. The teacher should provide the child with short but frequent practice sessions on day-to-day tasks. The child should be allowed to practice in a variety of situations and contexts. This should not only result in an increased rate of acquisition but also ensure a greater degree of retention.

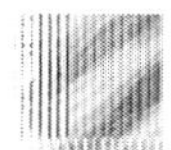

Core Concept

Distributed practice in a learning situation enhances the learning performance of children with intellectual disabilities.

Cipani and Spooner (1994) discussed the use of **naturally distributed trials**—that is, "trials that may occur as the skill would normally be performed in a natural school or home routine" (p. 89). Naturally distributed trials may improve both acquisition of a skill and its generalization to another setting (Westling & Fox, 2004).

Learning Concrete and Abstract Concepts

The more concrete the material, the more likely the child with intellectual disabilities will learn it. The child will grasp concepts more readily if the natural object, rather than a picture of the object, is present. Instead of reading and looking at pictures of buses, the child with intellectual disabilities will learn more and faster if given the opportunity to ride a bus in his or her local community.

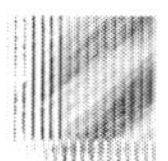

Core Concept

Children with intellectual disabilities are able to more easily grasp concrete versus abstract concepts in a learning situation.

Learning Sets and Generalization

Learning sets and generalization appear to be interrelated in the ability to solve problems. Whereas **learning set** refers to an individual's ability to learn how to learn, **generalization** happens when a child applies previously learned content or skills to a situation in which the information has not been taught. Generalization, then, is the ability to apply learning from previous experiences to new situations with similar components.

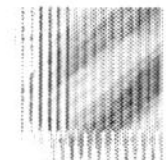

Core Concept

Children with intellectual disabilities develop learning sets at a slower rate than peers without disabilities.

Children with intellectual disabilities develop learning sets at a slower rate than same-age peers without disabilities. The formation of learning sets, however, can be facilitated in the classroom by providing successful learning experiences for the child and moving sequentially from easy-to-hard content. The following are some suggestions for working with the child with intellectual disabilities who is having difficulty in the development of generalization skills:

1. Age seems to make a difference in the ability to generalize learning for all children. Younger children generalize learning with greater ease than older children.
2. The child with intellectual disabilities will generalize more efficiently when both the initial task and the new task are very similar. Generalization is most effective if a considerable number of the operations involved in the first task can be performed as a unit in the new task.
3. Meaningfulness is extremely important to the person's ability to generalize. A more meaningful task is both easier to learn initially and easier to generalize to a second setting.

Educational Achievement

Core Concept

Children with intellectual disabilities will benefit from instruction in academic skill areas.

Children with mild intellectual disabilities require a systematic instructional program that accounts for differences in the rate of learning, but they may achieve as high as fourth- or fifth-grade level in reading and arithmetic. Reading is considered one of the weakest areas for these children, especially reading comprehension. Most children with intellectual disabilities read far below the average for children without disabilities (Katims, 2000).

A significant relationship appears to exist between measured intellectual capacity and reading achievement. A growing body of research, however, indicates that children with moderate to severe intellectual disabilities can be taught to read at least a protective, or survival, vocabulary—sometimes referred to as **functional reading.** In a functional reading program, children with intellectual disabilities develop meaningful vocabulary that facilitates inclusion in school and community settings (Browder & Snell, 2000). The goal is for "students to have enough of a sight word vocabulary to be able to scan printed materials and glean the key information needed in a given activity" (Browder & Snell, 2000, p. 526).

Children with intellectual disabilities are also deficient in math skills, but the majority of those with mild intellectual disabilities can learn basic addition and subtraction. However, these children will have significant difficulty in the areas of mathematical reasoning and problem-solving tasks (Beirne-Smith, Ittenbach, & Patton, 2002). Arithmetic skills are taught most efficiently through the use of money concepts. The immediate practical application motivates the student. Regardless of the approach used, arithmetic instruction must be concrete and practical to compensate for the child's deficiencies in reasoning ability.

ADAPTIVE SKILLS

The American Association on Mental Retardation (AAMR) (2002) identifies significant limitations in adaptive skills as important criteria for defining intellectual disabilities.

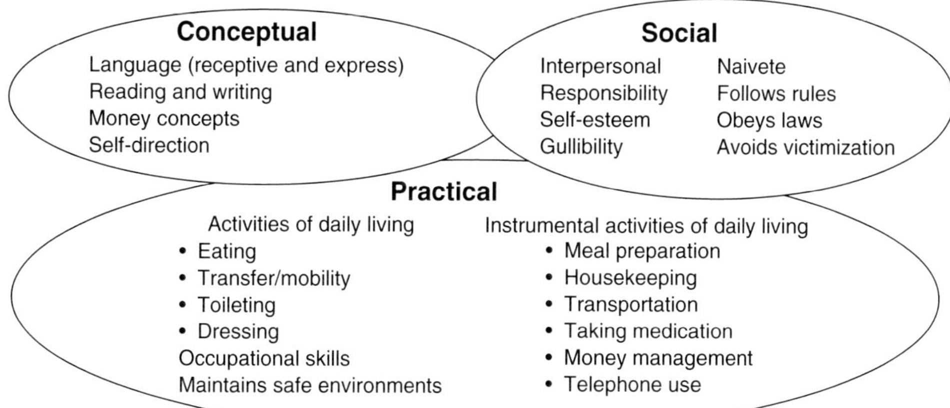

Figure 8–1
Examples of Conceptual, Social, and Practical Adaptive Skills

Source: Adapted from *Mental Retardation: Definition, Classification, and Systems of Supports* (10th ed., p. 42). Washington, DC: American Association on Mental Retardation.

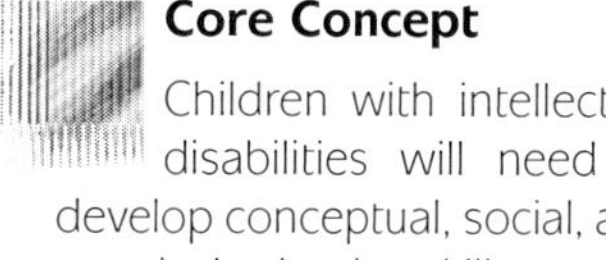

Core Concept

Children with intellectual disabilities will need to develop conceptual, social, and practical adaptive skills.

For an individual to meet the criterion for intellectual disabilities, limitations must occur in conceptual, social, and practical adaptive skills (see Figure 8–1 for examples of adaptive skills in each of these areas).

From an educational perspective, **adaptive skill development** may be defined as the ability (or lack thereof) to apply basic information learned in school to naturally occurring activities in the school, home, or community. Depending on the age of the child with intellectual disabilities, the need is to develop appropriate skills for coping in school, interpersonal relationships, language skills, and for taking care of personal needs.

The child with mild intellectual disabilities may have difficulty in both learning and applying adaptive skills for a number of reasons. As such, these children will need to be taught appropriate reasoning, judgment, and social skills that lead to more positive social relationships and personal competence.

Siperstein and Leffert (1997) studied the social acceptance of children with intellectual disabilities among peers with disabilities in general education classrooms. The researchers identified the characteristics of socially accepted and socially rejected students with intellectual disabilities. Characteristics of socially accepted children included a higher level of social skills. These children were not perceived by their peers without disabilities as aggressive in their behavior. The authors suggest there is value in recognizing and teaching the skills that distinguish between those children who are accepted and those who are not.

Interacting with peers is important for the intellectual and social development of children with intellectual disabilities.

Lee, Yoo, and Bak (2003) also investigated the quality of social relationships among children with mild intellectual disabilities and peers who were not disabled and reported similar results. These authors found that the children without disabilities did perceive of their classmates with intellectual disabilities as friends. However, they had concerns that limitations in communication and some behavior problems made it difficult to maintain a friendship with a child who had an intellectual disability.

Adaptive skill deficits for children with more severe intellectual disabilities may include head rolling, body rocking, twirling, teeth grinding, and inappropriate vocalizations. Children with severe intellectual disabilities may also engage in self-injurious acts, including self-biting and head banging.

MOTIVATION

Core Concept

Children with intellectual disabilities can learn to become success strivers rather than failure avoiders.

Children with intellectual disabilities are often described as lacking motivation—an unwillingness or inability to initiate new tasks or complete existing ones, to take responsibility, and to be self-directed. In fact, this apparent lack of motivation may be more attributable to the way these children learn to avoid situations because of a fear of failure. The child with a history of failure in school may be afraid to take risks or participate in new situations. The result of failure is often **learned helplessness,** or the feeling that "no matter what I do or how hard I try, I will not succeed." To overcome learned helplessness, the child with intellectual disabilities needs to have experiences that have high probabilities for success. The opportunity to seek success, rather than avoid failure, is a very important learning experience for these children.

Prestige, success, and self-respect, which fulfill the need for esteem, may be formidable goals for children with intellectual disabilities. Although the child may never be able to match the accomplishments of their peers without disabilities, they can find considerable satisfaction and contentment in doing their personal best, in being well-liked by peers, and in contributing to a better life for themselves and their families.

PHYSICAL AND HEALTH CHARACTERISTICS

Physical Differences

The vast majority of children with intellectual disabilities do not differ from children without disabilities in their physical appearance. A positive correlation does exist, however, between severity of intellectual deficit and extent of physical differences (Horvat, 2000). Among children with mild intellectual disabilities, no differences may be evident because the disability is not usually associated with physiological factors. For children with moderate to severe intellectual disabilities, physical differences are more apparent and often can be traced to biomedical conditions (e.g., Down syndrome, hydrocephaly).

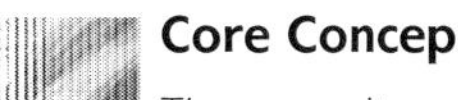

Core Concept

The severity of a child's intellectual disability is positively correlated with differences in the physical appearance.

Motor development of children with intellectual disabilities may be significantly below the norms for children who are not disabled. Children with intellectual disabilities are generally less developed in areas such as equilibrium, locomotion, and manual dexterity. Research has also suggested a higher prevalence of vision and hearing impairments among children with intellectual disabilities (Hardman et al., 2006).

Speech problems as well are more prevalent among children with intellectual disabilities (Beirne-Smith et al., 2002). The most common speech problems are articulation, voice, and stuttering problems (Hardman et al., 2006). Most children with severe intellectual disabilities have multiple challenges, exhibiting difficulties in nearly every aspect of cognitive and physical development.

Health Differences

Health problems for children with intellectual disabilities may be associated with either genetic or environmental factors. For example, there is a greater probability that people with **Down syndrome** will have a higher incidence of congenital heart defects and respiratory problems directly linked to their genetic condition (March of Dimes, 2004). On the other hand, some children with intellectual disabilities experience health problems due to environmental conditions. A significantly higher percentage of children with intellectual disabilities come from low

Core Concept

Several genetic and environmental factors can contribute to health problems for children with intellectual disabilities.

socioeconomic backgrounds in comparison to peers without disabilities. Children who lack proper nutrition and have not learned hygiene skills have a greater susceptibility to infections. Health services for families in these situations may be minimal or nonexistent, depending on whether they are able to access government medical support. As such, children with intellectual disabilities may become ill and are absent from school more often than their peers without disabilities.

EDUCATIONAL PROGRAMS AND SERVICES

The Individuals with Disabilities Education Act (IDEA)

Core Concept

The major provisions of IDEA are multidisciplinary and nonbiased assessment, a free and appropriate public education, the individualized education program (IEP), parental rights, and education in the **least-restrictive environment.**

Historically, the education of students with intellectual disabilities meant segregated programs and services. Before the 1960s, most special education services were available only in separate schools and classrooms that segregated the children with intellectual disabilities from their peers without disabilities. Additionally, special education was available primarily to the child with mild intellectual disabilities who was defined as "educable," a term implying that although the child had intellectual deficits, he or she still could benefit from some of the traditional academic curriculum taught in the public schools. Children functioning at lower levels (as determined solely by IQ tests) were usually excluded from public schools because they required "training" in such areas as self-help, language development, gross-motor skills, and academic readiness. The needs of children labeled "trainable" were not within the purview of the public education curriculum. For children with more severe intellectual disabilities, exclusion from the public schools was nearly universal. The pervading view was that these children needed habilitation, not education. Children with severe intellectual disabilities were often labeled "custodial," implying that care and management were the intended service outcomes.

The passage of the Education for All Handicapped Children Act (Public Law 94-142) in 1975 was the culmination of years of litigation in the United States dealing with discrimination against students with disabilities. Public Law 94-142 (renamed the **Individuals with Disabilities Education Act [IDEA]** in 1990) mandated that all eligible children with disabilities in the nation's schools must be provided a *free and appropriate public education* (FAPE). IDEA requires that these students, regardless of the extent or type of disability, receive at public expense the special education services necessary to meet their individual needs. **Special education** means specially designed instruction, at no cost to parents, provided in all settings (such as the classroom, in physical education, at home, and in hospitals or institutions). IDEA stipulates that students with disabilities are to receive any related services necessary to ensure that they benefit from their educational experience. **Related services** include

> transportation, and such developmental, corrective, and other supportive services (including speech-language pathology and audiology services, psychological

> services, physical and occupational therapy, recreation, including therapeutic recreation, social work services, counseling services, including rehabilitation counseling, orientation and mobility services, and medical services, except that such medical services shall be for diagnostic and evaluation purposes only) as may be required to assist a child with a disability to benefit from special education, and includes the early identification and assessment of disabling conditions in children. (2004 Amendments to IDEA, PL 108-446, Sec. 602[26])

IDEA requires that in order to be eligible for special education services, a child must meet two criteria. First, he or she must be identified as having one of the disability conditions identified in federal law or their counterparts in a state's special education law. One of these conditions is intellectual disabilities (referred to in the law as mental retardation). However, IDEA as reauthorized in 2004 also gives states and local education agencies (LEA) the option of eliminating categories of disability (such as intellectual disabilities or specific learning disabilities) for children up to the age of 9. For this age group, a state or LEA may define a child with a disability as

> (i) experiencing developmental delays, as defined by the State and as measured by appropriate diagnostic instruments and procedures, in one or more of the following areas: physical development, cognitive development, communication development, social or emotional development, or adaptive development; and (ii) who, by reason thereof, needs special education and related services. (IDEA 2004, PL 108-446, Sec. 602[3][B])

The second criteria for eligibility is the student's demonstrated need for specialized instruction and related services in order to receive an appropriate education. This need is determined by a multidisciplinary team of professionals and parents. Both criteria for eligibility must be met. If this is not the case, it is possible for a student to be identified as having a disability but not be eligible to receive special education services under IDEA. These students may still be entitled to reasonable accommodations or modifications in their educational program under Section 504 of the Vocational Rehabilitation Act and the **Americans with Disabilities Act (ADA).**

Originally, IDEA allowed states to exclude from the mandate all children under 5 years of age. In 1986, however, the provisions of the law were extended under Public Law 99-457, Education of the Handicapped Act Amendments, to children ages 3 to 5. Additionally, a new early intervention program for infants and toddlers was initiated.

In the 2000–2001 school year, nearly 6.5 million students with disabilities between the ages of 3 and 21 years were served under IDEA. Of these 6.5 million students, about 11% (612,978) are defined as having intellectual disabilities (U.S. Department of Education, 2002).

Specifically, federal requirements, as amended in the IDEA 2004, provide for the following:

- A free and appropriate public education
- Nondiscriminatory and multidisciplinary assessment of educational needs

- Development and implementation of an IEP for each student
- Parental involvement in the development of each student's educational program
- Education in the least-restrictive environment (LRE)

A Free and Appropriate Public Education (FAPE). Every student with a disability is entitled to a free and appropriate public education (FAPE) based upon individual ability and need. The FAPE provisions in IDEA are based on the Fourteenth Amendment to the U.S. Constitution, guaranteeing equal protection of the law. No student with a disability can be excluded from a public education based on a disability. In 1982, a major interpretation of FAPE was handed down by the U.S. Supreme Court in *Hendrick Hudson District Board of Education v. Rowley* (1982). The Supreme Court declared that an appropriate education consist of "specially designed instruction and related services" that are "individually designed to provide educational benefit." Often referred to as the "some educational benefit" standard, the ruling mandates that a state need not provide an ideal education but must provide a beneficial one for students with disabilities.

Nondiscriminatory and Multidisciplinary Assessment. The assessment provisions of IDEA require that students be tested in their native or primary language and that all evaluation procedures be free of cultural or racial discrimination. Assessment is to be conducted by a **multidisciplinary team** that works together in determining the needs of each child relative to a free and appropriate public education.

The Individualized Education Program (IEP). The IEP is developed by professionals from the multidisciplinary team, parents, and the student, where appropriate. The team should consist of the student's parents, at least one special education teacher, at least one regular (general) education teacher if the child is, or may be, participating in the general education environment, and a representative of the local education agency (LEA). The LEA representative must be qualified to provide or supervise the provision of specially designed instruction to meet the unique needs of children with disabilities. This individual must also be knowledgeable about the general curriculum and the availability of resources within the LEA.

At the discretion of the parents or the LEA, the IEP team may also include an individual who can interpret the instructional implications of evaluation results; other individuals who have knowledge or special expertise regarding the child may also participate in the IEP process, including related services personnel as appropriate and, whenever appropriate, the student with disability.

IDEA requires that each child's IEP include the following:

- Each child's IEP must include a statement of the child's present levels of academic achievement and functional performance, including how the child's disability affects the child's involvement and progress in the general education curriculum. For preschool children, the statement must describe how the disability affects the child's participation in appropriate activities.

- It must include a statement of measurable annual goals, including academic and functional goals, designed to meet the child's needs that result from the child's disability to enable the child to be involved in and make progress in the general education curriculum. The statement must meet each of the child's other educational needs that result from the child's disability. For children with disabilities who take *alternate assessments* aligned to alternate achievement standards, a description of benchmarks or short-term objectives is needed.
- It must include a description of how the child's progress toward meeting the annual goals described will be measured and when periodic reports on the progress the child is making toward meeting the annual goals will be provided.
- The IEP must include a statement of the special education and related services and supplementary aids and services, based on peer-reviewed research to the extent practicable, to be provided to the child, or on behalf of the child, and a statement of the program modifications or supports for school personnel that will be provided for the child to (a) advance appropriately toward attaining the annual goals, (b) be involved in and make progress in the general education curriculum and to participate in extracurricular and other nonacademic activities, and (c) be educated and participate with other children with and without disabilities.
- It must include an explanation of the extent, if any, to which the child will not participate with children without disabilities in the regular (general education) class.
- Last, the IEP must include a statement of any individual accommodations that are necessary to measure the academic achievement and functional performance of the child on state- and districtwide assessments. If the IEP team determines that the child should take an alternate assessment of student achievement, a statement of why the child cannot participate in the regular assessment must be provided. Finally, an alternate assessment must be selected that is appropriate for the child. (Adapted from IDEA, 2004, PL 108-446, Sec. 614[d])

Parental Involvement. IDEA requires parent involvement in the IEP process for two reasons. First, the requirement creates an opportunity for parents to be more involved in decisions regarding their child's education program. Second, the student and the family are protected from decisions that could adversely affect their lives. Families would be more secure in the knowledge that every reasonable attempt was being made to educate their child appropriately.

Provisions under IDEA for parents granted them rights to the following:

- Consent in writing before the child is initially evaluated
- Consent in writing before the child is initially placed in a special education program
- A request for an independent education evaluation if they think the school's evaluation is inappropriate
- A request for an evaluation at public expense if a due-process hearing decision is that the public agency's evaluation was inappropriate
- Participation on the committee that considers the evaluation, placement, and programming of the child
- Inspection and review of educational records and to challenge information believed to be inaccurate, misleading, or in violation of the privacy or other rights of the child
- A request for a copy of information from their child's educational record
- A request for a hearing concerning the school's proposal or refusal to initiate or change the identification, evaluation, or placement of the child, or the provision of a free appropriate public education

IDEA requires that schools regularly inform parents about their son's or daughter's progress in meeting IEP goals. For more information on working effectively with parents of children with disabilities, see the Tips for Professionals feature.

Education in the Least-Restrictive Environment (LRE). Students with disabilities are to receive their education with peers who are not disabled to the maximum extent appropriate which is known as the least-restrictive environment (LRE). To meet this mandate, IDEA regulations describe a **continuum of placements** to be made available, ranging from placement in regular classrooms with support services to homebound and hospital programs. Figure 8–2 presents educational service options for students with disabilities. Levels I through IV of the continuum involve inclusion of students with intellectual disabilities in a general education classroom with their peers without disabilities for all or some part of the school day. Levels V through VII emphasize placements ranging from full-time in a special education classroom to homebound and hospital instructional programs.

Inclusion in General Education Settings

Core Concept

Successful inclusion of students with intellectual disabilities in general education settings is dependent on the availability of appropriate services and supports.

An increasing number of educators are calling for a more *inclusive* educational approach for these students. Hardman and colleagues (2006) suggest that **inclusive education** may be defined as providing services and support appropriate to the needs of students with disabilities within general education settings. Peterson and Hittie (2003) describe this paradigm as "push-in" services. Whereas the traditional model for special education has been "pulling the student out of the general education class" to

Tips for Professionals

Increasing Parent Involvement

Jeffrey Thompson is the Disney 2004 Outstanding Elementary Teacher and Teacher of the Year. He teaches kindergarten at Evergreen Elementary School on the Fort Lewis Army Post in Washington, DC and works closely with the school's special education teachers. Below he shares some of his tips for developing effective collaboration among teachers and parents.

Relationships First, Education Second

- Start the year with a "parent-only" meeting before the first day of school. Parents often come to the classroom with preconceived ideas and fears. This is your opportunity to interact with parents without child interruptions and develop the parent-teacher relationship. Parents are able to focus on your words and interact with you and the other parents in the class. This meeting also allows you to set the expectations and tone for the year, relieve parent concerns, and establish a positive parent climate in your room. The underlying theme for this first meeting: that both educators and parents are the child's teachers. Schedule "parent-only" meetings through the year to build and maintain parent relationships, align teacher with parent, and maintain parent education.

Create a Partnership between Teachers and Parents

We can't expect academic assistance from parents if they don't understand the skills being taught. Understand that you are teacher to both student and parent.

- Provide weekly parent education tips that explain the concepts being taught and provide support materials that allow parents to help at home.
- Bridge the gap between home and school through thematic home projects.
- Provide parent homework and a method of weekly communication between parent and teacher.
- Record the efforts of parent involvement on each child's report card, so parents can see the importance of their work and the value you place on it.

Harness the Talents and Energies of Your Students' Parents

- Ask parents to chair and plan family events and class fundraisers. Empower them to make this their child's best year of learning. Their involvement establishes "buy-in" and a sense of ownership in the classroom.

Use Your Data to Establish Future Goals for Both School and Home

- Clearly communicate assessment goals and dates.
- Share the results of assessment with parents.
- Use a variety of assessment data to establish future goals for both home and school. Provide parents with the materials and education they need to assist their child.
- Collaborate with all specialists who work with your students, so all adults and parents work toward student success.
- Help parents set up graphic organizers and data collection sheets that indicate work completed and methods used at home. These graphic organizers provide indispensable parent documentation and will become a valuable tool for

continues on next page

continues from previous page

conferences when establishing resource needs as well as for future IEP and 504 meetings when new goals are established.

Encouragement vs. Praise

- Telling your students and parents that they are doing a great job is "hollow" praise. Offer encouragement rather than praise by giving specific examples of a job well done.
- Send home regular communication to all parents that details specific examples of parent-initiated creative teaching strategies and methods. Follow up with phone calls of encouragement and support. This motivates involved parents to continue working with their children and encourages less involved parents to become active members of the education process.
- Never give up . . . some parents take longer to become a member of your learning community. Celebrate student learning.
- Celebrate—provide regular events that showcase your students' learning and invite parents to participate.
- Use each event as an opportunity for parent education and encouragement while developing a community.
- End the year with a celebration of both student and parent successes, and solicit the parents' commitment to continue supporting their children throughout their academic careers.

Source: Adapted from "Strategies to Increase Parent Involvement That Really Work!" by J. Thompson, 2004. *CEC Today, 11*(2). Retrieved December 15, 2004, from http://www.cec.sped.org/bk/cectoday/strategies_1.html.

receive support, inclusive education focuses on "pushing services and supports" into the general education setting.

Inclusion may include full or partial participation in a general education class. **Full inclusion** of students with intellectual disabilities in a general education classroom is an approach in which all instruction and support services come to the student; the student is not pulled out of the regular class into a special education program. Under the full inclusion approach, a special education teacher and other support personnel collaborate with the general education teacher to meet the needs of the student with intellectual disabilities in the context of a class that is made up of primarily students without disabilities. In the **partial inclusion** approach, students may receive most of their education in the general education classroom but are pulled out into a special education program when the IEP team considers it appropriate to their individual needs.

The proponents of full inclusion argue that any pullout of students with intellectual disabilities into a separate special educational setting is not in the student's best interest. It results in a fragmented approach to instruction in which general and special educators do not work together and individual student needs go unmet (Lipsky & Gartner, 1999; Sailor, Gee, & Karasoff, 2000). Those opposing full inclusion suggest that the general education teacher does not have the training or expertise to meet the diverse needs of students with intellectual disabilities. These teachers are already significantly overburdened with large class sizes and little support to meet the needs of students without disabilities (Mills, Cole, Jenkins, & Dale, 1998).

Opponents also argue that specialized academic and social instruction can best be provided in a specialized (pullout) setting for which special educators have been specifically trained and have access to the specialized resources necessary to meet the needs of students with intellectual disabilities.

Two major professional and parent associations, The ARC and TASH, have taken positions on educating students with disabilities in general education classrooms. The ARC (2004) states in order for these students to participate in a democratic society, students with intellectual disabilities and related developmental disabilities must receive an education that includes individualized supports and access to a general education curriculum in inclusive settings with peers of the same age. (See the feature Should Students with Intellectual Disabilities Be Educated in General Education Classrooms?)

TASH, an international association of people with disabilities, their family members, and professionals, also advocates for educating students in a general education setting. The association states that every school community should provide "quality, inclusive education for all students with disabilities that is predicated on a shared vision of high expectations for all students and a commitment to a set of learning

Should Students with Intellectual Disabilities Be Educated in General Education Classrooms?

The ARC's position statement on education says the following:

- The Individuals with Disabilities Education Act (IDEA) requires that students with disabilities be educated to the maximum extent [appropriate] with students who are not disabled. Despite this law, many students . . . remain segregated in self-contained classrooms in separate schools, with limited or no opportunities to participate academically and socially in general education classrooms and school activities. Segregation of students in schools perpetuates the alienation of these students. Many do not have access to the same academic and extracurricular activities and services provided to other students. Frequently, these students leave school unprepared for adult life in the community.
- Additionally, many schools lack sufficient and/or trained educators and support personnel to provide an appropriate education. Despite some gains, special education programs continue to be under funded, particularly by the federal government. Some communities still oppose special education and seek to limit educational opportunities for students in special education. Indeed the education of students with disabilities has been under assault on numerous fronts by the press, school officials and the public.
- Individual Education Programs (IEPs) for students with intellectual disabilities must:
    - Be provided to the maximum extent possible with students who do not have disabilities.
    - Be constructed around an Individualized Educational Program that meets the student's needs and offers the necessary supports to ensure adherence to the IEP.
    - Be sensitive to linguistic, cultural, gender, and socioeconomic differences as well as individual family circumstances.

Source: From "Position Statement on Education" by The ARC, 2004. Retrieved December 28, 2004, from http://www.thearc.org/posits/educationpos.doc.

This student is progressing academically, although more slowly than peers without intellectual disabilities.

goals or standards that are strong, clear, understood, and put into practice" (TASH, 2005).

Whether full or partial inclusion, it is clear that the success of any inclusive educational program for students with intellectual disabilities depends on the availability of supports to both the student with intellectual disabilities and the general education teacher. These supports can be described as formal and natural. **Formal supports** may include the availability of qualified general and special education teachers, access to paraprofessionals and peer tutors, appropriate multilevel instructional materials, and **assistive technology** (e.g., talking computers, language boards). **Natural supports** are most often described as the student's family, friends, and classmates (McDonnell, Hardman, & McDonnell, 2003). McDonnell et al. suggest that success in inclusive programs depends on the availability of an array of natural supports within the general education setting, including peer tutors, and parent volunteers.

Core Concept

Placement in general education settings with support services includes both the consulting teacher and resource room models.

Needed Supports in General Education Classrooms. As depicted in Figure 8–2, placement at Level II means that the student remains in the general education classroom with support services. The classroom teacher is responsible for any adaptation that may be necessary for the student's success in this setting. Consequently, the teacher must have the skills to develop and adapt curricula to meet individual needs. Approximately 10% of students with intellectual disabilities are in a general education

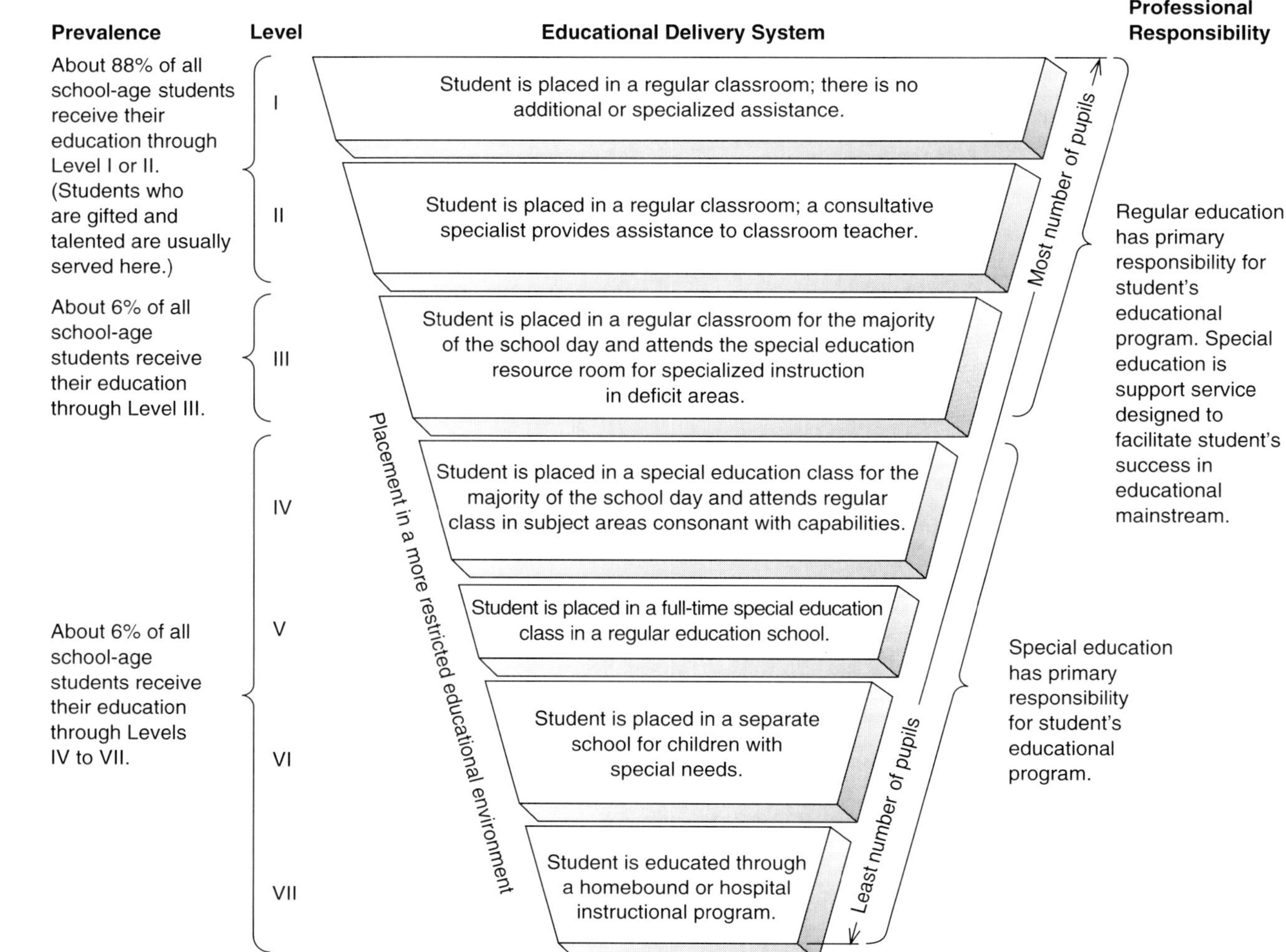
Prevalence
Level
Educational Delivery System
Professional Responsibility
About 88% of all school-age students receive their education through Level I or II. (Students who are gifted and talented are usually served here.)
About 6% of all school-age students receive their education through Level III.
About 6% of all school-age students receive their education through Levels IV to VII.
I
II
III
IV
V
VI
VII
Student is placed in a regular classroom; there is no additional or specialized assistance.
Student is placed in a regular classroom; a consultative specialist provides assistance to classroom teacher.
Student is placed in a regular classroom for the majority of the school day and attends the special education resource room for specialized instruction in deficit areas.
Student is placed in a special education class for the majority of the school day and attends regular class in subject areas consonant with capabilities.
Student is placed in a full-time special education class in a regular education school.
Student is placed in a separate school for children with special needs.
Student is educated through a homebound or hospital instructional program.
Placement in a more restricted educational environment
Most number of pupils
Least number of pupils
Regular education has primary responsibility for student's educational program. Special education is support service designed to facilitate student's success in educational mainstream.
Special education has primary responsibility for student's educational program.

Figure 8–2
Educational Service Options for Students with Disabilities

Source: From *Human Exceptionality: Society, School, and Family* (8th ed., p. 35) by M. L. Hardman, C. J. Drew, and M. W. Egan, 2006. Boston: Allyn & Bacon.

Competencies for General Education and Special Education Teachers in an Inclusive Classroom

The University of Northern Iowa's Department of Special Education outlines teacher competencies needed:

- Ability to problem solve, to be able to informally assess the skills a student needs (rather than relying solely on a standardized curriculum).
- Ability to take advantage of children's individual interests and use their internal motivation for developing needed skills.
- Ability to set high but alternative expectations that are suitable for the students; this means developing alternative assessments.
- Ability to make appropriate expectations for EACH student, regardless of the student's capabilities. If teachers can do this, it allows all students to be included in a class and school.
- Ability to determine how to modify assignments for students; how to design classroom activities with so many levels that all students have a part. This teaching skill can apply not just at the elementary or secondary level, but at the college level as well. It will mean more activity-based teaching rather than seat-based teaching.
- Ability to learn how to value all kinds of skills that students bring to a class, not just the academic skills. In doing this, teachers will make it explicit that in their classrooms they value all skills, even if that is not a clear value of a whole school.
- Ability to provide daily success for all students. Teachers have to work to counteract the message all students get when certain students are continually taken out of class for special work.

Source: From "Children That Learn Together, Learn to Live Together" by the University of Northern Iowa, Department of Special Education, 2004. Retrieved November 19, 2004, from http://www.uni.edu/coe/inclusion/standards/index.html.

classroom for the entire school day (U.S. Department of Education, 2002).

Because general educators are an integral part of a successful educational experience for the child with intellectual disabilities, it is important that they receive expanded university preparation in the education of children with disabilities. Needed skills include an understanding of how a disabling condition can affect the ability to learn academic skills or to adapt in social situations. The teacher must also be able to recognize learning or behavior problems and to seek out appropriate school resources that will facilitate the implementation of an appropriate individualized program. School districts also have a responsibility to the teacher and the child. Appropriate resources and consultative personnel must be available to assist the general education teacher, and time must be set aside for planning and coordinating activities for the child. (See the feature titled Competencies for General Education and Special Education Teachers in an Inclusive Classroom.)

The **consulting teacher,** sometimes referred to as a curriculum specialist, itinerant teacher, or master teacher, provides assistance to the classroom teacher in the general education setting. This specialist may help a teacher identify the child's specific problem areas and recommend appropriate assessment techniques and educational strategies. As support specialists, these special educators must:

- work with school personnel (including general educators, school principal, and related services personnel) and parents to identify the educational needs of students with disabilities.
- link student assessment information to the development of the IEP and access to the general curriculum.
- determine appropriate student accommodations and instructional adaptations.
- deliver intensive instruction using specialized teaching methods. (Hardman et al., 2006, pp. 78–79)

Consulting teachers are able to build mutually trusting relationships through positive interactions with other professionals, are responsive to others, and have a good understanding of the dynamics of social interaction. They view consultation as a learning experience for themselves as well as the professionals and students they serve. Effective consultants are also very concrete and specific in making suggestions to improve students' educational experiences, but are capable of looking at issues from broad theoretical perspectives. Finally, Lipsky and Gartner (1996) suggest that effective consultants are good researchers who know how to locate and use resources effectively.

Working with a consultant, general education teachers are supported in their own backyard, so to speak, with emphasis on adapting the classroom environment to the needs of the child with intellectual disabilities. If the child requires more support than a consultant can give, however, a more restricted setting, such as a resource room, may be necessary.

The consultant can also assist the classroom teacher in the implementation of a cooperative learning program between students with intellectual disabilities and their peers without disabilities. Peers can be a powerful support system within the classroom in both academic and behavioral areas. They often have more influence on their classmates' behavior than the teacher does. Peer support programs may range from creating opportunities in the class for students with disabilities to socially interact with their peers to highly structured programs of peer-mediated instruction. Peer-mediated instruction involves a structured interaction between two or more students under the direct supervision of a classroom teacher.

A student with intellectual disabilities placed at Level III in the cascade of services remains in the general education setting most of the school day and goes to a **resource room** for a portion of his or her instructional programming. Resource room placement still requires collaboration between general education teachers and other consulting professionals. Services may range from assisting a teacher in the use of tests or modification of curriculum to direct instruction with students.

The resource room also reflects a philosophy of sharing of responsibility between general education and special education. The resource room represents another effort to include children as much as possible into general education and still offer special education support services when needed. This approach allows the child to remain with children without disabilities for the majority of the school day while removing a great deal of the stigma associated with separate full-day special education classrooms.

The resource room teacher maintains a room within the school building and is a regular member of the school faculty. The special education teacher's function is essentially twofold. The first responsibility is to provide instructional support services to the child with a disability. These services may include orientation to the school for new students, tutorial services, counseling, and training of paraprofessionals if needed. A second function is to serve as a liaison between the classroom teacher and the child. The resource room teacher is responsible for facilitating each classroom teacher's understanding of the instructional and social needs of children with intellectual disabilities.

Core Concept

Students with intellectual disabilities may be educated in part-time special education classes in a general education school.

The Part-Time Special Education Classroom. The part-time special class (Level IV) involves the sharing of responsibility for the child by both general and special education teachers. The major difference between a part-time special class and a resource room is in the area of primary responsibility. In the resource room, the child with intellectual disabilities is primarily a student in the general education classroom with support services from special education. In the part-time special class, the students are assigned to a special education teacher and class and remain in the same room with the same teacher for a large portion of the day. During the remainder of the day, these students are included in as many general education activities as is appropriate to their needs. In most instances, the child remains in the special class for academic subjects. Inclusive classes are often less academically oriented and include music, shop, home economics, physical education, and art. Proponents of the part-time special class suggest that a student has the advantage of a nonthreatening academic setting, along with inclusion into the social mainstream.

Full-Time Special Education Classes and Schools

Some classes for children with more moderate and severe levels of intellectual disabilities are located in special classes or schools exclusively for students with intellectual disabilities.

Proponents of special classes and schools argue that they provide services for large numbers of children with intellectual disabilities and therefore offer greater homogeneity in grouping and programming for children. They also support this type of arrangement because it allows teachers to specialize in their teaching areas. For example, a teacher might specialize in reading for children with intellectual disabilities, another in math, and a third in music. In smaller programs with only one or two teachers, these individuals may have to teach subjects as diverse as art and home economics.

Core Concept

Students with intellectual disabilities may be educated in full-time special education classes in a general education school or in a special school.

Special classes and schools also allow for centralization of supplies, equipment, and special facilities for children with intellectual disabilities. Smaller, isolated programs may not be able to justify the purchase of expensive equipment used only occasionally, but the special school can justify expenditures based on more frequent use by a larger number of classes.

Research on the efficacy of special classes and schools reflect that regardless of the severity of their disability, children with intellectual disabilities benefit more from an inclusive education program where opportunities for inclusion with peers without disabilities are systematically planned and implemented (Gee, 1996; McDonnell et al., 2003) Additionally, in inclusive settings where there is access to needed supports, no substantiated detrimental outcomes have been found for students with severe disabilities. Systematically planned interactions between students with severe intellectual disabilities and peers without disabilities yield improved attitudes and social interaction (Gee, 1996).

INSTRUCTIONAL APPROACHES

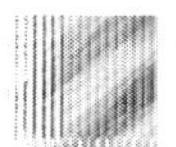

Core Concept

Learning in the school setting is a continual process of adaptation for students with intellectual disabilities.

Students with intellectual disabilities will learn if provided appropriate educational services and supports oriented to their individual needs. The individualized instructional program, based on annual goals, is a critical factor in ensuring appropriate education. The selection of curricula for students with intellectual disabilities, however, has been a problem for educators because of the students' heterogeneous needs. These students do not learn as quickly or as effectively as their peers without disabilities. As such, a "one size fits all" approach to teaching academic skills is often not appropriate. In the following section, we discuss some instructional approaches for children with intellectual disabilities that emphasize the acquisition of both academic and adaptive skills.

Teaching Academic Skills

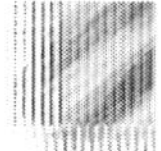

Core Concept

Instruction in academic areas may include a developmental or functional approach to learning.

The primary instructional approach in the elementary schools emphasizes learning of foundation skills in the basic academic areas. For example, reading is learned as a set of sequenced skills that can be divided into three phases: (a) the development of readiness skills (left-to-right sequencing, visual and auditory discrimination skills, and memory skills); (b) word recognition or decoding skills (breaking the code and correctly identifying the abstract symbols in sequence); and (c) reading comprehension (giving symbols meaning). Each step in the process is a prerequisite for the next, and the whole forms a framework for higher levels of functioning. Students with mild intellectual disabilities will require a systematic instructional program that accounts for differences in the rate of learning, but they can learn to read when given "rich, intensive, and extensive literary experiences" (Katims, 2000). In fact, these students may achieve as high as a fourth- or fifth-grade level in reading. In a 1996 study, Katims found that students with intellectual disabilities made significant progress in literacy programs that emphasized **direct instruction** (the direct teaching of letters, words, and syntactic, phonetic, and semantic analysis) in conjunction with written literature that was meaningful to the student, or from the student's own writings.

Some students with intellectual disabilities, however, may not efficiently acquire the necessary prerequisites within the time frame the schools prescribe. These children need significantly more time to learn academic skills. For others, instructional time may be better spent in such areas as personal management, mobility, or communication.

Another approach to learning academic skills is often termed **functional** and is consistent with an adaptive learning curriculum. In this approach, the basic academic tools are taught in the context of daily living activities and in the natural setting as much as possible (home, community). A functional life program in the area of reading focuses primarily on those words that facilitate adaptation in the child's environment. Functional mathematics may relate more to environmental needs like telling time or spending money. Whatever the academic area, a functional approach pairs the skill being taught with an environmental cue. Browder and Snell (2000) stressed that when attempting to functionalize learned skills, the teacher must use instructional materials that are realistic. Traditional materials—workbooks, basal readers, flash cards, and so on—are not practical because the student is unable to relate the materials to his or her world.

The curricular approaches discussed above are not necessarily mutually exclusive. A foundation approach can incorporate many functional elements to reduce the abstract nature of the academic subjects and facilitate efficient learning for the student with intellectual disabilities.

Teaching Adaptive Skills

Core Concept

Adaptive skills decrease an individual's dependence on others and increase opportunities for school and community participation.

Schools, which excluded many children with intellectual disabilities for the better part of this century, now face the challenge of providing an educational experience consistent with the individual needs of these children. Educational programming has been expanded to include the learning of adaptive skills. Teaching adaptive skills to children with intellectual disabilities is based on the premise that if these skills are not taught through formal instruction, they will not be learned. For children without intellectual disabilities, teaching these skills is often unnecessary because they are acquired through daily experiences.

Adaptive skill content areas for school-age children with intellectual disabilities include motor, personal management (self-care), social, communication, and functional academic skills. The development of gross- and fine-motor skills is a prerequisite to successful learning in other adaptive areas. Gross-motor-skills development relates to general mobility-balance and locomotor patterns. This includes neck and head control, rolling, body righting, sitting, crawling, standing, walking, running, jumping, and skipping. Fine-motor training includes learning to reach, grasp, and manipulate objects. For the child to develop motor skills, he or she must be able to fix on an object visually and track a moving target. The coordination of fine-motor skills and visual tracking (eye-hand coordination) is both a prerequisite to object-control skills that are required in vocational situations and a basis for learning leisure activities.

Personal management skills are essential to the child's independence at home and at school. The primary personal management areas are safety, dressing, hygiene, and eating. Westling and Fox (2004) describe a five-step task analysis for teaching a student to eat finger foods:

1. Reach to locate the food
2. Grasp the food
3. Lift the food from the table to the mouth
4. Put the food into the mouth
5. Chew and swallow the food

Dressing skills involve learning to button, zip, buckle, lace, and tie. Personal hygiene skills include toileting, face and hand washing, bathing, brushing teeth, and shampooing and combing hair. Eating skills include learning to finger feed, use proper utensils, drink from a cup, and serve food.

Instruction in social skills applies many of the self-care areas to the development of positive interpersonal relationships. Social skill training stresses appropriate physical appearance, etiquette, use of leisure time, and sexual behavior. Communication is closely related to social skill development because without communication there is no social interaction. The communication may be verbal or manual (e.g., sign language, language boards), but most important is that some form of communication be present.

Using Assistive Technology

Assistive technology includes any item, piece of equipment, or product system that can be used to increase, maintain, or improve the functional capabilities of students with disabilities (Public Law 100-407, Technology-Related Assistance for Individuals with Disabilities Act). There are several categories of assistive technology:

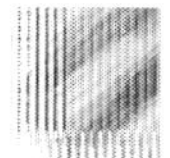

Core Concept

Students with intellectual disabilities will benefit from instruction that incorporates assistive technology devices or activities.

- Mobility (wheelchairs, lifts, adaptive driving controls, scooters, laser canes)
- Seating and positioning (assistance in choosing and using a wheelchair)
- Computers (environmental control units, word processors, software, keyboards)
- Toys and games (software, switch-operated toys)
- Activities of daily living (feeders, lifts, watch alarms, memory books)
- Communication (touch talkers, reading systems, talking keyboards (Wehman, 1997, p. 475).

Students with intellectual disabilities who have communication deficits or delays will benefit from assistive technology devices or activities that promote the

Tips for Professionals

Strategies for Augmenting Communication

There are many ways to augment communication including the use of communication boards. A communication board is a collection of images, including icons and photographs. When an image is pointed to or chosen, it sends a message to the person an individual is trying to communicate with. In turn, that choice evokes a response. For example, an icon of a stop sign can be used to represent the command "Stop." When pointed to, the "offender" knows to *stop* to honor the command.

When planning a communication strategy, it is important to start simply. Here are some everyday examples of ways to use a communication board or picture system to provide the opportunities to make choices.

Creating a Snack or Meal Time Menu

- Cut out labels from food packaging typically found in the refrigerator or pantry.
- Glue the labels on unlined index cards or poster board. Laminate the cards for extended use.
- Single hole punch them and place them on a metal ring, which can be purchased from a hobby or office supply store.
- Place the ring on the refrigerator or pantry door handle for easy access.
- Encourage the individual to thumb through the cards and select choices for drinks, snacks, etc.
- Consider grouping food groups together by using different colored poster board. For instance, put drinks on blue poster board, fruits on yellow, vegetables on green, desserts on red, and so on.

After a while, it can become tiring to make communication boards by cutting with scissors, copying, and pasting pieces of paper. A solution is to consider using Mayer-Johnson's Boardmaker™ software. Available for both Mac and Windows, Boardmaker™ is designed for finding, copying, and pasting icons quickly to design communication boards. Icons are provided for many trademark symbols for such things as Coca-Cola™ and McDonald's™, as well as numerous icons for various daily activities. Icons can be resized by the computer and placed in pre-made guides, or placed in customized ones. Communication boards can be printed in either color or black and white. And additional "libraries" can be created for personally drawn images, as well as digital or scanned photos. This provides easy accessibility, as well as the opportunity to use the images over and over again.

Source: From "Augmenting Communication" by K. Voss, July/August 1997, *Disability Solutions, 2*(2), pp. 7, 9.

use of **augmentative communication** strategies. Johnston (2003) suggests that communication aids are varied and may range from a laptop computer with voice output to pictures in a notebook or wallet. (For more information, see the Tips for Professionals feature.)

Core Concept

Culturally different children with intellectual disabilities need an educational experience that focuses on learning how to learn.

EDUCATING THE CULTURALLY DIFFERENT CHILD WITH INTELLECTUAL DISABILITIES

Children with intellectual disabilities come from many different cultural backgrounds. As such, teaching about different cultures and their value may be important in reducing racial and ethnic conflict and promoting respect and tolerance for these children. To meet the educational needs of culturally diverse children with intellectual disabilities, teachers must focus on learning how to learn, in addition to memorizing facts and acquiring basic skills. These children may have linguistic limitations both in their native dialect or language and in English. Thus, reading material should be primarily experience oriented so that children from different backgrounds can draw their own perceptions and experiences.

Gollnick and Chinn (2002) suggest that all teaching should be multicultural and that classrooms must be models for equity and social justice. For this to happen, educators must

- place the student at the center of the teaching and learning process.
- promote human rights and respect for cultural differences.
- believe that all students can learn.
- acknowledge and build on the life histories and experiences of students' microcultural memberships. (Gollnick & Chinn, 2002, p. 321)

The curriculum for the culturally different child with intellectual disabilities who is also living in poverty should include instruction on available resources for food assistance and medical care. In light of the limited financial resources of the child's family, effective money management and consumer skills must be emphasized. Finally, classroom teachers must believe in and communicate the basic tenet that people in this society exist in a pluralistic culture that values the intrinsic worth of every individual.

NEW ISSUES AND FUTURE DIRECTIONS

The No Child Left Behind Act and IDEA 2004

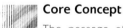

Core Concept

The passage of the No Child Left Behind Act (NCLB) in 2001 and the 2004 reauthorization of IDEA has moved education into an era of reform and restructuring that is unprecedented in our nation's schools.

With the passage of NCLB and IDEA 2004, there are several emerging issues that will affect access to an appropriate education for students with intellectual disabilities. The premise of NCLB and IDEA 2004 is that all students, including those with intellectual disabilities, will succeed in school. They will learn more than they are currently learning. If students don't succeed, then public schools are to be held accountable for their failure. The definition of success is determined by student proficiency on content (annual yearly progress) as specified by each state and measured by state performance standards. The promise of "all means all" includes students with intellectual disabilities. Therefore (at least in theory) students with intellectual disabilities are assured access to the curriculum upon which the standards were based, access to assessments that measure performance on the standards, and inclusion in the reported results that determine how well a school is meeting the established performance criteria. Although public policy provides the impetus for every student to learn and succeed, the critical issue is whether this promise becomes reality.

For students with intellectual disabilities, there are questions yet to be answered, such as:

- Are the characteristics of effective special education instruction for students with intellectual disabilities compatible with a standards-based approach to education?
- Will participation of students with intellectual disabilities in a standards-based curriculum result in higher academic achievement, or is failure an inevitable outcome?

As mandated in IDEA, students with intellectual disabilities must have access to the general education curriculum when appropriate, as well as participate in state or local performance assessments. The requirement raises some important curriculum issues as well. Will the general education curriculum be broadened to include the "life skills" appropriate to the needs of these students? On what basis will the decision be made to include or exclude students with intellectual disabilities from the general education curriculum? As these students participate in state or local performance assessments, will appropriate accommodations (such as more time to take the test or oral testing) be made available? If a student with intellectual disabilities is placed in an alternate assessment system, how will the schools be accountable for ensuring satisfactory educational progress?

Highly Qualified Special Education Teachers

University teacher education is critical to the success of effective educational programs for students with intellectual disabilities. During the past two decades, these programs have begun to expand their curricula to include more functional, community-based, and social inclusion instruction. University teacher education programs in special education are beginning to concentrate efforts on ways to facilitate collaboration with general education colleagues to address the needs of all students, including those with intellectual disabilities. These programs will need to assist potential special education teachers to organize and use school resources more effectively (such as peer tutors or paraprofessionals). Additionally, teacher education candidates from both elementary and secondary teacher programs, as well as potential school administrators, will require strategies that facilitate the success of students with intellectual disabilities in an inclusive public school setting. These strategies could include (a) functioning as a member of a multidisciplinary team, (b) supporting students with intellectual disabilities to function in the social network of the school, and (c) developing effective pedagogy for students in a regular education setting.

The passage of IDEA 2004 and its alignment with NCLB has further solidified the federal definition what it means to be a highly qualified special education teacher. IDEA states that the term "highly qualified" has the same meaning as applied to elementary, middle, and secondary teachers in NCLB (H.R. 1350 Sec. 602[10][A]). This means that new and veteran special education teachers at the elementary level must have subject knowledge and teaching skills in reading, writing, mathematics, and other areas of the basic elementary curriculum. New and veteran special education teachers at the middle and secondary level must have subject knowledge and teaching skills in academic subjects in which the teacher has responsibility for instruction (teacher of record).

As the new highly qualified standard for special education teachers goes into effect, there are several unresolved issues. Will "highly qualified" actually translate to "high quality"? Will the IDEA 2004 requirements to become a highly qualified special educator decrease the critical shortage of special education teachers? Or, will these shortages be exacerbated by driving away potential teacher candidates who don't see the benefit in meeting the additional subject matter requirements? Will service delivery for students with intellectual disabilities have to be modified with increasing dependence on highly qualified general educators to deliver instruction in core academic subjects while special educators serve in consultative roles? What impact will service-delivery modifications have on students' access to FAPE and their overall academic achievement?

Core Questions

1. Discuss various stages of development and periods of growth for children with intellectual disabilities.
2. How do the memory capabilities of children with intellectual disabilities compare with those of peers without disabilities?
3. Compare massed and distributed practice in relationship to the learning performance of children with intellectual disabilities.
4. Discuss several suggestions for working with children who have difficulty transferring what they have learned from one situation to another.
5. Identify examples of adaptive skills that children with intellectual disabilities may need to learn during the school years.
6. What are the major provisions of the Individuals with Disabilities Education Act?
7. Identify examples of the supports needed to facilitate the success of the child with intellectual disabilities in an inclusive school setting.
8. Describe adaptive skill content areas that children with intellectual disabilities may need to learn.
9. What are some of the questions regarding the potential impact of NCLB and IDEA 2004 on an appropriate education for students with intellectual disabilities?
10. Will the federal standard for what defines a highly qualified special education teacher translate into a high-quality teacher?

Roundtable Discussion

In this chapter, we have discussed many different aspects of what constitutes an appropriate education for children with intellectual disabilities in inclusive settings.

We also emphasized the need to provide the many supports required in the general education classroom if inclusion is to be successful.

In your study group, discuss the rationale for including children with intellectual disabilities in general education settings. Given the increasing support for the inclusion of children with intellectual disabilities in the general education setting, discuss ideas for planning appropriate instructional approaches and facilitating social interactions among children with intellectual disabilities and their peers without disabilities.

Parent and Professional Organization Positions on Key Issues in the Lives of People with Intellectual Disabilities

The inside front cover of this text presents a matrix that includes nine key issues in the lives of people with disabilities, the positions of various parent and professional organizations on each issue, and the chapter and page number where the information is addressed. Table 8–1 is a summary of the organizations and key issues addressed in this chapter.

Table 8–1
Key Issues and Organizations Discussed in This Chapter

Organization/Website	Key Issues Addressed	Chapter Heading
American Association on Mental Retardation (http://www.aamr.org)	Assessment issues	Adaptive Skills
The ARC—a national Organization on Intellectual Disabilities (http://www.thearc.org)	Inclusive education	Inclusion in General Education Settings
TASH, an international association of people with disabilities, their family members, and professionals (http://www.tash.org)	Inclusive education	Inclusion in General Education Settings

References

Agran, M., & Hughes, C. (1997). Problem solving. In M. Agran (Ed.), *Student-directed learning: Teaching self-determination skills* (pp. 171–198). Pacific Grove, CA: Brooks/Code.

American Association on Mental Retardation (AAMR). (2002). *Mental retardation: Definition, classification, and systems of supports (10th ed.).* Washington, DC: Author.

The ARC. (2004). *Position statement on education.* Retrieved December 28, 2004, from http://www.thearc.org/posits/educationpos.doc

Bebko, J. M., & Luhaorg, H. (1998). The development of strategy use and metacognitive processing in mental retardation: Some sources of difficulty. In J. A. Burack, R. M. Hodapp, & E. Zigler (Eds.), *Handbook of mental retardation and development* (pp. 383–407). New York: Cambridge University Press.

Beirne-Smith, M., Ittenbach, R. F., & Patton, J. R. (2002). *Mental retardation* (6th ed.). Upper Saddle River, NJ: Merrill/Prentice Hall.

Bonn, H., & Bonn, B. (2000a). In the best interests of the child. In S. E. Wade (Ed.), *Inclusive education: A casebook and readings for prospective and practicing teachers* (pp. 173–180). Mahwah, NJ: Erlbaum.

Bonn, H., & Bonn, B. (2000b). Part B of the case: "In the best interests of the child." In S. E. Wade (Ed.), *Preparing teachers for inclusive education* (pp. 209–211). Mahwah, NJ: Erlbaum.

Bray, N. W., Reilly, K. D., Huffman, L. F., Grupe, L. A., Fletcher, K. L., Villa, M., et al. (1999). Mental retardation. In W. Bechtel & G. Graham (Eds.), *A companion to cognitive science* (pp. 734–743). Malden, MA: Blackwell.

Browder, D. M., & Snell, M. E. (2000). Teaching functional academics. In M. E. Snell & F. Brown (Eds.), *Instruction of persons with severe handicaps* (5th ed.) (pp. 493–542). Upper Saddle River, NJ: Merrill.

Cipani, E., & Spooner, F. (1994). *Curricular and instructional approaches for persons with severe disabilities.* Needham Heights, MA: Allyn & Bacon.

Gee, K. (1996). Least restrictive environment: Elementary and middle school. In the National Council on Disability, *Improving the implementation of the Individuals with Disabilities Education Act: Making schools work for all children* (Suppl.), 395–425. Washington, DC: The National Council on Disability.

Gollnick, D., & Chinn, P. C. (2002). *Multicultural education in a pluralistic society* (6th ed.). Upper Saddle River, NJ: Prentice-Hall.

Haager, D., & Klinger, J. K. (2005). *Differentiating instruction in inclusive classrooms: The special educator's guide.* Boston: Allyn & Bacon.

Hardman, M. L., Drew, C. J., & Egan, M. W. (2006). *Human exceptionality: School, community, and family* (8th ed.). Boston: Allyn & Bacon.

Hendrick Hudson District Board of Education v. Rowley, 485 U.S. 176 (1982).

Horvat, M. (2000). Physical activity of children with and without mental retardation in inclusive recess settings. *Education and Training in Mental Retardation, 35*(2), 160–167.

Johnston, S. (2003). Assistive technology. In J. McDonnell, M. Hardman, & A. P. McDonnell, *Introduction to persons with moderate and severe disabilities* (2nd ed.) (pp. 138–159). Boston: Allyn & Bacon.

Katims, D. S. (2000). Literacy instruction for persons with mental retardation: Historical highlights and contemporary analysis. *Education and Training in Mental Retardation and Developmental Disabilities, 35* (1), 3–15.

Kittler, P., Krinsky-McHale, S. J., & Devenny, D. A. (2004). Semantic and phonological loop effects on visual working memory in middle-age adults with mental retardation. *American Journal on Mental Retardation, 109* (6), 467–480.

Lee, S., Yoo, S., & Bak, S. (2003). Characteristics of friendships among children with and without mild disabilities. *Education and Training in Developmental Disabilities, 38* (2), 157–166.

Lipsky, D. K., & Gartner, A. (1996). Inclusive education and school restructuring. In W. Stainback & S. Stainback (Eds.), *Controversial issues confronting special education: Divergent perspectives* (2nd ed., pp. 3–15). Boston: Allyn & Bacon.

Lipsky, D. K., & Gartner, A. (1999). Inclusive education: A requirement of a democratic society. In H. Daniels & P. Garner (Eds.), *Inclusive education, world yearbook of education, 1999* (pp. 12–23). London: Kogan Page.

March of Dimes. (2004). *Down syndrome.* Retrieved December 14, 2004, from http://www.modimes.org/professionals/681_1214.asp

McDonnell, J., Hardman, M., & McDonnell, A. P. (2003). *Introduction to persons with moderate and severe disabilities* (2nd ed.). Boston: Allyn & Bacon.

Mills, P. E., Cole, K. N., Jenkins, J. R., & Dale, P. S. (1998). Effects of differing levels of inclusion on preschoolers with disabilities. *Exceptional Children, 65,* 79–90.

Mithaug, D. E., Wehmeyer, M. L., Agran, M., Martin, J. E., & Palmer, S. (1998). The self-determined learning model of instruction: Engaging students to solve their learning problems. In M. L. Wehmeyer & D. J. Sands (Eds.), *Making it happen: Student involvement in education planning, decision making, and instruction* (pp. 299–328). Baltimore: Paul H. Brookes.

Peterson, J. M., & Hittie, M. M. (2003). *Inclusive teaching: Creating effective schools for all learners*. Boston: Allyn & Bacon.

Piaget, J. (1969). *The theory of stages in cognitive development*. New York: McGraw-Hill.

Sailor, W., Gee, K., & Karasoff, P. (2000). Inclusion and school restructuring. In M. Snell & F. Brown (Eds.), *Instruction of students with severe handicaps* (5th ed., pp. 1–30). Upper Saddle River, NJ: Merrill/Prentice Hall.

Shonkoff, J. P., & Phillips, D. A.(Eds.). (2000). *From neurons to neighborhoods: The science of early childhood development*. Washington, DC: Committee on Integrating the Science of Early Childhood Development, Board on Children, Youth, and Families, National Academies Press.

Siperstein, G. N., & Leffert, J. S. (1997). Comparison of socially accepted and rejected children with mental retardation. *American Journal on Mental Retardation, 101*(4), 339–351.

Smith, T. E. C., Polloway, E. A., Patton, J. R., & Dowdy, C. A. (2003). *Teaching students with special needs in inclusive settings* (4th ed.). Boston: Allyn & Bacon.

Sternberg, R. J. (2003). *Cognitive psychology* (3rd ed.). Florence, KY: Wadsworth.

TASH. (2005). *Position statement on inclusive, quality education*. Retrieved January 7, 2005, from http://www.tash.org/resolutions/res02inclusiveed.htm

Thompson, J. (2004). Strategies to increase parent involvement that really work. *CEC Today, 11*(2). Retrieved December 15, 2004, from http://www.cec.sped.org/bk/cectoday/strategies_1.html

University of Northern Iowa. (2004). Children that learn together, learn to live together. Cedar Falls, Iowa, University of Northern Iowa, Department of Special Education. Retrieved November 19, 2004, from http://www.uni.edu/coe/inclusion/standards/index.html

U.S. Department of Education, Office of Special Education Programs. (2002). *Twenty-fourth annual report to Congress on the implementation of the Individuals with Disabilities Education Act*. Washington, DC: Author.

Voss, K. (1997, July/August). Augmenting communication. *Disability Solutions, 2*(2), 5–10.

Wehman, P. (1997). Traumatic brain injury. In P. Wehman (Ed.), *Exceptional individuals in school, community, and work* (pp. 451–485). Austin, TX: Pro-Ed.

Westling, D., & Fox, L. (2004). *Teaching students with severe disabilities* (3rd ed.). Upper Saddle River, NJ: Merrill/Prentice Hall.

Chapter 9

The Adolescent with Intellectual Disabilities and the Transitional Years

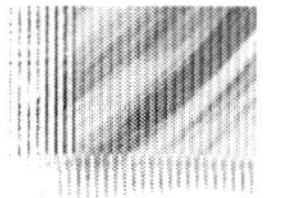

Chapter Preview

At the completion of this chapter, you will have a better understanding of services and supports for adolescents with intellectual disabilities, including:

- Components of an effective high school program for adolescents with intellectual disabilities that feature a comprehensive curriculum that focuses on employment preparation, the teaching of adaptive skills, and instruction academic skill learning when appropriate.
- Effective transition planning that is ongoing and focuses on opportunities to achieve valued postschool outcomes during the adult years.
- How to effectively involve both students and parents in the transition planning process.

Including Penelope in School and Community Life

Penelope is a 17-year-old student at Truman High School who also happens to have intellectual disabilities and needs special education services. She has attended her neighborhood elementary and middle school since kindergarten. Penelope loves Disney movies and going to the mall with her sister. She has learned to read some sight words (such as exit, restrooms, *and* danger*) as well as how to perform some basic functions on a hand-held calculator. These skills are very helpful in her school and community-based inclusion program at Truman High School. She is currently spending part of her day in employment training at a local grocery store. She enjoys going out into the community and has had employment training experiences in a hospital, a local community college, and a restaurant as well. She is also learning how to use and manage her money through her own checking account at a local bank. In addition to her community-based training, she attends high school classes in home economics, history, dance, and geography. Penelope loves to participate in school activities and is an active member of the ski club, bowling club, and a member of the Best Buddies high school chapter. Through Best Buddies, she has developed a number of friendships with peers who are not disabled as well as other students with disabilities in the school.*

- *Why do you think that Penelope's high school experiences include both classroom and community-based training?*
- *What are some other important experiences for Penelope as her parents and teachers plan for the transition from high school to adult life?*

Adolescence is a period of transition that encompasses personal, social, and educational experiences. Adolescents are suspended between childhood and adulthood for several years, attempting to free themselves from childhood but not yet ready to assume adult responsibilities. They work toward emancipation from the family unit while developing social and educational skills that help them gain greater acceptance in society. For adolescents with intellectual disabilities, educational goals during this period are directed toward employment opportunities and preparation for life as an adult.

The challenges of adolescence are intensified for the individual with intellectual disabilities. Many adolescents with mild intellectual disabilities will need some support to meet the demands of the environment. However, those with moderate and severe disabilities, such as Penelope in our opening vignette, will require an extensive support network of family, friends, and professionals. Penelope's educational experiences included not only learning from her high school teachers, but from professionals in the community, such as hospital staff, grocery store employees, and faculty from a local community college.

In this chapter, we consider educational supports and services for adolescents with intellectual disabilities. Our discussion focuses on expected outcomes of secondary education programs for students with intellectual disabilities, as well as on the elements of an effective high school experience. During the adolescent years, educational programs for students with intellectual disabilities primarily focus on the skills necessary to make the successful transition from school to adult life.

EXPECTED OUTCOMES OF SECONDARY EDUCATION PROGRAMS

A critical measure of the effectiveness of any educational program is the success of its graduates. Although 2005 marked the 30th anniversary of the passage of the Individuals with Disabilities Education Act, the opportunities afforded by this landmark legislation have not yet led to full participation of special education graduates in the social and economic mainstream of their local communities (National Organization on Disability [NOD] & Harris & Associates, 2004).

Results of several follow-up studies of special education graduates suggest that these adults were unable to participate fully in community activities, had little or no social life outside the family or primary care givers, and were isolated from peers with and without disabilities (Hasazi, Furney, & Destefano, 1999; Wagner & Blackorby, 1996). The vast majority of these adults were not employed. In fact, the 2004 NOD & Harris & Associates poll found that only 35% of people with disabilities reported being employed full or part time, compared to 78% of those who do not have disabilities.

Given that special education graduates are not fully accessing community services and programs, it is important to identify what should be expected of high school programs. Goals for these individuals are described most often as establishing social relationships with family and friends, access to services and activities within the local community, and employment (Hardman, Drew, & Egan, 2006; McDonnell, Hardman, & McDonnell, 2003). To be effective, a high school program for students with intellectual disabilities must be directed toward meeting each of these goals. Components of an effective high school program include a comprehensive curriculum that focuses on employment preparation, the teaching of adaptive skills for adult life, and instruction in academic skills where appropriate. Secondary education programs also should incorporate inclusion with peers who are not disabled, consistent parental involvement, and the implementation of systematic transition planning (AAMR, 2002; McDonnell et al., 2003).

EMPLOYMENT PREPARATION

The person with intellectual disabilities is often characterized as one who consumes services, rather than as one who contributes to the community. A consumer of services is dependent on the charity of others. Employment assists in removing this image and in placing the person in the role of contributor. Employment is important as a means to earn wages and, through wages, to obtain material goods that contribute to quality of life. Employment also confers personal identity and status.

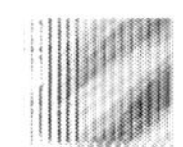

Core Concept

Employment is important not only for monetary rewards but also for personal identity and status.

From colonial days to the 21th century, the pervasive belief in the United States has been that everyone should have the opportunity to work. This belief, however, has not applied equally to all. For people with intellectual disabilities, access to employment training and placement has been negligible throughout most of U.S. history. Even today, many people with intellectual disabilities remain unemployed or underemployed (NOD & Harris & Associates, 2004).

Traditionally, many high schools have focused their employment preparation on a general assessment of student interests and strengths, and the teaching of vocational readiness skills in a classroom setting. This approach places high schools in a passive role in preparing students for employment. The instruction focuses more on general preparation rather than training for specific jobs.

In this section, we examine the issues surrounding employment preparation for people with intellectual disabilities, reviewing various approaches to training including career education, work experience, and **community-based training.** Our discussion begins with the legislative mandates that have played such a vital role in the development of employment services for citizens with intellectual disabilities.

Legislative Mandates for Employment Training

Federal legislation has given broad support to comprehensive employment preparation that is accessible to people with intellectual disabilities. These individuals have been eligible for vocational services under the Barden-LaFollet Act since 1943, but few received any services until the 1960s. The **Vocational Rehabilitation Act** of 1973 (Public Law 93-112) expanded access to vocational rehabilitation services. The act established vocational training as a mandatory service for all qualified persons with disabilities. **Section 504** of this act contains basic civil rights legislation for persons with disabilities, which makes it illegal to discriminate against these individuals in access to vocational training and employment. Subsection 84.11

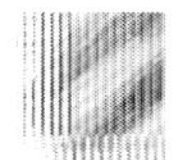

Core Concept

Federal legislation has had significant impact on employment training for adolescents with intellectual disabiities.

of the Federal Regulations for Section 504 states, "No qualified handicapped person shall, on the basis of handicap, be subjected to discrimination in employment under any program or activity to which this part applies."

Discrimination is prohibited in the following areas:

- Recruitment, advertising, and processing of applications
- Hiring, alterations in job status, rehiring
- Rates of pay and other forms of compensation
- Job assignments and classifications, lines of progression, and seniority
- Leaves of absence and sick leave
- Fringe benefits
- Selection and financial support for training, conferences, and other job-related activities
- Employer-approved activities, including social and recreational programs

The passage of this law did not mean that long-established negative attitudes toward people with disabilities suddenly disappeared. However, it was a first step toward opening new doors for people with intellectual disabilities. Career and vocational education for people with intellectual disabilities became more important than ever. Section 503 of the same act emphasizes the regulations for affirmative action to employ people with disabilities. If individuals with intellectual disabilities are properly educated and can perform competitively for jobs, the federal government stands behind these individuals both in promoting affirmative action in their employment and in prohibiting any discrimination in their hiring. It is critical to reemphasize that people with intellectual disabilities need to be educated and trained as competent employees. (See Chapter 10 for more information on nondiscriminatory practices in the employment of persons with intellectual disabilities under the Americans with Disabilities Act [ADA].)

In addition to reaffirming the civil rights of persons with disabilities, the Vocational Rehabilitation Act has several other objectives:

- To promote expanded employment opportunities for people with disabilities in all areas of business and industry
- To establish state plans for the purpose of providing vocational rehabilitation services to meet the needs of persons with disabilities
- To conduct evaluations of the potential rehabilitation of persons with disabilities and to expand services to them, as well as to those who have not received any or received inadequate rehabilitation services
- To increase the number and competence of rehabilitation personnel through retraining and upgrading experiences

In 1986, Congress passed new amendments to the Vocational Rehabilitation Act (Rehabilitation Act Amendments of 1986, Public Law 99-506) strengthening the act's mandate to serve individuals with the most severe disabilities. These amendments include provisions for supported employment (see Chapter 10 for a more detailed explanation of supported employment). This new paradigm in employment models for persons with intellectual disabilities is described in Section 103 of Public Law 99-506:

> Competitive work in integrated work settings for individuals with severe handicaps [disabilities] for whom competitive employment has not traditionally occurred, or for individuals for whom competitive employment has been interrupted or intermittent as a result of a severe disability, and who because of their handicap, need on-going support services to perform such work.

In 1992, Congress once again amended the Vocational Rehabilitation Act, encouraging stronger collaboration and outreach between the schools and rehabilitation counselors in transition planning. Greater collaboration between education and vocational rehabilitation are expected to benefit the student with intellectual disabilities in moving on to postsecondary education or in obtaining employment. The 1998 amendments to the Vocational Rehabilitation Act required greater linkages with public education in order to facilitate the transition of the student with a disability into postsecondary education and/or competitive employment.

Additional federal legislation, under the Carl Perkins Vocational and Applied Technology Education Act of 1990, has enhanced employment training opportunities for adolescents with intellectual disabilities. This act provides increased access for all students, including those with disabilities, to vocational education training during the high school years.

IDEA requires that all students with disabilities who are between the ages of 3 and 22 receive a free and appropriate education. The provisions of this act are the basis for current employment training for adolescents with intellectual disabilities. Research has clearly substantiated the need for appropriate employment preparation programs for adolescents with more severe intellectual disabilities prior to leaving school (Hasazi et al., 1999; Wehman & Kregel, 2005).

Career Education

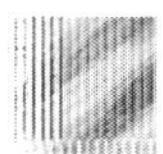

Core Concept

Career education focuses on preparation for life and personal social skills, in addition to instruction in occupational skills.

Career education begins in the early elementary years and continues throughout high school. Its purpose is to make work, either paid, or unpaid, a meaningful component of the student's life. The Division on Career Development and Transition, or DCDT (2002), of the Council for Exceptional Children describes career education as "a process that focuses on the life roles for individuals as students, workers, consumers, family members and citizens." DCDT suggests that career development is a cornerstone for a student's sucessful transition into adult life.

Several career education curriculum models have been developed, one of which is the life-centered career education model (Brolin, 2004). Brolin's model consists of several competencies, experiences, and stages clustered into three curriculum areas: daily living skills, personal-social skills, and occupational guidance and preparation. Brolin (1997) conceptualizes career education into four progressive and interrelated stages:

1. *Career awareness* begins at the elementary level and is intended to make students aware of the existence of work . . . and workers and how students will fit into the work-oriented society in the future.
2. *Career exploration* . . . emphasized at the middle school/junior high level, is intended to help students explore their interests and abilities in relation to lifestyle and occupations.
3. *Career preparation*, emphasized at the high school level, is a period for career decision making and skills acquisition.
4. *Career assimilation* is the transition of the student into postsecondary training and community-adjustment situations.

As a means to infuse career education into the general education program, Brolin (2004) developed the Life-Centered Career Education Curriculum (LCCE). Figure 9–1 provides a sample lesson plan from the *LCCE* in the area of occupational guidance and preparation.

Work Experience

Core Concept

Work experience provides opportunities for the student to participate in occupational activities under actual working conditions.

Work experiences vary according to the philosophy of each particular program. Some programs begin work experiences in the school setting and eventually ease the student into community settings; others may have the student work in the community immediately. The difficulty and the type of assignment are usually dependent on the needs and nature of each student. Before placements are made, each student's ability and interests are evaluated carefully. During the years spent in a vocational class, the student may have an opportunity to work in a variety of settings to maximize exposure to different types of job-related experiences and possibly allow the student to find the permanent placement he or she would like at the completion of school. The primary purpose of the work experience, however, is not to develop specific vocational skills but rather to enable the student to develop the work habits and interpersonal skills necessary to get and keep any job. If, in the course of the work experience, specific skills are acquired, these naturally could be helpful in obtaining specific jobs at the end of school. However, specific competencies must not be emphasized at the expense of the affective dimensions of vocational behavior.

Community-Referenced Employment Preparation

Core Concept

In community-referenced employment preparation, the demands of the work setting and the functioning level of the individual determine goals and objectives.

Community-referenced employment preparation, though similar to work-experience programs in some ways, has some very notable differences. Community-referenced preparation does not support the premise that people with intellectual disabilities must have acquired a certain level of skills prior to entering community work settings. This approach focuses directly on the activities to be accomplished in the community

Competency 17: Knowing & Exploring Occupational Guidance and Preparation.
Subcompetency: Identify remunerative aspects of work.

LCCE Objective: Discuss personal needs that are met through wages.

Lesson Objective: Students will identify major living expenses.

Instructional Resources: Living Expenses Worksheet.

Lesson Introduction: Your first paycheck will look like a large amount of money. But you must remember that your pay must cover many types of living expenses.

School Activity: **Time: 1 session**

Task:

1. Students work in small groups to identify categories for living expenses (for example, housing, transportation, clothing, and so on). List the categories on the board.

2. Students determine whether each expense category is an essential expense (need) or a nonessential expense (luxury). Essential expenses include items that one must have to live as an adult (for example, rent, food, transportation, medical care, clothing, utilities, and insurance). Discuss the types of insurance needed by adults and the reasons for the insurance. Nonessential expenses include tapes, compact discs, movies, and restaurant meals.

3. Students consider the difference between essential (needs) and nonessential (luxuries) expenses in class and arrive at a consensus regarding essential expenses.

4. Students complete the Living Expenses Worksheet.

Lesson Plan Evaluation:

Activity:	Students will complete the Living Expenses Worksheet.
Criteria:	Students will differentiate between essential and nonessential expenses and state three types of essential expenses.
Career Role:	Employee
Career Stage:	Exploration

Figure 9–1
Life-Centered Career Education Curriculum (LCCE)—Sample Lesson Plan in Occupational Guidance and Preparation

Source: From *Life-Skills Career Education Curriculum* by D. E. Brolin, 2004. Balston, VA: Council for Exceptional Children.

Sample Lesson Plan:
Daily Living Skills. Competency 5
Buying, Preparing, and Consuming Food

LESSON PLAN 4

LCCE Objective 5.20.3.: Identify different types and cuts of meat, fish, poultry, and vegetarian proteins.

Lesson Objective: Students will identify types and cuts of meat, fish, poultry, and vegetarian proteins.

Instructional Resources: Beef Cuts Worksheet (Student Workbook page 90) and **Pork Cuts Worksheet (Student Workbook page 91), Vegetarian Information Worksheet,** computer access, or information printed from the website.

Lesson Introduction: There are different sources for protein. Most families have some type of meat, fish, or poultry at least once a day. Usually families eat the same types or cuts of beef, pork, or poultry over and over. Vegetarians also have difficulty varying their protein choices. Today, we will talk about different kinds of meat, fish, poultry, and meat alternatives for vegetarians.

School Activity: **Time: 1 session**

Task:

1. Start a discussion with the class to find out what they know about protein choices.
   - Find out if any students know or are vegetarians.
   - Discuss with the students food choices and find out what they consider a source of protein for breakfast, lunch and dinner.

2. Draw a chicken on the board.
   - Ask students to name as many different parts of a chicken as they can and write them on the board.
   - Explain that poultry can be purchased in parts or whole.
   - Ask students to name their favorite part of the chicken.

3. Discuss the **Beef Cuts Worksheet (Student Workbook page 90)** and **Pork Cuts Worksheet (Student Workbook page 91)**
   - Have students go to the computer room/media center
   - Students go to the website.
     (Cattlemen's Beef Association) Students identify five cuts of meat, where they come from on the cow, and a brief description of how that cut of meat could be cooked.
   - Students then go to the website.
     (National Pork Board) Students identify five cuts of meat, where they come from on the pig, and a brief description of how that cut of meat could be cooked.

Figure 9–1
(continued)

- Discuss how the chicken chart on the board is similar to the beef and pork charts.
- Ask how many other meat types students have heard about.

4. Discuss fish as an alternative to meats.
   - Explain differences between shellfish and other kinds of fish.
   - Ask students to identify their favorites.

5. Discuss how not eating meat and fish is an alternative.
   - Hand out the **Vegetarian Information Worksheet**
   - Have students move to a computer lab/media center
   - Have students go to the website
     (Vegetarian Resource Group) or
     (University Health Services, University of California, Berkeley)
   - Tell students that they need to find out five points about the vegetarian lifestyle and identify five items that are protein alternatives for meat or fish, record this information on the worksheet.
6. Lead a class activity on the types and cuts of meat, fish, and poultry:
   - Have students pair off and each write down three favorite types and cuts of beef, pork, and poultry, a favorite shellfish, and other favorite fish.
   - List their choices on the board.
   - Tally how many times various items are identified.

Lesson Plan Evaluation:

Activity:	Students will identify cuts of meat, poultry, fish, and protein alternatives.
Criteria:	Each student will list five favorite cuts or parts of meat from beef, pork, and poultry, and will list one favorite shellfish and one favorite regular fish. Each student will identify three alternative proteins for vegetarians.
Career Role:	Family Member/Homemaker, Employee
Career Stage:	Awareness, Exploration

Figure 9–1
(continued)

work setting, rather than on the development of skills in the classroom. Consequently, goals and objectives eminate from the demands of the work setting considered in conjunction with the functioning level of the individual.

Research has clearly indicated that people with intellectual disabilities, including those with moderate and severe disabilities, can work in community employment settings with adequate training and support (McDonnell et al., 2003). TASH (2005b),

Transition planning and instruction will depend on the individual needs of the student.

an international association of people with disabilities, their family members, other advocates, and professionals, strongly advocates for employment in community settings where people with disabilities work alongside those without disabilities. The ARC, a national organization of and for people with intellectual disabilities, further recommends that these individuals are supported to make informed choices about their work and careers and have the resources to seek, obtain, and be successful in integrated community employment.

Effectively preparing adolescents with intellectual disabilities for community work settings requires a comprehensive employment training program in the high school. The critical characteristics of an employment training program based on a community-based approach to instruction include the following:

- A curriculum that reflects the job opportunities available in the local community
- An employment training program that takes place at actual job sites
- Training designed to sample the individual's performance across a variety of economically viable alternatives
- Ongoing opportunities for students to interact with nondisabled peers in the work setting
- Training that culminates in specific job training and placement
- Job placement linked to comprehensive transition planning, which focuses on establishing interagency agreements that support the individual's full participation in the community.

TEACHING ADAPTIVE SKILLS

Teaching adaptive skills to students with intellectual disabilities generally falls into three categories: socialization, **self-determination**/personal management, and recreational/leisure time. **Socialization training** includes developing positive interpersonal relationships with family and peers, as well as acquiring behaviors appropriate in a variety of community settings. Self-determination and personal management skills include the ability to problem-solve and make decisions, develop an understanding of sex-role expectations, and take care of personal appearance and hygiene. Recreation and leisure activities may vary considerably but may involve participation in sports, going to a movie or restaurant, or just "hanging out" with friends. It is important for adolescents with intellectual disabilities to become aware of their strengths and limitations as they interact with adults and peers in a social context.

Socialization

Access to social activities is a critical need for adolescents with intellectual disabilities. The challenges for these individuals include locating transportation, as well as planning and financing social activities.

Core Concept

Socialization training includes the development of positive interpersonal relationships with family and peers, as well as the acquisition of appropriate behaviors across a variety of community settings.

Transportation is a problem for many adolescents with intellectual disabilities. Some are unable to drive because they lack access to an automobile or because they can't pass driver's education. If the adolescent is unable to pass driver's training, the school must offer instruction in the use of public transportation. The ability to use public transportation may be important not only for social reasons but also for employment. If public transportation is not available, then parents, school staff, or volunteers must provide it. For those able to profit from it, driver's education is usually available in the high school. Driver's education may be perceived as controversial for the adolescent with intellectual disabilities. It has been argued that only the most capable students with intellectual disabilities should be encouraged to drive. These would include students who possess the coordination and ability to think critically in difficult situations and emergencies.

The adolescent with intellectual disabilities is often unable to take the initiative in planning social activities. As such, the responsibility to provide social activities rests with volunteer groups, local associations for people with intellectual disabilities (see the Best Buddies feature), and parents. Many social functions can be planned at school with the assistance of teachers and staff. If a university or college is nearby, special education and recreational therapy majors might be available to assist in planning and supervising functions.

Self-Determination and Personal Management

Adolescents with intellectual disabilities may need to learn the critical skills necessary to become more independent during the adult years. Personal management

Best Buddies

Making a Difference

Best Buddies is a nonprofit organization dedicated to enhancing the lives of people with intellectual disabilities by providing opportunities for one-to-one friendships and integrated employment. Founded in 1989 by Anthony K. Shriver, son of Sargent and Eunice Kennedy Shriver, Best Buddies is a vibrant, international organization that has grown from 1 original chapter to more than 1,000 middle school, high school, and college campuses. Best Buddies programs reach all 50 of the United States, and have active international programs in Australia, Canada, Colombia, Cuba, Egypt, Ghana, Hong Kong, Ireland, Kenya, Mexico, the Philippines, and Sweden. Around the world, more than 50,000 people volunteer for Best Buddies.

In addition to the traditional campus-based volunteer activities, and for those with limited personal time, Best Buddies helps people with intellectual disabilities connect with others through technology with its online friendship program, e-Buddies. Even though Best Buddies has grown tremendously in its short existence, most of the country still lacks programs to help people with intellectual disabilities become part of mainstream society. Best Buddies' goal is to bring friendship to every corner of the world, making Best Buddies programs active in every community and on every middle school, high school, and college campus.

For more information about Best Buddies, visit http://www.bestbuddies.org, call 1-800-89-BUDDY, or write Best Buddies, 100 S.E. 2nd Street, Suite 1990, Miami, FL 33131.

Source: Adapted from *About us*, 2005. Best Buddies. Retrieved February 14, 2005, from http://www.bestbuddies.org.

Core Concept

Adolescents with intellectual disabilities may need to learn skills necessary to speak up for themselves and manage their personal needs as they move into adult life.

skills include the ability to problem-solve and make decisions, develop an understanding of sex-role expectations, and take care of personal appearance and hygiene.

The ability to problem-solve and make life decisions is referred to as "self-determination." Definitions of self-determination focus on a person's ability to consider options and make appropriate decisions, and exercise free will, independence, and individual responsibility (University of Illinois at Chicago National Research and Training Center, 2005). Learning self-determination helps adolescents with intellectual disabilities to play a major role in choosing and achieving their goals as they make the transition into adult life; it also helps them to understand the barriers they may face. Ultimately, the student comes away from school with a more well-developed sense of personal worth and social responsibility. In supporting the right to self-determination, the AAMR (2005) states that people with intellectual disabilities must have opportunities and experiences that enable them to exert control in their lives and to advocate on their own behalf. See the Tips for Professionals feature.

Tips for Professionals

Promoting Self-Determination

Promote Choice Making

- Identify strengths, interests, and learning styles.
- Provide choices about clothing, social activities, family events, and methods of learning new information.
- Hold high expectations for youth.
- Teach youth about their disability.
- Involve children and youth in self-determination/self-advocacy opportunities at school, home, and community.
- Prepare children and youth for school meetings.
- Speak directly to children and youth.
- Involve children and youth in educational, medical, and family decisions.
- Allow for mistakes and natural consequences.
- Listen often to children and youth.

Encourage Exploration of Possibilities

- Promote exploration of the world every day.
- Use personal, tactile, visual, and auditory methods for exploration.
- Identify young adult mentors with similar disabilities.
- Talk about future jobs, hobbies, and family lifestyles.
- Develop personal collages/scrapbooks based on interests and goals.
- Involve children and youth in service learning (4H, Ameri-Corps, local volunteering).

Promote Reasonable Risk Taking

- Make choice maps listing risks, benefits, and consequences of choice.
- Build safety nets through family members, friends, schools, and others.
- Develop skills in problem solving.
- Develop skills in evaluating consequences.

Encourage Problem Solving

- Teach problem-solving skills.
- Allow ownership of challenges and problems.
- Accept problems as part of healthy development.
- Hold family meetings to identify problems at home and in the community.
- Hold class meetings to identify problems in school.
- Allow children and youth to develop a list of self-identified consequences.

Promote Self-Advocacy

- Encourage communication and self-representation.
- Praise all efforts of assertiveness and problem solving.
- Develop opportunities at home and in school for self-advocacy.
- Provide opportunities for leadership roles at home and in school.
- Encourage self-advocates to speak in class.
- Teach about appropriate accommodation needs.
- Practice ways to disclose disability and accommodation needs.
- Create opportunities to speak about the disability in school, home, church, business, and community.

Facilitate Development of Self-Esteem

- Create a sense of belonging within schools and communities.

continues on next page

continues from previous page

- Provide experiences for children and youth to use their talents.
- Provide opportunities to youth for contributing to their families, schools, and communities.
- Provide opportunities for individuality and independence.
- Identify caring adult mentors at home, school, church, or in the community.
- Model a sense of self-esteem and self-confidence.

Develop Goal Setting and Planning

- Teach children and youth family values, priorities, and goals.
- Make posters that reflect values and are age-appropriate.
- Define what a goal is and demonstrate the steps to reach a goal.
- Make a road map to mark the short-term identifiers as they work toward a goal.
- Support children and youth in developing values and goals.
- Discuss family history and culture—make a family tree.
- Be flexible in supporting youth to reach their goals; some days they may need much motivation and help; other days they may want to try alone.

Help Youth Understand Their Disabilities

- Develop a process that is directed by youth for self-identity: Who are you? What do you want? What are your challenges and barriers? What supports do you need?
- Direct children and youth to write an autobiography.
- Talk about the youth's disability.
- Talk about the youth's abilities.
- Involve children and youth in their IEP.
- Use good learning style inventories and transition assessments.
- Identify and utilize support systems for all people.

Source: Adapted from. "Self-Determination: Supporting Successful Transition" by C. D. Bremer, M. Kachgal, and K. Schoeller, 2003, *Research to Practice Brief of the National Center on Secondary Education and Transition, 2*(1), p. 3.

One area requiring considerable decision-making skills during adolescence is sexual behavior. Sexual interest is a defining characteristic of adolescence, and for high schools, it represents the difficult challenge of identifying what role, if any, the school will have in providing instruction in this area. Who is responsible for providing sex education? Whereas some individuals believe that sex education belongs in the school, others consider sex education primarily, if not exclusively, the responsibility of the parents. Sex education is one of the most controversial subjects confronting American public schools today. Teachers are hesitant to offer sex education without authorization. Peers are the only constant source of information about sex, but the ideas of adolescents are often distorted or highly inaccurate. This problem is certainly not unique to those with intellectual disabilities, but it may be more acute because they are often less able to locate accurate information. The adolescent with intellectual disabilities may not be able to read or comprehend the written information even if it is made available.

Personal appearance becomes increasingly important for the adolescent with intellectual disabilities.

In addition to changes in sexual function, puberty may also bring about changes in personal appearance. Acne frequently causes emotional scarring far more significant and permanent than any physical scarring. Adolescents who are not disabled have the advantage of being able to read and ask questions. Some go to a dermatologist to help protect their appearance. Adolescents with intellectual disabilities may have difficulty in locating necessary help. Some lack the financial resources to receive treatment from a dermatologist. Unable to care for themselves adequately and to maintain an acceptable appearance, adolescents with intellectual disabilities may find social acceptance very difficult. For students with skin problems who are unable to access a dermatologist, the school nurse should be able to provide the necessary information about skin care and treatment of acne. Beauty colleges that train cosmetologists are frequently willing to provide their services to teach students with intellectual disabilities how to shampoo and take care of their hair.

Unfortunately, some parents of children with intellectual disabilities make the assumption that their son's or daughter's intellectual limitations render physical appearance of little consequence. Yet most adolescents with intellectual disabilities strive constantly to be as much like their nondisabled peers as possible. They do not want to draw attention to the fact that they are different. Being less well groomed first draws attention and then hinders or even precludes social acceptance. Parents and teachers must be aware that looks usually have a bearing on self-concept and that programs and curricula must include attention to appearance in the education of adolescents.

Recreation, Sports, and Leisure

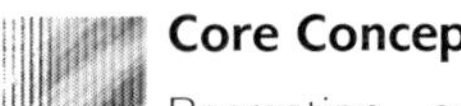

Core Concept

Recreation, sports, and leisure activities may contribute to the adolescent's emotional, psychological, and affective development.

The opportunity to participate in community recreation and leisure activities may vary considerably depending upon the age and severity of the individual's intellectual disabilities. For many adults with intellectual disabilities, television is the only consistent leisure experience (Hardman et al., 2006). However, this picture is changing for the better. Some agencies and communities are initiating new programs specifically for persons with intellectual disabilities. Many colleges and universities have developed special or adaptive physical education, recreation, and therapeutic recreation programs that prepare professionals to work with people who are disabled. Other programs, such as **Special Olympics,** are expanding throughout the United States and worldwide. Special Olympics provides children and adults with intellectual disabilities the opportunity to participate in sports training and competition. Special Olympics has expanded its traditional sports training and competition program to include Unified Sports. Unified Sports involves people with and without intellectual disabilities in integrated team sports. The goals of the program include the development of socialization skills and friendships among participants; enhanced self-esteem for athletes; and higher-level skills for participation in inclusive school and community sports. (For more information visit http://www.specialolympics.org.)

Although the development of structured leisure programs for adolescents with intellectual disabilities is encouraging, much remains to be done. It is disconcerting to realize that most free-time activities for adolescents with intellectual disabilities revolve around watching television. Yet, training programs in the development of leisure skills, like those used in therapeutic recreation, can be effective. The goal of therapeutic recreation is to help people with intellectual disabilities take advantage of leisure opportunities as a means to enhance their independence in the community (Hardman et al., 2006).

TEACHING ACADEMIC SKILLS

Core Concept

Academic skills enhance opportunities for independence in the classroom, family, and community.

For the adolescent with mild intellectual disabilities, academic skills may be a higher priority than for the student with more severe intellectual disabilities. This is because adolescents with mild intellectual disabilities may be better able to assimilate academic learning into their daily living and employment preparation activities. These students will need a systematic instructional program that accounts for differences in the rate of learning, but they *will* learn to read when given "rich, intensive, and extensive literary experiences" (Katims, 2000).

A functional academics program for students with intellectual disabilities includes instruction in reading, language, and mathematics. Reading programs at the secondary level often focus on functional skills related to employment (e.g., components of a job application form, reading classified ads), daily living (e.g., use of maps, telephone directories, catalogs), and leisure activities (e.g., movie listings, newspapers). The focus may also be on developing or expanding a student's reading vocabulary to enhance independence in the community. A functional vocabulary includes the ability to read building signs (e.g., push/pull, men/women, entrance/exit), street signs (e.g., walk/don't walk, stop, caution, railroad crossing), and common environmental safety words (e.g., *keep out, danger, poison, hazard, do not enter*).

Functional language programs focus on the use of expressive and receptive skills. Instruction in expressive language includes effective oral skills in carrying on a conversation, talking on the telephone, and responding to questions. Some degree of writing proficiency also may be necessary to enhance independence in community and employment activities. These skills range from the basic ability to write one's name to the more complex task of filling out a job application form. Receptive skills also are needed for daily conversations and job interviews. Good oral skills are not helpful if the individual is unable to understand what others say.

The intended outcomes for a functional mathematics program are generally basic management of personal finances, consumer skills, and telling time. A personal finance program instructs the adolescent in several areas, including budgeting money, establishing and using credit, taxes, insurance, and wages. Consumer skills include identifying coins and bills of all denominations, making change, and reading bus or train schedules and timetables.

The decision of whether to include functional academics as a component of a student's instructional program must be looked at in the context of each student's prioritized needs. As such, Browder and Snell (2000) recommend that six factors be addressed in deciding each student's program focus:

1. The student's preferences
2. The parents' preferences
3. The student's chronological age or how many years left in school
4. The student's current and future settings
5. The student's rate of learning academic skills
6. The student's other skill needs (p. 500)

TRANSITION PLANNING

Each year, approximately 50,000 adolescents with intellectual disabilities in the United States leave school and face life as adults in their local communities. The transition from school to adult life is not easy. Many adults with intellectual disabilities find that they cannot access services critical for success in the community (Hasazi et al., 1999; NOD & Harris & Associates, 2004). These individuals may face long waiting lists for employment and housing services.

Core Concept

Although effective educational and adult services will provide greater opportunities for individuals with intellectual disabilities in community settings, significant long-term changes may not result without transition planning.

Transition planning should include access to the general curriculum while facilitating the coordination and expansion of services within the community (Alberto, Taber, Brozovic, &

Elliot, 1997; McDonnell et al., 2003; National Center on Secondary Education and Transition [NCSET] and the Pacer Center, 2004). Professionals and parents have come to realize that a systematic transition planning process must begin during the school years and carry over into adulthood.

Under IDEA 2004, transition services for students with disabilities must be:

- Designed to be within a results-oriented process, that is focused on improving the academic and functional achievement of the child with a disability to facilitate the child's movement from school to post-school activities, including post-secondary education, vocational education, integrated employment (including supported employment), continuing and adult education, adult services, independent living, or community participation.
- Based on the individual child's needs, taking into account the child's strengths, preferences, and interests.
- Includes instruction, related services, community experiences, the development of employment and other post-school adult living objectives, and, when appropriate, acquisition of daily living skills and functional vocational evaluation. (IDEA 2004, PL 108-446, Sec. 602[34])

IDEA requires that, beginning at age 16 and updated annually, a student's individualized program should include appropriate measurable postsecondary goals based upon age appropriate transition assessments related to training, education, employment, and, where appropriate, independent living skills. The IEP must include a statement of **transition services** that relate to various courses of study (such as participation in advanced placement courses or a vocational education program) that will assist the student in reaching their goals. (IDEA 2004, PL 108-446, Sec. 614[d])

The critical components of transition planning include (a) effective high school programs that prepare students to work and live in the community, (b) a broad range of adult service programs that can meet the various support needs of individuals with disabilities, in employment and community settings, and (c) comprehensive and cooperative transition planning between educational and community service agencies in order to develop needed services for graduation.

The remainder of this section addresses a process designed to address the critical components of transition planning and to facilitate coordination and expansion of services within the community for each individual with intellectual disabilities.

Coordinating Transition Planning

The foundation for a formal transition planning process begins in as early as the preschool years and comes to fruition during high school. High schools must organize their programs and activities to produce outcomes that facilitate success for the individual during the adult years. Outcomes for the adult with intellectual disabilities include the ability to function as independently as possible in daily life. The individual should be involved in the economic life of the community, both in paid or unpaid work. He or she should also be able to participate in social and

Core Concept

Effective transition planning is ongoing and begins with goals and objectives established from the time the student enters school.

leisure activities that are part of community living. The role of school personnel includes assessing individual needs, developing an individualized transition plan (ITP) for each student, coordinating transition planning with adult service agencies, and participating with parents in the planning process (Hardman et al., 2006).

Determining Individual Need

For some adults with mild intellectual disabilities, support may be unnecessary following school. Others may need a short-term support network. For adults with moderate to severe intellectual disabilities, the support necessary to ensure appropriate access to community services may need to be long term and intense. An effective transition planning system must take into account both the short- and long-term service needs of the individual. McDonnell et al. (2003) suggest that to identify the level of support an individual will require, parents and school staff must look at the individual's performance during high school in a variety of areas (i.e., personal management, work, residential living, recreational and leisure time). Assessment in personal management includes such activities as shopping for groceries, using public transportation, crossing streets, and maintaining a schedule.

Core Concept

The needs of adults with intellectual disabilities are diverse and often vary with the severity of the condition and the demands of the environment.

Developing an Individualized Transition Plan

Approximately two years before the student leaves school, work should begin on a formal individualized transition plan (ITP). IDEA mandates that transition services must include a statement of the needed transition services, including, when appropriate, a statement of the interagency responsibilities or linkages (or both), before the student leaves school.

A person-centered transition plan serves several functions: (a) establishment of a formal working relationship between students, parents, and postschool case managers and adult service providers; (b) identification of the services and resources that will ensure meaningful employment and community participation; (c) access to services before graduation; and (d) identification of systems that will facilitate the maintenance of needed services (McDonnell et al., 2003). To address each purpose, students, parents, and professionals must work together to review potential services that are now or should be made available as the student leaves school. They identify activities that will facilitate access to these services and establish timelines and responsibilities for completion.

Core Concept

The purpose of transition planning is to establish a working relationship between students, parents, and adult service agencies in order to identify resources for employment and community participation prior to graduation.

Following are the components of an ITP:

1. *Employment training and placement.* Specify the type of training and placement most appropriate for the student. Determine how the resources between school and postschool service programs will be coordinated to

ensure that appropriate jobs are identified and that the student is trained for them.

2. *Residential placement.* Determine which residential alternative is the most appropriate for the student. If the family believes it is in the best interest of their son or daughter with intellectual disabilities to remain home for some time after leaving school, then appropriate family support services need to be in place. If the individual is to move into a residential placement immediately following school, then alternative living arrangements must be made.
3. *Leisure alternatives.* Identify the leisure activities most important to the student. Activities should be planned to ensure that the student has the necessary resources or skills to participate in the activities regardless of where he or she chooses to live after leaving school. Resources or skills include financing the activity, finding transportation, and locating a peer to accompany the student.
4. *Income and medical support.* Balance the potential array of service alternatives with the individual's supplemental security income program. Ensure that needed cash awards or medical benefits are not jeopardized by other services.
5. *Transportation.* Determine specific transportation needs for employment, residential, and leisure alternatives. Identify alternatives for each activity, the method of financing transportation, and strategies to coordinate transportation between school and adult service providers.
6. *Long-term support and care.* Identify the need for guardianship and/or specific trusts or wills. Parents will need legal assistance in drawing up these documents.

Involving Students and Parents in Transition Planning

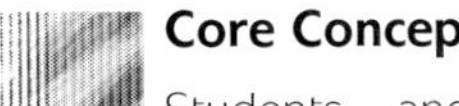

Core Concept

Students and parents must have the opportunity to fully participate in the transition planning process.

To be an effective tool for the future, transition planning must be built on a person-centered approach that values the input and participation of students and parents. They must be able to communicate interests and preferences, current skills levels across content areas, and future aspirations. Students and parents should be provided the opportunity to learn about critical components of adult service systems, including the characteristics of service agencies, and what constitutes a good program, as well as current and potential opportunities for employment and independent living (deFur, 1999; NCSET and the Pacer Center, 2004). (See Figure 9–2.)

There are several action steps in the development of a person-centered transition plan:

- *Choose a facilitator.* Parents and families begin the process of person-centered planning by choosing a facilitator. Facilitators must be good listeners with prior experience or training on person-centered planning. The role of the facilitator is to work closely with team members, including students, parents, school personnel, and adult services agencies in planning for the individual's life following school.

- *Design the person-centered planning process.* A personal profile is initially developed for each student with a disability reflecting his or her history or personal life story (critical events, medical issues, important relationships, etc.).
- *Implement the planning process.* Following the development and sharing of the personal profile, a meeting is held with team members to reflect on the individual's personal history and explore future opportunities for community participation, self-determination, and individual rights. Opportunities and challenges are discussed within the framework of a shared vision for the future. An action plan is developed with specific steps in the implementation of the shared vision.
- *Make the action plan a reality.* The team is periodically brought together to access progress in the implementation of the action, discuss what is working, and what requires more attention from the team if success is to be achieved. (NCSET and the Pacer Center, 2004)

Promoting Inclusion with Peers in High School Programs

Inclusion with peers who are not disabled is a critical factor in promoting successful community living for adults with intellectual disabilities. TASH (2005a) recommends that opportunities be available for secondary-age students with intellectual disabilities to participate in community and/or job skill development

From System Centered	To Person Centered
• Focus on labels	• See people first
• Emphasize deficits and needs	• Search for capacities, gifts
• Invest in standardized testing and assessments	• Spend time getting to know people
• Depend on professionals to make judgments	• Depend on people, families, and professionals to build good descriptions
• Generate written reports	• Gather information from people who know people well
• See people in the context of human service systems	• See people in the context of their local community
• Distance people by emphasizing difference	• Bring people together by discovering common experience

Figure 9–2
Moving from System-Centered to Person-Centered Transition Planning

Source: Adapted from *Person-Centered Planning* (p. 9) by B. Mount, 2000. New York: Graphics Futures.

Core Concept

The successful transition of the adult with intellectual disabilities to life in the community begins with inclusion during the school years.

programs as long as they do not impact negatively on participation and full membership in their high school community.

Inclusion during the secondary school years provides opportunities for peers without disabilities to develop positive attitudes about and friendships with a person with intellectual disabilities, as well as the skills needed to support people with disabilities during school, at work, and in neighborhood settings.

Opportunities for inclusion may take place in several contexts, including the general education classroom, in-school functions, and extracurricular activities. A peer support network (e.g., peer tutors, Best Buddies, Special Olympics Unified Sports) will facilitate the participation of students with intellectual disabilities in the life of the school. Peer tutors may assist the student in any context within the classroom, such as employment training, adaptive learning, or recreational, sports, and leisure activities. In a review of best practice indicators for educating learners with severe disabilities, several authors have suggested that the student with a disability *must* have access to the same environments as peers without disabilities (Giangreco & Doyle, 2000; Sailor, Gee, & Karasoff, 2000). As suggested by Hardman et al. (2006), successful inclusion includes instruction focused on valued postschool outcomes that will increase the competence of the student in the natural settings of family, school, and community. See the Tips for Professionals feature.

Tips for Professionals

Successful Inclusion in High School Programs

- Actively create and support opportunities for interaction between students with intellectual disabilities and their nondisabled peers. These should include opportunities to participate in high school content area classes as well as extracurricular activities (such as sports, clubs, school governance).
- Provide specific instruction to students with intellectual disabilities to increase their competence as they interact with students who are not disabled in natural settings.
- Ensure that highly trained teachers are available who are competent in the necessary instructional and assistive technology that facilitates social interaction between students with and without disabilities. Special education and general education teachers must work together to adapt subject matter in content classes (e.g., science or math) to the individual needs of students with intellectual disabilities.
- Ensure teachers have the support of the school administration to develop community-based programs that focus on students learning and applying skills side-by-side with nondisabled peers in community settings (such as grocery stores, malls, parks, work sites, etc).
- Support families who actively seek opportunities for nondisabled students to interact and become friends with their son or daughter who has intellectual disabilities. Help families locate resources that promote inclusion, such as Best Buddies or Special Olympics Unified Sports programs.

NEW ISSUES AND FUTURE DIRECTIONS

For adolescents with intellectual disabilities, the effective high school experience of the future will be comprehensive in its approach and involve a person-centered transition planning process oriented to individual needs, preferences, and inclusive environments. For this to happen, however, schools must develop transition planning that is outcome driven, focusing directly on providing access to natural environments to learn and apply different skills. Depending on individual student needs and abilities, transition planning must promote access to further education and/or preparation for life, including employment.

In the area of employment preparation, many high schools have focused more on getting the student ready by teaching vocational skills in the classroom, rather than in actual job settings. This emphasis places schools in a passive role, rather than an active one in which professionals prepare students and place them in jobs. The high unemployment rate for students with intellectual disabilities after they leave high school emphasizes the need for active involvement of school personnel in employment preparation. Graduates with disabilities who secure a job before leaving school are more likely to stay employed.

To facilitate employment preparation at the high school level in future years, it will be necessary for students, family, and adult service providers to be integrally involved in transition planning. School staff cannot, and should not, take on this task alone.

Core Questions

1. What are the three components of an effective high school program for adolescents with intellectual disabilities?
2. What basic civil rights were established under Section 504 of the Vocational Rehabilitation Act?
3. Distinguish between career education and work-experience programs.
4. Identify the components of a community-based employment preparation program.
5. What challenges face the adolescent with intellectual disabilities in attempting to manage personal needs?
6. What is the value of recreation, sports, and leisure activities?
7. Discuss the objectives of an academic skills program for an adolescent with intellectual disabilities.
8. Discuss the school's role in the transition planning process.
9. Why is inclusion with peers who are not disabled an important aspect of a quality educational experience for adolescents with intellectual disabilities?

Roundtable Discussion

In this chapter, we have discussed transition from school to the adult years for adolescents with intellectual disabilities. The purpose of transition planning is to match individual capabilities with the demands of adult life. In recent years, some professionals have advocated that educational programs for adolescents with more moderate to severe intellectual disabilities focus on performance required for successful adjustment to community life as adults and less on basic academics.

In your study group or on your own, design a transition plan for a student with intellectual disabilities. Take into account individual needs, preferences, and capabilities in relation to preparation for employment, residential living, and access to recreational and leisure experiences. You may choose to use the components of the transition planning process as discussed in this chapter as a guideline for the development of your plan.

Parent and Professional Organization Positions on Key Issues in the Lives of People with Intellectual Disabilities

The inside front cover of this text presents a matrix that includes nine key issues in the lives of people with disabilities, the positions of various parent and professional organizations on each issue, and the chapter and page number where the information is addressed. Table 9–1 is a summary of the organizations and key issues addressed in this chapter.

Table 9–1
Key Issues and Organizations Discussed in This Chapter

Organization/Website	Key Issues Addressed	Chapter Heading
American Association on Mental Retardation (http://www.aamr.org)	Transition planning	Self-Determination and Personal Management
The ARC—A national organization on intellectual disabilities (http://www.thearc.org)	Transition planning	Community-Referenced Employment Preparation
TASH, an international association of people with disabilities, their family members, and professionals (http://www.tash.org)	Community living and employment Inclusive education	Community-Referenced Employment Preparation Promoting Inclusion with Peers in High School Programs

References

Alberto, P. A., Taber, T., Brozovic, S. A., & Elliot, N. E. (1997). Continuing issues of collaborative transition planning in secondary schools. *Journal of Vocational Rehabilitation, 8*, 197–204.

American Association on Mental Retardation (AAMR). (2002). *Mental retardation: Definition, classification, and systems of supports* (10th ed.). Washington, DC: Author.

American Association on Mental Retardation (AAMR). (2005). *Policy statement on self-determination.* Retrieved February 21, 2005, from http://www.aamr.org/Policies/pos_self-determination.shtml

The ARC. (2005). *Position statement on employment.* Retrieved February 21, 2005, from http://www.thearc.org/posits/employmentpos.doc

Best Buddies. (2005). *About us.* Retrieved Feb 14, 2005, from http://www.bestbuddies.org

Bremer, C. D., Kachgal, M., & Schoeller, K. (2003, April). Self-determination: Supporting successful transition. *Research to Practice Brief of the National Center on Secondary Education and Transition, 2*(1), 1–5.

Brolin, D. E. (1997). *Career education: A competency-based approach* (5th ed.). Balston, VA: Council for Exceptional Children.

Brolin, D. E. (2004). *Life-skills career education curriculum.* Balston, VA: Council for Exceptional Children.

Browder, D. M., & Snell, M. E. (2000). Teaching functional academics. In M. E. Snell & Fredda Brown (Eds.), *Instruction of students with severe disabilities* (5th ed.) (pp. 493–542). Upper Saddle River, NJ: Merrill/Prentice Hall.

deFur, S. (1999). *Transition planning: A team effort.* Washington, DC: National Information Center for Children and Youth with Disabilities.

Division on Career Development and Transition, Council for Exceptional Children. (2002). *About DCDT.* Retrieved May 8, 2002, from http://www.ed.uiuc.edu/SPED/dcdt/aboutdcdt.html

Giangreco, M. F., & Doyle, M. B. (2000). Curricular and instructional considerations for teaching students with disabilities in general education classrooms. In S. E. Wade (Ed.), *Inclusive education: A casebook and readings for prospective and practicing teachers* (pp. 51–70). Mahwah, NJ: Erlbaum.

Hardman, M. L., Drew, C. J., & Egan, M. W. (2006). *Human exceptionality: school, community, and family* (8th ed.). Boston: Allyn & Bacon.

Hasazi, S. B., Furney, K. S., & Destefano, L. (1999). Implementing the IDEA transition initiatives. *Exceptional Children, 65*(4), 555–566.

Katims, D. S. (2000). Literacy instruction for people with intellectual disabilities: Historical highlights and contemporary analysis. *Education and Training in Mental Retardation and Developmental Disabilities, 35*(1), 3–15.

McDonnell, J., Hardman, M. L., & McDonnell, A. (2003). *Introduction to people with severe disabilities* (2nd ed.). Boston: Allyn & Bacon.

Mount, B. (2000). *Person-centered planning.* New York: Graphics Futures, p. 9.

National Center on Secondary Education and Transition (NCSET) and the Pacer Center. (2004, February). *Parent brief: Person-centered planning: A tool for transition.* Minneapolis, MN: Author.

National Organization on Disability (NOD) & Harris, L., & Associates. (2004). *National Organization on Disability/Harris survey of Americans with disabilities.* New York: Author.

Sailor, W., Gee, K., & Karasoff, P. (2000). Inclusion and school restructuring. In M. Snell & F. Brown (Eds.), *Instruction of students with severe disabilities* (5th ed., pp. 1–30). Columbus, OH: Charles Merrill.

TASH (2005a). *TASH resolution on inclusive quality* education. Retrieved January 28, 2005, from http://www.tash.org/resolutions/res02inclusiveed.htm

TASH (2005b). *TASH resolution on integrated employment.* Retrieved Feburary 21, 2005, from http://www.tash.org/resolutions/res02employment.htm

University of Illinois at Chicago National Research and Training Center. (2005). *Self-determination framework for people with psychiatric disabilities.* Retrieved February 14, 2005, from http://www.psych.uic.edu/UICNRTC/sdframework.pdf

Wagner, M., & Blackorby, J. (1996). Transition from high school to work or college: How special education students fare. In Center for the Future of Children, *Special education for students with disabilities, 6*(1) 103–120. Los Angeles: Center for the Future of children.

Wehman, P., & Kregal, J. (2005). *Intellectual and developmental disabilities: Toward full community inclusion.* Austin, TX: Pro-Ed.

Adulthood and Aging

Chapter 10

The Adult Years

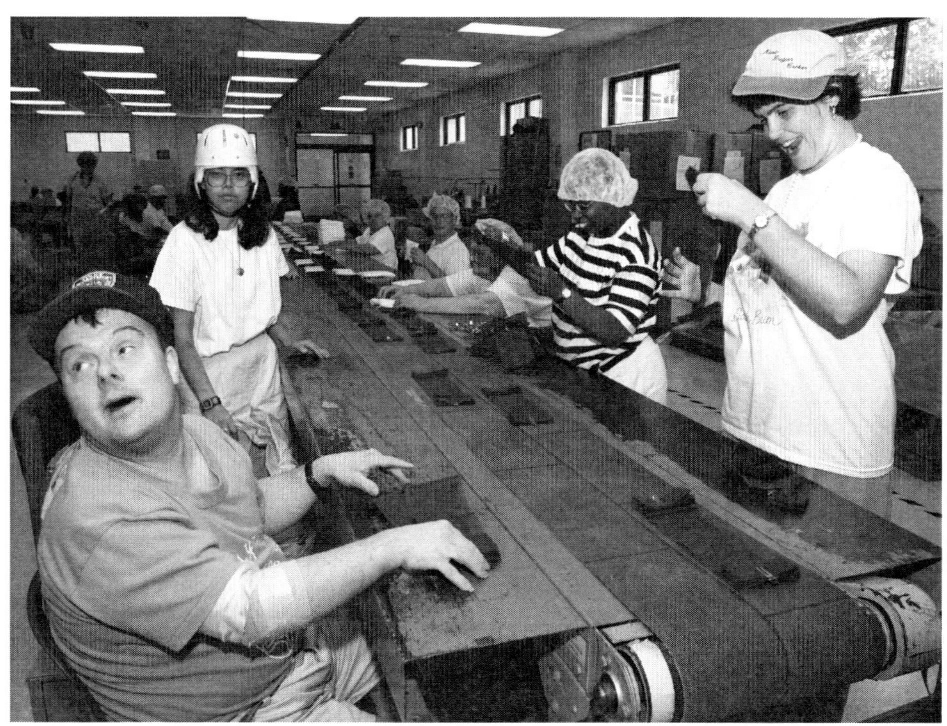

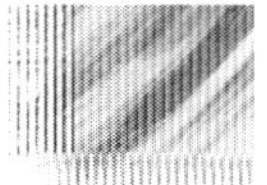

Chapter Preview

At the completion of this chapter, you will have a better understanding of services and supports for adults with intellectual disabilities, including:

- Why self-determination is so important in understanding how to speak up for oneself, and make informed lifestyle choices.
- The purpose and provisions of the Americans with Disabilities Act in ending discrimination against persons with disabilities.
- The importance of competitive employment, supported living, and community recreation/leisure opportunities, and why institutional living is widely viewed as detrimental to intellectual, psychological, and physical development.

Giving Steve a Chance to Work, Live, and Play in the Community

Steve is a person with intellectual disabilities and epilepsy who spent most of the first years of his life in a state institution. It was a place that frustrated Steve with all its rules—rules about when and what he would eat, where and when Steve would sleep, and what Steve would wear. During his stay in the institution, Steve developed a fierce sense of independence and fought against rules he saw as controlling his life. Now 45 years old and happily living on his own in an apartment in the southern part of the city, Steve makes most of the choices in his life with some help from a supported living staff of three trained individuals who are available 24 hours a day, 7 days a week, as needed. The staff also assists in daily tasks, including dispensing needed medications, personal hygiene, cooking at home, and arriving at work on time. Steve had a major fall down a flight of stairs in his early adult years while having a seizure. As a result, he lost a great deal of physical strength in one arm and both his legs. He is unable to walk or stand for any period of time. To accommodate Steve's needs, his supported employment program found him a job at a local restaurant for 4 hours a day where he can use his right arm and sit while cooking hamburgers for the lunch crowd. Steve has a job coach who trained him and now provides periodic assistance when there is a need to learn a new skill or practice on a previously learned one. He also gets help and moral support from his coworkers at the restaurant. Steve's mother and brother live within five miles of his apartment and spend time with him regularly at home, in the community, and on the phone. Steve is a big movie buff with an impressive collection of DVDs and videos. His favorite movies are Clint Eastwood and John Wayne westerns.

- *Why is it important for Steve to live and work in a community setting?*
- *What should Steve's supported living and employment staff do to assist him in the community but not make decisions for him?*

Early adulthood generally marks a time of transition from relative dependence to increasing independence and responsibility for one's life. Adults with intellectual disabilities are a paradox. They have achieved adulthood because they have lived long enough to deserve the distinction. However, many of these individuals are unable to be completely independent. This is true for Steve. He was still in a state institution when he was 21 years old where his life was regimented with routine and few choices. He was completely dependent on caregivers for his meals, his clothes, and determining how he would spend his leisure time. Today, he leads a more independent life but still needs periodic support from supported living staff and his family. He does, however, make most choices about his life, including deciding on the clothes he wears, the food he eats, and the places he goes for fun and recreation.

What does society expect of an adult? An adult works, earns money, and buys the necessities of life and as many of the pleasures as he or she wants or can afford. Adults socialize, often marry, perhaps have children, and try to live as productively and happily as possible. However, adults with intellectual disabilities may face significant challenges in accomplishing life tasks and goals. They may be unable to find or hold a job, particularly without a formal support system in place. If jobs are available, wages may be so low that even the basics of life may be out of reach. What if the adult with intellectual disabilities has no one to socialize with, no one to love or be loved by? What if he or she must become dependent on parents for mere existence and the parents die or become too old to help? There are many such "what ifs" for these individuals who may simply exchange the pressures of adolescence for new and sometimes more difficult ones.

There is little available research on the lives of adults with intellectual disabilities (Hardman, Drew, & Egan, 2006; Yamaki & Fujiura, 2002). Most studies have focused on children with intellectual disabilities and their lives at school. It was not until 1973 that the Association for Retarded Children (ARC) changed its name to the Association for Retarded Citizens (now The ARC—a national organization on intellectual disabilities). Although this association has long campaigned for the rights of all people with intellectual disabilities, the name change reflected a growing recognition of the need to emphasize support at all stages of life. Interestingly, one thing we do know from the limited research available on adults with intellectual disabilities is that they require ongoing support from family, friends, neighbors, and coworkers. This support is needed throughout life in order to live and work successfully in a community setting (American Association on Mental Retardation, 2002; Tymchuk, 2001; Tymchuk, Lakin, & Luckasson, 2001). The individual will probably be an adult three times as long as he or she is a child or an adolescent. Therefore, it seems only appropriate for us to devote more time to the needs and nature of adults with intellectual disabilities.

In this chapter, we consider supports and services for adults with intellectual disabilities. Our discussion focuses on life in the community, making competent and self-determined choices, the deteriments of institutional living, working in competitive employment with various types of support, and new issues and future directions.

COMMUNITY LIVING

In its most fundamental form, successful adult living may be defined as (a) earning a living, (b) having access to further education when desired and appropriate, (c) personal autonomy and independence, (d) interaction with friends and community participation, and (e) ongoing involvement within the life of the family. As one reaches the age of majority, there are decisions that have to be made relative to each of these five areas. What kind of career or job do I desire? Should I further my education to increase my career choices? Where and with whom shall I live? How shall I spend my money? Whom do I choose to spend time with? Who will be my friends? While most people face these choices as a natural part of growing into adult life, the issues facing adults with intellectual disabilities and their families may be very different.

Making Adult Choices: Competence and Self-Determination

Everyone is considered mentally competent—that is, able to make rational and reasoned choices about their lives—at the age of majority, unless legally determined otherwise. The legal presumption of mental competence removes from parents the obligation and power to make decisions for their adult child, a power that until this point in life could not be usurped unless it was abused. For professionals, this means no longer seeking parental advice or consent on issues related to the person who has reached the age of majority but respecting the rights of the individual as an adult. Respecting these rights involves the obligation to maintain confidentiality from parents and others if the person so desires.

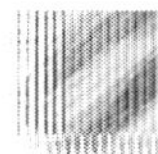

Core Concept

Self-determination involves people with intellectual disabilities speaking up for themselves, making their own lifestyle choices, and being able to act on them.

While the legal presumption is that everyone is competent at the age of majority, this supposition can be overturned or set aside by the courts in certain circumstances. An adult can be deemed incompetent through a process known as adjudication. In adjudication, those seeking to have the individual declared incompetent must provide a preponderance of evidence that the person does not have the capacity to make rational choices:

- Does the person have the capacity to consistently make rational and reasoned decisions that are in his or her best interests and those of others whom the individual has direct contact with?
- Is the individual partially competent and thus able to make some rational decisions at varying levels of complexity?
- Is the individual totally incompetent and thus unable to make any reasoned decisions on his or her behalf?

Determining incompetence is a very sensitive and complex process. It is further complicated by judicial criteria that is sometimes unclear as to what differentiates complete or partial competence from total incompetence. It is important to remember that competence is not an all-or-nothing proposition. Certainly, few people are completely competent in everything; correspondingly, few people are totally incompetent as well. Any decision to remove or reduce an individual's right to make choices must be weighed very heavily since such rights are fundamental to adult status from a legal, moral, and practical standpoint.

One of the first challenges facing families when their son or daughter with intellectual disabilities reaches the age of majority is weighing the right to self-determination against the mental competence to make reasoned choices. As discussed in Chapter 9, self-determination focuses on a person's ability to consider options and make appropriate decisions, and exercise free will, independence, and individual responsibility (University of Illinois at Chicago National Research and Training Center, 2005). Self-determination is an extension of a concept first introduced in the 1960s that became widely known as "the principle of **normalization.**" First articulated in Scandinavia (Nirje, 1969) and later expanded on in the United States (Wolfensberger, 1972), normalization means people with intellectual disabilities have access to the conditions of everyday life that are as close as possible to those of people without disabilities in mainstream society. Normalization does not mean just providing a normative situation, like a home in the community. Without supports, the individual with intellectual disabilities may not be able to meet the demands of the community.

Wolfensberger (2000) suggested a rethinking of the term *normalization* and introduced the concept of **social role valorization (SRV),** giving value to the individual with intellectual disabilities. He stated, "The key premise of SRV is that people's welfare depends extensively on the social roles they occupy; people who fill roles that are positively valued by others will generally be afforded by the latter the good things of life, but people who fill roles that are devalued by others will typically get badly treated by them" (p. 105). The goal is to seek more positive roles and experiences for people who are devalued. Strategies to accomplish this goal would enhance the individual's social image or perceived value in the eyes of others and enhance individual competence within society.

In the 21st century, the term *self-determination* embodies the view that persons with intellectual disabilities should act as the primary causal agent in their lives and be able to make choices and decisions about their quality of life without interference (Mount, 2000; Silverstein, 2001). Making self-determination a reality is not always easy. Parents, although advocating strongly for a son or daughter's independence, may face situations where the adult with intellectual disabilities may make a decision with which the family does not agree or is viewed as "risky." It may take considerable strength for parents or other family members to accept and support such choices.

Self-determination may be characterized by several factors, including (a) optimal challenge and empowerment, (b) autonomy, (c) competence, (d) involvement, (e) acknowledgment of individual feelings, and (f) self-regulation (Agran, Blanchard, & Wehmeyer, 2000; Morgan, Ellerd, Gerity, & Blair, 2000; Wehmeyer, 2002). Activities that optimally challenge students are those that are neither too easy nor too difficult. Excessive repetition, overlearned tasks, or activities far beyond a person's achievement level decrease motivation. The issue of optimal challenge is particularly salient to people with intellectual disabilities. These individuals often require repeated exposure to a task to learn a skill.

Development of opportunities to express preference, make choices, and experience the outcomes of these choices are characteristics of environments that support autonomy and empowerment. Unfortunately, many professionals have not focused on developing these opportunities (Nerney, 2004). As stated by Brown, Gothelf, Guess, and Lehr (1998), "For years, professionals decided what was best for people with disabilities and their families. Now . . . the field is moving away from an emphasis on care taking and fitting people to pre-existing services toward an emphasis on personal control, flexible support, and a rich, varied lifestyle" (p. 27).

Competence and involvement are considered basic human needs. Competence involves understanding how to attain various outcomes and being efficacious in performing the required actions to achieve these outcomes. This notion is also referred to as self-efficacy—that is, having confidence in being able to perform a particular task. Involvement may be defined as the level to which an individual develops secure and satisfying connections with others in his or her social environment. The most desirable outcomes for individuals are achieved when involvement occurs in conjunction with support for autonomy and competence. Self-determination may be also enhanced by acknowledging the individual's views and preferences. While everyone has to engage in tasks they see as uninteresting, self-determination is strengthened when a reason for participation is provided and the individual's questions or concerns are acknowledged.

Although providing opportunities for an individual to make choices and decisions is paramount in developing self-determination, it is also important for parents and professionals to assist in (a) identifying options from a range of alternatives, (b) identifying the associated consequences, (c) selecting and implementing options, (d) evaluating results, and (e) adjusting future directions. Self-regulation techniques are skills supportive of autonomy. The development of these skills is a complex and long-term process. Instructional programs that promote self-determination must begin laying the groundwork early in the child's life.

One strategy to create opportunities for people with intellectual disabilities to learn and apply self-determination skills in work and community life and thus to enhance their perceived value is legislative reform. One such major reform effort came to fruition in 1990 with the passage of the Americans with Disabilities Act.

The Americans with Disabilities Act (ADA)

Core Concept

The purpose of the Americans with Disabilities Act is to end discrimination against persons with disabilities in private-sector employment, public services, public accommodations, transportation, and telecommunications.

The Americans with Disabilities Act, or ADA (Public Law 101-336) mandates that barriers of discrimination against people with disabilities in private-sector employment, in all public services, and in public accommodations, transportation, and telecommunications are to be eliminated. The ADA requires businesses that serve the public to remove architectural barriers, such as curbs on sidewalks, narrow doorways, or shelving and desks, which prevent access by a person with a disability. The business community must provide "reasonable accommodations" to people with disabilities in hiring or promotion practices, in restructuring jobs, and in modifying equipment. Under the ADA, all new public transit facilities (e.g., buses or train stations) must be accessible, and transportation services must be available to people with disabilities who cannot use fixed bus routes. The ADA also requires that public accommodations (e.g., restaurants, hotels, retail stores) and state and local government agencies are accessible to people with disabilities. By the year 2010, all Amtrak train stations must be accessible. Telecommunication devices for people who are deaf must be made available by all companies that offer telephone service to the general public.

The ADA's purpose is to provide people with disabilities an "equal playing field" as they seek access to the same opportunities afforded those who are not disabled (Hardman et al., 2006). As important as this law is to people with disabilities, including those with intellectual disabilities, it is only social policy. The law must be translated from policy into daily practice as an accepted way of life for communities across the United States if it is to be truly successful in breaking down discrimination.

The National Organization on Disability (NOD) and Harris & Associates (2004) conducted a survey of how people with disabilities perceived their lives 14 years after passage of the ADA. Overall, the survey results suggested that although people with disabilities remain at a significant disadvantage in several key areas (e.g., income, social life, transportation, health care), progress is steady and gaps are being closed. (See the Closing the Gap feature.)

Most individuals take many areas of everyday living for granted, such as shopping, crossing streets, making daily purchases, and getting transportation. Yet unless people with intellectual disabilities receive the necessary support in these areas, their opportunities certainly will be very limited. In the following sections, we address various aspects of life in the community. These include supported living, parents or siblings as primary caregivers, community participation, marriage and sexuality, and adjustment to community life.

Closing the Gap

People with Disabilities and the ADA

- Only 35% of people with disabilities reported being employed full or part time, compared to 78% of those who do not have disabilities.
- Three times as many live in poverty with annual household incomes below $15,000 (26% versus 9%).
- People with disabilities remain twice as likely to drop out of high school (21% versus 10%).
- They are twice as likely to have inadequate transportation (31% versus 13%), and a much higher percentage go without needed health care (18% versus 7%).
- People with disabilities are less likely to socialize, eat out, or attend religious services than their nondisabled counterparts.
- Not surprisingly given the persistence of these gaps, life satisfaction for people with disabilities also trails, with only 34% say they are very satisfied compared to 61% of those without disabilities.

Source: From *National Organization on Disability/Harris Survey of Americans with Disabilities* by National Organization on Disability (NOD) & Harris & Associates, 2004. New York: Author.

Supported Residential Living

In this new century, many people with intellectual disabilities, along with their families and professionals, are advocating for nationwide expansion of small community-based places to live. The American Association on Mental Retardation (AAMR) and The Arc have adopted identical positions on an individual's right to live in the community. "All people with [intellectual disabilities] have a right to live in communities of their choosing and be fully included with people who do not have disabilities. Children belong with their families. Adults should control where and with whom they live, with increasing opportunities to rent or buy their own homes (AAMR, 2005b; ARC, 2005b).

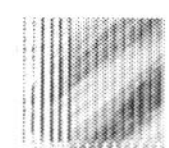

Core Concept

Small community living models for adults with intellectual disabilities include group homes, semi-independent homes and apartments, and foster care.

As is true for people without disabilities, community supports for people with intellectual disabilities should promote personal autonomy, social inclusion, and choice of lifestyle. For the vast majority of individuals with intellectual disabilities, **supported living** is the most appropriate residential arrangement. McDonnell, Hardman, and McDonnell (2003) identify five critical characteristics of a supported living model:

1. An emphasis on living, not programming. Supported living provides people with intellectual disabilities the opportunity to live in the same arrangements as people without disabilities. The focus is on supporting choices about where and how they want to live.
2. Accountability for lifestyle outcomes. The focus is on quality of life and achieving significant lifestyle outcomes, such as inclusion in the social network of the neighborhood and community, use of community resources, and empowerment in making lifestyle choices.
3. Diversity of residential options. People with intellectual disabilities choose where and how they want to live. Supported living promotes personal choice in selecting a living alternative.
4. Individually determined support. The level of support is dependent on individual need. Service programs must be flexible enough to accommodate the unique needs of different people.
5. Broad technology of residential support. Supporting people with intellectual disabilities in their homes will require the expertise of a number of professions who work together to meet the needs of each person.

Several types of community residential programs have been developed over the years. In this chapter, we discuss three widely used residential models for adults with intellectual disabilities living in the community: group homes, semi-independent homes and apartments, and foster care.

Group Homes. Considerable variation is found in organization and alternatives within the group home model. A small group home is usually a community residence with 2 to 4 persons living in a single dwelling. A large group home may have as many as 8 to 15 or more residents.

Living arrangements for adults with intellectual disabilities may involve several options.

Trained professionals usually provide support to persons with intellectual disabilities living in these homes, regardless of the size. In some instances, a house director works on a full- or half-time basis to handle logistics. Many group homes now are employing shift workers who are on duty for four to seven days at a time as a team. Small group homes are usually more integrated into residential neighborhoods. The homes emphasize programs that provide daily living experiences as similar as possible to those of individuals without disabilities. Government funding supplemented by fees paid by the residents or their family members usually finance these homes.

Semi-Independent Homes and Apartments. The semi-independent home or apartment represents the least restrictive of all supervised residential models (see the feature "The Keys Are Mine"). Several variations on the semi-independent home or apartment have been developed over the years:

1. *Apartment clusters.* Comprised of several apartments fairly close together, they function to some extent as a unit and are supervised by a resident staff member(s) who lives in one of the apartment units.
2. *Single co-residence home or apartment.* This consists of a single home or apartment in which an adult staff member shares the dwelling with one or more roommates who have intellectual disabilities.

"The Keys Are Mine"

When I lived at Lake Owasso State institution in Minnesota you had to ask for everything: "Can you let me out?," "Can I have a can of pop?," "Can I stay up a little bit longer?"

When I moved into a group home, I had to follow all of the rules. I had to go to bed at a certain time, and when I was in bed, I had to be asleep; that was that. I lived with two other guys. We were being watched all the time, 24 hours a day, seven days a week.

Two years ago I got married. My wife and I moved into our own apartment. Now that I have my own place, I make the decisions. I have my own keys. I can let myself out, and let myself back in. Now I can come and go when I want. I can make my own food, and I decide whether I want to have breakfast or lunch, when I'm ready for a snack. We can invite friends to stay over. My wife and I decide when the staff come over. They help us with some things but we make our own decisions.

Source: From "The Keys Are Mine" by K. Otley, 2004, *Guidebook on Consumer Controlled Housing*. Minneapolis: Arc-Minnesota and the Institute on Community Integration.

3. *Single home or apartment.* This consists of a home or apartment owned and/or occupied by an adult with intellectual disabilities whom a nonresident staff member assists. This is the most independent kind of living arrangement in the model.

These three variations provide different degrees of independence, and individuals living in this type of residential model require fewer supports than those living in other residential models. Most residents are responsible for or contribute to apartment maintenance, meal preparation, and transportation to place of employment.

Foster Family Care. The purpose of foster family care is to provide a surrogate family for the individual with intellectual disabilities. One goal of foster family care is to integrate the individuals into the family setting, with the assumption that within the family environment, the individual will learn adaptive skills and work in a community setting. One concern with this model is that a person with intellectual disabilities living in a surrogate family may assume a dependent, childlike role and become overprotected. In general, these placements offer residents adequate productive daytime activities and opportunities to manage their physical environment, both fundamental components of normalization. Those who operate the foster homes generally receive a per capita fee from the state. These settings often accommodate about one to six adults. Activities and quality of care are, to some extent, at the discretion of the provider.

Sheltered Villages. Another setting that some states consider a community residential alternative is the sheltered village. Sheltered villages for adults with intellectual disabilities usually are located in rural areas; they are secluded and spread over several buildings. Although rules, activities, and relative freedom within each sheltered village vary, they do have one common characteristic: isolation from the outside community. The rationale is that residents are better off in isolation than exposed to the potential failures, frustrations, and demands of the outside world. Many of these facilities are private, and a number are church supported.

Living with Parents and Siblings

While supported living facilitates opportunities for adults with intellectual disabilities to live on their own, some people never move away from their primary family. Parents or siblings may be the individual's primary support for a lifetime.

Approximately 60% of people with intellectual disabilities live under their families on and off throughout their lives (Fujiiura, 1998). Living with parents or siblings during the adult years may result from a lack of formal resources for the family or from the family's personal decision to keep the individual at home (Parish, Selzter, Greenberg, & Floyd, 2004). This is not to say that parents who choose to keep their adult son or daughter at home aren't in need of government-funded supports and services. In fact, parents of children with intellectual disabilities have lower rates of employment, larger families, and lower rates of social participation when compared to parents of children without disabilities (Seltzer, Greenberg, Floyd, Petee, & Hong, 2001). These parents often need respite care, in-home assistance, and counseling/training services.

Respite Care and In-Home Assistance. Respite care and in-home assistance provides relief and help for parents attempting to cope with the challenges of an adult with intellectual disabilities living in the home. In-home respite care may involve a paid companion spending some time with the adult who is disabled. Out-of-home respite care may be provided by parent cooperatives, day care centers, community recreational services, and families who are licensed to take adults with disabilities into their home for a limited period of time. Respite services provide the opportunity for family members to engage in social and recreational activities outside the home, thus reducing feelings of social isolation. As an example, in-home assistance could come from a professional homemaker who might reduce the family's time in dealing with household management tasks or a personal attendant who might help with daily routines.

Extended family members are also sources of respite care and in-home assistance. These family members may periodically help with meals, clean the house, provide transportation, or just listen when everyone is overwhelmed. Hardman et al. (2006) suggest that grandparents and other extended family members are a critical resource for helping parents who choose to keep an adult family member at home.

Counseling and Training. In addition to respite care and in-home assistance, families may also receive counseling services and training to help them cope with the daily stress of caring for an adult with intellectual disabilities. Counseling services and family training programs often focus on the relationships and interactions between and among the members, not just on the adult with intellectual disabilities. Such an approach, referred to as a **family systems perspective,** is based on the premise that all parts of the family are interrelated. Each family is unique and can be understood only by observing the interactions and relationships among its members (Turnbull & Turnbull, 2001).

Sibling Roles. While some attention has been paid to the role of parents during the adult years, little has been written about sibling responsibilities. During adulthood, sibling concerns center on:

> Who is going to take care of my brother or sister?
> When my parents die, who will be responsible?
> Am I going to have to take care of my brother or sister all of my life?

Hanna and Midlarsky (2005) found that siblings not only believe that families should be responsible for the care of a family member with intellectual disabilities, but actually engage in emotional support. In a longitudinal study of families who had adults with intellectual disabilities still living at home, Krauss, Seltzer, Gordon, and Friedman (1996) found that many siblings remained very actively involved with their brothers or sisters well into the adult years. These siblings had frequent contact with their brothers or sisters and were knowledgeable about their lives. In addition, they played a major role in their parents' support network. Approximately one in three of these siblings indicated that they planned to reside with their brother or sister at some point during adult life.

In a study of brothers and sisters of adults with intellectual disabilities, Orsmond and Seltzer (2000) found some interesting gender differences. Sisters of adults with intellectual disabilities tended to score higher in the areas of caregiving and companionship, while brothers' responses depended on the gender of their sibling with intellectual disabilities. Males with a brother who had intellectual disabilities were more emotionally responsive than males with a sister who had a similar condition.

The reality is that sibling roles with a brother or sister who has intellectual disabilities may vary considerably, depending on the attitudes and values of their parents, their own attitudes about responsibility, and the proximity to their brother or sister (Orsmond & Seltzer, 2000). There are siblings who develop negative feelings very early in childhood and carry these feelings through to adult life. These siblings grew up resenting the time and attention parents gave to their disabled brother or sister, eventually becoming bitter and emotionally neglected adults. Such negative feelings often result in guilt that further isolates the individual from the primary family. Adult siblings, resentful of their brother or sister, may actively disengage themselves from parents and the disabled family member for long periods of time. However, some siblings play a crucial role during adult life, providing ongoing support to parents and spending time with their brother or sister who has an intellectual disability.

Recreation and Leisure in a Community Setting

Some adults with intellectual disabilities have busy and active work schedules. For these individuals, recreational and leisure activities provide a much-needed change

Core Concept

Recreational and leisure activities are an important source of pleasure and relaxation for the adult with intellectual disabilities.

from daily work schedules. Brown (2000) indicated that adults with intellectual disabilities are most active socially and physically in their mid-20s. This activity level declines fairly rapidly during the ensuing years and opportunities for recreation and leisure experiences in the community diminish with time. Adults with intellectual disabilities are too often lonely and inactive without access to any meaningful leisure activities. Jobling (2001), in a review of literature on health and physical activity, reported that adults with intellectual disabilities "lack physical exercise and tend to favor sedentary activities" (p. 314). Typical sedentary activities include watching television, listening to music, and looking at books and magazines. As expressed by Brown, a decline in exercise and leisure activity through the adult years is "of grave concern because this decline can have a marked effect on health and community integration" (p. 31). Community recreational experiences must be developed and supported if people with intellectual disabilities are to have satisfying lives beyond work and home life. Therapeutic recreation is a profession concerned specifically with this goal: using recreation to help people adapt their physical, emotional, or social characteristics to take advantage of leisure activities more independently in a community setting. Some communities are initiating new recreation and leisure programs that will include people with intellectual disabilities as well as providing more support for programs that are well established (such as Special Olympics).

Marriage and Sexuality

Core Concept

Many individuals with intellectual disabilities desire and value marriage and sexual intimacy.

As suggested by The ARC (2005c), "people with [intellectual disabilities] like all people, have inherent sexual rights and basic human needs. These rights and needs must be affirmed, defended, and respected." However, as reported by Reiss (2001), the vast majority of these individuals do not marry and will not become parents. The idea of people with intellectual disabilities getting married, having interpersonal relationships, expressing their sexuality, and bearing children has been historically unacceptable to much of society. The sexuality of these individuals is often ignored despite the fact that many are capable of learning social and sexual skills. As adults in the community, people with intellectual disabilities are free, in many instances, to conduct their personal lives as they choose. The results of their interpersonal relationships may depend on the instruction and training they receive regarding sexual behavior. The sexual behavior of people with intellectual disabilities is learned and directly affected by their ability to make appropriate decisions and reduce their risk of abuse. These individuals must receive appropriate sex education that is focused on informed consent, sexual hygiene, and abstinence or contraception, depending on personal values. It is well documented that people with intellectual disabilities are at a significantly higher risk of sexual exploitation than their peers without disabilities. In fact, the rates of sexual abuse of people with intellectual disabilities are the highest among all disability areas and are four times the national sexual assault rate. Without abuse prevention training and the fostering of independent skills in self-regulation, assertiveness, and decision making, people with intellectual disabilities are often powerless to act on their own behalf (Khemka & Hickson, 2000; Sullivan, 2000).

Another issue concerning sexuality and people with intellectual disabilities is the practice of sterilization. For most of the 20th century, sterilization was viewed as a means of eliminating or curtailing intellectual disabilities, preventing individuals with intellectual disabilities from having unwanted children or preventing them from having children because of their alleged incompetence (Edgerton, 2001; Tymchuk, 2001). In 1927, Justice Oliver Wendell Holmes issued his famous opinion for the Supreme Court, which upheld a state compulsory sterilization law: "Three generations of imbeciles are enough" (*Buck v. Bell,* 1927). The Holmes opinion resulted in a marked increase in the practice of sterilization. The prime targets for compulsory sterilization appear to have been individuals with intellectual disabilities who were in the process of being released from institutions. During the period of institutionalization, sterilization was considered a prerequisite to release. Unless there was strong objection, the surgery was routinely performed. By 1935, people with intellectual disabilities constituted 44% of those sterilized in this country; by 1946, the percentage had increased to 69%. The rate of sterilization had increased through 1937 but leveled off by 1942. The rate of sterilization decreased dramatically after World War II, when it was revealed that Adolf Hitler's "final solution" (Operation T4) had actively terminated the lives of people with intellectual disabilities. Hitler used sterilization as a means to "purify" the human race and put these "wretched people" out of their misery (see the feature Operation T4).

The concern of discriminatory sterilization should not be limited exclusively to people who have been institutionalized. The question of whether society has the right to impose sterilization on any individual with intellectual disabilities has great relevance for parents, professionals, and the individuals themselves. Today, sterilization is still legal in the United States but requires a court order that the person with intellectual disabilities is presumed incompetent to make his or her own decisions and to parent children (Brown, 2002).

Research on Adjustment to Community Living

Studies of people with intellectual disabilities in community settings date back to 1919. Fernald (1919) studied individuals discharged from an institution over a 25-year period and found considerable variability in their adjustment to community life. In the 1930s and 1940s, several studies compared the community adjustment of individuals with intellectual disabilities with control groups of people without disabilities. Many of these studies suggested that the majority of persons with intellectual disabilities were able to make acceptable adjustments to community life.

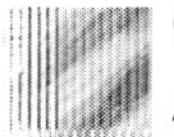

Core Concept

Adults with intellectual disabilities are capable of self-sufficiency and social adaptation within the community.

Operation T4

The Extermination of People with Intellectual Disabilities in Nazi Germany

Forced sterilization in Germany was the forerunner of the systematic killing of [people with intellectual disabilities and the mentally ill]. In October 1939, Hitler initialed a decree which empowered physicians to grant a "mercy death" to patients considered incurable according to the best available human judgment of their state of health. The intent of the so-called "euthanasia" program, however, was not to relieve the suffering of the chronically ill. The Nazi regime used the term as a euphemism: its aim was to exterminate the mentally ill and [people with intellectual disabilities], thus "cleansing" the Aryan race of persons considered genetically defective and a financial burden to society.

The idea of killing the incurably ill was posed well before 1939. In the 1920s, debate on this issue centered on a book co-authored by Alfred Hoche, a noted psychiatrist, and Karl Binding, a prominent scholar of criminal law. They argued that economic savings justified the killing of "useless lives" ("idiots" and "congenitally crippled"). Economic deprivation during World War I provided the context for this idea. During the war, patients in asylums had ranked low on the list for rationing of food and medical supplies, and as a result, many died from starvation or disease. More generally, the war undermined the value attached to individual life and, combined with Germany's humiliating defeat, led many nationalists to consider ways to regenerate the nation as a whole at the expense of individual rights.

In 1935 Hitler stated privately that "in the event of war, [he] would take up the question of euthanasia and enforce it" because "such a problem would be more easily solved" during wartime. War would provide both a cover for killing and a pretext—hospital beds and medical personnel would be freed up for the war effort. The upheaval of war and the diminished value of human life during wartime would also, Hitler believed, mute expected opposition. To make the connection to the war explicit, Hitler's decree was backdated to September 1, 1939, the day Germany invaded Poland.

Fearful of public reaction, the Nazi regime never proposed a formal "euthanasia" law. Unlike the forced sterilizations, the killing of patients in mental asylums and other institutions was carried out in secrecy. The code name was "Operation T4," a reference to Tiergartenstrasse 4, the address of the Berlin Chancellery offices where the program was headquartered.

Physicians, the most highly Nazified professional group in Germany, were key to the success of "T4," since they organized and carried out nearly all aspects of the operation. One of Hitler's personal physicians, Dr. Karl Brandt, headed the program, along with Hitler's Chancellery chief, Philip Bouhler. T4 targeted adult patients in all government- or church-run santeria and nursing homes. These institutions were instructed by the Interior Ministry to complete questionnaires about the state of health and capacity for work of all their patients, ostensibly as part of a statistical survey. The completed forms were, in turn, sent to expert "assessors"—physicians, usually psychiatrists, who made up "review commissions." They marked each name with a "+" in red pencil, meaning death, or a "2" in blue pencil, meaning life, or "?" for cases needing additional assessment. These medical experts rarely examined any of the patients and made their decisions from the questionnaires alone. At every step, the medical authorities involved were usually expected to quickly process large numbers of forms.

The doomed were bused to killing centers in Germany and Austria—walled-in fortresses, mostly former psychiatric hospitals, castles, and a former prison—at Hartheim, Sonnenstein, Grafeneck, Bernburg, Hadamar, and Brandenburg. In the beginning, patients were killed by lethal injection. But by 1940, Hitler, on the advice of Dr. Werner Heyde, suggested that carbon monoxide gas be used as the preferred method of killing.

Experimental gassings had first been carried out at Brandenburg Prison in 1939. There, gas chambers were disguised as showers complete with fake nozzles in order to deceive victims—prototypes of the killing centers' facilities built in occupied Poland later in the war.

Source: From "*Mentally and Physically Handicapped: Victims of the Nazi Era, 1933–1945.*" The United States Holocaust Memorial Museum, Washington, DC. Retrieved April 20, 2005, from http://www.ushmm.org/education/foradults/index.php?content=resource/.

Community participation for adults with intellectual disabilities may be similar to those for the rest of us.

Studies in the 1960s suggested that even in later years of life, community adjustment was considered successful (Baller, Charles, & Miller, 1966; Kennedy, 1966). In the 1970s, several studies (Bellamy, O'Conner, & Karan, 1979; Close, 1975; Gold, 1973) demonstrated that under carefully controlled conditions, even people with severe and profound intellectual disabilities are capable of self-sufficiency and social adaptation within a community setting. In the 1980s, investigations (Conroy & Bradley, 1985; Haney, 1988; O'Neill, Brown, Gordon, & Schonhorn, 1985) focused on the feasibility of small community living situations for people with moderate and severe intellectual disabilities.

The 1990s was a decade of expansion in supported community living alternatives for persons with intellectual disabilities. Significant advances were made in understanding the factors that promote successful inclusion into community living (Braddock, Hemp, Rizzolo, Parish, & Pomeranz, 2002; McDonnell et al., 2003). Much remains to be done, however, to use the information available effectively and to identify more specifically those variables associated with success in community programs.

Anthropologist Robert Edgerton has studied the postinstitutional lives of people with intellectual disabilities in community settings for more than four decades (Edgerton, 1967, 2001; Edgerton & Bercovici, 1976; Edgerton, Bollinger, & Herr, 1984). In a review of the research on the community adjustment of individuals with mild intellectual disabilities, Edgerton (2001) made several observations:

- While many people with mild intellectual disabilities drop out of sight after they exit school, available research indicates these individuals remain in need of a wide array of government and natural (family, friends) supports.
- Follow-up studies suggest that high percentages of people with intellectual disabilities who were released from institutions made positive adaptations to community living. However, there is little agreement among researchers about why some individuals do well and others fare badly in the community.
- The recent trend to study and improve quality of life in the community for people with intellectual disabilities is a positive development for policy planners and service providers. Quality-of-life indicators include social relationships, employment, self-determination, autonomy, recreation and leisure, personal competence and independent living skills, social status, financial well-being, and sense of subjective well-being.
- While some progress has been made in improving quality of life, many people leaving institutions still have considerable difficulty making the transition to community environments. Initially, they have difficulty establishing close social relationships and complain of loneliness in their leisure time and frustration on the job. Transportation and health care are recurring problems, and many are not satisfied with their living arrangements. However, in time, those who remain in the community tend to improve; they made some friends and express greater satisfaction in their lives.

INSTITUTIONAL LIVING

Core Concept

For individuals with intellectual disabilities, institutional living is widely viewed as detrimental to intellectual, psychological, and physical development.

Institutions for persons with intellectual disabilities go under many different labels—hospital, colony, or school. Characteristics of an institution include the following: (a) All aspects of life go on in the same place and under the same single authority; (b) activities are carried on in the immediate company of others, all of whom are treated alike and required to do the same things together; (c) a system of explicit formal rulings and a body of officials govern tightly scheduled activities; (d) social mobility is grossly restricted; (e) work is defined as treatment, punishment, or rehabilitation; and (f) a system of rewards and punishments takes place in the individual's total life situation.

For most of the 20th century, government support for residential living was directed to large congregate care settings (institutions, nursing homes). The deinstitutionalization movement of the 1970s came about because many institutions for those with intellectual disabilities had become dehumanizing warehouses with no adequate treatment programs (Braddock et al., 2002). For persons with intellectual disabilities, institutional living is widely viewed as a detriment to intellectual, psychological, and physical development. TASH (2005a), an association of people with disabilities, their family members, other advocates, and professionals, has called for the closure of institutions because such places discriminate against people with disabilities by removing them from their homes, schools, and neighborhoods.

As we move through the first decade of the 21st century, people with intellectual disabilities, their families, and professionals are advocating for smaller community-based residences within local neighborhoods and communities. In the past 20 years, spending for smaller community residences increased sevenfold (Braddock et al., 2002). People with intellectual disabilities and their families are also advocating for choice, individualization, and a focus on the abilities of people rather than on their disabilities. The most harmful aspect of institutional living is the emphasis on a restrictive regimen, with no attempt to personalize programs or living conditions to the needs of the residents (Hardman et al., 2006).

The legal and moral debate continues regarding what is a good or bad institution or whether there is a need for any large residential facility for persons with intellectual disabilities. Some institutions for those having intellectual disabilities have attempted to provide a more familylike environment for the resident instead of restricted dormitory living conditions. Changes include efforts to provide private or semiprivate bedrooms, family dining facilities, individual clothing and hairstyles, and private possessions. Neither parents nor professionals have agreed on criteria for determining whether any institution is an appropriate living and learning environment for any person with intellectual disabilities. We can say, however, that the accomplishments of institutions in the past century add up to very little.

The institution model has been more concerned with social management than with the physical and psychological growth of the individual with intellectual disabilities. Across the United States, these large public facilities continue to serve fewer and fewer residents each year, and a number of states have closed or are moving toward closure of large institutions. Braddock et al. (2002, p. 1) reported that "since the 1970s, many states have vigorously reduced their reliance on institutional facilities and developed community residential settings." Today, of the individuals with intellectual disabilities living outside the family home, only 19% are in public or private institutions, and this percentage continues to decrease. In 2000, 125 institutions in 37 states in the United States closed, compared to one institutional closure in 1970. Additionally, the cost of institutionalization continues to increase. The average daily cost for a person with intellectual disabilities in a publicly funded institution is now $321 compared to $45 in 1977 (Braddock et al., 2002).

COMMUNITY EMPLOYMENT

Community employment for persons with intellectual disabilities is a laudable goal. Employment is important for many reasons beyond monetary rewards, including adult identity, social contacts, integration with peers, and the perception of

Core Concept

Three alternatives for community employment are available for persons with intellectual disabilities: employment with no support services, employment with time-limited support services, and employment with ongoing support services.

contributing to society. Several professional and parent associations working on behalf of people with intellectual disabilities support the development of inclusive community-based employment opportunities. TASH (2005b) indicates that "employment of people with intellectual disabilities must be in regular employment settings where they work along side people without disabilities. . . . Job selection and retention must be based on the choice of the individual." The AAMR (2005a) and The ARC (2005a) also support competitive employment for people with intellectual disabilities, suggesting that these individuals should be "supported to make informed choices about their work and careers and have the resources to seek, obtain, and be successful in integrated community employment."

However, in spite of the support for community employment, research on adults with intellectual disabilities clearly indicates that these people are underemployed or unemployed (NOD & Harris & Associates, 2004). The high unemployment rates of people with intellectual disabilities seem to be attributable to several factors. First, traditional employment models have been oriented either to no training after leaving school or to short-term training programs with the expectation that the individual will not need ongoing support while on the job. Second, the emphasis has been on sheltered or protected work settings where the individual is placed for training but does not earn significant wages. The person with intellectual disabilities may remain in such settings for most, if not all, of his or her adult years.

There are, however, some good reasons to be optimistic about competitive employment for people with intellectual disabilities. Research knowledge is expanding, and more emphasis is placed on employment with both state and national policymakers (Kregel, 2001; McDonnell et al., 2003). Kregel (2001) suggests that several factors have contributed to this increased optimism and expectations:

- The passage of the ADA has helped reduce employment discrimination and promote career opportunities for people with intellectual disabilities and other disabilities.
- There has been a rise in the contingent workforce—those who are self-employed, temporary, contracted, and part-time workers. Along with a good economy, this has provided new and exciting alternatives to many individuals who previously faced little or no job opportunities or had been channeled into dead-end career choices.
- **Supported employment** has proven to be a highly successful rehabilitation alternative that has allowed tens of thousands of individuals with intellectual disabilities to participate in the economic life of their local communities.
- A generation of students with intellectual disabilities have benefited from improvements in special education programs, particularly the recent emphasis on efforts to improve the transition of students from school to adult services and employment settings.

- Business and industry are recognizing the value of employees with disabilities and are developing innovative programs to recruit, train, accommodate, and retain workers with intellectual disabilities.
- The national strategy of using Medicaid funds as the primary mechanism for residential and employment services for people with intellectual disabilities has led to a rapid rise in community-based program expenditures in many states.

The concept of competitive employment for persons with intellectual disabilities has changed dramatically in recent years. In the following sections, we discuss three competitive employment models: employment with no support services, employment with time-limited training and support services, and employment with ongoing support services.

Employment with No Support Services

The adult with intellectual disabilities may be able to locate and maintain a community job with no additional supports from public or private agencies. The individual finds a job independently either through contacts made during school vocational preparation programs or through such sources as a job service, want ads, family, and friends. For the person with mild intellectual disabilities, competitive employment without support is most often possible if adequate employment training and experience have been available during the school years.

A major concern of professionals preparing individuals with intellectual disabilities for competitive employment is identification of characteristics related to employment success. If these characteristics can be identified, employment training programs can be developed during the school years to emphasize the positive characteristics that tend to enhance job success.

Employment with Time-Limited Training and Support Services

After the individual with intellectual disabilities finishes school, he or she may have access to several services on a short-term basis, including vocational rehabilitation, vocational education, and on-the-job training. Time-limited services are generally intended for people believed to be capable of self-support after the services have been completed. Vocational rehabilitation is the best known time-limited employment service.

Vocational rehabilitation is a federally funded program intended to help persons with disabilities obtain employment. Under the Vocational Rehabilitation Act of 1973 (as amended in 1998), federal funds are passed to the states to provide services in counseling and job placement. Chapter 9 provides a detailed discussion of the purpose, eligibility, and programs under the Vocational Rehabilitation Act.

Employment with Ongoing Support Services: The Supported Employment Model

Supported employment is defined as work in an integrated setting for individuals with severe disabilities (including those with intellectual disabilities) who probably will need some type of continuing support and for whom competitive employment traditionally has not been possible (Wehman, West, & Kregel, 1999). McDonnell et al. (2003, p. 337) identify four characteristics of supported employment as mandated in federal legislation (the Developmental Disabilities Assistance and Bill of Right Act [Public Law 98-527] and the Vocational Rehabilitation Amendments of 1986 [Public Law 99-506]:

1. Supported employment is paid employment. Supported employment is intended to be paid employment rather than a training program. Supported employment is focused on obtaining positions for people that provide high wages, job security, job advancement, and acceptance by coworkers without disabilities. This stands in sharp contrast to traditional employment programs for persons with severe disabilities, which emphasize the development of the prerequisite skills assumed to be necessary for competitive employment.
2. Continuous versus time-limited support. Traditional competitive employment services for persons with disabilities have been structured to provide time-limited support to program participants. In contrast, supported employment acknowledges the ongoing support needs of persons with severe disabilities in the job site. This support may range from monthly telephone contacts with the employer to make sure the person is succeeding to day-to-day supervision on the job site.
3. Inclusive versus segregated service delivery. A critical feature of supported employment is its emphasis on the inclusion of persons with disabilities in typical businesses and industries. Supported employment assumes that the opportunity to interact with people without disabilities is an important outcome of work. These interactions create opportunities to develop social relationships with peers that will support not only individuals' job performance but also their participation in other aspects of community life.
4. Flexibility. Supported employment is not a single program; rather, it is an assortment of assessment, training, monitoring, and support strategies that can be used to help people succeed in their jobs. Program providers are encouraged to design services so that they are tailored to unique needs of the individual.

In a relatively short time, supported employment has become a viable alternative for rehabilitation training and employment of individuals with severe disabilities. Research on the effectiveness of supported employment services has documented the success of this delivery system (Braddock et al., 2002; Kregel, 2001; Morgan, Ellerd, Jensen, & Taylor, 2000).

Although the efficacy of supported employment services has been well documented, the growing fear is that the rapid expansion of this employment service delivery system will result in failure to safeguard the essential elements of the concept. As expansion continues, the need for trained personnel in administrative and job coach positions is more acute.

Although earnings are primary to the success of supported employment, they are not the sole indicator of quality. In addition to wages, work should take place in socially inclusive settings rather than in segregated facilities. Job placement in an inclusive setting allows the individual to learn appropriate social and vocational skills side by side with peers without disabilities and to apply the skills in the environment. The employer and coworkers also learn about the potential of the individual with disabilities as a reliable employee and friend.

Support on the job must also be continuous, based on individual need, and not time limited. Time-limited services terminate after the individual completes training and enters the workforce. Unlike time-limited services, continuous services are made available as needed. Support does not end with placement in an employment setting or after a specified time for follow-up. Services are provided on the job and consist of whatever support is necessary to maintain employment. Continuous supports include job development, job placement, ongoing postemployment training, skill maintenance and generalization, and follow-up services. The amount and type of continuous support are related to individual need, job demand, and the organizational structure of the supported employment program.

Supported Employment Within the Framework of Community Living

Supported employment should be viewed in the larger context of supported living. Supported living is an opportunity for people with intellectual disabilities to live in a home wherever they want and with whomever they choose while receiving the support needed. Supported employment fits within the framework of a supported life network for people with intellectual disabilities. Services and supports are defined by individual preference, need, and opportunities for inclusion within the life of the community (see the Tips for Professionals feature).

The goals for each person within a supported life network include increased independence, inclusion within the community, and productivity. Services must reflect these individualized goals, which will result in a better quality of life for the person with intellectual disabilities. Services that focus directly on increasing independence promote higher adaptive skill levels and greater opportunities for choice in residence, recreation, and employment. Services that support community integration will result in greater access to and participation in the community, including generic community services and programs such as restaurants, swimming pools, theaters, and parks. Services that focus on increasing the individual's productivity move the individual from consumer to contributor through identity in the workforce, wages to spend in the community, and taxpayer status. Supported employment is a service that increases productivity and is defined as wage-generating work with an emphasis on continuous support determined as much as possible by the individual and congruent with other aspects of the person's supported living network. People with intellectual disabilities can live and work successfully in as many different situations as individuals without disabilities. Work and living options are constrained only by inadequate support.

Tips for Professionals

Inclusion in Supported Employment and Supported Living Programs

- Business and industry in local communities can actively create and support opportunities for the employment of people with intellectual disabilities. Local businesses could look into innovative programs that focus on the recruitment and hiring of people with intellectual disabilities while at the same time meeting the needs of the business.
- Family and friends may seek ways to help the adult with intellectual disabilities become more actively involved in the life of the local community through participation in supported employment, friendship, and recreational programs (such as Best Buddies, Special Olympics Unified Sports, the YMCA, or the YWCA), organized religious programs, civic programs (such as volunteering and service), and neighborhood social activities (going to movies, shopping, dining out). Instruction and assistance to the adult with intellectual disabilities could be provided in order to increase their competence as they interact with people who are not disabled in natural settings.
- State and local supported living programs could assure the availability of highly trained staff competent in the necessary instructional and assistive technology that facilitates inclusion and social interaction between people with and without disabilities. These programs could develop community-based activities that focus on continuous learning and applying skills side by side with people who are not disabled in places such as grocery stores, malls, parks, employment sites, and so on. Families need to be supported as well as they seek opportunities, resources, and programs that promote inclusion of the adult with intellectual disabilities in a community setting.

Structural Features of Supported Employment

The development of supported employment as the basic structure of a vocational service system for individuals with intellectual disabilities has several implications: (a) the evaluation of the employment program based on client outcomes, (b) the elimination of the continuum of employment alternatives based on the "getting people ready" philosophy of vocational services, and (c) the development of training and advocacy services that are directly linked to employment success.

The success of an employment service may be evaluated in several ways. For example, in the vocational rehabilitation system, success is determined by closure of an individual's file, based on completion of training and job placement and maintenance for a specified length of time. Other means of evaluation relate more to the process of establishing a vocational service than to client outcomes. Process questions may include the following: Is the client eligible for the vocational service? Is an individualized work plan in place? Is the work plan consistent with a standardized vocational assessment of the individual? Does the plan contain goals and objectives? These questions are concerned with ensuring that a standardized process is in place that is consistent across all programs.

Although supported employment does not ignore process questions, its primary focus is on results for the individual. Does the vocational service provide good employment outcomes for the individual served? Measures for success are meaningful wages and benefits, access to services and resources in natural settings, contact with peers who are not disabled, and job security. Where more conventional vocational services emphasize a broader rehabilitation function, supported employment focuses on work and wages. Because employment outcomes are the key variables in the evaluation process, programs must become more effective in identifying, developing, and maintaining work opportunities.

The traditional philosophy of "getting people ready" (the flow-through model) for jobs is not consistent with the supported employment concept. The basis for supported employment is that the support needs of each person determine job training and placement. Individual functioning level and performance demands in a given work environment are matched. In addition, supported employment takes into account the job's compatibility with the individual's life needs as well as consideration for family values and constraints. The underlying principle of supported employment is not to move people to less restricted job placements as a result of training but to provide the necessary resources to support individuals in their current work site.

The purpose of supported employment is to achieve community-integrated employment for the person with intellectual disabilities. Therefore, all training programs and advocacy efforts must be directed toward this goal. Developing skills for various job tasks is only one component of a supported employment training program. Program training objectives might include riding the mass transit systems, personal hygiene, self-regulation, and evaluation of work performance. These objectives facilitate the individual's participation in the social network of the business.

Supported Employment Models

There are three basic models of supported employment: individual placement, the community work crew, and the enclave. Each model differs in terms of long-term support and intensity, training, support structure, organizational strategy and business base, number of workers per site, and levels of integration (see Table 10–1).

In the individual placement model, a job coach gives each person intensive one-on-one training aimed at successful performance of specific job tasks and social behaviors around the job setting. Initial training is usually continuous throughout the workday but may be reduced eventually to no more than an hour or less per day. The job coach may be responsible for as many as eight employees at sites throughout a community. Training and assistance also may be available through coworkers willing to support the individual in completion of job tasks or to act as friends in the workplace. The type of work available in individual placements varies from entry-level custodial or food service jobs to jobs in high-technology industries.

A community work crew usually consists of two to eight individuals with disabilities who are supervised by a crew supervisor. Work crews generally perform service jobs (e.g., custodial, food service) that are contracted with two or more businesses, industries, or private individuals. Training and support from the crew

Table 10–1
Features of Supported Employment Models

Model	Number of Workers with a Disability	Types of Support
Individual	1	An employment specialist provides training and ongoing support often in conjunction with coworkers at the job site. Support is gradually faded across time. The specialist is hired by an employment service program.
Work Crew	2–8	Continuous training and ongoing support is provided by a job coach and/or coworkers at the job site. The job coach is employed by an employment service program.
Enclave	2–8	Continuous training and ongoing support is provided by a job coach and/or coworkers. The job coach may be hired by the host company.

Source: From *Introduction to Persons with Severe Disabilities* (p.338) by J. McDonnell, M. Hardman, and A. McDonnell, 2003. Boston: Allyn & Bacon.

supervisor may be continuous and long term, focusing on completion of the service task and fostering community-integration activities. Work crews are usually mobile, moving from site to site in the performance of their contract. Under such circumstances, integration with individuals who are not disabled may be difficult to achieve. Systematic efforts must be made to create opportunities for social interaction between work crew members and people without disabilities.

In the enclave model, two to eight individuals with disabilities work in an industrial or business setting alongside people without disabilities. The enclave usually is supervised by a single staff person trained in the requirements of a host company or industry. Job support is usually continuous and long term; training focuses on production tasks, appropriate behaviors on the job, and community integration. Jobs include manufacturing and small-item assembly. Opportunities for social interaction with peers who are not disabled occur in the work area, during breaks, and at lunch. It is possible, however, for enclaves to be physically isolated within a business operating on different work, break, and lunch times. Conscious efforts are sometimes necessary to integrate enclaves within the workforce.

All three supported employment models give training in specific job skills at the work site. On-the-job training involves job analysis, development of systematic training programs, and the use of effective training strategies. The primary difference between the models in relationship to on-the-job training is the number of individuals being trained at a time. For example, in the individual placement model, training is always one on one. In a work crew, any number of individuals may be trained together.

In summary, the three supported employment models provide the opportunity for individuals with intellectual disabilities to work successfully in community employment settings with adequate training and long-term support. Since the passage of IDEA, research and demonstration programs clearly have made improvements in employment training and placement for persons with intellectual disabilities. Supported employment is being used successfully to place and maintain individuals with intellectual disabilities in jobs in the community. Research findings clearly indicate that ongoing training and assistance in the job setting are more effective than vocational services in segregated settings.

The components of an effective community employment program include (a) placement in a job that is consistent with the abilities and interests of the individual, (b) on-the-job training that includes direct instruction by a trained professional and that enables the individual to perform all skills the job calls for, (c) continuous assessment and monitoring of the individual's job performance, and (d) availability of systematic follow-up services to ensure skill retention years after the initial placement.

SHELTERED EMPLOYMENT

Sheltered employment includes sheltered workshops, day habilitation, and work activity centers. Sheltered workshops are characterized by training and jobs for people with intellectual disabilities that are based on short-term contracts with local businesses and are assembly line in nature. The job tasks are broken down into small tasks that result in a product.

Core Concept

The purpose of a sheltered workshop is to prepare the person with intellectual disabilities for competitive employment or to provide a terminal sheltered job.

Some sheltered workshops operate exclusively for clients with intellectual disabilities; others serve a wider variety of individuals with disabilities, such as those with visual impairments, cerebral palsy, or emotional disturbance. Some are operated by national programs, such as Goodwill Industries of America and Jewish Vocational Service agencies. Other workshops are community based and may be supported by the United Fund, religious groups, private endowments, or public schools. Typically, sheltered workshops restore or repair clothing or household articles and then sell them. Items come from collections or strategically located depositories. Other workshop revenue comes from contracts with various businesses or industries. Workshop clients usually are compensated on a piecework basis.

Over the years, the sheltered workshop model has been criticized as a segregated approach that provides low wages and fails to move people with intellectual disabilities into less restricted employment settings (Kregel, 2001). Questions have been raised about the value of sheltered work for individuals who earn little. From a purely economic standpoint, the justification for maintaining services for these individuals is questionable. Their wages are so low as to be of next to no value even to themselves, and their productivity is so low that their contribution to the employment field also may be considered nearly negligible. Workshops have been criticized also for not having systematic procedures to evaluate the production capabilities of clients and for failure to provide vocational tasks consistent with their clients' range of capabilities.

In many respects, the sheltered workshop contradicts any focus on community living and gainful employment. Industry employs workers to turn out a product. In the sheltered workshop, the product is often the means to produce workers. And for many workers, the sheltered setting becomes the permanent work setting.

Day habilitation and work activity centers are intended to provide programming that will prepare the person for more advanced work, preferably in a competitive employment situation. The results, at least for people with intellectual disabilities, have not reflected the stated intent. Current rates of progress in day activity and work activity programs suggest that people with intellectual disabilities will spend the better part of their adult lives being "prepared" for competitive employment.

NEW ISSUES AND FUTURE DIRECTIONS

Historically, human services programs for adults with intellectual disabilities have focused primarily on protection and care. The objective of such programs was to protect the individual from society and society from the individual. This philosophy resulted in services that isolated the individual in large institutions and that offered physical care in place of preparation for life in a heterogeneous world. With the international movement of the past two decades to educate students with disabilities in the public school system, new goals have become clear: (a) employment, useful work, and valued activity; (b) personal autonomy, independence, and adult status; (c) social interaction, community participation, leisure, and recreation; and (d) valued roles within the family.

Society must recognize that expectations for adults with intellectual disabilities are no different from those for people without disabilities. Although the characteristics of a "quality life" are certainly individual and personal, several indicators seem to be widely accepted in Western society. These are as follows: All people are empowered to make their own choices about adult living, including selecting friends, where they will live, and what jobs they will hold. Empowerment has three aspects: control of the environment, involvement in community life, and social relationships. Quality of life can be assessed by the answers to such questions as "Do you have a key to the house in which you live?" (controlling the environment), "Do you earn enough money to pay for your basic needs, including housing and food?" (involvement in the community), and "Do you have the opportunity of interacting with friends and neighbors?" (social relationships).

Each person is valued as an individual capable of personal growth and development. As such, everyone is treated with dignity and has the opportunity to participate in all aspects of community life. Participation in community life includes access to adequate housing, opportunities to exercise citizenship (e.g., voting), access to medical and social services as needed, and access to recreational and personal services (e.g., parks, theaters, grocery stores, restaurants, public transportation).

Each person has the opportunity to participate in the economic life of the community. Work is important for reasons beyond its monetary rewards—for example, social interaction, personal identity, and contribution to the community. Work removes the individual from being viewed solely as a consumer of services. Important personal needs include adequate and fair compensation, safe and healthy environments, development of human capacities, growth and security, social integration, constitutionalism (the rights of the worker and how these rights can be protected), the total life space (the balanced role of work in one's life), and social relevance (when organizations act in socially irresponsible ways, employees see their work and careers as less valuable).

Several indicators of a "quality of work life" have been identified by assessing the degree of employee satisfaction with the work process. These indicators include (a) adequate and fair compensation, (b) safe and healthy environments, (c) development of human capacities, (d) growth and security, (e) social integration, (f) affirmation and protection of worker rights, and (g) a balance between work and personal life. In the light of the such indicators, the question is whether there should be separate standards of quality for persons with intellectual disabilities. In fact, quality indicators do differ for the more conventional models of employment preparation for people with intellectual disabilities (day habilitation, sheltered workshops, work activity centers).

Sheltered workshops are designed as protected places for long-term employment, and people with intellectual disabilities may be placed in these settings with little or no reassessment of their competitive employment potential. Supported employment differs significantly from conventional work programs. The goals for people with intellectual disabilities in a supported employment program are the same as those for people without disabilities: What income does the job provide? What kind of lifestyle does the income allow? How attractive is the work life (coworkers, challenge, safety, status)? How good is job security?

Core Questions

1. Define and discuss the principle of normalization. Why is self-determination described as an extension of the normalization principle?
2. Describe three widely used community residential models for adults with intellectual disabilities.
3. Identify supports needed by parents or siblings who live with an adult family member with intellectual disabilities.
4. Why is knowledge regarding sexuality especially important for persons with intellectual disabilities?
5. Summarize the research on the adjustment of persons with intellectual disabilities to community living.
6. Why is institutionalization considered detrimental to the intellectual, psychological, and physical growth of the individual?
7. Discuss some of the reasons for high unemployment among persons with intellectual disabilities.
8. Define and discuss the concept of supported employment.
9. What are some of the criticisms of sheltered employment?

Roundtable Discussion

The principle of inclusion emphasizes that the person with intellectual disabilities should have the same opportunities and access to services as individuals without disabilities. It is much more than just the opportunity to live or work in the community because it means providing the support services necessary to assist the individual in successfully meeting the demands of adult life.

In your study group or on your own, discuss the range of activities and services that must be available for an adult with intellectual disabilities to live and work successfully in the community. How would you ensure that these supports are available?

Parent and Professional Organization Positions on Key Issues in the Lives of People with Intellectual Disabilities

The inside front cover of this text presents a matrix that includes nine key issues in the lives of people with disabilities, the positions of various parent and professional organizations on each issue, and the chapter and page number where the information is addressed. Table 10–2 is a summary of the organizations and key issues addressed in this chapter.

Table 10–2
Key Issues and Organizations Discussed in This Chapter

Organization/Website	Key Issues Addressed	Chapter Heading
American Association on Mental Retardation (http://www.aamr.org)	Community living and employment Community living and employment	Supported Residential Living Community Employment
The ARC—a national organization on intellectual disabilities (http://www.thearc.org)	Community living and employment Community living and employment Quality of life	Supported Residential Living Community Employment Marriage and Sexuality
TASH, an international association of people with disabilities, their family members, and professionals (http://www.tash.org)	Community living and employment Community living and employment	Institutional Living Community Employment

References

Agran, M., Blanchard, C., & Wehmeyer, M. L. (2000). Promoting transition goals and self-determination through student-directed learning: The self-determined learning model of instruction. *Education and Training in Mental Retardation and Developmental Disabilities, 35,* 351–364.

American Association on Mental Retardation (AAMR). (2002). *Mental retardation: Definitions, classification, and systems of supports* (10th ed.). Washington, DC: Author.

American Association on Mental Retardation (AAMR). (2005a). *Policy statement on employment.* Retrieved April 25, 2005, from http://www.aamr.org/policies/pos_employment.shtml

American Association on Mental Retardation (AAMR). (2005b). *Policy statement on housing.* Retrieved March 15, 2005, from http://www.aamr.org/policies/pos_housing.shtml

The ARC. (2005a). *Position statement on employment.* Retrieved April 20, 2005, from http://www.thearc.org/posits/employmentpos.doc

The ARC. (2005b). *Position statement on housing.* Retrieved March 15 2005, from http://www.thearc.org/posits/housingpos.doc

The ARC. (2005c). *Position statement on sexuality.* Retrieved March 15 2005, from http://www.thearc.org/posits/sexualitypos.doc

Baller, W. R., Charles, C., & Miller, E. (1966). *Mid-life attainment of the mentally retarded: A longitudinal study.* Lincoln: University of Nebraska Press.

Bellamy, G. T., O'Conner, G., & Karan, O. (1979). *Vocational rehabilitation of severely handicapped persons: Contemporary service strategies.* Baltimore: University Park Press.

Braddock, D., Hemp, R., Rizzolo, M. C., Parish, S., & Pomeranz, A. (2002). *The state of the states in developmental disabilities: 2002 study summary.* Boulder: Coleman Institute for Cognitive Disabilities and the Department of Psychiatry, University of Colorado.

Brown, A. J. (2002, June). Informed consent key to sterilization of mentally retarded. *MassPsych.com, 10*(5). Retrieved from http://www.masspsy.com/columnists/brown_9910.html

Brown, R. I. (2000). Learning from quality of life models. In M. P. Janicki & E. F. Ansello (Eds.), *Community supports for aging adults with lifelong disabilities* (pp. 19–40). Baltimore: Paul H. Brookes.

Brown, F., Gothelf, C. R., Guess, D., & Lehr, D. (1998). Self-determination for people with the most severe disabilities: Moving beyond chimera. *Journal of the Association of Persons with Severe Handicaps, 23*(1), 17–26.

Buck v. Bell. 274 U.S. 200 (1927).

Close, D. W. (1975, May). *Normalization through skill training: A group study.* Paper presented at the Annual Convention of the American Association on Mental Deficiency, Portland, OR.

Conroy, J. W., & Bradley, V. J. (1985). *The Pennhurst Longitudinal Study: A report of five years of research and analysis.* Philadelphia: Temple University Developmental Disabilities Center.

Edgerton, R. B. (1967). *The cloak of competence.* Berkeley: University of California Press.

Edgerton, R. B. (1993). *The cloak of competence* (Rev. ed.). Berkeley: University of California Press.

Edgerton, R. B. (2001). The hidden majority of individuals with mental retardation and developmental disabilities. In A. J. Tymchuk, K. C. Lakin, & R. Luckasson (Eds.), *The forgotten generation: The status and challenges of adults with mild cognitive limitations* (pp. 3–20). Baltimore: Paul H. Brookes.

Edgerton, R. B., & Bercovici, S. M. (1976). The cloak of competence: Years later. *American Journal of Mental Deficiency, 80,* 485–497.

Edgerton, R. B., Bollinger, M., & Herr, B. (1984). The cloak of competence: After two decades. *American Journal of Mental Deficiency, 88* (4), 345–351.

Fernald, W. E. (1919). After-care study of the patients discharged from Waverly for a period of twenty-five years. *Ungraded, 5,* 25–31.

Fujiiura, G. T. (1998) Demography of family households. *American Journal on Mental Retardation, 103,* 225–235.

Gold, M. W. (1973). Research on the vocational rehabilitation of the retarded: The present, the future. In N. R. Ellis (Ed.), *International review of research in intellectual disabilities* (Vol. 6, pp. 97–147). New York: Academic Press.

Haney, J. I. (1988). Toward successful community residential placements for individuals with intellectual disabilities. In I. W. Heal, J. I. Haney, & A. R. Novak Amado (Eds.), *Integration of developmentally disabled individuals into the community* (2nd ed., pp. 125–168). Baltimore: Paul H. Brookes.

Hanna, M. E., & Midlarsky, E. (2005). Helping siblings of children with mental retardation. *American Journal on Mental Retardation, 110*(2), 87–99.

Hardman, M. L., Drew, C. J., & Egan, M. W. (2006). *Human exceptionality: School, community, and family* (8th ed.). Boston: Allyn & Bacon.

Jobling, A. (2001). Beyond sex and cooking: Health education for individuals with mental retardation. *Mental Retardation, 39* (4), 310–321.

Kennedy, R. A. (1966). *A Connecticut community revised: A study of the social adjustment of a group of mentally deficient adults in 1948 and 1960.* Hartford: Connecticut State Department of Health, Office of Mental Retardation.

Khemka, I., & Hickson, L. (2000). Decision-making by adults with mental retardation in simulated situations of abuse. *Mental Retardation, 38* (1), 15–26.

Krauss, M. W., Seltzer, M. M., Gordon, R., & Friedman, D. H. (1996, April). Binding ties: The roles of adult siblings of persons with mental retardation. *Mental Retardation 34* (2), 83–93.

Kregel, J. (2001). Promoting employment opportunities for individuals with mild cognitive limitations: A time for reform. In A. J. Tymchuk, K. C. Lakin, & R. Luckasson (Eds.), *The forgotten generation: The status and challenges of adults with mild cognitive limitations* (pp. 87–98). Baltimore: Paul H. Brookes.

McDonnell, J., Hardman, M. L., & McDonnell, A. (2003). *Introduction to persons with severe disabilities* (2nd ed.). Boston: Allyn & Bacon.

Morgan, R. L., Ellerd, D. A., Gerity, B. P., & Blair, R. J. (2000). That's the job I want: How technology helps young people in transition. *Teaching Exceptional Children, 32* (4), 44–49.

Morgan, R. L., Ellerd, D. A., Jensen, K., & Taylor, M. J. (2000). A survey of community placements: Where are youth and adults with disabilities working? *Career Development for Exceptional Individuals,* 23, 73–86.

Mount, B. (2000). *Person-centered planning* (p. 9). New York: Graphics Futures.

National Organization on Disability (NOD) & Harris & Associates. (2004). *National Organization on Disability/Harris survey of Americans with disabilities.* New York: Author.

Nerney, T. (2004). *Lost lives: Why we need a new approach to quality.* Ann Arbor, Michigan: Center for Self-Determination.

Nirje, B. (1969). The normalization principle and its human management implications. In R. B. Kugel & W. Wolfensberger (Eds.), *Changing patterns in residential services for the mentally retarded* (pp. 179–195). Washington, DC: President's Committee on Mental Retardation.

O'Neill, J., Brown, M., Gordon, W., & Schonhorn, R. (1985). The impact of deinstitutionalization on activities and skills of severely/profoundly retarded multiply handicapped adults. *Applied Research in Mental Retardation, 6,* 361–371.

Orsmond, G. I., & Seltzer, M. M. (2000). Brothers and sisters of adults with mental retardation: Gendered nature of the sibling relationship. *American Journal on Mental Retardation, 105* (6), 486–508.

Otley, K. (2004). "The keys are mine." *Guidebook on Consumer Controlled Housing.* Minneapolis: Arc Minnesota and the Institute on Community Integration.

Parish, S. L., Selzter, M. M., Greenberg, J. S., & Floyd, F. (2004). Economic implications of caregiving at midlife: Comparing parents with and without children who have developmental disabilities. *Mental Retardation, 42* (6), 413–426.

Reiss, S. (2001). People with a dual diagnosis: America's powerless population. In A. J. Tymchuk, K. C. Lakin, & R. Luckasson (Eds.), *The forgotten generation: The status and challenges of adults with mild cognitive limitations* (pp. 275–298). Baltimore: Paul H. Brookes.

Seltzer, M. M., Greenberg, J. S., Floyd, F. J., Petee, Y., & Hong, J. (2001). Life course impacts of parenting a child with a disability. *American Journal on Mental Retardation, 106* (3), 265–286.

Silverstein, R. (2001). An overview of the emerging disability policy framework: A guidepost for analyzing public policy. In A. J. Tymchuk, K. C. Lakin, & R. Luckasson (Eds.), *The forgotten generation: The status and challenges of adults with mild cognitive limitations* (pp. 323–346). Baltimore: Paul H. Brookes.

Sullivan, P. M. (2000). *Violence and abuse against children with disabilities.* Omaha, NE: Center for Abused Children with Disabilities, Boys Town National Research Hospital.

TASH (2005a). *Resolution on desinstitutionalization.* Retrieved March 21, 2005, from http://www.tash.org/resolutions/res02deinstitut.htm

TASH (2005b). *Resolution on integrated employment.* Retrieved April 23, 2005, from http://www.tash.org/resolutions/res02employment.htm

Turnbull, A. P., & Turnbull, H. R. (2001). *Families, professionals, and exceptionality: A special partnership* (4th ed.). Upper Saddle River, NJ: Prentice Hall.

Tymchuk, A. J. (2001). Family life: Experiences of people with mild cognitive limitations. In A. J. Tymchuk, K. C. Lakin, & R. Luckasson (Eds.), *The forgotten generation: The status and challenges of adults with mild cognitive limitations* (pp. 249–274). Baltimore: Paul H. Brookes.

Tymchuk, A. J., Lakin, K. C., & Luckasson, R. (2001). Life at the margins: Intellectual, demographic, economic, and social circumstances of adults with mild cognitive limitations. In A. J. Tymchuk, K. C. Lakin, & R. Luckasson (Eds.), *The forgotten generation: The status and challenges of adults with mild cognitive limitations* (pp. 21–38). Baltimore: Paul H. Brookes.

United States Holocaust Memorial Museum. (2005). *Mentally and physically handicapped: Victims of the Nazi era, 1933–1945*. Retrieved April 20, 2005, from http://www.ushmm.org/education/foradults/index.php?content=resource/

University of Illinois at Chicago National Research and Training Center. (2005). *Self-determination framework for people with psychiatric disabilities.* Retrieved February 14, 2005, from http://www.psych.uic.edu/UICNRTC/sdframework.pdf

Wehman, P., West, M., & Kregel, J. (1999). Supported employment program development and research needs: Looking ahead to the year 2000. *Education and Training in Mental Retardation and Developmental Disabilities, 34*, 3–19.

Wehmeyer, M. L. (2002, September). Promoting the self-determination of students with severe disabilities. (ERIC Document Reproduction Service #E633). Retrieved April 1 2005, from http://www.ericec.org/digests/e633.html

Wolfensberger, W. (1972). *Normalization: The principle of normalization in human services.* Toronto: National Institute on Mental Retardation.

Wolfensberger, W. (2000). A brief overview of social role valorization. *Mental Retardation, 38*(2), 105–123.

Yamaki, K., & Fujiura, G. T. (2002). Employment and income status of adults with developmental disabilities. *Mental Retardation, 40*(2), 132–141.

Chapter 11

The Older Person with Intellectual Disabilities

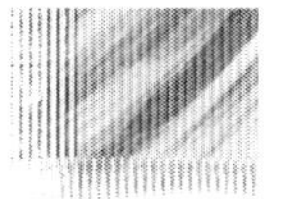

Chapter Preview

In this chapter we move further into the latter phases of the lifespan. Human development in this portion of life presents a number of challenges for all of us. The issues on the table for those with intellectual disabilities during this part of life often magnify those faced by the older population in general. This chapter will examine some of the matters of importance to the older person with intellectual disabilities. You will encounter:

- Some very basic questions about who is considered old and some of the challenging issues faced by those conducting research on elderly individuals with intellectual disabilities.
- Examination of age-related changes in mental, social, and personal functioning of older people with intellectual disabilities and how they impact the lives of these individuals and those around them.
- Discussion of services available and living arrangements employed for elderly people with intellectual disabilities.

Moving Is Frightening

Grace was worried about moving—all her friends were here and moving to a new place was unsettling. She hadn't thought about it until the other day when the doctor came for her regular check-up and had talked to her about moving. Grace didn't really know why she needed to move. Her friends weren't moving. The doctor hadn't talked to them about moving but he had talked to Grace about it. So she guessed that she would move—from the supported living center where she had lived for the past 10 years to another one. The doctor had talked about why she would be moving but Grace didn't remember what he had said. She had always done what she was supposed to do and this was what she was supposed to do—because the doctor said so.

Grace's story is becoming increasingly familiar. She has moderate intellectual disabilities and has lived for some time in a supported living facility with several of her friends. Her health is still good but Grace is having increasing difficulty taking care of herself, even with the help of the staff of the home. There have been more lapses in her medication regime and in a few cases she has had seizures because she hadn't taken her meds. She simply needs more supervision than is possible in her current placement, so her doctor has recommended that she be moved to a nursing home where greater care can be exercised regarding her ongoing needs.

Most of the residents of her new home are somewhat different from Grace. They have spent most of their lives in a different environment and have been in an assisted living circumstance for only the last few years. Grace has spent almost all her life in a group living arrangement of some type. And there is another significant difference—Grace's 55th birthday will be next month. Her new roommates have an average age of 79. In one sense Grace has been integrated into a portion of the community without intellectual disabilities. What Grace cannot know, however, is the risk that seems present in the new environment. Nursing home abuse and neglect may place Grace's well-being in greater jeopardy than lapses of medication.

- *What are your thoughts regarding Grace's life and what the future holds for her? Although this story is told through her eyes and with a limited awareness, the place that she lives is one where people generally reside who are substantially older.*
- *What do you tell Grace as a friend? How do you go about explaining to her that she needs to move? Her doctor has spoken with her, but what are the elements of your message on a personal basis?*

Grace's story is only the first of many dilemmas we will encounter as we discuss the latter portions of the life phases. The study of elderly people with intellectual disabilities continues the progression through the developmental cycle. In some ways, the content of this chapter extends the material in Chapter 10, although the focus is altered to suit the group. Distinguishing between the aged and adults is not as simple as it may appear. There is, however, legitimate reason to give special attention to the latter part of adulthood—the final phase of the life cycle. Interest in aging and geriatrics has grown dramatically in the past decade. This growth may be partially because society can afford to be increasingly humanitarian. Another reason, however, is the highly visible presence of an increasing number of older persons. As medical sophistication has progressed and survival needs have been satisfied, the longevity of the general population has increased (Foos & Clark, 2003; Freeman, 2004; McNamara & Williamson, 2004). Technological advancements and changing attitudes have resulted in increasing research on those with intellectual disabilities just as it has the general population (e.g., Botsford, 2004; Jacquemont et al., 2004; Searcy et al., 2004).

AGING: WHAT DOES IT MEAN? WHO IS AN OLD PERSON?

Certainly, these are questions most people can answer. An old person is perhaps one's grandmother or grandfather. An old person may be one who is retired. But a child's definition of an old person is very different from that of a 45-year-old. For the most part, people's perceptions of age involve specific examples from personal experience or individual conceptualizations. One does not have to probe very far to see that answers vary a great deal. It follows that the conceptual basis from which a behavioral scientist operates also must vary. If aging is considered from a physiological viewpoint, it looks very different from its appearance from a cultural standpoint (IASSID, 2005). Different individuals and characteristics emerge from the different definitions, and the problem is compounded further by different attitudes, philosophies, social views, and public policy perspectives (Leonardo, Resick, Bingman, & Strotmeyer, 2004; Quadagno, 2005; Wang, 2004). What appears on the surface to be a rather uncomplicated question is not so simple on further consideration.

This chapter focuses on the aging of the population of people with intellectual disabilities. We have emphasized throughout this volume that people with intellectual disabilities represent one part of the complete spectrum of humanity. Although they are different from those without intellectual disabilities in some respects, they are similar in many others. To ignore this fact is to be blinded by either attitude or lack of information. The process of aging must be given attention for the elderly with intellectual disabilities, as well as for the population in general. The major emphasis of both research and service for those having intellectual disabilities has largely fixed on childhood and more recently has included more focus on adolescence. One only need scan the literature that has accumulated over the years to note that attention and research on many conditions, including intellectual disabilities, declines dramatically as one progresses up the age scale (e.g., Hardman, Drew, & Egan, 2006; Phelan, Anderson, LaCroix, & Larson, 2004; Zigman et al., 2004). Children with intellectual disabilities do, however, grow up, and they grow old and die.

RESEARCH ON AGING AND INTELLECTUAL DISABILITIES

In comparison with many areas of behavioral science, relatively little study of aging in populations with intellectual disabilities has been conducted. In fact, the information available has been so limited that it was characterized in earlier editions of this book as nearly nonexistent. With rare exceptions (e.g., Kaplan, 1943), little interest in this area has been evident until recently. Although the need is still urgent for additional study, aging is gaining priority (e.g., Bergman & Boker, 2005; McCallion & McCarron, 2004; McDonnell, Hardman, & McDonnell, 2003).

We mentioned the lack of clarity about identifying the elderly with intellectual disabilities. Some of the reasons for this lack of clarity receive additional attention in this section. We review research in an attempt to explore how the elderly with intellectual disabilities are both like and unlike their peers without disabilities. Because we have limited research data on older people with intellectual disabilities, we sometimes use those without retardation as a reference group.

Methodological Problems

A number of factors contribute to the paucity of research in the area of aging and intellectual disabilities. Some involve lack of interest and an uncaring attitude toward the population, although such perspectives appear to be changing. Others involve the methodological problems of conducting research on aging in general and with the population having intellectual disabilities specifically (e.g., Bergman & Boker, 2005; Hultsch, 2004; McKee, 2004).

> **Core Concept**
>
> Problems in research methodology have contributed to the relative lack of information on elderly individuals with intellectual disabilities. Some problems relate to aging research generally; others arise specifically from intellectual disabilities.

Some of the methodological problems encountered in investigations on aging involve fundamental difficulties in research design (Goodwin, 2005; Sofaer, 2005). These difficulties represent serious impediments to increasing knowledge on aging. Consequently, we need to examine these design problems before we can interpret existing data on the elderly and on the process of growing old.

Two of the most common approaches to studying aging are the cross-sectional design and the longitudinal design. **Cross-sectional studies** sample subjects from several age levels (say, ages 40 to 49, 50 to 59, 60 to 69, and 70 to 79) and compare certain measures among groups. **Longitudinal studies** select a single group of subjects and follow it through the years to compare behaviors at different ages. Each approach compares attributes at different ages to determine how the aging process affects them. Although on the surface these approaches appear suited to their purpose, problems have arisen that make reliable interpretation of data difficult.

The cross-sectional design is by far the more convenient procedure because all subjects are assessed at approximately the same time. A sample of subjects at each level is selected, and the investigator records the desired data. Data then are compared among age levels to find any differences among groups. The problem is that the investigator may incorrectly attribute differences to aging (e.g., Bergman & Boker, 2005; Goodwin, 2005; Nussbaum & Coupland, 2004). Although observed differences may be caused by age differences, other explanations also are possible. Differences between the group that is 40 and the group that is 70 years old, for example, could be the result of sociocultural change over the 30 years that have passed since the older group was 40. It is quite likely (and observations of the past 25 years would confirm) that many social and cultural changes have occurred in such a period of time, creating cohort differences among groups that are not due to aging. People with intellectual disabilities also may be affected by the enormous changes in treatment over the years. Differences among groups may be from aging, different sociocultural influences, different treatments, or combinations of all three. Researchers on aging must be cautious in their interpretations in order to determine age-related and other contextual information in cross-sectional research (Bigby & Balandin, 2004; Goodwin, 2005).

Longitudinal investigations are not plagued by the problem of sociocultural change in the same fashion as cross-sectional studies. Because the same sample is followed through a period of years (even a lifespan), generation gap differences are not as potent. It cannot be denied, however, that a given person changes behaviors in response to altered sociocultural influences. A more serious difficulty is the problem of sample attrition during the period of the study. Because subjects inevitably are lost during the investigation, the sample available at age 70 years is likely to be quite different from the initial sample at 40 years. Thus, differences might result because the composition of the sample has changed, rather than from the effects of age. This difficulty has been called "experimental mortality" and is an inherent design problem of longitudinal studies (Gelfand & Drew, 2003; Hultsch, 2004). An additional difficulty of longitudinal studies is that the researcher may die before the investigation is over. This misfortune sometimes leads to the use of retrospective studies that do not directly assess status at earlier ages but rely on reports based on the subjects' memory or that of others close to them. Such studies are rife with problems of reliability and accuracy.

These methodological problems are serious threats to the soundness of research on the effects of aging. They do not, however, imply that the study of aging is impossible or should not be undertaken. It is merely important that one keep them in mind when reading and interpreting research on the elderly. Obviously, at times, research results need to be interpreted cautiously in order not to generalize beyond the data or to make unsound inferences based on preliminary findings.

Identifying the Older Person with Intellectual Disabilities

Core Concept

Identifying the elderly with intellectual disabilities has been difficult because of disagreement on who is old and problems in actually finding such individuals.

Investigators studying the aging process in intellectual disabilities face even more difficulties than those who study aging in general. Because little research has focused specifically on this population, little information is available for use as a point of departure. Although progress has been made recently in research on the elderly in general, and those with intellectual disabilities, difficulties are still inherent in identifying, detecting, and analyzing data on such individuals (Lifshitz & Merrick, 2004; McCallion & McCarron, 2004; Schaie & Willis, 2002).

Researchers are forced to address some fundamental questions as they consider investigating aging in intellectual disabilities. One of the basic questions immediately raised was mentioned earlier: Who is an old person with intellectual disabilities? Among people with intellectual disabilities, age ranges for the elderly have varied considerably and have been rather arbitrary. Ages as young as 40 and 55 years have appeared in the literature—hardly what some would consider old. Some current research on people with intellectual disabilities still investigates age ranges younger than most would consider old in the general population. In some cases such investigation is focused on particular cause categories where decline seems to appear earlier, such as Down syndrome (e.g., Carmeli, Kessel, Bar-Chad, & Merrick, 2004; McCallion & McCarron, 2004; Zigman et al., 2004). However, early literature in intellectual disabilities often carried an assumption that a person with intellectual disabilities living to 45 or 50 years of age may be considered old. This assumption was based on the view that people with intellectual disabilities may be subject to double or triple jeopardy regarding the normal loss pattern associated with advancing age. This does not mean that the aging process (physiologically) is necessarily more rapid in the population with intellectual disabilities. In part this assumption is and remains based on such factors as where the person resides and what services are available and used (Ruckdeschel & Katz, 2004). Factors such as poverty, marital status, life crises, gender, services available, and housing or living status are important considerations in the study of aging (Brady, 2004; Feld, Dunkle, & Schroepfer, 2004; Schaie & Willis, 2002). Agreement about who is old among people with intellectual disabilities remains a problem, as it does for many researchers in gerontology (Leonardo et al., 2004; McDonnell et al., 2003).

Noting that identifying the elderly with intellectual disabilities is not simple, we find that a related task is thereby complicated—determining the size of the population. Determining demographic information and various associated characteristics for older people with intellectual disabilities and other disabilities remains as research to be undertaken (Carmeli et al., 2004; Foos & Clark, 2003; McCallion & McCarron, 2004). Estimates vary widely with the nature of the population studied, the age used as a lower limit, and the procedures employed for calculating prevalence.

If age 65 is used as the cutoff, a prevalence rate of 1% generates 350,000 individuals who might be considered elderly with intellectual disabilities (U.S. Census Bureau, 2001). Estimates based on a younger age, like the mid-50s, would clearly result in a much larger number. Thus our beginning question of what is considered old among people with intellectual disabilities is an important one. Without a clear point of demarcation, policy matters related to service will lag.

Because of the absence of a firm knowledge base regarding this group, variability in the data raises some extremely interesting questions about aging and intellectual disabilities. Where are the elderly with intellectual disabilities? Perhaps the use of population percentage projections is inappropriate for this group, although no particular logic explains why. Are they hidden or invisible because of a lack of services and, therefore, not on anyone's records? Do they have a shorter lifespan? Have they adapted to the point that they are no longer evident as having intellectual disabilities? These types of questions are central to the study of aging in those with intellectual disabilities, and definitive answers remain among the forthcoming.

CHARACTERISTICS OF THE OLDER PERSON WITH INTELLECTUAL DISABILITIES

The absence of a complete picture of elderly people with intellectual disabilities is not surprising. Problems encountered in the study of aging generally are compounded by additional complications specific to the population with intellectual disabilities. Interest in this area is growing, however, and some evidence is accumulating about the characteristics of this population. We examine two broad areas: mental functioning and social and personal functioning.

Core Concept

Age-related changes in mental functioning of older people with intellectual disabilities are of great interest and often are compared with changes in peers without intellectual disabilities.

Mental Functioning

Mental functioning includes a number of specific cognitive skills. At this time, we are unable to discuss all of these skill areas separately because the accumulated body of research pertaining to older people with intellectual disabilities is relatively immature. Although we know more about the older population without intellectual disabilities, some comparisons are only broadly inferred because of limited data.

Mental functioning is a performance domain that often is assumed to decline with advancing age, and some research supports this assumption (e.g., Brehaut, Raina, & Lindsay, 2004; Kanfer & Ackerman, 2004; West, Welch, & Knabb, 2002). Most people would agree that older people they know are frequently less mentally alert and generally not as mentally capable as younger individuals. Additionally, people often compare the present functioning of a particular older person with recollections of his or her functioning when younger—a comparison fraught with error for many reasons. Although many questions about this perception are unanswered, it is a widely held view in our culture.

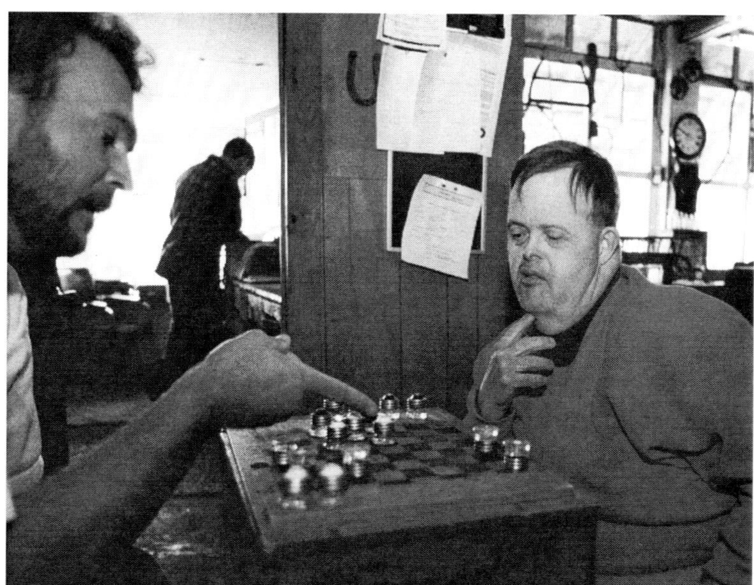

Elderly people with intellectual disabilities may engage in a variety of activities to enrich their lives.

This perspective appears to have substantially influenced research on aging, which often seems to presume that aging erodes cognitive ability. Although it may be true that a decline in mental functioning occurs as age increases, when such a perspective unduly influences scientific investigation, the resulting knowledge base may be biased. Consequently, we must be cautious in interpreting results as they now exist. Although evidence does suggest that some areas of mental functioning decline with aging, this is not a universal pattern of performance, and the type of decline varies greatly among individuals (Brehaut et al., 2004; Schooler, Mulatu, & Oates, 2004; Strough & Margrett, 2002). For example, the type of memory that stores information as abstract symbols and relations between them is known as secondary memory. This type of memory performance does seem to decline in older people. In other mental performance areas, however, such a trend does not appear. Thus memory performance includes several different dimensions and some of these, but not all, seem to show a decline that is necessarily related to aging (Brehaut et al., 2004; Kanfer & Ackerman, 2004; Li & Schmiedek, 2002). Table 11–1 presents a summary of certain typical myths regarding aging and mental functioning, along with abstracted research evidence pertaining to that area of performance.

One question related to our particular focus concerns the influence of aging on older people with intellectual disabilities. Do such people experience a further or marked decline in mental functioning as they age? Does the rate of mental decline occur in a fashion similar to that for peers without intellectual disabilities? Precise answers to these questions remain elusive even with more attention being paid to populations of elders with intellectual disabilities. Some common beliefs about decline

Table 11–1
Myths About Aging and Mental Functioning

Myth	Best Available Evidence
Most old persons suffer from severe memory impairments and cannot remember such basic information as the names of their loved ones and where they live.	Secondary memory does decline significantly with increasing age, but usually not to this extent. Memory impairments of this magnitude typically result from severe illnesses, such as Alzheimer's disease or other dementias. Memory declines in healthy middle-aged and elderly adults are likely to take the form of absent-mindedness, such as forgetting what one said an hour ago and repeating it to the same listener or deciding to do something 10 minutes from now and then forgetting to do so.
Most middle-aged and elderly adults conform to the maxim, You can't teach an old dog new tricks.	Although it is true that the rate of learning is often slower with advancing age, most of the research suggests that people of all ages can learn and remember information if allowed enough time. Because memory problems may contribute to difficulty in learning, specialized methods of instruction may be particularly helpful to older learners.
Because of age-related declines in memory and learning, most older people should not be given complicated and challenging jobs.	Although older adults frequently perform more poorly on difficult memory tests, most jobs probably do not have high demands to remember novel information. Furthermore, as people gain experience in a job, they are likely to increase their level of performance regardless of any memory limitations they might be experiencing.
There is a universal decline in intelligence with increasing age. Thus, you are very likely to suffer serious and widespread deterioration in intellectual ability during your old age.	Some intellectual abilities do show significant decrements as we grow older, especially after middle age. But the declines in other abilities are small and do not appear to have much effect on our daily functioning. Age-related changes in intelligence test scores may not accurately reflect true changes in intelligence because of cohort effects, extraneous variables, selective attrition, and/or other methodological problems. The majority of elderly adults do *not* suffer extreme deterioration in intelligence, although some losses may be expected in such areas as perceptual integration, response speed, and certain aspects of memory.
If you have not made any creative contributions by about age 40, you probably never will.	Creativity does tend to peak prior to middle age, but numerous important creative works have been produced during the latter part of the creator's life.

Source: From *Adult Development and Aging: Myths and Emerging Realities* (3rd ed., pp. 129, 146) by R. Schulz and T. Salthouse, 1999, Upper Saddle River, NJ: Merrill/Prentice Hall. Adapted by permission.

in mental functioning also have influenced the field of intellectual disabilities. These views generally presume not only a general decline of intelligence with age but also a more rapid decline in the intellectual disabilities population. However, solid research evidence on the general nature of intellectual change as a function of age is unclear.

Research literature in intellectual disabilities suggests that the elderly in this population appear to mirror many of the same cognitive trends of their counterparts who do not have intellectual disabilities although in some cases they appear at a younger age (Lifshitz & Merrick, 2004). In some cases impairments do seem to appear at a higher rate in older people with intellectual disabilities, although this is a heterogeneous population with many different influences causing their reduced intellectual functioning (Brehaut et al., 2004; Lifshitz & Merrick, 2004). Some subgroups appear to show a decline in cognitive capacity with age; the performance of other subgroups seems related to specific detrimental influences other than aging, such as depression (Bergman & Boker, 2005; Das, 2003; Lifshitz & Merrick, 2004). For example, evidence is accumulating that older adults with Down syndrome are affected by Alzheimer's disease or Alzheimer's-type dementia more frequently and at an earlier age than their peers without retardation (Zigman et al., 2004). It is worth noting, however, that despite this susceptibility, not all elders with Down syndrome show evidence of Alzheimer's disease. This will be of interest as genetic research proceeds along the line in the Eye on Technology feature.

Thus older individuals with intellectual disabilities appear to have mental functioning trends similar to those of people without intellectual disabilities, although rates may be higher and some subgroups more vulnerable than others. Like most groups, specific health problems may influence cognitive performance and other functioning, and the specific effects of aging alone are difficult to identify (Brehaut et al., 2004; Kanfer & Ackerman, 2004). It should be emphasized that focused research on some of the more specific cognitive skills noted for general populations (e.g., secondary memory) have yet to be investigated. It is also important to underscore

Eye on Technology

Genetic risk for Alzheimer's disease creates significant memory problems even for those who do not have intellectual disabilities. Genetic evidence is beginning to accumulate that even carriers of the genetic elements are significantly impacted. A study at the University of New Mexico indicated that older adults between 60 and 87 were subject to a very strong impact of this genetic make-up even without the development of the actual disease. Carriers had significantly worse memory performance than those who were not carriers. Both genetic and memory research will be important moving forward for older adults with intellectual disabilities.

Source: From "Older People with the 'Alzheimer's Gene' Find It Harder to 'Remember to Remember' Even When They're Healthy," by the American Psychological Association, 2005. APA Online. Retrieved January 23, 2005, from http://www.apa.org/releases/alzheimersmemory.html, © APA, adapted with permission.

the need for longitudinal research to isolate more clearly the effects of age from the cohort effects found in cross-sectional studies. With rare exceptions, research to date on aging in older people with intellectual disabilities has predominantly employed cross-sectional methodology.

Interpreting these research results warrants caution for a variety of reasons. Situational factors, such as the testing itself, can substantially alter an individual's performance. The immediate circumstances or environment may cause enhanced or diminished performance, depending on the individual and the situation. Such influences have long been recognized by psychologists and those in the field of gerontology (e.g., Gelfand & Drew, 2003; Neiss & Almeida, 2004; Schaie & Willis, 2002). Special care should be taken with elderly people when professionals interact, as suggested in the Tips for Professionals feature.

One factor that may well result in declining test scores is an apparent increase in cautiousness observed in older people in general. Behavior occasionally interpreted as increased cautiousness, however, might also be viewed as test anxiety in

Tips for Professionals

Procedural Guidelines: Conducting Evaluations of Dementia and Age-Related Cognitive Decline

The American Psychological Association has issued guidelines for clinical interviews with elderly clients particularly regarding age-related cognitive declines. They include the following:

a. Psychologists obtain the client's self-report and subjective impressions regarding changes in memory and cognitive functioning. This information can be obtained through informal interview or through formal memory complaint questionnaires. . . .
b. Psychologists are aware that self-reported memory problems often do not correspond to actual decreases in memory performance. . . . Frequently, persons with significant cognitive dysfunction are not aware of the problem. . . .
c. It is important, when possible, to obtain behavioral descriptions and subjective estimations of cognitive performance from collateral sources such as family and friends. This information can be obtained either through clinical interview or through memory complaint questionnaires. It is important to be particularly alert to discordance between self and family reports. . . .
d. It is important to take a careful history. The time of onset and nature and rate of the course of the difficulties provide information important to differential diagnosis. The clinical interview provides an opportunity to assess for the presence of deleterious side effects of medication, substance abuse, previous head injury, or other medical, neurological, or psychiatric history relevant to diagnosis. Obtaining a family history of dementia is also important.
e. Depression in elderly persons can mimic the effects of dementia.

Source: From *Guidelines for the Evaluation of Dementia and Age-Related Cognitive Decline* by APA Presidential Task Force on the Assessment of Age-Consistent Memory Decline and Dementia, *American Psychologist*. 1998 Dec Vol 53(12) 1298–1303, © APA, adapted with permission.

the elderly. Such a characteristic often stands out most prominently in tasks with a time limit. It may also come into play in situations that have the potential to produce additional anxiety by their very nature, such as the presence of a nonroutine authority figure (the psychometrician). Both of these conditions often exist in a testing situation. If older people with intellectual disabilities exhibit the same situational anxiety as older people in general (and there is no reason to expect that they would not), the timed responses required by testing may have a substantial negative influence on their scores. They simply may fail to respond within the allotted time and respond but more slowly (Bergman & Boker, 2005; Hagen, 2003; Schaie & Willis, 2002). In fact, the presence of a psychometrician may create some special concern for the elderly person with retardation. A mental test is an important occurrence in the life of such a person—an event that is likely to have a significant personal history. The possibility is also good that much of that history has not been particularly pleasant. A number of disagreeable or troubling associations may be made with the presence of a psychometrician and the process of a psychological test. All of these matters may contribute to anxiety and serve to suppress test performance.

A number of factors may contribute to the apparent decline in mental functioning by older people with retardation. It should be noted once again that these points are largely speculative because research on these topics comes mainly from the general field of gerontology, rather than from the field of intellectual disabilities. For example, age deficits tend to be evident on tasks that are paced, tasks that require a constant switching of attention, and tasks that involve free recall, rather than recognition. Such research remains to be systematically conducted with subjects having intellectual disabilities. However, there is little reason to believe that similar studies done with this population would not produce similar results. The tasks noted are also reminiscent of the activities included in an intelligence test.

Cognitive performance in elderly people also seems to be negatively influenced by self-perceptions of poor health, emotional impacts, and by symptoms of depression (Backman et al., 2004; Schaie & Willis, 2002). In these areas the individuals' actual health status also seems to influence cognitive functioning, although here too the evidence suggests individual differences and variability regarding the type of health problems. For example, some cardiovascular problems do not seem related to mental functioning, while chronic bronchitis does have a negative impact. There are some data suggesting that stress-related circumstances may relate to poor health, although separating out other risk factors is difficult (Faragher, Cooper, & Cartwright, 2004; Salthouse & Nesselroade, 2002; Steiler & Cooper, 2004). The concept of cumulative effects of multiple risk factors on a person's functioning is emerging as health care workers, psychologists, and gerontologists view some trends of declining performance with age. General trends appear to support enhanced life qualities, including cognitive functioning, in later years, trends associated with higher exercise and activity patterns and healthy lifestyle practices (Larson & Wang, 2004; McDowell, Kerick, Santa-Maria, & Hatfield, 2003; Schaie & Willis, 2002). However, it is also clear that advancing age leads to more complex health problems, with multiple symptoms that seem to interact and sometimes exacerbate each other. These matters and communication challenges also brought on by advancing age lead many physicians to dread treating elderly patients (Adams et al., 2002; Quadagno, 2005).

Another area of cognitive or mental functioning that has generated some interest in aging research is rigidity—a reduced ability to change as situations or tasks are altered. This, too, is among the characteristics that are commonly associated with aging (Kanfer & Ackerman, 2004; Strough & Margrett, 2002). It may be related also to the performance of tasks that require one to switch attention, as noted previously. Intellectual disabilities has also played a role in theories about cognitive and behavioral rigidity in addition to the perception that there is an increasing tendency to exhibit rigid behavior (e.g., Das, 2003; Urv, Zigman, & Silverman, 2003). Much of the empirical evidence suggests both cognitive and motivational elements play roles in rigid behavior. Increasing chronological age generally seems related to increased rigid behavior, and increased mental age relates to decreased rigidity (Bergman & Boker, 2005; Kanfer & Ackerman, 2004). Further research is needed to delineate this aspect of mental functioning. Additionally, research specifically on older people with intellectual disabilities needs to be undertaken. Early research suggested that those with intellectual disabilities are particularly susceptible to the formation of learning sets, diminishing their ability to transfer training well. Although this susceptibility seems related to rigidity, further study is needed.

Social and Personal Functioning

Core Concept

The social and personal functioning of elderly people with intellectual disabilities provides some extremely interesting areas of study. Evidence currently is confusing and, in some ways, may challenge the normalization principle.

Social and personal functioning is a very broad theme and potentially covers an enormous range of topics. This type of section heading is useful in the current discussion for two reasons. First, we still are examining performance areas for which the body of research evidence still is accumulating and information regarding subtopics is relatively scarce. Second, social and personal functioning, though a broad subject, relates to normalization, an important concept for those working in intellectual disabilities (O'Neill & Heathfield, 2004).

We presented the principle of normalization in earlier chapters of this volume. Essentially, it reflects the general concern for educating, placing, and treating individuals with intellectual disabilities as normally as possible. Normalization emerged in the literature during the late 1960s and early 1970s and is related to the least restrictive alternative concept. It has continued to be of interest in a variety of conceptual formats and under some divergent terminology (e.g., social valorization, inclusion) (Hardman et al., 2006). Normalization ideas have a number of applications as we consider the quality of life for older people with intellectual disabilities (Ludlow, 2002; Schalock & Felce, 2004; Thompson, Ryrie, & Wright, 2004).

Many aspects of one's quality of life relate to personal health and an ability to function in the environment. Personal health and health care have become topics of vital concern as the general population has become older (IASSID, 2005; McCullough & Laurenceau, 2004; Turner, 2004). Some general indicators are that the health status of those with intellectual disabilities does not compare favorably with their counterparts without disabilities, although these indicators are not necessarily age related (Carmeli et al., 2004; McCallion & McCarron, 2004; Schalock & Felce, 2004). For example, general mortality rates appear higher for those with intellectual disabilities and seem to be related to severity of retardation. In some cases, underlying causation of the intellectual disabilities appears associated with death, which would be expected in circumstances in which the etiology is physiologically based. However, much of the research addressing these topics is plagued with methodological limitations like those outlined in the beginning of this chapter. Sound longitudinal investigation is needed to delineate more adequately the age-related variables affecting this group as they grow older. Such information is vital as policymakers plan for the future of cost-effective health care delivery to those with intellectual disabilities (Hawkins, Eklund, James, & Foose, 2004; McCallion & McCarron, 2004).

Mental health problems, such as depression, seem to emerge more frequently in older populations and have been the focus of increased study in such groups (Harpole & Williams, 2004; Morano & DeForge, 2004). As usual it is difficult to separate the various influences in such research. Does depression really appear more frequently with increased age or are the various other maladies associated with becoming older more linked to such mental health states (e.g., reduced independence, physical limitations, fewer social relationships)? Interest in depression and other psychopathologies and their relationships to intellectual disabilities also appears in the literature with increasing frequency, although direct analysis of the relationship needs attention (Krauss, Gulley, Sciegaj, & Wells, 2003; Strydom & Hassiotis, 2003). It is unlikely that the factors of aging, intellectual disabilities, and the emergence of depression or other mental health difficulties represent relationships that are linear or easily investigated.

Additional questions of interest remain regarding the quality of life of the elderly with intellectual disabilities (Carmeli et al., 2004; McCullough & Laurenceau, 2004; Turner, 2004). What are their social and personal lives like? Where do their support systems lie? These are difficult questions for older people generally, and the picture for those with intellectual disabilities is not an appealing one. The variety of supports tend to be different and of variable effectiveness for those with intellectual disabilities (McCallion & McCarron, 2004; Schalock & Felce, 2004; Wilkinson & Janicki, 2002). For many people without intellectual disabilities, growing older means an increased dependence on informal support systems, as well as on governmental agencies. Family members often shoulder a significant burden of support and caregiving (Hardman et al., 2006; Keen & Knox, 2004; Shu, Lung, & Huang, 2002). However, for those older individuals with intellectual disabilities, the family may not be available for a variety of reasons (IASSID, 2005). In many cases, no spouse is available to provide care and support because the person was not married, and siblings may not be a reliable source of care and support. Although it is promising to see social agency networks increasingly serving elderly people with intellectual disabilities, such assistance may be a poor substitute for family support (Lifshitz & Merrick, 2004; McCallion & McCarron, 2004; Parish, Pomeranz-Essley, & Braddock, 2003). Further, family support networks for older people with intellectual disabilities may be limited. There is a serious need for additional systematic research on the family structures of older citizens having intellectual disabilities. Likewise the

Tips for Professionals

Inclusion for Older People with Intellectual Disabilities

- Focus on the individual needs and preferences of the older person with intellectual disabilities in developing an individualized program plan, analyzing interpersonal needs, behavioral and health supports, and the benefits to be achieved by interaction with the broader community.
- Functional analysis is likely to provide the most helpful evaluation for community placement. Chronological age or other markers for living decisions are unlikely to provide much guidance in designing living goals for the older person with intellectual disabilities.
- Review program elements that are successful for inclusion of younger people with intellectual disabilities (e.g., friendship and recreational programs) to explore ways these programs might be altered for the older person with intellectual disabilities.
- Analyze community resources (e.g., health care, social services, recreational) for inclusive supports that may be included as elements of the individual's program planning.
- Analyze the family's capacity for care and financial support as an element of developing an inclusive living program for the older person with intellectual disabilities.

planning of services may involve further complications as one considers family circumstances intertwined with the individual needs of the older person with intellectual disabilities. The Tips for Professionals feature summarizes some inclusion tips for consideration in designing what might be an individualized family service plan (IFSP) and individualized program plan (IPP) for such a person.

Adaptive behavior skills become increasingly important as a greater numbers of adults, including older adults with intellectual disabilities, are moved from institutions to community living arrangements (AAMR, 2002; Hewitt et al., 2004; Salvatori, Tremblay, & Tryssenaar, 2003). This is an area of escalating interest and concern among professionals working in intellectual disabilities, since therapeutic services may be less available or require more individual initiative outside of an institutional setting (e.g., Hill, Thorn, Bowling, & Morrison, 2002; Holburn, Jacobson, Schwartz, Flory, & Vietze, 2004; Podgorski, Kessler, Cacia, Peterson, & Henderson, 2004). Problem solving in the interpersonal domain is a skill that is likely to be of heightened importance as one lives in a community setting and represents a set of skills where age differences are clearly evident. Older adults appear to employ different social strategies and have quite different perspectives of the world than their caregivers. Some features of the social circumstances of elderly adults suggest less desirable situations (e.g., diminished interpersonal contact and support) and behavioral profiles that do not promote interpersonal contact as a group (Hooyman & Kiyak, 2002; Schaie & Willis, 2002). As we have found in other areas, individual and cultural differences clearly have nearly preemptive influences, and changes in adaptive behavior are not evident in all investigations (Leung, Wu, Lue, & Tang, 2004;

Marx & Cohen-Mansfield, 2003; Rogers & Delewski, 2004). These topics must, however, be the focus for future research as we observe the juncture of increased lifespans and community living for our citizens with intellectual disabilities, a circumstance that increases the importance of interpersonal competence and life decision making.

Research has demonstrated a decline in adaptive behavior functioning in Down syndrome subjects as a function of aging. Such evidence, however, may include some significant other influences beyond aging effects. For example, this particular population has also been shown repeatedly to be affected by a relatively early onset of Alzheimer's disease or Alzheimer's-type dementia (e.g., Zigman et al., 2004). The presence of such a condition may certainly contribute to behavior that most would consider to be nonadaptive. Not surprisingly, adults with intellectual disabilities seem significantly influenced by their environmental circumstances. Social relationships, autonomy, and health matters emerge as themes of increased importance to older adults with disabilities. Further, those in community living arrangements seem involved in generally higher participation or activity levels than those in institutional circumstances (Salvatori et al., 2003; Washburn, Sands, & Walton, 2003). Current evidence is as complicated as the settings in which the research must necessarily be undertaken. However, solid rigorous research methods now in use allow and promote such investigation (Bergman & Boker, 2005; Bigby & Balandin, 2004; Gelfand & Drew, 2003). Further research on the personal and adaptive functioning of elderly people with intellectual disabilities is extremely important, particularly in community settings.

A comprehensive picture of the social and personal functioning of the elderly person with intellectual disabilities is still not available. Many dimensions of this topic remain relatively unexplored. The emergence of community living as a preferred alternative for many with intellectual disabilities opens new areas needing investigation. Although some elements of the family circumstances for older people with intellectual disabilities may seem rather depressing, other pieces of data provide much more hope (Poston et al., 2003).

PROGRAMMING AND FUTURE RESEARCH

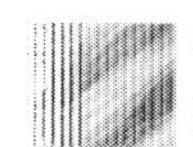

Core Concept

Service programs and living arrangements for elderly people with intellectual disabilities also raise interesting questions about normalization.

The development of programs for older people with intellectual disabilities varies greatly throughout the nation. Reports of state service plans range from programs that are already implemented to circumstances in which policies have yet to be articulated (Parish et al., 2003). As noted earlier, however, the nearly standard and strong impetus is for educating, placing, and treating individuals with intellectual disabilities as nearly normally as possible. Some of the positive outcomes of such placements prompt further interest in these types of arrangements. Future programming plans increasingly must anticipate changes in this population as health care of all types continues to improve. Additionally, there may well be some additional risks generated by the normalization of living arrangements for adults and older citizens with intellectual disabilities. To some degree, normalization brings with it some of the self-inflicted hazards that we all live with on a daily basis such as health problems resulting from lifestyle issues.

Community living arrangements for adults with intellectual disabilities have raised considerable controversy periodically. Objections often come from neighborhood residents who are fearful for the physical well-being of their families or who believe that the value of their property will be reduced by the proximity of facilities for people with retardation. These arguments have been the most prominent in objections to community living placements. However, we must also consider an issue that surfaces only occasionally in the heat of such controversy—the well-being of the individual.

Evidence is accumulating that demonstrates advantages of community living for those with intellectual disabilities. In some cases, such living arrangements require alterations in the way service is conceived and provided. Modification of staffing arrangements in group homes, for example, allows for the additional health care services that may be required by older residents experiencing some added physical needs with age. New relationships are being suggested between service providers and clients in order to promote some citizens with disabilities being able to live most productively in the community. We are learning more regarding what is needed and are beginning to see even larger areas where additional research is required. The base of research information regarding living arrangements for the elderly with intellectual disabilities, though growing, remains limited when compared with that regarding the general population.

Considerable research is necessary for a better understanding of the elderly with intellectual disabilities in general. The empirical knowledge based on this population remains rather thin. We do not have a firm grasp on how many aged people with intellectual disabilities there are or where they are in general. Such information, plus a clear definition of what old means in this group, is fundamental to further research. It is difficult to describe characteristics and to prescribe programming coherently unless these basic questions are answered. Investigation of the aged population with intellectual disabilities is obviously a rich area of study for beginning researchers. It represents an area of specialization that promises an exciting career. Future researchers in this area will have to study both intellectual disabilities and gerontology and then synthesize the two for use with the elderly with intellectual disabilities. The research needed is unlikely to come from either intellectual disabilities or gerontology singly.

Who are the elderly with intellectual disabilities, and what are their characteristics? These were general questions with which we began this chapter, and they have been answered only partially. The final part of the life cycle of the individual with intellectual disabilities has had little examination in comparison with earlier phases. We still do not know whether people with retardation tend to age more rapidly than their peers without disabilities. In individual cases (e.g., some individuals with Down syndrome), they do seem to become prematurely old, but what of the population as a whole? Certainly people of the ages under discussion in this chapter (i.e., the 50s) are not considered old in the general population. If, in fact, this population does age more quickly, it is not at all clear whether it results from factors related to intellectual disabilities or to environmental factors that may be associated with intellectual disabilities, such as poor health care. More likely, we are seeing a phenomenon that is a social construct; we see these people in a particular way and with certain expectations.

It is interesting to note that people with intellectual disabilities seem not to experience middle age to any marked degree. They often are thought of as being in an extended childhood and adolescent phase for a large part of their lives. This also is likely the result of how people have viewed them. It is a view that may well change as the literature on adults with intellectual disabilities grows, as it has begun to do.

When older people with intellectual disabilities are placed in nursing homes, they tend to be grouped with patients who are senile. This classification may be one factor that contributes to the invisibility of elderly people with intellectual disabilities. No one distinguishes their behaviors from those of elderly patients in general, so they lose their diagnosis of intellectual disabilities. Obviously, one must question whether such programming practices are appropriate for and in the best interests of these individuals. If the practices are appropriate and in the best interests of these individuals (a matter not yet determined), is it advisable to relabel these people with a term that carries such negative connotations? Intellectual disabilities is a complex problem that involves interaction of many forces and influences. It is a problem that society has at least partially created, and society must address it. The life of the aged individual with intellectual disabilities continues to reflect these interacting variables.

NEW ISSUES AND FUTURE DIRECTIONS

A number of questions have been examined in this chapter, several of which began the chapter and remain only partially answered. The literature available on the latter part of the lifespan has expanded in recent years. The future of services to the elderly with intellectual disabilities, however, depends heavily on consolidating knowledge about this population. Policymakers have a difficult time enacting legislative support for a problem that has an undetermined size, and there remains a great deal to be learned about the size and age distribution of this group. Although the literature has grown, the results also remain mixed in terms of identifying their special problems. Issues like these are vital to our knowledge base on older people with intellectual disabilities and our ability to serve them.

We are also somewhat confused about what we should do with older people in general, let alone those with intellectual disabilities. The aging of our population presents a variety of problems, and some of those matters become very personal when they involve an individual in our own family. We become increasingly torn as we watch the evening news of late and learn about the sexual assault of 77-year-old Virginia Thurston in what was supposed to be a safe place, a nursing home (CBS News, 2004). That could be our mother. Abuse of residents in nursing homes is more widespread than most ever thought. For example, Connecticut alone recorded over 3,400 complaints in the two-year period from 1998 to 2000. Nearly 70% of Connecticut's nursing homes had complaints and almost half (47%) had actual abuse (Allen, Kellett, & Gruman, 2004). Multiply this by a national sample and there are a large number of elders not receiving desired care. As individuals we may have made some decisions that are effective to some degree. But as a population there is much that needs attention about our older citizens, and policies and services for them will also impact that segment that has intellectual disabilities. It is little wonder that we expressed concern for Grace in the opening vignette.

There are also ethical concerns that may be particularly relevant to this age group (Field & Behrman, 2004). Some of the dilemmas that recur with older

Bill of Rights for the Elderly Person with Mental Retardation

1. The right to an adequate standard of living, economic security, and protective work.
2. The right to humane services designed to help them reach their fullest potential.
3. The right to live as independently as they are able in the community of their choice, in as normal a manner as possible.
4. The right to an array of services that is generally available to other elderly groups.
5. The right to choose to retire. In addition, the opportunity to retire "to something," rather than just "from something."
6. The right to participate as a member of the community, having reciprocal interdependency.
7. The right to be considered a person and not merely "elderly" or "retarded."
8. The right to protected, personal well-being and to a qualified guardian, when required.
9. The right to be involved in setting one's goals and in making one's decisions. The right to fail, if necessary.
10. The right to a positive future, and having enough involvement with life to prevent a pre-occupation with death.
11. The right to be romantic, not asexual.
12. The right to sufficient activity and attention to permit continued integrity of self, individual identity, and purpose.
13. The right to an interesting environment and lifestyle, with availability of sufficient mobility to provide a variety of surroundings.
14. The right to live and die with dignity.

Source: From "The Elderly Mentally Retarded Developmentally Disabled Population: A Challenge for the Service Delivery System" by P. D. Cotten and C. L. Spirrison, in S. J. Brody and G. E. Ruff (Eds.). *Aging and Rehabilitation* (pp. 159–187), 1986. New York: Springer. Copyright 1986 by Springer-Verlag New York, Inc. Reprinted by permission.

individuals having intellectual disabilities illustrate certain similarities and differences between this group and the general population of elderly people. One dilemma of particular note is competence to refuse recommended treatment—an issue that recently has received more widespread attention (Aveyard, 2004; Lemme, 2002; Schwartz, 2005). However, one important difference in older people with intellectual disabilities is that they may be considered incompetent by reason of mental ability irrespective of age. Does this factor really make such individuals less competent to refuse treatment? This question remains unanswered but is one that faces care providers in a very real, perhaps personal way when considering an individual with whom they have formed a service relationship (Nelson, 2003). These are no longer hypothetical issues when real people are involved.

The future of services for elderly people with intellectual disabilities is still relatively uncharted territory. Balancing real life with the hypothetical ideal presents many challenges for people working with this population. It is important to think carefully as we enter these unknown areas, to draw on the desirable as professionals develop service plans that will work within the constraints of society's ability to provide. Twenty years ago Cotten and Spirrison (1986) articulated many elements of a desirable quality of life for the elderly with intellectual disabilities. These are presented in the feature Bill of Rights for the Elderly Person with Mental Retardation as a bill of rights that might be desirable for all elderly people.

Core Questions

1. How have the general methodological problems encountered in conducting gerontological research contributed to problems in the investigation of the elderly with intellectual disabilities?
2. Why might elderly people with intellectual disabilities be characterized as an "invisible" group?
3. What effect does invisibility have on social services for the elderly with intellectual disabilities?
4. How does disagreement about who is old contribute to research difficulties on elderly people with intellectual disabilities?
5. The general perception of older people is that they have a reduced level of mental functioning. Does this perception hold for older individuals with intellectual disabilities?
6. Do people with intellectual disabilities decline in mental functioning more rapidly than people in the general population?
7. What factors, other than reduced mental functioning, may enter the picture in terms of mental performance for older populations?
8. Why do some people object to community-based living arrangements for older individuals with intellectual disabilities?

Roundtable Discussion

Throughout this volume, the notions of mainstreaming and normalization have been much in evidence at many stages of the life cycle. In some ways, these principles represent an imposition of what one group (intellectual disabilities professionals) believes is best for another group (people with intellectual disabilities). When people reach the level of old age, these considerations take on other meanings and may require additional planning.

In your study group or on your own, examine the principles of mainstreaming and normalization with regard to the elderly with intellectual disabilities. Consider that the notions seem more complicated by the fact that some older people with intellectual disabilities have been institutionalized for many years. How might this influence their perceptions of satisfaction? How do these matters influence the way you might plan services for elderly people with intellectual disabilities during the next decade?

Parent and Professional Organization Positions on Key Issues in the Lives of People with Intellectual Disabilities

The inside front cover of this text presents a matrix that includes several key issues in the lives of people with disabilities, the positions of various parent and professional organizations on each issue, and the chapter and page number where the information is addressed. Table 11–2 on page 338 is a summary of the organizations and key issues addressed in this chapter.

Table 11–2
Key Issues and Organizations Discussed in This Chapter

Organization/Website	Key Issues Addressed	Chapter Heading
American Association on Mental Retardation (http://www.aamr.org)	Testing and assessment	Mental Functioning
International Association for the Scientific Study of Intellectual Disabilities (http://www.iassid.org)	Aging and terminology Family support Quality of life	Aging: What Does It Mean? Who Is an Old Person? Social and Personal Functioning Social and Personal Functioning

References

Adams, W., McIlvain, H., Lacy, N., Magsi, H., Crabtree, B., Yenny, S., et al. (2002). Primary care for elderly people: Why do doctors find it so hard? *The Gerontologist, 42,* 835–842.

Allen, P. D., Kellett, K., & Gruman, C. (2004). Elder abuse in Connecticut's nursing homes. *Journal of Elder Abuse and Neglect, 15,* 19–42.

American Association on Mental Retardation (AAMR). (2002). *Mental retardation: Definition, classification, and systems of supports* (10th ed.). Washington, DC: Author.

American Psychological Association. (2005, January 23). Older people with the "Alzheimer's gene" find it harder to "remember to remember" even when they are healthy. *APA Online.* Retrieved from http://www.apa.org

Aveyard, H. (2004). The patient who refuses nursing care. *Journal of Medical Ethics, 30,* 346–350.

Backman, L., Wahlin, A., Small, B. J., Herlitz, A., Winblad, B., & Fratiglioni, L. (2004). Cognitive functioning in aging and dementia: The Kungsholmen project. *Aging, Neuropsychology, and Cognition, 11,* 212–244.

Bergman, C. S., & Boker, S. M. (2005). *Methodological issues in aging research.* Mahwah, NJ: Erlbaum.

Bigby, C., & Balandin, S. (2004). Issues in researching the ageing of people with intellectual disability. In E. Emerson, C. Hatton, T. Thompson, & T. R. Parmenter (Eds.), *The international handbook of applied research in intellectual disabilities* (pp. 221–236). Hoboken, NJ: Wiley.

Botsford, A. L. (2004). Status of end of life care in organizations providing services for older people with a developmental disability. *American Journal on Mental Retardation, 109,* 421–428.

Brady, D. (2004). Reconsidering the divergence between elderly, child, and overall poverty. *Research on Aging, 26,* 487–510.

Brehaut, J. C., Raina, P., & Lindsay, J. (2004). Does cognitive status modify the relationship between education and mortality? Evidence from the Canadian Study of Health and Aging. *International Psychogeriatrics, 16,* 75–91.

Carmeli, E., Kessel, S., Bar-Chad, S., & Merrick, J. (2004). A comparison between older persons with Down syndrome and a control group: Clinical characteristics, functional status and sensori-motor function. *Down Syndrome: Research and Practice, 9,* 17–24.

CBS News. (2004, November 15). *Abuse in the nursing home.* Retrieved from http://www.cbsnews.com/stories/2004/11/15/eveningnews/main655704

Cotten, P. D., & Spirrison, C. L. (1986). The elderly mentally retarded developmentally disabled population: A challenge for the service delivery system. In S. J. Brody & G. E. Ruff (Eds.), *Aging and rehabilitation* (pp. 159–187). New York: Springer.

Das, J. P. (2003). Cognitive aging and Down syndrome: An interpretation. In L. M. Glidden (Ed.), *International review of research in mental retardation* (Vol. 26, pp. 261–306). San Diego, CA: Academic Press.

Faragher, E. B., Cooper, C. L., & Cartwright, S. (2004). A shortened stress evaluation tool (ASSET). *Stress and Health: Journal of the International Society for the Investigation of Stress, 20,* 189–201.

Feld, S., Dunkle, R. E., & Schroepfer, T. (2004). Race/ethnicity and marital status in IADL caregiver networks. *Research on Aging, 26,* 531–558.

Field, M. J., & Behrman, R. E. (2004). *Ethical conduct of clinical research involving children.* Washington, DC: National Academies Press.

Foos, P. W., & Clark, M. C. (2003). *Human aging.* Boston: Allyn & Bacon.

Freeman, P. B. (2004). Sensitivity to Alzheimer's disease. *Optometry: Journal of the American Optometric Association, 75,* 541–542.

Gelfand, D. M., & Drew, C. J. (2003). *Understanding child behavior disorders* (4th ed.). Belmont, CA: Wadsworth.

Goodwin, C. J. (2005). *Research in psychology: Methods and design* (4th ed.). Hoboken, NJ: Wiley.

Hagen, B. (2003). Gerontological nursing research: A challenging but rewarding field. *CJNR: Canadian Journal of Nursing Research, 35,* 175–180.

Hardman, M. L., Drew, C. J., & Egan, M. W. (2006). *Human exceptionality: School, community, and family* (8th ed.). Needham Heights, MA: Allyn & Bacon.

Harpole, L. H., & Williams, J. W., Jr. (2004). Assessment and management of depression in older adults. *Primary Psychiatry, 11,* 31–36.

Hawkins, B. A., Eklund, S. J., James, D. R., & Foose, A. K. (2004). Adaptive behavior and cognitive function of adults with Down syndrome: Modeling change with age. *Mental Retardation, 41,* 7–28.

Hewitt, A. S., Larson, S. A., Lakin, K. C., Sauer, J., O'Nell, S., & Sedlezky, L. (2004). Role and essential competencies of the frontline supervisors of direct support professionals in community services. *Mental Retardation, 42,* 122–135.

Hill, R. D., Thorn, B. L., Bowling, J., & Morrison, A. (2002). *Geriatric residential care: Clinical theory and practice.* Mahwah, NJ: Erlbaum.

Holburn, S., Jacobson, J. W., Schwartz, A. A., Flory, M. J., & Vietze, P. M. (2004). The Willowbrook Futures Project: A longitudinal analysis of person-centered planning. *American Journal on Mental Retardation, 109,* 63–76.

Hooyman, N. R., & Kiyak, H. A. (2002). *Social gerontology: A multidisciplinary perspective* (6th ed.). Boston: Allyn & Bacon.

Hultsch, D. F. (2004). Introduction to special issue on longitudinal studies of cognitive aging. *Aging, Neuropsychology, and Cognition, 11,* 101–103.

International Association for the Scientific Study of Intellectual Disabilities (IASSID). (2005). *Aging SIRG mission.* Retrieved from http://www.iassid.org

Jacquemont, S., Farzin, F., Hall, D., Leehey, M., Tassone, F., Gane, L., et al. (2004). Aging in individuals with the *FMR1* mutation. *American Journal on Mental Retardation, 109,* 8.

Kanfer, R., & Ackerman, P. L. (2004). Aging, adult development, and work motivation. *Academy of Management Review, 29,* 440–458.

Kaplan, O. (1943). Mental decline in older morons. *American Journal of Mental Deficiency, 47,* 277–285.

Keen, D., & Knox, M. (2004). Approach to challenging behaviour: A family affair. *Journal of Intellectual and Developmental Disability, 29,* 52–64.

Krauss, M. W., Gulley, S., Sciegaj, M., & Wells, N. (2003). Access to specialty medical care for children with mental retardation, autism, and other special health care needs. *Mental Retardation, 41,* 329–339.

Larson, E. B., & Wang, L. (2004). Exercise, aging, and Alzheimer disease. *Alzheimer Disease and Associated Disorders, 18,* 54–56.

Lemme, B. H. (2002). *Development in adulthood* (3rd ed.). Boston: Allyn & Bacon.

Leonardo, M. E., Resick, L. K., Bingman, C. A., & Strotmeyer, S. (2004). The alternatives for wellness centers: Drown in data or develop a reasonable electronic documentation system. *Home Health Care Management and Practice, 16,* 177–184.

Leung, K. K., Wu, E. C., Lue, B. H., & Tang, L. Y. (2004). The use of focus groups in evaluating quality of life components among elderly Chinese people. *Quality of Life Research: An International Journal of Quality of Life Aspects of Treatment, Care and Rehabilitation, 13,* 179–190.

Li, S. C., & Schmiedek, F. (2002). Age is not necessarily aging: Another step towards understanding the "clocks" that time aging. *Gerontology, 48,* 5–12, 22–29.

Lifshitz, H., & Merrick, J. (2004). Aging among persons with intellectual disability in Israel in relation to type of residence, age, and etiology. *Research in Developmental Disabilities, 25,* 193–205.

Ludlow, B. (2002). Handbook on quality of life for human services practitioners. *Developmental Disabilities Bulletin, 30,* 221–225.

McCallion, P., & McCarron, M. (2004). Ageing and intellectual disabilities: A review of recent literature. *Current Opinion in Psychiatry, 17,* 349–352.

McCullough, M. E., & Laurenceau, J. P. (2004). Gender and the natural history of self-rated health: A 59-year longitudinal study. *Health Psychology, 23,* 651–655.

McDonnell, J., Hardman, M., & McDonnell, A. (2003). *Introduction to persons with severe disabilities.* Boston: Allyn & Bacon.

McDowell, K., Kerick, S. E., Santa-Maria, D. L., & Hatfield, B. D. (2003). Aging, physical activity, and cognitive processing: An examination of P300. *Neurobiology of Aging, 24,* 597–606.

McKee, K. J. (2004). The perspectives of people with dementia. Research methods and motivations. *Aging and Mental Health, 8,* 381–382.

McNamara, T. K., & Williamson, J. B. (2004). Race, gender, and the retirement decisions of people ages 60 to 80: Prospects for age integration in employment. *International Journal of Aging and Human Development, 59,* 255–286.

Marx, M. S., & Cohen-Mansfield, J. (2003). Hoarding behavior in the elderly: A comparison between community-dwelling persons and nursing home residents. *International Psychogeriatrics, 15,* 289–306.

Morano, C. L., & DeForge, B. R. (2004). The views of older community residents toward mental health problems. *Journal of Mental Health and Aging, 10,* 45–64.

Neiss, M., & Almeida, D. M. (2004). Age differences in the heritability of mean and intraindividual variation of psychological distress. *Gerontology, 50,* 22–27.

Nelson, L. J. (2003). Respect for the developmentally disabled and forgoing life-sustaining treatment. *Mental Retardation and Developmental Disabilities Research Reviews, 9,* 3–9.

Nussbaum, J. F., & Coupland, J. (2004). *Handbook of communication and aging research* (2nd ed.). Mahwah, NJ: Erlbaum.

O'Neill, R. E., & Heathfield, L. T. (2004). Educational supports. In E. Emerson, C. Hatton, T. Thompson, & T. R. Parmenter (Eds.), *The international handbook of applied research in intellectual disabilities* (pp. 445–458). Hoboken, NJ: Wiley.

Parish, S. L., Pomeranz-Essley, A., & Braddock, D. (2003). Family support in the United States: Financing trends and emerging initiatives. *Mental Retardation, 41,* 174–187.

Phelan, E. A., Anderson, L. A., LaCroix, A. Z., & Larson, E. B. (2004). Older adults' views of "successful aging"—How do they compare with researchers' definitions? *Journal of the American Geriatrics Society, 52,* 211–216.

Podgorski, C. A., Kessler, K., Cacia, B., Peterson, D. R., & Henderson, C. M. (2004). Physical activity intervention for older adults with intellectual disability: Report on a pilot project. *Mental Retardation, 42,* 272–283.

Poston, D., Turnbull, A., Park, J., Mannan, H., Marquis, J., & Wang, M. (2003). Family quality of life: A qualitative inquiry. *Mental Retardation, 41,* 313–328.

Quadagno, J. S. (2005). *Aging and the life course* (3rd ed.). Burr Ridge, IL: McGraw-Hill.

Rogers, A., & Delewski, C. (2004). Elders with serious and persistent mental illness (SPMI): Assessing needs, resources, and service utilization. *Journal of Gerontological Social Work, 43,* 19–36.

Ruckdeschel, K., & Katz, I. R. (2004). Care of dementia and other mental disorders in assisted living facilities: New research and borrowed knowledge. *Journal of the American Geriatrics Society, 52,* 1771–1173.

Salthouse, T. A., & Nesselroade, J. R. (2002). An examination of the Hofer and Sliwinski evaluation. *Gerontology, 48,* 18–21.

Salvatori, P., Tremblay, M., & Tryssenaar, J. (2003). Living and aging with a developmental disability: Perspectives of individuals, family members and service providers. *Journal on Developmental Disabilities, 10,* 1–19.

Schaie, K. W., & Willis, S. L. (2002). *Adult development and aging* (5th ed.). Upper Saddle River, NJ: Prentice Hall.

Schalock, R. L., & Felce, D. (2004). Quality of life and subjective well-being: Conceptual and measurement issues. In E. Emerson, C. Hatton, T. Thompson, & T. R. Parmenter (Eds.), *The international handbook of applied research in intellectual disabilities* (pp. 261–279). Hoboken, NJ: Wiley.

Schooler, C., Mulatu, M. S., & Oates, G. (2004). Occupational self-direction, intellectual functioning, and self-directed orientation in older workers: Findings and implications for individuals and societies. *American Journal of Sociology, 110,* 161–197.

Schwartz, R. J. (2005). *Law and aging: Essentials of elder law* (2nd ed.). Upper Saddle River, NJ: Prentice Hall.

Searcy, Y. M., Lincoln, A. J., Rose, F. E., Klima, E. S., Bavar, N., & Korenberg, J. R. (2004). The relationship between age and IQ in adults with Williams syndrome. *American Journal on Mental Retardation, 109,* 231–236.

Shu, B. C., Lung, F. W., & Huang, C. (2002). Mental health of primary family caregivers with children with intellectual disability who receive a home care programme. *Journal of Intellectual Disability Research, 46,* 257–263.

Sofaer, B. (2005). *Qualitative methods in health services and policy research*. Hoboken, NJ: Wiley.

Steiler, D., & Cooper, C. L. (2004). Short communication: French version of the Occupational Stress Indicator (OSI): Preliminary assessment of reliability and validity. *Stress and Health: Journal of the International Society for the Investigation of Stress, 20,* 231–237.

Strough, J. N., & Margrett, J. (2002). Overview of the special section on collaborative cognition in later adulthood. *International Journal of Behavioral Development, 26,* 2–5.

Strydom, A., & Hassiotis, A. (2003). Diagnostic instruments for dementia in older people with intellectual disability in clinical practice. *Aging and Mental Health, 7,* 431–437.

Thompson, D. J., Ryrie, I., & Wright, S. (2004). People with intellectual disabilities living in generic residential services for older people in the UK. *Journal of Applied Research in Intellectual Disabilities, 17,* 101–108.

Turner, L. (2004). Life extension research: Health, illness, and death. *Health Care Analysis, 12,* 117–129.

Urv, T. K., Zigman, W. B., & Silverman, W. (2003). Maladaptive behaviors related to adaptive decline in aging adults with mental retardation. *American Journal on Mental Retardation, 108,* 327–339.

U.S. Census Bureau. (2001). The 65 years and over population: 2000. *Census 2000 brief.* Washington, DC: U.S. Department of Commerce, Economics and Statistics Administration, U.S. Census Bureau, C2KBR/01-10.

Wang, D. (2004). Service delivery and research considerations for the 85 population. *Journal of Gerontological Social Work, 43,* 5–17.

Washburn, A. M., Sands, L. P., & Walton, P. J. (2003). Assessment of social cognition in frail older adults in its association with social functioning in the nursing home. *Gerontologist, 43,* 203–212.

West, R. L., Welch, D. C., & Knabb, P. D. (2002). Gender and aging: Spatial self-efficacy and location recall. *Basic and Applied Social Psychology, 24,* 71–80.

Wilkinson, H., & Janicki, M. P. (2002). The Edinburg principles with accompanying guidelines and recommendations. *Journal of Intellectual Disability Research, 46,* 279–284.

Zigman, W. B., Schupf, N., Devenny, D. A., Miezejeski, C., Ryan, R., Urv, T. K., et al. (2004). Incidence and prevalence of dementia in elderly adults with mental retardation without Down syndrome. *American Journal on Mental Retardation, 109,* 126–141.

Family and Social Issues

Chapter 12

Families

Chapter Preview

At the completion of this chapter, you will have a better understanding of:

- The impact of the child with intellectual disabilities on the family.
- The importance of ongoing and effective communication among professionals and parents.
- The role of parent and professional associations in providing valuable information and support to the family.
- The importance of a parent and professional partnership in meeting the needs of a family member with an intellectual disability.

My Child Is NOT Retarded!—Part I

When my son was 18 months old, he was being diagnosed in many different ways to try to label his various idiosyncracies. Nothing felt quite right and my son didn't fit the rigid molds of these "labels." I was going out of my mind. I went through many emotions. First, I thought "What have I done to cause this?" Then I went into my I-can-fix-this mode. I searched the Internet. I read books. Finally, I was referred to the coordinator of a support group for mothers of children with special needs. I didn't realize it at the time, but this unsuspecting group of mothers would literally change the way I perceived my life, and more importantly, children with disabilities, including my own son.

Nervous and extremely self-conscious, I attended my first meeting. When the mothers introduced themselves and the diagnoses of their children, I was convinced that I had taken a wrong turn Autism? Cerebral palsy? Down syndrome? Other names were so long and obscure even the acronyms sounded like I fell head first into my alphabet soup. Intellectual disabilities? My child is NOT retarded! He's smart, very smart, gifted in fact! I was NOT like these other women, and they couldn't possibly help me. At least that is what I thought. (Berry, 2003, p. 16)

(To be continued)

- *What are some of the emotions experienced by this mother that eventually lead her to a support group of parents who have children with special needs?*
- *What do you think this support group will have to offer this mother as she moves through the many different reactions to her son's diagnosis?*

The family is the oldest and most enduring of all human institutions. Today, the family is characterized as a diverse and evolving social system. Married couples constitute only 52% of family households, and approximately 20% of all children are living in single-parent families with the mother as the head of the household. Additionally, 10% of families live in poverty and 8% of family members between the ages of 5 and 20 have an identified disability (U.S. Census Bureau, 2005). As noted by McDonnell, Hardman, and McDonnell (2003, p. 55), "The reality is that the traditional family consisting of a mother, father, and children all under one roof is now only one of many different family constellations that may range from single-parent households to formal family support systems (such as foster care).

Regardless of its structure, the family is centered on an emotional bond between parents and children. Family systems exist for various reasons, including the need for security, belonging, and love. Many individuals see children as an extension of themselves; others perceive their children as a means to attain some degree of immortality.

The arrival of any child usually represents a change in lifestyle for a couple. Financial issues may concern new parents. Recreational and social activities have to be modified. Travel over long distances may become difficult because of expense and inconvenience. Housing needs may change significantly. The small apartment that once seemed most adequate suddenly becomes confining.

The list of changes in lifestyles brought on by a new child often seems endless. However, the "inconvenient" aspects of parenthood are overshadowed by the sheer joy and pleasure that the child brings to the new parents. Diaper changing and sleepless nights tend to fade away with the first smile, the first step, and the first spoken word. With these accomplishments, parents begin to envision the fruition of their dreams and hopes of parenthood: healthy, bright, capable, beautiful children doing all the things the parents did or wished they could have done.

For parents of children with disabilities, dreams and hopes for the future are often put on hold. The birth of a child with intellectual disabilities may cause parents to view themselves as failures in what they consider one of their fundamental purposes in life. For some parents, these feelings and the loss of self-worth are temporary. For others, these emotions may last a lifetime. What can be said with certainty is that the process of adjustment for parents is continuous and distinctly individual (Turnbull & Turnbull, 2001).

No response, reaction, or feeling can be considered typical, mature, good, or bad. Reactions are based on emotions, and for the parents, the magnitude of their feelings and reactions is as great as they perceive the challenges facing them.

In this chapter, we address the impact of the child with intellectual disabilities on the family. The needs of the child, the parents, and the siblings are discussed in the context of the needs of the family unit and of its relationship with professionals.

THE IMPACT OF THE CHILD WITH INTELLECTUAL DISABILITIES ON THE FAMILY

Core Concept

Parents of children with intellectual disabilities may have many reactions, ranging from awareness to acceptance.

Intellectual disabilities may be apparent at birth or may become evident only with the passage of time. As parents recognize differences in the development of their child, their reactions can be highly variable. Some move through distinct phases; others exhibit no emotional pattern (Fine & Simpson, 2000; Hastings & Taunt, 2002).

From Awareness to Acceptance

One of the first authors to suggest that parents of children with intellectual disabilities move through a series of stages or phases was Rosen (1955). He addressed five stages through which parents of children with intellectual disabilities may progress from the time they first become aware of a child's differences until acceptance of the condition. Rosen's five stages are referred to throughout this chapter: (a) awareness of differences or delays in the child's growth and development, (b) recognition that the condition is intellectual disabilities, (c) search for a cause for the intellectual disabilities, (d) search for a cure, and (e) acceptance of the child.

It is important to emphasize that although some parents go through distinct periods of adjustment, others cope without passing through any set of sequential reactions. The severity of the intellectual disabilities is a factor in this adjustment process. A child with mild intellectual disabilities may not have any physically distinguishing characteristics, and thus the parents may be unaware that the child has intellectual disabilities until the school suggests that the child is not keeping up academically. The degree of impact, frustration, or disappointment, however, does not necessarily correlate directly with the degree of intellectual disability. Nonetheless, parents of children with severe intellectual disabilities sometimes find it easier to acknowledge differences because the child's disability is highly visible; thus, acknowledgment (not necessarily acceptance) generally comes quickly.

The religious background of the parents may affect their attitude toward intellectual disabilities. Etiology and age of onset are also important factors. For the parents of children with severe intellectual disabilities, awareness and recognition of the condition may come simultaneously. Parents of children with mild intellectual disabilities become more aware of their child's condition gradually as the child fails to develop or progress as anticipated. Learning difficulties may be more obvious to parents with other children who have typical development.

Although some delays in development may be apparent in the early childhood years, the identification of children with mild disabilities does not usually occur until the child is in elementary school. When the parents are informed that their child has intellectual disabilities, they may acknowledge and accept the condition or resort to a variety of defense mechanisms to aid in coping. The initial impact may take several forms. It may result in transient stress for the parents, or it may have a permanently debilitating effect on the marriage and family unit (Fuller & Olsen, 1998; Gray, 2002). However, it is also true that some families with a child who has a disability have no more frequent problems than those who do not. In fact, *parents may report greater emotional support for one another and strong family relationships* (Poston et al., 2003).

Fathers and mothers may react very differently to the child with intellectual disabilities (Hardman, Drew, & Egan, 2006). The mother may take on the role of physical protector and guardian of the child's needs, while the father may take a more reserved role. Although many fathers may cope by withdrawing and internalizing feelings, others may become more involved in caregiving and contribute substantially to the well-being of the child (Simmerman, Blacher, & Baker, 2001).

The presence of a child with intellectual disabilities need not create a family crisis. Professionals can help the family adjust by examining resources, including role structure and emotional stability.

Core Concept

Parents may go through denial, especially during the initial stage of adjustment.

Denial

Some parents may minimize the degree of disability or simply deny that any differences exist. They may close their minds to their child's limitations or explain their child's limitations by implying laziness, indifference, or lack of motivation. Denial can be both useless and destructive—useless because refusal to accept the reality of a child's disability does not make the child's differences disappear, and destructive because it can impede the child's own acceptance of limitations and prevent needed services and supports. Denial provides self-protection against painful realities.

Parental denial is frustrating to professionals. Parents may refuse to recognize the conditions for what they are; consequently, the needed supports and treatment frequently are delayed and sometimes never provided. The Individuals with Disabilities Education Act (IDEA) requires parental consent before placement of a child in special education, so the child with intellectual disabilities whose parents deny that the condition exists will be excluded from receiving the specialized instruction he or she may need. Denial also may deprive the child of necessary medical treatment, which only adds to the frustration of professionals endeavoring to assist the family.

Professionals must be aware of the extreme emotional stress placed on the family and realize that for the time being, this reaction may be the only one possible for the parents. With time, patience, and continued support, professionals eventually may help parents face the situation and begin making accommodations for the child in their family (Fine & Nissenbaum, 2000). Eventually, parents may come to realize that the birth of a child with intellectual disabilities need not stigmatize their lives or cast any doubts on their integrity as adequate parents or human beings.

Core Concept

Parents may project blame for the child with intellectual disabilities on others.

Projecting Blame

Another possible parent reaction is "projection." Parents blame others for the birth of their child with intellectual disabilities. Targets are frequently physicians, whom the parents associate with considerable futility and agony. For example, blame often is directed at the allegedly incompetent obstetrician:

> If only the doctors had taken better care of my wife (or me) before the baby was born, they would have known something was going wrong and could have prevented it.
>
> If only the doctor had not taken so long to get to the hospital, help would have been there early enough to keep something from happening.
>
> If they'd had enough sense not to use so much anesthesia . . .

Some parents may also blame the pediatrician for not properly attending to the child immediately after birth or failing to treat an illness or injury adequately. Most often, this blame is not justified. However, parental hostility may be well placed by inadequate and sometimes even improper counseling on the part of the physician. Although skilled in the medical aspects of their practice, physicians may be ill equipped to counsel parents; they know little about the resources available for supporting children with intellectual disabilities. Physicians must become more knowledgeable about community resources, including other parents, educators, clergy, family counselors, and so on. Parents may choose not to consult these individuals, but at the very least, they should be informed of their availability.

When the presence of intellectual disabilities is evident and can be diagnosed at birth, it is usually the responsibility of the attending physician to inform the parents. Some may see the task of telling parents that their child has intellectual disabilities as difficult at best. Physicians have been criticized for not assuming this professional responsibility in a sensitive, caring manner. The manner in which the physician counsels the parents may have a profound and long-lasting impact. Physicians cannot prevent the shock felt by parents as they learn of the child's disability, but they can lessen its impact. They can also provide parents with perspective and direction as they attempt to adjust their lives and make room for the child.

School personnel may also be open to criticism. Frustrated parents may project blame on educators for the perceived failure to teach the child properly.

Fear

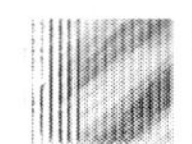

Core Concept

Parents may fear having other children, loss of friends, a lifetime of care, and impact on the family unit.

The unknown makes everyone anxious at one time or another. Anxiety, in turn, may generate fear. Parents of children with intellectual disabilities face so many unknowns that fear is a natural and common reaction. Some of these fears may seem completely unwarranted. Yet they are very real to parents and must be acknowledged, listened to with sensitivity, and responded to appropriately. Until parents receive adequate information, these fears persist. Unfortunately, answers to parent's questions may not be available, and anxiety persists. Some frequently asked questions include the following:

What caused this disability, and if we choose to have other children, will they have intellectual disabilities too?

How will our friends and relatives feel about the child and us?

Will we always have to take care of the child, or is independence possible someday?

What will this do to our family?

Who will take care of the child when we are no longer able?

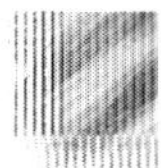

Core Concept

Parents of children with intellectual disabilities may blame themselves for their child's condition.

Guilt

Human nature generally dictates that when something goes wrong, the blame must be attached somewhere. When parents of children with intellectual disabilities are unable to blame someone else, they may blame themselves. They may look for and find something in their lives or their behavior that they believe is responsible. When people look hard enough, a seemingly logical reason appears. The result is guilt.

Guilt is insidious and debilitating. Assuming blame does not eliminate the child's disability, and the negative emotions associated with guilt are extremely difficult to dispel. Professionals working with parents who are experiencing feelings of guilt are most often successful when they support them in channeling their energies into more productive areas.

Grief and Mourning

Core Concept

When parents realize that their child has intellectual disabilities, they may react with grief or mourning.

Grief is a natural reaction to situations that bring extreme pain and disappointment. We all grieve when we lose something that we cherish or value. The birth of a child with intellectual disabilities represents the loss of hope for a healthy son or daughter. Parents of an infant with a disability often experience recurrent sorrow and frequent feelings of inadequacy that persist over time. For some parents, the grief is chronic, and they need considerable time to adjust to the fact their child has intellectual disabilities. For others, the feeling of being victimized evolves into the view that they are a "survivor" of trauma (Gray, 2002).

The birth of a child with intellectual disabilities represents the loss of the parents' positive self-image. To the parents, the event may seem more like a death. They may harbor death wishes toward the child, particularly when the child becomes burdensome and they wish to end their ordeal. In rare instances, parents institutionalize a child who is diagnosed as having intellectual disabilities, announce that the child was stillborn, and even place an obituary notice in the newspaper. Some parents, preoccupied with thoughts of "when the child dies" or "if the child should die," unconsciously wish for the child's death. These parents may deny their death wishes if confronted, as they are unable to acknowledge these hidden desires on the conscious level. Other parents, however, are consciously aware of their death wishes and may or may not be willing to express these feelings publicly.

Core Concept

Parents may choose to isolate themselves because of their feelings of shame and guilt.

Withdrawal

At times, we all want and need to be alone. We can be alone physically or have others around us and still feel isolated. We may choose to shut others out of our thoughts, giving us a kind of freedom to think by ourselves, rest, and meditate in our private world. Solitude can be therapeutic.

Although therapeutic in some instances, withdrawal is also potentially damaging. Parents may withdraw from friends, relatives, coworkers, or activities that may facilitate the healing process. By withdrawing, parents can construct a protective barrier or space and silence against outside pain, if not against the hurt inside. Staying away from social functions protects against "nosy" questions about the children and the family. By keeping away from restaurants and other public places, the family avoids critical eyes staring at the child who is different.

Rejection

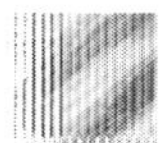

Core Concept

Parents may show rejection of the child through strong underexpectations of achievement, unrealistic goals, escape, and reaction formation.

Parental rejection has such a negative connotation that anyone who has been described as rejecting is frequently stereotyped as an incompetent parent and devoid of basic humanity. In everyday life, there are many instances between parents and children in which the child's behavioral patterns exceed the parents' tolerance. Parental rejection is expressed in four common ways:

1. *Strong underexpectations of achievement.* Parents so devalue the child that they minimize or ignore any positive attributes. The child often becomes aware of these parental attitudes, begins to have feelings of self-worthlessness, and behaves accordingly. This process is often referred to as a **self-fulfilling prophecy.**
2. *Setting unrealistic goals.* Parents sometimes set goals so unrealistically high that they are unattainable. When the child fails to reach these goals, parents justify their negative feelings and attitudes on the basis of the child's limitations.
3. *Escape.* Another form of rejection may include desertion or running away. It may be quite open and obvious, as when a parent leaves the family and moves out of the home. Other types of desertion are more subtle: The parent is so occupied with various responsibilities that he or she has little, if any, time to be at home with the family. This could take the form of "demanding special projects at the office" or perhaps the requirements of "various responsibilities at church." Other parents place the child in a distant school or institution even if comparable facilities are available nearby. It is important to emphasize here that placement of a child into an institution is not necessarily equated with parental rejection.
4. *Reaction formation.* When parents deny negative feelings and publicly present completely opposite images, this may be classified as **reaction formation.** Negative feelings run contrary to the parents' conscious values, and they cannot accept themselves as anything but kind, loving, warm people. For example, parents who resent their child with intellectual disabilities may frequently tell friends and relatives how much they love their child.

Parents are often in an untenable position when dealing with professionals. If they express honest feelings of not accepting their child, they are condemned as rejecting parents. If they profess genuine love for their child with intellectual disabilities, they may be suspected of manifesting a reaction formation.

Searching for a Cause

When parents recognize and acknowledge the condition of their child, they may immediately seek to find a cause. Most often this search leads to either a theological or medical explanation.

Theological Explanations. In times of perceived crisis, people frequently turn to religion for comfort, security, and sanction. Some seek assurance that they are not to blame; others seek some help in picking up the "broken pieces of their lives." In order to be sensitive to the needs of parents, clergy must have accurate training and information. Intellectual disabilities within a family unit may precipitate a theological crisis. The birth of a child with intellectual disabilities may either weaken or strengthen religious beliefs, and the particular faith of the parents may affect their response.

Family acceptance may be a function of religious affiliation. Catholics consider redemption a continual process, so humanity continually experiences suffering for its sins. This does not imply that the advent of a particular child results from the sins of the parents but rather that it is an expiation for all humankind. Methodists believe that the child with a disability is a function of nature missing its mark. The Church of Jesus Christ of Latter Day Saints (Mormons) believes that individuals with intellectual disabilities are part of the divine plan; their premortal existence was as whole spirits, and their presence on earth is merely temporal and for a short time, in comparison to eternity. The Jewish faith assigns no particular theological explanation, simply stating that the event occurred.

Explanations within specific denominations or religious groups may vary according to the theological interpretation of each religious leader. We wish only to point out that there are divergent theological views. Considering these divergent views, one can begin to understand why parental reactions differ with religious affiliation. Some devout parents view the child with intellectual disabilities as a religious responsibility. Some even look on themselves as martyrs, ready to accept the responsibility as a God-given cross to be borne patiently and submissively.

Religious leaders must have a grasp of the issues involved in counseling parents of children with intellectual disabilities. It is important for these leaders to understand clearly the theological implications in their own minds. A plan for counseling parents in the light of the theological implications must be formulated. Through this plan, a religious leader may assist parents better to deal with feelings of anxiety and guilt. If religious institutions are to reflect the social conscience of society, they must undertake affirmative action to educate congregations about children with intellectual disabilities and to provide effective programs for them.

Medical Explanations. For some parents, it is the physician who first delivers the news that the child has intellectual disabilities (such as a newborn with Down syndrome or other genetic condition). Parents want a medical opinion on the child's condition, the prognosis for the child, and the possibility of having a second child with intellectual disabilities. The odds, the risks, and the possible consequences should be clearly articulated. After the information is given, the decision of whether to have another child is that of the parents.

There are several considerations when providing comprehensive medical counseling and services to persons with intellectual disabilities and their families:

1. The physician in community practice (e.g., general practitioner, pediatrician) must receive medical training in the medical, psychological, and educational aspects of people with intellectual disabilities.
2. Physicians must be more willing to treat patients with intellectual disabilities for common illnesses when the treatment is irrelevant to the patient's specific disability.
3. Physicians need not become specialists in specific disability areas but must have enough knowledge to refer the patient to an appropriate specialist when necessary.
4. Physicians must not expand their counseling role beyond medical matters but must be aware of, and willing to refer the patient to, other community resources (Hardman et al., 2006).

Acceptance

Acceptance means recognizing the child as an individual with feelings, wants, and needs. The child has the potential to enjoy life and to bring enjoyment to others. As each child with intellectual disabilities grows into adolescence and adulthood, realistic and attainable goals are set. The attainment of these goals brings satisfaction, pride, and pleasure to both parents and child.

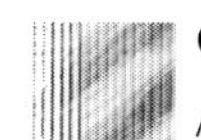

Core Concept

Acceptance of the child is a critical step in the healing and growing process for parents.

The process for parents to reach self-acceptance may be filled with pain, frustration, and self-doubt. Although some parents may never reach acceptance, they can experience positive feelings as they attempt to move in that direction. With acceptance, the family is able to better endure crises and, in the process, grow stronger, wiser, and more compassionate. (See the feature Offer Yourself Hope When Others Don't.)

SUPPORTING THE FAMILY

Parents of children with intellectual disabilities exhibit the same range of emotions and behaviors as parents of children without disabilities. However, parents of children with intellectual disabilities may differ from other parents in that they often have an ongoing and extensive need for both formal and informal support networks.

Formal and Informal Family Support Networks

Formal family supports are provided by society (usually the government) and include education, health care, income maintenance, employment training and placement, and housing. These formal supports may extend into parent training and information centers, **respite care,** in-home assistance, and counseling services to help address the challenges of daily life as well as planning for the future.

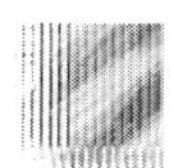

Core Concept

Families need government-sponsored services, as well as the assistance of an informal support network of family and friends.

Offer Yourself Hope When Others Don't

How do you respond when a trained, seasoned, experienced doctor tells you that your newly-born child will not amount to much more than a doorstop? This was our experience when we were informed that our son, Danny, was born with Down syndrome. Such news is not what is needed when the child is but five hours old and nothing but hope and promise are on the minds of the parents. We had two responses. The first was immediate; the second continues to this day and will, in all likelihood, continue as long as we are an influence on Danny's life.

The notification process is the single most important factor in parents' ability to cope and manage with the blessing of a child with special needs. And make no mistake about it—these children are blessings. Raised properly, they can teach us more about lives and ourselves than any course or textbook, and in raising them properly, we are directly contributing to society's understanding of these children so that they, too, can make a meaningful contribution with and of their lives. . . .

We were treated as being the paramount of ignorance. Our doctor "greeted" us with the following introduction: "Hi, I'm from the Human Genetics Department at Children's Hospital, and your son—What's his name? Danny? How nice. Your son has Down Syndrome."

The next hour was an exercise in mental torture, but it needn't have been. The good doctor gave us the physiological signs indicative of Danny's diagnosis, but we parried every indicator she gave with physical features in both mother and father that could also provide some explanation. . . . That hour was spent with a litany of "he can't," "he won't," and "he'll never," not exactly what a parent needs to hear on the first day of their new child's life.

That notification imparted a grieving process that could have been mitigated had it been handled better. . . . My wife and I learned that, while grieving is a collective journey, so is it an individual one. But although the grieving was made much more difficult by the way in which we were told, it also crystallized our reaction as parents, and particularly my reaction as a father, as to how we were going to proceed with Danny's development.

This resolve hardened at the doctor's concluding remark. "Try not to think of him as a Down's baby who is also your son," she said, "but as your child who just happens to have Down Syndrome." Well, now. Rarely have I shook as I did when she uttered that fateful advice. In an emotional and vocal crescendo, my voice raised with rage as I uttered each syllable, responding, "I do not need you to tell me how I should think about my son." . . .

A startling revelation ended the grieving process, at least for me, and began my own steps towards recovery. If the doctor could be so callous towards our opinions, why couldn't I be likewise towards hers? And at that point, I resolved to ignore the predictions and treat Danny as I would had he not had Down syndrome or any other disability. Nothing, of course, could change the reality of Danny's condition. Try as we might to hold out against the diagnosis, the blood tests confirmed what the doctor had told us. Danny, indeed, had Down syndrome.

Like any father, I had high dreams, hopes and aspirations before my son was born; why couldn't I have them afterwards? . . . I started Danny on that path by raising him not as if he had Down syndrome, but as if he hadn't. Games, rough-housing and reading became part of our daily regimen, but to that developmental diet we added two important ingredients: prayer and holding. Prayer helped us in ways beyond description, and we soon found that, as Danny developed his motor skills, he began folding his hands and joining us in the best way he could. The smile that came over his face each time we prayed reminded us that God had not abandoned us, even though we thought otherwise during his first few weeks of life.

Thus far, only one of the dire predictions we heard over two years ago has had any merit. Danny's speech is somewhat delayed, but that is the only aspect of his development that is. In fact, in some gross motor skills, he is ahead of where "normal" two-year-olds should be. What Danny can say should not be confused with what he can communicate. He has an understanding that the spoken word is our primary vehicle for communication, but when a voice within screams to converse with those around, some method will be found to break through whatever physical barriers exist. Danny has hurdled through this temporary encumbrance by displaying a remarkable ability to grasp sign language. It has become his second vocabulary.

As Danny is halfway between his second and third birthdays, we have also discovered that he need not fear playing baseball. The boy can throw, and it's not just balls: pens, pencils, blocks, car keys, crystal and china have all experienced the discovery of flight at his hands. To be certain, it was "dad play" that launched him on this particular trajectory, but for someone who was predicted to have low muscle tone and delayed physical development, whatever frustrations we may experience at this particular tendency have been replaced with our hope for the long-term ramifications.

Source: Adapted from "Offer Yourself Hope When Others Don't" by J. E. Sullivan, 2005. The Father's Network. Retrieved May 1, 2005, from http://www.fathersnetwork.org/page.php?page=641.

Informal supports extend beyond government-sponsored programs and include the natural supports provided by the extended family (e.g., grandparents), friends, and neighbors. Natural supports may include in-home assistance, housecleaning, and transportation from extended family members or friends. McDonnell et al. (2003) suggested that "the nature and type of support will be unique to the individuals involved, and be dependent on a mutual level of comfort in both seeking and providing acceptance" (p. 60).

Providing Information to Parents

It is critical for parents to know they have the support of those who care about them. For professionals working with families, support implies recognition of each family member's individual needs.

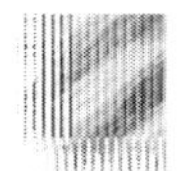

Core Concept

Parents of children with intellectual disabilities must have their needs and feelings acknowledged when communicating with professionals.

Parents need to receive accurate information from professionals that is meaningful rather than jargon-based. Professionals need to develop communication skills for positive interaction that avoids "talking down" to parents. When professionals believe parents lack sufficient experience or background to understand the information, interactions become confusing and disappointing to everyone. Such situations can be avoided when professionals value parent input and participation, assist them in understanding diagnostic information on their child, and actively involve them in decision making. (See the Tips for Professionals feature.)

The Role of Parent and Professional Associations

Parent and professionals associations, such as The ARC, the American Association on Mental Retardation (AAMR), and TASH are comprehensive sources of information for

Parental acceptance of a child with intellectual disabilities facilitates a healthy interaction which promotes the child's development.

Tips for Professionals

Providing Information to Parents

- Provide feedback in a private, safe, and comfortable environment.
- Keep the number of professionals to a minimum.
- Begin by asking parents their feelings about the child's strengths as well as weaknesses.
- Provide evaluation results in a jargon-free manner, using examples of test items and behavioral observations throughout.
- Be sensitive to viewing the child as an individual and a "whole" child when reporting various evaluation results.
- Allow the parent time to digest the results before planning begins.
- Be sensitive to linguistically different families and the use of interpreters.
- Prepare for the session with other professionals, clarifying any possible conflicts before the meeting.
- Use conflict resolution strategies to clarify any conflicts with families.

Source: Adapted from *Interactive Teaming: Enhancing Programs for Students with Special Needs* by V. I. Correa, H. A. Jones, C. C. Thomas and C. V. Morskink. 2005. Upper Saddle River, NJ: Prentice Hall.

Core Concept

Parent and professional organizations provide valuable information and support to parents.

families with a child who has intellectual disabilities. The ARC is an organization that works on behalf of people with intellectual disabilities and their families, advocating for the rights of people with disabilities at all levels of government. The association promotes community supports and services that are person and family-centered. The ARC provides direct support for families by providing advice and support on services available within their local community. For more information, visit The ARC website at http://www.thearc.org.

The AAMR promotes policies, practices, research, and human rights for people with intellectual disabilities. This professional association publishes many resources that may be valuable to families in the areas of community support, effective education practices, health care, positive behavior supports, and social services. For more information, visit the AAMR website at http://www.aamr.org.

In addition to the many family resources provided by The ARC and AAMR, both associations have taken strong positions on the need for family-centered supports in the community. Specifically:

- Family supports should be responsive to the needs of the entire family unit, flexible enough to accommodate unique needs, and enabling and empowering for families to make informed decisions.
- Because each family is unique, family support cannot be viewed only as services offered by professionals (e.g., respite) or as a single program (e.g., cash subsidy). Rather, it must comprise a flexible network of public services plus other supports capable of bending to meet individual family needs.
- Family supports must allow for diverse approaches. No single approach to supporting families is likely to work with all families. Differences in family type, culture, income, and geographic location require diversity in the approaches. To be most effective, support services must be consistent with the cultural preferences of individual families.
- Supports are most effective when their source is closest to the family. The supports should give families control of the services they need.
- Families should be assisted in weaving together the multiple existing sources of help and the informal networks into a cohesive circle of support to meet the needs of both child and family. Families need informational, financial, and emotional support to promote full inclusion and enhance their family's quality of life. (AAMR, 2005; The ARC, 2005).

TASH (formerly known as the Association for Persons with Severe Handicaps) is an international association of people with disabilities, their family members, other advocates, and people who work in the disability field. TASH members are concerned with dignity, civil rights, education, and independence for all individuals with disabilities. The association provides a number of resources to families in the areas of community living, public policy, health, employment, and inclusive education. TASH (2005) has also taken a strong position on the need for families of children with disabilities to have maximum control over their personal assistance and other supports, independent of service agencies. Families should also have the right to choose the type of support needed and wanted and how that support will be provided. For more information on TASH, visit the website at http://www.tash.org.

Other community resources in addition to AAMR, The ARC, and TASH may be available to assist parents. For example, some communities have organized "parent-to-parent programs" that assist parents who recently have given birth to a child with

My Child Is NOT Retarded—Part II *(continued from part I on page 345)*

My child is NOT retarded! . . . I was NOT like these other women, and they couldn't possibly help me. At least that is what I thought.

After the first hour, I put away my pride and began to actually listen. I was like these women and they were like me. They were scared, concerned, caring, and often funny. Their children may have problems different from my child, but the process, the parent-child dynamic, the advocating for the best interest of the child, all that was the same. The more I listened, the more I realized their children shared common symptoms with my child. I wasn't along in the world where a child never sleeps or cannot stand to have certain foods and textures touch him. Instead of trying to declare myself as different, I looked for things we had in common and I asked questions and searched for answers.

I was so lucky to have a room full of wise and experienced mothers to help me. If one didn't know the answer surely the next mother would. I don't believe I have ever gone to a meeting and left without learning something that could help my child. It may be advice on education. It may be a solution to our sleep issues. It may be new and different drugs and treatments others have success with. If nothing else, it might be a hug or a simple word of support. (Berry, 2003, p. 17)

a disability or have learned of their child's disability. (See the feature My Child Is NOT Retarded—Part II.)

On the national scene, there are several advocacy programs for people with a disability. These include the Disability Rights Education and Defense Fund, which was established to advance the civil rights of individuals with a disability through guiding and monitoring national public policy. The Developmental Disabilities and Bill of Rights Act established a protection and advocacy system in every state for persons with a developmental disability. State protection and advocacy systems are authorized to pursue legal and administrative remedies to protect the rights of persons with developmental disabilities who are receiving education and treatment in a given state. For parents of school-aged children with disabilities, more than 100 training and information centers (PTIs) have been funded by the U.S. Department of Education. These centers assist parents in communicating effectively with education professionals, participating in educational decision making, and obtaining information about options, programs, services, and resources available at the national, state, or local level. (For more information and location of PTIs in each state, go to http://www.dssc.org/frc/TAGuide/pti.htm.)

Core Concept

A positive relationship among parents and professionals is important to the success of children with intellectual disabilities in the school setting.

Building a Parent-Professional Partnership in the Schools

Schools are most successful when they establish positive relationships with the family (Berry, 2003). Children are first and foremost members of a family unit. As they grow older their learning experiences extend beyond the family into the school and finally into the vast environment we call community. As children mature, they are nurtured across a variety of environments in which one context influences and interrelates with the others. A home-school partnership is a critical building block in providing an appropriate and successful educational experience for the child with intellectual disabilities. There are two components to establishing and maintaining an effective home-school partnership. First, both professionals and parents must understand and respect each other's needs, differences, and constraints. Second, communication between school and home must occur often, and in an atmosphere of openness and mutual trust.

By getting to know the family and taking the time to learn about their attitudes and beliefs, the school sends a message of respect. Collaboration will be most successful when both parents and educators:

- acknowledge and respect differences in values and culture
- listen openly and attentively to concerns
- value varying opinions and ideas
- discuss issues openly and in an atmosphere of trust
- share in the responsibility and consequences for making a decision

Everyone benefits from a home-school partnership. Children benefit because their learning can be taught and applied across both school and home environments. As communication between parents and educators increases, student progress can be more readily evaluated and reinforced. Additionally, opportunities to solve difficult learning or social challenges will often occur early enough in the situation that a positive solution may be possible. As participating members of the collaborative team, parents learn the attitudes and skills necessary to work effectively with their child in areas such as communication, behavior, and academics. Parents feel valued as equal members of the team, and in turn a positive attitude toward the school is developed and fostered. Educators also profit from working closely with parents. Through interacting with parents, teachers gain access to critical information about the needs and ability level of the child.

A successful parent-professional partnership requires a two-way communication process where information is openly shared, input is valued, and a mutually acceptable resolution is reached. Implied within the partnership is mutual respect for one another.

Family Support Programs

Family support programs are a critical resource in helping parents and siblings meet the challenges of everyday life (Romer, Richardson, Nahom, Aigbe, & Porter, 2002). These programs "identify family needs and locate formal and informal resources that support those needs while assisting families to mobilize their own resources" (p. 191). These authors further recommend the hiring of family support workers acting as advocates to help families locate and use community resources, including respite care, recreation programs, health care services, and public transportation. As Shin (2002) indicates, families with a child who has intellectual disabilities often face significant challenges that go far beyond their physical and material resources.

Core Concept

Community supports, including respite care, recreation, health services, and public transportation, can be a major asset to families of children with intellectual disabilities.

A healthy family environment is very important for all children.

These families make Herculean efforts to organize the family and reach out for the resources that will help them meet the needs of their child. The availability of these resources and the willingness of the family to make use of them are critical if parents and siblings are to meet the challenges and demands of everyday life.

NEW ISSUES AND FUTURE DIRECTIONS

> **Core Concept**
>
> Positive relationships among professionals and parents of children with intellectual disabilities need to be strengthened as we move through the 21st century.

The field of intellectual disabilities continues to experience dynamic change as we move through the early years of the 21st century. Educational, medical, and social services are expanding with new and innovative approaches. Such developments as inclusive education, fetal surgery, and supported employment are bringing about significant positive outcomes in the lives of people with intellectual disabilities and their families. One issue, however, has remained unchanged over the years: the necessity to reinforce and expand the parent-professional partnership in meeting the individual needs of people with intellectual disabilities. No single issue has received more lip service without achieving results, indicating that such partnerships require considerably more nurturing. In the field of education, for example, active participation by parents in educational decision making continues to be inconsistent despite the mandate for parental involvement in IDEA.

The Center on Education Policy (Mandlawitz, 2003) reported mixed results from parents of students with disabilities in regard to satisfaction with schools. Although some parents indicated that the IEP process worked well overall, others suggested they had "a diminished voice" in the decision-making process and were struggling to get needed services.

There are many potential barriers to parent participation in special education, including low parental attendance at IEP meetings, the scheduling of meetings at times that are inconvenient to parents, a lack of adequate skills and available information for parents, an overall devaluing of parent input into the decision-making process, inadequate preparation of professionals to work with families, and time constraints (Brown, 2005; Powell & Graham, 1996).

The use of educational jargon and highly technical language by education professionals may also prevent parents from fully participating in their child's education. Language issues may become even more complex for parents from culturally different backgrounds. As such, appropriate oral and written communication is critical to ensuring parent involvement (Choi, Nisbett, & Norenzayan, 1999; Gollnick & Chinn, 2002). While federal law requires written communication to be in the parents' native language, this may not always be the case. Harry, Allen, and McLaughlin (1995) report that important documents are sent home to parents in English, contain unfamiliar words, and are presented to parents with little or no feedback regarding their understanding of what has been written.

It is time to reevaluate the nature of the parent-professional partnership and to move beyond rhetoric. Specific activities need to be explored that will maximize positive relationships. Positive parent-professional relationships are essential in the areas of (a) developing IEPs and adult service programs, (b) keeping parents informed about educational and community services, and (c) supporting organized parent advocacy (McDonnell et al., 2003). Organized parent advocacy moves beyond advancing personal interests to supporting change for all people with intellectual disabilities. The history of intellectual disabilities is replete with examples of parent advocacy. Nearly all significant changes in services to people with intellectual disabilities have occurred as a result of it. As such, it is imperative for professionals to continue to support and participate in this effort. Parent advocacy now and in the future is absolutely necessary if professionals are to bring about services and supports focusing on individual need.

Core Questions

1. Discuss the various stages of parent adjustment to a child with intellectual disabilities.
2. Discuss common parental reactions to a child with intellectual disabilities.
3. In searching for a cause for their child's intellectual disabilities, parents often seek either theological or medical explanations. Compare and contrast these two areas of explanation.

4. Identify parent and professional organizations that may assist and support parents of children with intellectual disabilities.
5. Identify strategies for establishing a partnership among professionals and parents to meet the needs of children with intellectual disabilities.
6. What community supports must be available for families of children with intellectual disabilities?

Roundtable Discussion

In this chapter, you have learned about stages that parents progress through in adjusting to a child who has intellectual disabilities as well as various reactions. Review and discuss parental reactions to the child with intellectual disabilities.

In your study group, organize a role-playing activity. Assign participants to role-play parent reactions and the role of professionals in supporting parents who face the challenges of raising a child with intellectual disabilities.

Parent and Professional Organization Positions on Key Issues in the Lives of People with Intellectual Disabilities

The inside front cover of this text presents a matrix that includes nine key issues in the lives of people with disabilities, the positions of various parent and professional organizations on each issue, and the chapter and page number where the information is addressed. Table 12–1 is a summary of the organizations and key issues addressed in this chapter.

Table 12–1
Key Issues and Organizations Discussed in This Chapter

Organization/Website	Key Issues Addressed	Chapter Heading
American Association on Mental Retardation (http://www.aamr.org)	Family support	The Role of Parent and Professional Associations
The ARC, a national organization on intellectual disabilities (http://www.thearc.org)	Family support	The Role of Parent and Professional Associations
TASH, an international association of people with disabilities, their family members, and professionals (http://www.tash.org)	Family support	The Role of Parent and Professional Associations

References

American Association on Mental Retardation. (2005). *Policy statement on family support.* Retrieved May 10, 2005, from http://www.aamr.org/Policies/pos_fam_support.shtml

The ARC. (2005). *Position statement on family support.* Retrieved May 10, 2005, from http://www.thearc.org/posits/familysuppos.doc

Berry, J. O. (2003). *Supported families.* Norman: University of Oklahoma Health Sciences Center, Center for Learning and Leadership/UCEDD.

Brown, P. C. (2005). *Involving parents in the education of their children.* Retrieved February 13, 2005, from http://www.kidsource.com/kidsource/content2/Involving_parents.html

Choi, I., Nisbett, R. E., & Norenzayan, A. (1999). Causal attribution across cultures: Variation and universality. *Psychological Bulletin, 125,* 47–63.

Correa, V. I., Jones, H. A., Thomas, C. C., & Morskink, C. V. (2005). *Interactive teaming: Enhancing programs for students with special needs.* Upper Saddle River, NJ: Prentice Hall.

Fine, M. J., & Nissenbaum, M. S. (2000). The child with disabilities and the family: Implications for professionals. In M. J. Fine & R. L. Simpson (Eds.), *Collaboration with parents and families of children with exceptionalities* (2nd ed., pp. 3–26). Austin, TX: Pro-Ed.

Fine, M. J., & Simpson, R. L. (2000). *Collaboration with parents and families of children with exceptionalities* (2nd ed.). Austin, TX: Pro-Ed.

Fuller, M. L., & Olsen, G. (1998). *Home-school relations: Working successfully with parents and families.* Boston: Allyn & Bacon.

Gollnick, D. M., & Chinn, P. C. (2002). *Multicultural education in a pluralistic society.* Upper Saddle River, NJ: Merrill.

Gray, D. E. (2002). Ten years on: A longitudinal study of families of children with autism. *Journal of Intellectual and Developmental Disability, 27,* 215–222.

Hardman, M. L., Drew, C. J., & Egan, M. W. (2006). *Human exceptionality: school, community, and family* (8th ed.). Boston: Allyn & Bacon.

Harry, B., Allen, N., & McLaughlin, M. (1995). Communication versus compliance: African-American parents' involvement in special education. *Exceptional Children, 61*(4), 364–377.

Hastings, R. P., & Taunt, H. M. (2002). Positive perceptions in families of children with developmental disabilities. *American Journal on Mental Retardation, 107,* 116–127.

Mandlawitz, M. (2003, February). *A tale of three cities: Urban perspectives on special education.* Washington, DC: Center on Education Policy.

McDonnell, J. M., Hardman, M. L., & McDonnell, A. P. (2003). *Introduction to persons with severe disabilities* (2nd ed.). Boston: Allyn & Bacon.

Poston, D., Turnbull, A., Park, J., Mannon, H., Marquis, J., & Wang, M. (2003). Family quality of life: A qualitative inquiry. *Mental Retardation, 41*(5), 313–328.

Powell, T. H., & Graham, P. L. (1996). Parent-professional participation. In National Council on Disability, *Improving the implementation of the Individuals with Disabilities Education Act: Making schools work for all of America's children* (Suppl., pp. 603–633). Washington, DC: National Council on Disability.

Romer, L. T., Richardson, M. L., Nahom, D., Aigbe, E., & Porter, A. (2002). Providing family support through community guides. *Mental Retardation, 40*(3), 191–200.

Rosen, L. (1955). Selected aspects in the development of the mother's understanding of her mentally retarded child. *American Journal of Mental Deficiency, 59,* 522.

Scherzer, A. L. (1999). Coming to an understanding: Can parents and professionals learn to be more realistic about a child's disability? *Exceptional Parent, 29*(8), 22–23.

Shin, J. Y. (2002). Social support for families of children with intellectual disabilities: Comparison between Korea and the United States. *Mental Retardation, 40*(2), 103–118.

Simmerman, S., Blacher, J., & Baker, B. L. (2001). Fathers' and mothers' perceptions of father involvement in families with young children with disabilities. *Journal of Intellectual and Developmental Disability, 26,* 325–338.

Sullivan, J. E. (2005). *Offer yourself hope when other's don't.* The Father's Network. Retrieved May 1, 2005, from http://www.fathersnetwork.org/page.php?page=641

TASH. (2005). *Resolution on services and supports in the community.* Retrieved May 11, 2005, from http://www.tash.org/resolutions/res02supports.htm

Turnbull, A. P., & Turnbull, H. R. (2001). *Families, professionals, and exceptionality: A special partnership* (4th ed.). Upper Saddle River, NJ: Prentice Hall.

U.S. Census Bureau. (2005). *American fact-finder.* Retrieved May 5, 2005, from http://factfinder.census.gov/servlet/SAFFPeople?_sse=on

Chapter 13

Social and Ethical Issues

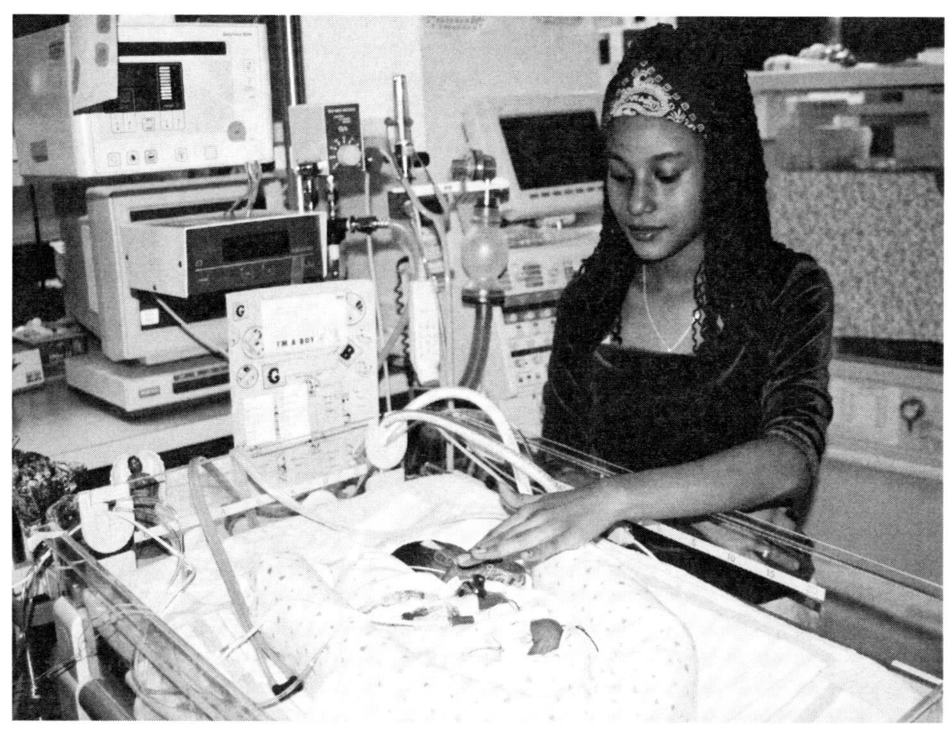

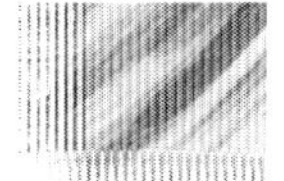

Chapter Preview

At the completion of this chapter, you will have a better understanding of:

- social and ethical dilemmas in the field of intellectual disabilities, including issues in which individual rights are balanced against the need for scientific information and the complexities of appropriate treatment.
- society's responsibility in meeting the health care, social, and educational needs of individuals with intellectual disabilities.

"Martha, Your Unborn Baby Has Down Syndrome"

Author Martha Beck wrote the book Expecting Adam, *the true story of the birth of her son, John, a child born with Down syndrome. In the following excerpt, Martha relates the telephone call she received from the health clinic with the results of her amniocentesis indicating that her unborn baby has Down syndrome.*

> *"Hello, Martha?"*
> *"Speaking." I recognized the voice.*
> *"It's Judy Trenton," she said. "From University Health Services."*
> *"Right," I said. "Hi, Judy."*
>
> *I was pleased that she had called me by my first name. Most of the clinic personnel called me Mrs. Beck, which made me feel like an aged hausfrau. I now understand that Judy's first-name familiarity was a dangerous signal, a clear sign that I should slam down the telephone receiver and run away fast.*
>
> *"I have some . . . not so good news for you," said Judy. She sounded strange, robotic. "The results from your amniocentesis are in, and they show that you are carrying a Down syndrome fetus."*
>
> *I didn't say anything. I felt as though I was falling through space. What I remember most about that moment are the details of the room: the maroon quilt on the futon, the clutter of papers on the desk, the smoke smudges on the wall. The smudges had been there ever since Food Shak burned. No matter how we scrubbed at them they won't come off.*
>
> *"Martha?" Judy Trenton's voice wasn't so dispassionate anymore. Now she sounded a little frightened.*
> *"Martha? Martha, are you there?"*
> *"I'm here," I whispered.*
>
> *Judy said something else. I don't remember what. I didn't hear her because there was someone else speaking to me at the same time—or perhaps I should say something. . .*
> *"Martha? Martha? Martha?"*
> *"Yeah."*
>
> *Judy's voice had lost its mechanical timbre. Now she sounded almost desperate. "Do you still feel the same way about . . . about not terminating*

the pregnancy?" she said. "There's still time if you want to change your mind. Not much, but there is still time."

I took a long breath. Everything I had ever striven for, every hope I'd ever hoped and dream I'd ever dreamt, seemed to be poised like a delicate Faberge egg between the tips of my fingers. (Beck, 1999, p. 182–183)

- *Upon learning that her unborn fetus has Down syndrome, Martha Beck and her husband, John, face an ethical dilemma. Should Martha have an abortion or should the pregnancy continue to full term?*
- *The answers in this dilemma are not simple. What is your viewpoint on how a decision should be reached in the difficult dilemma facing John and Martha?*

Attitudes toward and treatment of people with intellectual disabilities have always reflected the prevailing philosophies of human existence and human worth. These philosophies are the source of ethics; the rules that guide or govern conduct and define what is "good or bad."

There are periods in history in which some practices were unquestioned because they were accepted as being in harmony with the best interests of society as a whole. Contemporary civilization, however, has publicly deplored practices as euthanasia, or mercy killing, and has described them as inhumane and barbaric. At the same time, many loudly denounced actions have quietly continued. Only in the past three decades have public statements and examinations of these practices been forthcoming, breaking the silence on such social taboos. As public awareness has increased, many people have been shocked not only by the actions and conditions that exist but also by the realization that in many ways this is a hypocritical society. Our task is to progress from shock to a serious examination of fundamental values concerning what is right and important in society and to determine the most effective means to achieve the desired outcomes. Society will have to balance these considerations with the ability and willingness to expend limited resources.

BACKGROUND

Core Concept

Complex social and ethical issues that impact the lives of people with intellectual disabilities often become questions of individual versus societal rights.

It is important to explore philosophical foundations as we examine complex social and ethical issues. Our daily activities seldom include any conscious consideration of philosophy, and for some, it has become fashionable to express indifference or even unfavorable attitudes about its place in contemporary civilization. Regardless of how we define philosophy, each of us operates on the basis of some set of guiding principles that are the basis for a code of ethics governing our behavior.

Two philosophic positions frame our discussion: **utilitarianism** and **deontology.** They represent polarized viewpoints of the rights and worth of individuals. Utilitarianism is based on the premise that any action is "right" if it leads to the greatest good for the greatest number of people (Veatch, 2003). The utilitarian theory holds that the "end justifies the means." An individual has only those rights granted by the larger society. Where utilitarianism is based on consequences that lead to the greater good, deontology (derived from the Greek word for duty) suggests that some acts may be wrong and others right independent of their consequences (Beauchamp & Childress, 2001).

Neither philosophy in its purest form is workable within a society. Strictly following utilitarianism leads to a tendency for the group with the greatest power to continue in power and often to expand that power by substantially limiting the rights of those with less power. Pure deontology is also problematic. As the rights of some are maintained, the rights of others are diminished. Where on the continuum between these two extremes can a society exist comfortably? This is an enormously difficult question but one that must be seriously addressed if professionals are to ensure individual rights without unduly taxing society in general. One topic discussed in this chapter, **euthanasia,** is defined in *Merriam Webster's Collegiate Dictionary* (2005) as "the act or practice of killing or permitting the death of hopeless or injured individuals in a relatively painless way for reasons of mercy." The practice of euthanasia was dramatically brought into the public eye over three decades ago in case of Karen Ann Quinlan, a 22-year-old New Jersey woman whose life was being maintained by means of an artificial support system. For nearly a full year from the time of her admission to the hospital in April 1975, she remained comatose, her life apparently wholly sustained by a respirator and tube feeding. At the time of the New Jersey Supreme Court decision in March 1976, it was the opinion of all individuals involved that no medical procedures were available to facilitate her recovery and that termination of artificial support would result in almost immediate death. This case entered the courts because of a disagreement between Karen's family and the attending medical personnel. After much agony and soul-searching, her parents had requested that the life support system be terminated. Her physicians refused to take this action, but the courts sided with her parents. Following cessation of life support, Karen continued to survive in a comatose state. She died in June 1985, more than 10 years after she initially was admitted to the hospital.

The issues raised for Karen Ann Quinlan continued into the 21st century with the case of Terri Schiavo. In February 1990, Terri's heart stopped beating temporarily, and oxygen was cut off to her brain, causing severe brain damage and requiring that she receive sustenance through a feeding tube. Some physicians described her condition "a persistent vegetative state." During the next 15 years several court cases ensued when her husband, as legal guardian, sought to have the feeding tube removed on the basis of what he believed that Terri would have wanted. Terri did not have a living will. Ultimately, the case came down to a legal battle between her husband who sought removal of the tube and her parents who pleaded for government intervention and court action to keep the tube in tact. The feeding tube was removed under court order in April 2005 and Terri died within a few days. As was true for Karen Ann Quinlan, the question in this case was who has the decision to decide? Many people argue that this is a personal, family decision; others see it as a matter that ultimately must be decided by the courts. (See the feature Point of View: All Lives Are Equal Under the Law.)

Point of View: All Lives Are Equal Under the Law

The following point of view was written by Steven Eidleman, executive director of The ARC.

Terri Schiavo died on April 1 [2005]. Her fate was a topic of intense debate for months, and it is clear now that her death will not end the dialogue. . . . The case of Terri Schiavo raises a number of troubling questions for Americans. For people with disabilities and their families, the case represents a "slippery slope" and raises the possibility that the right to life of people with significant intellectual and/or physical disabilities might one day be questioned. . . . Today, there are thousands of people with disabilities who use feeding tubes. For them, a feeding tube is not life support or heroic intervention, but the normal way they get food and water. When they are hospitalized for any reason—however minor—they risk having their normal means of eating and drinking being classified as "extraordinary treatment" or "life support." . . .

The disability community today is troubled by the possibility that Terri Schiavo's life—and death—may cause legal protections for people who have guardians to be dismantled, making it easier for guardians to kill by withholding food and water. There must be a way to balance a person's right to expressly refuse treatment against a person's right not to be deprived of life without due process of law. Due process of law must appreciate the wishes and interests of people with disabilities, even if their lives are devalued by other people. Today, we fear that is not the case.

Terri Schiavo's wishes were not documented, and her husband and family had many conflicts. Advocates for people with disabilities would never have wished to deprive Terri Schiavo of her right to self-determination regarding the end of her life, had her wishes been documented in a living will and/or power of attorney. But they were not.

Given these ambiguities, the disability community feels that the courts should have ruled on the side of sustaining her life, not allowing her to die. The disability community, from many years of grappling with these issues, feels that in such cases, it is best to assume that life is preferable over death. This is the position of 26 national disability groups, many of which represent people like Terri Schiavo who have guardians. . . .

We must, as a society, stop using the term "persistent vegetative state." Too many people with significant disabilities have been called "vegetables," and this needs to stop. It is beyond demeaning. It is dehumanizing. In fact, some of the people who use the term most freely are doctors, and what often comes next is a discussion of the death or warehousing of the individual with such a pejorative label.

For a person with serious disabilities, the debate should not be about whether or not they are going to "get better" someday. Disability is a fact of life, every day of our lives. Millions of Americans are disabled, and for millions more, it is just a matter of time. None of us is guaranteed an able body or mind for life.

People with disabilities sometimes have wonderful lives, and sometimes they have lousy lives. They are just like other Americans. Just because a person has a significant disability does not mean that he or she does not love life. It does not mean that they should be assumed to be better off dead.

Terri Schiavo's case is every family's nightmare. But disability doesn't have to be a nightmare. Even if our nation disagrees on how we define compassion, we must certainly agree that all lives are equal under the law. (Eidelman, 2005)

The topic of euthanasia clearly warrants considerable attention. More directly related to our discussion, however, is the practice of euthanasia with individuals having intellectual disabilities. For the most part, attention has focused on euthanasia with newborns who have or appear to have intellectual disabilities at birth. This usually involves a request on the part of the parents to withhold some routine surgical or medical treatment needed for the infant to survive. If the physician agrees, the newborn usually dies. The practice of withholding treatment is far more widespread than most people realize. In the past, it was not typically open for public discussion. Nearly 30 years ago, however, Robertson (1975) characterized it as "common practice for parents to request, and for physicians to agree, not to treat" infants with birth defects (p. 214). Duff and Campbell (1973) investigated the background of 299 consecutive deaths that were recorded in a special-care nursery and found that 43 of them involved withholding of treatment. This figure represents over 14% of the sample studied. Euthanasia and withholding of treatment are topics that are now more openly discussed, although they remain controversial (Veatch, 2003). Although one's initial reaction to euthanasia may be straightforward—that it is morally wrong—unfortunately, it is not quite that simple. The issue is rife with complexities from many perspectives that we will discuss more fully later in this chapter.

A concept that plays a significant role in societal dilemmas is known as **competing equities**—that is, as the rights of some individuals are emphasized, inevitably the rights of others are diminished. The issue of competing equities enters into several treatment controversies. Some contend vigorously that it makes little sense to expend the extraordinary resources necessary to maintain life support for a terminally ill patient when resources are so badly needed by others. It is argued that valuable resources such as expensive equipment and medical talent should be deployed to generate the greatest benefit to society. People with this utilitarian viewpoint would cut the resources available for citizens who are terminally ill or aged or have intellectual disabilities.

For others with a "deontological" point of view, there is a call to maintain life support for infants who have severe disabilities at birth. This position often is based on the infants' right to life, which from the deontological perspective cannot be abridged by anyone. Competing equities are evident as one considers the potential conflict between the rights of the infants and the rights of the parents. Some have argued that the psychological, social, and economic burdens imposed by the care of a child with intellectual disabilities are so extreme that parents should have the right to choose another alternative, particularly when extraordinary life support measures are involved. Thus, the rights of parents and the rights of infants with disabilities present potentially conflicting situations without easy answers (McDonnell, Hardman, & McDonnell, 2003).

It is evident from this brief overview that there are myriad social and ethical issues that could be addressed in this chapter. The issues present complexities and controversies that defy simple solution. It is not the purpose of this chapter to present answers or to assume that one position is better than another. In most cases, the proponents on both sides are not only earnest in their viewpoints but also well armed with legitimate arguments to support their convictions.

Although many ethical issues are not limited to a given age-group, some patterns relate to different stages of the life cycle. The remainder of the chapter is organized in a life cycle format. Discussions focus on prenatal ethics and issues and those particularly relevant to early childhood, the school years, and adulthood. Certain issues, such as competing equities, transcend life cycle stages and are examined as appropriate.

ETHICAL ISSUES THROUGHOUT THE LIFE CYCLE

The Prenatal Period

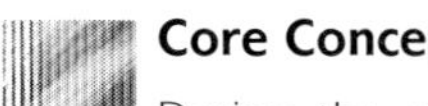

Core Concept

During the prenatal period, ethical questions focus on prevention through genetic screening and counseling as well as prenatal assessment procedures.

The prenatal period presents some uniquely difficult ethical questions. Historically, the concept of preventing or eliminating intellectual disabilities has been considered by society as laudable goal. However, the means to achieve this goal (e.g., abortion, withholding treatment, or genetic screening) have been considerably more controversial.

Genetic Screening and Counseling. Some professionals believe that genetic screening and counseling should be routine when high-risk situations exist. Others view genetic screening and counseling as interference in individual rights and freedom to reproduce by choice. These objections strike particularly sensitive chords when they relate to conditions associated with ethnic or family origins (e.g., sickle cell anemia, Tay-Sachs disease). It is understandable how such procedures could be viewed as discriminatory and aimed at reducing the reproduction of certain ethnic groups. Such an interpretation, however, goes far beyond the purpose typically defined and associated with genetic screening and counseling.

Genetic screening is a search for certain genes that are predisposed to disease, already diseased, or may lead to disease in future generations of the same family. Genetic screening involves research that examines a population in search of certain genetic characteristics that relate to disease or that may cause some disease or defect in offspring. Today, the majority of women who are pregnant undergo an ultrasound examination of their unborn baby between 16 and 24 weeks of pregnancy. The primary purpose of this examination is to ensure the unborn child is progressing normally. If this is not the case, parents may choose additional screenings and seek **genetic counseling.** Resta (2001) suggests that a genetic counselor must be able to (1) comprehend the medical facts, including the diagnosis, probable course of the disorder, and the available management; (2) appreciate the way heredity contributes to the disorder, and the risk of recurrence in specified relatives; (3) understand the alternatives for dealing with the risk of occurrence; (4) choose the course of action that seems appropriate to them in view of their risk, their family goals, and their ethical and religious standards, to act in accordance with that decision; and (5) make the best possible adjustment to the disorder in an affected family member and/or the risk of recurrence of that disorder (p. 1). The genetic counselor must be prepared to answer all questions openly and completely for the parents to become informed about the problem they face.

The fundamental purpose of screening and counseling is to ensure that parents or potential parents are thoroughly informed about the genetic disorder. It is not the counselor's task to make a decision for them. If this purpose is adhered to, the argument of discrimination and interference with individual rights is largely disarmed. It would seem that parents are even better prepared to exercise their rights if they are fully aware of the potential outcomes and options. As with most emotionally charged issues, however, this point of view does not prevent some from continuing to put forth arguments against **genetic screening** and counseling.

Prenatal Assessments. There are many procedures available for prenatal screening, including **amniocentesis, chorion biopsy, fetoscopy,** and **ultrasonography.** Each procedure brings the potential for an ethical dilemma. For example, if the assessment indicates that the fetus either has or is likely to have a defect, one alternative is abortion. Perhaps no single topic receiving public attention is as controversial as abortion. Some people argue vigorously that abortion is murder. This notion is based on the view that human life exists from the time of conception or shortly thereafter. On the other side of the issue are those who maintain that abortion should be an option for any woman under any circumstances. This viewpoint is based on the proposition that a woman has the right to be in control of her body and that being forced to continue an unwanted pregnancy violates that right.

When abortion is approached in relation to disabilities, however, perspectives may change. Some people hold fast to their blanket opposition to abortion, but their numbers are fewer when a fetus with a disability is at issue. Some who do not favor abortion by virtue of religious or personal philosophy are ready to accept it in the context of disabling conditions. In many cases, this shift in perspective is not limited to intellectual disabilities but applies to any disabling condition.

Those who support the option of aborting a fetus with a disability argue that the quality of life for such an individual is likely to be so diminished that no one would choose to live under such circumstances. Furthermore, the family may face immediate and continuing financial, psychological, and social burdens that are extreme and detrimental (McDonnell et al., 2003). As such, parents should have the option to decide. The opposing view counters with the right of the unborn fetus to life regardless of the consequences for others.

This dilemma is irreconcilable because the disagreement is so fundamental. Society is faced with competing equities that probably cannot be resolved to the satisfaction of both sides. More important, the conflict presents a very difficult dilemma for parents.

The Early Years

Ethical issues during the early childhood years (birth to 5 years of age) may involve agonizing dilemmas that have no easy or simple solutions. Each developmental period is critical to a child's overall growth. The neonatal period (the first 2 months after birth) is often described as the most dangerous time in a person's life. During this period, infants who are diagnosed as having intellectual disabilities may be vulnerable to euthanasia and the withholding of medical treatment.

Core Concept

During the early years, ethical dilemmas are troubling to many because they often deal with the life or death of a child with intellectual disabilities.

Euthanasia and the Withholding of Medical Treatment. The differing viewpoints on abortion, discussed earlier in this chapter, continue into the early years with dilemmas associated with euthanasia and the withholding of medical treatment. For most situations, the decision is whether to prolong life rather than perform euthanasia. The two concepts have different meanings that are important from legal and moral standpoints. Euthanasia suggests mercy killing, or the beneficent termination of a life that might otherwise continue. Failure to prolong life suggests not artificially extending life that would naturally end. These differences, though subtle, clearly become part of the controversy.

From a legal standpoint, the distinction between euthanasia and the decision not to prolong life is the difference between acts and omissions. Euthanasia involves the act of terminating a life that would continue if the act were not committed. Not to prolong life, however, involves omission—the physician, by failing to act, permits death to occur.

As we examine our values on euthanasia and the withholding of medical treatment, several questions emerge. How are such decisions made? Who makes such decisions and under what circumstances? For whom are these decisions made? As suggested by Boyle (2001),

> Any discussion of these issues must recognize the tragedy that underlies these situations: the loss of newborn life, the short-term and long-term health problems of survivors, the disabilities that many infants will face, and the emotional cost to families and clinicians. . . . The decisions are often very difficult. However, we should be extremely concerned if the discussion ever becomes routine or we are comfortable with all the decisions. (p. 36)

In most cases, the debate on ethical dilemmas focuses on infants with severe disabilities evident at birth. However, the term "severe" may be broadly defined and is subject to differing interpretations. How do these differing interpretations translate to the real world? The classic Johns Hopkins case of the 1970s helps illustrate.

In the Johns Hopkins case, substantial debate transpired over the severity of an infant's disability. The incident occurred at Johns Hopkins Hospital with a 2-day-old full-term male infant who had facial characteristics and other features suggesting Down syndrome. No cardiac abnormalities were evident, but the infant began vomiting shortly after birth. X-ray examination indicated duodenal atresia (a congenital absence or closure of a portion of the duodenum). This condition can be surgically corrected with negligible risk. The infant reportedly had no additional complicating factors other than Down syndrome. Is Down syndrome an example of a severe disabling condition? Some would answer with a resounding yes. Others would not, noting a wide range of capabilities for children with Down syndrome. After discussion with the parents, surgical correction of the duodenal atresia was not performed and all feeding and fluids were discontinued. Fifteen days later, the infant died of starvation and dehydration.

Many ethical issues are raised by the Johns Hopkins case. One can question the humaneness of permitting an infant to starve to death over a 15-day period. This is a particularly difficult question because the decision not to operate made it impossible for the infant to receive food and fluids in a normal manner. However, the issue concerning the degree of disability represented by Down syndrome is equally troubling. It is highly questionable whether Down syndrome can be described as a terrible or tragic disability.

Table 13–1
Resolutions on the Withholding of Medical Treatment from Infants with Intellectual Disabilities

AAMR and The ARC	TASH
People with [intellectual disabilities] . . . must have dependable, high quality health care in the community and affordable, comprehensive health insurance.	All people, regardless of their disabilities, have a right to life, liberty, and protection from treatment that causes pain or death. TASH strongly opposes the position that it would be in the best interest of any person to die rather than live with a disability.
Disability must not be a factor in the decision to provide, delay, or withhold treatments or to provide or receive organ transplants. The person's medical condition and welfare must be the basis for the decision.	TASH strongly opposes any cessation of nutrition or hydration for people regardless of the severity of their disabilities.
Treatment must be high quality and not denied on the basis of [intellectual disabilities].	

Sources: The American Association on Mental Retardation (2005); The ARC (2005); TASH (2005a).

Several national organizations (The ARC, the AAMR, and TASH) have strongly opposed the withholding of medical treatment when the decision is based on the individual having disabilities. These organizations hold that everyone is entitled to the right to life, and society has an obligation to protect people from the ignorance and prejudices that may be associated with disability. See Table 13–1 for more information on each organization's position regarding the withholding of medical treatment from infants with intellectual disabilities.

Withholding Treatment and Issues of Informed Consent. The questions surrounding who makes life-and-death decisions, and under what circumstances are not easily answered. Adult status gives each individual the right to be fully informed about proposed medical treatment. It is generally agreed that adults have the legal right to accept or reject any treatment. However, when the patient is a minor or not judged to be mentally competent, the decision process is vastly altered. In the case of infants with disabilities, parents have the right to **informed consent** but do not have sole decision-making prerogatives (Gelfand & Drew, 2003; McDonnell et al., 2003). When the parents' decision is at odds with the physician's, it is subject to legal review.

The act of consent is not simple. Although consent has specific meanings in a variety of contexts, the ramifications of consent often require legal interpretation. Three elements of informed consent must be considered: capacity, information, and voluntariness. For the most part, these elements must be present for effective consent. It is also important to realize that consent is seldom, if ever, permanent and

Consent is never a simple matter and presents parents with some very difficult issues.

may be withdrawn at almost any time (Dinerstein, Herr, Phil, & O'Sullivan, 1999; Turnbull, 1978).

Capacity is defined in terms of three factors: (a) the person's age, (b) the person's competence, and (c) the particular situation. A person under the age of majority (generally 18 years) is legally incompetent to make certain decisions. Likewise, it is clear that an infant does not have the developed mental competence to understand and give consent. Thus, in terms of capacity, the parents or legal guardians have the authority to consent for an infant.

The *information* provided to parents must also receive careful consideration.

> The focus is on "what" information is given and "how" it is given since it must be effectively communicated (given and received) to be acted upon. The concern is with the fullness and effectiveness of the disclosure: is it designed to be fully understood, and is it fully understood? The burden of satisfying these two tests rests on the professional. (Turnbull, p. 8)

Clearly, the giving or withholding of consent rests primarily with the parents, but such decisions are the joint responsibility of parents and medical personnel. For effective information to be present, the physician must ensure that the information about the infant's condition is fully understood.

Voluntariness may appear to be a straightforward concept. However, subtle influences in the process of giving or withholding consent make it far from simple. The person must give consent of his or her own free will, without pressure or coercion of any form from others. This requirement places even greater responsibilities on the physician. Information must be complete and without explicit or implicit inclusion of personal judgment. This guideline may be particularly difficult because physicians typically are viewed as authority figures by the lay public, and they certainly are not without their own feelings or beliefs in such situations. It also may be that parents are highly vulnerable to persuasion immediately after the birth of an infant with a disability.

Decisions regarding withholding treatment from infants with disabilities are extremely complex and controversial. Perhaps nowhere is the concept of competing equities so evident. The rights of the infant and the rights of the parents may be in direct conflict. Such conflict is not new to those who work with children who have intellectual disabilities and their families. What may be unique is the stark realization that the decisions being made involve a degree of gravity that is totally unfamiliar to most people.

The School Years

Ensuring a Free and Appropriate Education. The Individuals with Disabilities Education Act (IDEA) requires that every eligible student with a disability receive a free and appropriate public education (FAPE). Although the term *appropriate education* is at the heart of this federal legislation, its specific meaning has been open to legal and moral interpretation. A major interpretation of FAPE was handed down by the U.S. Supreme Court in *Hendrick Hudson District Board of Education v. Rowley* in 1982. The Supreme Court declared that an appropriate education consists of "specially designed instruction and related services" that are "individually designed" to provide "educational benefit." Often referred to as the "some educational benefit" standard, the ruling mandates that a state need not provide an ideal education but must provide a beneficial one for students with disabilities. Although the Supreme Court provided some guidance on FAPE, the question of what constitutes "educational benefit" for each child remains an issue of contention for parents and schools.

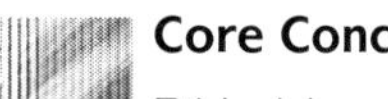

Core Concept

Ethical issues during the school years may focus on the right to a free and appropriate public education (FAPE), the use of aversive procedures in changing behavior, and informed parental consent.

Since its passage, IDEA has been primarily focused on "access to education" rather than improving results for students with disabilities. The focus on "access" has lead to a disproportionate emphasis on what is referred to as "paper compliance," in which resources are concentrated more on making a child's program look appropriate on paper than on ensuring effective instruction. Paper compliance has detracted from the effectiveness of instruction, the fundamental purpose of the legislation. However, one can understand some of the reasons why it occurs. For the most part, schools have not been well equipped to implement IDEA on a widespread basis. It is broad legislation, which, if interpreted and implemented as intended, would require significant resources in most school districts. The law is a prescriptive piece of federal legislation that from the viewpoint of many school administrators is being imposed on them without adequate funding. This perspective also reflects the

Table 13–2
TASH Resolutions on Positive Behavior Support and the Use of Aversive Procedures

Positive Behavior Support	The Use of Aversive Procedures
• Educational and other support services applied in situations involving problem behavior must: 1. be developed in collaboration with the individual in a respectful and culturally sensitive manner that facilitates self-determination; 2. be based on a functional behavioral assessment of the internal and external variables that may be affecting the person's behavior; and 3. use the findings of [behavioral be effective attempt to identify the assessments] to develop constructive and comprehensive approaches to assist the individual to address the circumstances that adversely affect his or her behavior.	• Although it has been believed that [aversive] procedures are necessary to control dangerous or disruptive behaviors, it has now been irrefutably proven that a wide range of methods are available which are not only more effective in managing dangerous or disruptive behaviors, but which do not inflict pain on, humiliate, dehumanize or overly control or manipulate individuals with disabilities. • Alternative approaches that are proven to individual's purposes in behaving as he or she does and offer support and education to replace dangerous or disruptive behaviors with alternative behaviors that are positive and will achieve the individual's needs.
• Supports should be provided in a manner that maximizes access to, and participation in, the full range of typical home, school, and community settings, in order to maximize the individual's personal well being.	• [All] persons with disabilities [have the right] to freedom from overly restrictive procedures and from aversive or coercive procedures of any kind.

Source: TASH (2005b, 2005c).

concern that the law dictates how education will be conducted at the state and local levels. IDEA continues to raise questions about federal intervention in states' rights.

Using Aversive Procedures to Change Behavior. Behavioral principles have long been employed to achieve educational progress with children who have intellectual disabilities. In some cases, application of such principles has involved the use of punishment or aversive consequences to change inappropriate behavior. Such techniques have received considerable attention as being both unethical and unnecessary (TASH, 2005b). See Table 13–2.

Aversive procedures are viewed by many professionals and parents as restrictive because they do not use contingencies that exist in natural settings. This makes it difficult for the individual with intellectual disabilities to generalize behavior learned to more community settings. Thus, questions also arise concerning generalization and effectiveness of instruction, further highlighting the questionable use of aversive techniques. A variety of positive approaches to behavioral support have been demonstrated as effective alternatives in recent years as concern has emerged regarding the ethics of aversive treatments (Eber, Sugai, Smith, & Scott, 2002; Horner, Albin, Sprague, & Todd, 2000). See Table 13–2.

Ensuring Informed Parental Consent. IDEA grants parents several rights to ensure their involvement in the education of the child with an intellectual disability. These include, but are not limited to, consenting to (a) an initial evaluation that could lead to the provision of special education services, (b) the child's individualized education program, and (c) a change in educational placement.

Parental consent must include the three elements of capacity, information, and voluntariness. Consent is seldom, if ever, permanent and may be withdrawn at nearly any time. One element of consent that may be altered somewhat in the context of the school years is "capacity." Legally, the capacity to consent rests with the parents and not the child. Good practice, however, would suggest that a blanket assumption of incapacity throughout the school years may not be in the child's best interest. Specifically, adolescents with intellectual disabilities may be quite capable of participating in the consent process. Depending on the situation, adolescents may be able to give consent directly or concurrently with a third party, such as the parents. The burden of obtaining informed consent rests heavily with the professional, a situation that may create a certain amount of discomfort but that must prevail if the rights of individuals with intellectual disabilities are to be adequately protected.

The Adult Years

Core Concept

Ethical issues during the adult years often focus on the right of the individual to marry and have children.

The emergence of ethical issues during the adult years is not surprising. Questions of marriage, reproduction, and sterilization become considerations during this time in life. As with the other issues discussed in this chapter, these topics are highly controversial.

Sterilization. Controversy surrounding sterilization has existed throughout history. One way to approaching this issue is to examine how and why people with intellectual disabilities are treated differently from nondisabled individuals. Historically, several arguments have been used to justify the sterilization of people with intellectual disabilities (Brown, 2002; Hardman, Drew, & Egan, 2006). For the most part, these arguments can be summarized in the following paragraph.

Sterilization is in the best interests of all concerned, including the person with intellectual disabilities, their family, and society as a whole. There is also, however, strong opposition to sterilization, including concerns about (a) the potential misuse of legal authority to sterilize, (b) the rights of the individual with intellectual disabilities, and (c) the manner in which the process is undertaken. Each of these presents serious societal and legal issues that warrant further examination.

Sterilization advocates claim that the practice is in the best interest of society. This proposition exemplifies, perhaps more clearly than any other issue, utilitarian versus deontological philosophical positions. As advocated by proponents to sterilization, one benefit to society involves preventing disabilities. Sterilization would decrease the number of individuals requiring extra services from society and would lessen the cost burden for such care on taxpayers. This argument is clearly utilitarian; such savings, if they were to occur, could be redirected to societal needs perceived as having a greater return in investment.

From a practical perspective, the view that sterilization would prevent intellectual disabilities doesn't appear to hold true. If sterilization is viewed as preventing only the transmission of inferior or damaged genetic material, the reduction in incidence is quite minimal. Intellectual disabilities that can be attributed directly to genetic causation represent a very small proportion of all cases. Environment plays a significant role in the etiology of intellectual disabilities. Furthermore, those individuals whose intellectual disabilities can be attributed to genetic causes are more likely to be functioning at lower levels and significantly less likely to bear children.

Sterilization advocates argue that society must be willing to set aside the right of the individual to have children in order to preserve the greater good. Yet, the importance of the right to have children has been noted in legal interpretations of the Constitution. For example, in 1921, the Michigan attorney general issued an opinion, based on the Constitution, that held that the right to have and retain the power of procreation was second only to the right to life itself. It is generally accepted that such a fundamental individual right can be abrogated only on a voluntary basis by the individual involved. Given this fundamental right to have children, how have compulsory sterilization laws come to exist in some states? Obviously, in these situations the state deemed that its interests superseded the rights of people with intellectual disabilities.

The competence of the individual with intellectual disabilities is also an issue in regard to sterilization. The basic question is whether an adult with intellectual disabilities has the mental competence to understand sterilization and its implications. This question is unanswerable in a general sense. It is more logical to consider each case individually, depending on the person's level of functioning.

In regard to consent for sterilization, it seems logical that parents or legal guardians would consider such decisions in cases where the person with intellectual disabilities was deemed by the courts not competent to make such a decision. The assumption is that these individuals have in mind the best interests of the person with intellectual disabilities. Yet, the tendency has been for the courts to intervene and review parental decisions regarding consent for sterilization. The courts want to ensure that each individual's best interests are protected and is the sole determining factor influencing the decision to sterilize. This presents a difficult dilemma, one that makes the consent process extremely complicated. To ensure objectivity, the court must hear information and arguments on both sides. This duality requires that advocates for both sides are present in court and be equally informed and articulate. It further requires that the arguments include all relevant information, and that the information presented be limited to the issues pertaining to the best interests of the individual.

This brief discussion represents only a small subset of the complex issues related to consent for sterilization. The discussion demonstrates how issues can become extremely complicated as attempts are made to protect individual rights. It also raises

Courts continue to play important roles in the lives of those with intellectual disabilities.

other social questions that are not easily answered: Do the parents' rights and interests have no value? What about the interests of the state? Competing equities take center stage in situations in which the rights and interests of all parties are not in harmony.

Marriage. In the United States, many states still have laws restricting the right of people with intellectual disabilities to marry (Pietrzak, 1997). Why do such laws still exist? Are they aimed at the protection of the individual, or are they for the protection of society? From a historical perspective, Wolfensberger (1975) discussed restrictive marriage laws as a means for society to prevent intellectual disabilities. Credence for the perception certainly arises from the widespread negative attitudes toward sexual expression and marriage among people with intellectual disabilities. Wolfensberger cited an 1895 bill passed by the Connecticut House of Representatives:

> Every man who shall carnally know any female under the age of forty-five years who is epileptic, imbecile, feeble-minded, or a pauper, shall be imprisoned in the State prison not less than three years. Every man who is epileptic who shall carnally know any female under the age of forty-five years, and every female under the age of forty-five years who shall consent to be carnally known by any man who is epileptic, imbecile, or feeble-minded, shall be imprisoned in the State prison not less than three years. (p. 40)

Historically, it does seem that society's interests have been paramount. Some of these old laws remain on the books today. Are current laws merely more carefully disguised attempts to protect the best interests of society, or are they really aimed at achieving some balance between the rights of individuals and the greater good? Strong arguments can be made on both sides, and some limited research related to the topic appears periodically (e.g., Reiss, 2001).

Core Concept

Research and professional ethics in intellectual disabilities involve a wide variety of issues in which individual rights must be balanced against the need for scientific information and the complexities of appropriate treatment.

RESEARCH AND PROFESSIONAL ETHICS

Research is important to further our understanding of people with intellectual disabilities in family, school, and community contexts. However, research also raises many concerns regarding confidentiality, invasion of privacy, and risk. A careful balance must be struck between an investigator's need to probe and the subject's right to be protected. For these people, special care must be taken in the areas of consent, privacy, and harm. Likewise, issues of deception (e.g., explicit lying to subjects as well as omitting details about the study) remain controversial in intellectual disabilities, as they do in all behavioral sciences (Krathwohl, 2004). Certain medications and other treatments inherently pose some risk, and inappropriate applications may be harmful. All these considerations make research on intellectual disabilities challenging. Such safeguards as institutional review boards (sometimes referred to as human subjects committees) used by universities and other agencies to monitor research are vital to protecting subjects and to maintaining a balance between the needs of scientists and subjects' rights. Likewise, many professional associations and societies have ethics committees and codes of ethics to guide their members.

Research is not the only area in which professional ethics comes into play in the field of intellectual disabilities. Schools, health care centers, and other agencies must be careful to administer the most effective interventions possible while simultaneously remaining conscious of the rights of people with intellectual disabilities. In some cases, the intervention may involve some risk, as is the case with

Tips for Professionals

A Code of Ethics for Special Educators

Special education professionals:

- are committed to developing the highest educational and quality of life potential of individuals with exceptionalities.
- promote and maintain a high level of competence and integrity in practicing their profession.
- engage in professional activities which benefit individuals with exceptionalities, their families, other colleagues, students, or research subjects.
- exercise objective professional judgment in the practice of their profession.
- strive to advance their knowledge and skills regarding the education of individuals with exceptionalities.
- work within the standards and policies of their profession.
- seek to uphold and improve where necessary the laws, regulations, and policies governing the delivery of special education and related services and the practice of their profession.
- do not condone or participate in unethical or illegal acts, nor violate professional standards.

Source: Council for Exceptional Children (2005).

some medications. Once again, people with intellectual disabilities are at risk and more vulnerable than others who are not disabled. It is vital that professionals be adequately trained and qualified to deliver instruction or an intervention being employed. It is essential that government agencies, as well as professional associations, remain vigilant to ensure the well-being of people with intellectual disabilities by closely adhering to a code of professional ethics. (See the Tips for Professionals feature.)

NEW ISSUES AND FUTURE DIRECTIONS

Earlier chapters in this book examined the beginning of the life span in terms of normal development and the spectrum of intellectual disabilities. Society is faced with many ethical dilemmas in this early phase of the life cycle, including abortion, euthanasia, and withholding of treatment. More than three decades since the U.S. Supreme Court decision in *Roe v. Wade*, abortion remains a volatile, controversial social question that continues to appear in the news and in the courts. It will continue to do so in the future, as will issues surrounding the withholding of medical treatment from seriously ill newborns.

Advances in medical technology are constantly presenting new and equally controversial topics for the early phase of the life cycle. Geneticists are rapidly developing the capability to determine many aspects of a person's genetic makeup through genetic engineering. This capability holds great potential for the prevention of conditions that have known genetic causes. However, genetic engineering also raises serious questions. To what degree is society ready to have some people determine the genetic makeup of others? Genetic engineering will clearly raise new ethical issues (see Human Genome Project, 2005).

The final phase of the life cycle will also present challenging issues for professionals in the field of intellectual disabilities. More than ever before, people with intellectual disabilities are living longer and becoming part of the growing senior population. Questions about how society will care for these individuals and what their lives will be like in the community are being raised more than ever before (see Gettings, 2001). Quality of life issues and dying with dignity are becoming more visible within society, testing our ability to better understand the complete cycle of human development. As those with intellectual disabilities are included more fully into society, questions arise regarding how to provide the services and supports needed to ensure their participation in family, school, and community life.

Core Questions

1. How do utilitarianism and deontology philosophies contribute to our understanding of the rights of people with intellectual disabilities?
2. Discuss the concept of "competing equities." How does it apply to people with intellectual disabilities?

3. What is the role of genetic counseling in the prevention of intellectual disabilities? Abortion?
4. Selective withholding of medical treatment for infants with intellectual disabilities remains in practice even today. Who should make these judgments about such life-and-death decisions?
5. Special education for children with intellectual disabilities often costs more than educational services for their peers who are not disabled. To what degree, if any, do you think parents of children without disabilities should be held responsible for the increased costs of educating children having intellectual disabilities? What is the basis of your view?
6. Sterilization of adults with intellectual disabilities is often justified on the basis of the general welfare of society and the state. How might the best interests of the state and those of the individual be in conflict? Whose interests should prevail? Why?
7. How did early marriage laws place society's interests above those of the individual with intellectual disabilities? Has this changed? Explain your reasoning.
8. How does the interdisciplinary nature of the study of intellectual disabilities contribute to professional ethical dilemmas?

Roundtable Discussion

Ethical dilemmas are often reduced to the fundamental question of individual versus societal rights embodied in utilitarianism and deontological philosophies. These perspectives are found throughout the study of intellectual disabilities. In your study group or on your own, examine the study of intellectual disabilities, considering both individual and societal interests. Think in terms of prevention of intellectual disabilities, abortion, withholding of treatment, provision of services and supports, sterilization, and research. What is your philosophical view? Does your position shift, depending on age of the person with intellectual disabilities or the severity of their condition? Do you feel comfortable with your position(s)? Why?

Parent and Professional Organization Positions on Key Issues in the Lives of People with Intellectual Disabilities

The inside front cover of this text presents a matrix that includes nine key issues in the lives of people with disabilities, the positions of various parent and professional organizations on each issue, and the chapter and page number where the information is addressed. Table 13–3 is a summary of the organizations and key issues addressed in this chapter.

Table 13–3
Key Issues and Organizations Discussed in This Chapter

Organization/Website	Key Issues Addressed	Chapter Heading
American Association on Mental Retardation (http://www.aamr.org)	Bioethics Quality of life	Euthanasia and the Withholding of Medical Treatment
The ARC, a national organization on intellectual disabilities (http://www.thearc.org)	Bioethics Quality of life	Euthanasia and the Withholding of Medical Treatment
TASH, an international association of people with disabilities, their family members, and professionals (http://www.tash.org)	Bioethics Quality of life Bioethics Quality of life	Euthanasia and the Withholding of Medical Treatment Using Aversive Procedures to Change Behavior

References

American Association on Mental Retardation. (2005). *Policy statement on family support.* Retrieved May 10, 2005, from http://www.aamr.org/Policies/pos_healthcare.shtml

The Arc. (2005). *Position statement on health care.* Retrieved May 10, 2005, from http://www.thearc.org/posits/healthcarepos.doc

Beauchamp, T. L., & Childress, J. E. (2001). *Principles of biomedical ethics* (5th ed.). Oxford: Oxford University Press.

Beck, M. (1999). *Expecting Adam.* New York: Times Books.

Boyle, R. J. (2001). Ethics in the neonatal intensive care unit and beyond. *Infants and Young Children, 13*(3), 3–46.

Brown, A. J. (2002, June). Informed consent key to sterilization of mentally retarded. *MassPsych.com, 10*(5). Retrieved from http://www.masspsy.com/columnists/brown_9910.html

Council for Exceptional Children. (2005). *CEC Code of Ethics for educators of persons with exceptionalities.* Retrieved May 14, 2005, from http://www.cec.sped.org/ps/ps-ethic.html

Dinerstein, R. D., Herr, S. S., Phil, D., & O'Sullivan, J. L. (1999). *A guide to consent.* Washington, DC: American Association on Mental Retardation.

Duff, R., & Campbell, A. (1973). Moral and ethical dilemmas in the special-care nursery. *New England Journal of Medicine, 289,* 890–894.

Eber, L., Sugai, G., Smith, C., & Scott, T. (2002). Wraparound and positive behavioral interventions and supports in the schools. *Journal of Emotional and Behavioral Disorders, 10,* 171–180.

Eidelman, S. (2005). *All lives are equal under the law.* Retrieved May 3, 2005, from http://www.aapd-dc.org/News/Schiavo/watchSchiavo.html#opinion

Gelfand, D. M., & Drew, C. J. (2003). *Understanding child behavior disorders* (4th ed.). Belmont, CA: Wadsworth.

Gettings, R. M. (2001). Renegotiating the social contract: Rights, responsibilities, and risk for individuals with mild cognitive limitations. In A. J. Tymchuk, K. C. Lakin, & R. Luckasson (Eds.), *The forgotten generation: The status and challenges of adults with mild cognitive limitations* (pp. 39–54). Baltimore: Paul H. Brookes.

Hardman, M. L., Drew, C. J., & Egan, M. W. (2006). *Human exceptionality: School, community, and family* (8th ed.). Boston: Allyn & Bacon.

Horner, R. H., Albin, R. W., Sprague, J. R., & Todd, A. W. (2000). Positive behavior support. In M. E. Snell & F. Brown (Eds.), *Instruction of students with severe disabilities* (pp. 207–243). Upper Saddle River, NJ: Merrill.

Human Genome Project. (2005). *Human Genome Project Information*. U.S. Department of Energy Office of Science. Retrieved May 15, 2005, from http://www.ornl.gov/sci/techresources/Human_Genome/home.shtml

Krathwohl, D. R. (2004). *Methods of educational and social science research: An integrated approach* (2nd ed.). Long Grove, IL: Waveland Press.

McDonnell, J., Hardman, M., & McDonnell, A. (2003). *Introduction to people with severe disabilities* (2nd ed.). Boston: Allyn & Bacon.

Merriam Webster's Collegiate Dictionary. (2005). Retrieved May 9, 2005, from http://www.mirriam-webster.com/

Pietrzak, P. (1997). Marriage laws and people with mental retardation: A continuing history of second class treatment. *The Institute of Law, Psychiatry and Public Policy—The University of Virginia, 17*(1 & 2). Retrieved May 16, 2005, from http://www.ilppp. virginia.edu/DMHL/Issues/brookv17.html

Reiss, S. (2001). People with a dual diagnosis: America's powerless population. In A. J. Tymchuk, K. C. Lakin, & R. Luckasson (Eds.), *The forgotten generation: The status and challenges of adults with mild cognitive limitations* (pp. 275–298). Baltimore: Paul H. Brookes.

Resta, R. G. (2001). *Genetic counseling: Coping with the human impact of genetic disease*. Access Excellence: The National Health Museum (U.S. Department of Health and Human Services, Public Health Services, National Institutes of Health, National Cancer Institute). Retrieved from http://www.accessexcellence.org/AE/AEC/CC/counseling_background.html

Robertson, J. A. (1975). Involuntary euthanasia of defective newborns: A legal analysis. *Stanford Law Review, 27*, 213–269.

TASH (2005a). *Resolution on nutrition and hydration*. Retrieved May 11, 2005, from http://www.tash.org/resolutions/ res02nutrition.htm

TASH (2005b). *Resolution on positive behavioral supports*. Retrieved May 13, 2005, from http://www.tash.org/resolutions/res02behavior.htm

TASH (2005c). *Resolution opposing the use of aversive and restrictive procedures*. Retrieved May 13, 2005, from http://www.tash.org/resolutions/res02aversive.htm

Turnbull, H. R. (Ed.). (1978). *Consent handbook*. Washington, DC: American Association on Mental Deficiency.

Veatch, R. M. (2003). *The basics of bioethics* (2nd ed.). Upper Saddle River, NJ: Prentice Hall.

Wolfensberger, W. (1975). *The origin and nature of our institutional models*. Syracuse, NY: Human Policy.

Glossary

Accommodation. A term used by Jean Piaget to describe the adaptation of an individual to the environment as he or she develops intellectually.

Adaptive fit. Compatibility between demands of a task or setting and a person's needs and abilities.

Adaptive skill development. The ability (or lack thereof) to apply basic information learned in school to naturally occurring daily activities.

Amblyopia. A condition in a child who is unable to see a single object when looking at it with both eyes (binocularity).

Americans with Disabilities Act. A federal law mandating that barriers of discrimination against people with disabilities in private-sector employment, all public services, and public accommodations, transportation, and telecommunications be eliminated.

Amniocentesis. A prenatal assessment of a fetus that involves analysis of amniotic fluid to screen for possible abnormalities.

Assimilation. A term used by Jean Piaget to describe an individual's modification of the environment to fit his or her perceptions during intellectual development.

Assistive technology. Any item, piece of equipment, or product system that can be used to increase, maintain, or improve the functional capabilities of students with disabilities.

Augmentative communication. Adapting existing vocal or gestural abilities into meaningful communication; teaching manual signing, static symbols, or icons; and using manual or electronic communication devices.

Blissymbols. A rebus system developed by C.K. Bliss that ties a specific symbol to a word. There are four types of Blissymbols: pictographic, ideographic, relational, and abstract.

Career education. An educational process that focuses on the life roles for individuals as students, workers, consumers, family members, and citizens.

Cephalocaudal developmental trend. A developmental trend where the fetus develops more rapidly in the head area "(*cephalo-*)" first, with maturation in the lower extremities "(*caudal*)," or "tail," following.

Chorion biopsy. A diagnostic procedure for pregnant women to determine whether the fetus has chromosomal anomalies. It involves collecting a small sample of chorion cells for karyotyping.

Community-based training. Training that focuses directly on the activities to be accomplished in the community work setting rather than on the development of skills in the classroom. Consequently, goals and objectives develop from the demands of the work setting considered in conjunction with the functioning level of the individual.

Consulting teacher. A special education professional who provides assistance to the general education classroom teacher or the child while the child remains in the general education classroom. This specialist may help a teacher identify the child's specific problem areas and recommend appropriate assessment techniques and educational strategies.

Continuum of placements. As per federal law (IDEA), educational placements for students with disabilities ranging from general education classrooms with support services to homebound and hospital programs.

Cranial nerves. Distinct neural pathways that provide for the specialized sensory function and motor performance of the sensory and other essential organs and surrounding muscle structure.

Criterion-referenced assessment. A model of assessment that does not place the individual's performance in comparative context with either other students or a normative standard. Such assessment focuses on specific skills and looks at absolute level of performance.

Cross-sectional studies. Investigations that sample subjects from several age levels to compare behaviors at different ages.

Curriculum-based assessment. A model of evaluation that uses the objectives of the student's curriculum as the referent or criterion for evaluating progress. The objectives associated with the curricular activities represent the standard for success as the youngster's performance is assessed.

Deontology. A philosophy based on the premise that some acts may be wrong and others right independent of their consequences. As the rights of some are maintained, the rights of others are diminished.

Down syndrome. A condition resulting from a chromosomal abnormality that results in unique physical characteristics and varying degrees of intellectual disabilities.

Erythroblastosis fetalis. A blood incompatibility condition between mother and unborn baby where the mother has a negative Rh blood factor and the infant a positive Rh factor. The mother develops antibodies that destroy the infant's blood cells, leading to serious consequences during fetal life and the neonatal period.

Euthanasia. The act or practice of killing or permitting the death of hopeless or injured individuals in a relatively painless way for reasons of mercy.

Family systems perspective. Counseling services and family training programs that focus on the relationships and interactions between and among the members.

Fetal alcohol effect. A condition in which the fetus is injured by maternal alcohol consumption. This involves less severe damage than found in fetal alcohol syndrome but developmental problems are clearly evident.

Fetal alcohol syndrome. An alcohol-induced fetal injury resulting from alcohol consumption by the mother during pregnancy.

Fetoscopy. A procedure for examining the unborn baby using a needlelike camera that is inserted into the womb to video scan the fetus for visible abnormalities.

Formal supports. Government-funded services that support the education of students with intellectual disabilities. Formal supports may include qualified general and special education teachers, paraprofessionals, appropriate multilevel instructional materials, and technology aids.

Formative evaluation. An evaluation framework where assessment focuses on the next step in an instructional program rather than a desired ultimate behavior.

Full inclusion. All instruction and support services come to the student with intellectual disabilities; the student is not pulled out of the general education class into a special education program.

Functional reading. Reading that involves learning a protective or survival vocabulary.

Galactosemia. An inherited metabolic disorder in which galactose accumulates in the blood because of deficiency of an enzymes catalyzing its conversion to glucose.

Generalization. The ability to apply learning from previous experiences to new situations with similar components.

Genetic counseling. Counseling to ensure that parents or potential parents are thoroughly informed regarding possible genetic disorders in their unborn or new born child. A counselor's role is to inform the parents and not to make a decision or coerce them in any way.

Genetic screening. A search for certain genes that are predisposed to disease, already diseased, or may lead to disease in future generations of the same family.

Genotype. Refers to the genetic message makeup of an individual; genotype is established at conception by the combining of sperm and ovum.

Gestational age. A measure of fetal maturity that begins at the time from conception. For example, a baby born prior to gestational age of about 35 to 37 weeks is preterm.

Growth matrix. The result of interactions between heredity and environment. The growth matrix is more than a simple combination of phenotype and genotype. The growth matrix changes as interactions occur between the organism and its environment.

Hydrocephalus. A condition characterized by exceptionally large head size.

IDEA (Individuals with Disabilities Education Act). A federal law mandating that all eligible children with disabilities in the nation's schools be provided a *first and appropriate* public education. IDEA requires that these students, regardless of the extent or type of disability, receive at public expense the special education and related services necessary to meet their individual needs.

Inclusion. An educational placement approach for children with disabilities that involves educating a significant number of such children in general education classrooms.

Inclusive education. Participation and support that the student with intellectual disabilities receives in the general educational setting.

Information-processing theories. How a person processes information from sensory stimuli to motor output.

Informed consent. Consent given that contains the critical elements of capacity (competence of the individual to make a decision), information (designed to be fully understood and asking whether it is fully understood), and voluntariness (without pressure or coercion of any form).

Intelligence quotient (IQ). A summary of a person's intellectual capacity originally derived by dividing an individual's mental age by his or her chronological age and multiplying the result by 100. IQ is now calculated using standard deviation.

Interdisciplinary. A model of collaboration between disciplines that attempts to develop "knowledge bridges" among professions. From these efforts, subdisciplinary areas, such as social psychology, sociolinguistics, and neuropsychology, have developed.

Karyotype. A classification of photographed human chromosomes obtained from a blood or skin sample.

Learned helplessness. The feeling that no matter what one does or how hard one tries he or she will not succeed.

Learning. Refers to changes associated with specific practice or instruction.

Learning set. The ability to learn how to learn.

Least-restrictive environment (LRE). Requires that all students with disabilities receive their education with nondisabled peers to the maximum extent appropriate.

Life-Centered Career Education (LCCE) Curriculum model. Instructional program that teaches 22 major life skill competencies across the four stages of career development.

Longitudinal studies. Investigations that select a single group of subjects and follow it through the years to compare behaviors at different ages.

Maturation. Any development or change in the status of a behavioral trait that takes place in the absence of specific experience, such as instruction.

Mental age (MA). A means of expressing a child's intellectual development. An MA score represents the average performance of children with a given chronological age.

Mosaicism. A condition resulting in Down syndrome where the cells of the individual's body are of a mixed type: some contain trisomics, while others are normal.

Multidisciplinary. A model of collaboration between disciplines wherein various professions approach a particular condition from their own focus (e.g., psychological aspects of intellectual disabilities or medical aspects of intellectual disabilities).

Multidisciplinary team. As described in IDEA, a team of professionals and parents who work together to determine the needs of each child relative to a free and appropriate public education. The team should consist of the student's parents, at least one special education teacher, at least one general education teacher if the child is or may be participating in the general education environment, and a representative of the LEA.

Myelinization. Refers to the development of a sheathlike material that covers and protects the nervous system.

Natural supports. Family, friends, and classmates.

Naturally distributed trials. Learning trials that may occur as the skill would normally be performed in a natural school or home routine.

Neonate. A term applied to the baby during the first 2 months after birth.

Neurological system. The human system composed of the brain, spinal cord, and peripheral neurons.

Normalization. People with intellectual disabilities have access to the conditions of everyday life that are as close as possible to those of nondisabled people in mainstream society.

Norm-referenced assessment. An assessment model whereby an individual's score on an instrument is viewed in comparison with some standard or group norm.

Partial inclusion. Students with intellectual disabilities may receive most of their education in the general education classroom but are "pulled out" into a special education program when the multidisciplinary team considers it appropriate to their individual needs.

Phenotype. The observable result of interaction between the genotype and the environment.

Phenylketonuria (PKU). An inherited human metabolic disease that is characterized by the inability to oxidize a metabolic product of phenylalanine. The condition can result in intellectual disabilities if left untreated.

Phonology. The system of speech sounds that an individual utters.

Precipitous birth. Delivery of a baby after a labor of less than about 2 hours that can cause some injury to the baby.

Proximodistal gradient. Refers to the growth trend wherein more rapid growth and development occur near the center of the organism "*(proximo-)*," with extremities "*(distal)*" maturing later.

Reaction formation. Denying negative feelings and publicly presenting completely opposite images.

Readiness. A developmental state that exists when a child is at a point in development (including previous maturation and learning) where he or she might be expected to profit from a particular situation or experience (such as instruction).

Related services. As defined in IDEA, services necessary to ensure that the child benefits from their educational experience (e.g., transportation, speech and language, occupational therapy, and so on).

Resource room. Educational placements in which the student with intellectual disabilities remains in the general education classroom most of the school day and receives specialized instruction in a special education class for a portion of his or her instructional programming.

Section 504. (of the Vocational Rehabilitation Act). A section of federal law that indicates that no qualified handicapped person shall, on the basis of handicap, be subjected to discrimination in employment.

Self-determination. The ability to problem-solve and make decisions, develop an understanding of sex role expectations, and take care of personal appearance and hygiene.

Self-regulation. The ability to regulate one's own behavior.

Sheltered employment. Includes sheltered workshops, day habilitation, and work activity centers. Sheltered workshops are characterized by segregated training and jobs for people with intellectual disabilities that are based on short-term contracts with local businesses and are assembly-line in nature.

Short-term memory. The ability to recall material over a period of seconds or minutes.

Social intelligence. The concept of a person's ability to effectively perform in areas of interpersonal interaction and forming relationships, communication, and self-regulation and reacting appropriately to the subtle cues in one's environment. Overlaps and in some usages is synonymous with *social competence* or *personal competence*.

Social role valorization (SRV). Giving value to the individual with intellectual disabilities. The goal is to seek more positive roles and experiences for people who are devalued.

Socialization training. Instructional approach focused on developing positive interpersonal relationships with family and peers as well as acquiring behaviors appropriate in a variety of community settings.

Special education. Specially designed instruction, at no cost to parents, provided in all settings (such as in the classroom, in physical education, at home, and in hospitals or institutions).

Special schools. Schools that are exclusively for students with disabilities.

Summative evaluation. An evaluation model that involves assessment of terminal or ultimately desired behaviors and evaluates a child's performance at the end of a given program.

Supported employment. Work in an integrated setting for individuals with severe disabilities (including those with intellectual disabilities) who probably will need some type of continuing support and for whom competitive employment traditionally has not been possible. Supported employment is characterized by wages, continuous support as needed, inclusion with nondisabled people, and flexibility in training, monitoring, and support strategies.

Supported living. A living arrangement that provides support to people with intellectual disabilities in a community setting. Supported living includes small group homes, semi-independent homes and apartments, and foster care.

Tabula rasa. Refers to human developmental theories that emphasize the prepotency of environmental influences.

Transdisciplinary. A model of collaboration between disciplines that was conceived as an effort to overcome some of the problems with other models. This approach emphasizes the role of a primary therapist, who acts as the contact person for service provisions, so the number of professionals with direct child contact is minimal.

Transition services. Services provided to students with intellectual disabilities that facilitate their transitioning out of school and into adult life.

Translocation. A type of chromosomal difficulty resulting in Down syndrome where some of the chromosomal material of one pair detaches and becomes attached to another chromosome.

Trisomy. A condition where an extra chromosome occurs in Group G. This is the most common cause of Down syndrome.

Turner syndrome. A condition where 45 chromosomes are present with only a single X sex chromosome: also known as gonadal aplasia.

Ultrasonography. A prenatal evaluation procedure that employs high-frequency sound waves that are bounced through the mother's abdomen to record tissue densities. Ultrasound may be used as a prenatal assessment to locate fetal abnormalities.

Utilitarianism. A philosophy based on the premise that any action is right if it leads to the greatest good for the greatest number of people. The utilitarian theory holds that the end justifies the means. An individual has only those rights granted by the larger society.

Vocational Rehabilitation Act. A federal law establishing vocational training as a mandatory service for all qualified persons with disabilities.

Work experience. A method of training in which the student may participate in occupational activities in the community under actual working conditions.

Name Index

Subject Index